D0886518

REAR ADMIRAL DAVID D. PORTER

KENNETH P. WILLIAMS

GRANT RISES IN THE WEST

From Iuka to Vicksburg, 1862–1863

INTRODUCTION TO THE BISON BOOKS EDITION
BY BROOKS D. SIMPSON

UNIVERSITY OF NEBRASKA PRESS
LINCOLN

♾ The paper in this book meets the minimum requirements of American
National Standard for Information Sciences—Permanence of Paper for Printed
Library Materials, ANSI Z39.48-1984.

First Bison Books printing: 1997
Most recent printing indicated by the last digit below:
10 9   8   7   6   5   4   3   2   1

Library of Congress Cataloging-in-Publication Data
Williams, Kenneth P. (Kenneth Powers), 1887–1958.
[Lincoln finds a general. Volume 4]
Grant rises in the West. From Iuka to Vicksburg, 1862–1863 / Kenneth P.
Williams; introduction to the Bison Books edition by Brooks D. Simpson.
p. cm.
Originally published as v. 4 of Lincoln finds a general. New York: Macmillan,
1952.
Includes bibliographical references (p.) and index.
ISBN 0-8032-9794-7 (pa: alk. paper)
1. Grant, Ulysses S. (Ulysses Simpson), 1822–1885—Military leadership.
2. Command of troops. 3. Vicksburg (Miss.)—History—Siege, 1863.
4. United States—History—Civil War, 1861–1865—Campaigns. 5. Mississippi—History—Civil War, 1861–1865. I. Title.
E672.W733 1997
973.7′344—dc21
97-7005 CIP

Reprinted from the original 1956 edition, titled *Lincoln Finds a General: A
Military Study of the Civil War*, vol. 4, *Iuka to Vicksburg*, by the Macmillan
Company, New York. Reprinted by arrangement with Scribner, an imprint of
Simon & Schuster Inc.

To
The Memory
of
My Wife

INTRODUCTION

Brooks D. Simpson

On the afternoon of 18 May 1863, two men sat on horseback on a rise overlooking the city of Vicksburg, Mississippi. One, with red beard and lively eyes, barely able to contain himself, squirmed in anticipation; the other, somewhat shorter, calmly puffed away at a cigar as he looked over the ground around him. Behind them columns of blue-clad soldiers marched by, moving into position; in the distance their counterparts worked feverishly to prepare their defenses for an anticipated assault. At last the red-head could wait no longer. Turning to his companion, he exclaimed. "Until this moment I never thought that your expedition would be a success; I never could see the end clearly; but *this* is a campaign,—this is a success if we never take the town."

Ulysses S. Grant said nothing, but perhaps his face betrayed a small smile. After all, William T. Sherman rarely admitted that he had been mistaken.[1]

Some two months later, after Vicksburg had fallen, someone else also admitted to having been in error about Grant's plan, and shared that information with the Union commander. The writer had no problem with Grant's decision to cross the Mississippi River south of Vicksburg; once across, however, he thought it would have been better had Grant marched south to join forces with another Union army, under the command of Nathaniel Banks. Instead, when Grant "turned northward east of the Big Black, I feared it was a mistake. I now wish to make the personal acknowledgment that you were right, and I was wrong." That the signature at the bottom of the letter read "A. Lincoln" suggested the true significance of the admission of error.[2]

Most people overlook the fact that what scholars acknowledge as Ulysses S. Grant's most remarkable campaign—one worthy of rank among the best in American and world history—was undertaken by a man under a cloud, his plans questioned by the two men usually assumed to be among his staunchest supporters. His ultimate success in compelling the capitulation of the Confederate citadel obscured the fact that he nearly lost his command in the process. That Grant's greatness is evident in hindsight offers no clue as to how events unfolded as they did, or why Grant—and not John A. McClernand or William S. Rosecrans—emerged as the coming man a year after Henry W. Halleck's efforts to avoid placing Grant in command along the Mississippi proved fruitless.

It must be said that hindsight influences Kenneth P. Williams's account of this critical year in Union military fortunes between the Appalachian Mountains and the Mississippi River valley. "The main theme of this volume is Vicksburg," he announces in his preface. He would leave for a subsequent volume the story of Rosecrans's operations versus Braxton Bragg in the aftermath of Stones River. Indeed, this volume would have been much stronger had Williams decided to hold back his treatment of Buell in Kentucky and Rosecrans in Tennessee for the fifth volume of *Lincoln Finds a General**; one senses that he viewed these chapters as distractions from the main work at hand—tracing Grant's emergence as the premier Union field general. If Williams designed his enterprise as a Yankee counterpart to Freeman's *Lee's Lieutenants*, it might have been advisable to follow Freeman in concentrating on one army at a time.

It is one of the oddities of Civil War military history that the most successful Union field army, the Army of the Tennessee, lacks a compelling history. Historians devoted to the Union cause, led by Bruce Catton, have lavished much more attention upon the Army of the Potomac. It might come as somewhat of a surprise that the author of *Mr. Lincoln's Army, Glory Road*, and *A Stillness at Appomattox* (the last a winner of the Pulitzer Prize) hailed not from Massachusetts or New York but from Michigan (although Catton's fondness for the Iron Brigade in *Glory Road* betrays his regional roots); it would not be until Catton took it upon himself to carry Lloyd Lewis's biography of Grant through the Civil War years that he gained a full appreciation of the war west of the Blue Ridge Mountains. Indeed, the historiography of the Army of the Potomac's operations and of the abilities of its leaders is a rich one, even if in many cases the issues raised reiterate the themes sounded by William Swinton and other chroniclers of the immediate postwar period. It is somewhat more surprising that the Army of the Cumberland attracts more than its share of attention, although a survey of the biographies of two of its leading generals, Rosecrans and George H. Thomas, suggests that the old rivalry between that army and its cousins on the Tennessee remains a vibrant one. Peter Cozzens's recent trilogy covering Stones River, Chickamauga, and Chattanooga, while giving due attention to Confederate leaders and soldiers, still derives its

---

*This book was originally published as volume 4 of *Lincoln Finds a General*, a projected seven-volume work of which only 5 volumes were completed.

thematic unity from its celebration of the generals and men of the supposedly neglected Army of the Cumberland: here and there one can detect more than a hint of the same need to praise the Cumberlanders and disparage their erstwhile colleagues.

In contrast, the Army of the Tennessee and its signature campaign at Vicksburg have suffered from relative neglect. To be sure, something of that army's progress can be gleaned from Catton's *Grant Moves South*, Lloyd Lewis's *Sherman: Fighting Prophet*, and John Marszalek's *Sherman: A Soldier's Passion for Order*, but we still lack substantial biographies of many of the army's leading officers, including McClernand and James B. McPherson. And the literature covering the Vicksburg campaign is little better. The text of Edwin Bearss's detailed trilogy plows through the *Official Records* with the occasional detour into other sources: its dense narrative challenges all but the most devoted readers. Yet it clearly towers over Earl S. Miers's flimsy if readable overview, *The Web of Victory* (1954), one of Kenneth Williams's favorite targets. Most people either ignore or are ignorant of Samuel Carter's *The Final Fortress: The Campaign for Vicksburg, 1862–1863* (1980), which stands as the best single-volume history available. It is, in fact, a matter of some amazement that what has been termed one of the great campaigns of military history continues to suffer such neglect—all the more so since a fresh look at it could integrate the themes of politics, civil-military relations, emancipation and black enlistment, and the treatment of southern whites with an analysis of the military campaign itself to present a new type of campaign history that transcended the battlefield proper to explore the multiple facets of warmaking. Thus, to learn about how Ulysses S. Grant and the Army of the Tennessee went about the business of capturing Vicksburg, one could not do better than to turn first to this volume of Williams's series.

There was nothing inevitable about Grant's triumph—or Vicksburg's coming to represent the focal point of Union operations in the West. For as Williams's narrative opens in the summer of 1862, it appeared that the Army of the Ohio (the predecessor of the Army of the Cumberland) would play the decisive role by clearing Tennessee, capturing Chattanooga, and penetrating the Confederate heartland. In contrast, Grant found himself entangled in the responsibilities of a commander of occupied territory, torn between pacification and punishment. Halleck, skeptical of Grant's abilities as a military commander, had initially looked elsewhere for someone to head the District of West Tennessee; it would not be until October that Halleck elevated Grant to department command.

Nor, for all the talk of Grant's vaunted ability to learn from his mistakes, did he show great promise as a general during the last six months of 1862—which is one reason why so many of his biographers give short shrift to this time period (William McFeely dismisses Iuka and Corinth in a handful of sentences in his rush to get to Vicksburg from Shiloh, while in *Grant Moves South* Catton devotes two chapters carrying the story forward from July to the end of October 1862). One might have thought that his failure to execute a coordinated attack by two separate columns at Iuka might have demonstrated to him the difficulties of such an operation, but he resorted to the same approach at Corinth and the first drive on Vicksburg, with less than satisfactory results. Grant himself would later claim that in his retreat from Oxford in December 1862 he learned that his army could live off the land, but even Halleck had raised that possibility two months before. And, of course, Grant committed one of his most serious blunders when on 17 December he issued orders barring Jews from his department. Williams hems and haws over this incident (pages 178–79), seeing in the general's decision to get rid "of a recognizable group of offenders" a reflection of his practical bent of mind. Surely there are better ways to explain what even Julia Dent Grant termed "that obnoxious order."[3]

And one looks for a more balanced treatment of the relationship between Grant and his most troublesome subordinate, John A. McClernand. McClernand's efforts to gain an independent command ensnared him in a world of ambiguous orders and sharp practice, although perhaps this was just retribution for his never-ending quest for fame and recognition. He never quite understood the inherent contradiction in the instructions which gave him an independent command under Grant—orders that never in fact made him truly independent of Grant. For this he had no one to blame but Abraham Lincoln and Secretary of War Edwin M. Stanton: nevertheless, his underhanded efforts to displace Grant do much to temper whatever sympathy one might have for him. Here and there one finds people willing to plead McClernand's case and claim that Grant and others treated him unfairly. A good deal of this constitutes little more than revision for revision's sake, mistaking fresh interpretations for persuasive ones. Nevertheless, there is some truth to the charge that Grant did not always treat McClernand justly, either at the time or in his postwar commentaries. Of course, in light of what McClernand said about him, all this proves is that Grant was a human being, sensitive to slights and criticism, to deviousness and character assassination.

During 1862 Grant had lost whatever trust he ever had in McClernand,

and thereafter was unwilling to give him a break—something made embarrassingly obvious when he initially criticized the expedition against Arkansas Post as a "wild goose chase" undertaken by McClernand, only to reverse himself once he learned that it was actually Sherman's idea. If McClernand did not exactly distinguish himself at Port Gibson and at Champion's Hill, one must remember that Grant, who was well aware of his subordinate's shortcomings (having seen McClernand at Belmont, Fort Donelson, and Shiloh), could have supervised him better. And, on 22 May, when Grant questioned the accuracy of McClernand's reports of success in taking enemy fortifications, he should have gone to see matters for himself. Men died that day because Grant did not do so; his subsequent recountings of the import of McClernand's dispatches rested upon questionable renderings of their content. But no one can shuffle through McClernand's correspondence with Grant, Lincoln, and others without coming to the conclusion that in the end he got what he so richly deserved. If the men of the Thirteenth Corps distinguished themselves during this campaign—and they did—it was in spite of and not because of their immediate commander.

What made McClernand a threat rather than a nuisance to Grant was the politician-general's relationship with Abraham Lincoln. It is one of the wonders of Civil War historiography that somehow the president escapes censure from most historians for his role in matters concerning McClernand. T. Harry Williams admitted that he could not explain the president's reasoning, weakly concluding that perhaps "Lincoln's powers of human evaluation were not as sharp as usual." That Lincoln sanctioned McClernand's concept of an expedition against Vicksburg (however much the actual orders muddled it) demonstrates that his faith in Grant was less than complete. To warp a phrase that Lincoln in all probability never actually uttered, he believed he could well spare Grant.[4]

That Lincoln embraced McClernand's plan and failed to do anything more than gently hint he did not welcome the general's derogatory missives about his colleagues—and that in February 1864 he actually reinstated McClernand as a corps commander—reveals at the least a serious blind spot in the president's handling of his generals. Praise for "Lincoln's clear-sighted unwillingness to allow partisan concerns to interfere with decisions critical to the army" must be muted when one recalls that McClernand, a War Democrat, cited the political advantages of his project in bolstering support for the war effort in the Old Northwest. Yet even Grant, in reflecting on the Vicksburg campaign, chose to overlook the president's meddling, claiming that Lincoln's support for him was "constant."[5]

Actually, as Grant well knew, he was close to losing his command in the spring of 1863. Efforts to open up water passages north and west of the city had failed; newspapers reported that many of his men were sick or dying; whispers circulated that he was drinking. Cincinnati newspaper editor Murat Halstead did not mince words. "How is it that Grant who was behind at Ft. Henry, drunk at Donelson, surprised and whipped at Shiloh and driven back from Oxford, Miss., is still in command?" he thundered in a message to Secretary of the Treasury Salmon P. Chase. "Our noble army of the Mississippi is being *wasted* by the foolish, drunken, stupid Grant." The editor elaborated in a second letter, declaring that Grant was "a jackass in the original package. He is a poor drunken imbecile. He is a poor stick sober, and he is most of the time more than half drunk, and much of the time idiotically drunk." As Cadwallader Washburn, brother of Grant's congressional patron, Elihu B. Washburne, put it, "All of Grant's schemes have failed. He knows that he has got to do something or off goes his head."[6]

The arrival of visitors from Washington confirmed Grant's suspicions that the administration was considering a change in commanders for the Army of the Tennessee. Charles A. Dana came at the behest of Secretary Stanton, supposedly to inspect problems with paymasters; Adjutant General Lorenzo Thomas was interested in raising black regiments. Both men were also to report to Washington about Grant, and Thomas allegedly bragged that he carried authorization to remove him on the spot. Fortunately, Grant had already commenced the movement that would in the end bring him success, causing even Lincoln to proclaim it "one of the most brilliant in the world."[7]

Between the beginning of April, when Grant decided to put his plan into motion, and the end of May, when he settled down to besiege Vicksburg, he demonstrated that he was a general who knew when to take calculated risks, respond to circumstances, improvise when necessary, all the time remaining calm and focused. In so doing he met Carl von Clausewitz's definition of military genius as that "which rises above all rules." Those critics who claim that Grant was a plodding butcher who won by sheer superiority of numbers know nothing of this campaign, for Grant moved quickly against a superior enemy force, defeated it in detail, and did so while suffering fewer losses (less than ten thousand for the entire campaign through Vicksburg's surrender) than did Lee in any number of battles. As Williams so eloquently puts it, "Vicksburg is Grant."

Readers will note several characteristics about Williams's approach to his topic. He concentrates upon the varied aspects of command, as befits a former officer who saw service in World War I. Discipline and drill, the problems of logistics and communication, the need to coordinate movements and work with naval counterparts—all were part of the task of directing military operations. So were governing occupied regions, responding to the problems and opportunities presented by emancipation, and corresponding with civil superiors. That Williams devotes a good portion of his narrative to these topics might disappoint those readers who crave the excitement of battle, pure and simple. But in fact these are essential elements to the successful practice of command. Williams reminds us how hard it is to be a good commander—and in so doing provides a useful corrective to the notion that there is nothing difficult about being a general. In later years Grant, demonstrating his skill at aphorism, sought to dispel the myths of generalship and strategy by insisting, "The art of war is simple enough. Find out where your enemy is. Get at him as soon as you can. Strike at him as hard as you can and as often as you can, and keep moving on." More recently, William McFeely reminded his readers of "how simple war is, concluding merely that "to make war is to kill."[8]

In breaking down generalship to its fundamentals, Grant demonstrated his ability to distinguish between the important and the unimportant; his remark reminds us of why so many people praised him for his uncommon common sense. But to assert that war is simple is simpleminded. If the whats of strategy seem self-evident, the hows are not always so apparent. After reading Williams one is struck by the truth of Clausewitz's observation that while everything in war is simple, the simplest thing can be very difficult to do—something that even the armchair warrior, armed with that most valuable of weapons (hindsight), might keep in mind. Break down Grant's aphorism. How does a general find out where the enemy is, and what the enemy's intentions are—especially when he has to sift through contradictory reports and rumors? How does a general get his forces to the field of battle—and how does he make sure that the enemy will be there? What about coordination, supply, and communication? And, once in battle, how does a general make sure that he will be able to strike as hard as he can and as often as he can—while avoiding, deflecting, or absorbing the blows of the enemy? How does one prepare to pursue a defeated foe—or rally one's own forces after a setback?

War may appear simple, but it is not. Good generals are hard to find; exercising command capably is a demanding task. Grant realized this. "There is a desire upon the part of people who stay securely at home to read in the morning papers, at their breakfast, startling reports of battles fought," he once observed. "They cannot understand why troops are kept inactive for weeks or even months. They do not understand that men have to be disciplined, arms made, transportation and provisions provided." The art of war might seem simple, but its successful practice was difficult indeed, and great artists even rarer.[9]

Williams does not conceal his preference for some generals and his dislike for others. McClernand comes in for particularly rough treatment, but Williams reserves some of his choicest turns of phrase for William S. Rosecrans, who comes off as imperious and bombastic, and whose personal bravery on the battlefield obscured his inability to manage his army in combat. He treats Henry Halleck rather gently, although the narrative reveals that Halleck was much better at offering advice from a desk than in exercising command on the field, and that he viewed his mission as one of offering advice, repeating maxims that were little more than truisms, and relaying information and assessments of the political environment rather than actually coordinating the Union war effort (his efforts to reinforce Grant during the siege of Vicksburg proves a notable exception) or pursuing an overall plan. In contrast, Williams showers Grant, Sherman, and Philip Sheridan with plaudits.

The narrative and analysis suffers from several flaws. Relying upon printed sources, most notably the *Official Records*, Williams refrained from serious archival research, thus overlooking valuable information and evidence that would support (or contradict) his conclusions. His relentless efforts to discredit Sylvanus Cadwallader's *Three Years with Grant*, which had then just appeared in print, proved excessive and betrayed his commitment to protect Grant's reputation. In places his foreshadowing becomes heavy-handed; his judgments and characterizations of various generals are not always impartial; some of his speculations about what might have happened in different circumstance or with different generals are dubious at best.[10]

In fact, Williams is so interested in explaining how Grant triumphed that he fails to ask why that victory was of such importance to the Union cause. As several authors have suggested, some of the traditional responses do not withstand scrutiny. While the capture of the city helped secure Union navigation of the entire Mississippi River, one still had to control both banks of that waterway to guarantee safe passage of transports and warships. For some time the trans-Mississippi Confederacy had operated as a nation unto itself, and would continue to do so quite well. That Union military planning continued to include operations in this region resulted in a major diversion of resources from the main task at hand of conquering the Confederate heartland from Virginia through the Carolinas, Georgia, and Alabama. As the flow of most supplies within the Confederacy across the Mississippi actually ran from east to west (and not the other way around), the impact upon Confederate logistics was unclear, especially as illicit traffic and smuggling continued along the river. Thus, according to Herman Hattaway and Archer Jones, "the loss of the Mississippi was purely a loss of prestige and a psychological defeat"—and in conquering the area the Union also inherited the need to garrison it. The greatest material gain was in the capture of some thirty thousand Confederate soldiers as well as cannon and ammunition—and even here one must add that a sufficient number of the paroled Confederates soon took up arms again without being exchanged, which contributed to the collapse of the agreement governing prisoner exchanges.[11]

One need not minimize the impact of psychological victories or defeats, especially when democracies wage war. But Vicksburg was important for another reason. In taking the city, Ulysses S. Grant cemented his place in the front rank of Union leaders. Here and there people might continue to entertain doubts about him, but never again did he have to worry about retaining his command. Future advancement continued to hinge upon subsequent developments, for it was far from clear that Grant was destined to become general in chief—but defeat here would have closed off that option. Indeed, in failure Grant might well have faded away—and William T. Sherman might have gone with him. For all the endless speculation about why the Union triumphed or the Confederacy collapsed, it is hard to envision exactly how the Union would have triumphed had it been deprived of the services of these two generals. Because of Vicksburg, when Lincoln again went about finding a general, he now knew where to look.

Reservations aside, Williams's study tracing the emergence of Grant remains essential reading to anyone who seeks a better understanding of the war along the Mississippi. At the time it appeared, it offered an essential corrective to critical and usually uninformed criticisms of Grant's generalship. It explodes the stereotype of Grant as a plodding, unimaginative butcher who won by sheer din of superior numbers and establishes the general's credentials as one of history's great captains, while offering readers a more sophisticated understanding of the complexity of command. Not bad for a professor of mathematics—which, by the way, is the career Grant had imagined for himself. In that fact we might find a clue as to the empathy between scholar and subject.

NOTES

1. Adam Badeau, *The Military History of U. S. Grant*, 3 vols. (New York: Appleton, 1881), 1:281.

2. Bruce Catton, *Grant Moves South* (Boston: Little, Brown, 1960), 489.

3. John Y. Simon, ed., *The Personal Memoirs of Julia Dent Grant* (New York: Putnam, 1975), 107.

4. T. Harry Williams, *Lincoln and His Generals* (New York: Knopf, 1952), 194. Brooks D. Simpson, "Alexander McClure on Lincoln and Grant. A Questionable Account," *Lincoln Herald* 95 (fall 1993): 83–86, questions whether Lincoln ever uttered the words, "I can't spare this man; he fights."

5. Mark E. Neely, Jr., *The Last Best Hope of Earth: Abraham Lincoln and the Promise of America* (Cambridge MA: 1993), 90; Ulysses S. Grant, *Personal Memoirs*, 2 vols. (New York: C. L. Webster, 1885–86), 1:460.

6. Catton, 395; Murat Halstead to Salmon P. Chase, 1 April 1863, Chase Papers, University Press of America (microfilm); Shelby Foote, *The Civil War: A Narrative*, 3 vols. (New York: Random House, 1958–74), 2:216–17.

7. Williams, 230.

8. T. Harry Williams, *McClellan, Sherman, and Grant* (New Brunswick NJ: Rutgers University Press, 1962), 105; William McFeely, *Grant: A Biography* (New York: Norton), 78. I am indebted to Mark Grimsley for reminding me of the McFeely remark and its import.

9. Carl von Clausewitz, *On War*, Michael Howard and Peter Paret, eds. and trans. (Princeton NJ: Princeton University Press, 1976), 119; Grant to Jesse Root Grant, 17 November 1861, in John Y. Simon et al., eds., *The Papers of Ulysses S. Grant*, 20 vols. to date. (Carbondale: Southern Illinois University Press, 1967–), 3:227.

10. On the controversy surrounding Cadwallader's book, see my introduction to the Bison Books edition of *Three Years With Grant* (1955; reprint, Lincoln: University of Nebraska Press, 1996).

11. Herman Hattaway and Archer Jones, *How the North Won: A Military History of the Civil War* (Urbana: University of Illinois Press, 1983), 421–22.

CONTENTS

ILLUSTRATIONS

MAPS

PREFACE

T HE MAIN theme of this volume is Vicksburg. But Buell's campaign and Rosecrans's operations that culminated at Murfreesboro, which were briefly described in former volumes, are here also given in detail.

The Buell campaign is one which I think has been frequently misunderstood, chiefly because of the persistent but false claim that his movement against Chattanooga was hampered by Halleck's requirement that he rebuild the railroad as he advanced. Buell goes to the sidelines in this volume, not to reappear. Although some of his characteristics were sensed by Lincoln when he had him relieved of command, even the extensive testimony before the Buell Commission did not tell the entire story. Buell revealed himself fully in messages that were not presented to that body. Although Thomas gave damaging testimony, he did not put into the record the letter in which he strongly urged Buell to inspect the McMinnville position, after it was known that Bragg had crossed the Tennessee in the vicinity of Chattanooga.

While it is customary to begin the Murfreesboro campaign with at most an introductory paragraph or so about Rosecrans's activities at Nashville, a whole chapter is devoted to that period. This has been done in order to show some of the aftermath of the Kirby Smith-Bragg invasion of Kentucky, and to afford Rosecrans an opportunity to reveal certain of his characteristics. He was a difficult subordinate and showed a tendency to boastfulness and self-esteem that does not augur well for the future.

Some attention is given to operations west of the Mississippi, for the Vicksburg campaign cannot be fully appreciated without knowledge of what transpired in that vast area. No adequate military study of the war there has, so far as I know, ever been made. It would be a difficult theme, but an important one. West of the Mississippi there was plenty of drama; there was bitter enmity between different civilian groups, both North and South; there was friction between commanders and civil authorities; and there was an extensive irregular warfare in addition to the operations of regularly constituted forces. The military operations cannot be fully appraised unless administration and logistics are duly considered. Unfortunately such matters possess little of the spectacular, and are too frequently neglected, even by writers who may appreciate their importance.

The appendix contains a discussion of Cadwallader's *Three Years with Grant,* as edited by Benjamin P. Thomas. More should be said, for the book is a symbol—a disturbing symbol of eagerness for the sensational without careful investigation whether it be true or not. It is very probable that the book would never have been published if it had not been for Cadwallader's Satartia story, which is completely disproved by the *Official Records.* Certain it is that there are so many and such serious errors in the work that nothing of import in it that is not already known to be true can be accepted.

Assistance in the preparation of this volume has come to me from a number of persons. Dr. C. Percy Powell of the Manuscripts Division of the Library of Congress and Dr. W. Neil Franklin of the National Archives have once more been helpful. In addition, Dr. Richard G. Wood, Mr. Ray Flynn, and Mr. J. O. Kane of the War Records Branch of the Archives, have found useful material in that great storehouse of records. The Library of Congress kindly furnished prints of Mathew Brady photographs.

Special thanks are due Mr. Charles E. Shedd, Jr., Historian of the Shiloh National Military Park, for a personal reconnaissance of the region west of Corinth and a report on the principal roads that existed at the time of the battle. Helpful answers to queries about Sherman's attack at Chickasaw Bluffs came from Mr. James R. McConaghie, Superintendent of the Vicksburg National Military Park. Several questions about the Battle of Murfreesboro were sent to Mr. Charles S. Dunn, Superintendent of the Chickamauga and Chattanooga National Military Park, and information compiled by Mr. James R. Sullivan, Historian at the park, was sent to me, as well as some tracings of maps.

I have to thank Mr. Robert G. Sanner, Historian of the Manassas National Battlefield Park, who had previously been at the Appomattox memorial, for efforts he made to discover who was actually present in the McLean parlor at the time of Lee's surrender to Grant, after that question had arisen in considering the reliability of Sylvanus Cadwallader.

I am indebted to Miss Charlotte Capers, of the Department of Archives and History of the State of Mississippi, and to Mrs. Eva W. Davis, of the Old Court House Museum at Vicksburg, for helpful answers to questions. Miss Margaret A. Flint, reference librarian of the Illinois State Historical Library, put material at my disposal that made two visits to Springfield very profitable. Miss Ethel L. Hutchins, of the Cincinnati Public Library, gave assistance to me during a visit to consult newspaper files.

Nearer at home, I have received assistance from various persons during visits at the Indiana State Library and continuing help from the staff of the Indiana University Library.

With Miss Joan Doyle, a graduate student at the Louisiana State University, I had a profitable conversation on the subject of General Butler, while she was on a visit to Bloomington. I have had many stimulating talks on the war with Mr. James R. H. Spears, a graduate student in this university, who has also aided in checking and looking up material for me, both locally and in Washington.

Recognition is given in notes for information which was secured from Mr. William H. Townsend, of Lexington, Kentucky, and Mr. Henry P. Stearns, of the Taft School, Watertown, Connecticut. A letter from Mr. D. Alexander Brown disposed of a question about Grierson's raid. Mr. Brown's admirable book on that famous operation is one that can be read without the fear that accuracy is sacrificed for the spectacular and the dramatic. In conversation and in letters, Major General U. S. Grant, 3rd, communicated information that has been very useful.

A seemingly simple question as to the existence or nonexistence of some ten miles of railroad in western Tennessee led to considerable correspondence, which, however, left the matter unsettled, part of the conflicting evidence being outlined in a note. For material and letters on this question I am indebted to Mr. C. H. Mottier, Vice-President and Chief Engineer of the Illinois Central Railroad, Colonel Robert S. Henry and Mr. C. J. Corliss of the Association of American Railroads, Mrs. Gertrude Morton Parsley of the Tennessee State Library and Archives, Judge William H. Swiggart, Vice-President of the

Atlantic Coast Line Railroad, and Mr. W. M. Miles, an attorney of Union City, Tennessee.

The manuscript for this volume, as for the preceding volumes, was critically read by Professor John M. Hill, Colonel Herbert G. Esden, and Major General E. F. Harding, and I owe a debt to all of them for comments and appraisals. My editor, Mr. Cecil Scott, alone read all the notes and followed revisions made after the entire work had been completed. Many improvements came from his suggestions, and his counsel on large points that I referred to him was particularly helpful.

The death of my wife shortly before proofs were received deprived me of a helper whose devotion to the work was beyond measure. She was E. L. W. of earlier dedication pages and she possessed an enviable feeling for language and a passion for accuracy and thoroughness. Professor Hill assisted me greatly with the proofs at a time when aid was something more than merely welcome.

K. P. W.

Department of Mathematics
Indiana University
Bloomington
June 11, 1956

ACKNOWLEDGMENTS

Permission to quote copyrighted material is acknowledged to publishers and authors as follows: Association of the United States Army —*American Campaigns* by Matthew F. Steele (1951); The Atlantic Monthly Press—"Meade's Headquarters, 1863–1865" by George R. Agassiz, copyright, 1922, by the Massachusetts Historical Society; Dodd, Mead & Company—*The Generalship of Ulysses S. Grant* by Colonel J. F. C. Fuller, copyright, 1929, by Dodd, Mead & Company, Inc.; Duke University Press—*James Parton; The Father of Modern Biography* by Milton E. Flower, copyright, 1951, by Duke University Press; *Encyclopaedia Britannica*—"U. S. Grant" by C. F. Atkinson, copyright, 1940, by *Encyclopaedia Britannica, Inc.;* Indiana Historical Bureau—*Indiana Politics During the Civil War* by Kenneth M. Stampp, copyright, 1949, by the Indiana Historical Bureau; The Jewish Publication Society of America—*American Jewry and the Civil War* by Bertram W. Korn, copyright, 1951, by The Jewish Publication Society of America; Alfred A. Knopf, Inc.—*Three Years with Grant* by Benjamin P. Thomas, copyright, 1955, by Benjamin P. Thomas, *The Web of Victory* by Earl Schenck Miers, copyright, 1955, by Earl Schenck Miers; B. H. Liddell Hart—*Sherman* by B. H. Liddell Hart, copyright, 1929, by Dodd, Mead & Company, Inc.; Little, Brown & Company—*The Fremantle Diary,* edited by Walter Lord, copyright, 1954, by Walter Lord; Longmans, Green & Co., Inc.—*Leonidas Polk, Bishop and General* by William M. Polk, (1915), *Grant, Lincoln and the Freedmen* by John Eaton, (1907); The Louisiana Historical Quarterly—"New Orleans under General Butler" by Howard B. Johnson, Volume XXIV; Louisiana State University Press—*With Sherman to the Sea* edited by O. O. Winther, copyright, 1943, by Louisiana State University Press; The Neale

Publishing Co.—*The Life of John A. Rawlins* by James Harrison Wilson, (1916); W. W. Norton & Company—*Memoirs of a Volunteer, 1861–1863* by John Beatty, copyright, 1946, by W. W. Norton & Company; The University of North Carolina Press—*General Jo Shelby* by Daniel O'Flaherty, copyright, 1954, by The University of North Carolina Press, *Pemberton, Defender of Vicksburg* by J. C. Pemberton, copyright, 1942, by The University of North Carolina Press; G. P. Putnam's Sons—*Letters of Ulysses S. Grant* by Jesse Grant Cramer, copyright, 1912, by Jesse Grant Cramer; The State Company—*Braxton Bragg, General of the Confederacy* by Don C. Seitz (1924); University of Texas Press—*Ploughshares into Swords* by Frank E. Vandiver, copyright, 1952, by University of Texas Press; Yale University Press—*A Volunteer's Adventures* by John W. De Forest, copyright, 1946, by Yale University Press.

The letter from Lincoln to Grant which appears as one of the endpapers of this volume is reproduced from *A Personal History of Ulysses S. Grant* by Albert Deane Richardson, Hartford, Connecticut, 1868. The original letter is in the Ferdinand Dreer Collection of the Historical Society of Pennsylvania.

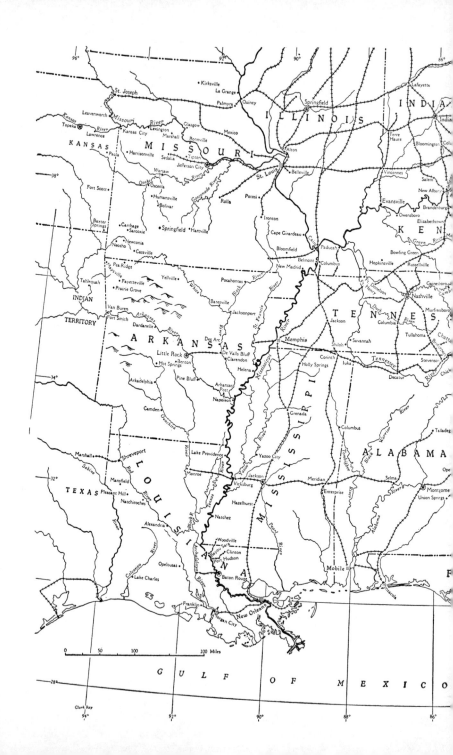

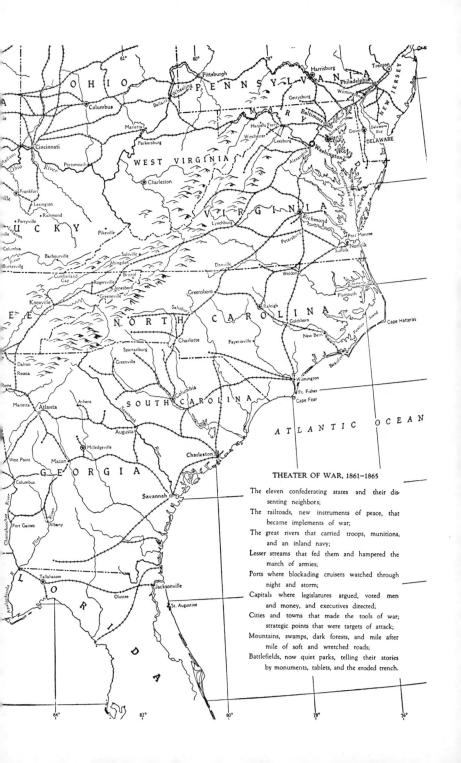

THEATER OF WAR, 1861–1865

The eleven confederating states and their dissenting neighbors;

The railroads, new instruments of peace, that became implements of war;

The great rivers that carried troops, munitions, and an inland navy;

Lesser streams that fed them and hampered the march of armies;

Ports where blockading cruisers watched through night and storm;

Capitals where legislatures argued, voted men and money, and executives directed;

Cities and towns that made the tools of war; strategic points that were targets of attack;

Mountains, swamps, dark forests, and mile after mile of soft and wretched roads;

Battlefields, now quiet parks, telling their stories by monuments, tablets, and the eroded trench.

Executive Mansion,

Washington, July 13   1863.

Major General Grant
  My dear General

    I do not remember that you
and I ever met personally, I write this now as
a grateful acknowledgment for the almost inestimable service you have done the country.— I
wish to say a word further. When you first
reached the vicinity of Vicksburg, I thought you
should do, what you finally did— march the
troops across the neck, run the batteries with the

manoeuvre, and when you got below; and I never had any
faith, except a general hope that you knew better
than I, that the Yazoo Pass expedition, and the
like, could succeed. When you got below, and
took Port-Gibson, Grand Gulf, and vicinity, I
thought you should go down the river and join
Gen. Banks; and when you turned Northward
East of the Big Black, I feared it was
a mistake. I now wish to make the personal acknowledgment that you were right, and I was wrong.

Yours very truly
A. Lincoln

GRANT RISES IN THE WEST

CHAPTER I

A SEASON OF REVERSES

What I cannot do, of course, I will not do; but it may as well be understood, once for all, that I shall not surrender this game leaving any available card unplayed.

Lincoln to Reverdy Johnson

THE MIDSUMMER months of 1862 were, Grant recorded later, the most anxious period for him of the entire war. He was deep in enemy country, faced by a determined, resourceful foe, while regular and irregular bands of cavalry threatened his rear. The summer was hot and dry; because low water made the Tennessee River all but worthless as a supply line dependence had to be placed upon the railroad that ran back to Columbus, Kentucky. On the 140 miles of track were many bridges and culverts, and strong forces were necessary to protect it and reduce guerrilla damage to what could be repaired quickly. Railroads, even when rebuilt, could not always be used because of lack of equipment. On July 7 Sherman had complained to Halleck that he had had to haul supplies to Moscow from Memphis by wagon. Being without a locomotive, the recollection that his division had captured five had made him fretful. "Don't get angry," was Halleck's unruffled reply. "We are doing everything for you in the range of human possibility. If you knew how hard everybody here has been working you would not grumble." [1]

Supply difficulties would be lessened and an important point held securely by having Sherman move to Memphis; and in the message in which he bade farewell to Sherman before leaving Corinth for

[1]

Washington on July 17 to become General in Chief, Halleck said, "You will soon receive orders from General Grant to march yours and Hurlbut's divisions to Memphis." A directive by Sherman the next day put his command in motion on the 18th "at early daylight." Discipline was stressed; but the general had the comfort of his men in mind when he wrote: "The march will be steady and no long stretches. . . . Should the days be hot it is better to wait for the first halt before making coffee. . . . With these rules and care on the part of officers having charge of wagon trains there is no difficulty in making the day's march in six or seven hours, divided between the cool of the morning and evening." Knowing that his men were looking forward to duty in Memphis, Sherman promised that as soon as camp was established "as large an amount of liberty will be given to all good soldiers as is consistent with their duty, and ample opportunity afforded them to see the city with all 'its sights.' " [2]

In Memphis, Sherman found Lew Wallace's Third Division of Grant's old Army of the Tennessee, now under Brigadier General Alvin P. Hovey, Wallace having asked for a leave of absence. "Fully qualified to fill the place of the former commander," had been Grant's comment to Halleck, when he replaced one Hoosier lawyer by another. The day after his arrival, in accordance with instructions from Grant, Sherman dispatched Hovey with all his infantry to Helena, Arkansas, the touch of urgency in his order indicating that there may have been some uneasiness about Curtis's situation.[3] This left Sherman with 16,000 troops; and although Grant did not need to worry about feeding the men and the many animals that steamboats could easily supply, he lost two fine and ably commanded divisions as an immediate potential force against the enemy.

The railroad between Chewalla and Grand Junction seems not to have been rebuilt, and that between Grand Junction and Memphis was abandoned to the pleasure of the guerrillas on July 15 because of lack of rolling stock. Soon communication with Sherman by wire was lost to Grant, and messages had to go to Columbus, Kentucky, and down the river by boat. Providing security toward the north were 10,000 men, operating under McClernand out of Jackson, Tennessee, and 7,500 at Columbus, Cairo, and Paducah. The balance of 12,000 men of the Army of the Tennessee was at Corinth. It consisted of C. F. Smith's old Second Division, temporarily under Brigadier General Richard Oglesby, and Prentiss's old Sixth Division, commanded at the moment by Brigadier General John McArthur, the two division corps—not officially so designated—being commanded by Major General Edward O. C. Ord, who was graduating from West Point along with Halleck when Grant was entering, and who had recently been assigned to the West after service in Virginia.

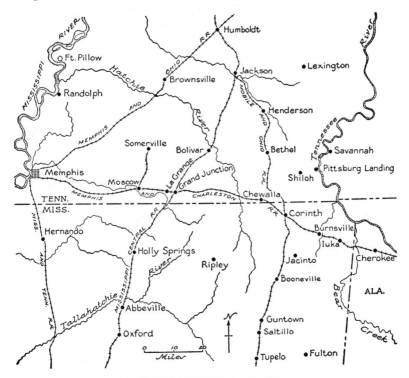

A MUCH DISPUTED REGION

Rosecrans's Army of the Mississippi—a part of Grant's command—with a total present of 32,000, held a front of some thirty-five miles, with its left in Alabama at Cherokee and its right in front of Corinth. The chief concentration was at Jacinto, where there were 13,000 men, consisting of the Fourth Division under Brigadier General Jefferson C. Davis, and the Fifth Division, commanded by Brigadier General Gordon Granger. Rosecrans himself had his headquarters at Iuka, a small county seat and spa near Mississippi's highest point.[4]

When the Federal southward advance stopped, the initiative passed to the Confederates. From his headquarters at Tupelo, Braxton Bragg, like Grant, was directing two armies, but his force was not weakened by the withdrawal of large detachments to guard long supply lines. Hardee now commanded the Army of the Mississippi, while Price had the smaller Army of the West. Bragg had 68,000 men present on July 16; though this was 10,000 fewer than Grant possessed, the difference was well compensated by Bragg's situation in friendly territory.[5]

It had been Earl Van Dorn, whom Curtis had defeated at Pea Ridge in March, who had brought the Army of the West from Arkansas; but on June 20 an order from Richmond put him in command of the Department of South Mississippi and East Louisiana, and he had hastened toward Vicksburg, where Brigadier General Martin L. Smith was in immediate command. From Jackson, Mississippi, Van Dorn issued an order providing, among other things, for the organization of the Partisan Ranger service. After saying that the officers would be held to strict account for the discipline of the irregulars, he opined, "An undisciplined rabble is not dangerous to the enemy, is extremely injurious to the neighborhood where it may be stationed, and is a disgrace to any country." Burning of fences and the killing of stock were two acts the Mississippian specifically proscribed.[6]

Van Dorn reached Vicksburg on the 28th, the day after Federal Brigadier General Thomas Williams broke ground on the canal across the point opposite Vicksburg in the hope of securing a passage that would avoid the batteries at that place. The working party consisted of about 1,200 Negroes. Williams's brigade of troops came, it may be recalled, from the command of Major General Benjamin Butler at New Orleans. As Helena was now in the possession of Unionists, Van Dorn had to contemplate the possibility of a land force from up the Mississippi joining the one from below, just as the naval force that was vigorously bombarding Vicksburg consisted of Davis's gunboats that had descended the river, and of the fleet and mortars that Farragut had brought northward. It looked as though grim work might be ahead, and Van Dorn's order taking command ended: "Let it be borne in mind by all that the army here is defending the place against occupation. This will be done at all hazards, even though this beautiful and devoted city should be laid in ruins." [7]

Originally Bragg's department had extended only as far south as the thirty-third parallel, which gave Vicksburg comfortably to Van Dorn. But the day after Van Dorn reached the city, Jefferson Davis wiped out the illusive parallel as a boundary line and gave all of Van Dorn's territory to Bragg, so that Van Dorn found himself reduced to a district commander, comforted, however, with a presidential assurance that the merger had not been dictated by "want of confidence" in him. In all, Van Dorn had about 14,000 officers and men present in his different subdistricts. Watching over the Gulf, Bragg had a force of some 9,000 in the vicinity of Mobile under Brigadier General John H. Forney.[8]

Viewing the situation from Bladon Springs, Alabama, where he was resting and recuperating, was General Pierre G. T. Beauregard. Recently he had received from Colonel Thomas Jordan, his old chief of staff, who was now serving Bragg in like capacity, a quite disturbing letter telling of efforts to make him the scapegoat for the outcome of the Battle of Shiloh. Said the faithful colonel, "I have my eyes on an officer, high in rank, of this army, who, I think is disposed to give aid and comfort to your enemies for the sake of his own selfish ends and gain." Not being certain, Jordan would not name the man, but he whetted curiosity by saying, "I hear around me murmurs of the smaller conspirators, and can trace the leaders too, I think; the cue came from Richmond." Though he must have been incensed, Beauregard does not seem to have been made less zealous for his cause, and on July 19 he sent Forney a friendly letter with seven suggestions and the postscript, "Should the enemy come to Mobile while I am here, and you have need of my assistance, I would gladly serve on your staff as a volunteer aide." [9]

Across the Mississippi at Opelousas, a small old town with a strong French touch, Governor Thomas O. Moore, dispossessed of Baton Rouge by Farragut's warships, was operating a state government. On June 12 he had written to President Davis that Louisiana west of the river had resources and men, provided they were not taken "by too literal enforcement of the conscript law." He had already charged that the capture of the forts below New Orleans had been facilitated by "the disgraceful conduct of officers who had charge of their defense," and he now said: "The army of Butler is insignificant in numbers, and that fact makes our situation more humiliating. He has possession of New Orleans with troops not equaling in number an ordinary city mob." [10]

Soon Secretary Edwin Stanton was reading a long address by Governor Moore to the people of his state, a copy of which Butler had obtained on a visit to Baton Rouge. The Federal general had already acquired a reputation for harsh rule, but he evidently felt himself a mere amateur, for he described Moore's address as "more remarkable than any document of the kind" he had ever read. In it Moore repeated orders he had already issued, saying, for example, "Tories must suffer the fate that every betrayer of his country deserves." To classify mere sympathy for the North with harmful acts against the South is hard to condone—yet that is what Moore's pronouncement virtually did. At the end, however, the governor revealed himself to be a strong man. No heed should be given to rumors of foreign intervention in favor of the Confederacy—"To believe them is to rely on them." He concluded with timeless words: "Help yourselves. It is the great instrument of national as well as of individual success." [11]

While Moore was tightening up on Louisianians still dominated by affection for their old flag, and assuring Secessionists that their cause would triumph, Richmond was sending Brigadier General Albert G. Blanchard to command camps of instruction for conscripts beyond the Mississippi. He had some trouble getting across the river; but, embarking in a skiff at midnight, he eluded the Federals and on July 12 reached Monroe, which had been named by Davis as his headquarters. After looking the situation over, the Massachusetts-born West Point classmate of Robert E. Lee, Ormsby Mitchel, and Joe Johnston reported gloomily to George W. Randolph, Davis's new War Secretary: "Everything is in trouble here." There were no conscripts to train; and it would be weeks before any arrived. There were practically no arms, and the seizure by Confederate officers in Mississippi of weapons provided by the State of Louisiana was having a bad effect. There was no cavalry, Texan horsemen having been ordered to Arkansas. Artillery to defend Louisiana's many navigable streams was lacking, and the Yankees could go almost where they wished.[12]

To add to difficulties there was confusion over command, with bewildering districts and departments, leading back to the Richmond War Office.[13] Who commanded what was not always clear. The troubled Blanchard forwarded to Randolph a long order issued at Little Rock in early June by Major General Thomas C. Hindman, covering conscripts, which Blanchard thought contained three illegal provisions. The laws of economics were also being tampered with, and

Blanchard enclosed a list of prices on articles for his district. Beef at $0.10 a pound, butter at $0.20, chickens at $2.40 a dozen, and 12 eggs for $0.15, suggest a desperate effort to bolster a collapsing market. But the prices were ceilings.[14] Support prices were an invention for the future.

Before Halleck had been called to Washington, Rosecrans—on July 5—had sent him a note with a startling thought: Bragg's main body was moving toward Chattanooga or Atlanta, with cavalry covering the left flank and rear. Rosecrans was sending Sheridan out that night to investigate the situation. At the moment Sheridan's stock was high, for on the 1st he had handsomely defeated a greatly superior force that had attacked his two regiments at Booneville. It was a small engagement, but it revealed an aggressive, resourceful, courageous, and skillful combat leader. Now Sheridan was having his own ideas as to the enemy's plan, and he ended a dispatch of the 5th to Granger—whose division contained the cavalry of the Army of the Mississippi—"I believe they will go to Atlanta, but it is only an impression." Halleck naturally did not accept too quickly the idea that Bragg was departing, and in the note in which he told Sherman not to get ruffled about supplies he thought it was Bragg's intention to cut off communications with Buell, who, it will be remembered, had started to move from Corinth toward Chattanooga on June 10.[15]

Grant had hardly settled in command when a message from Rosecrans gave new intelligence. Among other things a strong column was moving toward Mobile and Richmond, while another under Price had gone toward Chattanooga or Rome. Cavalry and guerrillas were screening everything, and between the opposing armies there was "a desert country of dry ravines and rough ridges" that made movements by the enemy most practical toward the west or east. Five days later— July 23—Grant began his first report to Halleck by saying that in spite of the greatest vigilance by the cavalry "nothing absolutely certain of the movements of the enemy has been learned." But a move away from Tupelo had surely been made, though doubt obscured both direction and intent. The very unanimity of statements of deserters and escaped prisoners made Grant suspicious: they might have been misled for the purpose of deceiving. Their stories indicated that a large force had moved toward Chattanooga on the 7th, while Price in a speech at Tupelo on the 17th had promised his Missourians that he would take them home by way of Kentucky. Grant summed up, "I do not regard this information of special value, except as giving an idea of points to watch and see if these statements are verified." [16]

Uncertainty was resolved on the 28th in a dispatch from Rosecrans:

> Sheridan has returned from the front. Has captured a captain of cavalry and some thirty letters on a private mail carrier. They show the enemy moving in large force on Chattanooga. Has sent the letters up. They had 19 miles to come. Will dispatch you when they arrive.

The next day brought a detailed report, with two dispatches from Sheridan, and a digest of the interesting letters of Southerners that Rosecrans had been perusing. Grant soon had a telegram on the way to Halleck: "Information just in from Colonel Sheridan, who attacked and defeated 600 rebels from Ripley this morning, says large force leaving Saltillo for Chattanooga by rail. Wagons moved across the country. . . . The Hatchie northwest of Bolivar is now occupied by rebels. McClernand is there with about 6,000 men." [17]

On the 30th Rosecrans and four other brigadier generals in the Army of the Mississippi sent directly to the General in Chief a telegram that said good brigadiers were scarce, and added: "The undersigned respectfully beg that you will obtain the promotion of Sheridan. He is worth his weight in gold." Halleck needed no urging in the case of the officer already riding at the head of Granger's second brigade, for on July 6 he had concluded his telegram to Stanton announcing the victory at Booneville: "I respectfully recommend Colonel Sheridan for promotion for gallant conduct in battle." [18] Bravery and skill in combat, ability to get information: such were qualities that Sheridan had quickly revealed. They weigh heavily when one appraises a general.

Because of Sheridan's enterprise Grant and the Washington High Command knew of Bragg's move seven days after the Confederate general had—on July 21—sent Davis a warning telegram well calculated to surprise him: "Will move immediately to Chattanooga in force and advance from there. Forward movement from here in force is not practicable. Will leave this line well defended." Two days passed before Bragg wrote a letter to Adjutant General Cooper that gave the real reason for the shift and outlined the object of the adventure. From Kirby Smith, Bragg had, he explained, learned that Buell was approaching Chattanooga. Bragg was hastening there with 35,000 effectives, by rail through Mobile, while artillery, cavalry, engineers, and trains went overland by way of Rome, Georgia. After joining Smith he hoped to strike an effective blow through Middle Tennessee, gaining Buell's rear, dividing the Federal forces, and defeating them in detail. Behind him he was leaving Van Dorn with 16,000 effectives and Price with an equal number. Perhaps to lessen anxiety over northern Mississippi, Bragg said the enemy in his front numbered "not less than 10,000." Though skillfully worded, a general for once did not magnify the enemy in his vicinity. But, as Bragg had previously said the scarcity of water was a reason for not advancing against Grant, he knew the Federals were immobilized by the same condition, as well as harassed by guerrillas.[19]

Bragg's decision was a bold one, and represented a sudden change of purpose, for as late as July 20 he still seemed to intend to block Buell's advance in front while his main force moved against Buell's rear, quite as Halleck had thought probable. In all his thinking he was undoubtedly influenced by a misunderstanding of his responsibilities because of Richmond's secretiveness in the matter of department command. Believing that Chattanooga was in his territory, Bragg had sent Major General John P. McCown's division of 3,000 effectives there in late June, and it was the departure of this force that had brought to Federal headquarters at Corinth the first report of an eastward movement by the Confederates. Although a Department of East Tennessee had been created in early spring, with headquarters in Knoxville and with Kirby Smith in command, Bragg asked the latter on July 20 if he were not "still, as formerly, a part of General Johnston's [Albert Sidney Johnston, whose death at Shiloh had brought command first to Beauregard, then to Bragg] old department and hence embraced within my command." [20]

One might argue that Bragg should not have started on his great enterprise without first getting approval of the Confederate President. But Davis could hardly be expected to interpose until he had more information than was contained in Bragg's telegram of the 21st; and as Bragg said in his letter that he was personally leaving Tupelo on the 24th, he virtually presented his superiors with a campaign already begun. Because time was pressing and a certain minimum of success seemed certain, Bragg said in his letter of the 23rd, "In any event much will be accomplished in simply preserving our line and preventing

a descent into Georgia, than which no greater disaster could befall us."
In a friendly letter to Beauregard he combined a prediction and a
hope: "Before they [the Federals] can know of my movement I shall
be in front of Buell at Chattanooga, and by cutting off his transportation may have him in a tight place." [21]

While Bragg was taking the cars at Tupelo on the 24th, Kirby Smith
was writing to him at length. He explained that his department had
been organized independently of the "army of the West," but he did
not inform Bragg—in case Richmond had let him know—that on the
18th the War Department had transferred to him a little bulge into
Georgia that had previously belonged to Bragg. He stated he did not
believe the Federals would attempt anything in Mississippi and
Alabama, citing "the character of the country" as well as the climate
as "insurmountable objects." Instead, they would try to get possession
of East Tennessee, so as to make it a "base for fall and winter operations." He asked if Bragg could not shift the main body of his command "to this department," and take command in person. Time still
was available, he said, "for a brilliant summer campaign"; there
would be a good and secure base, and abundant supplies. The Tennessee River could be crossed at any point by steam and ferryboats,
"and the campaign opened with every prospect of regaining possession
of Middle Tennessee and possibly Kentucky."

The matter of mountains and poor roads was entirely forgotten by
Smith, who, in addition to being in an optimistic frame of mind, was
generously inclined, saying he would "cheerfully place" his command
under Bragg's orders. His First Division, under Brigadier General
Carter L. Stevenson, numbering 9,000 effectives, was, he said, "well
organized and mobilized and in good condition for active service."
Momentarily it was opposing the estimated 10,000 well intrenched
Federals at Cumberland Gap under George Morgan. His Second Division, under Brigadier General Henry Heth, was at Chattanooga, along
with McCown's 3,000 men that had come from Bragg.[22]

The letter could certainly be called a promising one, and when
Bragg picked it up en route it must have raised his spirits and made
him eager to send Buell's invading Bluecoats reeling toward the Ohio.
At any rate, when the two generals met they could proceed with their
plans with an extraordinary unanimity of mind—until Bragg suggested that Smith do something he did not approve, or Smith put forward an idea that Bragg did not fancy.

As Bragg's columns of cavalry, guns, and wagons moved through dust and heat over bad and mountainous roads, and troop trains carried his infantry toward Mobile and Chattanooga on the first stage of the long trek to a bloody rendezvous with Buell in Kentucky, the Federals were liquidating their first effort against Vicksburg as a failure.

By early July it was apparent that digging a practicable canal across the point opposite Vicksburg would be a much greater task than had been expected. In giving Williams instructions on June 6, Butler had told him to make the cut about four feet deep and five feet wide, adding, as if the project were a simple one, "The river itself will do the rest for us." But on July 4 Williams reported that the soil was clay, down through the six to seven feet that had already been dug. No matter how strong the current, the river would not wash the clay, and he might have to go four feet deeper before reaching sand. Though the river was falling, some driftwood had come past, and the *Missouri Republican* of June 28 had said the Missouri was in flood. Williams, therefore, was hopeful for a rise, and he pronounced the project a great one worthy of success. By July 11, when the bottom of the canal had been carried a foot and a half below the river level, sudden cave-ins at several places prevented the letting in of water, as had been intended, within twelve hours. While his canal was then thirteen feet deep and eighteen wide, Williams had "encountered at least a temporary failure." He proposed to collect an additional force of Negroes and tools and make a real canal, thirty-five to forty feet wide, with a bottom adjusted to the lowest level that could be expected in the river. This, however, would require three months.[23]

Smarting under the humiliating and brilliant exploit of the Confederate ram *Arkansas* on July 15, Lieutenant Colonel Alfred W. Ellet, successor to the command of his late brother's ram fleet, had written on the 20th to Flag Officer Davis, suggesting that an effort be made to destroy the *Arkansas,* now lying beneath the Vicksburg batteries. He would, he said, himself take one of the rams with a small and select crew and make the attempt, if Farragut and Davis would vigorously attack the enemy shore guns.[24]

Details were worked out in a conference between the three officers, and as light broke on the 22nd the gunboat *Essex,* with William D. Porter in command, came down the river and headed for the enemy ram, followed by Ellet in the *Queen of the West.* At close range the

Essex put a shot into the target that killed seven men and wounded six, but she herself took heavy punishment and the blow she delivered was a glancing one. Though the *Queen* had no guns with which to pound the *Arkansas* as she closed, she was moving rapidly, and the blow she dealt was far heavier than that of the *Essex.* Her sharp prow penetrated the Confederate craft, making the *Arkansas* career and roll heavily. After maneuvering for another strike, the *Queen* withdrew from the heavy fire concentrated upon her. Though badly damaged, she had not lost a man.[25]

There were brave and skillful men on the three vessels, and the six wounded and seventeen unhurt companions of the seven dead on the *Arkansas* might not have liked the second sentence in the report of the encounter in the telegram which Van Dorn sped to Richmond: "An attempt made this morning by two ironclad rams [the *Queen* was unarmored] to sink the *Arkansas.* The failure so complete that it was almost ridiculous. Several men were, however, killed by a shot entering one of the ports." Though not destroyed, the *Arkansas* was in need of repairs; and Stanton promptly congratulated Ellet and his crew and recommended the water-fighting colonel for a brigadiership. Presently Ellet urged that the War Department build for him "one strong, heavy iron-plated gunboat and ram," so that he would be more independent and not under the necessity of applying for cooperation.[26] The *Arkansas* had made him a believer in armor and gunfire.

The day after the failure to destroy the *Arkansas,* Farragut was cheered by receiving a telegram that Welles had sent on the 18th: "Go down the river at discretion. Not expected to remain up during the season. Messenger on the way with dispatches." Williams could hardly have regretted the necessity of withdrawing with his brigade, which was "numerically little reduced by disease, effectively greatly so." The futility of his mission is revealed by the gloating words of Van Dorn's telegram to President Davis: "Canal will be a failure. Nothing can be accomplished by the enemy unless they bring overwhelming number of troops." Down the river with the ocean fleet, the five transports and the mortars, went the gunboats *Essex* and *Sumter.* In bidding adieu to Farragut, his navy colleague Davis wrote, not too cheerfully: "We are having a dark hour like those who have gone before us. Our trust is in God and the justice of our cause." Never did a prompt departure pay better, for on the 25th Welles, humiliated by the performance of the *Arkansas,* sent by way of Cairo an urgent dispatch, the second of whose two sentences was, "That vessel must be destroyed at all hazards." [27]

Not content with the departure of the Federals, Van Dorn at once sent Major General John C. Breckinridge with 5,000 men to retake Baton Rouge. Making the move rapidly by rail, the former Vice President of the United States detrained at Camp Moore, sixty miles east of his objective, and set out on foot to drive the National forces from the Louisiana capital. Although his command included regiments from Alabama, Mississippi, and Louisiana, his men suffered badly from the extreme heat, and August 4 found him ten miles from Baton Rouge with only 3,000 effectives and 200 Partisan Rangers.

General Williams, back in Baton Rouge with his recuperating brigade, was well advised of the enemy's approach, and received his attack at dawn on the 5th along a line closer to the town than the camps of some of his regiments. His left was forced back, but the naval support for which he had asked was at hand, the fire of the *Essex* doing much to halt the enemy. About ten o'clock Williams passed to the offensive and soon afterward fell—the second of about forty Federal generals to be killed in action. Later the *Kineo* and *Katahdin* joined in the battle, throwing shells over the town into the enemy, their fire being adjusted by signals from a naval officer on the tower of the statehouse.[28] In April, Farragut had passed the forts below New Orleans in a terrific action against the forts as well as against enemy vessels, and had then presented Butler with a captured city.[29] Now, three months later, guns of his ships had prevented a defeat of the only troops Butler had had in action.

Each side lost 84 killed, but the total Confederate casualties were the greater. While both Breckinridge and Williams probably had about 2,500 men on the field, the former had parts from some eighteen regiments against the seven of the Federals. The badly wounded commander of Breckinridge's Second Division fell into Federal hands, and three colonels leading brigades were casualties. Among the Confederate killed was Lieutenant Alexander H. Todd, brother of Mrs. Lincoln.[30]

The *Arkansas* was to have cooperated with Breckinridge by trying to clear the river of Union craft, but repeated engine trouble had prevented her keeping the rendezvous. Informed of her presence not far up the river, Porter on the morning of the 6th moved upstream to engage her. About ten o'clock he sighted her and opened fire at long range. The Confederate ram, unable to maneuver, and with her vulnerable stern downstream, was fired and abandoned by her crew. About noon she blew to pieces.[31]

The Confederates were more than a little vexed that Porter should state or even insinuate that the guns of the *Essex* were the direct cause of the burst of flames that he so joyfully witnessed. Rightly they insisted that the matches that brought her doom had been lighted by her own commander. But the summer months were lean, unhappy ones for the Yankees, and they naturally applauded the explosion above Baton Rouge that had taken from the scene the craft that had tarnished the prestige of their fleets. Truthfully they could say that the *Arkansas* had committed suicide only because her destruction by the *Essex* was certain. Nor could protests by Southerners keep them from believing that her engine trouble was at least partly due to the hard but well-deserved bump given her by Ellet's sturdy and venturesome *Queen of the West*.[32]

Though the Federals now had complete mastery of the waters of the great river, Baton Rouge was evacuated two weeks later, Butler feeling that his small force was too much dispersed. Once again a long stretch of the Mississippi was open for the Confederates to draw much needed supplies from the region to the west, and Earl Van Dorn was so much encouraged that he even had visions of retrieving New Orleans.[33]

While Butler was yielding Baton Rouge to the Confederates, a former political enemy, who for three weeks had been scrutinizing certain aspects of his administration, was writing a report that would give the general scant pleasure. Of the coming investigation by a special emissary from the State Department, Butler had been informed in a letter from Stanton dated June 10. After commending Butler for his "vigorous and able administration," the War Secretary stated that the Honorable Reverdy Johnson, Senator from Maryland, was being sent to New Orleans to "investigate and report upon the complaints made by foreign consuls against the late military proceedings in their respective cases." [34]

Johnson was courteously received by Butler upon his arrival on July 7, and was soon at work in an office in the Custom House. The interchange of correspondence shows that Butler cooperated well with the Senator, as the latter wrote in his report to Secretary Seward in Washington on August 19 (he left New Orleans on July 30). But Johnson found against Butler in his seizures of extensive foreign funds in banks, as well as holdings of sugar and cotton. It softened the verdict but little when Johnson referred to Butler's patriotic zeal and alluded to circumstances well calculated to awaken Butler's suspicion as to the real owners of money or goods. Johnson did, however, state that some consuls had been at fault through entertaining erroneous ideas as to their powers, believing themselves public ministers when, because of "the absence of treaty stipulations," they were in reality merely "mercantile agents, authorized to protect the commercial interests of their fellow-subjects." The discovery of their error, Johnson said, "almost at once led to friendly official intercourse with the major general." [35]

But Butler never forgot that he had been overruled, and in his memoirs he called Reverdy Johnson a "Baltimore secessionist." [36]

If Johnson's visit led to a rebuke to Butler, it also brought one to Johnson from Lincoln, so sharp as to be startling. The Marylander brought it upon himself by reporting the actions of General John W. Phelps, not in themselves a subject of dispute with foreign countries. Phelps commanded the one of Butler's three brigades that was in the vicinity of New Orleans, and Lincoln was well aware of his strong views on abolition, for on June 18 Butler had forwarded to him a long document that his subordinate had written three days before, in which Phelps said, "It is then for our President, the Commander-in-Chief of our Armies, to declare the abolition of slavery, leaving it to the wisdom of Congress to adopt measures to meet the consequences." Phelps requested that the paper be sent to Washington, saying he left his commission—he was a regular officer—at the President's disposal. In his covering letter Butler explained that Phelps evidently wished to make a test case of an incident that he was reporting, and said that if the non-Phelps policy that he himself was then following were endorsed, Phelps was "worse than useless," but if the views Phelps expressed were adopted he would be invaluable, for he was "a good soldier, of large experience, and no braver man lives." [37]

In the reply that Lincoln wrote to Johnson's protest, one finds the difficulties that had beset the President revealed in great clarity. But the distinguished Democrat and Maryland lawyer could hardly have relished finding that he had been written down a year before as a counselor of timidity and appeasement. The letter read:

My Dear Sir: Yours of the 16th by the hand of Governor Shepley is received. It seems the Union feeling in Louisiana is being crushed out by the course of General Phelps. Please pardon me for believing that is a false pretense. The people of Louisiana—all intelligent people everywhere—know full well that I never had a wish to touch the foundations of their society or any right of theirs. With perfect knowledge of this they forced a necessity upon me to send armies among them, and it is their own fault, not mine, that they are annoyed by the presence of General Phelps. They also know the remedy; know how to be cured of General Phelps. Remove the necessity of his presence. And might it not be well for them to consider whether they have not already had time enough to do this? If they can conceive of anything worse than General Phelps within my power, would they not better be looking out for it? They very well know the way to avert all this is simply to take their place in the Union upon the old terms. If they will not do this should they not receive harder blows rather than lighter ones? You are ready to say I apply to friends what is due only to enemies. I distrust the wisdom if not the sincerity of friends who would hold my hands while my enemies stab me. This appeal of professed friends has paralyzed me more in this struggle than any other one thing. You remember telling me the day after the Baltimore mob in April, 1861, that it would crush all Union feeling in Maryland for me to attempt bringing troops over Maryland soil to Washington. I brought the troops notwithstanding, and yet there was Union feeling enough left to elect a Legislature the next autumn, which in turn elected a very excellent Union U. S. Senator. I am a patient man, always willing to forgive on the Christian terms of repentance, and also to give ample time for repentance; still I must save this Government if possible. What I cannot do, of course, I will not do; but it may as well be understood, once for all, that I shall not surrender this game leaving any available card unplayed.[38]

Johnson had little more than departed from New Orleans when Butler was engaged in an argument with Phelps, because the uncompromising Vermonter claimed he would be a slave driver if he put escaped Negroes to work upon military defenses. Finally, on August 5, Butler wrote to Phelps that he had forwarded his resignation to the President, but that he could not give him a leave of absence while action was pending, because of the shortage of officers. He urged that work by the colored refugees was in accordance with his understanding of the recent law of Congress, and said: "Will you or will you not employ a proper portion of the negroes in cutting down the trees which afford cover to the enemy in the front and right of your line? I pray you to observe that if there is anything wrong in the order that wrong is mine, for you have sufficiently protested against it; you are not responsible for it more than the hand that executes it; it can offend neither your political nor moral sense." [39]

Phelps's resignation was accepted, the effective date being August 21, a day on which the Confederate War Department issued an order branding him a felon to be held in confinement for execution in case he should be captured, because he—like Hunter in South Carolina— had armed and drilled slaves.[40] Of more permanent significance was the letter Phelps had caused Lincoln to write, with its solemn assurance of inflexible purpose.

From Vicksburg Flag Officer Davis withdrew his gunboats to Helena, where Curtis was. The newspapers had duly elaborated on that general's long march from northwest Arkansas, with a force reduced by the dispatch of troops to the Army of the Mississippi in front of Corinth. His objective at first had been Little Rock; but because the Confederate strength was gaining in his front, and because his long supply line was subject to interruptions, he had turned toward the Mississippi and Helena. At one time he reported that his trains had to go sixty miles for forage. On July 29, after his force had been raised to about 18,000 by the addition of Hovey's division from Grant's army, Curtis reported that he was ready to move on Little Rock, whether or not gunboats could negotiate the low water of the Arkansas River. Captured enemy mails had made some very interesting reading. General Pike, commanding the Confederate Indians, had tendered his resignation. The letters of this scholarly and poetically inclined general were "gloomy" and expressed the belief that the Indians were "very doubtful" in their devotion to the South. General Hindman, Curtis said, was reporting thirty regiments from Arkansas and some from Louisiana and Texas, but they were poorly armed. In a previous dispatch Curtis had described the great excitement in the state because Texas Rangers were rounding up Arkansas conscripts. As July ended he reported the interception of another package of letters that told of the move of 25,000 to 50,000 Confederates to Chattanooga. Their health was good, but one brigade had mutinied and stacked its arms, while another "forced them to remain rebels." [41]

Helena was a productive center, and a correspondent wrote that

General Pillow "of unenviable notoriety" owned three plantations nearby with three hundred slaves, who had been set free. On the hills overlooking the river was the fine mansion of General Hindman, which was now Federal headquarters. Some of the local people professed low regard for the Confederate commander, who had earned a commission for conspicuous bravery in the War with Mexico, and had practiced law at Helena before he went to Congress in 1856. His slaves had also been freed. Many released Negroes were going out with government teams and escorts, claiming cotton as theirs by right of hard work. Curtis, said the correspondent, permitted the cotton to be taken and sold for the benefit of the Negroes, in case their masters had been convicted of disloyalty. The general himself used fewer words in describing the situation to Halleck:

I have given free papers to negroes who were mustered by their rebel masters to blockade my way to my supplies. These negro prisoners were the most efficient foes I had to encounter; they are now throwing down their axes and rushing in for free papers. It is creating a general stampede in this region of cotton and contempt for Yankees. The slaves are mutinous, but do not abuse their masters. Society is terribly mutilated, and masters and slaves are afraid of famine.

Presently Curtis found his camp so "infested" with rapacious traders, "secessionists, and spies," that he had to restrict cotton buying to a few who could be restrained as "sutlers under military law." [42]

No move against Little Rock was made, though Hovey went as far as Clarendon on the White River, an enemy force retreating across the stream. Cavalry reconnoitered toward the state capital, but there was no encounter. Newly intercepted letters put Hindman at Little Rock with 25,000 well equipped men. Because Curtis's army was in good health, but not strong enough for a move inland, in accordance with permission from Halleck he set to work to fortify Helena with guns from Birds Point, Columbus, and Fort Pillow. An important decision by the High Command was communicated to him on August 8: "It is decided that no land expedition will be moved on Vicksburg at present." [43]

As the Federal column under Curtis was moving toward Helena, Brigadier General John M. Schofield, commanding in Missouri, redeployed much of his force of 17,000 volunteer and militia troops into the southern part of the state to guard Curtis's supply line. Suddenly, about July 20, there was a great outbreak by guerrillas, well planned and directed. Said Schofield in his excellent report on his stewardship of the crucial state, "A large number of Missourians in the rebel army were sent home with commissions to raise and organize troops for the rebel army." From those who were captured or voluntarily surrendered themselves, information about this underground apparatus was ascertained, and Schofield wrote that persons involved reported that from 30,000 to 50,000 Missourians were enrolled, organized, and assembled at designated places, to rise at an appointed signal. Having surprised and eliminated small defending Federal units, they were to cooperate with an invading force from Arkansas.[44]

The outbreak was especially bad in the vicinity of Palmyra, the old trouble spot, and about the time the *Arkansas* was being blown to pieces Lincoln was reading a letter Senator Orville Browning had written from Quincy, Illinois, which began: "Northern Missouri is again in revolt. The condition of affairs there is quite as bad as at any time." It was all due, said Browning, to the removal of John M. Glover and his regiment of cavalry, currently guarding Curtis's base at Rolla. How much may depend upon the character of a single man was made clear by the Senator's tribute to the colonel: "All loyal men love and respect him; all traitors hate and fear him." The evening before a physician from La Grange, Missouri—"no alarmist, no sensationalist"—had come to Browning, asking aid in protecting citizens of his town from "robbery and murder" at the hands of a gang estimated at from 200 to 300 men. Though not so much as a company of troops was available, the men of Illinois were not deaf to the pleas of their neighbors, and at 2:00 A.M. a band of 160 armed citizens had left Quincy and crossed the river. Realizing the burdens of his close friend in the White House, Browning concluded, "God bless, strengthen, and sustain you." [45]

To Schofield it seemed that every Secessionist in North Missouri was taking up arms, and he feared he could not prevent a general insurrection. By calling out the entire state militia, by skillful organization and direction, as well as effective leadership by subordinate officers, Schofield brought the situation under control, though he presently had to meet an effort at invasion from northwest Arkansas. But no fewer than eighty skirmishes occurred in the state during July and August alone. At Kirksville, on August 6, Colonel John McNeil with

1,000 cavalry and six guns decisively defeated the largest of the guerrilla bands—led by Joseph C. Porter—so that by casualties and desertions it was reduced from 3,000 men to 800.[46]

Northern officers had difficulty drawing a line between the Partisan Rangers officially recognized by the Confederate government and the guerrillas it did not nominally encourage, though some Southern officers—notably Price—were active in raising guerrilla bands. No matter by what name he might be called, a man not in uniform could, if his unit was broken and scattered in a contest, hide his weapons and soon be nonchalantly gathering eggs or industriously working in the garden with a hoe fresh from the hands of his accommodating wife. Lacking both discipline and regular supply arrangements, irregular units tended to help themselves to what they wanted. Colonel G. N. Fitch, a Federal who had issued a proclamation about which General Hindman had complained, wrote to the general that his protest ill became one who had authorized the formation of irregular units "to operate at will." Said the colonel, "You must be aware that your captains of tens will soon become little else than highway banditti, more terrible to citizens of your own State than to soldiers and sailors of the United States." In a letter to General Breckinridge, Commander Isaac Brown, the courageous captain of the *Arkansas* and a former officer of the United States Navy, eschewed fancy words and spoke bluntly of "Confederate guerrillas." [47]

While the invading Federals had no Partisan Rangers, they were matching the Confederates by employing Indians, and along with the news of the uprisings in Missouri there came word of the halting of the Indian expedition that had penetrated into the territory of the Cherokee Nation as far as the Arkansas River.

Indians loyal to the Union had fled to Kansas after October 28, 1861, when the Cherokees had finally yielded to the blandishments of Confederate representatives and had cast their lot with the seceding states. Two regiments of Indian Home Guards were formed from the refugees, and these with some 5,000 white troops started southward about the middle of June from the general vicinity of Fort Scott, Kansas. Colonel William Weer, commanding the expedition, was enthusiastic over his native Americans, and on the eve of departure wrote to Brigadier General James G. Blunt, who was directing the recently created Department of Kansas: "To-night they have a grand 'war dance.' They have all taken their medicine and consider themselves bullet-proof." But he had not been on the march very long before he reported: "Sickness and mortality are increasing among the Indians; they seem incapable of endurance." [48]

The expedition pushed on, causing much alarm among the Cherokees who had guessed wrong. Though Weer wrote that his Indians were behaving well, he had to admit that it was difficult "to repress outrages perpetrated after Indian fashion." After some skirmishes Weer, on July 9, was on the Arkansas River twenty-five miles southwest of Tahlequah, Indian Territory, his train far behind due to the rapidity of his march. While Blunt was reporting optimistically to Stanton on the 20th, Colonel Frederick Salomon, of the Ninth Wisconsin, brother of the governor of the state whence the regiment came, was writing to Blunt that he had put Weer in arrest and had taken command of the expedition. His charge that the expedition was threatened by separation from supplies and by enemy movements on the left, and that Weer refused to heed the judgment of a council of war, coincided with a report a correspondent of the *New York Tribune* wrote on July 22, a dispatch not published until August 10 when big headlines told of Pope's battle at Cedar Mountain. The reporter described the coup on the Arkansas as unprecedented, and said it would be called mutiny. But nothing happened to Salomon, who fell back toward Kansas—nothing, except prompt promotion to a brigadiership. Nor did the deposed Weer fare too badly, for he soon had another brigade.[49]

Just about everything in the catalogue of military possibility happened during those hot dry summer months of 1862.

Everything, that is, except a good clear-cut victory for the North. The situation had indeed altered. In May, Horace Greeley, gloating over Farragut's dispatches from New Orleans, had headed an editorial "A Deluge of Victories." By midsummer he was in despair, even before Bragg's bold move had become a dangerous threat. The failure of McClellan at the very gates of Richmond had intensified the feeling that had developed in Congress and throughout the North during the winter and spring. Three days after Lincoln, in mid-May, had set aside General Hunter's order emancipating slaves in Florida, Georgia, and South Carolina, as a usurpation of power, he addressed to the people of the border states a proclamation reminding them that Congress had pledged remuneration for liberated slaves, and saying: "I do not argue; I beseech you to make the arguments yourselves. You cannot, if you would, be blind to the signs of the times." On July 17 he signed with some reluctance—largely because of phraseology—amendments to the Confiscation Act, which constituted a complete reversal of the policy of the government. It went much beyond the new article of war adopted in March, which made a dead letter of Halleck's famous General Order 3 by providing penalties against anyone who would use the armed forces "for the purpose of returning fugitives from service or labor who have escaped. . . ." [50]

The change in public sentiment was well illustrated by a very long letter that Robert Dale Owen wrote to Stanton, and that was given to the press. He was, he said, no radical, and he did not regret that there had been no declaration of emancipation a year before. But he said, "Stand where we are, we cannot; and to go on is less dangerous than to retrace our steps." He desired emancipation to be general, not confined only to "the slaves of Rebels." However, loyal slaveowners were to be compensated. In conclusion, Owen wrote: "I feel assured that final success awaits us in pursuing such a path. And I see no other road out of the darkness." A few days later Horace Greeley addressed his famous appeal to Lincoln, presumptuously heading it "The Prayer of Twenty Millions." To his surprise, Lincoln replied by telegraph on August 22, not exactly meeting the issue Greeley had raised, but skillfully flanking him in memorable words that expressed the principles that had guided him and would continue to do so. No more than the public who read the letters did Greeley know that Lincoln a month before had presented to his Cabinet the draft of a proclamation on emancipation; but on the astute suggestion of Secretary Seward, Lincoln had put it aside, waiting for a Federal victory of such magnitude that the proclamation would not appear to be an act of sheer desperation.[51]

Corinth had one very considerable advantage as headquarters for Grant's District of West Tennessee. It possessed no attractions for reporters. They naturally congregated at Memphis, for "the sights" that Sherman had promised good soldiers could also be enjoyed by gentlemen of the press. The Gayoso Hotel, with accommodations for six hundred, was famous, and although many of the best families had departed, the city that had numbered 23,000 inhabitants in 1860 still had facilities for entertaining journalists when they grew weary with their heavy responsibilities. There was the possibility of diversion even in languid morning hours, for a stroll to the waterfront might reveal a noble steamer arriving or departing, or an ironclad provokingly doing nothing, when it should be shooting at Rebels.

When William Howard Russell, distinguished correspondent of the *Times* of London, visited Memphis in June, 1861, he was amazed by the lofty stores, the warehouses, the rows of shops, and most of all by the handsome buildings on the broad esplanade along the river. Though the American reporters in Memphis in the summer of 1862 may never have written the word "esplanade" and may have had ideas of city comfort and elegance acquired only in Eastern seaboard cities, they knew they were more happily situated than they would be in Corinth, which Russell libelously said consisted of a wooden grogshop and three log shanties, the acropolis being represented by a grocery store.[52]

Sherman towered above the reporters in Memphis in intelligence and incurable honesty; in addition he could use language in a way to excite their envy. This did not save him from being soon in conflict with the press, as he had been previously, in Kentucky. The reporters had to write something and, as Sherman was fighting no battles, his administration was their sole theme. In a long letter on August 1, Albert D. Richardson, one of Greeley's aces, claimed that Sherman was supplying the Confederacy. Salt, medicines, and even ammunition were, he said, passing quite freely through the lines, while Unionists were being discriminated against in favor of the disloyal. Sherman had, the *Tribune* man conceded, eminently won his promotion at Shiloh, but fighting and legislating were quite different things, "and (to characterize it very mildly) the eccentricities of his administration" were working grievous injustice. It is not likely that Richardson appreciated the difficulties of the situation, or even that he was always well informed about matters he reported with such assurance. Two days before his tirade he had revealed how his mind worked. The telegraph office had, he said, been closed because Sherman "did not deem telegraphic communication of sufficient importance to send out a cavalry force and protect the line, though the manager of the telegraph believed two companies would be sufficient." Then Richardson stated that it was rumored that Confederates were moving to plant a battery at old Fort Pillow above Memphis. If they did not do so, said the *Tribune* man, it would be from sheer lack of enterprise, for there was a gap all the way to Grand Junction—a fifty-mile stretch that two companies of horsemen could protect, if Sherman would only let them!

What was needed, according to Richardson, was a "vigorous general, fit for the field." And Greeley's authority on military matters could name him: Frémont would delight the volunteers; Banks would inspire confidence; Lew Wallace "would be sure to hurt someone." [53]

The hot days, however, had some satisfaction for Sherman, for an order came from Grant to arrest and send to the Alton penitentiary the correspondent for the *Chicago Times*. The man wrote a long appeal to Grant and asked Sherman to "stay proceedings" until Grant could be heard from. This Sherman declined to do, explaining to the correspondent that "persons writing over false names were always suspected by honorable persons." To Grant, Sherman said, "I regard all these newspaper harpies as spies and think they could be punished as such." A week later he blistered both reporters and newspapers in a personal letter to the colonel of the Fifth Ohio Cavalry: "Military men are chained to a rock, whilst the vultures are turned loose. We must be silent, whilst our defamers are allowed the widest liberty and license. We dare not speak the truth unless the truth be palatable to the crowd." [54]

CHAPTER II

BUELL, LOGISTICS, AND BRAXTON BRAGG

> Once concentrated, we may move against the enemy wherever
> he puts himself if we are strong enough.   *Buell to Thomas*

In mid-August, Grant lost two divisions of the Army of the Mississippi to Buell. This was no surprise to the Confederates, for Kirby Smith had said in his letter of July 14 to President Davis, "I see by the Northern papers that three divisions of Grant's army are to operate in East Tennessee in connection with Buell's corps." [1]

In reporting to Washington that the divisions were on the way, Grant said reconnaissance far to the south showed the country so dry he did not believe the enemy could attack. But upon Rosecrans's noting that he was now left with a small army to guard the eighty miles of railroad to Decatur, Grant asked Halleck if he might not give it up beyond Tuscumbia. The answer was, however, to try to keep communications open with Buell. Five days later—August 22—Halleck telegraphed that Clarksville, Tennessee, which a Federal colonel had disgracefully surrendered to guerrilla bands on the 18th, must be retaken. Grant replied the same day that such an order had been given to the commander at Fort Donelson "yesterday," and that his chief of staff would go there "to-morrow" with further instructions. But Grant's request that some cavalry be sent to him by Curtis to handle guerrillas in western Tennessee was denied, though Halleck promised, "I will send you more cavalry as soon as we can get it." [2]

From its inception, Washington was enthusiastically behind Buell's thrust toward Chattanooga. In fact, in a telegram of June 11 briefing

Halleck—then still at Corinth—on the situation in Virginia, Stanton said, "The President is greatly delighted with your own contemplated movements mentioned in your telegram two days ago." One must believe that the War Secretary was reporting accurately and that he fully realized his sentence indorsed the stopping of any advance southward in Mississippi, for Halleck had stated he did not intend to pursue the enemy further but would "send all forces not required to hold the Memphis and Charleston Railroad to the relief of Curtis in Arkansas and to East Tennessee," if the plan was approved by the War Department.[3]

It was, of course, expected at the time that Vicksburg could be taken by the Farragut–Butler operation from New Orleans. Thus, with a notable advance from the north on both sides of the Mississippi, one can understand why Lincoln was satisfied to have matters stabilized there for the present, while a strong army was thrown into East Tennessee. That was the region which for upward of a year he had earnestly sought to have occupied, in spite of acknowledged difficulties; and now at last his Western commander was starting a large, well disciplined force eastward. The cutting of the vital railroad that led from Virginia to northern Georgia, and the liberation of Unionists now held in unhappy submission to the Confederacy, seemed to be imminent. It will be recalled that when Halleck received on June 30 the order—soon canceled—to send 25,000 men to the East, he suggested that the Chattanooga expedition "be abandoned or at least be diminished." This must not be done, Lincoln emphasized in his reply, adding, "To take and hold the railroad at or east of Cleveland, in East Tennessee, I think fully as important as the taking and holding of Richmond." [4]

When Halleck on June 9 verbally ordered Buell to march, the objective was not definitely assigned, Buell asking for some leeway in the matter; but two days later Halleck wrote to him that, after considering everything fully, he was satisfied that the "line of operations should be on Chattanooga and Cleveland or Dalton instead of McMinnville." With an eye toward enemy reaction he said, "By moving on Chattanooga you prevent a junction between Smith and Beauregard [who had not yet been relieved by Bragg] and are on the direct line to Atlanta. Smith must abandon East Tennessee or be captured." [5] Though the campaign was far from working out that way, it is notable that Halleck saw, while Buell did not, that it was important to try to interpose his army between the enemy forces and prevent their union.

The four divisions with which Buell started the move were commanded by Brigadier Generals Alexander McD. McCook, William Nelson, Thomas L. Crittenden, and Thomas J. Wood, and had an aggregate present on June 10 of 28,358 officers and men. Each division had three brigades (in general of four regiments) and three batteries, except Crittenden's, which had two brigades and two batteries. While Buell's cavalry brigade numbered only 1,557, he had unbrigaded mounted regiments of nearly double that strength, several of which were on duty in Tennessee. When the order for the movement was given, Wood's division, with elements as far east as Bear Creek, was assisting and protecting eight companies of the First Michigan Engineers and Mechanics, which were rebuilding the railroad. The remaining two companies of the Michigan regiment were with the division of Ormsby Mitchel, which, it may be recalled, had seized Huntsville, Alabama, on April 11.[6] Mitchel was now holding the railroad from Athens around through Huntsville to the vicinity of Stevenson, while he also had troops occupying an advanced position along Battle Creek fifteen miles east of that place. The division of George Thomas had not yet been returned to Buell's control; George Morgan's division was on the eve of starting the move that led to the Confederate evacuation of Cumberland Gap on June 18 with the prompt occupation of that highly strategic position by Morgan's command.

One of the great myths of the war is that Buell's move on Chattanooga failed because Halleck required him to rebuild the Memphis and Charleston Railroad as he advanced. Misled probably by an exaggerated statement in the long paper that Buell presented to the Military Commission investigating his campaign, and not having before it the important dispatches sent at the time, the Commission declared that repair of the road had made a prompt advance impossible. While Halleck magnified the role the line eastward had played in supplying Buell, he was entirely correct when he wrote in his indorsement upon the Commission's report that Buell had not been delayed by repairing the railroad.[7]

The divisions of McCook and Crittenden crossed the Tennessee River at Florence, marched as rapidly as they could on the road through Athens, and did no work whatsoever on the railroad. Nelson's division, after making some repairs on the line near Iuka, followed those of McCook and Crittenden without any interval of time. Wood's division alone advanced along the railroad, one of its three brigades aiding and protecting the engineers, and it arrived at Decatur

THE REGION OF BUELL'S ADVANCE FROM CORINTH

only two days after the head of the other column had passed through Athens. This completed the repair of the road, and it is impossible to believe that Buell initially protested Halleck's requirement that he put it in condition. In a dispatch to Mitchel on June 12 from his headquarters near Corinth, Buell said, "I expect the road will be repaired between this point and Decatur in a week." No less optimistic was his chief of staff, Colonel James B. Fry, when he replied on the same day to a message from Brigadier General Jeremiah T. Boyle in Louisville. After the Battle of Shiloh, Boyle had been sent back to Kentucky where he was now military governor, and he had just asked for the return of his old brigade to help keep order in the Bluegrass commonwealth. Said Fry with regard to Buell's pending operations, "It is expected that they will effectually quiet the rebellious element in Kentucky and Tennessee and render the command in Kentucky secondary and unimportant." [8]

On this same June 12 Buell informed Halleck that he expected McCook and Crittenden to begin crossing at Florence on the 16th and that he hoped they would "get over in three days." But the large ferry that had to be constructed was not finished until the 22nd, and then Buell was immobilized by fear of an attack from 10,000 Confederates reported southeast of Iuka. Not until the 24th did he inform Halleck that a cavalry reconnaissance had found no signs of the enemy except small bodies of enemy horsemen. "It appears," said the unabashed general, "that these have everywhere told that they were the advance guard of a large force, and no doubt in this way the reports of an advance on this line have gained such general circulation as to give them color of truth." The scare being over, Buell could add, "My troops are now moving steadily forward." [9]

The 27th found Buell at Athens; McCook had already passed through en route for Huntsville; Crittenden was camping four miles to the east of the town and Nelson three to the west. While the Elk River—wide and rather deep at the time—had been forded with little difficulty, a failure was discovered in supply arrangements instituted at Florence. From that place a train of two hundred wagons had been dispatched on the 20th to Reynolds, ten miles north of Pulaski on the Nashville-Decatur railroad. These would augment Mitchel's wagons which were hauling supplies around breaks in the line, caused principally by the enemy's destruction of the 700-foot bridge over Elk River and the very long and high trestle near the tunnel north of Athens. Guarding the wagon train was the Second Indiana Cavalry, commanded by Colonel Edward M. McCook. (A cousin of General McCook, he was one of the Scotch-Irish "fighting McCooks" from Ohio, whose devotion to the Union was shown by the service of eight brothers, their father, and five first cousins.) While the actual rail breaks were confined to a stretch some twenty-five miles long, McCook had a forty-mile trip each way in order to use a good ford over Elk River and to avoid the high hills. [10]

In accordance with previous instructions, Buell had expected to find 200,000 rations for men and 150,000 for animals at Athens. But no forage whatever was found. Army service trains that had moved with the troops, including the 100-wagon ammunition train, were unloaded and the wagons added to those hauling from Reynolds, until McCook had about 450. On reaching Huntsville, Fry telegraphed to Captain J. D. Bingham, Nashville quartermaster, rather sharply and said, "Send forward grain." Buell, however, took no notice of the disappointment in his first dispatch to Halleck, likewise sent on June 29: "I arrived here yesterday afternoon, and am engaged in preparations for advancing, the principal of which is the means of crossing," referring of course to reaching the south bank of the Tennessee somewhere in the vicinity of Bridgeport.[11]

The next day Buell informed Halleck that the engineers had finished repairing the railroad to Decatur and were awaiting orders. This dispatch alone shows how false is the claim that Buell had been delayed by repairs to the railroad. Recalling that McCook and Crittenden had been held up for a week by the building of the ferry at Florence and by Buell's alarm over the 10,000 imaginary Confederates, his statement to the Commission that the opening of the railroad "occupied the *troops* [italics supplied] until about the last of June"[12] was hardly ingenuous.

The request from Buell to Halleck that the engineer regiment be now released to his full control was immediately granted, in accord with Halleck's statement on June 12, "Rest assured that I shall do everything in my power to facilitate your movement."[13]

Neither Bingham nor commissary officer Robert Macfeely at Nashville nor quartermaster Thomas Swords at Louisville was in a position to meet the sudden demand for supplies that Buell had placed on them on June 14. Some two weeks later, when troops had to go on half-rations, Fry would reproach Macfeely and tell him he had warned him on June 2 to be ready. If Fry had reread the telegram he had sent to Macfeely on June 3, he would have seen that while he had told the latter to see how supplies could be brought forward, he had specifically told him not to transport any to Nashville for fear of alerting the enemy to Buell's impending move. On the 11th Bingham telegraphed to Fry that the Cumberland was falling and that there were only three and a half feet of water over the shoals below the city, with the prospect that in a few days there would be but thirty inches. The only two boats running were expected on the 14th with a paltry hundred tons of freight. Then on the 16th Bingham warned, "The Louisville and Nashville Railroad has not enough rolling stock to bring forward all the supplies."[14] Thus as June ended we find Buell expecting to sustain his army of nearly 40,000 men and hundreds of animals, by three hundred miles of railroad, on which, in addition to a severe shortage of engines and cars, there was a forty-mile wagon haul. Yet at Eastport, only eight miles from Iuka, which was only seventy miles by repaired road from Decatur, there was an abundance of what he needed.

That those seventy miles of track were open had in the end been due to an explicit order by Halleck, for although Buell had initially spoken to Mitchel approvingly about repairing the line, he had, as was often his habit, shifted his position. In a long message to Halleck, on June 17 he said the road had been greatly overrated, being not only useless for transporting troops but neither essential nor the most convenient means for supplying troops in Tennessee. Actually, the question with which he was faced was that of supplying troops in Alabama, for practically all of the route to Chattanooga lay in that state. Halleck did not accept the proposal to halt the repairs, though it was not until the 21st that he told Buell he was not satisfied with the progress of the work, and stated peremptorily that "the road to Decatur must be put in running order with all possible dispatch." [15]

On the 24th Buell gave Thomas (partially released to him) instructions about guarding the railroad, and the next day, in response to a specific inquiry from Halleck as to rolling equipment, he reported that a locomotive and nine cars which had been off the track had reached Tuscumbia "yesterday," and that he also had an engine and six cars that had been landed at South Florence. Though he pronounced the second locomotive positively unsafe, he said it had been patched—all the motive power captured in the vicinity of Corinth had had to be repaired—and had been "put to light use between this place and Decatur." Then, he complained, "We have been obliged to detail men from these commands to run these trains." [16]

Buell felt differently about that stretch of track and those two trains when he found that Swords, Bingham, and Edward McCook had not done the impossible. On June 29—the day Fry reproached Bingham—Fry directed Thomas to put at least 150 wagons at work hauling forage from Eastport to Iuka for forwarding to Decatur, adding, "The two trains of cars you have will just about accomplish the work." Then bad news came from Tuscumbia. All three of the engines Thomas had found upon arriving that morning had broken down (where the third one came from is not clear, but hardly matters). The next day Buell personally telegraphed to Thomas: "We are without forage. Apply for other engines, stating the importance, and let me know with what result. If you fail in that, use relays of mules or horses to bring trains through." In a message to Halleck asking if other engines could not be spared, Buell said, "I made other arrangements for provisions, but calculated on the Iuka road for forage and we are suffering for it." Fry on his part, with thoughts turned all the way to the Ohio, telegraphed to Swords, "Instead of 200 tons it will be necessary for the Louisville and Nashville and Nashville and Decatur Railroads to transport 300 tons a day." [17]

The evidence is strongly against Buell's having intended to draw forage from Iuka for anyone but Thomas after he left Florence.[18] It augured poorly for his campaign when he complained about detailing a few soldiers to operate trains. It was worse when he resorted to a false statement to his superior because he found himself in difficulty.

July began as cheerlessly as June had ended. Halleck could furnish no more engines; two that had been repaired had "been smashed by guerrillas." Almost tauntingly, Thomas telegraphed, "If I can get an engine to-night or to-morrow morning I will send you a train of forage at once." [19] (He evidently did not think well of trying to haul the train by horses or mules.) No way was now left to obtain the forage except by taking an engine across the river at Decatur and sending for it.[20]

Though he had engineers who asked for work, Buell telegraphed to Thomas: "The transfer of engines from this side of the river to the other would cost more trouble and time than it would be worth. By the time an engine can be put on the track our dependence on Eastport will have ceased." He was, however, still in hopes that Halleck would obtain another locomotive somewhere. The next day—July 2, the day a telegram arrived for Mitchel to report in Washington, much to his own and Buell's satisfaction—Buell telegraphed to Halleck that an engineer officer had told him it would take three days to transfer an engine; and the necessary rope was wanting. However, *if Halleck desired,* Buell would have an engine carried across; but he informed his superior that there was "scarcely a sufficiency" of engines to meet requirements north of the river.[21] Once more the clear, indubitable record is almost unbelievable. But this was just the beginning of an unbelievable campaign that still had nearly four months to run.

On July 4, perhaps as a salute to Independence, Buell ordered that an engine be transferred. The work proceeded slowly, for on the 9th Fry received from Colonel Abel D. Streight, commanding a regiment in Wood's division, now camped north of the river, a message informing him that on arriving at Decatur early the preceding afternoon, he had found the necessary boat only "partially framed." Being a good expediter, the colonel could add, "Since then we have completed the boat, launched it, and she has made a successful trip with her valuable cargo." Two days before the engine *Sam Cruse* made its short water voyage to then dash westward to get Thomas's waiting cars, Buell repeated Fry's injunction to Swords about the necessity of increasing railroad capacity to three hundred tons. His message ended: "We are living from day to day on short supplies and our operations are completely crippled." [22]

More than two-thirds of the specified tonnage was needed for animal subsistence, and the question arises: Was not forage available locally? One of Buell's leading defense witnesses was Lieutenant Colonel Francis Darr, his chief commissary officer, and he testified to scouring the country with but small results. Much, of course, depended upon locality and the enterprise of individual officers. While Crittenden reported on July 1 that he had been unable to procure forage near Athens, Wood said in a dispatch to Fry on the 10th from Mooresville (nearly across the river from Decatur), "I telegraphed you to-day to have a train sent down to move some of the corn which my command has collected here." [23] Wood apparently had more than enough for his own division for a few days at least.

Horses must have been getting along with much less than the book allowed: fourteen pounds of hay and twelve oats a day. The lowly mules, apparently discriminated against with a nine-pound allowance of grain, may have been doing better—they hauled the grain; and though their drivers might speak harshly to them, they would be remorseful and indulgent at mealtime. Buell could have read with profit what Halleck had written fifteen years before about the difficulty of subsisting animals during a campaign, precisely because of the difficulty of transporting forage: "The commanding officer of troops should always use his best endeavors to obtain his forage by purchase of the inhabitants, or by requisition on the local authorities." Forage for animals would produce less distress among noncombatant inhabitants than subsisting men on the country, and certificates should always be given when there was seizure rather than cash purchase.[24]

But Buell had not marched with the intention of using local resources as much as possible, even for animals. He objected to forceful requisitions in general, not only because it was troublesome and tended to injure discipline, but because he held the view that a mild policy might win Southerners to the Union cause. When the Louisville commissary officer suggested on July 16 that dependence be placed on local flour and beef, Fry snapped back: "What do you mean by not seeing your way clear if we use hard bread and salt meat. . . . We only eat about 75 tons a day." The country could not furnish flour, he said; and if it could, there was no necessity for depending upon it. Two days later General Sooy Smith sent Fry an extensive list of supplies that could be obtained near Tullahoma within ten days and said he would have them collected. Buell replied approvingly, except as to the 2,500 bushels of wheat, which he said he did not want. But four days later he told Smith to buy the thousand barrels of flour he had reported for sale at Manchester. Smith was not on detail to hunt provisions. He was in charge of guarding bridges, but kept his eyes and ears open—and probably, like soldiers with less rank, spent some of his spare time thinking of past meals and possible future ones. To the Manchester flour he soon added two hundred barrels from a mill near Tullahoma. In the fall Braxton Bragg not only supported his army in that general area, but exported supplies.[25] In July, however, the year's corn crop was still green, and its availability for forage was lessened.

By the middle of the month supplies had ceased to reach Nashville by river, except for a trickle transferred to small boats and hauled over the shoals. On the 12th Buell reported to Halleck that the difficulty of getting freight across the river at Decatur and the likelihood of interruption of the railroad back to Iuka made the line "useless as a channel of supplies for this army." Still, he pronounced it "highly desirable and even important to keep the road open as a means of communication and as a line of outposts." Anticipating Halleck's permission, Thomas had been ordered to send a train over the line twice daily, with a guard of forty men equipped to repair wires and minor breaks in the track. As all bridges had to be protected, it was a costly road to operate for the limited purpose Buell contemplated. Why the engineers had not been promptly put to work improving the ferry at Decatur, which Buell later described as "very inefficient," is difficult to understand. The ferry was an improvisation by Captain John B. Yates, who commanded the two companies of engineers that had been with Mitchel. Nothing was apparently done to better it until August

23, when the colonel of the engineer regiment was directed to hasten to Decatur with a company to put the ferry in the most efficient condition practicable—and to "bring tools if required." [26]

In early July the bulk of the engineers were put to work repairing the Nashville–Decatur railroad. A month previously Mitchel had had all of his mechanics on that line while a force based on Nashville repaired the road north of the break. On June 11 Buell had ordered both groups of workmen transferred to the crucial route through Murfreesboro to Stevenson because it could be completed first. But about July 4—unwisely it would seem—he reversed priority.[27]

And what about preparations to cross the river, of which Buell had spoken in his first telegram to Halleck from Huntsville? On July 1 he had closed a dispatch with the words, "We are working on a bridge," and the previous day Mitchel had in fact ordered Yates to put all sawmills between Huntsville and Stevenson at work to provide lumber for pontoons and a bridge floor. Yates was a defense witness for Buell before the Commission, and after referring to Mitchel's order to open mills he said, "But it was impossible to get the men to work at them; they were afraid of guerrillas running in upon them at night." To this he added the amazing statement that "it was considered dangerous to start" the mills. Two men, he said, had been taken prisoners after one mill had been put in operation. Yates's statements were made under oath and upon questioning by Buell, who did not bring out that any effort was made to give protection to workmen, or that he seized and operated the mills instead of merely detailing men to assist, as Yates indicated was done.

Only two of the five mills in the region were put in operation, for, according to Yates, there were not only too many guerrillas but there was too little water. Other troubles also arose, for it was necessary on one occasion to send to Nashville for a circular saw. The colonel of the engineer regiment was, Yates admitted under cross-examination, dissatisfied with his slowness in starting sawmills, though he never complained of the manner in which he operated the railroad. [28]

When a few guerrillas could hamper sawmill operations, and Buell could calmly accept it as a valid excuse, it is not difficult to predict what would happen to his operations when the enemy appeared in force at Chattanooga.

Mitchel had expected that troops would be sent forward by railroad as soon as Buell reached operating track, for the situation on his eastern front had become threatening before Buell left Florence. Encouraged, apparently, by the prospects of Buell's advance, Mitchel

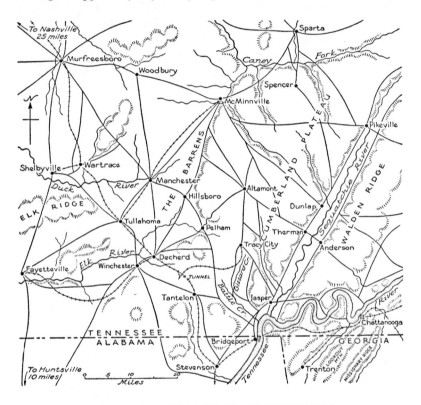

THE HARD APPROACH TO CHATTANOOGA

had told him on June 12 that he would occupy Jasper, and he soon had a partial brigade under Colonel Joshua Sill, a regular officer, in that important position. Then on the 21st he forwarded to Buell a dispatch that Sill had sent him at noon saying he was falling back to Battle Creek because the enemy had seemingly crossed the Tennessee in some force. While Sill stated that it might be well to accumulate more force at Stevenson, he was not in a panic, for he said, "If we ascertain that we are mistaken as to the enemy strength we will again advance; the distance is only 5 miles." In commenting, Mitchel pointed out that if he were compelled to fall back from Stevenson, the bridge he had just finished fourteen miles west of the town and the one he had started to rebuild at its edge would have to be again replaced. He concluded: "I have no troops at any point that can be spared to re-enforce Colonel Sill. Cannot you possibly send at once a brigade forward to Decatur and I will send them by rail to Stevenson." [29]

Though some commanders would have had a brigade on a forced march for Athens within a few hours, Buell replied the next day about "the reported movements of the enemy in this quarter," and bade Mitchel collect his detachments from every point where they could be spared. Then he proclaimed: "It seems to me far more probable that the enemy has crossed with a small than with a large force. The latter could retreat less easily before the superior force he must soon expect to meet. His object is, I think, to destroy your works." The reasoning that he proffered Mitchel would have applied much better to himself, for a Confederate force advancing toward Iuka would have been in immediate peril. Halleck, upon receiving from Nelson a copy of the message which had frightened Buell, not only quickly released Thomas to Buell, but ordered Rosecrans to move a division eastward by the Jacinto road to strike the reported Confederate force in the flank, promising more aid if that did not suffice.[30]

On that troubled Sunday word went back to Buell from Mitchel that a train had been fired upon and wires cut between Huntsville and Stevenson. Mitchel was sending an armed train to protect the line. The next day he reported he was shifting ammunition from other batteries to stock Sill's guns and was determined to hold the Battle Creek position if possible. He seemed to be doing all he could for himself, for he said, "Our re-enforcements will commence to go forward tomorrow from here [Huntsville]." Informed by Buell that he would probably have some troops in Athens by June 25—which would probably have been the case but for the subsequent alarm—Mitchel ended a long dispatch on the 24th in a manner that showed he thought Buell realized the aid railroads could be in war: "Please give me all the notice you can, that we may be ready to transport your troops." [31]

But McCook's men trudged on over the hot, dusty road. On Independence Day Fry directed Brigadier General Richard W. Johnson, temporarily commanding the division, then in camp west of Huntsville, to take up the march for Stevenson the next day. It looked like a conditioning exercise for new recruits, for he said, "March at the rate of about ten miles a day." Four days later a brigade was picked up by rail and carried forward to guard and assist in opening the railroad to Nashville.[32]

That same day—July 8—Buell received a disturbing telegram from Halleck. The enemy was moving troops from Tupelo and Okolona. While there was doubt as to where they were going, some believed them bound for Chattanooga. After stating that a few days might remove the uncertainty, Halleck said:

> The President telegraphs that your progress is not satisfactory and that you should move more rapidly. The long time taken by you to reach Chattanooga will enable the enemy to anticipate you by concentrating a large force to meet you.
>
> I communicate his views, hoping that your movements hereafter may be so rapid as to remove all cause of complaint, whether well founded or not.[33]

While Lincoln may not have appreciated some of the difficulties in Buell's operation, he would seem to have been intuitively conscious of the "about 10 miles a day" order.

It required a six-word dispatch from Halleck on the 11th, "I want to hear from you," to bring a long answer from Buell on the same day. It was written in good temper and gave a picture of his situation and plans. Buell also said, "The advance on Chattanooga must be made with the means of acting in force; otherwise it will either fail or prove a profitless and transient prize." While he elaborated on the number of wagons required to make the forty-mile haul around the break in the railroad, he did not even intimate that he had lost so much as an hour because of repairing the Memphis and Charleston Railroad west of Decatur. After saying, "The dissatisfaction of the President pains me exceedingly," Buell closed by requesting that his dispatch be communicated to him.[34]

The next day the sun seemed to be breaking through. "The road to Stevenson will be done to-day and trains can come through to-morrow. Send supplies to Stevenson as rapidly as possible," said Fry in a dispatch to the hard-working Nashville commissary and quartermaster officers. From now on, mere subsistence should not be controlling. Furthermore, there arrived sometime on the 12th a dispatch from Halleck indicating that Buell had written effectively:

I can well understand the difficulties you have to encounter and also the impatience in Washington. In the first place they have no conception of the length of our lines of defense and of operations. In the second place the disasters before Richmond have worked them up to boiling heat.

Halleck did not state that he was transmitting Buell's message as requested, but said, "I will see that your movements are properly explained to the President." Then he asked for all information that could be given of the enemy.[35]

When it came, the news was startling, for it told of John Morgan's first raid into Kentucky.

To George Morgan at Cumberland Gap, with whom there was swift telegraphic communication, Fry sent an excellent message. Lack of cavalry in Kentucky rendered it difficult to check the raider, and George Morgan must look to his own line of communications. The telegram had a striking ending: "Morgan is said to have 2,000 cavalry; he probably has not to exceed 1,000."[36] Had such ability to appraise the enemy continued to prevail at the headquarters of the Army of the Ohio, all might have been well.

Then came Sunday the 13th and the capitulation of the Federal force at Murfreesboro to Nathan Bedford Forrest after his ugly threat to "have every man put to the sword." The blow did not prevent Buell from ordering Crittenden to advance to Battle Creek, from where the men of Mitchel's division—now under Lovell H. Rousseau—had evidently been withdrawn and replaced by Milo Hascall's brigade of Wood's division. "Economize with your supplies to the last degree," was Buell's injunction when he informed Crittenden of the blow against Murfreesboro and the threat to the line of communications. "I march in the morning at 2 o'clock for Battle Creek," was Crittenden's assurance that he would heed the order to reach that place "early."[37]

The next day, quite as if the pontoons might soon be ready, Fry telegraphed to a Cincinnati captain to send calkers and materials to Louisville, specifying that they go by rail. To the adjutant at Nashville he telegraphed, "We are living from hand to mouth"; and apparently forgetting that a little over a month previously Bingham had sent word about the very low and dwindling Cumberland, he said, "Tell Colonel Swords to use the river from Louisville to Nashville and get plenty of boats." When almost simultaneously word came that supplies in Nashville were exhausted, appeal was made to Thomas to send some to Decatur; and an exasperated Fry telegraphed to Swords at Louisville on the 15th: "The general is discouraged at having to urge this matter. The army will starve unless there is more activity in throwing forward supplies." Swords had an explanation—as quartermasters usually do. The railroad had been wholly occupied by General Boyle in moving troops to forestall John Morgan; furthermore, two collisions during the past week had crippled four locomotives.[38]

A telegram that arrived on the 15th from Colonel John Miller, commanding at Nashville, eased matters considerably. Forrest had retired to McMinnville, and Miller made an excellent appraisal: "They were not over 2,000 strong." Now there was no danger of an attack on Nashville, Franklin, or Columbia, as had been feared. Casting up the situation for Halleck, Buell said, "I had taken the precaution to place some twelve regiments on that route, until it should be securely established." But he ended with a touch of resolution, "We will go to work again."[39]

Still no order went to Nashville to have civilian officials require the bringing in of supplies, or to levy on the countryside.

Under Mitchel's régime local resources had been called upon when John Morgan's raid on Pulaski in May had destroyed a supply train. Colonel John Beatty, who was on duty in Huntsville, wrote approvingly in his diary, "Our boys find Alabama hams better than Uncle Sam's side meat and fresh bread better than hard crackers." Quickly and unfavorably impressed by Buell's conciliatory policy, Beatty recorded with pleasure that Rousseau discarded it under Buell's very nose. On the 18th he wrote gloomily that the star of the Confederacy appeared to be rising, and that he doubted not but that it would continue to ascend until the rose-water policy then being followed gave way to one more determined and vigorous. A week later Andrew Johnson, military governor of Tennessee, would write to Stanton from Nashville, "I hope the Secretary of War will cause the commanding general of this department to issue an order similar to that of General Pope in Virginia in regard to subsisting, &c., on the enemy." Buell's view that a mild, benevolent policy would swing Southerners away from the Confederacy was vigorously denied before the Commission by William G. Brownlow, the strong Union journalist-parson of Knoxville: "They attribute our forebearance toward them to cowardice and think we are afraid of them. It disheartens and discourages the Unionists." [40]

It was July 29 when the first train steamed at last into Stevenson on the direct line from Nashville, though, except for the change of railroad-repair priority, some could doubtless have come before Forrest's blow. On the train there were 210,000 rations. A comparable amount followed the next day, and troops went back on full allowances. Even before Halleck had left Corinth for Washington on the 17th, Thomas had been released to join Buell, and the end of the month found him en route to Decherd. In the meantime Nelson and Wood had taken positions at McMinnville and places on or near the important rail line. McCook had joined Crittenden at Battle Creek and had taken over command. Marching had taken its toll of leather, and he telegraphed to Fry, "If you can, for God's sake send me all the shoes to spare and at once." [41]

In addition to Thomas there came out of the West warnings of Bragg's move to Chattanooga: first on the 20th from Grant; then more definitely on the 28th from Rosecrans, as a result of Sheridan's capture of the mail bag. As July ended, McCook sent army headquarters a portentous report:

One of my men just in. General Bragg arrived at Chattanooga Tuesday evening [the 29th]. On the same evening two trains came in with soldiers. Railroad agent says he has orders to furnish cars for 30,000 as fast as he can. One brigade left for Knoxville on Tuesday evening. No crossing at Chattanooga. The re-enforcements were ordered to cross the river. Order countermanded. The river above Chattanooga will soon be fordable.

McCook's agent had good contacts: Bragg, it may be recalled, had told Cooper that he would take 35,000 effectives from Mississippi. [42]

Here was a new and urgent problem for the new General in Chief, who only four days before had handed Stanton a memorandum about his visit of investigation to the idling Army of the Potomac. What he told the President and the Secretary about Buell's prospects and the over-all situation in the West cannot be known, but the collapse of McClellan's thrust at Richmond must have made the High Command still more eager for success in East Tennessee. The reply that went to Huntsville was prompt, brief, and suggestive of an unyielding purpose: "I have directed General Grant to be prepared to re-enforce you if you should find the enemy too strong at Chattanooga." [43]

A week passed and Buell received a sharp prod, brought on by his unwisely suggesting Sherman as commander for a district composed of Kentucky, Ohio, Indiana, and Illinois that Halleck had just told him was being discussed. Sherman was fit, Buell said in reply; and he could spare no one from his own command. His willingness to deprive Grant of his best subordinate may have nettled Halleck, who answered with an immediate No. That would have made a good dispatch in itself, but Halleck took occasion to remind Buell of the "great dissatisfaction" with his slowness. Now he pointed it up: "It is feared that the enemy will have time to concentrate his entire army against you." [44]

Buell's prompt reply contained the news that the railroad from Nashville to Decatur was now open, the first train having passed the day before. In speaking of the enemy's facility for movement, he said, "If I could have reached Chattanooga in two weeks I should probably have met the same force as now." [45] Whether Beauregard would or could have made in late June the fast transfer of troops that Bragg made beginning in late July is very much open to question. But the statement destroys any remaining claim that Buell blamed his predicament on Halleck's requirement that he rebuild the railroad west of Decatur.

Having disposed of bygones, Buell got down to the future in a message the next day—August 7. He put the enemy strength in East Tennessee at 60,000, though he said he was prepared to find it less. His own force, exclusive of George Morgan, numbered 46,000 effectives; but because of the necessity of protecting Nashville and the railroads he had but 31,000 men for a forward move. These could be increased to 36,000 if the road from Nashville through Athens to Decatur were given up. The lumber was all cut for the pontoons he expected to use near Bridgeport, and for four days the mechanics had been working on them, after being previously engaged on roads. Buell proposed to march on Chattanooga "at the earliest possible day," unless he learned the enemy's strength rendered it imprudent. No objection can be made to that qualification, but it is to be noted that he followed it with a sentence to which no strings were tied: "If, on the other hand, he should cross the river I shall attack him, and I do not doubt that we shall defeat him." [46]

The pontoon situation was worse even than Buell had indicated.

On the 10th Fry telegraphed to the Nashville quartermaster that nails purchased three weeks before had not arrived, nor had the oakum and the pitch. Quick-acting Bingham soon replied that he had found the nails and oakum, and the next train would take them to Stevenson. But the pitch had eluded him. He had heard, however, that eight barrels of it were at some station "between here and Huntsville," and the train conductor would look for them. All this makes it appear as if the engineer officer was exaggerating a little when he told the commission that the delay in the pontoons—finished about August 20—was solely due to the inadequacy of the sawmills. Buell on his part made the revealing statement, "I do not pretend that the failure to complete the bridge in time was the cause of my not moving to Chattanooga." [47] Apparently he had not desired to throw a bridge before he had a large accumulation of supplies. A strongly held bridgehead might have made Bragg think Buell was a general with resolution and not one who could easily be induced to retreat.

On the day after Bingham found the nails and oakum—August 11—Buell learned from Thomas that Nelson—who was operating under Thomas's supervision—had on the 10th sent a flag of truce to Sparta, where it was ascertained that John Morgan had left the town on the morning of the 9th, taking the road to Kentucky with 1,800 cavalry and four guns. Word was flashed to Swords and Symonds at Louisville to push forward supplies to the full capacity of the railroad (a very questionable thing to do at that moment), for Morgan probably meant to strike again at the line where his July efforts had been frustrated.[48] Such indeed was his purpose, and this time he was to be amazingly successful.

In the early morning of the 12th he captured the five companies guarding Gallatin, the Federal investigating officer reporting, "Not a gun was fired by any of those to whom the safety of the command was intrusted, and everything goes to show that they were either asleep or shamefully neglecting their duty." Two bridges and thirty cars, most of them containing forage, were destroyed, while 125 men and upward of 100 badly needed horses were captured. But the real catastrophe was the seizure of the tunnel seven miles north of the town and the burning of its timber work by pushing blazing cars into its interior, so that the dirt caved in. Morgan, however, did not get off without being hurt, for Colonel Miller brought a force from Nashville by rail and attacked him. With no injury to his own men, Miller killed six of Morgan's, including two captains, one with the well known name of Breckinridge.[49]

Said the jubilant Braxton Bragg in reporting the Gallatin success to Richmond: "The first blow in General Smith's expedition." [50]

Well could Jefferson Davis feel that the plan that Kirby Smith had described on August 11 in a long letter from Knoxville was starting auspiciously. Pleased over the receipt of Bragg's approval of his suggested strike toward Lexington, Smith said: "My advance is made in the hope of permanently occupying Kentucky. It is a bold move, offering brilliant results, but will be accomplished only with hard fighting, and must be sustained by constant re-enforcements." Five days later George Morgan broke the news in a short dispatch to Fry: "Smith is advancing by way of Big Creek and Huntsville [Tennessee]." A previous telegram had prepared the way for this announcement and had said the invasion would probably comprise 12,000 or 15,000 men in all. But Morgan was not disturbed; he could stay where he was for five weeks, while Smith could not possibly remain in his rear for three. Buell passed the news of the 16th to Halleck, directed Morgan to hold his position and trust to other troops to open his communications, told Grant that Kirby Smith was headed for Kentucky or Nashville, with other offensive movements to be expected, and queried about the two promised divisions. At 5:00 P.M. Grant replied that the divisions of Paine and Davis were being sent. His notable readiness to meet another's wishes, even when it was to his own disadvantage, was revealed by the ending, "Also have ordered block-houses to be built at principal bridges." Even the signature was designed to cheer the troubled Buell. The customary initials and subscribed rank were omitted, and it was just a friendly "Grant." [51]

Buell administered first aid to Kentucky by dispatching Nelson, a major general since July 17—as were also McCook and Crittenden—to take command, the superseded Boyle being assuaged with the assurance that there would be "work enough and honor enough for all." Doubtless more rank was needed in the Bluegrass State, and Buell evidently thought his choice a good one, for he ended his second letter of instructions to Nelson: "The credit of the selection will be mine. The honor of success will be yours." As a matter of fact, Nelson's tendency toward hasty and harsh language poorly qualified him to deal with the intense alarm and excitement certain to develop. Only four days before Buell ordered Nelson northward, John Beatty had put him down in his diary as "ardent, loud-mouthed, and violent," while Rosecrans in Mississippi would presently speak in a letter to Halleck of "Bully Nelson." [52]

After some difficulty Nelson reached Louisville late in the morning of August 23, a mere hour after Major General Horatio G. Wright had reached the city to take command of the new Department of the Ohio, in accordance with orders from Washington. Nelson's appeal to Halleck as to what he should do brought instructions to remain and give assistance to Wright. Generals, however, were not enough; six days previously Halleck had asked Governor Morton of Indiana and Governor Tod of Ohio to send troops to Kentucky as speedily as possible, as Buell and Boyle had similarly requested on the 15th. Answers were prompt. Unless disappointed in clothing and camp equipage, Ohio would send four or five regiments by the 20th. Morton was starting 1,000 men that night, 7,000 "to-morrow," while 16,000 in camp would be available when armed. Shortage of officers was troubling Morton. For some regiments he had appointed temporary officers of experience, but he asked Stanton, "Can Lieutenant-Colonel King, Nineteenth Regulars, have leave of absence for this purpose— say fifteen days? Will you answer at once?" [53] The governor wanted green men at least to be well led.

Halleck had quickly passed to Buell the word that Tod would send five regiments by the 20th. But this cheering sentence was followed by two of unmitigated harshness: "So great is the dissatisfaction here at the apparent want of energy and activity in your district, that I was this morning notified to have you removed. I got the matter delayed till we could hear further of your movements." Buell's prompt reply does him credit. He asked that Halleck not interpose on his behalf. On the contrary, he requested that he be relieved if dissatisfaction could not cease, saying, "My position is far too important to be occupied by an officer on sufferance. I have no desire to stand in the way of what may be deemed necessary for the public good." He closed:

We are occupying lines of great depth. They are swarming with the enemy's cavalry and can only be protected by cavalry. It is impossible to overrate the importance of this matter. Three months ago I represented to the Department the necessity for eight more regiments of cavalry in Tennessee and Kentucky.[54]

Halleck's message at least caused Buell to try to use more effectively the troops he had. At the head of a special force he put Brigadier General Richard W. Johnson, then commanding one of McCook's brigades. Kentucky-born, Johnson had graduated from West Point in 1849, the outbreak of the war finding him in the Fifth U.S. Cavalry. Five cavalry regiments were now put under him, as well as an infantry brigade and a battery at Murfreesboro, with no fewer than one hundred wagons to transport "infantry rapidly or for other contingencies." His rendezvous point was Murfreesboro and his mission was to "protect Nashville, and destroy the enemy's cavalry and guerrillas." He was given a nice compliment by Buell, doubtless in part an exhortation: "The army will feel that its communications are safe with your energy and judicious management, my confidence in which has induced me to trust to you this all-important duty." But seldom has disaster struck more swiftly.[55]

On the 19th Johnson, at Cookeville with about 700 troopers from four regiments, learned that Morgan with perhaps 800 men was at Hartsville. He moved against Morgan the next day, only to discover that the Confederates had returned to Gallatin. On the 21st he pressed on, and in the encounter that resulted Johnson at first had the advantage. But the superiority of a single large well-knit and experienced regiment over a new agglomeration of four small commands soon showed, and Johnson was not only forced back, but he and a part of his command were captured in an effort to reach the south side of the Cumberland.

The victory stimulated the secession sentiment of the community, and John Morgan wrote: "Recruits are daily and hourly arriving. The population seems at last to be thoroughly aroused and to be determined on resistance." But he had to say to his men: "We have to mourn some brave and dear comrades. Their names will remain in our hearts; their fame outlives them." Before the fight on the Hartsville road, Morgan had destroyed every bridge to within eight miles of Nashville, and he considered that his earlier work on the tunnel had been so good that it could never be repaired, "the rocks having fallen in every direction." [56] In delivering this judgment, John Morgan was venturing beyond his field of competence.

With the Cumberland reduced to little more than a creek and with the railroad cut, Buell would be forced to live on the country as soon as accumulated supplies were exhausted. But even before Morgan had blocked the tunnel, and probably in anticipation of the order he would write to put into effect the recent Confiscation Act, Halleck had directed Buell to take on forced requisition such supplies as the country afforded, "causing receipts in all cases to be given, the payment or non-payment to be determined on hereafter." Here the new point was the possibility that receipts might not be honored. The general order that followed a week later, on August 15, drew a clear line between taking property for public purposes and pillage for private gain or use, the latter being punishable by death, as was the entering of a "private house for that purpose." Accurate returns were to be made of all property taken by foraging parties, and penalties for an unlawful act were to be the same "whether the offence be committed in our own or in an enemy's territory." [57]

Besides the stern compulsion of the situation, Buell's attitude to the new order should have been influenced by the killing on August 6 of Brigadier General Robert McCook. A brother of Alexander McCook, he had been colonel of the Ninth Ohio when its charge broke the enemy at Mill Springs. He was sick and riding in an ambulance toward Decherd when an attack was made upon his escort, the shot that gave him the quickly fatal wound coming from the pistol of a horseman who rode past the vehicle. In reporting the incident the next day, Thomas wrote, "His regiment were very much enraged, and before they could be stopped burned and destroyed some four or five farm-houses; but Colonel Van Derveer, by great exertions, succeeded in subjugating them to discipline before night, and they are quiet now." [58] Though not an act to emblazon in the record of hard marches and great battles by the Ninth, the uncontrollable fury of the Buckeye soldiers showed their affection and admiration for the man who had led them on the bleak January Sunday.

From Alexander McCook—whose request to take his brother's body home had been refused because of the situation—there came to Buell on Friday, August 22—the day after Johnson's humiliating defeat—the message:

Three of my spies came to me this morning . . . and said: Bragg in command; Cheatham's division crossed the river on Friday last; up to Wednesday thirty-three regiments had crossed; six regiments crossed last night. Hardee is there and is crossing to-day. General Withers is crossing at Harrison; had crossed eleven regiments on Wednesday. General

Cheatham is in command of Polk's corps. General Polk second in command. . . . The troops that are crossing are well armed and have good artillery. The advance of the enemy has reached the top of Walden's Ridge. . . . This news is reliable. The enemy intend marching upon McMinnville. . . .

(On the 15th Bragg had informed Smith, "We begin crossing the river to-morrow and shall push ahead.") [59]

Buell without delay shifted his headquarters to Decherd and directed that all trains be employed to transfer to that place the subsistence accumulated at Stevenson and Huntsville. Thomas's division was still at Decherd, but he himself had been sent to McMinnville personally to supervise Wood's and Nelson's divisions—the latter now under Jacob Ammen, recently made a brigadier. On being informed of McCook's report, Thomas immediately strongly urged Buell to concentrate at McMinnville. Bragg could be met there advantageously if he moved directly on Nashville, or be struck at Sparta in case he went through that place.[60]

The next day—the 23rd—Buell replied that it was impossible to assemble at McMinnville. It was necessary either to concentrate in advance and assume the offensive, or fall back ultimately to Murfreesboro. Believing a forward move the best plan, he directed Thomas to make a forced march to Altamont, although Thomas had previously informed him that there was neither forage nor water at that lofty place. McCook likewise was directed to march to Altamont with his division and that of Crittenden, while Schoepf, now commanding Thomas's division, was given the same objective. But certain precautionary measures were taken. Rousseau at Huntsville and Negley at Athens were ordered to prepare to fall back by rail on Nashville, the sick at Huntsville to be left with twenty days' rations. The commander at Stevenson was confidentially alerted to vacate at a moment's notice and was told, "Let engineers quietly prepare pontoons for burning, and when you leave destroy everything that cannot be brought away." To the commanders of the two divisions Grant had sent went urgent orders to "move by forced marches on Nashville." [61]

When no sound of battle had come from the direction of Altamont by the 25th, Fry seemed vexed with the enemy and telegraphed Rousseau: "No fight. Bragg is very slow. If he wants one he can have it. We are all ready." With the army commander thirty miles away, it is not clear how the degree of readiness was determined. Actually, at 5:00 P.M. Thomas was writing from the mountaintop: "The enemy no nearer than Dunlap. It is reported there is one brigade there and one at Pikeville." Wood had been unable to get any guns onto the plateau, and Thomas deemed it next to impossible for a large army to cross at Altamont because of the scarcity of water—only one spring—and forage, "and the extreme difficulty of passing over the road." He was going back to McMinnville; aware by now of Buell's futility, he added, "As I mentioned in one of my dispatches, I regard McMinnville as the most important point for occupation of any." In replying two days later, Buell did not reprove Thomas for returning without orders, but fatuously told him that from the east the "road is very good and the mountain quite easy of ascent." More than that, the descent to the west was "easy enough by four roads, all diverging from Altamont." [62]

Unconvinced by Thomas's report, Buell on the 27th ordered McCook, then at Pelham—where General James Steedman afterward testified he heard McCook remark, "Don Carlos won't do; he won't do"—to be ready to march with his and Crittenden's divisions at three o'clock the next morning for Altamont, the object being "to observe the enemy and impede his progress across the mountain." Two days later Thomas telegraphed to Fry that he wished to fortify McMinnville, and asked for an engineer officer. Pointedly he said, "I would suggest to General Buell that a trip to this place might assist him very much in maturing his plans of operations." At noon of the same day McCook wrote from Altamont, "The country is a desert and stripped of everything." His half-rations would be gone by the 31st; uncomplainingly he commented, "I must get some somewhere." [63]

Already Buell had sent 21,000 rations to McCook. Now he ordered him back from the inhospitable mountain, while at Decherd Provost Marshal Beatty wrote in his diary: "I am weak, discouraged, and worn out with idleness. . . . The whole army is concentrated here, or near here; but nobody knows anything, except that the water is bad, whisky scarce, dust abundant, and the air loaded with the scent and melody of a thousand mules." [64]

By the 30th Thomas had given up urging a concentration at McMinnville and seemed reconciled to a retirement to Murfreesboro, if Bragg was moving on that place through Sparta, as seemed indicated by reports that he was concentrated along the Sequatchie Valley.

While the order that Buell issued was probably not influenced by Thomas, it was a careful piece of work that should have guided the movement without confusion—though not without the agony of heat and dust. One sentence was something of a giveaway: "In case, however, the enemy should not press upon Altamont and McMinnville the troops at those points will delay as long as they can do so and still have a day's march between them and the enemy's advanced guard, if indeed the enemy should follow at all." [65]

Six full days before this, Bragg had written to Smith that he looked for Buell "to recede to Nashville" before offering battle. The prophecy was to prove true, and Buell admitted it in a letter to Governor Andrew Johnson on the 30th. After casting up the situation, he said: "These facts make it plain that I should fall back on Nashville, and I am preparing to do so. I have resisted the reasons which lead to the necessity until it would be criminal to delay any longer." [66] So it was not really to be Murfreesboro—that was a fiction for his generals.

Thomas could not have been very hopeful that Buell would strike a blow from Murfreesboro, for although Buell had written to him on the 28th that Murfreesboro was the nearest point from which his "whole strength" could be thrown against the enemy, and that that was where he was going, he had ended with a sentence having an escape clause at both ends: "Once concentrated, we may move against the enemy wherever he puts himself if we are strong enough." [67]

Buell's dispatch of the 28th is also important because it gave his latest estimate of Bragg's army. On the 24th he had told Halleck that it probably consisted of "not less than 60,000 men, independently of irregular cavalry and the force operating toward Kentucky in rear of Cumberland Gap." On the 28th Thomas had sent him a report from a scout named Smith, who, as Buell knew, Thomas had sent out on the 25th "to put in operation a system of spies." Three days later Smith's brother came in with the information that Bragg was in the valley of the Tennessee with 40,000 men, awaiting his train before crossing the mountain. In replying, Buell spoke of reports that put Bragg in the Sequatchie Valley with his entire force; but he added, "I estimate that it may be as low as your informant reports." [68]

On the 26th a very good order had been sent to Captain Macfeely, Nashville commissary officer; good, but much overdue: "Don't lose a moment in collecting all the wheat you can and in making flour. Get all the beef cattle and other supplies you can as rapidly as possible.

Apply to Colonel Miller for such military aid as you need." The war was getting very grim. A scant ten days earlier Fry had transmitted to the Nashville adjutant Buell's order that staff officers should not restrict themselves to "the business hours known to peaceful times." [69]

CHAPTER III

KENTUCKY, CINCINNATI, AND
A GLANCE AT CORINTH

Where do you understand Buell to be and what is he doing?

Lincoln to Boyle

WHILE Buell was issuing his retirement order, the two brigades of new men forming Nelson's "Army of Kentucky" were being virtually wiped out by the veteran regiments of Kirby Smith in a battle near Richmond, Kentucky.* When night came the Federals who had not been killed, wounded, or captured were fugitives, individually seeking safety. But there had been times on that hot day when the regiments of men only two or three weeks in service, and only three days under the hard instruction of their brigadiers—Mahlon Manson and Charles Cruft—stood to their work like veterans and delivered volleys that were terrific. Though they were too green to be maneuvered well, many of them, after twice breaking in panic, were rallied to fight yet once more. And the force to which they gave battle, and which at times recoiled before their rifles, was not only well seasoned; it exceeded them in numbers.

Nelson, who had arrived late, was wounded, and Manson, who had brought on the action by advancing to meet the Confederates, again took charge. He organized a rear guard that behaved well, then a small advance guard that removed some enemy horsemen from the

---

* A map of central Kentucky is given on p. 122.

road. Slowly in the failing light of this August 30 the column moved back toward Lexington, proudly bringing nine of the twelve guns the novice cannoneers had served so well. But there was to be no escape. The weary men walked into an ambush.

At an early hour the Confederate commander had sent his cavalry on a wide detour around Richmond to seize the roads to Lexington. From about four o'clock they had been engaged in the easy and pleasant task of picking up stragglers. Now, as night was falling, Colonel J. S. Scott's 850 men poured well directed volleys from a cornfield into what he called the Federal main body of 5,000 men. Many fell; some thousands surrendered; the others fled. In attempting to escape, Manson was captured after his horse was killed.[1]

Just how Nelson got to Lexington he did not reveal in the dispatch he sent the next day—Sunday, August 31—to Wright, whose headquarters were now in Cincinnati, a dispatch which ended, "What the motive of General Manson was in bringing on an action under the circumstances, and marching 5 miles to do so, I will leave him to explain to you."[2] It was apparently Nelson's intention to take position at or near Lancaster, in the belief that Smith would not move on Lexington with a force under his flank. If so, that is where he should have been, or Manson should have been clearly instructed before Nelson left Richmond on a tour of inspection, as to his superior's purposes under different contingencies.

The incompleteness of the intelligence that spread through the North on Sunday increased the suspense. But there could be no hope that the first report was a gross exaggeration, for the concluding sentence of Wright's message to Halleck about Nelson's defeat had an awful finality: "At any rate his force has been routed." Lincoln turned to Boyle in Louisville: "What force and what the numbers of it which General Nelson had in the engagement near Richmond yesterday?" Seven to eight thousand, Boyle answered, and all new levies, except one regiment, while the enemy had fifteen to twenty thousand. "We need drilled troops and drilled artillery," was an indisputable appraisal. Prayers may have been uttered, as work on the fortifications about Covington and Newport, begun a year before by Ormsby Mitchel and Charles Whittlesey, was pushed forward. But before invoking supernatural aid, Halleck ventured to try a new governor, telegraphing to Austin Blair, "All Michigan troops not already started for Washington will be subject to General Wright's orders."[3]

At McMinnville, George Thomas likewise had a troubled Sunday, but to Buell he reported a complete victory: "Succeeded in deciphering order for concentrating. It was a hard problem. Whoever put it up must have been asleep, as no particular route was followed and a great many words were omitted." [4]

Though the roads to Cincinnati and Louisville were open, Kirby Smith did not advance beyond Lexington, except for small forces sent to Frankfort and Cynthiana. Lexington was the place he had announced as his objective in letters that went to Braxton Bragg and Jefferson Davis informing them of the lack of supplies in the region about Barbourville. The people there had also shown open hostility for the Confederate banners instead of embracing the tired men who had marched over hard mountains to free them from Lincoln rule. At Lexington there was not only plenty to eat but real friendliness. Furthermore, the clashes below Richmond could not have encouraged Smith to risk an attack upon a superior force of the new Union levies in intrenched lines. He had been content to issue an order that ended, "To-morrow being Sunday, the general desires that the troops shall assemble and, under their several chaplains, shall return thanks to Almighty God, to whose mercy and goodness these victories are due." [5]

The captured regiments were paroled, returned to their states, exchanged and, with the exception of a three-month regiment, were soon back in service. Four of them would be in the line with which Grant invested Vicksburg. But the Seventy-first Indiana was captured again before the end of the year. After being once more paroled and exchanged, it was prudently reorganized as cavalry. Astride their horses the Terre Haute Hoosiers saw the war through without a mishap, and with much honor. [6]

Such things the people of the North could not foresee as they read the details of the Richmond battle. But as they watched the almost unbelievable retreat of the Army of the Ohio, many must have taken solace in the thought that Mahlon Manson, even when commanding raw regiments, had not been afraid to march to meet the enemy.

As September came, Thomas wrote to Buell that Scout Smith was back from Dunlap. The total enemy force he now put at 45,000; some said they were coming toward McMinnville, others that they were headed for Kentucky. While the arms of the Confederates seemed generally good, they were short of provisions and spirits appeared low. The next day Thomas sketched a forward move and said, "I have studied the roads, and am now convinced that this is our best plan of attack." [7]

Thomas's dispatch was addressed to Murfreesboro, but Buell was already in Nashville, from where, at 1:55 P.M. the same day—September 2—he wrote to Halleck that it was beyond question that Bragg had crossed the Tennessee with 45,000 to 50,000 men. Apparently Buell thought Scout Smith had underestimated, whereas he had actually increased Bragg's army by 50 per cent. According to Buell the Confederate general had made demonstrations looking to a crossing of the mountains, and certain facts justified the belief that Bragg was moving up the Sequatchie Valley with the object of entering Kentucky. One of Grant's divisions had arrived, Buell reported, and the other was expected within a few days. His hope and program were given in the sentences: "I believe Nashville can be held and Kentucky rescued. What I have will be sufficient here with the defences that are being prepared, and I propose to move with the remainder of the army rapidly against the enemy in Kentucky." [8]

The General in Chief, who was trying to straighten out matters in front of Washington after Pope's defeat, threw up his hands in a one-sentence reply: "March where you please, provided you will find the enemy and fight him." [9]

Even without the 10,000 men Grant had sent, Buell had 46,000 present for duty south of the Cumberland, and Major General Lew Wallace, president of the commission, subscribed the statement:

The commission cannot justify the falling back from Murfreesborough to Nashville, but is of opinion that it was General Buell's duty from that point to have attacked the rebel army before it crossed the Cumberland, and it is the [their?] belief that had that course been pursued Bragg would have been defeated.[10]

At daylight of September 7 Wood crossed the Cumberland at Nashville and started with his division for Bowling Green. He made seventeen miles that day, camping where water was neither good nor abundant, and ended his report to Buell, "Every piece of information I get indicates Bowling Green as the destination of Bragg's command." As Wood's column began its march, Bragg at Sparta was ending a dispatch to Polk, "Forrest reports the enemy rapidly evacuating Nashville, so that we must push to head him off." Forrest, recently made a brigadier, had really been anticipating. But Buell, who on the 8th urged both Rousseau (commanding Ormsby Mitchel's old division) and Crittenden forward—as well as Wood—expressed to the latter some doubt that Bragg was going to Bowling Green.[11]

Buell's fate depended upon securing the large supply of provisions which had been accumulated at Bowling Green. Although foraging about Nashville had resulted in a goodly supply of meat and flour, shelves were bare of many items. On the 10th Fry sent almost frantic messages for the forwarding to Nashville from Bowling Green of "500,000 rations of coffee, the same of sugar, the same of beans." They were to go by train to Mitchellville (just below the Kentucky border), there to be transferred into one hundred wagons emptied of their divisional loads, and hurried to Nashville with the right of way over everything.[12]

Something that can challenge even sugar and beans in military importance was speeding to Nashville through McCook from the hard-marching Wood—intelligence about the enemy. Near Gallatin he had employed "a reliable Union man" to get information. The man had just returned from Gainesboro with the report that the Confederates, under Bragg, Hardee, and Cheatham, 35,000 strong, had crossed the Cumberland on Sunday the 7th and were moving by forced marches toward Glasgow, Munfordville, and on to Louisville. Said Wood: "I regard the information as entirely reliable. I cannot mention all the corroborative circumstances in this brief note." The last sentence testified to his conviction: "I will get to Bowling Green to-night, though I have marched 22 miles to-day." The heading of the dispatch showed Wood still had 12 miles to march—miles that would lengthen in the dark.[13]

Replying to a dispatch from Lincoln on the 12th that had ended with the simple but devastating sentence, "Where do you understand Buell to be and what is he doing?" Boyle placed him in Nashville, with part of his army at Bowling Green, and he summed up: "Bragg reported at Burkesville and Columbia advancing into the center of the State. I do not believe any of the reports of an early attack at any point. They can, and I hope will, be driven out before they attack."[14]

On the same day an excellent intelligence summary sped from Louisville to Colonel Anson Stager, in charge of telegraph affairs at

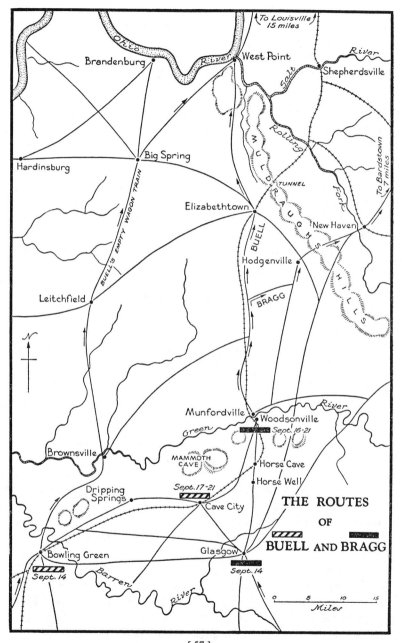

THE ROUTES

OF

BUELL AND BRAGG

Cleveland. From time to time the superintendents of the wires at Cincinnati and Louisville gave the colonel reports that unquestionably went to T. T. Eckert, supervisor of the communication center at the War Department. Sam Bruch at Louisville summed up the situation thus:

> Large portion of Buell's army is now at Bowling Green; more following. Buell himself still at Nashville. Bragg's advance said to be at Glasgow. Rebels cut telegraph faster than I can put it up to Nashville. Kirby Smith said to be at Frankfort.[15]

Bruch was a little behind time as to Buell, for Buell had left Nashville the day before, although not soon enough to suit Rousseau, senior general at Bowling Green, who had sent forward by a locomotive a dispatch that told Fry: "You ought to be here. Pardon me, but you have to be here." Rousseau was inaccurate when he made the gloomy statement that the rations were not at Bowling Green. Then he corrected. They were there: 1,200,000 of them, except bread. But flour could be had, and Rousseau was "preparing to bake for the whole army." [16]

Buell arrived the next day—September 14—with two more divisions to join the three already at Bowling Green. Thomas had been left in Nashville with his own division, Negley's (which had been the occupying force), and Paine's, lately arrived from Mississippi with Brigadier General John M. Palmer as temporary commander. On the evening of the 13th a message had been sent for Thomas to hasten forward with his own division and that of Palmer—unless he deemed it more prudent to leave the latter. Bragg would be concentrated at Glasgow not later than the next day, said Fry, who gave the situation a dramatic touch: "If Bragg's army is defeated Nashville is safe; if not, it is lost." As Thomas believed the city locally threatened, he left Palmer and hurried forward with only his own command.[17] The information about Bragg had been such that it would seem that Thomas should not have been left at Nashville in the first place.

While alarm was now to mount in Louisville, people were breathing more easily in Cincinnati, just as they were in Washington since the direct threat to the capital had vanished with Lee's move across the Potomac into Maryland. Late in August, Lew Wallace, on a leave status but helping to raise Indiana's quota of the 300,000 volunteers Lincoln had called for on July 2, had offered his services to Wright, and after Nelson's arrival he had been given immediate command of the Cincinnati area. On September 6 Wright had relaxed a little on Cincinnatians, who had been tied up tightly by Wallace's proclamation of martial law. The next day, however, he cautioned the governors of Ohio, Indiana, Illinois, and Wisconsin not to lessen their exertions to send troops. It would be necessary, he said, to relieve George Morgan at Cumberland Gap, or he would be starved out. "Enemy reported in strong force at Falmouth on the road to this city," was the sentence by which the general sought to keep tired governors at their desks.[18]

On the 10th Wright went into a panic, calling upon Tod, ill at Columbus, at 2:30 A.M. to rush him all the armed men he could.[19]

"They will pour in upon you by thousands," replied the governor. Though green, every Minute Man would have a weapon, two days' food, and a blanket; and there would be 50,000 of them, said Tod to Stanton. Not only did Wright call on Louisville for troops, but in a dispatch to Buell saying that Kirby Smith was in front of Cincinnati with 15,000 to 30,000 men, he asked Buell to attack his rear—quite as if Braxton Bragg could be easily brushed aside. Boyle dispatched a regiment and promised others when he got transportation. But he was far from happy about it, and told Wright that the latter's troops could whip the enemy in his front if they did not get panic-stricken.[20]

Telegraph instruments soon rattled with protests about weakening Louisville: to Wright and Halleck from Governor James Robinson, to Lincoln from Boyle. Halleck telegraphed sensibly to Wright; Lincoln told him he could not judge the propriety of what was being done, but pleaded for a rational answer that would quiet the governor and others in Louisville. To Fellow-Kentuckian Boyle, Lincoln said bluntly enough, "With all possible respect for you I must think General Wright's military opinion is the better." The unabashed Boyle replied, "I concur with you that General Wright's military opinion is better than I ever thought mine to be, but I can know facts as well as the ablest military man." [21]

A week earlier Wright had received from Grant a telegram saying that Gordon Granger was being hurried northward; artillery and cavalry were marching to Paducah; infantry was going by rail to Columbus, Kentucky, as fast as the capacity of the road allowed. Depleted now by the loss of a third division, Grant stood ready to do even more: "My old regiments are very much reduced from the number of engagements they have been in. I will spare them, however, if required." [22] In ordering Granger to Louisville, Halleck was playing cards well, for the small, well trained division would be a good nucleus for new organizations. Veteran regiments from the Battle of Pea Ridge and the advance on Corinth would quiet fears; names like Gordon Granger and Phil Sheridan would stimulate morale.

Major General C. C. Gilbert, in command in Louisville by reason of an unconventional promotion by Wright, had telegraphed both to Lincoln and to Wright on the 12th, briefly but effectively. "The enemy must destroy Buell's army or cast it off to the west a long distance before attempting the capture of Cincinnati," was reasoning Lincoln would appreciate. Gilbert added that if Buell's communications with Louisville were secured, there could be no attack on Cincinnati except by way of Kanawha and western Virginia. And in protesting the sending of Granger to Cincinnati, the infantryman ended in a manner that surpassed the best sentences constructed by Engineer Wright: "Granger's division is of the utmost importance as a head to the force now here, and a head it must have before it can move to co-operate with Buell, whose forces now show themselves at Bowling Green." [23]

But Wright was not convinced. He telegraphed to Gilbert: "Kirby Smith is in our front and threatening our lines. Have regiments ready to come here instantly on call." His alarm is made the more surprising by a dispatch sent him on September 12 by Wallace. Referring probably to a recent skirmish at Fort Mitchel, a work protecting Covington and situated on the Lexington pike, the literary Hoosier wrote:

The skeedaddle is complete; every sign of a rout. If you say so I will organize a column of 20,000 men to pursue to-night. Granger's batteries will likely be here to-morrow; if not, they can follow and overtake me. Say the word.[24]

Taking the field with the new troops in an aggressive move was nothing to be undertaken hastily, and it is not surprising that Wright did not order Wallace to proceed. But he seemed a trifle apologetic the next day when he ended a telegram to Lincoln: "Louisville has not been threatened at all, while Kirby Smith's force did approach to within 8 miles of Cincinnati. He is now retreating from before the force hastily collected." This brought an answer the next day that showed Wright he was serving under a man who was most appreciative, if somewhat exacting: "Thanks for your dispatch. Can you not pursue the retreating enemy and relieve Cumberland Gap?" [25]

As Lincoln saw the enemy swiftly reconquer large portions of two states, the Gap seemed very precious.

On the day Wright telegraphed to Lincoln about the enemy's retreat—September 13—he also sent a circular to the editors of the six Cincinnati newspapers, complaining that articles of a seditious and treasonable character, as well as statements conveying to the enemy information of military movements and positions, had been published in some of their papers. This was to stop; a repetition of the offense would "necessarily be immediately followed by the suppression of the paper in which such articles shall be published and the arrest and confinement of the proprietors and writers concerned in the same." [26]

Entirely unknown to Wright, Grant, a little more than a month earlier, had written to his father, then living in Covington, that he did not expect or want the support of the Cincinnati press. Its course, he said, had been so remarkable since the beginning of the war that he feared its endorsement would cause the people to mistrust his patriotism.[27]

Also on September 13, Governor Tod was telegraphing to Stanton:

The Minute-men or Squirrel Hunters, responded gloriously to the call for the defense of Cincinnati. Thousands reached the city and thousands more were *en route* for it. The enemy having retreated all have been ordered back. This uprising of the people is the cause of the retreat. You should acknowledge publicly their gallant conduct.

Please order Quartermaster Burr to pay all transportation bills upon my approval.[28]

But not all the emergency men went home promptly. A few days later Brigadier General A. J. Smith, recently assigned to the troubled West, would send a plea to Lew Wallace that might have shocked David Tod: "Cannot I get rid of the Squirrel Hunters? They are under no control." [29]

The dispatch that Buell sent to Halleck on the 14th from Bowling Green by way of Evansville revealed the difficulty of his situation. Bragg was virtually between him and Louisville, and there was danger that he would form a junction with Smith. But he held out a promise of a sort by saying he would "commence to move against Bragg's force on the 16th." [30]

The Confederate commander on his part—happy in the discovery that none of the Federal forces had passed Bowling Green—intended to rest his command, and prepared to strike Buell in the flank if he proceeded further northward. He had cause for the gratification he recorded in his report: without firing a gun he had the Federals in a difficult position and had "compelled the evacuation of Northern Alabama and Middle Tennessee." [31] Not often has boldness and hard marching accomplished more. But an agressive subordinate was now to shape events.

Quietly, at 11:30 P.M. of the 12th, the Confederate brigade of James R. Chalmers had moved into the sleeping town of Cave City and soon had possession of the telegraph office, the post office, and the depot. Chalmers's mission was security and reconnaissance, but the next day he found some wheat in addition to intercepting telegraph dispatches. One from Gilbert revealed that 500 men were being sent by rail to reenforce Munfordville, together with five days' rations for 3,000 men. It was late on the 13th when an officer from the staff of Colonel John S. Scott appeared, the same Scott whose cavalry had ambushed the Federals at Richmond. Earlier in the evening Scott had sent to Colonel John T. Wilder of the Seventeenth Indiana, commanding at Munfordville, a summons to surrender. The reply was a sharp refusal. Would Chalmers, asked Scott's officer, help to capture the unaccommodating Federals? They numbered only 1,800, were all raw troops, and were cut off from aid by his destruction of the railroad. [32]

The idea appealed to Chalmers, and soon he was in motion for the objective ten miles away—a position that could be a trap for the defenders because Green River separated small Munfordville on the north bank from smaller Woodsonville on the south. It was shortly after daylight of the 14th when Chalmers opened his attack, and after three hours of hard fighting he sent a note complimenting Wilder on his stout defense, but demanding unconditional surrender. No help could come to him, said the Confederate, while he himself had the potential support of Bragg's entire army. Said Wilder in reply: "Thank you for your compliments. If you wish to avoid further bloodshed keep out of the range of my guns. As to re-enforcements, they are already entering my works. I think I can defend my position against your entire force; at least I shall try to do so."

Indeed, 446 men of the Fiftieth and Seventy-eighth Indiana, under Colonel Cyrus L. Dunham, were close at hand. When their train was derailed during the night, six miles away, they had taken to the woods and fields, forded the river between the pontoon and railroad bridges, and were greeted by hearty cheers from the men then in action.[33]

Chalmers had had enough. After an exchange of courteous notes with Wilder about the care of the dead and wounded—far heavier for the Confederates than for the Federals—he withdrew. Conscience, however, disturbed him, and in a report written the next day at Cave City he said he feared his action might have incurred the censure of headquarters. He was right. A longer effort at explanation four days later received an indorsement by Bragg condemning the attack as "unauthorized and injudicious." [34] Though at the time he so wrote Bragg was looking for scapegoats, it would be impossible to dispute his description.

Unwilling to allow the impression of a setback to rest on the minds of his men, Bragg, on the evening of the 15th, set his army in motion with a scant supply of provisions but with the intention of throwing his full strength against the little band of offending Unionists. Hardee moved directly through Cave City and invested the position from the south, while Polk crossed the river a few miles above and deployed on the north. There was some fighting; and soon after 5:00 P.M. a message from Bragg told the Federal commander it was time to capitulate, for he was surrounded by an overwhelming force. An exchange of notes followed, the Federals not believing that Bragg would bring his entire army to capture a small garrison. Finally Wilder asked proof of a superior force. In reply the canny Bragg said the only evidence he would give beyond the statement that it exceeded 20,000 would be to use it. He then demanded an unconditional surrender, saying it would be enforced, and appointing an hour for a decision. Thereupon six colonels and a captain went into conference. Against such a number as Bragg claimed, they could not contend. But because of the possibility that Bragg was bluffing, the council voted unanimously not to capitulate upon the evidence they had. Wilder sent back word that it was of no use to parley; he had to know what force Bragg had. Presently he requested, and received, permission to see Bragg in person. Unbowed in the presence of a full general, the Hoosier argued for an hour; and when Simon Bolivar Buckner—who had recently been exchanged and who was commanding one of Hardee's divisions—joined in, Wilder made him admit he had twice failed to carry the Federal line by assault.

As wearying midnight approached, the stubborn Federal commander was taken by Buckner on a tour of the Confederate lines to the south while his adjutant was afforded a visit to those on the north. The colonel counted 46 guns, the lieutenant 26; and of the total, 54 were in position to open fire. Then Wilder gave up, though apparently without apology for the annoyance he had caused. In the small hours of the 17th he signed articles of capitulation, and at six o'clock his command marched out "with all the honors of war, drums beating and colors flying." They were paroled and the next day started toward Bowling Green, officers wearing their side arms.[35]

In the dispatch that Bragg sent promptly to Richmond—but which was not received until the 26th—there was no indication that the capture had been carried out to bolster the morale of his army after the sharp defeat of one of its brigades by green troops. After counting booty: 4,000 prisoners, 4,000 small arms, guns, and copious munitions, Bragg said, "My junction with Kirby Smith is complete. Buell still at Bowling Green."[36]

The unusual operation established that John T. Wilder was not an officer who panicked. In reporting to Gilbert his refusal of Scott's demand for surrender, Wilder said, "I shall fight anything that comes." And Gilbert spoke advisedly when, in relaying the message to Wright on the 14th, he said, "Colonel McCook, who knows Wilder, says Scott cannot take him unless it is an attack in very strong force."[37] The McCook referred to was a brother of Alexander and Robert, and truer words were never spoken. When queried by the Court of Inquiry as to why he had not escaped with his force before he was completely invested, Wilder said he could have done so on the afternoon of the 16th, but had been directed by Gilbert to hold the position as long as possible. The Court put no blame on him.[38]

From Scout Wash Miller, sent by Wilder to Bowling Green on the 13th, Buell learned the next day that Munfordville was threatened. Not knowing whether Buell had personally arrived, Wilder had instructed Miller to report to whoever commanded, but to try to find General Wood, to whom his reliability was known. (Munfordville was strongly Unionist.) Though Miller gave Buell information, he transmitted no request for help, for Wilder had not so instructed him. He was back in Munfordville on the 16th with the report that no aid could be expected from Bowling Green. Nor can Buell be blamed for not immediately rushing forward. The town was under Gilbert's orders, and Bragg's army was Buell's true objective. Buell argued cogently but tiresomely in the paper he later submitted in his defense that it was illogical for Bragg to give up Glasgow and go to Munfordville. Neither he nor McCook, who branded the move a piece of impudence that hazarded Bragg's army, divined the reason behind the Confederate general's move.[39] And it would have taken a very astute commander indeed to say, on learning of Chalmers's repulse, "That will make Bragg throw his entire force on Munfordville."

But as Buell rested his army and waited for Mitchell's division, he should certainly have ordered his cavalry to keep a close eye on the enemy. This he did not do; and when he began his promised move against Bragg on the afternoon of the 16th he did not know that the Confederates had begun to leave Glasgow the evening before. The news was brought to him during the night, and the next day his army marched to Cave City and Horse Well. When word came of the surrender of Munfordville, the Federal commander was faced with the cruel necessity of a new appraisal and a new decision. A message to Gilbert indicated that the prevailing opinion was that Bragg would head rapidly for Louisville, in expectation of quickly overpowering the new troops. Should this prove true, Buell promised, he would be close behind the enemy. His own belief, however, was that Bragg would not strike northward, but would make a stand either at Green River or Muldraugh Hill, with the latter his probable choice. Buell put the enemy at from 30,000 to 40,000, spoke of the likelihood of a junction of Bragg and Smith, said Cincinnati was not in danger, urged that troops be concentrated at Louisville without delay, and ended impressively, "I expect to be at Green River early to-morrow." [40]

It was a good message. But what happened? Bragg had concentrated on the south rather than on the north side of Green River; and by maneuvering Buckner's division in front of Buell he frightened him into passivity. In his postwar article Buell put his own effectives at 35,000. Inasmuch as Bragg could not have had over 27,000, we have the ironic coincidence that on the same day—September 18, 1862—both McClellan and his good friend Buell were afraid to attack an inferior force that had its back to a river. If unwilling to take the offensive because of uncertainty as to relative numbers, Buell could at least have pressed up close to Bragg's lines, for he knew that at worst they were about evenly matched, and he should have been confident of repelling any attack by the enemy.[41]

If Buell had felt for an opening, the 20th would have been a day of opportunity. Polk marched northward at daybreak, and heavy pressure would have resulted in nothing but disaster for the part of the Confederate army still south of Green River. The uneasiness which Bragg must have felt during the night had disappeared by 6:00 A.M. of the 21st, when, from a point fifteen miles north of Munfordville, he wrote to Polk:

> Do not push your troops to-day. As I hear nothing from the rear it is presumed we are not pressed, and, in any event, our troops are jaded so that too great a pressure will be worse than a fight with superior numbers. Send ahead and see if subsistence or forage in small quantities can be had for our wants to-night, say 5 miles beyond Hodgenville.[42]

Thomas had arrived on the 20th, and Buell pushed forward a battle line on the 21st, only to find that the enemy had left. Then, while his great train of empty wagons moved by a road to the west, Buell followed the Confederates until they turned off toward Hodgenville, leaving the Army of the Ohio to continue northward unmolested. In a message on the 24th, reporting to Stager that every able-bodied man in Louisville had had a rifle or shovel placed in his hands, Sam Bruch said, "Pontoon bridge being built to move over if necessary." But Nelson showed confidence in a dispatch that told Buell a bridge had been thrown for him over Salt River, and rations sent to Brandenburg; he even talked of attacking Bragg when Buell had brought him "to bay." Nelson was manifestly feeling more cheerful when at a later hour he telegraphed to Wright:

> Maj. Gen. Thomas L. Crittenden has crossed Salt River with the advance of Buell's army, consisting of 12,000 men and six batteries of artillery. Louisville is now safe. We can destroy Bragg with whatever force he may bring against us. God and liberty.[43]

Vacillation and caution had of course damaged morale. "A spirit of impatience began to develop itself in Cave City when we came in striking distance of the enemy," was the testimony of a colonel before the commission, while General Steedman said, "I frequently heard officers express doubts of General Buell's loyalty." Such officers brushed aside timidity and prudence as explanations, and said simply, though with no evidence except his behavior, "General Buell did not desire to whip Bragg." [44]

In Corinth, matters were taking a different shape.*

On August 31, the black Sunday in Washington when there was a telegram from Sam Bruch with the sentence, "Indications are General Buell will fall back on Nashville," when Wright telegraphed about the defeat at Richmond, and when the plans for McClellan's divisions to take effective aid to Pope crumbled, Halleck had telegraphed to Grant, "Could you send any more troops into Tennessee or Kentucky, east of the Cumberland, without risking your own positions; if so, from what points can you best spare them?" Grant replied the next day that he was weak and that, being threatened from Humboldt to Bolivar, he deemed it unsafe to spare more troops unless the railroad east of Bear Creek was abandoned. If that were done he could send a division from Tuscumbia or beyond. It was a very helpful message for a High Command to receive, and on September 2 Halleck wired, "Railroad east of Corinth may be abandoned, and Granger's division sent to Louisville, Ky., with all possible dispatch." When repeated because of garbling, Grant was told to inform Wright at Cincinnati when Granger would arrive. The reply was: "I am hurrying Granger all practicable. Your dispatch was explained by one from General Boyle." [45]

The threat to his rear and flank to which Grant had referred included a sharp attack on Bolivar on August 30 followed by a move across the Hatchie at Brownsville by a force reported as considerable. To hold his rear more securely and to compensate for loss of troops in his front, Grant directed Sherman to send a division to Brownsville. The order had to go through Columbus; but there was no delay when the dispatch boat reached Memphis, and Sherman soon had Hurlbut on the march. At the new location Hurlbut became a very important strategic reserve, for he could be moved either to Jackson or to Bolivar, allowing troops at those places to be shifted by rail to Corinth. The Jackson district was now commanded by Brigadier John A. Logan, McClernand having been sent to help the governor of Illinois raise troops (and, as will appear later, to carry on intrigue of his own

* For places in the remainder of the chapter, see maps, pp. 3, 38.

devising). In reporting his new dispositions to Washington, Grant said that he would probably move his headquarters to Jackson, from where by means of a courier to Brownsville he could communicate with Sherman "in seven or eight hours in case of necessity." [46]

But Grant did not leave Corinth, for there were increasing reports of enemy activity, from residents, from deserters and, best of all, from cavalry. Rosecrans was called in from Iuka, and early on the 16th Grant sketched the situation to Halleck. The enemy had been hovering around for ten days or more "in reported large force." Grant had been watching closely and concentrating his troops. "All are now in good shape," he said. Six thousand men had been brought from Bolivar, Hurlbut moving up to fill the vacancy. Price was to the southeast; Van Dorn and Breckinridge were reported ready to join him for an attack; but, Grant said, they probably could not arrive for four days. They might be merely covering a move to get Price into East Tennessee. The dispatch ended: "If I can I will attack Price before he crosses Bear Creek. If he can be beaten there it will prevent either the design to go north or to unite forces and attack here." [47]

Presently there was a message from Rosecrans forwarding a short note from Colonel J. A. Mower, who was at Burnsville with the Eleventh Missouri. People in the vicinity were saying that Price was at Iuka with a strong force. The colonel was not certain that this was true, but he said, "I am going to see." Cavalry officers, Rosecrans added, believed Price was on the Fulton and Iuka road; scouts were out to get the facts. The next day a telegram came from Halleck:

Do everything in your power to prevent Price from crossing the Tennessee River. A junction of Price and Bragg in Tennessee would be most disastrous. They should be fought while separated. [48]

Mower sent another note to Rosecrans, who passed it to Grant:

I am going to send in a prisoner who gave himself up to our skirmishers yesterday. He gives some very valuable information. According to his statement Price is trying to draw our troops out from Corinth, when Van Dorn and Breckinridge will attack that place. [49]

When interviewed by Rosecrans—who described him as an "Irish Texan"—the man stuck to his story: "Breckinridge and Van Dorn are to leap into Corinth from the west as soon as we get out after Price." Rosecrans naturally had doubts about this, but he believed the statement that Price was in Iuka with all his force, headed for the Tennessee Valley, and that he had directed the issuance of five days' rations. Soon a cavalry patrol that had been close to Iuka without encountering pickets brought Rosecrans an Englishman and an Arkansas schoolteacher, both of them Confederate captains. They too located Price in Iuka, with details as to his forces. Yet another accession to the Rosecrans Confederate collection—in this case a simple deserter—gave the situation a new twist: Breckinridge had surely gone to Holly Springs and would move on Bolivar.[50]

It is not surprising that Grant said in a letter to his father that day— September 17—"I now have all my time taxed," or that he had scarcely the chance "for looking over the telegraphic columns of the newspapers." But he must have known that Lee had invaded Maryland, that Kirby Smith was at Lexington, and that Bragg's objective was not clear. He realized that at such a time it would be calamitous if Corinth were lost and the Federals in West Tennessee were forced back. Though no position was probably more threatened, he reassured his father: "I expect to hold it and have never had any other feeling either here or elsewhere but that of success." He criticized his father for denouncing other generals, the report having been brought to him by officers returning from leave. People naturally inferred the father was echoing what the son had written. Jesse Grant also had unwisely—though naturally—been defending his son from attacks, especially common about Cincinnati, where Whitelaw Reid's florid and grossly exaggerated story about Shiloh had first been published. Though trying to help him, Jesse had, Ulysses said, done him more harm than had any enemy. That would not be a pleasant thought for his loyal father; but the soldier who was confident of success was also undisturbed about his record: "I require no defenders and for my sake let me alone."[51]

The day must have been well-nigh spent when Grant read a dispatch, headed "Jacinto—9:30 p.m.," that General Hamilton had sent to Rosecrans: "Price and his whole force are in Iuka. We have captured a lot of prisoners, wagons, mules, and ordnance stores. Some of the prisoners just from Iuka."[52]

An assured target seemed located at Iuka, though mystery still obscured Rosecrans's old Academy classmate Earl Van Dorn, who in March had struck Curtis at Pea Ridge from an unexpected direction. Actually, conflicting purposes and a misconception about Rosecrans's mission had actuated the Confederates. Price, under orders from Bragg to move rapidly to Nashville, had ended a letter to Van Dorn written at Guntown on the 9th with the enticing thought: "Of course nothing could please me more than that you should unite your army to mine and move in command of the combined armies for Nashville." Van Dorn, however, wanted no part in such a program, his mind being set on an operation in West Tennessee. On August 25 he had sent a message to Breckinridge laden with hopeful sentences: "A brilliant field is before us yet. Let us start as soon as possible. Set your officers to work. We have transportation sufficient and everything necessary." But the summons brought no joy to the Kentucky-born former Vice President, and on the 13th he lamented to a political friend, "I groan and obey." [53]

While Breckinridge was groaning, Price was waiting for the moon to rise to light his pathway into Iuka, where his advance guard had that day come in contact with the last units of Rosecrans's army. The Federals were engaged in removing stores, and hastened away, leaving many undestroyed. Price now had to reconsider everything, for Bragg's order had plainly been predicated on the belief that all of Rosecrans's command would move to the support of Buell. He now gave up the Nashville march and decided to join Van Dorn, to whom he telegraphed on the 14th: "Rosecrans has gone westward with about 10,000 men. I am ready to co-operate with you in an attack upon Corinth. My courier awaits your answer." [54]

As Price filled his wagons with the gratifying abundance left by the hurrying Yankees, and waited to learn Van Dorn's pleasure, Grant made his decision to attack Iuka, and on the 17th he began a directive to Ord, "We will get off all our forces now as rapidly as practicable." Rosecrans, informed by Grant as to how Ord was to move, issued an order saying his army would move with five days' rations, three cooked, 100 rounds of ammunition per man, 40 on the person, "short rations" for animals, a minimum of wagons, "a few hospital stores," and specifying, "The ambulances will accompany the troops." [55]

Like McClellan along Antietam Creek and Buell between the Barren and the Green rivers, Price was again in a state of indecision. A fresh telegram from Bragg dated the 12th had arrived with a new plea that he move northward. But as it put Rosecrans at Nashville with a part of his army, it was plain that Bragg was still thinking from a false premise. No reply to his dispatch of the 14th having been received from Van Dorn, Price sent him another message, quoting the telegram from Bragg, and saying, "I cannot remain inactive any longer, and must move either with you against Rosecrans or toward Kentucky." [56] Grant would soon help the perplexed general reach a decision.

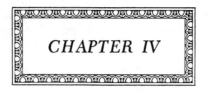

CHAPTER IV

IUKA AND CORINTH

> I have strained everything to take into the fight an adequate
> force and to get them to the right place. *Grant to Halleck*

GRANT's operation against Price was ambitious: he hoped to capture
a large part of the Confederate command by columns totaling about
17,000, while he estimated the enemy at possibly 15,000. Only a
complex and risky envelopment could be successful, and the desired
result was not obtained because of a delay of several hours in Rosecrans's column, an adverse wind that kept the noise of battle from
reaching Grant, and the decision by Price not to remain and fight a
second day. Grant passed no censure on the error in Rosecrans's
march and only praised him for his fighting, while in his *Memoirs* he
said his subordinate had suggested the plan. As always, the responsibility of decision was the commanding general's, and in making a
suggestion Rosecrans was doing no more than the operation section
of a modern staff habitually does. General Hamilton, whose division
led Rosecrans's advance, put it well in a postwar article. After noting
that Price had concentrated at Iuka, this classmate of Grant, who
after eight years in civil life had returned to service at the head of a
Wisconsin regiment, wrote: "As soon as definite information was had
of this position of Price, Grant took immediate steps to beat him up.
A combined attack was planned, by which Rosecrans with his two
divisions (Hamilton's and Stanley's) was to move on Iuka from the
south, while Ord, with a similar column, was to approach Iuka from
the west." [1]

After providing a small garrison for Corinth, Ord could furnish from his two depleted divisions less than 4,000 men for the operation against Price, whom Rosecrans had called an "old woodpecker" in a dispatch on the 17th warning Grant that the Missourian must be watched. To strengthen Ord, troops were temporarily drawn from Bolivar in an excellent example of "economy of force." Within twenty-four hours after Grant had sent a message for the troops to "come on," empty cars held at Jackson had been moved to Bolivar, had picked up Brigadier General Leonard F. Ross and his infantry, had returned to Jackson and delivered enough men at Corinth to raise Ord's movable command to 8,000—this in spite of a wreck between Bolivar and Jackson causing several hours' delay.[2] The first objective of this force was Burnsville, well over halfway to Iuka.

A dispatch on the 17th announced to Grant the personal arrival at Jacinto of Rosecrans, and said that as soon as Stanley's division arrived he would "move on to near Barnett's, probably tonight." That would put the southern force within about eight miles of Iuka. But it did not work out that way. The long drought had been partially broken, and Rosecrans reported the next day, "The rain and darkness prevented Stanley from making progress until this morning." He still expected, however, to be concentrated by 2:00 P.M. and would move forward that night. Grant reached Burnsville before noon of the 18th and at 6:45 P.M. he acknowledged receipt of another message from Rosecrans saying he intended to move up as close as possible that night, concealing his movements. Then as Ord drew the enemy's attention, Rosecrans would "move in on the Jacinto and Fulton roads, massing heavily on the Fulton road, and crushing in their left and cutting off their retreat eastward." Rosecrans was in an expansive humor and expectant of handsome results.

After explaining Ord's position, Grant replied, "Make as rapid an advance as you can and let us do tomorrow all we can." The security of Corinth was much in his mind. Detachments were being left at Rienzi and Jacinto to give warning of an enemy approach from the south, and Hurlbut had been moved from the vicinity of Brownsville to Bolivar with directions to demonstrate toward Holly Springs to attract the attention of Confederates known to be north of that place. Remembering that deserters had predicted Van Dorn would strike at Corinth while the Federals moved against Price, Grant told Rosecrans, "It may be necessary to fall back the day following [tomorrow]."

He also foresaw the possibility of disappointment, saying he thought the nearness of the cavalry which Ord had encountered and driven back indicated an intended retreat, the horsemen being "a force to cover it." [3]

Under such circumstances it was disappointing to receive after midnight a dispatch from Rosecrans, saying that, through the fault of a guide, Stanley's division had followed that of Ross for some miles on the road to Burnsville and had not arrived at Jacinto until after dark. Rosecrans's leading infantry was only eight miles out, and Stanley would have a march of twenty miles. "Shall not therefore be in before one or two o'clock, but when we come in will endeavor to do it strongly," was the best that Rosecrans could now promise.

The difficulties of a converging operation were manifesting themselves. In addition to rain and human error, the thick, impenetrable country made it impossible to keep close contact with Rosecrans's tardy advance, and all messages—according to Grant's words—"had to pass around near to Jacinto, even after he had got on the road leading north." Ord, on schedule in every way, was in the field early on the 19th, and had the divisions of Ross and McArthur six miles from Iuka, ready to advance, the one from the west, the other from the north. His Second Division, now under Brigadier General Thomas A. Davies, was, however, held at Burnsville, ready to entrain at a moment's notice for return to Corinth. About 10:00 A.M. Ord received from Grant a copy of the last dispatch from Rosecrans with a covering note: "You will see that he is behind where we expected him. Do not be too rapid with your advance this morning, unless it should be found that the enemy are evacuating." [4]

Ord sought to turn the irritating delay to advantage by indulging in psychological warfare. At some time during the previous evening Grant had received from the telegraph superintendent at Cairo a dispatch summarizing messages on the wires about the Battle of Antietam. After describing the action the dispatch said: "Longstreet and his entire division prisoners. General Hill killed. Entire rebel army of Virginia destroyed, Burnside having re-occupied Harper's Ferry and cut off retreat." The battle had been sanguinary, and the message ended cheerfully, "Latest advices say entire rebel army must be captured or killed, as Potomac is rising and our forces pressing the enemy continually." It would be interesting to know what Grant thought about this telegram that came while he was receiving disappointing word from Rosecrans. But he indulged in no appraisal when forwarding it to Ord with instructions that it be "read early in the morning to the troops under your command." Ord did more than that. He sent it to Colonel Mortimer D. Leggett of the 78th Ohio, with the note:

Can you not get the inclosed dispatch from Cairo to the general commanding the enemy in front? I think this battle decides the war finally, and that upon being satisfied of its truth General Price or whoever commands here will avoid useless bloodshed and lay down his arms.

There is not the slightest doubt of the truth of the dispatch in my hand. This by permission of General Grant.[5]

Colonel Leggett got the note through, but Sterling Price, of whom Rosecrans had spoken a little disparagingly, did not on his part have a very flattering idea of Yankees, and in his report he wrote, "I replied to the insolent demand through the commanding officer of my cavalry advance." The absence of a signature over the words "Colonel, Commanding Cavalry," in the message that came to Leggett, as well as the wording, suggests that the message was written by none other than Price himself. After questioning the accuracy of the Cairo dispatches, it said that neither the Confederate commander nor his men would "ever lay down their arms—as humanely suggested by General Ord—until the independence of the Confederate States shall have been acknowledged by the United States." [6]

Rosecrans had finished with his delays, and at daylight he took up the march toward Barnett's with his two divisions and six batteries, the spirits of his troops elevated by the news from the East. Strangely enough it was his medical director, not a troop commander, who recorded: "On the 19th the roads were in splendid order, hard, and entirely free from dust. The men marched with ease and in fine order, none lagging and very few straggling." Hamilton had the advance, following behind eight companies of the Third Michigan Cavalry in light marching order, Captain L. G. Willcox commanding, while the Second Iowa Cavalry gave flank protection. When they were about eight miles beyond Jacinto, Willcox detected "indications of the presence of rebel cavalry," and just before Barnett's was reached a volley greeted his horsemen as they crested a hill. It looked to the captain as if there were substance in the opposition, and, quite as the textbooks admonish, he worked rapidly to clear it up and allow "the uninterrupted march of the main body." Twenty dismounted troopers under a captain were thrown into the woods on one side of the road, and a similar number under a lieutenant into a cornfield on the other side, while dismounted men from two companies advanced along the road. After a running fight of four miles, a mounted charge broke the enemy detachment that had rallied at a house on a hill; but a charge by the reformed Confederates regained the position and forced the Federals back. Hamilton's infantry was pressing close, and Willcox withdrew to let the rifles of the foot soldiers take over. Three companies of the Fifth Iowa were deployed and soon cleared the situation. After they had pushed the hostile detachment from position to position for several miles, the Hawkeye soldiers turned over their tiring task to four companies of neighbors from the Twenty-sixth Missouri. At a road junction on the brow of a hill about two miles from Iuka the main body was halted and the skirmish line was pushed rapidly forward. The hour was about four o'clock, and a sharp battle was only a very few minutes off.[7]

The skirmishers had advanced some four hundred yards when they were greeted by a volley from a battle line the enemy had just deployed across the road, for until three o'clock Price had had his entire command in position to block Ord. Soon the first Confederate brigade of six regiments that had been hurried to the south was joined by another of four; then two more were brought up, so that the eighteen regiments of the division of Brigadier General Henry Little, as well as two batteries, were available to contest the advance of the seventeen regiments and six batteries of the Federals. The initial advantage was with the Confederates, for the uneven and wooded country made deployment of the Federal column extremely difficult. Hamilton, who was just behind the line of skirmishers, saw the danger and as quickly as possible got three regiments of his leading brigade into position, as well as the Eleventh Ohio battery. With this force he opened the battle for the Federals. The balance of his division was soon put in line, and in due course the first brigade of Stanley's division, though all on a restricted front.[8]

The Southerners pushed the attack, and the Federals were forced back until the guns of the Ohio battery were captured, but not until 16 of its men had been killed and 35 wounded beside their pieces. Among the Confederates to fall was General Little, killed early in the action. When darkness came there were 141 Federal dead, 127 of them from the leading brigade, that of Colonel John B. Sanborn. In fact, in one entire division the casualties, with the exception of the Eleventh Missouri, had been negligible.[9]

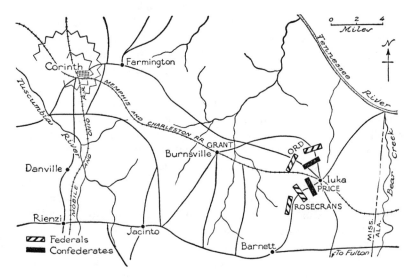

BATTLE OF IUKA, SEPTEMBER 19, 1862

Rosecrans, Ord, and Price each had two divisions, but the total Federal and Confederate strengths were about the same.

Rosecrans apparently never explained why he had not adhered to his purpose—reiterated in a note to Grant at 6:00 A.M. of the 19th— to advance up the Fulton as well as the Jacinto road. The change may have been fortunate, for contact between the two columns would have been almost impossible until near the town, and one cannot tell how Rosecrans would have handled the difficult situation which might have developed unless he had held back his leftmost column until coordination was assured. As things were, he rearranged his troops with the expectation of another day of battle, and at 10:45 P.M. wrote a note to Grant describing briefly what had happened, adding, "The ground is horrid, unknown to us, and no room for deployment. Could not use our artillery at all. Fired but few shots." Then, speaking as if he were the commander, a habit he not infrequently affected, he said, "Push in onto them until we can have time to do something. We will try to get a position on our right which will take Iuka." [10]

Grant must have been much pleased when about 4:00 P.M. Edward Ord reported to his headquarters. This Maryland-born soldier was, like Grant, an officer who would remain calm in all circumstances and who would always be a gentleman. Though he had had no combat experience in the Mexican War—being on duty in California—he quickly revealed aggressive talents and the quality that would attach him to a superior—dependability. Like Sheridan, he would be one of the little group in the parlor at Appomattox when Grant sat down to write a historic document.

On this September 19 Ord reported that the enemy was showing a bold front toward Burnsville and northward, with skirmishing throughout the day four miles to the east. He agreed with Grant that the last reports from Rosecrans made it undesirable to launch an attack until further word was received as to the whereabouts of the Jacinto column. Grant directed him, however, to move his entire force forward to within four miles of Iuka, "and there await sounds of an engagement between Rosecrans and the enemy before engaging the latter." At six there came to Ord's hand a dispatch that Ross had written at four: "For the last twenty minutes there has been a dense smoke arising from the direction of Iuka. I conclude that the enemy are evacuating and destroying the stores." In accordance with Grant's instructions Ord moved forward, but not a sound of the sharp battle to the south did he hear, for all day there was a wind "freshly blowing in the direction of Iuka." [11]

From Brigadier General Dabney H. Maury, commanding Price's Second Division, we learn that in the late afternoon he was ordered from his position west of Iuka and took post where he could support Little in his battle with Rosecrans. He added significantly that the Federals at once moved into the place he gave up. Knowing the qualities of Grant and Ord, one cannot doubt that a hard attack would have been made on Price's rear if the sound of battle had reached Ord after he left his chief.[12]

It was 8:35 on the morning of the 20th when Grant received Rosecrans's message of the night before. He at once wrote to Ord, "Get your troops up and attack as soon as possible. . . ." The injunction was, however, not needed. Ord, hearing artillery, had already pushed forward "with all possible dispatch." Almost simultaneously with the arrival of Rosecrans's courier there appeared two members of Grant's staff, and very embarrassed colonels they must have been. They had joined the southern column about noon the day before and had been present during the engagement. Eager to get word back to their chief, they had sought to shorten distance by cutting through, but—said the general in his report—"became lost and entangled in the woods and remained out overnight." [13]

The gunfire that Ord heard was from a few shells that Stanley had thrown into the town when upon advancing he found the enemy had departed except for a rear guard. At 9:45 Rosecrans sent a dispatch to Grant saying the Confederates were retreating with all possible speed; Stanley was following and Hamilton would endeavor to cut them off from the Fulton road. Using the tone of an ill-tempered commanding general, he concluded, "Why did you not attack this morning?"

The message came to the hands of James McPherson, now a brigadier, who evidently was with Ord. He opened it, and gave it to Ord, who wrote on it the indorsement:

We are out of rations to-night. We didn't hear any sounds of battle last p.m. Started with sounds of first guns for town. General McArthur got tangled up among the hill roads and caused me some delay, but I was within 3½ miles at 7 a.m. Took position there as per order till I could hear from General Rosecrans.[14]

The disappointed Ord was at once ordered back to Corinth, leaving, however, a brigade to garrison Iuka.[15] The move would provide food for his men and thwart any leap into the town by the zealous Van Dorn.

Not until he reached Iuka did Grant learn that the Fulton road was entirely open. He had been told in Rosecrans's early message of the morning before, "Cavalry will press in on the right to cut off their retreat." Then in the dispatch that Rosecrans sent soon after noon Grant had read, "Cavalry gone east toward Fulton road one hour," so he must have thought the plan to bar the enemy's avenue of escape was being carried out. The force referred to in the 12:40 P.M. message consisted of the Second Iowa Cavalry and two troops of the Seventh Kansas, and it did reach the Fulton road and followed it northward for a distance, destroying some tents, commissary stores, and two wagons. But it retired in time to reach Barnett's by dark. This force, especially if equipped to fell trees, could certainly have hampered Price's retirement during the night and might have led to the results that Grant had hoped for. The fault must have been in Rosecrans's orders, for he warmly praised his cavalry commander in his report. The next day he sent horsemen by another road to try to get just such a position ahead of the retiring enemy as had been held and relinquished.[16]

In the report which Grant sent immediately to Halleck he too optimistically said he thought the pursuing troops would break up the enemy badly "and possibly force them to abandon much of their artillery." At a point about eight miles from Iuka the Confederates waited in ambush for their pursuers; and though a Northern officer described the resulting clash quite differently than the Southern rearguard commander the pursuit seems to have been then abandoned with no greater results than the destruction of a few hundred small arms. Toward Rosecrans, Grant was more than generous when he said, "I cannot speak too highly of the energy and skill displayed by General Rosecrans in his attack and the endurance of the troops under him." Ord's command was described as zealous and eager for combat. But there was no boasting in the mildly climactic ending of this first battle report that Grant made direct to Washington: "I have reliable information that it was Price's intention to move over east of the Tennessee. In this he has been thwarted." [17] This made good reading in the North.

It was not strange that Grant did not learn of Price's change of plan, especially since the latter's chief of staff—who emphasized the excellent condition, equipment, training, and discipline of the Confederate force—later insisted that Price should have marched toward Nashville before Grant could attack him, in spite of the fact that Bragg's order for such a move was based upon a false premise. In his report Price stated that he had made dispositions to renew the battle on the 20th; but, knowing that his trains would be endangered even if he were victorious, of which he "had but little doubt," he determined to make the move upon which he "had already agreed with General Van Dorn." Significantly, the message that announced his final decision also said, "Enemy concentrating against me." [18]

If Price was indebted to a friendly wind,[19] he also owed much to the fact that Phil Sheridan had departed. One must believe that Sheridan would have seen that proper orders for the Fulton road were given him by Rosecrans, the first of the five subscribers to the statement, "He is worth his weight in gold."

After Price had disappeared to the south, Rosecrans turned his thoughts toward his old classmate Van Dorn, and so eager was he that after reaching Jacinto he stayed up until 1:00 A.M. of the 21st to write to Grant:

> If you can let me know that there is a good opportunity to cross the railroad and march on Holly Springs to cut off the forces of Buck Van Dorn I will be in readiness to take everything. If we could get them across the Hatchie they would be clean up the spout.[20]

This may have been the proper way for Rosecrans, the man fourth from the top in a class of fifty-six, to speak of Van Dorn, the man who had been fourth from the bottom. Or Rosecrans may have felt he owed himself some handsome promises in the first dispatch he signed as a major general—a promotion long overdue.[21]

The facts about the situation in the direction of Holly Springs were coming to Grant from Hurlbut, whose demonstration southward from Bolivar was precisely for the purpose of attracting the attention of Van Dorn. Messages arrived on the 21st describing the advance of Brigadier General Jacob Lauman's five-regiment brigade, reenforced by two six-gun batteries and covered by four hundred cavalrymen. An enemy force was known to be at Davis's Mill, seven miles south of Grand Junction, and Lauman returned rather hastily because of movements on his left flank. After sending Grant a message that revealed apprehension, Hurlbut telegraphed reassuringly, "General Lauman's command has returned all safe. . . ."[22]

Hurlbut was having all the worries of a detached commander, and the next day he telegraphed that an "intelligent deserter" had brought word that a strong force—20 regiments, 5 batteries, and 1,000 cavalry—under Van Dorn had moved north from Davis's Mill and would probably spend the night near Van Buren, where there was good water. Since they were said to be carrying only one day's rations, it was of course possible that the Confederate commander wanted nothing more than to give men and animals a deep, refreshing drink and a sleep in new surroundings, while puzzling the Federals a little. But one could not be sure, and Hurlbut felt that unless they fell back they would certainly attack. After requesting orders, he gave the assurance, "I shall of course hold this place, unless ordered to the contrary, to the last extremity." He ended with a piece of general news: "Breckinridge, with one of his brigades, has gone to Chattanooga." This was a near scoop, for it was not until two days later that Breckinridge issued an order at Meridian directing the movement to Chattanooga of two brigades, one of Kentuckians, one of Tennesseans—three regiments each.[23]

Grant handled the threat to Bolivar by returning the troops he had brought from there to Corinth, and the next day Hurlbut could telegraph happily: "Two loads of Ross' troops have come; the others will not be in before night. The enemy have unquestionably, from all reports, fallen back to Davis' Mill, about 10,000 strong. Cavalry are out in pursuit." [24]

With Bolivar free of danger, Grant was able to give attention to a possible offensive move. On the 18th Halleck had wired to him:

General Butler telegraphs me from New Orleans that the enemy is constructing two iron-clad vessels high up the Yazoo River, and thinks they can be reached by a small land force from Memphis or Helena. Consult with General Steele and the commander of the flotilla and, if possible, destroy these vessels before their completion.[25]

Brigadier General Frederick Steele had been in command at Helena since late August when Curtis departed on leave, the position being made permanent when Curtis was appointed on September 19 to head the newly reconstituted Department of the Missouri, with headquarters at St. Louis.[26] On the morning of the 22nd—even before matters had cleared at Bolivar—Grant assured Halleck: "Will try to set an expedition on foot for the destruction of rebel boats on the Yazoo," and had queried, "Do I understand that I am to have the co-operation of Steele's forces—cavalry particularly?" The next afternoon Halleck replied: "Arrange with General Curtis at Saint Louis in regard to Steele's co-operation. New troops will be sent you as they can be spared." This dispatch Grant picked up on the 24th at Jackson. That he was anticipating and was eager for further cooperation with the force at Helena was indicated by the promptness with which he wrote:

The enemy being driven from his position in front of Bolivar by the rapid return of troops drawn from there to re-enforce Corinth, and everything now promising quiet in our front for a short time, I shall go to Saint Louis in person to confer with General Curtis.[27]

Before he put these words on paper Grant surely recalled that he had been suspended from command a bare six months before, partly because of a perfectly justified trip to Nashville to confer with Buell. Telegrams had been flowing freely between him and Halleck since the latter went to Washington, but they were all coldly official. No reply had come to Grant's dispatch after the Battle of Iuka, which told Halleck he need worry no more about Price's possible advance into Tennessee. Thus there was no change in the attitude of his superior toward him. What about absenting himself under such conditions as now existed? Though he did not wait for permission, as a cautious person would have done, Grant pleaded his case a trifle, ending with the statement that, not having been well, he thought the trip would be of benefit.

He was off the same day, wiring to Halleck from Columbus to ask if he had authority to give a short leave of absence to General Quinby "to arrange for his family." "Do as you deem best with General Quinby," was the response of the General in Chief, who, in spite of the heading on Grant's wire, addressed him at Corinth. After inquiring as to Price, Halleck queried, "Do you hear anything from Nashville or Buell's army?" From this it would seem that Wright's dispatch to Halleck at 6:45 P.M. of the 24th, based on Nelson's message announcing that the advance of Buell's army had crossed Salt River, had not arrived by the morning of the 25th. Halleck's telegram reached Grant in St. Louis on the day it was sent. Answering at once, Grant had to say, "I do not hear a word from Buell's army." After again assuring Halleck that Price would not go to Tennessee, he added, "I understand that Breckinridge has gone by way of Mobile and Chattanooga." Once more he indicated that Bolivar was safe, and he closed: "I wrote from Jackson the object of my coming to Saint Louis. Will leave in the morning." [28]

No record seems to exist of the conversation between Grant and Curtis, but a revealing statement in a telegram from Grant to Halleck will be mentioned presently. Grant may have made a report of his visit in a letter he wrote to Sherman on the 27th from Columbus. Unfortunately, this letter is not in the records, though Sherman's reply shows that it had to do with the expedition to the Yazoo. [29]

While Grant was away, John Rawlins had moved headquarters from Corinth to Jackson. From his new location Grant issued on the 29th an order putting Brigadier General Grenville M. Dodge temporarily in command of Columbus and the area that included Forts Henry and Donelson. This thirty-one-year-old general, who would rise to a position of considerable importance before the end of the war, and who later became one of the country's great railroad builders, had come into service at the head of the Fourth Iowa Infantry. At the Battle of Pea Ridge he had commanded a brigade with distinction and had been wounded. Throughout the summer he had been at Trenton, twenty-five miles above Jackson, and the *Official Records* afford evidence of his alertness and energy in protecting the railroad from the ravages of guerrillas. He was also apt at forwarding information, and it was probably a report from him confirming the departure of Breckinridge that caused Grant to pass the word to Halleck with some confidence. A deserter from the Seventh Kentucky, known personally to Dodge, had come in with several fellow soldiers as well as a good budget of information. While Breckinridge was doubtless happy to get away from under the command of Van Dorn, he would not have been cheered by Dodge's report, which Grant was reading the day before he himself issued his entraining order at Meridian.[30]

In his first appraisal of the situation after his St. Louis outing, Grant made an error. A telegram he sent to Halleck from Corinth on September 30 stated that Price was at Ripley and Van Dorn at Somerville—eighteen miles west of Bolivar. His misplacement of the Mississippi general caused him to remark, "It looks as if Van Dorn was trying to effect a lodgment on the Mississippi." As the mistake was soon corrected, the most important statement in the dispatch was: "If Helena troops could now be sent across the river I think they would meet with no difficulty in getting to Grenada, and perhaps down on to the Yazoo." This certainly indicates that Grant had been unsuccessful in planning cooperation with Curtis. That officer, however, should not be hastily criticized. The new department which he had just been given was in an unsettled condition. With a fresh threat to southwestern Missouri developing and enemy forces assembling at Little Rock, he could hardly agree to send forces east of the Mississippi for the purpose of destroying two uncompleted vessels which, according to Sherman, would in any case be blockaded for five months because of low water in the Yazoo.[31]

It is vexing not to know what new reports came in—but come they certainly did, and the next day Grant had the situation correctly appraised. Corinth, from where he again telegraphed, was, he said, clearly to be the point of attack, "and that from the west or southwest." Price, Van Dorn, Villepigue, and Rust—Breckinridge's successor—were together. "My position is precarious," Grant said in closing, "but hope to get out of it all right." [32] Not a single man could come to him from outside; everything would depend upon his ability to concentrate—but not prematurely—forces necessarily dispersed to hold captured territory. The destruction of Grant and the redemption of western Tennessee was at the moment a major point in Confederate strategy. He had been stripped to aid Buell, now safe in Louisville, and with his diminished command he alone must save the remnant of Federal success of the winter and spring. Did the Washington High Command worry when it read the serious but uncomplaining sentence? Probably not.

Simultaneously there was going to Richmond a message from Van Dorn at Pocahontas, and a practiced writer of communiqués could not have begun better: "I have made union with General Price and am now before Corinth." He hoped to break Grant piece by piece, for he wrote, "It is said two divisions are left at Corinth." Elaborating, he stated: "Expect to take Corinth; move division to [Chewalla] in the morning to feel position and strength, and to cut, with cavalry, the railroad to Jackson, Tenn." [33] Isolate; then devour.

It was true that Grant had left two divisions of the Army of the Tennessee—the Second and Sixth—at Corinth, when he shifted Ord to command at Jackson and Bolivar. But Rosecrans also had the divisions of Hamilton and Stanley, and they were closed in toward Corinth in accordance with instructions from Grant, who also directed the recall of the garrison at Iuka. Thus, there would be 23,000 men in Corinth when Van Dorn struck. In addition, Corinth was intrenched. Though it is not clear at what figure Grant put the enemy, he assumed the Confederates exceeded his four divisions. Grant incorrectly believed that Van Dorn thought him capable of concentrating his forces in time to meet the Confederate attack.[34]

A dispatch from Stanley to Rosecrans on the 1st—relayed to Grant—told of prisoners taken by a cavalry patrol to the Hatchie, and said: "Reported rebel force 40,000. Prisoners don't know where they are going." Van Dorn's own soldiers had been bewildered by his march to Pocahontas; and Rosecrans, doubting that he would venture an attack on Corinth, hoped he would seek to neutralize the position and pass northward, giving him "an opportunity to beat the masking force and cut off their retreat." To clear the situation he ordered Colonel John M. Oliver's brigade of the Sixth Division—now under Brigadier General Thomas J. McKean—to proceed to Chewalla, where one regiment and a cavalry company were already posted. Oliver reached the heights near the little town just before dark; learning that the cavalry pickets had been fired upon, he soon had a line of battle of two regiments and two guns, well covered by pickets, while six companies explored a road running south to the bottoms along the Tuscumbia River.[35]

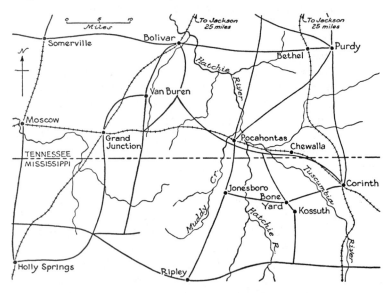

THE REGION WEST OF CORINTH

As day broke on the 2nd, Oliver's patrols began working the roads; before long, contact developed, light at first, then heavier. The enemy was in force and resolute, and when night came Oliver, after resisting as stoutly as he could and as much as his orders directed, found himself back at a point about seven miles from Corinth. There he set up for the night with his front alertly guarded.[36]

Though Van Dorn's effort at deception ended when he turned eastward at Pocahontas, he knew that he would push on in the morning with the hope of making a one-day conquest of Corinth and its imagined 15,000 defenders. Rosecrans, however, could not yet be certain the Confederate advance was more than a masking effort. In his 1:30 A.M. order of the 3rd he went as far as facts warranted, when he spoke of "indications of a possible attack on Corinth immediately." To be prepared, he deployed three divisions northwest and north of the town, in the order, left to right: McKean, Davies, Hamilton. Stanley was held in reserve.[37] Probably in accordance with previous instructions, a line was taken along the outer batteries erected by Halleck, which were well within the original works constructed in the spring by Beauregard. But in that position the divisions did not long remain.

At about 7:30 A.M. Oliver's pickets were driven in and the enemy struck his main line, to be at first repulsed. But the power in the advance being soon apparent, the colonel, pursuant to his instructions, fell back slowly until he occupied a favorable position near and north of the Memphis and Charleston Railroad and a little in advance of the old Confederate defensive line.* There he met General McArthur, who had been sent to appraise the situation. McArthur reported—according to Rosecrans—that the position "was of great value to test the advancing force," and he was accordingly ordered "to hold it pretty firmly with that view." "Pretty firmly" is a little vague; and before long McArthur had his own brigade in action with that of Oliver, and in due course two regiments, and then the third, of the brigade of Colonel Silas D. Baldwin of Davies's division. Davies evidently considered the position important, but Rosecrans spoke ambiguously about McArthur "contesting the ground almost as for a battle." [38]

Even before he had received McArthur's and Oliver's appeal for help, Davies had sought to aid Oliver by asking and receiving permission to move forward and occupy the old Confederate works to the north. Then came an order from Rosecrans "not to let the enemy penetrate beyond the rebel breastworks." Advancing to that line, Davies put the brigade of Brigadier General Pleasant A. Hackleman on the right and that of Richard Oglesby on the left, the latter reaching out toward Baldwin's brigade, which was with McArthur. Davies's division was one of battle-tested regiments: with two of them Grant had seized Paducah; two were Belmont regiments; most had been at Fort Donelson; all had been at Shiloh. But so depleted was the divi-

* See map, p. 92.

sion by wastage, absentees, and men on special duty, that Davies had on the field only 2,924 infantrymen and 264 artillerymen—officers and men. A small force it was, to hold the two-mile line between the Memphis and Charleston Railroad and the Mobile and Ohio, and entirely inadequate to give security to McArthur's right flank.* McArthur, however, held on until noon, repulsing many efforts to dislodge him. Then, with his right and rear threatened, he began his retirement. Davies was forced to conform, and at 1:00 P.M. Rosecrans realized "that the enemy were in full strength and meant mischief." [39]

An hour later Rosecrans addressed a one-sentence circular to division commanders: "For fear of a misunderstanding in relation to my orders, I wish it distinctly understood that the extreme position is not to be taken till driven to it." Though intended to banish misunderstanding, the dispatch increased it. Hamilton wrote later that neither he nor Davies understood it. Davies received the order while retiring to a line seven hundred yards in front of Fort Robinett, his fourth battle line, one with flanks protected and his men in the edge of a wood with a good field of fire. But there was little respite. Again and again the enemy attacked, to be driven back by musketry and the fire of the eleven guns still remaining. When the artillery ammunition was exhausted, the batteries were sent to Corinth to replenish, the infantry remaining to break further attacks with their rifles—the old infantry of C. F. Smith and W. H. L. Wallace. After Hackleman and Oglesby had both been gravely wounded, reenforcements—several times requested—arrived: Colonel Joseph Mower's brigade of Stanley's division. The fresh men were put in line, and during a lull Davies withdrew his hard-pressed regiments and retired to a line resting on Fort Robinett, to be joined there by his guns with replenished caissons and limbers.[40]

The troops on the left, fighting stubbornly, fell back upon McKean's third brigade of four Iowa regiments commanded by Colonel Marcellus M. Crocker, which had made a forced march the day before from Iuka and had been resting a mile west of Corinth. The line they formed, and held, enabled McKean to withdraw Oliver and McArthur to the vicinity of Corinth. With them came Baldwin's brigade, which passed into the town and rejoined Davies.[41]

While this heavy fighting was going on west of the Mobile and Ohio

* The map on p. 92 shows the region of the action. The positions of units changed rapidly.

Railroad, Hamilton was unengaged to the east. To keep connection with Davies, he retired from his position in the old Confederate line which he had reached about ten o'clock, changing front so as to face westward. Various messages came to him from Rosecrans, some not too clear, some too detailed for a division commander as competent as Hamilton. An order that bore no hour, but which Hamilton later said reached him about 3:30 P.M., explained that Davies had apparently fallen back "behind the works, his left being pressed in," and ordered Hamilton, if the retirement continued, to make a flank movement, "falling to the left of Davies when the enemy gets sufficiently well in so as to have full sweep. . . ." Hamilton wrote upon the back: "Respectfully returned. I cannot understand it." Presently a staff officer arrived and explained that Hamilton was to take position opposite Davies's *right,* and at five o'clock an order arrived which ended, "If you see the chance, attack fiercely." [42]

In accordance with what Rosecrans seemed to wish, Hamilton prepared to attack westward, Sullivan's brigade on the south and the first brigade, now under Brigadier Napoleon Bonaparte Buford, on the right. It was Buford, it may be recalled, who as colonel of the Twenty-seventh Illinois, became separated from the bulk of Grant's force at Belmont and required special embarkation. Now, according to Hamilton, Buford diverged too far to the right, one of his regiments becoming engaged with a few enemy skirmishers. Sullivan, however, with three regiments numbering only eight hundred men, advancing as directed through some extremely difficult terrain, took the enemy by surprise and captured eighty-two prisoners. The Confederates rallied and opened two batteries on him, whereupon Sullivan, unable to use any guns himself and unsupported by Buford, retired with the approval of Hamilton. The latter believed the demonstration aided Davies materially, and Sullivan made bold to write in his report, "Our advance was so entirely unexpected by the enemy that, had we been supported as intended, I may be pardoned for stating that in my opinion the fight of the succeeding day would not have occurred." [43]

The force of 22,000 men which had driven the Federals back close to Corinth on the left and center had marched about eight miles before it deployed in line of battle in front of Beauregard's old intrenchments. There were three divisions: Major General Mansfield

Lovell's—brought by Van Dorn—and those of Hébert and Maury, still under Price. No time was needed for reconnaissance, the country being familiar to Van Dorn—as he explained in his report—so that the force was ready for battle by 10:00 A.M., in the order, right to left, Lovell, Maury, and Hébert. The Memphis and Charleston Railroad was the boundary between Lovell and Maury. Nine of the eleven brigades were in line with only two in reserve, an arrangement not auguring well for the quick decision Van Dorn hoped for. Though he believed himself superior in numbers, the terrain was bad and he had no strong reserve with which to attack the inner intrenchments. The terrific fighting of Davies's division, outnumbered three to one between the converging railroads, forced the deployment of at least one of the reserve brigades by four o'clock. Though Van Dorn lamented that there had not been one more hour of daylight,[44] when the fighting ended the unused power was clearly with Rosecrans: Hamilton's division, one brigade of Stanley's, and one of McKean's that had had but one regiment in action.

The heat had been intense—like that of a midsummer day. Men were casualties not only to bullets but to the sun. Canteens were empty, so that during lulls there could be no refreshing drinks of tepid water. But for the care of their wounded the Federals were fortunate in having the two hotels in Corinth. Together in one room Davies found his three brigade commanders; while he was present Hackleman died. It was a night with a brilliant moon, which facilitated the moving of men already weary almost unto death: Van Dorn, to try again for victory; Rosecrans again to defend, until he saw an opening. At 11:30 Rosecrans, who had sent a dispatch to Grant near midday, wrote again. Only Davies's troops had, he said, been "really engaged." The battle in fact was "bushwacking" because the troops did not know the ground, though many had been stationed in the vicinity. He ended: "If they fight us to-morrow I think we shall whip them. If they go to attack you we shall advance upon them. General Hackleman killed." [45]

Because the wires leading northward had been cut, Rosecrans's message went by courier over moonlit forest roads. But Grant knew a battle was in progress, and he was making efforts to turn a repulse into a catastrophe for Van Dorn. From Bethel, where Colonel Isham

N. Haynie commanded, a dispatch had arrived on the 2nd reporting the return of a scouting party that had been within a mile of Pocahontas and had "captured 3 of Price's men and 2 spies, citizens." The invading force was put at from 30,000 to 35,000. Messages on the 3rd told Grant of the destruction of railroad track, bridges, and the telegraph to Corinth, and a contraband was reported as asserting "the rebels say they go to Corinth and then to join Bragg's army." Finally Grant had this from Haynie:

> The two couriers sent last night are here; got to Corinth safely; delivered dispatches; were attacked to-day coming back; lost one horse wounded. They are fighting at Corinth; rebels investing it close at hand. Couriers lost dispatches sent me by General Rosecrans. The general told the courier if he lost them it was not much.[46]

In early afternoon McPherson, who was in charge of railroads and had been in Columbus when word came of the destruction of the track near Corinth, reported to Grant; and there could hardly have been a more welcome person. Before long he was on the way to Bethel with 270 men of the Engineer Regiment of the West. Presently the telegraph brought an order of momentous import to him: Grant had made him a troop commander. Two regiments would be sent from Jackson during the night. McPherson was to take command of them, as well as of the two already advancing southward from Bethel, and "proceed without delay and with all possible dispatch to Corinth" and report to Rosecrans.[47]

For two days Hurlbut had been waiting at Bolivar with alerted troops. But not until the Confederates were definitely committed against Corinth did Grant dare throw him against their rear. "My column will move at 3 o'clock a.m. in marching order with three days provisions. . . . A line of couriers will be kept up to General Ross, who will telegraph to you," was Hurlbut's response when at last he was released. In another dispatch he reminded Grant that it was forty-six miles to Corinth, and said: "On reaching Davis' Bridge I shall of course know whether the enemy are repulsed or not; if not repulsed, I propose to cut through; if repulsed, to destroy their line of retreat in this direction." Grant knew the man who had commanded the Fourth Division at Shiloh could be relied upon, while from Haynie's telegram he knew his message to Rosecrans had been delivered.

Though the message does not survive, Grant stated in his report that he informed Rosecrans about the move from Bolivar, "and directed him to follow up the enemy the moment he began to retreat." [48]

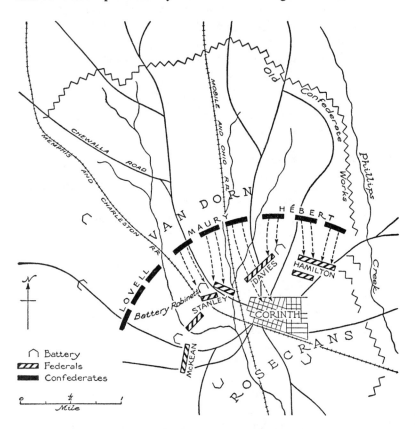

BATTLE OF CORINTH, OCTOBER 4, 1862, 9:00 A.M.

On the 3rd the Federals had been driven back from positions along the old Confederate works. Van Dorn's attack on the morning of the 4th was held, and a counterstroke initiated by Hamilton led to a Federal victory.

Day was just breaking when the Confederate artillery opened upon the Union line, drawn in close to Corinth. "It was grand," wrote Napoleon Buford. "The different calibers, metals, shapes, and distances of the guns caused the sounds to resemble the chimes of old Rome when all her bells rang out." But Van Dorn thought not of chiming bells but of the infantry which was supposed to move forward, yet did not. His plan contemplated that Hébert would attack heavily and early on the left; Lovell would tarry a while on the right, with skirmishers feeling the enemy, until Hébert was heavily engaged; then he would roll the Federal left back into town while Maury in the center moved "quickly to the front and directly at Corinth." [49]

But Hébert was sick, and hours passed before Van Dorn learned the fact and named Brigadier General Martin E. Green to command the left. According to Rosecrans, the enemy gunfire had been silenced by seven o'clock and it was two hours later when his own skirmishers, exploring the woods to the front, proclaimed by their fire that the enemy was in great force. Soon heavy columns appeared, bearing down first on Davies in the right center, then on Stanley to his left. Davies's division gave way, its break-up precipitated in part by the runaway caissons and limbers of a captured battery belonging to Hamilton, on Davies's right. Davies, who was born in New York, and who was a classmate of Lee, Joseph Johnston, and Ormsby Mitchel, wrote in his report:

The Confederates took possession of the earthwork, captured the seven guns left in it, and held our whole line. Some few of them advanced beyond it some 50 yards, but the troops having gallantly rallied, drove back the enemy with slaughter, recaptured the guns, charged the enemy from the whole line, directing a most murderous fire upon them, punishing them most severely for their temerity, and in the most splendid style made, I think, a suitable apology for, and corrected, unassisted, their fault.

Advancing beyond their old line, some of Davies's men were struck by the shot and shell from a Union battery that was firing over the town. The general himself had a narrow escape, and he wrote in his report, "I sent two orderlies in succession to the commander of this battery, begging him to reserve his fire for the enemy." [50]

At about eleven o'clock Colonel John W. Fuller, commanding a four-regiment Ohio brigade of Stanley's division, saw the enemy approaching through the woods in four close columns, their objective Battery Robinett. His men had not been engaged the day before, but the full fury of desperate attacks was to fall upon them today. Nine of the thirteen line officers of the Sixty-third Ohio and 45 per cent of the brigade were killed or wounded. The Forty-third lost Colonel

J. L. Kirby Smith, pronounced by Fuller "the most accomplished officer of the brigade." Only five years out of West Point, he "fell while giving commands as if at parade." Stanley, despairing of "words to describe this model soldier," wrote, "The best testimony I can give to his memory is the spectacle I witnessed myself, in the very moment of battle, of stern, brave men weeping as children as the word passed, 'Kirby Smith is dead.'" The guns of Robinett were not served by certificated artillerymen, but by infantrymen, and Stanley recorded how they reverted to former attachments in this hour of heavy battle: "The old soldiers of the First Infantry quit their cannon and picked up their old trusty muskets and prevented the enemy crossing the parapet with the bayonet." Not far beyond the ditch there fell Colonel William P. Rogers of the Second Texas, the gallant leader of the assault.[51]

On the right, Hamilton met the attack mostly by artillery fire, and when this checked the enemy he ordered his whole line to advance. Within minutes those who had seemed so nearly defeated had won the battle. "Our lines melted under their fire like snow in thaw," wrote Captain E. H. Cummins of Van Dorn's staff, while the general himself—who incorrectly attributed the sudden change in the battle to "fresh troops from Iuka, Burnsville, and Rienzi, that had succeeded in reaching Corinth in time"—said, "Exhausted from loss of sleep, wearied from hard marching and fighting, companies and regiments without officers, our troops—let no one censure them—gave way. The day was lost." But Van Dorn was equal to the occasion, quite as he had been at Pea Ridge; and he promptly ordered Lovell, whose division was about to advance against the Federal left, to at once shift a brigade to the center to cover the retirement of the army.[52]

The hour was not yet twelve, and according to Stanley it was announced early in the afternoon that a pursuit would be made. Thus it was probably early when Hamilton received from Rosecrans the brief message, "Hurlbut is in rear of the rebels. Prepare for an advance movement." Hamilton had not been heavily engaged—Buford had only one officer and six men killed in his five regiments and two batteries—and McKean had engaged in nothing but occasional artillery fire. But the pursuit which should have been pushed without delay was postponed. Rosecrans would appear to have been exhausted and a little unsettled, for only thus can one condone his riding to Davies's division and publicly accusing it of being "a set of cowards." The enemy strength in its sector and its casualties—800 killed and wounded out of 3,000 engaged—refute the charge, which, to his credit, Rosecrans did not repeat in his report or his subsequent account of the battle. In the latter he took credit that not until 4:00 A.M. of the 4th—not 3:00 A.M. as he said in his report—did he lie down to get some rest, only to be aroused by the artillery a half-hour later.[53] Apparently his essential orders had been given before midnight; his division commanders were all professionally trained (four out of four as against Grant's one out of six at Shiloh); they needed no supervision. Four hours of sleep might have protected Rosecrans from the danger of collapse when the excitement of battle ended.

To McPherson, who reached Corinth at four o'clock, Rosecrans must have seemed indifferent both to his opportunity and his duty. The two regiments from Jackson had reached Bethel at daybreak, and the cars carried them twelve miles farther south before they were detrained. Over a road that led eastward so as to skirt the Confederate army, the march was started to the sound of distant cannonading, "the men stepping out at a quick pace, notwithstanding the intense heat of the day and the prospect of a march of 15 miles before them, all hoping to get in in time to take part in the contest." The two regiments that had left Bethel the day before were picked up where they had halted, and the augmented command was hurried forward by its aggressive brigadier. McPherson had talked with Grant only the afternoon before; he knew the mission of the men he led and that Grant thought Hurlbut would be in peril if there were not a prompt pursuit from Corinth. A little rest after those hard fifteen miles, a little water, and his men would have been ready to push on. But he was ordered to bivouac for the night.[54]

The Bolivar column—some 5,000 strong, with regiments stripped to their ammunition wagons and a single one for baggage—halted at five o'clock on Muddy Creek, west of Pocahontas. In spite of some resistance, it had covered close to twenty-five miles. A few days later Hurlbut said in an order to his troops: "The march was arduous, the undertaking desperate. My orders were to reach Rosecrans at all hazards and relieve him or perish." A message reporting progress had been sent to Grant before noon; in the one dispatched after the halt, Hurlbut said, "We have driven in the pickets of [the] enemy up to Davis' Bridge, where my cavalry encountered two regiments of rebel cavalry at sunset and fell back." After saying he would push on as rapidly as possible but did not believe he could reach Corinth the next day, Hurlbut closed, "A citizen reports Davis' Bridge destroyed; if so, the game is up, and I shall return to save my own command." [55]

Hurlbut's dispatch did not arrive until the 5th, but on the 4th Grant received some Corinth news from Haynie. A courier had reached the town, but, though he must have had a dispatch for Rosecrans, he brought none back. Being curious, he hovered around the general and picked up fragments of conversation between Rosecrans and a colonel. The picture he gave Haynie was somewhat distorted: Price had fallen back, but not Van Dorn; the latter had sixty or seventy guns; if Van Dorn held his position Rosecrans would open on him with his siege guns. "As the courier came on here he heard cannon about 9 o'clock," was the concluding sentence of Haynie's telegram.[56] While Rosecrans was normally careful to keep his superior informed, he seems to have made no report at this important time. Having been ordered to pursue the enemy promptly, he perhaps did not wish to reveal that he was waiting until the morning to start.

The hard-marching Bolivar force secured Davis's Bridge before it could be destroyed, but not without bold and sharp fighting that won praise from Edward Ord. Arriving at seven-thirty on the morning of the 5th, he assumed command, and for the first time he saw the aggressiveness of the Army of the Tennessee. The road to the Hatchie was "narrow and winding, through swamp and jungle," and cut by ridges. Veatch, whose brigade was leading, had gone only a short distance when he met cavalry resistance. Deploying a short battle line, he pushed ahead; after advancing two or three miles his own horsemen reported hostile infantry and guns, and soon he was hit by "grape, canister, and shell." The enemy was driven from ridge to ridge, and a four-gun battery was taken; at the bridge two hundred prisoners were gathered in. "The river and the bridge were gained, but the fight was not ended," wrote Veatch. Ord told him to cross the "miserable bridge"—Ord's description—and form line beyond. The Fifty-third Indiana led the way, but after crossing, it received fire which threw it into confusion, the ground being too restricted for deployment. With some difficulty the Fifteenth Illinois crossed and moved in good order to the other side of the road; regiments of Lauman's brigade followed.[57]

At 2:10 P.M. Ord dictated a short dispatch to Rosecrans, to be forwarded by Grant: "We have been fighting all a.m. and have driven the enemy across Davis' Bridge, on the Hatchie; they are contesting the ground at every point, and Van Dorn's forces are increasing rapidly. If you can possibly produce a diversion do so." The aide who wrote added a postscript: "General Ord is wounded and General Hurlbut is in command." Writing to Grant at 6:00 P.M. from a hospital at Pocahontas, Ord spoke highly of Hurlbut, Veatch, and Lauman, adding that the crossing of the bridge under grape and canister from three batteries "proved that wherever their officers dare lead them the men will go." A habitual concealer of his feelings, Grant must have felt deeply when he read Ord's report about his subordinates: "Gallant officers! So much praise of them is entirely unnecessary." [58]

When he resumed command Hurlbut had the advantage of knowing the ground, having once encamped on the hill the enemy occupied, which he now took after a half-hour's fighting. Batteries quickly put in position smashed the head of a column that sought to seize one of them; and under cover of a demonstration the enemy withdrew about 3:30 P.M. Hurlbut did not pursue because of shortness of provisions and the necessity of caring for wounded, prisoners, and captured munitions. From prisoners he learned of the Federal victory at Corinth and could well feel that his paramount duty was to hold securely the road to Pocahontas. Four troops of the Fifth Ohio Cavalry did, however, keep sufficient contact with the retiring enemy to discover that he had changed his route and was crossing the Hatchie at Crum's Mill, seven miles above Davis's Bridge. [59]

The courier who had eavesdropped on Rosecrans reported to Haynie that at 2:00 P.M. of the 4th Rosecrans had ordered "three regiments and some batteries out in that direction"—northwest of Corinth. He was inaccurate in some particulars, but the reconnaissance that McArthur conducted showed what could have been accomplished by a vigorous pursuit by McPherson's regiments and other troops that had not been heavily engaged. After marching with two regiments up the Kossuth turnpike far enough to learn the enemy was not in that direction, McArthur turned northward. Presently he discovered the enemy rear guard and followed it for a distance of four miles. Turning northward again he picketed a line as far as the Mobile and Ohio Railroad, inclosing the Confederate hospitals and capturing about three hundred prisoners in addition to fifty wounded officers and five hundred wounded men, his command "remaining under arms without food or rest till morning." When day came McArthur was joined by the remaining regiments of his brigade, a battery, and the four-regiment brigade of Oliver, who at 2:00 A.M. had been ordered "to assist him in the pursuit of the enemy." Leaving his own two regiments under the colonel of the Twenty-first Missouri to guard prisoners and salvage arms and material, McArthur pushed on.

At a distance of seven miles from Corinth, McArthur was met by two hundred of the enemy under a colonel "bearing a flag of truce." If Rosecrans had been personally in the lead, a message could have gone at once to Van Dorn that his dead would be cared for. As it was, McArthur was detained for three hours, long enough, as he discovered presently, to allow the three brigades of Lovell to get away. After he resumed his march he came up with McPherson, who, with his small division augmented by a battery and five companies of cavalry, had crossed over from a road to the north; and thereupon McArthur fell in behind this force.[60] It would clearly have been possible to have put McPherson, McArthur, and Oliver in position on the 4th to attack Lovell's rear guard early on the 5th.

In spite of Rosecrans's delay in starting and the lengthy pursuit order issued on the 5th—probably to confirm and extend verbal instructions of the day before—march directions were inadequate, and all four divisions met on the same road. Few things will make a general more articulate than a tight road jam; and although it was Sunday the convergence of four divisions should have produced something historic in the way of military eloquence. By changing a few words in Hamilton's proper sentence, "Much confusion and delay occurred from want of a commander," one might get an accurate picture of the exasperating situation. Rosecrans, on learning of the tie-up, wrote to McKean sharply: "Halt your train, turn it out, and park it. I am told it is a mile long. . . . You are in the way of the other divisions." Stanley, reporting his guide did not know the roads, received the message: "Dispatch received; will send you another guide. You should have taken the road to the right. . . ." A half-hour later a second message repeated the promise of a new guide and told Stanley to advance rapidly and if possible to overtake McPherson. But a message to the latter explained that the main column had fallen "behind-hand" and ordered him to halt until support arrived.[61]

A sequence of dispatches was sent to Grant. The first told of McArthur's advance, of the plans for the general pursuit, and of the muddled march. Rosecrans's rested mind traveled across the Missis-sippi and he advised, "Now is the time for Steele to pitch in, while they are all looking this way." A second report gave his answer to Van Dorn about burying the dead, and queried: "Where is Hurlbut? Now is the time to pitch in. If they stand this side of Chewalla we shall fight where there is no water." A final message saying that the leading troops had reached Chewalla ended: "Progress very slow. McKean in the way. Order us forage at once or our animals will starve." [62]

In two telegrams to Halleck, Grant did the best he could with his information: The enemy under Van Dorn, Price, and Lovell had been repulsed at Corinth with heavy loss and was in full retreat; McPherson had arrived; there were from seven hundred to one thousand prisoners, besides the wounded; Ord had crossed the Hatchie, taking guns and prisoners; much of Rosecrans's force had reached Chewalla. The second message ended: "At this distance everything looks most favor-able, and I cannot see how the enemy are to escape without losing everything but their small-arms. I have strained everything to take into the fight an adequate force and to get them to the right place." [63]

As Grant's quiet sentences sped to the nation's distant, eager capital, couriers were searching moonlit woods and fields for five division commanders, to deliver Rosecrans's nine o'clock circular:

Am coming out to Chewalla with car-load of water. No news from any of you for several hours. Ord has been heavily engaged with the enemy at Davis' Bridge. We must push on as lightly as possible. Baggage has, I understand, interfered with your progress, which certainly has not been remarkable. We must push ahead as soon as the men get a little rest, and be with them by daylight. Send messengers to Chewalla report-ing your position.[64]

Early the next morning—October 6—McPherson, who had been stopped short by the enemy rear guard just east of the Tuscumbia, found the Confederates withdrawn and the bridge destroyed. In less than an hour a temporary structure that would carry artillery and

cavalry was ready, and the pursuit was continued. It was soon discovered that Van Dorn, having lost Davis's Bridge, had turned southward on a road that led to Bone Yard, where he could pick up the
Corinth-Jonesboro road that crossed the Hatchie at Crum's Mill. The
route was strewn with all sorts of equipment, including six caissons

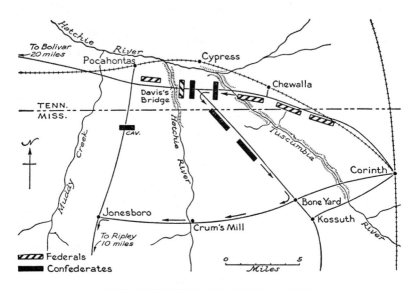

VAN DORN ESCAPES FROM A TRAP

and a battery forge. In one place felled trees blocked the road, but
they were soon removed by McPherson's engineers, while his weary
men got some rest and a good meal—a midafternoon "breakfast,"
according to Colonel Michael Lawler. At 10:30 P.M. McPherson
reached Jonesboro and bivouacked for the night, to take the road
again early the next morning. Advance was slow because of the necessity of thorough reconnaissance and frequent cavalry skirmishing.
Not until the 8th did he arrive at Ripley with his main body, though
some cavalrymen entered the town near midnight, soon after the departure of the enemy for Holly Springs.[65]

Van Dorn had been able to give his men some rest on the 7th, and
from Ripley he sent a telegram giving Richmond his version of his
misadventure. His defeat was due, he said, to the arrival of "fresh
reenforcements" for the Federals. Though this was not so, he cor-

rectly stated that the Bolivar force had cut his intended line of retreat and compelled him to turn southward. "Bloody affair," he said. "Enemy still threaten. Will fight him at all points. There are about 40,000 men still in West Tennessee. We will have hard fighting." There was something ominous in the determined attachment of the Yankees for the corner of Jefferson Davis's beloved Mississippi, and he wrote on Van Dorn's message: "Read. It will be necessary to re-enforce, if possible, at once." [66]

The 7th found Rosecrans personally at Crum's Mill in a spirit of high hope. All he needed was the chance, and the Confederate cause in the whole state would be about crushed. That was the general tenor of a dispatch he wrote to Grant at 2:00 A.M. He explained what Hurlbut and Sherman should do, talked of pushing the enemy to Mobile and Jackson (Mississippi), directed Grant, "Beg the authorities North to send us more troops," and listed other things that should be done. One item in the impassioned recital surely did not surprise Grant. Just before his concluding exhortation, "Telegraph Quinby to come or send him down with all you can," Rosecrans wrote: "A civilian must take the place of McPherson. He is needed in the field; he adds twenty per cent. to any troops he commands." But this had already been cared for. In a letter Grant wrote to Halleck two days before, he said, "I would feel more strengthened today if I could place McPherson in command of a division than I would to receive a whole brigade of the new levies." [67]

In making good on bold promises Rosecrans had done as badly at Corinth as at Iuka, and it is hard to reconcile his thinking in the early hours of October 7 with the statement in his report that the Confederates numbered, "according to their own authorities, 38,000 men." Deducting even his grossly exaggerated figures for their losses, Van Dorn would still be decidedly the superior. In a later message to Grant on the 7th Rosecrans spoke of the enemy meeting "the 9,000 exchanged prisoners," and though he said he thought the Confederates were scattered he added significantly, "They have much artillery." The 15,000 prisoners recently exchanged at Vicksburg—many of whom Grant had captured at Fort Donelson—were an element in the situation very difficult to appraise. Hurlbut had telegraphed to Grant on the 3rd that they were arriving at Davis's Mill, and Grant could not know that there had been delay in arming them. Price testified at the Court of Inquiry that later heard the charges brought against Van Dorn, that he had favored delaying the attack on Corinth until the returned prisoners were received. He also revealed the belief that, together with another unit, they made a reenforcement of 12,000 to 15,000 which the retreating army received upon arrival at Holly Springs.[68]

All things considered, Grant acted soundly on the 6th when, on learning that Van Dorn was across the Hatchie, he ordered Hurlbut back to Bolivar and directed Rosecrans to return to Corinth. But so vigorously did the latter protest the order that Grant told him to remain at Ripley while he consulted Halleck. It was a questionable procedure, for the General in Chief was too involved in other theaters to give much attention and too remote to understand the situation. Grant, however, did not wait for Washington to decide the Rosecrans case, and a second telegram to Halleck ended: "On reflection I deem it idle to pursue further without more preparation, and have for the third time ordered his return." [69]

The telegraph was working rapidly on October 8, and before the day ended Grant had this from Halleck: "Why order a return of our troops? Why not re-enforce Rosecrans and pursue the enemy into Mississippi, supporting your army on the country?" Grant replied that an army could not "subsist itself on the country except in forage." Moreover, Rosecrans had already been reenforced with everything at hand, even at the risk of raids against the railroads. (Six regiments had been withdrawn from guarding them.) Referring probably to the exchanged prisoners, Grant said he had information that reserves were on the way to the enemy and that there were fortifications to which he could return. Prophetic of the calamity that would within a year befall Rosecrans when operating on his own responsibility, Grant cautioned, "Although partial success might result from farther pursuit disaster would follow in the end." Then came a sentence that revealed his full subordination to his superior and his complete acceptance of the responsibility of command: "If you say so, however, it is not too late yet to go on, and I will join the moving column and go to the farthest extent possible." [70]

It was certainly unfortunate that there was not a cordial relationship between Grant and Halleck. The fault lay with the latter, for Grant's good regard, professional and personal, for his superior had been put into the record before the battle at Corinth. In a letter to

Congressman Washburne a few days after Halleck's departure for the East in July, Grant had said that there could be no better selection for Secretary of War or for General in Chief, with headquarters in Washington, adding the comment: "He is a man of gigantic intellect and well studied in the profession of arms. He and I have had several little spats but I like him and respect him nevertheless." [71] Halleck certainly saw that Grant's final telegram disposed of the question of further pursuit of Van Dorn; and he should have so informed him. Otherwise, Grant might hold Rosecrans at Ripley, and a telegram approving and commending his judgment was the only proper ending for the case.

One must note, however, that other fronts were demanding attention from the High Command: McClellan was tarrying in Maryland and asking for three or four thousand hospital tents; Pope had been raising questions as to operations against the Indians in the northwest; Curtis had just inquired about putting the troublesome Jim Lane—of whom Halleck so strongly disapproved—in command of three Kansas regiments he had raised, saying Blunt had recommended it because Lane would "scare the rebels in Southwest Missouri and Arkansas very much." The Department of the South was demanding consideration because of a change of commanders. Ormsby Mitchel, the new commander, had on September 20 written to Halleck, sketching the situation and asking if he might not be strengthened by his old division and another one composed of new levies. In view of Mitchel's known vigor, here was the question of turning the theater into a more active one. In a letter to Stanton on the same day, Mitchel had reported that officers and men were prejudiced against the Negroes because they thought them the recipients of more favors from the government than were the soldiers. Mitchel's suggestion for the difficulty was the subordination to the department commander of the officers in charge of Negroes and the plantations being operated.[72] On this question of high policy Halleck would certainly be consulted.

Enclosed with Mitchel's letter to Halleck was a copy of a recent report of the department medical director that could not be passed on to the Surgeon General and then forgotten. There had been an outbreak of yellow fever with eight deaths in a detachment of a single regiment. It looked as if the scourge might be under control, and Mitchel had spoken hopefully in his letter. But in addition to military operations and the Negro question, the possibility of a serious epidemic in the Department of the South was a matter for concern at Army Headquarters in those first days of October. Before the month had ended, Mitchel himself would die of the dread disease.

It was a war of great magnitude, with many troublesome theaters for a General in Chief to direct with a staff of seven officers—only one of them a general—and sixteen enlisted men—eleven of whom were privates. In the 46 days between July 29 and September 12 Halleck sent 421 telegrams to 100 different persons. Grant was the recipient of 21, McClellan, Pope, and Burnside exceeding him with 65, 42, and 33, respectively. The originals of the telegrams received by Halleck in the 16 days between August 28 and September 12 make a bound volume of 524 pages.[73] Letters also were numerous, sometimes long, hard to read, requiring time to assimilate, and some, like that of Mitchel, raising questions of much import. While a telegram rounding out the Corinth matter should have gone to Grant, it must be admitted that Halleck was short-handed and overburdened.

With all the different theaters Lincoln also was concerned, but while he read many of the telegrams that came, the number of dispatches he sent was small in comparison with those that went from Halleck. On October 8 Lincoln sent to Grant the first of the numerous telegrams he addressed to him. He extended congratulations to all concerned in the "recent battles and victories," expressed regret at Hackleman's death, bespoke his anxiety for Oglesby, "an intimate personal friend," and asked, "How does it all sum up?" [74]

When "summed up" Corinth is found to have been one of the hardest of the smaller battles of the war. About 21,000 men were engaged on each side, and the killed and wounded were in good balance—if one accepts, as is now generally done, the Confederate figures about themselves, and not those of Rosecrans—the Federals having 2,196 and Van Dorn, 2,470. But the attacker's "missing" were nearly six times those of the defenders—1,763 to 324. Total casualties at the Hatchie were: Hurlbut, 570; Van Dorn, 605.[75]

In his postwar article Rosecrans said, "If Grant had not stopped us, we could have gone to Vicksburg." Perhaps no more fatuous statement about the war was made by one with good grounds to know better. It was two hundred miles to Vicksburg by straight line, and Rosecrans was to discover at Chickamauga what can happen when an army advances deeply into enemy country. He gave in full Grant's second dispatch to Halleck about having ordered him back for the third time, but not the far more important final message. Nor did he refer to a report he passed on to Grant soon after he returned to Corinth. Said the general who a few days before had been so eager to press on: "A rumor is gaining currency among the secesh that Johnston [Joseph E.] with 40,000 men from Virginia, has arrived at Oxford." Such an actually accomplished reenforcement was out of the question, but the report might have been an exaggeration of a lesser move in progress. Certainly Rosecrans did not consider it mere idle gossip, for he said: "It must receive prompt attention. . . . Tell Sherman to put spies in motion; I will do the same to find out all I can." [76]

In the matter of the participation of the Bolivar force, Rosecrans was something less than accurate, and it is difficult to believe it was not by design. The rear blow, as he portrayed it, was entirely Hurlbut's idea—not something Grant had ordered and timed. Since Rosecrans did not reveal that he knew on the 4th that the move was being made, one sees the importance of his previously noted message to Hamilton on that day: "Hurlbut is in rear of the enemy. Prepare for an advance movement." And this raises an interesting question. When Rosecrans postponed pursuit he must have believed that Van Dorn would either voluntarily turn southward before he reached Davis's Bridge or be compelled to do so by Hurlbut; otherwise he was acquiescing to the possible destruction of the Bolivar force.[77] Grant's instructions to follow the enemy to Bolivar if he drove Hurlbut back that far [78] did not deprive Rosecrans of following the sound principle for a pursuit—get ahead of or strike the enemy flank, while a part of your force presses and engages his rear. Such would be the way in which Grant would later pursue Lee from Petersburg, and the doctrine is so obvious that Rosecrans cannot be excused because there was in his headquarters nothing like a modern field manual on operations.[79]

If two or even three of Rosecrans's divisions had taken the Bone Yard Road early on the 5th while the balance of his command followed McPherson, there would have been no snarled-up march; the southern column could have moved from Bone Yard toward Davis's Bridge if necessary,[80] but would actually have intercepted Van Dorn's column—train and reserve artillery leading—after it turned southward.[81] Then Rosecrans might have realized the satisfaction of seeing his old classmate really "go up the spout." [82]

The battle Rosecrans fought and won naturally raised the esteem in which he was then justly held. Some may have seen a resemblance in the engagement to Second Bull Run, where Pope had recently been defeated. In the first day of that battle Pope had heavily assailed Lee's left under Jackson, and though Stonewall was not driven from his position he had held it by a narrow margin. Again the next morning Pope attacked, like Van Dorn at Corinth, only to be later routed by a heavy counterstroke against his left, as was Van Dorn. And as Longstreet anticipated Lee's actual order to throw himself on the Federal left, so Hamilton chose the moment for the launching of the telling blow at Corinth. But there were differences. At Bull Run night had come before the battle was over; at Corinth it was barely noon. At the earliest possible moment Lee put Jackson in motion to march around and try to get behind Pope. At Corinth, Grant had Hurlbut block the Confederates' rear avenue of escape; but Rosecrans—following the Iuka pattern—left the side door open.

CHAPTER V

BATTLE IN KENTUCKY;
DECISION IN THE WHITE HOUSE

I sincerely wish war was an easier and pleasanter business than it is, but it does not admit of holidays.

Lincoln to Thomas H. Clay

IN HIS final report on his Kentucky campaign Bragg said that when he marched to Bardstown he expected to be joined by Kirby Smith for a prompt move against Louisville. Why was this not done? Before answering this important and interesting question we return to Munfordville, for it is there that Bragg's actions first come under criticism. Joseph Wheeler, then only a colonel commanding Hardee's cavalry brigade, but a lieutenant general when the war ended, contended in a well-known article that a single supreme commander could have achieved a signal victory over Buell south of Munfordville on September 18. All that would have been necessary, according to Wheeler, would have been to order Kirby Smith to that place to establish a preponderance of force. Horn, quoting General Basil Duke, who rode with John Morgan, is more severe. He indicts Bragg for not fighting Buell even without the aid of Smith, saying the conclusion is inescapable that Bragg was unequal spiritually to the responsibility of precipitating a battle. Bragg's claim of scarcity of supplies, according to Horn, was an afterthought invented as a cloak for timidity. One of Bragg's officers went so far as to say that Bragg had Buell "in the hollow of his hand." [1]

That Bragg was subject at times to irresolution, and could swing quickly from confidence to pessimism, is well agreed upon; and he definitely broke down before this campaign ended. But he was not timid when he stayed on the south side of Green River on September 17 and threw Buckner's division into Buell's face and made him forget his announced intention of being at the river early on the morning of the 18th. Neither Buell nor Bragg had ever directed an engagement, though both had splendid troops and good subordinates. Buell had a sufficient edge in numbers for victory and should have won if Bragg had carried the battle to him. Under such circumstances it is going too far to say that the weaker had the stronger "in the hollow of his hand."

Wheeler implies that Bragg would have had Smith present if the latter had not been an independent department commander; Horn, that Smith was virtually operating under Bragg's orders, but that Bragg simply did not instruct him "to join up." Though there is conflict in the criticisms, both are nullified by the fact that it was a hundred miles from Lexington to Munfordville, and orders to Smith would have had to be dispatched well before Bragg reached Glasgow, even assuming that Smith was concentrated and ready to move—which he was not. Surely it would have been the height of folly for Bragg to order Smith to join him without knowing the aspect of affairs about Lexington and elsewhere to the north.

On the very day that Bragg moved from Glasgow to Munfordville an excellent report was written by Smith, and its contents must be noted in order to do justice to the two generals.

Smith was becoming alarmed because of the Federal concentration at Cincinnati, the arrival of part of Grant's army—Granger's division—and the indications that the Federals were preparing to advance. Calling his position very hazardous, he suggested that he might indeed have to fall back upon Bragg for support. But he saw this as a calamity, for many of the supplies he had amassed must then be destroyed, while recruiting would have to be stopped in the surrounding country. The sacrifice would, however, be necessary unless Bragg could join him before the arrival of the rest of Grant's army, which Smith not unnaturally expected. Louisville was, Smith thought, the point to strike for; and he did not believe the destruction of the force presently there would be especially difficult.[2] One cannot tell when Smith's dispatch reached Bragg, but it must have influenced him.

That he, just arrived in Kentucky and unoriented about the situation, should have deferred to Smith, who had been there for two weeks, was both natural and proper.

Bragg's statement in his dispatch to Richmond announcing the capture of Munfordville, that his junction with Smith was complete, was not accurate; and only the intention of moving toward Lexington without delay could justify the exaggeration. In the congratulatory order he issued on the same day—September 17—he told his soldiers that their fruitful victory "crowns and completes the separate campaign of this army." Only a short time could be given for repose. Then it would be necessary to resume the "march to still more brilliant victories." The next day, Bragg noted, had been set aside by the President as one of thanksgiving and prayer, and on that day he issued an order ending, "The troops will be ready to move at daylight to-morrow." But rumors that Buell was advancing caused a day's delay, though the trains started on the 19th.[3]

Suppose that upon receiving Smith's dispatch, Bragg had ordered him to destroy his unmovable stores and march to Munfordville, while he waited behind Green River with a good bridgehead on the south bank and with the purpose of attacking the Federals. Buell would unquestionably have learned of Smith's march, and he would only have had to fall back across Barren River and occupy the fortifications Hardee had constructed during the previous fall and winter. The Michigan Engineers, who had been put to work late in August on the railroad north of Nashville, had repaired the Confederate fortifications and built new platforms for ten guns. With supplies on hand for twenty to thirty days, Buell would have been in no great difficulty—though Bragg would. Buell did not have to use the Munfordville route to Louisville, and it was reported to Bragg that he was advancing by the road he did in fact use for his empty train.[4] If both armies had remained near Bowling Green, Central Kentucky would have soon been redeemed by advances from Cincinnati and Louisville, and what shape the campaign would then have taken cannot be even surmised.

Probably the ablest officer in Bragg's army was General Hardee, and the final sentence in a message he wrote to Wheeler at Bardstown on the evening of the 23rd is good proof that he thought no serious error had yet been committed. Said Hardee, "Our affairs, except our men being jaded, are prosperous."[5] It would not be long before

Hardee would take strong exception to Bragg's actions, but for the moment he was well pleased.

It was George Morgan who was largely instrumental in causing the plans of the Confederate generals to miscarry. Throughout the summer he had made Cumberland Gap impregnable under the directions of Lieutenant W. P. Craighill, an engineer officer of great ability sent by Stanton, and he had constructed ample storehouses for provisions and for arms for East Tennesseans. He promptly blocked the gaps through which Smith had moved, and claimed that he unsuccessfully tried to get a fight with Stevenson by having his bands play "Dixie" as a provocative act. But because his stores were insufficient for a protracted siege, and the country was exhausted, on the night of September 17 Morgan successfully evacuated the position, blowing up his magazine and burning the warehouses with upward of 6,000 small arms. Stevenson flashed the word to General McCown—commanding at Knoxville since Smith's departure—who had received that very day from Secretary Randolph a telegram saying that Major General Sam Jones had been ordered to send all troops possible in order to complete the investment of the Gap. "Your troops not needed," McCown quickly told the Chattanooga general.[6]

Morgan's successful 200-mile march to the Ohio through a mountainous country, with a superior force in his front and one equal to him in his rear, was one of the feats of the war; and it was that march which helped to save Louisville. Not planned as a diversionary operation, it nevertheless was such to an eminent degree, and in his report Bragg categorically said it was responsible for Smith's failure to join him.[7]

Kirby Smith's gyrations were one of the amusing features of the campaign—though not to the soldiers who marched and countermarched—and must be narrated in some detail in order to appreciate that general.

Spies had brought Smith word of Morgan's intention to evacuate the Gap, and on the 18th he directed Humphrey Marshall, who had entered Kentucky from the east, to concentrate as quickly as possible at Mount Sterling. Through that place the spies had placed Morgan's line of retreat. "His forces are completely demoralized, and I think it will be an easy matter for you to capture them," said the general who had delivered the knock-out blow to Irvin McDowell at First Bull

Run. Morgan did not, Smith said, have over 6,000 men; and he would so dispose his own force as to aid, if that were necessary. But Bragg was advancing on Louisville and had written him to be ready to cooperate by the 23rd. That was an additional reason for Marshall to hasten.[8]

A longer letter was written on the same day to Bragg, in answer to one of the 15th received that morning—which unfortunately does not seem to have survived. The brigades of Preston Smith and Cleburne, said Kirby Smith, would be at Shelbyville on the 22nd, ready for Bragg's orders to effect a junction. But someone was giving Smith poor information, for he also said that stores and supplies were being moved from Louisville into Indiana and that everything indicated an intention to evacuate "on the approach of our troops." He was no longer afraid of a Federal advance from Covington and was withdrawing his own force thrust in that direction so as to be well concentrated. George Morgan's movements indicated Manchester, Booneville, and Mount Sterling as his probable line of retreat, and Smith asserted, not realizing how he would entrap himself, "I shall be on the lookout for them." [9]

All this indicated that the great adventure was prospering and would soon pay off, with Louisville the grand prize. Then Smith added a touch of humor, in view of what had transpired before. On the 14th McCown had wired to Cooper: "General E. K. Smith calls for arms for the Kentuckians flocking to his standard. Could arm 20,000 men if he had arms. Can I get them from Richmond? None here. General Smith (date 5th, from Lexington) says Kentucky is rising *en masse*." Telegrams were promptly sent in search of weapons for the eager Bluegrass Secessionists, and wagons for arms were added to the money train about to start for Lexington under guard of convalescents. But arms were difficult to come by, Georgia reporting she could offer the Kentuckians "only pikes and knives." And now the day after Sam Jones sent this news to Bragg, Smith wrote to him: "I have still some 10,000 stand of arms—the trophies of the Richmond battles. The Kentuckians are slow and backward in rallying to our standard. Their hearts are evidently with us, but their blue-grass and fat-grass are against us." [10]

It was, however, not just the "slow and backward" Kentuckians who were to prove Smith's undoing; it was the Federals. Once more Smith began to fear an advance from Covington, this time with

Morgan coming on his rear. A letter to Bragg on the 19th said he would hold his command ready to cooperate in the movement on Louisville—"if needed." But everything he heard convinced him "of the inability of the enemy to hold the place" against Bragg's force; therefore he respectfully asked Bragg to consider the exposed condition in which he would leave the valuable region where he was. The next day reports from his signal corps indicated that there were only 6,000 of the enemy in Louisville on the 18th. Though troops were coming from Cincinnati and 1,000 Negroes were building fortifications, he was informed that, since the fall of Munfordville, there was little hope of holding the city. A "rapid movement" and the place would be Bragg's. Thus Smith bowed himself out of the Louisville scheme.[11]

Such were the messages that Bragg received when he reached Bardstown, from where Forrest wrote at 7:00 A.M. of the 22nd to Polk, acknowledging an order just received to make a demonstration on West Point at the mouth of Salt River, and to break up the railroad between Elizabethtown and Louisville. Forrest's reputation for aggressiveness makes his reply the more impressive: "It will be impossible for me to carry out your orders on account of the condition that my horses are in." It was an exhausted army, whose power was largely spent. Not suspecting this, Smith had written the day before to Marshall, "I feel every confidence in the ability of General Bragg to take Louisville and in our ability to hold this section." But his own front was nevertheless disturbing the Bull Run hero, and he halted Cleburne and Preston Smith, then moving to join Bragg, so that they could go to the aid of Henry Heth's division north of Lexington, if he were pressed from Covington.[12]

Unfortunately, the letter that Bragg wrote to Smith on the 21st from near Hodgenville is also missing; but Smith, in his reply two days later, said he regarded the defeat of Buell before he made a junction with the Louisville force as a military necessity. Forgetting that he had blamed the apathy of the Lexingtonians on "their blue-grass and fat-grass," he now said Buell's army was "the great bugbear to these people," and until it was defeated there could not be much hope for Kentuckians to swell the Confederate ranks. Cleburne and Preston Smith—3,000 strong—were stated as being at Frankfort with orders to proceed without delay to Bloomfield. The balance of Smith's force—8,000 in infantry alone—would move the next day to Frankfort, to support Bragg's operations against Buell. The whole thing is bewildering; but the opening sentence in a dispatch that Hardee wrote to Wheeler in the early evening of the 2nd from New Haven makes it look as if it might have been believed that Buell would not continue straight to Louisville by the Elizabethtown road, but would swing eastward after Bragg. Hardee said, "It is necessary that you should watch Buell, to see where he goes and to divine his intentions." Indeed, it appears that Smith thought Buell was almost tramping on Bragg's heels, for he wrote to Marshall, "As General Bragg may have a hard battle at any time with Buell I have ordered Heth with all his command to march immediately for Frankfort." [13]

What about the gap toward Covington that would be left when Heth hastened westward? Humphrey Marshall was ordered to move from Mount Sterling to Paris and keep a bright eye northward. What then about George Morgan's threat from the south? At the moment this danger appeared to have vanished, for Morgan had not been reported north of Manchester. John Morgan was now called upon peremptorily to clear up the situation about his troublesome namesake. As early as the 19th he had been ordered to probe the reports of the Federal advance; and if they proved unfounded he was to "push toward Manchester and destroy all the mills and grain at that point." The famous Lexington cavalry leader had reported on the 22nd from near Irvine, and an order now went to him "to ascertain definitely whether the forces of the enemy in the neighborhood of Manchester are a foraging party or whether the Gap is really evacuated." [14]

John Morgan measured up to his assignment and sent word next day that the Cumberland Gap force had passed through Booneville at 11:00 A.M. of the 23rd, with the evident intention of crossing the Kentucky River at Proctor. The force numbered from 6,000 to 8,000 men, had upward of 36 guns, but only 100 cavalry. Prisoners stated they were headed for Maysville on the Ohio River. Such was John Morgan's report. Thereupon Kirby Smith, reversing everything once more, hurried Marshall back to Mount Sterling and arrested Heth in his westward trek with orders to make forced marches to the same place. Marshall was told that Smith would be there himself before the concentration was complete and was directed to have his cavalry get all stock out of the way of the advancing Federals and do everything to slow them down. In the dispatch informing Bragg of the startling reversal, Smith said, "Stevenson, I think, must be on Morgan's track." [15]

It looked as if things were shaping for another impressive harvest of Federal prisoners—something better than Richmond, something better than Munfordville. These were not green levies, but seasoned troops who were walking into the trap. And among them were those six regiments of exasperating East Tennesseans who loved the Union. What a present for Jefferson Davis!

In his message to Bragg, Smith mentioned the possibility of Morgan turning eastward after crossing the Kentucky River and making for Salyersville and Louisa. In that case he would "push him with the cavalry, and, leaving him to the ruin and demoralization that would overtake his army in that wild, mountainous country," would dutifully return to the support of Bragg. The next day he conjectured to Marshall about his approaching victim: "Unless he abandons his artillery I think he will be compelled to advance from Proctor upon Mount Sterling. Everything in his front has been burned at Proctor, and his army is in a reduced condition." [16] This, however, was only wishful thinking.

When George Morgan pointed out his proposed route—one that turned northeastward at Proctor and ran to Greenup—to his topographical engineer, a former state geologist of Kentucky intimately familiar with its topography, and asked the question, "Can I take my division by that route to the Ohio River?" the answer had been, "Yes, possibly, by abandoning the artillery and wagons." Morgan only partly accepted this judgment, and wrote in his postwar article, "I therefore determined to retreat by the red-chalk line, and at all hazards to take my artillery and wagons with me." But he did not fail to employ deception. A few men, under an officer who carried written authority to purchase supplies, were sent toward Mount Sterling. It was of course intended that they should be captured, and they were probably among those who named Maysville as the Federal destination.[17]

Unfortunately, Kirby Smith laid aside his pen as he waited to capture his old adversary at the Gap, so there is no record of his disillusionment. But on the 25th Bragg wrote a long letter to General Cooper that was anything but cheerful. Having noted his arrival in Bardstown on the 22nd, Bragg said: "The long, arduous, and exhausting march renders it necessary for my troops to have some rest. They will therefore remain several days." He regretted the circumstances that made his move to Bardstown necessary, for it had enabled Buell to reach Louisville, where Bragg said a very large force had been concentrated. In addition to Buell and the new levies, the armies of Grant, Rosecrans, and Curtis were there, and his tendency to find fault with others was revealed in blame of Price and Van Dorn. Toward the Kentuckians he was bitter: "We have 15,000 stand of arms and no one to use them. Unless a change occurs soon we must abandon the garden spot of Kentucky to its cupidity. The love of ease and the fear of pecuniary loss are the fruitful source of this evil." (This would be a surprise after McCown's statement that Smith had reported the state rising en masse and in need of arms.) At the end Bragg cheered up a little. Price and Van Dorn might still do something; and he trusted that Smith's dispositions would result in George Morgan's destruction or capture.[18]

On the first day of October, Bragg wrote more optimistically from Danville to Polk, left in command at Bardstown. Stevenson had arrived "with 8,000 fine troops." George Morgan had made a turn to the right, and it was doubtful whether Kirby Smith could head him off; but John Morgan was in his rear, gathering prisoners and wrecking trains. "His command is ruined for any useful purpose," was Bragg's consoling thought. He spoke of steps preliminary to the investment of Louisville—a grandiose idea indeed—and balanced the happy thought, "The country and the people grow better as we get into the one and arouse the other," by saying the accumulation of supplies at Danville was not as great as he had hoped. In the last sentence, good news struggled valiantly with bad: "Breckinridge has failed, but General Preston joined me last night. He has great influence here and will forward our recruiting." [19]

Recruiting was certainly uppermost in Bragg's mind, and to understand this campaign fully one must examine how the Confederates sought to match the new levies of the Federals.

On the eve of leaving Barbourville, Kirby Smith had indicated to Jefferson Davis that if there were not substantial support from the "loyal citizens of Kentucky," there would have to be reenforcements from East Tennessee. And in his dispatch to Cooper a month later, Bragg said, "Kentucky and Tennessee are redeemed if we can be supported, but at least 50,000 men will be necessary, and a few weeks will decide the question." With Lee recuperating from his heavy loss on Antietam Creek, there were neither trained troops nor newly impressed men to spare from the East. Breckinridge, however, was at last soon to arrive in Knoxville, but with only 2,500 men—all that Van Dorn would let him bring from Mississippi. An equal number of exchanged men were following, and Maxey had accumulated 4,000 at Knoxville.[20] The sum total of all these reenforcements was small compared with the number Bragg had set.

Though Richmond apparently never intended to support the campaign by new troops, it was not entirely without a plan, for Secretary Randolph wrote near the end of August that if Kentucky were secured the conscript act would be enforced. But the hold on the state was now too limited and too shaky to resort to such means to swell Bragg's ranks. What then about East Tennessee, whence Smith had indicated reenforcements should come, but where he himself, on Presidential authorization, had suspended the act because of the violent reaction that had greeted its passage? The vexing question fell to McCown, and Smith had little more than won the battle at Richmond, Kentucky, when he spoke up boldly to Secretary Randolph: "The conscript law should be enforced at once." [21]

Disillusionment came quickly, and on September 16 McCown reported to Smith, "Governor Harris' and General Bragg's conscription orders have thrown the whole country into a feverish state, and I do not think I overestimate when I say thousands are stampeding to the mountains and to [George] Morgan." A night's sleep did not make the situation brighter, and a telegram to Randolph ended: "Many counties will have to be conscripted by military force. What must be done with the Union leaders?" In passing the message to the President, Randolph commented that McCown seemed to have no policy and recommended nothing. (He perhaps had had his fill of recommending.) After himself shedding responsibility by saying a prescription for Union men could not be written in Richmond because of lack of knowledge, Randolph added, "Will it not be well to send a discreet person to confer with General McCown and Governor Harris in reference to this difficult subject." [22]

It is not likely that there was in Richmond a "discreet person" waiting idly for a hard assignment, and the Secretary or President soon had a better idea. McCown was sent to join Smith in Kentucky, and Sam Jones was ordered to Knoxville from Chattanooga and elevated to the command of the Department of East Tennessee by a telegram that plainly told him his chief duty was the "execution of the conscript law in East Tennessee." The promotion must have been pleasing, but Jones, who had demonstrated energy in taking steps to rebuild the Bridgeport bridge, could hardly have relished the new task thrust upon him. However, he wasted no time in regrets, saying to Randolph in a long letter of September 24, "The work of enrolling conscripts is going on and I hope soon to have a number of them in camps of instruction." He was clearly hopeful that Lincoln's recent Emancipation Proclamation had played into Southern hands, and he reported it had alienated some former Unionists, naming one who now proclaimed that all chance to save the Union was gone, and who was actually urging all men remaining in the Confederacy to take up arms in its defense. But dropped into the letter was the interesting confession: "A regiment which was raised some time since of men who were suspected of being disloyal, but who were permitted to choose between volunteering and being sent to prison, proved, as I am informed, utterly worthless and was soon disbanded." [23]

On the last day of the month Jones attacked the problem by a proclamation, quite as Kirby Smith six weeks before had tried to induce the East Tennesseans to desert the Union army by the promise, "You will receive a fair price for any arms, ammunition, and equipments you may bring back with you." But three days later Jones wrote to the War Secretary that he found "the disloyalty and disaffection to the Government much more general and bitter" than he had expected. At his suggestion, a former ardent Unionist broke into print on the iniquities of Lincoln. No European despot, he proclaimed, would dare to exercise the powers that Lincoln had boldly usurped in less than two years. Emancipation was of course the worst offense, and the address of T. A. R. Nelson reached its climax in the statement, "If he can thus take our negroes, why may he not take our lands and everything else we possess and reduce us to a state of vassalage to which no parallel can be found save in the history of the Middle Ages." [24]

The new and eloquent Secessionist was unable to convince even his own family, and presently Lincoln, ignoring the castigation of himself, wrote to Andrew Johnson: "David Nelson, son of the M.C. [Member of Congress] of your State, regrets his father's final defection, and asks me for a situation. Do you know him? Could he be of service to you or to Tennessee in any capacity in which I could send him?" [25]

Not many East Tennesseans were enthusiastic about emancipation, but memories of Confederate harshness made denunciation of Lincoln's "tyranny" a little hollow. But with the Gap gone, the Unionists no longer had a convenient sanctuary. Never again could Stanton be stirred by a message such as had come from George Morgan a few days after he had seized the priceless pass: "A moment ago 13 Virginians came in, and when I welcomed them back to the old flag every eye was dimmed with tears." [26]

Safety had descended upon Louisville, but there still was drama.

On September 24 Halleck had addressed to Colonel F. C. McKibbin, one of his aides, a letter that began, "As the bearer of the accompanying dispatches you will proceed by the most practicable route to the army of General Buell in the field." It flowed freely, and though the first sentence was long and contained three "ifs," it was as clear as crystal. There were three more "ifs" before the letter closed. Contingencies are always hard to handle, and catastrophe can result if the writer is not skillful. Halleck was.

Following the pattern used by Lincoln when he removed Frémont, the order provided for the replacement of Buell by Thomas, but not if Buell had fought a battle, or was about to, or Thomas was not close at hand. McKibbin carried three papers: the short, formal War Department general order creating a new Department of the Tennessee and putting Thomas in command; a short note from Halleck to Buell, directing him to go to Indianapolis and await orders; and a letter of instructions from Halleck to Thomas. Though in friendly tone, there was a grimness in the letter. The General in Chief had been *directed* to say that the government expected "energetic operations." Disregarding state and department lines, Thomas was to find the enemy "and give him battle." And Halleck enjoined him to live on the country as much as possible, so as to cut down on transportation, the cause, he said, of "the immobility of our armies." [27]

McKibbin had no more than left the capital when word came that Buell's head of column was nearing Louisville, and on the 27th Halleck wired to McKibbin at Cincinnati not to deliver his dispatches until further orders. But the colonel was hard to locate, and two days later a telegram went to Louisville: "Await further orders before acting." Noon had barely passed when the reply was in: "The dispatches are delivered. I think that it is fortunate that I obeyed instructions. Much dissatisfaction with General Buell. There is no probability of a fight within a week." [28]

When Halleck showed McKibbin's dispatch to Stanton, the stern War Secretary no doubt let the equally grave General in Chief see a telegram written at Springfield, Illinois, at nine o'clock: "Twelve regiments under orders for Louisville." [29] The North may have been frightened, but it did not hold back. It turned on the power, great power, and in an amazingly short time. Its leaders were men of stature who meant to win, not to negotiate.

But Washington had a grave decision to make, for at 11:45 A.M. Thomas telegraphed:

> Colonel McKibbin handed me your dispatch, placing me in command of the Department of the Tennessee. General Buell's preparations have been completed to move against the enemy, and I therefore respectfully ask that he may be retained in command. My position is very embarrassing, not being as well informed as I should be as the commander of this army and on the assumption of such a responsibility.[30]

In this there is no suggestion that injustice was being done to Buell, and one can raise a question about Thomas. He knew that preparations alone do not suffice; and though Buell had pushed his army well after it left Munfordville he had previously shown there was no real, unyielding aggressiveness in him. Thomas should have known the general situation, for Buell had recast his army into three corps, with Thomas second in command. Not Buell's fitness for his position, but some doubt about himself, is what Halleck may have read into Thomas's message. In answering, he explained that the order—which he had no power to change—had been written before Buell reached Louisville, and that two telegrams holding it up had not reached McKibbin in time. He requested that his message be shown to Buell, and concluded, "You may consider the order as suspended till I can lay your dispatch before the Government and get instructions." But Thomas had had an hour or so as official army commander, for Buell wired at 2:30 P.M. that he had turned over command and was preparing to "repair to Indianapolis and await orders." [31]

Faced by the telegrams from McKibbin and Thomas, the decision would have been trying enough, but a Senator and three Congressmen—John J. Crittenden, Garret Davis, Robert Mallory, and George W. Dunlap—moved into the picture with a telegram to Lincoln that coupled a tragic happening at the breakfast hour that day with their views of Buell. Crittenden's was the powerful name, but the others were not to be lightly dismissed. Their message began: "We grieve to announce to you that this morning General William Nelson was killed in a rencounter with General Davis. About the same time intelligence was received that General Buell was superseded and directed to pass over to General Thomas his command. These two events have caused great regret and something of dismay." [32] It was their business to keep in touch with popular feeling, and it may have been presumed they spoke with authority as to public regard for Buell, which they pronounced high, and that the esteem they ascribed to the army reflected the testimony of Crittenden's son. But the Congressmen's presentation was contrary to testimony later given to the Court of Inquiry, and it was certainly counter to the report by McKibbin. Halleck had been holding out for Buell against Lincoln and Stanton; now, ironically, his aide, after a close look at the situation, reported it was time for a change.

But with Thomas reluctant and four leading Kentucky politicians protesting, what happened was inevitable. The order changing commanders was suspended "by authority of the President." Buell, in acknowledgment to Halleck, said, "Out of sense of public duty I shall continue to discharge the duties of my command to the best of my ability until otherwise ordered." [33]

In Cincinnati George Morgan was the center of interest. On the day when Louisville was buzzing over the killing of Nelson and Buell's escape from removal, a courier rode in with a dispatch from Colonel H. Blair Wilson, commanding the Forty-fourth Ohio at Maysville. At Mount Sterling there was, said the message, a concentration of 16,000 Confederates plus 30 guns and Kirby Smith, all for the purpose of cutting off George Morgan. The information had been gleaned from a dozen sources; and Wilson said, "If the above is not all entirely reliable then I don't believe there is a loyal man in Kentucky." [34]

When Wright, on the 24th, received the first report that Morgan had left the Gap, he was dubious, and queried Nelson. His statement, "Morgan has supplies for from seventy to eighty days and feels secure," in a message to Halleck on the 18th was to do much mischief, for it brought from the General in Chief on the 28th the direction that the abandonment of the Gap "be promptly inquired into and reported on." Unfortunately, amid the press of other matters, it was five months before the question was cleared up and Washington recognized the necessity of Morgan's action.[35]

As October arrived, Wright was pessimistic and wired to Buell: "I see no salvation for Morgan except an advance on your part to force Smith to join Bragg. I shall push forward what force I have at once in the hope that this may save him." But within hours there were convincing reports that Morgan was safe, and at 10:30 P.M. of the 3rd Wright flashed to Washington the word of his arrival at Greenup with all his command. Impossible as the route had seemed, Morgan lost neither gun nor wagon, and his total casualties were only about eighty men. After having annoyed him in the rear, John Morgan passed to his front and made himself disagreeable by felling trees across the road. But the work of his zealous troopers proved useless, and George Morgan wrote, "On three successive evenings so closely did we push him that we drove him from his hot supper." [36]

It was also on October 3—late in the afternoon—when Washington learned that Buell was on the march. Welcome news this was, because only the day before Halleck had nudged him by saying there was apprehension that if he did not act promptly the enemy might move on Cincinnati, now held by only a few green regiments. "My troops have been in motion since yesterday," said Buell's answering dispatch. He had occupied Shepherdsville, Mount Washington, Taylorsville, and Shelbyville. Bragg's force, Buell said, was mainly at Bardstown, but he was collecting supplies at Danville and might concentrate at that place.[37]

The corps of the reorganized army—each of three divisions—were commanded by McCook, Crittenden, and Gilbert, the latter wearing the stars of a major general though he was entitled only to those of a brigadier. McCook's old division, now under Brigadier General Joshua W. Sill—seen formerly at Jasper and Battle Creek in command of a brigade of Ormsby Mitchel's division—was marching on Frankfort, to cover Louisville and perplex the enemy. The remainder of the army was moving in three columns toward Bardstown, McCook being far enough to the left to support Sill if necessary. In all there

122

were about 60,000 men, but many of the regiments were levies of the summer that had been rushed to Kentucky. Some veteran brigades had been augmented by a single new regiment, but the eight regiments of Brigadier James G. Jackson's two-brigade division were all inexperi-

CENTRAL KENTUCKY

enced. Furthermore, eight of the twelve regiments in the new division of Sheridan—now a brigadier—had known neither heavy marching nor battle. Left behind at Louisville was Brigadier General Ebenezer Dumont's four-brigade division, the largest in Buell's command. His 15,000 men—some very recent arrivals at Louisville—were to follow Sill toward the state's capital city of Frankfort.[38]

When he cast up the total enemy strength upon arriving in Louisville, Buell was commendably conservative. Fifty thousand "effective men" was the figure for Bragg that he reported to Halleck on September 25. That numbers alone do not measure combat effectiveness Buell well knew, and he correctly described the hostile soldiers as "inured." By the time Buell marched, the arrival of Stevenson and other smaller detachments had—or soon would—put the Confederate Kentucky Expeditionary Force at an over-all total of about 60,000 men.[39] The recruits being present as replacements, the entire command could be regarded as well seasoned. Thus Buell would be at a disadvantage in an engagement if both forces were concentrated, and his hope lay in deceiving the Confederates by the column advancing on Frankfort.

A rapid movement was not planned, perhaps because of the presence of green regiments—though a good way to keep undisciplined men out of mischief is to tire them out. McCook, in order to get water, moved to Taylorsville in one day instead of the allotted two. Steedman, commanding a brigade in Gilbert's corps, testified that that general repeatedly halted his column to warn of the danger of being cut off. Sheridan in later years indicated that the advance was leisurely. The enemy evacuated Bardstown on the 4th, and the Federals entered that evening. The next day McCook, who had already rested two days at Taylorsville, said in a report from Bloomfield to Thomas, the second in command: "There were about 50 or 100 cavalry in my front on the Springfield pike this morning. They ran at 10:30 back to Springfield. I informed General Buell that I would not move to-day. Please keep me advised of your movements, so that I can co-operate. I am in blissful ignorance." [40]

In the afternoon of the 7th, as Gilbert's column approached Perryville from Springfield, the enemy was observed in some force on the ridge beyond Doctor's Creek, with the apparent intention of offering resistance. Under Buell's personal direction the divisions of Mitchell and Sheridan were partially deployed, while that of Schoepf was held in reserve. In accordance with an order issued just before the previous midnight, McCook was in march for essentially the position Gilbert had now reached. It had been hoped he would arrive by the evening of the 7th, but because of the road and security necessities he had only reached Mackville. A courier was sent to find him, with an order to march at 3:00 A.M. The order of near midnight of the 6th had not only directed McCook to move to a concentration point; it had told him to send instructions to Sill to make forced marches toward Perryville—provided the enemy had left Frankfort.[41]

Crittenden's corps, with which Thomas was riding as a sort of super corps commander, was converging on Perryville by the road from Lebanon, and at 7:00 P.M. Fry wrote Thomas a letter in which essential information and orders were overburdened with instructions almost affronting to the second in command of the army. The enemy was reported as at and near Perryville in strong force, and the chief of staff said bravely, "We expect to attack and carry the place tomorrow." Thomas was to march at three o'clock precisely; if possible all canteens were to be filled, and the men were to be told to drink sparingly. Every officer in fact was to "caution his men on this point." [42]

Only an hour previously Thomas had written to Buell from Haysville, ten miles from Perryville. He too had discovered that the country was dry, and he was moving to camp on a stream two and a half miles away, where an abundance of water was reported. "It will," he said, "only throw us about 1½ miles farther from Perryville." Without any discernible prompting from Buell or Fry, Thomas had learned there were 200,000 pounds of pork at Lebanon, owned by a professing Unionist, which could be obtained at any time by sending for it. In addition, he had been told that Maxey's brigade had left Lebanon that day for Danville by a road a little to the south; and he made bold to ask, "Shall I send and intercept him now or capture him hereafter?" [43]

There surely was no good reason why short dispatches could not have gone both to McCook and to Thomas well before dark. When messengers who had set forth in the night to find McCook did not return, Fry fretted; and at 4:00 A.M. of the 8th he sent another dispatch—shorter, because he no doubt was tired. But the purpose of attacking that day seems to have gone—gone in those early morning hours which test the heart of a commanding general. Defense, rather than offense, is suggested by the injunction, "You must get within supporting distance to-day." But the messenger sent at eight the previous evening had arrived—reaching his target ten miles away six and a half hours after he had started.[44] As his message spoke of attack, it would hasten McCook.

And at 3:00 A.M. Thomas was writing to Buell that the instructions of the evening before had just come to hand; he had given the necessary orders to Crittenden and would "take position before Perryville as soon as possible." The roads over which they had marched the day before were pronounced "exceedingly rough and tortuous," and it was eleven o'clock when the camping place was reached. The ending suggests Thomas was a little troubled: "As soon as I decided to make Rolling Fork I dispatched messengers to your headquarters, who must have reached you before this." [45]

For four long months Buell had been marching and maneuvering, while dealing also with a difficult supply problem. His army had covered hundreds of miles. He had been repeatedly censured for slowness—in some instances perhaps unfairly—and had recently escaped removal about as narrowly as is possible. But on the afternoon of the 7th his army was nearing concentration in front of the enemy. Then slowness in issuance and delivery of orders—due certainly in part to a tendency toward verbosity—intruded upon and threatened all that had been gained by the wearying marches.

The Confederate force in front of Buell consisted only of Hardee's "wing" and half of Polk's—three divisions, totaling about 15,000 effectives, plus Wheeler's and Wharton's small cavalry brigades.[46] Nor were the rest of the Confederates in Kentucky hastening to join them; they were marching northward—if not already there—because of a fantastic misconception as to where lay the mass of the Federal army.

The bewilderment and vacillation through which both Bragg and Kirby Smith passed during those early October days must be traced a little, though no one has ever set it all in order. Initially the trouble came from Bragg's involvement with political considerations. At Danville he had met Richard Hawes, the new Confederate claimant to Kentucky's gubernatorial chair, the first, George W. Johnson, having been killed at Shiloh. On September 17 Sam Jones reported that Hawes and his council were setting forth that evening from Chattanooga to join the army in Kentucky. Apparently Hawes was behind time, for the next day Smith, after suggesting to Bragg that a provisional government should be instituted, queried, "Where is Governor Hawes?" But once in Bragg's hands the party moved with military precision; yet in a letter to Polk written while en route, the general—as was his wont—added a rather sour touch: "We reach Lexington this morning and Frankfort on Friday. Enthusiasm is unbounded, but recruiting at a discount; even the women are giving reasons why individuals cannot go." [47]

Collapse in recruiting was certainly not due to lack of rhetorical appeals. On September 24 Buckner had issued a very long address "To the Freemen of Kentucky." Two days later Bragg stepped across the Ohio with a scarcely shorter pronouncement "To the People of the Northwest," and his "To the People of Kentucky" was scarcely in type when he met the would-be governor.[48]

But the jubilation in Frankfort was not conducive to good military judgment, and Buell's thrust of Sill toward that place was timely indeed. Bragg was deceived into believing it was the main Federal advance, and early in the afternoon of the 2nd he reported the move to Polk with an order to put the entire available force at Bardstown in motion to strike the enemy in flank and rear. When Polk received the message twenty-four hours later he knew Bragg was seriously in error as to Buell's main movement, and after fortifying himself by calling a meeting of his wing and division commanders he decided not to obey the order, but to act on a previous one, authorizing him to retire toward Bryantsville. A note to Polk on the 3rd revealed that Bragg was still poorly informed about the location of the Federal army, but a dispatch the next day began a little better: "We shall put our Governor in power soon and then I propose to seek the enemy." While Bragg supposed Buell would move on Frankfort as the nearest route to the supply accumulation at Lexington, he added, "but it may be he hopes to strike you alone." Then Bragg enjoined Polk to use every means to get information and report often. A 1:30 P.M. postscript was the really important part of the message: "Enemy in heavy force advancing on us; only 12 miles out. Shall destroy bridges and retire on Harrodsburg for concentration and then strike. Reach that point as soon as possible." [49]

This made sense, and the next day Smith wrote to John Morgan that the army was concentrating at Harrodsburg. But the movements seem to have been arrested. At 11:00 P.M. of the 6th Polk, who had personally gone to Harrodsburg, leaving Hardee in command of the retiring column, sent to Bragg a report that closed with a sentence which the latter later claimed was the chief cause of his undoing: "I have directed General Hardee to ascertain, if possible, the strength of the enemy which may be covered by his advance. I cannot think it large." Polk's son said his father meant that it was merely the Federal advance guard or covering force that was not large.[50] But that is not what the bishop-general said, and Bragg had a point when he claimed that Polk had represented that the main body of the enemy advance on Perryville was not large—though it would seem likely that corrective oral statements may have been made.

No one wavered on historic October 7 more than Kirby Smith, whose command post was at McCoun's Ferry. The fifteen surviving dispatches that he and staff officers wrote cannot be put into harmony because they do not show the hours. In one to Bragg he said, "The extended position of the enemy from Springfield to Frankfort offers an opportunity for cutting his center toward Taylorsville and falling on either of his wings." His own concentration at Versailles was advantageous for such a move, he said, though it had been made in the expectation that the Federals would cross the Kentucky River at Frankfort. From Versailles, Stevenson wrote that Cavalryman Scott reported 20,000 of the enemy had crossed, and Heth was hurried in that direction from Salvisa with the instructions to tell his men there would be a battle. But in a message definitely written in the evening Smith told Bragg, "The enemy has made no move from Frankfort, nor do I think they have crossed the river in very large force." [51]

Like Bragg, Kirby Smith "did not know the score," and it was all a fine illustration of the fact that when one side starts an offensive move and employs a diverting column, the enemy may be much bewildered.

At 5:40 P.M. Bragg got a glimmer of the truth, and "in view of news from Hardee" wrote a note to Polk—both generals being in Harrodsburg—modifying a circular issued in the morning that had directed the movement of the whole army toward Lexington. Polk was now ordered to go back to Perryville with Cheatham's division, join Hardee, give the enemy battle immediately, rout him and move to the support of the rest of the army at Versailles. While this recognized that the Federals approaching Perryville were not to be ignored, it still did not correctly appraise them, and Bragg's order was as bad as could be. When Hardee read the circular and a copy of the note to Polk which arrived with it, he was horrified. He voiced his protest in a remarkable note to Bragg that bore the hour 7:30 P.M. Said the writer of the book on tactics: "Do not scatter your forces. There is one rule in our profession which should never be forgotten; it is to throw the masses of your troops upon the fractions of the enemy. The movement last proposed will divide your army and each may be defeated, whereas by keeping them united success is certain." Hardee urged Bragg to strike with his whole force first to the right and then to the left, or reversely. But it is to be noted that he did not so much as intimate that the force confronting him was the main Federal army. A postscript added that he favored striking "this force first," not because of its size, but because of the position of Bragg's depots.[52]

Thus Hardee failed to drive home the essential fact. And Braxton Bragg kept stubbornly to his purpose.

As with other small streams, there was not a trickle in Doctor's Creek. But here and there were pools, and during the night of October 7–8 Gilbert ordered Sheridan to seize the hills beyond so as to have a water supply. The task was handed to Colonel Dan McCook, another brother of General McCook, in command of a brigade of four regiments "fresh from their homes." Sheridan recorded that the mission was accomplished "very handsomely after a sharp skirmish at daylight." A battery was soon in position to hold the captured hill, and Sheridan moved forward a brigade that contained three veteran regiments, as well as another battery. Thus he was well prepared when the enemy a little later sought to regain the lost ground, and he drove them back across Chaplin River, a more ample stream that flowed through Perryville, to which Doctor's Creek was tributary. Finding himself well in advance of his assigned position, Sheridan retired; and by late morning he had his entire division well located in rifle pits along a good crest. Messages from Gilbert, flashed to him by flags, had told him not to bring on an engagement. Sheridan's reply was that he did not intend to, but that it looked as if the enemy did. In his report Gilbert said that "toward the middle of the day indications pointed toward a general engagement." Certain it is that soon afterward he ordered Mitchell and Schoepf forward so that they could support Sheridan.[53]

Buell later wrote that his "staff-officers had been at the front till dinner-time." Their synchronized stomachs served notice of emptiness at the same hour and they returned to headquarters, not one having sufficient curiosity or sense of responsibility to remain and keep an eye on developments. The little group must have arrived almost simultaneously with General McCook, who said it was 12:30 when he reported. The head of his corps had appeared upon the left about two hours before and was taking position so as to prolong Sheridan's line, from which he was separated by perhaps 350 yards, because of a bend in Doctor's Creek. After receiving Buell's instructions to make a reconnaissance to Chaplin River to get water, and Fry's statement that Hardee was in Perryville with two divisions, McCook rode back to his command. He could hardly have left when Captain O. A. Mack appeared with a report from Thomas: two of Crittenden's divisions were in position on the right, about two and a half miles from Perryville, while the third was two miles to the rear on the road (information as of 12 o'clock, as Mack had wandered a little in search of headquarters).[54]

One must criticize Thomas for not reporting in person. Fry's message of the evening before, which Thomas had received at 3:00 A.M., had said, "When the column has got into position you will please report in person at these headquarters with all the information you may have been able to obtain, and instructions for the further movements will be given." The proper location for Crittenden's third division would have been in reserve, not in line, and the fact that it was still in march was no excuse for Thomas's not reporting at army headquarters at the very earliest moment possible. He had been informed of an intention to attack this day, and as second in command he should have wanted to be something more than a companion or prompter to a corps commander. Not only did he have an explicit order to report, he knew Buell's weakness; and he should have realized that his presence might be highly important, might greatly influence instructions that would be given. Thomas had heard artillery fire before Mack left, and the captain testified that he heard so much of it while in transit that he believed an action was under way. He also thought he had heard volleys of musketry previous to the time he set out for headquarters, though of this he could not be certain. Army headquarters explained his reports of artillery as nothing serious.[55] But it is easier to brush off a captain than a major general who is second in command.

What were Buell's intentions now? The detention of Mack until three o'clock and the character of the instructions he took back to Thomas make it appear that the plan to attack on the 8th had been abandoned, and this in spite of the fact that McCook was told Perryville was held only by Hardee. The next day, in a telegram to Halleck, Buell said McCook "came up on the Mackville road about 10 o'clock," adding, "It [McCook's division] was ordered into position to attack and a strong reconnaissance directed." [56] This almost looks as if an attack was intended that day. But Buell could have meant tomorrow, or perhaps the day after—or the next week. One will never know because the enemy suddenly called the tune.

"I went forward in person, examined the ground, and saw the water," was McCook's statement to the Court of Inquiry. Continuing, he said he explained to Generals Jackson and Terrill—the latter commanding a brigade in Jackson's division—the line he desired held; pointing to Chaplin River, he told Terrill he wanted skirmishers advanced to its edge as soon as his battle line was formed. "I'll do it, and that's my water," said Terrill in reply. The coveted stream was only 600 yards away, and there seemed nothing to interfere except 400 or 500 enemy cavalrymen at some distance on the other side. A few shots from a battery scattered them. The advance toward the water had barely started when Polk, very reluctantly, but on explicit orders from Bragg, gave up the "defensive-offensive" he had planned and launched a hard attack near two o'clock.[57]

On his right, concealed by hills east of Chaplin River, Polk had Cheatham's division deployed powerfully in column of brigades. Then came Hardee's command in the order Buckner and Anderson. Cheatham's heavy blow struck the green regiments of Terrill's brigade. Jackson, who was with them, was killed almost at the first volley. Terrill valiantly sought to steady his men against the overpowering onslaught, and Cheatham's losses were evidence of the destructiveness of their volleys. But under the heavy musketry and artillery fire to which they were subjected, Terrill's men broke and he also was killed. Because of a fortunate error in march order, Starkweather's brigade—four old regiments and one new one—of Rousseau's division had been at the rear of McCook's column, and Starkweather had taken position to the left and rear of Terrill, some distance to the left of Webster's brigade of Jackson's division, which was behind the center of the two veteran regiments that Rousseau had in line. Starkweather was in the very spot where he was needed. His batteries scattered enemy cavalry threatening the flank, and the guns and musketry of the old regiments broke and drove back Donelson's brigade of Cheatham's division after desperate fighting.[58]

Rousseau's remaining two brigades—commanded by Colonels Harris and Lytle—fought with great stubbornness, but were forced back largely because the enemy, advancing up the low ground that separated Lytle from Gilbert, took them in flank and rear. In retiring they were strengthened by Webster's new brigade, which fought well, though Webster himself was mortally wounded. Timely help came to

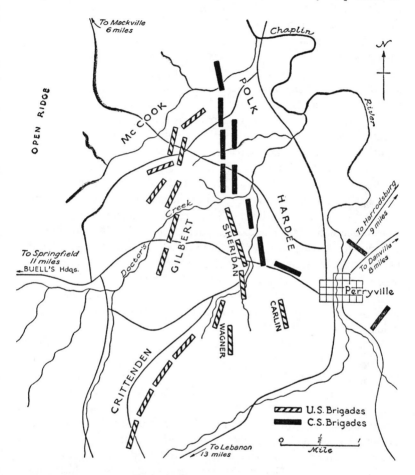

BATTLE OF PERRYVILLE, OCTOBER 8, 1862

The country was rolling but generally open. Polk, commanding in Bragg's absence, drove back McCook's corps. A large part of Buell's much superior army was not engaged because he was unaware that a battle was being fought. The Confederates withdrew during the night.

Rousseau from the right: Colonel Michael Gooding's brigade of Mitchell's division. "Pea Ridge men," Rousseau called them, adding,

"It was a gallant body of men." Gooding wrote that for two hours his two old regiments and his new one opposed Wood's Confederate division of fifteen regiments and ten guns. "Fiercer and fiercer grew the contest and more dreadful became the onslaught," was his comment. Steedman also brought his brigade of Schoepf's division to aid McCook's stricken corps, now forced back a mile from its initial position with loss of some fifteen guns. Evening, however, was at hand; and Steedman engaged only the artillery that was with him, claiming it silenced an enemy battery and dismounted two guns.[59]

The brisk attack the enemy made against Sheridan was quickly checked, though at the price of fairly heavy casualties in some of his regiments. Sheridan then advanced his line, calling on Mitchell to support his right. After moving forward as far as seemed prudent because of the falling back of McCook, he directed his artillery fire leftward across the intervening valley, so as to aid the First Corps. Mitchell answered Sheridan's call by ordering Colonel William Carlin to advance with his brigade. And advance he did. After breaking the enemy with a sharp charge, Carlin pursued him closely for two miles into Perryville itself. There another charge shattered the reformed men of Anderson's division. After capturing an ammunition train of fifteen wagons and two caissons, Carlin took position to the west of the town, his battery engaging hostile guns on the other side of the village until night closed in.[60]

Within something like supporting distance of Carlin was a brigade of Wood's division of Crittenden's corps, commanded by Colonel George D. Wagner. Wood had sent him to aid Sheridan, and Wagner told the Court that one of Gilbert's aides wanted him to move to the edge of the town, or even into it, but that he declined because he had been "informed during the day that there was a large force in front of General Crittenden's main body," and he feared the enemy might get in his rear. But he accompanied the aide to Wood's headquarters, joining in the plea for sufficient support to enable them "to hold the town during the night." Wood seemed to think the idea attractive, and with Gilbert's officer went to Crittenden, while Wagner returned to his command. He received no further orders, but testified that while in the rear he heard confirmation of the report that there was a large force in front of W. S. Smith's division on the extreme right.[61]

What actually was in front of Crittenden? Perhaps twelve hundred of Wheeler's cavalrymen and a couple of guns! With a sharp charge

Wheeler had scattered Colonel Edward McCook's cavalry that headed Crittenden's column, driving them back upon the infantry, after which he took position on the Confederate left. In a congratulatory order to his command two weeks later, Wheeler said, "And upon the memorable field of Perryville alone and unsupported, you engaged and held in check during the entire action at least two infantry divisions of the opposing army." Crittenden himself put in the record the fact that he had 20,000 to 23,000 men, but apparently not even a stout skirmish line had been pushed forward to discover what was really in front.[62] Well did Wheeler's boldness and skill pay off in the face of an army which had been so indoctrinated with caution that even curiosity was rare. (It is notable that the only aggressiveness displayed that day was by Sheridan and Carlin, both from the Army of the Mississippi, as were the "Pea Ridge men," whose fighting thrilled Rousseau.)

Not until four o'clock in the afternoon did Buell learn that a hard battle had been raging and that McCook was being driven back. When artillery fire increased toward noon, Buell's adjutant had asked Fry if they were not going forward, only to be told that the guns were merely protecting the captured water pools. Because of the direction and intensity of the wind, the heavy musketry firing had not been heard; but Buell's statement that he supposed "information of anything of serious import" would have been communicated to him is no excuse whatever.[63] He should have been forward. Never before had he deployed the new Army of the Ohio, and he should have wanted to see his men—so many of whom were new—going into position; and he should have wanted them to see him. The afternoon hours of this day were laden with a rare opportunity, and he missed it because he lacked the controlling instinct of a real field soldier. If the lameness from a fall with his horse had been actually incapacitating (he made no reference to it himself), he should have sent Captain Mack galloping back to Thomas with orders to inspect the whole front and send him a report, remaining himself in an advanced position behind the center. Service in the Adjutant General's office had probably habituated Buell to having information sent to him. One recalls also that he had remained at Decherd after ordering a concentration of his army at Altamont in the expectation of a battle at that place with Bragg's main force.

And why was it that his elaborate signal corps installations did not give him prompt word of the attack? A flag station had been set up on a hill near headquarters, an intermediate one toward Perryville, one near Sheridan's command, and a fourth close to Rousseau's headquarters. Before Station 4 was compelled to move, word of the attack was flashed by one of its lieutenants to Sheridan's station, whence it went to the rear. But the commander of the signal detachment, Captain Jesse Merrill, told the Court of Inquiry that the message was "merely an exchange of ideas" within the corps—family gossip, as it were. It was not official. If one general had wanted to tell another general something, the line was open, said Captain Merrill. It seems unbelievable, but things more unbelievable in communication of information have happened since that day. So it came about that it was from a hard-riding staff captain sent by McCook for help, who was passed quickly by Schoepf to Gilbert and by him to headquarters, that Buell learned he was fighting a battle. Posthaste the army adjutant was sent with orders to Gilbert, who ordered Steedman's brigade to McCook, as previously indicated, Gilbert having on his own initiative already lent Rousseau the "Pea Ridge men." [64]

Buell's only really commendable action was a prompt order for an attack by Crittenden. But the hour was growing late for a reward such as could have been reaped by an advance at two o'clock. The Second Corps was composed of three seasoned divisions, with only an occasional raw regiment; and Carlin's twilight success was proof that a vigorous advance could quickly have brushed Wheeler's horsemen aside and closed on the rear of the three attacking divisions. After they had been destroyed, the way would have been open for a move northward to where the rest of the Confederate army was futilely marching and countermarching. Time was of the essence, and again time was lost. It took the aide, who set out promptly enough, two hours to find Thomas, whom he finally met coming back to his headquarters. There the two ate supper, while Thomas debated whether it was intended he should attack at night. A full moon, as a matter of fact, made the night just about as light as day, as both the aide and General McCook testified. [65]

Thomas, who had heard artillery but no musketry to the east, shared Crittenden's view that the enemy was in strength in their front; and with that thought in his head and food in his stomach he sent back word that he would "advance in the morning with the first sound

of an action on the left." Buell testified that at six-thirty he changed
his instructions and wrote to Thomas "to press his command forward
as much as possible that night and be prepared to attack at daylight
in the morning." [66] However, the second in command was not to
enjoy the full repose that good digestion requires. Buell's evening
message summoned him to headquarters, where along with Buell he
learned directly from McCook the story of the day.

While men were falling in a battle where casualties were very high
for the number engaged—the Federal killed and wounded numbering 3,696, the Confederates 3,145—Lincoln was commenting favorably about the marching of the Army of the Ohio and pronouncing
a timely aphorism on war. His inspired statement grew out of a new
assignment for George Morgan's division. On the day after Morgan
reached the Ohio, Wright (in accordance with instructions from
Halleck) ordered him to Point Pleasant to join General Jacob Cox,
who was returning with the Kanawha Division after its participation
in the Battle of Antietam, to clear the Confederates from western
Virginia. On the 8th a telegram came to the President from Thomas
H. Clay, of Cincinnati, protesting that loyal Kentuckians had just
waited upon him with the request that Morgan be sent to their state.[67]
Lincoln's reply had a touch of sharpness. Clay could not, he said,
have considered the result of what he asked: a precedent that would
"break up the whole army." No special reward was due Morgan's
men, and Lincoln asserted that Buell's old troops "now in pursuit of
Bragg" had done more hard marching recently—a questionable statement from certain viewpoints. Standing squarely behind his General
in Chief, the President said, "On Morgan's command, where it is now
sent, as I understand, depends the question whether the enemy will
get to the Ohio River in another place." But the dispatch had a sentence as striking as the pithy "How does it all sum up?" that went this
day to Grant in the telegram of congratulations for Iuka and Corinth.
Quite as if he had watched Buell dawdle on a day of battle, Lincoln
said, "I sincerely wish war was an easier and pleasanter business than
it is, but it does not admit of holidays." [68]

"Pursuit of Bragg" was in Buell's mind in only a timid way when
he conferred with Thomas and McCook in the early hours of the 9th.

The signal corps having apparently opened a station on the right, toward 1:30 A.M. Thomas sent Crittenden the message:

"Have your different divisions ready to attack at daylight. Issue orders at once."

"I am all ready. My post will be to the rear of the center of the line," was Crittenden's reply. Then he waited, waited "a long time" for the order he expected.

At eight o'clock Fry sent the message: "Have you commenced the advance? What delays the attack?" No attack had ever been ordered, and the cautious habit that had led to the insertion of the words "ready to" had lost three precious hours.[69]

To recount in detail what now followed would be only tiring. Bragg, recognizing at last that he was confronted by virtually Buell's entire army, had his troops withdrawn at midnight to a position near the road to Harrodsburg, to which place he personally rode at 5:00 A.M. to hurry forward the divisions and brigades under Kirby Smith. Polk followed, and with the units that had attacked so fervently the day before he formed a line of battle about eight miles from Perryville. Buell stopped just beyond the town, though he quickly obtained good information about the Confederates, and by a quick movement could have thrown an overpowering force upon the enemy. He waited for Sill, who had eluded Smith at Lawrenceburg, but against whose rear that disappointed general had dispatched some annoying cavalry. At 9:00 P.M. of the 10th Sill wrote to Buell from Willisburg, "The rain to-day has prevented our making the march intended. We will be at Perryville *without fail* to-morrow, I think." [70]

Rain or no rain, the Confederates concentrated on the 10th; and now the advantage lay with them because their force was one of seasoned troops. Bragg, however, had virtually collapsed, in a manner which Polk's son said was "simply appalling to Smith, to Hardee, and to Polk." In a letter to his wife, Bragg wrote that he was disgusted with the Kentucky men. The women were really magnificent—but the men would "cravenly submit to any rule." "Why then," said the disillusioned North Carolinian, "should I stay with my handful of brave Southern men to fight for cowards who skulked in the dark to say to us, 'We are with you; only whip these fellows out of our country, and let us see you can protect us, and we will join you.' " [71]

So, turning his back on the fairest prospect he had during the entire campaign, Bragg started his "handful" of 60,000 for Cumberland

Gap, where in anticipation of a retreat he had on September 29 directed that 100,000 rations be sent, in addition to 200,000 at London. (Thoughts of a possible retirement had also flickered through the mind of Kirby Smith when, three days earlier, he had ordered McCown to build a bridge at Cumberland Ford. George Morgan's retreat not only made that route the best for communication, but, added Smith, it "may become the line of retreat of this army in case of accident.") When the Confederates moved out of Harrodsburg on the 11th, Buell's cavalry bravely moved in. And an hour and a half later—at 4:00 P.M.—Lincoln, who could well have feared the worst after Buell's report of the 9th, telegraphed to Boyle, "Please send any news you have from General Buell to-day." After waiting twenty-four hours he pressed again: "We are very anxious to hear from General Buell's army. We have heard nothing since day before yesterday. Have you anything?" [72]

At 5:30 Boyle did the best he could, saying in a fairly long dispatch: "My understanding is that Buell is pressing the enemy. Heavy fighting reported at Harrodsburg." The truth was soon out, and the Buell Court of Inquiry thought "pressing" was hardly the correct word. Their findings concluded:

The evidence establishes that General Buell received information on the night of the 11th that Bragg had crossed the river [Dix River] to Camp Dick Robinson; yet he made no determined movement with the main body of his army until 12 o'clock on the night of the 13th. From the morning of the 9th to the night of the 11th he waited to learn whether the enemy would cross the river; that being definitely known, he lost two days before taking any decisive action. Finally, on the night of the 13th, as stated, he started Crittenden's corps through Danville toward Crab Orchard. It was then too late; Bragg, with his column and all his train, had passed the point of interception. To this delay we are compelled to attribute the escape of the rebels from Kentucky.[73]

On the 17th Lincoln could read a long dispatch that Buell had sent Halleck the day before. In it Buell said he thought it best to abandon the pursuit because of the difficulty of the road—it was very rough and abounded in "difficult defiles"—and the barrenness of the country. He proposed to move with his main force directly to Nashville, which Negley had reported as threatened. He broached the subject of being relieved by saying it was probably as convenient a time for making a change as any could be. Having said that, one can pardon him a little for asserting that his army—whose proportion of raw troops he overstated—had "defeated a powerful and thoroughly disciplined army in one battle," and then had "driven it away baffled and dispirited at least, and as much demoralized as an army can be under such discipline as Bragg maintains over all troops that he commands." In a reply sent in the early hours of the 18th, Halleck generously acknowledged the victory, but spoke strongly against a move to Nashville. "The great object to be attained is to drive the enemy from Kentucky and East Tennessee. If we cannot do it now we need never to hope for it." [74]

The busy telegraphers now had a line to Buell's headquarters seven miles from Crab Orchard, and Halleck's message passed one in which the field commander said, "There can, however, be no perfect security to Kentucky until East Tennessee is occupied." Avidly the General in Chief pounced upon the sentence and retorted: "The capture of East Tennessee should be the main object of your campaign. You said it is the heart of the enemy's resources; make it the heart of yours. Your army can live there if the enemy's can." After stating that the President directed that the army enter East Tennessee "this fall," and that it should move while the roads were passable, he added the oft-quoted sentence, "He does not understand why we cannot march as the enemy marches, live as he lives, and fight as he fights, unless we admit the inferiority of our troops and of our generals." [75]

On that same Sunday Brigadier Charles Cruft, commanding a brigade in Smith's division of Crittenden's corps, which was leading the pursuit, wrote a report that would have bolstered Lincoln's faith in the Federal troops. Said the Hoosier volunteer, who had been with Grant at Donelson and Shiloh and had done so much in three days to train one of the brigades that fought at Richmond, "My officers and men are in good spirits, and all willing and desirous of undertaking any expedition." Eating was not too difficult, for he said, "Have now about 100 cattle (very fine) in camp and more coming," while a postscript added, "Some 2,000 or 3,000 cattle were driven past here yesterday afternoon, taking Goose Creek road. These might be captured or stampeded by pursuit." [76]

Soon Cruft was sent to destroy the salt works on Goose Creek near Manchester, which the Confederates had worked to advantage during their occupancy. This Cruft did, as well as the stock on hand, after permitting all loyal persons in the region—which was practically everyone—to remove all they needed. In reporting the expedition, General Smith wrote:

The noble conduct of some of those interested in the works, especially of Mrs. Garrard, who expressed her entire willingness that not only that valuable property, but all else that she had and her husband (a colonel in our service) owned, might be destroyed if such destruction would help to restore the Union, constrains an earnest recommendation that prompt restitution be made for the damage done.[77]

While Lincoln did not know of the sacrificing devotion of the Kentuckians at Manchester, he read, before receiving Buell's reply, a warning telegram from Governor Morton about sentiment in another quarter:

An officer just from Louisville announces that Bragg has escaped with his army into East Tennessee, and that Buell's army is countermarching to Lebanon. The butchery of our troops at Perryville was terrible, and resulted from a large portion of the enemy being precipitated upon a small portion of ours. Sufficient time was thus gained by the enemy to enable them to escape. Nothing but success, speedy and decided, will save our cause from utter destruction. In the Northwest distrust and despair are seizing upon the hearts of the people.[78]

The next day—October 22—brought Buell's long and able presentation of the very real difficulties involved in entering East Tennessee, together with the statement:

The spirit of the rebellion enforces a subordination and patient submission to privation and want which public sentiment renders absolutely impossible among our troops. To make matters worse on our side, the death penalty for any offense whatever is put beyond the power of the commanders of armies, where it is placed in every other army in the world. The sooner this is remedied the better for the country. It is absolutely certain that from these causes, and from these alone, the discipline of the rebel army is superior to ours.[79]

Halleck replied that the government wanted East Tennessee occupied, leaving to Buell the choice of route, but urged that it cover Nashville and prevent another raid into Kentucky. Morton's warning seems reflected in the ending: "Neither the Government nor the country can endure these repeated delays. Both require a prompt and immediate movement toward the accomplishment of the great object in view—the holding of East Tennessee." [80]

It was only an interim or stop-gap directive, for the Administration must have already decided that "Don Carlos won't do; he won't do." His successor was not to be George Thomas, who had begged off from the responsibility of command a month before, but William Rosecrans. The telegram that Halleck sped that same day to Corinth was short: "You will immediately repair to Cincinnati, where you will receive orders. Telegraph your arrival. Go with the least possible delay." [81]

While Rosecrans was getting his effects together, an old friend of Lincoln's, now a "very important person," must have been preparing to leave the President's home town to pay him a visit. In Indianapolis he was to be joined by another man who, like himself, had the heavy responsibility of raising and forwarding regiments and keeping his finger on the public pulse. After reading the newspapers and writing the following, he could go home:

Indianapolis, Ind., October 25, 1862—10.40 a.m.
His Excellency the President:

We were to start to-night for Washington to confer with you in regard to Kentucky affairs. The removal of General Buell and appointment of Rosecrans came not a moment too soon. The removal of Buell could not have been delayed an hour with safety to the army or the cause. The history of the battle of Perryville and the recent campaign in Kentucky has never been told. The action you have taken renders our visit unnecessary, although we are very desirous to confer with you in regard to the general condition in the Northwest, and hope to do so at no distant period.

Rich'd Yates,
Governor of Illinois,
O. P. Morton,
Governor of Indiana.[82]

Apparently the governors appreciated the chances that Buell had bungled on October 8 and 9.

When Rosecrans reached Cincinnati toward noon of the 28th, he found a long letter from Halleck with two inclosures. One was an order from the Secretary of War, putting him in command of the new Department of the Cumberland, composed of the part of Tennessee east of the river of that name and any portions of northern Alabama and Georgia that the Federal forces might occupy. In accordance with the recently legalized corps organization, the troops he would command were designated the Fourteenth Army Corps. The other inclosure was a short note from Halleck addressed to Buell, stating that the President directed him upon its presentation to turn over his command to Rosecrans and repair to Indianapolis—but humanely saying nothing about extending felicitations to the Hoosier governor.[83]

Ohio's governor was so slow in getting into the act that it looks as if he kept newspapers out of both his household and his office. Although the replacement of Buell by Rosecrans was announced on the 25th, Tod telegraphed to Stanton on the 30th: "For the first time since my connection with the service I feel it my duty to advise as to the disposition of officers in the field. With one voice, so far as it has reached me, the army from Ohio demand the removal of General Buell." By suppertime the Buckeye executive could relax over one of the War Secretary's smooth-flowing and adequate dispatches:

Eight days ago General Buell was superseded by General Rosecrans under order of this Department. I had been urging his removal for two months; had it done once, when it was revoked by the President. But Rosecrans is probably in command of the army in Kentucky to-day, and will retain that command if he proves worthy, as I believe he will. I am glad to find your opinion, although much later, concurs with my own.[84]

Rosecrans had indeed been in command since morning. The telegram he sent to Halleck from Louisville at six in the evening gave a good picture of the situation. The army was on the march to Bowling Green and Glasgow, and he would join it in two days. The railroad bridge over Salt River would be finished the next night, and provision trains could go as far as Franklin. Bragg's force was reported as scattered over East Tennessee, while at Murfreesboro there were said to be 9,000 enemy "of all sorts." Then followed a second message with a refreshing touch:

I find we have here eight regiments of cavalry. Would be able to do wonders under an able chief. Brigadier-General Stanley, besides being an able and indefatigable soldier, is a thorough cavalry officer. He can do more good to the service by commanding a cavalry than an infantry division. I beg you for that reason to send him to me. You know the expense of cavalry, and what the rebel cavalry has done. Stanley will double our forces without expense.[85]

"Rosy" was starting well when he gave his first attention to countering the enemy cavalry, whose marches had been so spectacular and so effective. At the moment, John Morgan was embarking on another exploit. Just as he had initiated the campaign by destroying the Gallatin tunnel and presenting to Buell the specter of empty stomachs, so now he ended it by a raid around Buell's army that opened on the 19th with the capture of Lexington and some three hundred newly arrived Federal cavalry. Eluding efforts to intercept him, he destroyed several trains of supplies for Buell's army; and as the month ended he rode out of the Bluegrass State toward Springfield, Tennessee, twenty-five miles north of Nashville.[86] It was adding insult to injury, and the new Federal commander intended that such escapades be stopped. Lincoln had never read such a sentence as the last one Rosecrans wrote. He could well have asked to have it verified that he was awake and that the telegrapher had made no mistake. Double a force without expense! That looked like a promise of magic. The right commander of cavalry can, however, be something of a magician.

But what about the plan of operations that Halleck set down for Rosecrans in his long letter of the 24th, read four days later in Cincinnati? East Tennessee was still the real target, but Halleck was realistic, saying the difficulty of the roads, the pressure of the enemy upon Nashville, the position in which he found Buell's army, and the problem of supply might compel him to select Nashville for a base. Though this relaxed on the prescription given Buell, the letter ended, "Neither the country nor the Government will much longer put up with the inactivity of some of our armies and generals." [87]

Rosecrans had no choice; he must move to the Tennessee capital, precisely for the reasons Halleck mentioned. Buell's army was already heading in that direction when Rosecrans assumed command, and the enemy was arriving at Murfreesboro. To that place Forrest had been sent in the last week of September. Though his command was small, and on one occasion a portion of it was roughly handled by a surprise attack, he hampered the foraging activities of the Federals at Nashville. Toward the end of October, Breckinridge reached Murfreesboro with the men brought from Mississippi; and previous to that, Bragg had issued at Knoxville an order for his entire army to move there—Kirby Smith remaining in his own department. The railroad from Chattanooga having been put in order, the movement could be made with considerable dispatch.[88]

Thus, the great campaign of marches in stifling heat and dust ended, with a real trial of strength in battle yet to be made. Bragg had fallen far short of all he hoped for, but he had achieved more than the minimum he set down in his letter to Cooper of June 23. There is much to admire in his generalship up to the time he marched from Munfordville. After that he was totally inadequate, and he shrank from the test of battle when at last he had his entire force united.[89]

On his part, Buell constantly displayed the same timidity that appeared when he arrived at Nashville in February and became so fearful of Sidney Johnston's returning to attack him that he reached beyond his own command and borrowed C. F. Smith from Grant without so much as saying "by your leave." His sending Sill toward Frankfort was admirable, as was his summoning him to Perryville by forced marches while Dumont moved forward to take over the threatening feint. Though both Bragg and Smith were deceived, Buell was too lacking in the qualities of a combat commander to spring the trap. Not often does a general have the chance to bungle so fair a prospect.

In a sense, the war was precipitated by the written instructions that Buell gave to Robert Anderson at Fort Moultrie on December 11, 1860, authorizing the movement of his command to Fort Sumter if he had "tangible evidence" that the South Carolinians designed "to proceed to a hostile act." One can warmly commend that, and still be galled by Buell's unabashedly querying Crittenden at the Court of Inquiry as to whether it was known when they marched from Louisville at what point the enemy "could probably be *brought* to battle."[90] Though Buell was perfectly loyal, it was not strange that some of his subordinates, as well as citizens of the North, diagnosed his trouble as unwillingness to harm the Confederates. Unjust criticisms of Buell have, however, been balanced by bizarre efforts to excuse him. Thus even at the present time it is asserted that Buell was a scapegoat or the victim of the Committee on the Conduct of the War.[91] Claims that even ignore Lincoln's early dissatisfaction with Buell's operations hardly require comment.

CHAPTER VI

AUTUMN ALONG THE RIVER

Generosity and benevolence to the poor and distressed are characteristics of good soldiers.   *Sherman*

War and commerce with the same people! What a Utopian dream!   *Hovey*

A T GRANT's headquarters in Jackson the last weeks of October were a time of uncertainty as to the enemy's strength and design. Replying on the 17th to a telegram from Halleck that told him inferentially his old District of West Tennessee had been made into a department, Grant said that another hostile attack was inevitable in the near future and that reinforcements were needed to keep up the confidence of his men. Six days later Rosecrans warned: "Beware of Bragg; it is nearly time for a few carloads of his troops to arrive. Depend upon it unless Buell is sharper than heretofore we shall have the devil to pay here." [1]

It was at ten that very night—October 23—that Rosecrans acknowledged Halleck's order to report at Cincinnati. His going would bring pleasure not only to himself but to Grant, for the two officers were touching each other's nerves. A dispatch, now lost, that Grant sent Rosecrans on the evening of the 21st evidently complained of a leak of news from the latter's headquarters. Rosecrans replied spiritedly at 10:30: "There are no headquarters in these United States less responsible for what newspapers and paragraphists say of operations than mine. This I wish to be understood to be distinctly applicable to the affairs of Iuka and Corinth." Then he bristled: "After this declaration I am free to say that if you do not meet me frankly with a declaration that you are satisfied I shall consider my power to be useful in this department ended." [2]

Still vexed the next day, Rosecrans reported his troubles to Halleck in a reply to a friendly letter Halleck had written to him on the 1st. After noting that orders of September 17 for him to report to Wright at Cincinnati were still valid, he stated he was "very sorry to say that ever since the battle of Iuka there has been at work the spirit of mischief among the mousing politicians on Grant's staff to set up in his mind a feeling of jealousy." Success in such efforts was indicated, he averred, by the telegram Grant had sent the evening before, and Rosecrans quoted the near ultimatum with which he had terminated his reply. Continuing his attack, he said:

I am sure those politicians will manage matters with the sole view of preventing Grant from being in the background of military operations. This will make him sour and reticent. I shall become uncommunicative, and that, added to a conviction that he lacks administrative ability, will complete the reasons why I should be relieved from duty here, if I can be assigned to any other suitable duty where such obstacles do not operate.

After an adroit reference to the Battle of Iuka, there was a still more adroit ending: "But I must close this personal letter, wishing you were here to command." [3]

It was not a pretty letter, and it shows that Rosecrans held himself in no way culpable for not blocking the road to Fulton at Iuka, or for delay and mismanagement of the pursuit after Corinth, so that Hurlbut's hard fight for Davis's Bridge did not end in disaster for Van Dorn.

Halleck's telegram the next day to report to Cincinnati must have seemed to Rosecrans almost Heaven-sent. But a sharp reprimand promptly followed. Though he had said in his reply that the order would "be promptly obeyed," Rosecrans was still in Corinth on the afternoon of the 25th, when he telegraphed to Lincoln asking that a Lieutenant Lyford be given him as a member of his staff. The next day Halleck wired:

Your telegram of yesterday to the President has been sent to the War Department. Your conduct in this matter is very reprehensible, and I am directed to say that unless you immediately obey the orders sent to you you will not receive the command. [4]

Strange indeed was the reply that the "astonished" Rosecrans sent from Cairo at 11:40 on the morning of the 27th. His telegram had only meant, he said, that he "could not get conveyance from Cairo before this morning," and he did not want to idle there.[5] Thus Rosecrans, one of the inconsistent figures of the war, headed for Cincinnati under a smarting rebuke from the General in Chief. But he may not have been sufficiently honest with himself to recall his dispatch to Halleck on the night of the 23rd and to see that the interpretation he offered of his telegram to Lincoln was sheer dissemblance. However, when he reached Louisville he was at his best and, as noted, made an excellent appraisal of the situation.

News of Rosecrans's departure did not go to Sherman at Memphis until the 29th, when Colonel Hillyer, one of Grant's aides, wrote: "Rosecrans has been ordered to Cincinnati to receive further orders. This is greatly to the relief of the general, who was very much disappointed in him. This matter the general will explain to you when he sees you." Detailed elaboration was, however, not needed, for Sherman wrote three days later in a report to Rawlins, "I note the general's allusion to Rosecrans, and was somewhat surprised, though convinced." In his *Memoirs* Grant indicated he believed that Rosecrans's ability would show itself in an independent command, but that he had determined to relieve him on the day he was ordered away, because of inability to get him to obey orders.[6]

Although Grant was now rid of a subordinate who would not carry out instructions thoroughly, trouble was building up behind him through the machinations of McClernand. We have seen the deviousness of this officer on a small scale in the fall of 1861; we have observed his taking advantage of Grant's trip from Cairo to Department Headquarters to write a report of the January demonstration ordered by Halleck, an act of crass impertinence, whose purpose could only have been to glorify himself and outshine C. F. Smith and Grant. The letter that went to Lincoln soon thereafter was laden with boasts of what he could do if given the opportunity, and the one after Shiloh was hardly disingenuous. Two months later he wrote: "Give me a field of independent action, give me Arkansas south of the Arkansas River, western Louisiana, Texas and the Indian Nation. Give me this as a Department and let one volunteer officer try his abilities."[7] (McClernand seemed to forget that part of the region he wanted was in the department commanded by Ben Butler, a volunteer and brother Democrat.)

After he had gone home in midsummer to aid in recruiting, McClernand had proceeded to Washington, and when Lincoln visited McClellan at Antietam in early October, McClernand went along. Two of the mementos of the occasion are photographs by Brady, showing Lincoln with checker-shirted Allan Pinkerton upon his right hand and heavily bearded John McClernand upon his left. "Lincoln between two troublemakers," would be a fitting caption.

Lincoln could hardly have known that Pinkerton was spying upon him for the benefit of McClellan, or have suspected that this head of intelligence would hasten to report to the army commander what the President had said about him during the trip back to Washington.[8] But he should have been able to take the measure of McClernand and avoid a situation from which he would eventually extricate himself only with embarrassment.

The documents in the McClernand case begin with a very long letter that he wrote to Lincoln under a Washington date line of September 28. In view of his previous unsolicited letters, his opening sentence of apology may be disregarded. While Lincoln may have been "pleased to invite" the letter, he surely did not have to urge it upon a bashful caller who had dropped in for a cup of tea. McClernand's trip could have had no other purpose than to persuade Lincoln to give him an independent command with orders to take "the comparatively insignificant garrison at Vicksburg" and open the Mississippi. A force of at least 60,000 was set down as needed for his whole design, the first step of which was a short ascent of the Yazoo to get behind the coveted goal.[9]

In a letter to Stanton of October 10 the size of the force was whittled down to 20,000. McClernand, however, wanted some of Grant's seasoned men, and asked that Brigadiers Ross and Morgan Smith be given him as division commanders. In addition, he wanted Lieutenant James H. Wilson as engineer officer. This Academy graduate of 1860 hailed from Shawneetown, Illinois, a small Ohio River town, was currently in Washington, and McClernand thought Wilson would welcome an assignment to his staff.[10]

The order that set the design in motion was written by Stanton on the 21st and was marked confidential. It directed that McClernand "organize the troops remaining in Indiana, Illinois, and Iowa," and those "to be raised by volunteering or draft," and send them to Memphis or Cairo, or elsewhere if so directed by Halleck. When they should exceed in number the requirements for the operations of Grant's command, an expedition would be organized by McClernand to take Vicksburg and open the Mississsippi to New Orleans.

Stanton's final sentence could hardly have been pleasing to McClernand: "The forces so organized will remain subject to the designation of the general-in-chief, and be employed according to such exigencies as the service in his judgment may require." [11] Over two months were to pass before Grant would see this document in a copy sent him by McClernand. The important final sentence did not appear, but there was this indorsement:

This order, though marked confidential, may be shown by General McClernand to Governors, and even others, when in his discretion he believes so doing to be indispensable to the progress of the expedition.

I add that I feel deep interest in the success of the expedition and desire it to be pushed forward with all possible dispatch consistent with the other parts of the military service.

A. Lincoln [12]

Three lawyers, McClernand, Stanton, and Lincoln, had indeed brewed a strange concoction. It would remain to be seen how Halleck, also a lawyer, but a soldier with a strong distaste for politically minded generals, and Grant, with a comparable dislike for intriguers, just elevated to department command and a field general par excellence, could handle the affair.

During his early July days in Memphis, Grant had turned his thoughts toward Vicksburg. In replying to Washburne's inquiry about Captain Henry Fitch, quartermaster at Memphis, he commented, after calling attention to the Corinth date line, "I was in hopes of another field, probably the taking of Vicksburg, but the call of Gen. Halleck to Washington made my recall necessary." What disturbed him now, as October approached its end, was not only the possibility of another enemy attack, but also the lack of a unified plan of operations for all Federal forces in the West. Two dispatches to Halleck on the 26th portray the situation fully. A short one dated 8:40 A.M. reported that the enemy was moving again, probably on Corinth, and closed, "Is it not possible to send the Helena force or some other re-enforcement here?" The other message, presumably a letter at a later hour, began:

You never have suggested to me any plan of operations in this department, and as I do not know anything of those of commanders to my right or left I have none therefore that is not independent of all other forces than those under my immediate command.

Continuing, Grant said that with no more troops than he then had—7,000 at Memphis, 19,000 from Union City southward, 17,500 at Corinth—he could do nothing but defend his positions, none of which he felt at liberty to abandon without permission. He suggested that the railroads from Corinth be destroyed in all directions by removal of the rails, and the line from Humboldt to Memphis be put in repair. If this were done, he would shift the Corinth force to Grand Junction and unite it with most of that currently at Bolivar. Then, with a small reenforcement from Memphis, he could move down the Mississippi Central Railroad and, he believed, force the evacuation of Vicksburg, as well as capture or destroy all boats on the Yazoo. What he clearly wanted was aggressive action in some form; and having sketched his own program, he said, "I am ready, however, to do with all my might whatever you may direct, without criticism."

Small as Grant's force was, it was he who was holding New Madrid on the west of the Mississippi, and Curtis had assumed command over Grant's detachments there, "cooly" informing him that he could not spare them. After so reporting, Grant closed with a sentence going to the heart of the matter: "I would respectfully suggest that both banks of the river be under one command." [13]

Although he did not mention it when he spoke of the Helena troops, Grant certainly had in mind that one of his old divisions had been there since July. Now its commander, Brigadier Alvin Hovey, was the senior officer, Curtis having become so alarmed over the possibility of Confederate moves into southern Missouri that he had hurriedly called Steele northward with half the Helena garrison and sent him to the vicinity of Ironton. Grant, it will be recalled, had made a hurried trip to St. Louis to see Curtis about obtaining cooperation from the troops at Helena, and it was the force at that place which in late September had caused deep anxiety to Martin L. Smith, Confederate commander at Vicksburg.

Writing to Van Dorn on September 30, Smith had said, "In the excitement and absorbing interest of events at a distance, I am seriously apprehensive that the safety of this important point may be, and actually is, overlooked." Since the departure of Breckinridge, there had never, he said, been a day when a successful attack could not have been made by the Helena force. So far only the "unaccountable inertness" of the Federals had been the Confederates' salvation; but it was not safe to believe that they would always be inactive. Smith had, he said, only 1,800 infantry, 200 cavalry, and six inexperienced field batteries, of which two were under marching orders. All this was presumably in addition to the personnel manning the heavy batteries, but the force was inadequate to guard the city from a land operation. Available reenforcements were practically nil, and there was no possibility of saving the position from a simultaneous move from Helena and New Orleans "and but a faint probability if attacked only from above." [14]

With Van Dorn and Price about to launch their disastrous attack against Corinth, this was doubtless the moment of Vicksburg's greatest weakness, and one must ask why no advantage was taken of it. The gunboats were still at Helena, although on the 25th their commander, Charles H. Davis, just made an Acting Rear Admiral, had personally left for Cairo to be present at the final transfer of the flotilla to the Navy Department.[15] For some weeks steamers with prisoners to be exchanged had been going to Vicksburg under gunboat convoy. Some information about the place must have been acquired, but it was Grant's view that the exchanged men would come north to reenforce Van Dorn and not stay in Vicksburg. Two days before Smith reported his weakness, McClernand, it will be recalled, wrote to Lincoln of the "comparatively insignificant garrison at Vicksburg"—wishing, however, to accumulate 60,000 men before starting his proposed operation.

The answer to the question lies in the success of Confederate offensive operations, which from Virginia to western Missouri had thrown the Federals on the defensive. Grant had been weakened to aid Buell; while to the west of the Mississippi, Curtis, deceived as to the magnitude of the threat to Missouri, had recalled much of Steele's force from Helena. Thus the possibility of a strong Federal offensive disappeared. The operations west of the river must be briefly considered.

After being recalled from a leave of absence, Curtis reported to Halleck on September 25 from St. Louis, "General Schofield thinks two large armies are moving on Missouri, but I think he overestimates the forces of the enemy." [16] Curtis, however, soon swung into general agreement with Schofield; and the Confederates had indeed greatly strengthened themselves in Arkansas during the past two months.

When Price and Van Dorn left Missouri in April, no Confederate force of consequence remained, and sentiment was turning to the Union as Secessionists felt they had been abandoned. But the arrival of troops from Texas and a flood of recruits from Missouri, together with the strict enforcement of conscription in Arkansas by General Hindman, had changed the picture. "Thousands of men have fled from Missouri during the past two weeks and joined the rebels in Arkansas," had been Schofield's report on August 12, the day after Governor Gamble had written that north of the Missouri the people were three to one hostile to the state militia. Schofield thought that an enemy force was being organized in the vicinity of Batesville, and Admiral Davis added touches to the picture of the Arkansas build-up. When departing for the north on September 25, he told Captain Phelps, left in command of the gunboats at Helena, "The transportation of arms, ammunition, and men from Mississippi to Arkansas is, as you are well aware, the service in which the rebels are at the moment busily engaged." He enjoined Phelps to try to stop such traffic.[17]

Unaware that Curtis had resumed command, Steele wrote to Halleck on September 26 that there was no large force threatening Missouri from Arkansas. He was certain that most of the Confederates under Holmes were in the vicinity of Little Rock. Schofield, currently at Springfield, had asked him to move on Batesville, but he added, "It is impracticable. My troops would starve. I shall move on Holmes directly. He seems standing off between me and Schofield." Steele's column would amount to about 12,000, but his heart was not in striking at Holmes. Thinking not of glory from an operation of his own, Steele closed, "This command could do splendid service in Mississippi." [18]

But this same day some sort of report reached Curtis that the Confederates were moving into both southeastern and southwestern Missouri, and he called north much of the Helena force. Vigorous opposition came immediately from John S. Phelps, Federal military governor of Arkansas, then at Helena. This man, who after the war was to be one of Missouri's most distinguished governors, had emigrated from Connecticut to Springfield, Missouri, in 1837, when it was a very small frontier town. Soon he was one of the most prominent lawyers in that part of the state, and from 1844 to 1860 he served in Congress, where he was highly respected as a skillful debater. At the head of the "Phelps Regiment" he had fought gallantly at Pea Ridge, and his brigade commander said in a report, "Of the activity, zeal, and energy of Colonel Phelps I cannot speak too highly." [19]

Though sick, Phelps was soon on a boat for Cairo, to say in a telegram to Halleck on October 1, "No large rebel force on borders of Missouri, therefore no immediate danger of invasion." He put the enemy at from 25,000 to 30,000 men with 42 to 50 guns, the principal concentration being near Little Rock. "If Steele and troops ordered shall leave Helena, residue must remain idle or be withdrawn; those left insufficient to move into Mississippi or Arkansas if Helena be retained," was his appraisal. And his recommendation: "Hope you will countermand General Curtis' order and order General Steele to move on enemy in Arkansas. Army pleased with Steele." [20]

Having heard from Curtis, to whom Phelps also telegraphed, about the threat of invasion, the General in Chief was in a difficult position. That he did not approve of what Curtis had done was plainly shown by his telegram the next day. Referring to Phelps's report about the order to Steele, Halleck warned, "I fear you will regret dividing his army, and that the part left at Helena will be useless or lost. Unless you find it absolutely necessary to withdraw General Steele he ought to operate from Helena." After stating that as soon as Cincinnati and Louisville were relieved, he could give Curtis more troops, and that the decision must remain his, Halleck closed, "At so great a distance I can only advise." [21]

But Curtis was in no humor for advice, and in his prompt reply he sought to justify his action by asserting that the move conformed to a suggestion Halleck had made to Schofield a fortnight before. Schofield, he added, was daily asking for reenforcements at Springfield, and was being strengthened by troops from Kansas under Blunt, whose department had been joined to that of the Missouri. But there was no way to augment the 2,000 men guarding the important Iron Mountain Railroad, or insure Schofield's communications, except by calling upon Steele. Troops taken from Helena could later be replaced, argued the apprehensive Curtis, who repaid Halleck for his closing truism with one equally worn: "Delays are dangerous." [22]

Schofield later tried to make it appear that Curtis's recall of Steele was contrary to his judgment, but the case rather goes against him. The Missouri situation alarmed Schofield, and when John Pope, banished for his failure at Second Bull Run to St. Paul and the Department of the Northwest—which included the states of Wisconsin, Minnesota, and Iowa, as well as the territories of Nebraska and Dakota—promptly started offensive operations against the rampaging Sioux, Schofield—then in St. Louis—made haste to telegraph Halleck: "General Pope is detaining the Iowa regiments you have ordered here. I beg of you do not let him take them from me." [23]

The Confederate threat to southwest Missouri was not mere bluff. Toward the end of September a part of the division of Colonel Douglas H. Cooper, numbering in all some 9,000 to 10,000 men, of whom 3,000 were Indians, occupied Newtonia, and on the 30th repulsed an attack by Federal Brigadier Salomon. It was a sharp engagement between about 4,000 on each side, in which casualties were relatively heavy and in which the war whoops of Indians increased the din of battle.[24] Schofield promptly reenforced Salomon, and on October 3 Blunt arrived with more Kansas troops. Though Schofield had only about 10,000 men and reports now put the enemy at from 13,000 to 20,000, he marched against Newtonia at once. Boldness paid off. Brigadier General James S. Rains had not reenforced Cooper, as had been reported, and on the 5th Schofield reported to Curtis that he had taken Newtonia and with 3,000 cavalry and artillery was pursuing the 7,000 Confederates who had hurriedly departed.[25]

Feeling certain that his command was better equipped and trained than the enemy force in northwest Arkansas, Schofield called up Brigadier General Francis J. Herron with the remaining troops at Springfield and marched southward. Blunt was sent in pursuit of one body of the enemy, and after some hard night marching defeated it on the morning of October 22 at old Fort Wayne, five miles south of Maysville, just over the line in Indian Territory. Although Schofield pushed his other column, he arrived at Huntsville (twenty-five miles east of Fayetteville) after the last of the Confederates had departed—according to report—for a rendezvous on the Arkansas River, where arms were being collected; whereupon he marched back to the vicinity of Pea Ridge. Within a few days his cavalry had some successful encounters in the direction of Fayetteville.[26]

While there had thus been an actual Confederate invasion of south-western Missouri, it was quite a different matter in the southeast. On October 13 the St. Louis correspondent of the *Chicago Times,* after saying that Steele's force was debarking from a fleet of steamboats twenty miles below St. Louis and would proceed immediately to Pilot Knob, near Ironton, and that the general himself was in the city, commented, "The rebels have played a successful game of deception." When the paper reached General Holmes at Little Rock, he clipped the item and sent it to Hindman, with the comment, "What he [Steele] has gone to Pilot Knob for I can't imagine, unless Curtis permitted himself to be alarmed and sent Steele there to resist an invasion." [27] But Curtis would continue under his delusion, and it would be two weeks before Halleck straightened out the situation with a sharp order.

Grant's contention that both banks of the Mississippi should be under one command would have been warmly seconded by Sherman. Though this restless general now found it hard to hire regular spies, he obtained considerable free information about the situation toward Oxford from persons coming to Memphis "on various pretexts." But his big task was the suppression of guerrilla activities, especially that of firing on steamers. In a letter to Grant on October 18, reporting that Brigadier General Edwin W. Price—son of Sterling Price—once captured and exchanged for General Prentiss, had now renounced the Confederacy and had "come in," Sherman said he intended to expel ten secession families for every boat fired upon and would visit summary punishment on all persons in the neighborhood of the act. "It may sometimes fall on the wrong head," admitted Sherman, "but it would be folly to send parties of infantry to chase these wanton guerrillas." [28]

In an indorsement to Halleck, Grant approved the policy, just three days after he had reported that he held Colonel William Falkner, three of his officers, and twelve men, captured in their disastrous stroke against Island No. 10. Actually, it was not W. C. Falkner, the well-known Mississippi Partisan Ranger, that Grant held, but W. W. Faulkner, his Kentucky counterpart, who had been operating both in his home state and in West Tennessee. Once in Federal hands Faulkner claimed he was a regular soldier entitled to exchange. Grant, however, said to Halleck, "I think the officers at least should be held." Sherman, not content with halfway measures against irregulars—but with no aversion to split infinitives—three days later sent Colonel Benjamin H. Grierson, Sixth Illinois Cavalry, northeasterly with a "select battalion" of four hundred troopers, his order saying, "The object is to completely destroy Falkner's band of guerrillas, already in confusion from their losses at Island 10." The Pittsburgh-born cavalryman, who had been a music teacher, then a storekeeper, before enlisting as a private, did not wipe out the band, but he killed 7, wounded some 20, and brought in 17 as prisoners, together with 22 horses and mules—all "without loss or injury of a man." [29] More important, Sherman now knew he had a cavalry colonel of rare ability. And within due time everyone would know it.

The policy of removing secessionist families as reprisals for the firing on boats brought protests from Memphis Secessionists, and one of the season's sizzling documents was Sherman's reply to a Miss Fraser:

. . . God himself has obliterated whole races from the face of the earth for sins less heinous than such as characterized the attacks on the Catahoula and Gladiator. . . . We will now wait and see who are the cruel and heartless men of this war. We will see whether the firing on the Catahoula and Gladiator is sanctioned or disapproved, and if it was done by the positive command of men commissioned by the Confederate Government, you will then appreciate how rapidly civil war corrupts the best feelings of the human heart.

Would to God ladies better acted their mission on earth; that instead of inflaming the minds of their husbands and brothers to lift their hands against the Government of their birth and stain them in blood, [they] had prayed them to forbear, to exhaust all the remedies afforded them by our glorious Constitution, and thereby avoided "horrid war," the last remedy on earth.

Your appeals to me shall ever receive respectful attention, but it will be vain in this case if General Holmes does not promptly disavow these acts, for I will not permit the families and adherents of secessionists to live here in peace whilst their husbands and brothers are aiming the rifle and gun at our families on the free Mississippi.[30]

A few days previously—on October 18—Sherman had informed Curtis that there had been no recent firings from the Tennessee side of the Mississippi, but that he might have to carry out reprisals on the west bank, causing Hindman and Holmes to threaten vengeance.

Already Sherman had informed Hindman that he would not allow firing on boats from the Arkansas shore to go unnoticed, at the same time reporting the firing with 12-pounder howitzer shells from the west bank upon two steamers loaded exclusively with goods for people in Memphis and West Tennessee. He warned Hindman not to carry out his threat of hanging some Federal officer-prisoners upon the false statements of interested parties: "You initiate the game, and my word for it you people will regret it long after you pass from earth." [31]

But Sherman grieved for more than the cruelty of civil war as he saw his own side turning the conflict to monetary advantage. In a letter congratulating Grant on the victories at Corinth and Pocahontas [Davis's Bridge], which had made the Memphis "secesh" change their tone, he said:

The great profit now made is converting everybody into rascals, and it makes me ashamed of my countrymen every time I have to examine a cotton or horse case. I have no doubt that our cause suffers from the fact that not only horses and cotton are bought of negroes and thieves under fabricated bills of sale, but that the reputations of even military men become involved. Still, as the Treasury authorities think it proper to allow trade and encourage the buying of cotton it is my duty not to interpose any obstacle. Whenever I do detect fraud I punish it to the fullest extent; and we have made large and valuable prizes, all of which I see go to the use of the United States.

Sad it was to Sherman that some of those he was trying to protect from guerrilla shells—the clerks and stevedores on the steamboats —smuggled anything by which they could make profit. [32]

The high-strung soldier was not, however, thrown into discouragement and gloom by realities, as he had been a year before. A message to Grant on the 22nd that put the enemy force at Holly Springs at 23,000, with cavalry in good order, "infantry only so so," clothing poor, blankets and shoes lacking, corn meal and beef in plenitude, "all else scarce," ended in a way that revealed the happy troop commander: "I am just going to review two of my brigades, which are in fine order." A letter to Hovey a few days later said his men were in good discipline as to drill, his honest pen adding, "They do rob and steal occasionally, to my mortification, but on the whole behave pretty well." The very next day a communication to company and regimental commanders began, "Generosity and benevolence to the poor and distressed are characteristics of good soldiers." It noted the suffering among Memphis families, reminded officers of the bountiful provision of the government for its troops, and urged that spare food and other articles be turned in at the headquarters of the Central Relief Committee: "By this process charity is done to the best advantage." [33]

Such was the situation beyond and along the great river when Grant informed Halleck of the apparent certainty of attack by the reenforced enemy—as well as of his tentative plans for a move southward. The next day—October 27—brought a dispatch from the General in Chief saying that the Governor of Illinois had been directed to send him as many troops as possible, but that Curtis was "begging" for reenforcements for Helena. Although the projected operation under McClernand, who had reached Springfield, Illinois, on the 25th was ostensibly secret, there had been a leak somewhere, and Grant's aide Colonel Hillyer wrote to Sherman on the 29th, "From newspaper and other reports it is probable that McClernand will go to Helena and lead whatever expeditions may move from there and report to Curtis." [34]

McClernand, however, had not secured the much-desired Lieutenant James H. Wilson, for on the 27th, McPherson, commanding now at Bolivar—Hurlbut having been shifted to Jackson—telegraphed to Rawlins: "You are a trump. I would rather have Wilson for my engineer than any officer I know. We are old friends; came home from California together last year." [35]

On November 2 Grant informed Halleck that he was concentrating five divisions at Grand Junction—three from Corinth and two from Bolivar—and if practicable would proceed to Holly Springs "and maybe Grenada," completing the railroad and telegraph as he advanced. He was leaving Jackson the next evening to take command in person, and he expressed the opinion that recent threats against Bolivar were to cover an enemy retreat. The column from Corinth was under Hamilton's command, who, when starting, reported, "Rosecrans carried off the maps that were most needed." Grant's move was promptly approved by Halleck, who said that the Governor of Illinois had promised ten regiments within the week, while Minnesota and Wisconsin troops should arrive soon. Pope had in fact told Halleck that sixteen regiments were available for operations down the river—regiments recently operating against Chief Sleepy Eyes and other chiefs. Halleck also informed Grant he had told Curtis to reenforce Helena, and if the command there was not able to move against Little Rock it could cross the river and threaten Grenada. The High Command seemed bent on clearing the Mississippi, for Halleck wrote, "A large force will ascend the river from New Orleans." [36]

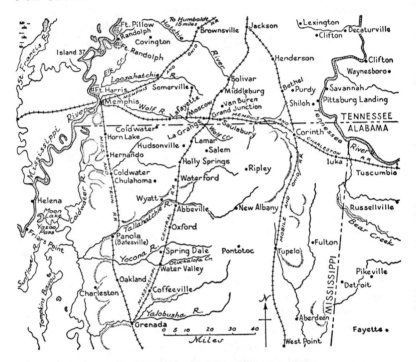

THE REGION OF GRANT'S ADVANCE

The telegram Halleck had sent to Curtis the day before had a sharpness that plainly revealed his displeasure with that general. Information from various sources had confirmed, he said, his previously expressed opinion that it had been a great error to bring Steele from Helena, and he asserted that the best way to clear northern Arkansas was to move from Helena upon Little Rock. It so happened that on this same November 2 Steele was writing Halleck a long letter in which he said that Helena was the proper point of departure, if operations were to be directed against Arkansas. For him to write directly was undoubtedly insubordinate, but he justified his action by opening with the statement that Schofield had told him Halleck had complained of not hearing from him while he was in command of the Army of the Southwest. After giving some explanations of his own conduct, he unburdened himself generally, ending by accusing Curtis of having instituted a policy with regard to slaves contrary to that directed by the President. As a grand climax to his letter he stated that the interests of a political party seemed to be currently directing military movements within the department.[37]

Alvin Hovey, the man on the spot at Helena, had only a few days before read an interesting report that could influence the decision with regard to a thrust at Little Rock. On October 21 he had sent Colonel Robert A. Cameron, of the Thirty-fourth Indiana, under a flag of truce with letters from Curtis and Sherman to General Holmes. The Hoosier kept his eyes and ears open and pinpointed Confederate forces in the region he traversed. While these forces were not impressive, a move on the Arkansas capital would be difficult because of lack of forage, which was so scarce beyond White River after the severe summer's drought that the enemy had dismounted part of his cavalry. From his conversation with the Confederate commander, Cameron learned of the bitter hatred for the Federal flag felt by the North Carolinian who had served in the regular Army from graduation at West Point in 1829 until a year and a half before. "We hate you with a cordial hatred," Holmes had said. "You may conquer us and parcel out our lands among your soldiers, but you must remember that one incident of history, to wit, that of all the Russians who settled in Poland not one died a natural death." The general's rancor matched the austerity of life in Little Rock. Salt hauled 250 miles was selling at $4 a bushel, while Yankee shoes smuggled out of Memphis or Helena were fetching $24 a pair. The quinine that leaked through was going for $20 an ounce.[38]

All things considered, Little Rock was not impressive as a military objective; and the Northerners at Helena had been spending so much time shaking with ague [39] that the last thing in the world any of them wanted was a parcel of Arkansas.

Just what were the enemy intentions and where would he concentrate? On October 18 Sherman had written to Grant, "Van Dorn and Price were both at Holly Springs yesterday, expecting Pemberton, who is to command all"—according to Edwin Price. The Confederate general mentioned in Federal correspondence in this theater for the first time—a Pennsylvanian by birth, and classmate of Bragg, John Reynolds, and Joe Hooker—had previously commanded at Charleston, where he had incurred the displeasure of Governor Pickens and the influential Rhetts. Because Beauregard's restored health made it possible for him to return to the city where he was something of an idol, a War Department letter of September 30 directed Pemberton to proceed to Jackson, Mississippi, and take command of a department consisting of Mississippi and the portion of Louisiana east of the Mississippi. Assistance to commanders of camps of instruction for conscripts was set down as one of his duties, and an ambitious program was given him. He was to get in touch with Major General Richard Taylor, commanding the part of Louisiana west of the river, "as speedily as possible and concert with him a joint plan for the defense of the river and the capture of New Orleans." [40]

Sherman's grapevine telegraph led him to report on the 21st that Pemberton had been expected at Jackson the day before, but he was not sure of his arrival. The next day he said, however, "Pemberton is now in command," information which Grant passed to Halleck, with the addition that Tilghman was in command of exchanged prisoners, and that Holly Springs was being intrenched and reenforced. While Pemberton's was a new face, Tilghman's was an old one. Grant had once sent him north as a prisoner—a fact that may not have seemed significant to the new commander when they met. Ten days later Lieutenant Commander Shirk of the *Lexington* telegraphed to Grant from Columbus. Sherman had requested him to report that he had confirmatory reports that the enemy was evacuating Holly Springs and was going south to Meridian and toward New Orleans and Mobile. But this idea was upset on November 8 when McPherson reported from Lamar that an escaped Federal had brought the information that there were 30,000 enemy infantry, artillery, and cavalry at Coldwater. The evacuation of Holly Springs had been begun, but Pemberton had returned on the 6th and canceled it; troops that had left had been ordered back.[41]

"Well done so far. . . . My hope rather favors their remaining at Holly Springs. The opportunity of attacking there is better than it would be with the Tallahatchie between," Grant said in reply from his new headquarters at La Grange. He promised to hold two divisions ready to support McPherson—who had reported sharp cavalry skirmishing—but cautioned against bringing on a general engagement. The next day McPherson reported the enemy in three groups totaling 30,000, so disposed as to block his further advance; therefore, in accord with contingent instructions from Grant, he would return to La Grange. Almost simultaneously, Hamilton, in command of the left wing, reported that a Confederate officer just arrived from Jackson, Mississippi, had said France and England had formally recognized the Confederacy. Was he purposely sent out to scare? Grant at least was having to learn the style of a new opposite number, though he had known Pemberton—newly made a lieutenant general—in Mexican days.[42]

Hamilton had something else of interest: "A letter from Wisconsin to-day advises me that the Wisconsin regiments in the State, as also those of Pope's command, are ordered to McClernand." Incredulous disapproval seems registered in the question, "Is that so?" Grant could hardly have answered with precision, though here an annoying factor enters the story. On November 8 Lieutenant James H. Wilson reported for duty at La Grange, and in the biography of Rawlins that Wilson wrote fifty-four years later he goes into detail as to what that officer told him almost immediately upon his arrival. If so, what Rawlins said was in part such as to reflect on him for having revealed it to a newcomer. But after fifty-four years, memory may deceive, and Wilson's incorrect statement that Grant was absent and in Memphis on November 8 proves that recollection played him badly. One cannot be certain how much Wilson knew of the McClernand scheme, which he says he soon explained. Without doubt he knew something, for McClernand's request to Stanton that Wilson be assigned to him, with the statement that Wilson was currently in Washington, implies a McClernand-Wilson conversation. Such a meeting would have been natural, for it was to Wilson's home town that McClernand's parents had brought him from his birthplace in Kentucky, and there it was that he had studied law and had been admitted to the bar. However, the young lieutenant could hardly have given Grant the answer to Hamilton's worried query, or Grant would not have referred in a letter to Sherman on the 14th to "the mysterious rumors of McClernand's command."[43]

The most interesting question is this: How did it happen that

Wilson was sent to Grant and not assigned to McClernand? It may have been Halleck's doing, either with or without knowledge of McClernand's request to Stanton.[44] One recalls that immediately upon ordering Grant up the Tennessee on January 30, Halleck sent McPherson to him as engineer officer. He highly approved of Grant's changing McPherson to field command, and he knew how important it was that McPherson's old position be well filled. That may have been all there was to it, and any special briefing of Wilson by the General in Chief about the McClernand scheme cannot be accepted as a fact without clear proof.

Grant had asked Halleck to have sixteen infantry regiments and all the artillery and cavalry sent to Sherman, while only sufficient reenforcements came directly to him to make up for organizations guarding railroads. When informing Sherman of this on the 6th, Grant had said he could make only independent moves until he was informed of "how all these other forces are moving, so as to make the whole co-operate." Two days later Halleck acted decisively, ordering Curtis to place Steele immediately in command at Helena again, and send him all troops that could be spared from the vicinity of Ironton. The morning of the 10th should have brought the General in Chief a telegram that Grant had sent the evening before. Reenforcements were arriving very slowly, only one regiment having reached Memphis. Said the restive general: "If they do not come more rapidly I will attack as I am." [45]

Five regiments and a battery had left Illinois for Memphis, while six or seven more would leave within a week, Halleck telegraphed in reply. Furthermore, other units would be sent from Ohio and Kentucky. Then the General in Chief stated, "Memphis will be made the depot of a joint military and naval expedition on Vicksburg." The McClernand operation of course came to Grant's mind, and he queried:

Am I to understand that I lie still here while an expedition is fitted out from Memphis, or do you want me to push as far south as possible? Am I to have Sherman move subject to my orders, or are he and his forces reserved for some special service? Will not more forces be sent here?

The answer that sped from Washington on the 11th was in a way as good as any field commander could have wished: "You have command of all troops sent to your department, and have permission to fight the enemy where you please." [46] But it confined Grant to a land move, for he had no authority over gunboats or transports.

Though new regiments had not been arriving, new Negroes had, whole families of them as well as individuals, fresh from slavery, some in tatters, some in silk, actuated often by blind hope, and sometimes encountering in Federal camps prejudice against their color more bitter than they had left. The situation was a menace to the operation of the Union army, and to it some attention must be given, though it interrupts the military narrative. Far too often some of Grant's great problems are shouldered aside by writers who would leave the impression that the number of Confederates on Pemberton's returns and the number of Federals on Grant's are adequate measures of advantages in the campaign that was beginning.

Even the fact that Pemberton was operating on interior lines within his own country is not always sufficiently stressed—yet it was worth thousands of men to him. He did not have to rebuild railroads and detach troops to guard them. Couriers could carry his messages without much danger; but dispatches between Grant and Sherman either had to go by way of Columbus or under a very strong escort. Always hovering about Union columns were enemy cavalry, regular or partisan, well acquainted with roads that often were mysteries to Grant's men. Thus while Grant was writing to Sherman on the 6th, Confederate Colonel W. H. Jackson, Van Dorn's chief of cavalry and the officer who had tried to capture Grant in June, was reporting from Mr. Robert's house, one mile from Coldwater.* After describing Federal moves, he said, "I think 40,000 will cover their entire force." [47]

That Grant could not know, but he did know that the mounting refugee problem must be straightened out. On November 11 he issued an order placing Chaplain John Eaton, of the Twenty-seventh Ohio, in charge of all contrabands. The man so designated had, like Grant himself, early become adept with horses, for his prosperous but thrifty New Hampshire father had taken him out of school at the age of five so that he might help plow. The boy having demonstrated a great yearning for knowledge by diligent and surreptitious study, the father gave him an academy education, after which the son earned funds for

---

* Of the two Coldwaters on the map on p. 158, it is the one southwest of Lafayette that is meant; but it is the one south of Hernando that survives.

four years at Dartmouth. In 1856, at the age of twenty-seven, Eaton was superintendent of schools in Toledo, Ohio, but presently gave up the position to study for the ministry, completing his seminary course just in time to become chaplain of the Twenty-seventh Ohio in the summer of 1861.[48]

In the fall of that year Eaton was captured when he remained with his colonel, ill with typhoid, at the time Curtis withdrew from Springfield. General Ben McCulloch was so well impressed with Eaton that he allowed him to accept invitations of Confederate commanders to preach to their soldiers, presumably upon the theme of spiritual rather than political salvation. After his release, Eaton had a meeting with Halleck in St. Louis, about as unhappy as the one Grant had when he first broached the move up the Tennessee to his glowering superior. After being in the operations against New Madrid and Island No. 10, Eaton was with Pope during the advance on Corinth, and with Rosecrans at Iuka—though his regiment was not engaged—and in the battle of Corinth, where his old regimental commander Colonel John W. Fuller handled a brigade with distinction.

Thus it was a well seasoned officer who read with surprise "amounting to consternation" the order that manifestly gave him an assignment of the hardest sort. Though battle-experienced, he trembled at the ending: "For further instructions the officer in charge of these labors will call at these headquarters." In the book he wrote some forty years later, Eaton told of the trepidation with which, in response to an orderly's direction, he knocked on a door in the house that was department headquarters. He was told to come in, and he wrote: "Upon entering the room the same quiet voice said to me, 'Have a seat, and I'll talk with you in a few moments.' Then, as I announced my name, the General added, 'Oh, you are the man who has all these darkies on his shoulders.'"

When the generals who were in conference with Grant filed out—with amused glances at the waiting lieutenant—it was Eaton's turn to draw a chair up to the central table. He at once urged that the order be revoked, marshaling—he thought—impressive reasons: scarcity of chaplains to look after the spiritual needs of his brigade; he was not experienced in command; he would come in conflict with officers when he took colored people from their camps; he would have to get Negroes to work in cotton fields, bringing inevitable conflict with speculators. Of course, it was an honest feeling of inadequacy that gave words to Eaton's tongue, but he wrote:

All that I said had no more effect upon that quiet, attentive face than a similar appeal might have had upon a stone wall. When my arguments were exhausted, the General simply remarked, "Mr. Eaton, I have ordered you to report to me in person, and I will take care of you." And so he did.

Day after day Eaton came to consult with Grant, and order followed order, with instruction to commanding officers, quartermasters, and commissaries, so that Eaton could get along with his task. The work which he started under Grant led ultimately to his appointment to head the Freedmen's Bureau and to close contact with Lincoln. And the general who appeared so indifferent to his appeals that day in La Grange, when President, made Eaton Commissioner of Education, a relatively new position, which he did much to fashion into one of great importance.[49]

Just before acting with so much wisdom and acumen in one difficult question, Grant had taken the first steps toward an unfortunate order in another. On November 9 he had telegraphed to Hurlbut: "Refuse all permits to come south of Jackson for the present. The Israelites especially should be kept out." This was not really discriminatory, and no one with imagination to picture the situation about La Grange would be bothered by it. But the next day Grant wired to Brigadier Joseph D. Webster, his former chief of staff, now general superintendent of railroads in Grant's department: "Give orders to all the conductors on the road that no Jews are to be permitted to travel on the railroad southward from any point. They may go north and be encouraged in it; but they are such an intolerable nuisance that the department must be purged of them." [50]

Grant was not the first to speak of the trading problem being aggravated by a special group. In a letter to Rawlins on July 30—which of course Grant read—Sherman indicated he had stopped activities of newly arrived "swarms of Jews." And he said in a dispatch to the Secretary of the Treasury, in which he protested the Department's trading policy, "The flock of Jews has disappeared, but will again overrun us." On the preceding day Curtis had written to Halleck about his camp being "infested with Jews." The speculators, however, were by no means confined to one faith, and no one could have made this clearer than Sherman when he told Grant that profit was making rascals of everybody. In a letter to Lincoln on November 9, replying to a recent dispatch in which the President had told Curtis that he had been accused of cotton speculation, that general had stoutly denied the charge, laying it at the door of "wealthy speculators" whom he would not allow to pass through his lines. For the offenders, however, he had used no special label.[51]

Grant's thoughts were taking a regrettable turn when he spoke of purging his department, for the department included a rear zone where there was neither cotton nor speculators. If the contemplated expulsion had been confined to the area near the front, one could hardly condemn it, especially in view of Grant's recent order promising severe punishment of his men for vandalism—issued just four days after one providing for the relief of distressed civilians. If one cannot praise the dispatch to Webster, one can give high praise to a letter written that day to Sherman, an uncommonly long one for Grant. There were twelve good military paragraphs, including one giving a breakdown of Pemberton's command. Then came a sentence that shows the difficulty with which command was exercised in those days when there were no high-ranking staff officers to share some of the burdens of their chief: "There were a number of matters I intended to write you when I commenced, but being interrupted so often I have forgotten them." Plenty, however, had been put down for Sherman to think about, and he was left with an assurance: "I will communicate with you again before the final start is made." [52]

Just as Negro refugees and unscrupulous and often clandestine traders were a vexatious by-product of the war to Grant, so the termination of the campaign against the Minnesota Indians brought to the Chief Executive the most difficult and painful of questions. On the very day of Grant's dispatch to Webster, Lincoln telegraphed to John Pope:

Your dispatch giving the names of 300 Indians condemned to death is received. Please forward as soon as possible the full and complete record of their convictions; and if the record does not fully indicate the more guilty and influential of the culprits, please have a careful statement made on these points and forwarded to me. Send all by mail.

The same day the governor of Minnesota urged that the execution of all the condemned Sioux be at once ordered, adding to the harsh recommendation the grim warning: "Private revenge would on all this border take the place of official judgment on these Indians." The President passed the telegram on for cogitation by Edwin Stanton.[53]

Having received the General in Chief's permission to do as he pleased, Grant passed the good news to Sherman on November 14 in a letter which said, "I am exceedingly anxious to do something before the roads get bad and before the enemy can intrench and re-enforce." No time was lost, but on the 23rd, just as Grant was returning from Columbus where he had given Sherman his final instructions in a personal meeting, Halleck telegraphed to him to report the number of men that could be sent down the river to Vicksburg, "reserving merely enough to hold Corinth and West Tennessee." In his reply the next day Grant said he had contemplated an attack on Pemberton and had given orders accordingly. Sherman was to move on the 26th and form a junction with him south of Holly Springs on the 30th. Steele had been asked to threaten Grenada; and Commodore David D. Porter, who had relieved Commodore Davis in command of the gunboat flotilla and whom Grant had met at Cairo on his trip to Columbus, had sent gunboats to open the mouth of the Yazoo. Never was language more temperate or more effective: "Must I countermand the orders for this movement? It is too late to reach Sherman or Steele before they will have moved." Halleck rallied behind his department commander: "Proposed movement approved. Do not go too far." [54]

The advance went well—Sherman with the right wing; McPherson, the center; Hamilton, the left wing. There were about 50,000 men, while the enemy was decidedly overestimated at something between the same figure and 40,000. In a dispatch to Sherman from Holly Springs on the 20th, Grant sketched the logistics. Rations—200,000 of them—were coming forward as the railroad was repaired, though there would still be a considerable wagon haul. At La Grange there was a stock of 800,000 rations that could be brought forward "in case of accident." Two trainloads of grain would be arriving soon, but it was desirable to keep it as a reserve, using first what could be found in the country. Information about the enemy was contradictory. A contraband who had left the Tallahatchie four days before had declared the enemy was cooking rations for a retreat, but a spy taken only the night before, who had been pumped by one of Hamilton's scouts "dressed in secesh uniform and put in prison with him," had stated the enemy meant to fight. A postscript said, "Bragg's forces are anxiously looked for." [55]

The contraband was right; and early on December 1 Grant telegraphed to Halleck from Waterford:

Our cavalry are now crossing Tallahatchie. Infantry will follow immediately. The rebels are evidently retreating. If so, I will follow to Oxford. Our troops will be in Abbeville tomorrow, or a battle will be fought. Sherman is up and will cross the Tallahatchie at Wyatt.[56]

The Grant-Sherman team was beginning to function. Halleck would soon perceive that these two vigorous soldiers had loyalty and confidence in each other and that their actions would never be tarnished by jealousy. The message was one he could have handed to the President with much satisfaction, and Lincoln, master of clarity and brevity, could have found in it something to admire besides the encouraging content.

Grant's silence on the subject suggests that he did not know that a supporting blow was actually being struck from Helena. Ten regiments of cavalry—2,000 strong—with some guns were ten miles from Grenada, the two-brigade division being commanded by Brigadier Cadwallader C. Washburn, brother of the Congressman (the general had not added a decorative "e" as had Elihu). Northward, Hovey had 5,000 infantry and 14 guns to serve as a rallying force in case Washburn should get into serious difficulty. On the afternoon of November 30 the cavalry had crossed the Mississippi and Tennessee Railroad and had come to within five miles of Grenada. Learning from Negroes that a large force of Confederates had moved by the Mississippi Central to Grenada, Washburn fell back with horsemen tired from long marches, and camped for the night, but not until he had sent forward a strong detachment to carry out demolitions on the rail line from Holly Springs, bridges having already been destroyed on the line from Memphis.

Failure of rations to arrive practically immobilized Washburn on December 1, and the next day incessant and hard rain played havoc with the roads. But on the 3rd, after being reenforced with 600 infantry, he had a brisk skirmish near Oakland with three enemy cavalry regiments totaling 1,264 men, which Washburn accurately appraised as numbering 1,500. As he had reports that there were similar columns to his north and south, the Federal commander did not press the issue, but went into camp in the Oakland square, where at midnight word reached him to return to Helena. (Steele felt that the object of the expedition had been accomplished.) In a report written at the mouth of Coldwater River, Hovey expatiated on the evils of trade with the enemy: "War and commerce with the same people! What a Utopian dream!" While the Hoosier lawyer's indictment covered all "unprincipled sharpers," he singled out Jews for special maledictions. Upon reaching the Mississippi after struggling through the heavy mud of the flat delta region, Hovey had another problem— "at least 500 contrabands of all sizes, shapes, shades, and condition" had attached themselves to his columns.[57]

While Washburn was withdrawing from Oakland, Grant wired to Halleck, "I have heard nothing from Steele's expedition, but from the precipitate flight of the enemy I think it must have been successful." High streams and heavy roads, however, slowed pursuit; and when the Helena troops started homeward, Van Dorn stiffened, throwing an infantry attack at Grant's cavalry advance in the vicinity of Coffeeville on the 5th. "The tactics of the enemy did them great credit," was Lloyd Tilghman's generous comment in a long report, while Van Dorn telegraphed to Pemberton: "Enemy came up to within 2 miles of town this evening. . . . He will be careful how he comes up again." [58]

In the early afternoon of the same day Grant sent a telegram from Oxford ending with a sentence calculated to force a decision from the High Command: "If the Helena troops were at my command I think it practicable to send Sherman to take them and Memphis troops south of mouth of Yazoo River and thus secure Vicksburg and State of Mississippi." The day was likewise notable because Grant issued his final order sending the assistant superintendent of telegraph lines out of his department because of noncompliance with instructions, in spite of the fact that he had direct access to Colonel Stager, who had the ear of Stanton.[59]

Monday, December 8, was a day of important decisions. On the 7th Halleck had telegraphed that the capture of Grenada, which he evidently expected would be accomplished by the Helena troops, would change plans with regard to Vicksburg. Specifically he said, "You will move your troops as you may deem best to accomplish the great object in view." Grant was to retain any of Curtis's troops that were in his department; call on the St. Louis quartermaster for such steamers as he might need; ask Admiral Porter to cooperate; and telegraph his plans.[60] More Grant could not have desired.

In a mid-morning reply on the 8th, Grant said he would send two divisions to Memphis in a few days, and he queried, "Do you want me to command the expedition on Vicksburg or shall I send Sherman?" He made the decision himself, and at 10:00 P.M. wired: "General Sherman will command the expedition down the Mississippi. He will have a force of about 40,000 men." After outlining how Sherman would operate, he said that he himself would occupy the Mississippi Central as far as Coffeeville, hold the Yalobusha with his cavalry, "and where an opportunity occurs make a real attack." [61]

Sherman, who was at Grant's Oxford headquarters, wrote at length to Porter. After describing the situation, the eager soldier said:

Time now is the great object. We must not give [the enemy] time for new combinations. I know you will promptly co-operate. It will not be necessary to engage their Vicksburg batteries until I have broken all their inland communication. Then Vicksburg must be attacked by land and water. In this I will defer much to you.

My purpose will be to cut the road to Monroe, La., to Jackson, Miss., and then appear up the Yazoo, threatening the Mississippi Central road where it crosses the Big Black.

Sherman was leaving Oxford the next day and hoped to be in Memphis with one of his divisions on Friday; he earnestly hoped Porter could meet him; he wanted Captains Phelps, Gwin, and Shirk—the sailors that Grant and he knew so well—to bring light-draft boats at once to assist in preliminary work; Porter to bring the large gunboats later, if there had to be delay. The dispatch ended: "General Grant's purpose is to take full advantage of the effects of this Tallahatchie success." [62]

Grant on his part wrote to Steele, telling of the authority granted him to retain the Helena force that had crossed the river, adding, "If these troops have gone back to Helena I wish you would return them to Friar's Point, or the most suitable place to march them directly upon Grenada, or embark them for Vicksburg, as I may decide upon." He needed information, and he said to his old classmate:

Please inform me by return couriers all you know about the present condition of our gunboats. You having been so long on the Mississippi

River looking toward Vicksburg are possessed of much information as to
the best method of attacking that point that I am not possessed of. I would
be glad to have your views.

Grant would also be pleased if Steele could accompany Sherman on
the river expedition.[63]

The next day brought a dispatch from Halleck with a disturbing
sentence: "The President may insist upon designating a separate commander; if not, assign such officers as you deem best." In closing he
said, "Sherman would be my choice as chief under you"—a statement that disclosed the General in Chief's confidence not only in
Sherman but also in Grant. In replying late in the afternoon, Grant
put at something like 1,200 the number of prisoners to date, and said
he had permitted many from the border states to take the oath and
go home. The message had this ending: "A letter from General
McClernand, just received, states that he expects to go forward in
a few days. Sherman has already gone. The enterprise would be much
safer in charge of the latter." [64]

Grant's message to Steele had been turned over by Sherman to
Colonel Grierson, who had ridden straight westward from Oxford with
his Sixth Illinois Cavalry. "He is the best cavalry officer I have yet
had. . . . I know that you will soon appreciate his merits," had been
Sherman's statement in a note to his chief. Much now depended upon
sureness of communication, and a single courier or a few horsemen
could not have prudently been sent into the guerrilla-infested country.
When Grierson reached Helena on the 12th (he had started on the
9th), Steele was no longer in command, having been replaced by
Brigadier General Willis A. Gorman. "Curtis will do everything in
his power to injure me because I denounced his d———d rascality,"
was Steele's explanation to Grant. But he was very happily accompanying the expedition. Gorman wrote that he would send a force a
little stronger than the recent Hovey expedition, and if Sherman believed it insufficient, he would take the responsibility of sending all his
command—12,000 infantry, 4,700 cavalry, 5 batteries—except what
was needed as a garrison. Gwin wrote about the navy—six ironclads,
four light-draft wooden boats, two rams—and Gorman reported that
the Confederates had a battery on the Yazoo fifteen miles from its
mouth, twelve by land from Vicksburg.[65]

Gorman's offer of full cooperation may or may not have been made
before the receipt of a dispatch from Curtis dated St. Louis, December

9, which began, "I am required to have most of the troops now at Helena ready for a down-river expedition." This fitted in well with the message from Grant, but the ending was new: "Blunt and Herron have fought a battle and won a victory at Fayetteville over Hindman." The battle, generally known as that of Prairie Grove, fought on the 7th, was a sharp one, and the victory was greatly to the credit of the Federal soldiers and their generals. Hindman had moved to attack Blunt in the vicinity of Cane Hill, ten miles southwest of Fayetteville. Learning that Herron was coming by forced marches to join Blunt, Hindman threw himself on the head of the latter's column shortly after it left Fayetteville. Herron, whose infantry had been marching thirty-five miles a day since it left Springfield, fought skillfully and hard for several hours, until Blunt, guided by the sound of heavy gunfire, struck the Confederate flank and rear. Fighting continued until night, and in the darkness Hindman retreated. On each side there were about 10,000 men (but the 3,000 Federal cavalry were not engaged); on each side total losses were about 1,300. "The results of your victory cannot be overestimated. The stake was an important one," said Blunt in his congratulatory order to the Army of the Frontier. But he did overestimate when he said, "Your victory has virtually ended the war north of the Arkansas River." [66] Within the foreseeable future, however, southwestern Missouri was safe, and such was the shock to the Confederate Arkansas command that Federal troops could with impunity be taken from Helena.

When Sherman started back to Memphis with Morgan Smith's division, he forgot the castigating order he had recently issued to his troops because of plundering, and fairly wept in an order taking leave of his other two divisions. (Grant kept two of Sherman's divisions instead of one, as he had first contemplated.) As one would expect, Sherman arrived on time and was soon energetically at work. He found that the divisions of A. J. Smith and George Morgan, recently arrived from Kentucky, had been little more than skeletons and had been filled up with new regiments. Counting Morgan Smith's division, brought from Oxford, Sherman had but 20,000 men, and he urged Gorman and Curtis to make Steele available with at least 10,000. To Gorman he said, "Grant is ready and impatient, and the enemy is shaken by their being outwitted at the Tallahatchie." [67]

Quartermasters were to have troubles aplenty with the logistical problem suddenly thrown on them. On the 10th, Robert Allen at St.

Louis wired to Stanton that Grant had asked for a million bushels of coal and he suggested that half of it be sent to Memphis and the other half to Cairo. To Grant, Allen telegraphed that the river was low and he did not know how fast the coal could be brought down; but steamboatmen had said wood could be chopped without too much delay. Transportation could not be secured for the troops within the time Grant had asked. On the 15th Colonel Lewis B. Parsons, who would make a great record in the transportation field before the war was over, wired to Halleck from Cairo that it had been impossible to get the boats to Memphis in the three and a half days that Grant had specified, but he hoped to be there not later than the morning of the 19th with sixty steamers and fuel enough to go to Vicksburg.[68]

In his dispatch of the 9th Halleck, repeating a warning given on the 5th, had said, "As it is possible that Bragg may cross at Decatur and fall upon Corinth the security of that place should be carefully attended to." Commanding at Corinth was General Dodge, careful and enterprising, and at noon on the 10th Grant passed to Washington a dispatch Dodge had just sent: Kirby Smith was at Murfreesboro (some of his troops were, but not the general), Breckinridge at Shelbyville, Bragg at Tullahoma, intending to stay there. Provisions were getting very scarce in the Tennessee Valley and north of it. That was reassuring. But the next day Rosecrans wired to Grant from Nashville, "Tell the authorities along the road to look out for Forrest." The warning was passed at once to Dodge and Brigadier Jeremiah C. Sullivan at Jackson. Simultaneously, in reply to a message from Grant, Colonel Haynie sent a report from Bethel—where he had been helpful during the Corinth battle. Forrest's forces were in and about Columbia. Haynie added: "Returned Confederates say the army is destitute and is coming on this way after supplies. Scouts start to-night to hunt main forces." [69]

Fully conscious of the responsibilities of a commander of a zone of communications, Sullivan on the 3rd had sent a message to eighteen commanders, alerting them against guerrilla bands. He put things clearly: "Guarding railroads and keeping communications open to the army is now the vitally important duty of troops in this district. Energy, courage, and daring are required of officers and men. . . . Disgrace will inevitably follow a defeat." On the 12th he reported to Grant that scouts from the Tennessee stated that Forrest's cavalry was coming from Columbia to strike Savannah. Grant passed the word to Porter with the query, "Can a light-draught gunboat get up there at this time?" The prompt reply from Cairo was hardly cheering. Two gunboats were working their way up the Tennessee, but could not get higher than Cuba Ford, fifty miles below Savannah. One of them was already aground.[70]

On the day Grant was seeking a gunboat to keep Forrest off his line of communications, he also issued an order to mitigate the suffering of Southern families from the havoc of war. It began:

Distress and almost famine having been brought on many of the inhabitants of Mississippi by the march of the two armies through the land, and humanity dictating that in a land of plenty no one should suffer the pangs of hunger, the general commanding directs that the following provision shall be made at all military posts within the State.

At all posts one or more loyal persons were to be authorized to sell "provisions and absolute necessaries for family use." In addition, special funds were to be provided by contributions, carefully administered and accounted for, and open to the scrutiny of the department inspector general.[71]

The next day, December 13, while Sherman was busy with plans for the river movement, Colonel Mizner, commanding Grant's cavalry at Water Valley on the Otuckalofa, sent dispatches with considerable enemy information. Price and Van Dorn, each with about 15,000 men, were in the vicinity of Grenada; Pemberton was there himself; Negroes were throwing up earthworks north of the Yalobusha; Lovell had gone to Richmond four days before. All this came from a captured courier carrying to a Confederate major at Horn Lake, eight miles south of Memphis, an order to destroy all cotton between the Tallahatchie and the Coldwater "and all other points accessible."[72]

To give greater security to his left flank, Grant wrote a note to Colonel T. Lyle Dickey, commanding his three-brigade cavalry division—located near Water Valley—that began, "I want you to strike the Mobile road as far south as possible and follow up north, destroying it all you can." Difficulties might defeat the object of the expedition; he wanted no great risk run, but left this to Dickey's judgment. Dodge would that day start a force of some 2,500 southward to cooperate. Knowing that Dickey would not turn the discretion given him into justification for nonperformance, Grant said, "If practicable you might continue north until you meet them and return by Pontotoc to the front." Simultaneously Mizner, who commanded the part of the cavalry that remained at Water Valley, was ordered to protect Dickey, "Should you discover any movement of the enemy toward Colonel Dickey appraise him of the fact or go to his assistance, as may seem best." [73]

On the 14th the operator at Columbus put on the wire a dispatch that had come upriver from Sherman. The latter was wondering if Grierson had arrived at Helena and whether he could depend upon 12,000 men from there. Said Grant in reply, "I have not had one word from Grierson since he left, and am getting uneasy about him." Well he might, after learning of the intercepted enemy courier bound for Horn Lake. But he told Sherman that the 21,000 men he had and 12,000 from Helena would "make a good force." The enemy, he said, was still along the Yalobusha; he was pushing down slowly, "but so as to keep up the impression of a continuous move." In a week he probably would have his headquarters at Coffeeville. It would be well if Sherman would get two or three small boats that could navigate the Yazoo, for Grant might have to draw supplies from it.[74] Optimist though Grant was, he was fully aware of the uncertainty of his lengthening rail line, which soon would be struck heavy blows.

The very next day, in fact, while Grant was resolving doubts by telling Sherman to use Halleck's order and assume command of the Helena troops if need be, Haynie transmitted to Sullivan a message just in from a captain of the First West Tennessee Cavalry (Union), stationed near Clifton: "Colonel Haynie: I inform you from a source believed to be reliable that a force is to cross the river at Clifton, supposed to be Forrest's cavalry, said to be 3,000 strong." Thus it was men in blue from the region where Forrest—former alderman and prosperous businessman of Memphis—lived who sounded the alarm. Soon after the long winter night had closed in with the heavy all-day rain still falling, Sullivan wired to Grant that Forrest was crossing both at Clifton and above, and he added, "Bragg's army is reported by scouts to be moving this way, through Waynesborough." Northward the report also went, and even before midnight Davies at Columbus telegraphed to Sullivan: "I will try to push forward the regiment here to-night. If not, they will leave in the morning." [75]

Prudently Grant waited before concentrating more strength about Jackson. A dispatch to Halleck the next day said nothing about

Forrest, but merely: "Bragg is said to be going toward the Tennessee River through Waynesborough. Rosecrans ought to push them and if possible gunboats ought to be sent up the Tennessee." Twenty minutes after this reached Washington late in the afternoon, Grant forwarded a message just received from Dodge. Agents who had left Shelbyville on the 8th reported that all of Bragg's army, including "most of cavalry," was to move to La Vergne, halfway point on the railroad between Murfreesboro and Nashville. Joe Johnston, the dispatch said, was in command of everything, and it was his intention to make a stand at La Vergne. All in all, the reports of the scouts were confirmed by West Tennessee and Arkansas deserters. "When these men left," the message said, "most of Forrest's cavalry was up on Cumberland River, west of Nashville." [76] Grant could feel he had done right in not concentrating troops against Forrest until he learned more.

A unique day followed. From Springfield, McClernand wired to Lincoln: "I believe I am superseded. Please advise me." A similar message to Stanton brought the reply: "Your telegram this moment received. It surprises me, but I will ascertain and let you know immediately." The promised second message told the worried McClernand that he had not been superseded but would have the First Corps of three "assigned to the operations on the Mississippi under the general supervision of the general commanding the department," Halleck being about to issue the order.[77] It was hardly a message to bring forth cheers, for John McClernand was not getting the independent command he had been intriguing for.

Repeating an earlier request, Brigadier Robert Allen, St. Louis quartermaster, telegraphed to Halleck that Grant wanted six locomotives, and queried, "Shall they be purchased?" (More will be told about this presently.) A second message said the body of the Memphis fleet would leave Cairo "to-night"; Parsons was going; he reported everything all right; there would be sixty-two steamers.[78]

Rosecrans, bustling about at 2:00 A.M., wired to Sullivan that Bragg, Withers, Cheatham, and Breckinridge were in Murfreesboro the day before, with Hardee at Triune, twelve miles west. No other than Jeff Davis had reviewed the troops on Saturday the 13th; he had said, "Middle Tennessee must, could, and should be held"; having thus proclaimed, Davis had left for Mobile. Forrest, whose horsemen were too numerous for Rosecrans's "little force," would probably make a raid across the river; but Rosecrans did not think anything more would be done.[79]

Gorman, writing to Curtis, said that the Arkansas River being up, gunboats and some of his command could move on Little Rock unless all his force was needed by Sherman. For his part, Sherman was writing to Gorman: "Nothing is now wanting but the transports; my troops here are ready and impatient." A boat from upriver had brought word that Bragg might interpose between Grant and Columbus, but Grant "ought to gain advantage by any such desperate move." The canny general added: "I rather suspect it is designed to draw us back from our purpose of going to Vicksburg. I shall disregard these signs unless orders come from Grant or Halleck." [80]

Sullivan was telegraphing to Grant that the Tennessee cavalry captain reported several thousand enemy cavalry—"estimated 10,000"—and a battery were seven miles west of Clifton. But since yesterday noon, Sullivan had had 600 cavalry and a gun section out with orders to go to Clifton; from them he had heard nothing at all.[81]

Assistant Secretary of the Navy Gustavus Fox was writing to Halleck that Porter had been instructed to send gunboats up the Tennessee, in accordance with Halleck's request of the morning.[82]

And Grant? He ordered Hamilton, commanding his left wing, to advance McArthur's division, and told McPherson, who had the right wing since Sherman's departure, to reconnoiter to Otuckalofa River, adding that he would probably move his headquarters to Spring Dale on Saturday (the 20th).[83] In addition he issued two general orders designed to keep matters in the rear under control as he moved southward. Since the year that was drawing to an end saw the promulgation of only fourteen general orders after Grant had been made a department commander, two in one day made Wednesday, December 17, quite exceptional.

One general order named Chaplain Eaton "General Superintendent of Contrabands for the Department," with power to designate such assistant superintendents as he thought necessary for the care of his charges. Although the proper commanders would have to detail the officers on whom Eaton put his finger, Eaton was being given wide authority. He must have proved himself during the past five weeks, and Grant obviously wanted him to have good assistants. Doubtless some of the provisions of the order were drawn up by Eaton himself on the basis of his experience, though one may be sure they were carefully studied by Grant. That a delicate matter was being dealt with was shown by the last sentence of the order: "In no case will negroes be forced into the service of the Government, or be enticed away from their homes except when it becomes a military necessity." [84]

The other order was not such a happy one, for it expelled Jews from the department within twenty-four hours. Actually, the order revealed conflicting thinking, the ending being superfluous: "No passes will be given these people to visit headquarters for the purpose of making personal application for trade permits." In a letter written the same day to Assistant Secretary of War C. P. Wolcott, Grant explained some of the methods of the offending Jews, indicating at the same time that "other unprincipled traders" were also violating the specie regulations of the Treasury Department, but saying nothing of a general order that had been or was about to be issued. The most important statement in the letter was the ending: "There is but one way that I know of to reach this case; that is, for the Government to buy all the cotton at a fixed price and send it to Cairo, Saint Louis, or some other point to be sold. Then all traders (they are a curse to the army) might be expelled." [85]

The storm that Grant's order provoked came largely from the uprooting of innocent and respected families in Paducah, who protested directly to Lincoln. Several persons, including Grant's father, who was in Oxford when the order was written, were to assert that it was issued upon specific instructions from Washington. In spite of the lack of any confirmatory documents, Korn, who has studied the question extensively, states that we are bound to accept the testimony as to Washington "promptings," and he comes close to putting the onus specifically upon Halleck. The dispatch that Grant had sent Webster five weeks before, is, however, fatal to a claim of Washington responsibility, and after Korn has introduced that message he has a new explanation: the expulsion order was the *"logical capstone of a policy of discrimination against Jews"* (emphasis Korn's) which Grant had deliberately formulated and pursued. Categorically Korn says of the order, *"It was no accident."* This conclusion is mitigated by the statement: "General Grant can in no wise be held responsible, personally and solely, for the anti-Jewish regulations which he dictated and signed. The causes, roots, pressures, and reasons go deep into the nature of the conditions in the Department of the Tennessee." [86]

It is not necessary to appeal to the "social climate" to explain Grant's order. He was fighting a hard war, and was trying to do so vigorously and with expedition, but found himself hampered by contrabands and cotton traders. He devised an excellent solution for the contrabands and he had the power to put it into effect. For the buyers he also thought he had the answer; but because he lacked authority to institute it he sought to lessen his problem by getting rid of a recognizable group of offenders. Grant was usually practical.

One cannot say how many innocent families in Paducah and elsewhere suffered because of the expulsion order. For them there can be only regret and sympathy. Awareness of them should have prevented such a sweeping order. But there need be neither regret nor sympathy for actual traders who had to leave the forward army zone until the order was revoked. Of course, they and their friends pointed to buyers not forced to leave, and a cry of discrimination was inevitable. It was even natural that it should be said that Grant wished to favor the traders who remained. But the final sentence of his letter to Wolcott proves such a contention is entirely unfounded.[87]

Guerrillas, contrabands, and cotton traders would have been sufficient problems over and above those normal to an offensive military operation. But there was also that of confiscated property. Grant's order about pillaging had pointed out that the Confiscation Act gave no license to soldiers as individuals, and an order of November 26 dealt specifically with the seizure and disposal of property, as well as its accountability. On the seizure question Sherman was almost leaning over backward. In the postscript to a letter to Halleck he spoke of the old Memphis navy yard, where the Confederates had founded cannon, constructed gun carriages, built wagons, and fabricated other military equipment. Then the general whose name to many is a synonym for wanton plundering and destruction wrote, "Though donated by Congress to the city of Memphis, I think it is fairly liable to confiscation, but I have only taken certain parts of it for necessary workshops, taking accurate inventories of tools and materials." [88]

Probably before noon of the 18th Grant knew for certain that Forrest was west of the Tennessee, his telegram to Colonel William W. Lowe at Fort Henry saying 3,000 men were already across. A concentration from different points in the direction of Jackson was at once ordered, and Grant's military philosophy was revealed in a telegram to Sullivan: "Have you made preparations to get forces from Corinth? Don't fail to get up a force and attack the enemy. Never wait to have them attack you." At 7:10 P.M. Sullivan wired, "My cavalry was whipped at Lexington to-day." After saying it was reported that the enemy had from 10,000 to 20,000 men and was still crossing the river, Jeremiah Sullivan again showed a casual manner: "I will try to find their number by daylight." [89]

Colonel Fuller, ordered at nine o'clock to move his infantry brigade from Oxford to Jackson, was on the way at midnight with one regiment; a second was to follow in two hours; the other two would stand by awaiting cars. In a telegram to Porter, Grant said he understood there were now four feet of water in the Tennessee; gunboats would be of immense value. He put the enemy at from 5,000 to 10,000 and said: "I hope my force will be able to drive to the river. I have been concentrating troops all day to meet them." Porter had already gone down the Mississippi, but the fleet captain at Cairo replied that five light-draft gunboats drawing three feet had left the Ohio on the 15th with orders to go up the Tennessee on the rise. But he reminded: "They are only musket-proof." [90]

That Grant was hoping to turn the enemy venture into an enemy disaster was shown by a dispatch informing McPherson that Forrest and Napier (T. Alonzo Napier) were across the river and near Jackson: "I have directed such a concentration of troops that I think not many of them will get back to the east bank of the Tennessee. They will probably succeed, however, in cutting the road and wires so as to interrupt communications north for a day or two." [91] It proved to be much too optimistic an appraisal. To the end Grant would never see any situation as lacking opportunities. That was one reason why he was a very great general. Perception, however, is not sufficient for a commander. He must exploit opportunities quickly and fearlessly. That too Grant did.

A commander must also put full responsibilities upon his subordinates and encourage the offensive spirit. Here is what Grant wrote to Dodge on the 8th: "When you are satisfied the enemy can be attacked and repulsed without endangering the post from other parties, do it. You can judge the propriety of attacking at Guntown better than I can." Then followed a sentence that showed his understanding of a good subordinate's feelings. At the moment, Lew Wallace was under orders to return to Grant, and Grant said to Dodge, "General Wallace will probably relieve you in a day or two. A division then awaits you here." [92] Dodge knew Grant's standards for a field commander and he must have been deeply touched.

A general must also build in subordinates the feeling that they will not be forgotten. We have seen Grant tell Mizner, "Should you discover any movement of the enemy toward Colonel Dickey apprise him of the fact or go to his assistance, as may seem best." To Dodge he telegraphed: "Keep me informed of appearances around you. Should you be advanced upon by any considerable force I will reenforce you." One can not exaggerate the significance of such messages, with their simple, clear sentences. Even in minor matters Grant showed himself the master. Here was the ending of a note to Hamilton dated November 28: "Detail four good companies of cavalry, well commanded, to remain at Holly Springs until they receive orders from me. I want to send them to communicate with Sherman." [93] Subordinates should always feel their commander knows what he wants. Grant's subordinates never doubted.

Grant kept in mind the possibility of misunderstandings and confusion arising from the passing of messages. On November 11 he telegraphed to Hamilton: "I have directed five companies of cavalry to report to Colonel Lee in the morning, and sent a communication for you to furnish a brigade and battery, just as your dispatch states you have done." This prevented a possible double detail of troops. Another message to Hamilton on the same day ended, "My dispatch to you was in consequence of the superintendent of telegraph reporting that all the troops had left Davis' Mill." [94] Now Hamilton had the picture of the situation as Grant saw it.

For himself, Grant wanted definite information. Thus on the 12th he telegraphed to Hamilton:

Have you sent forward more than one brigade? My instructions were that if Wolf River Railroad Bridge is still standing, and Holly Springs and Lumpkin's Mill deserted, as I understand they are, these two divisions were to be pushed forward. Answer if the two divisions have already gone. If so, I want telegraph office pushed forward and a brigade sent to Davis' Mill.

It is hardly necessary to say that Hamilton replied with a careful report.[95]

Not merely on troop commanders did Grant keep a friendly, observant eye. He showed officers in charge of technical matters that he knew just what they were doing, and he complimented them for their achievements. On December 3 he sent a dispatch to Colonel George G. Pride, addressed to Hudsonville, Mississippi. Colonels could not have been so abundant at that little place as to require identification, but under the name was spelled out a title that reminded the recipient that he held a very responsible position: "Chief Engineer Military Railroads." The dispatch read:

Colonel: Am glad to hear you are progressing so well with your work. Push on the repairs to the Tallahatchie. It is the intention to rebuild the Tallahatchie Bridge, and Quinby has been directed to commence getting out timber to that end.[96]

Of course Pride had had difficulties. But now he was repaid in the best of all coin—the army commander's approval. Yet he could not slow up, thinking materials would not be ready when he got to the Tallahatchie. In fact, he now had reason for pushing hard. Colonel Pride could hardly want a lot of timber ready and unnecessarily waiting for the arrival of his men to use it.

In connection with those six locomotives that Allen told Halleck Grant wanted, there is quite a story, worth the telling, for it shows a part of Grant's plan often overlooked, and reveals his well conceived and effective persistence.

In a letter to Congressman Washburne on November 7, Grant said, "Once at Grenada I can draw supplies from Memphis, and save our present very long line." On the 12th he wrote to Halleck that if it were intended to let his column push on down the Mississippi Central and supply itself by the Mississippi and Tennessee road after reaching Grenada, it would be necessary to have "six additional locomotives as early as possible," three of them to be sent to Memphis. Of the eighteen serviceable engines out of the total of twenty-two that Grant had, three, he said, were in the shops about half the time. The next day he raised his request for locomotives to twelve, saying, "Will you direct them ordered?" Looking forward to the problem of keeping them in condition, he asked, "Can I not have an ordnance officer from Saint Louis ordered to Memphis?"[97]

On the 15th Halleck replied that twelve additional locomotives could not be procured without seriously deranging other lines. Furthermore, he said it was not advisable to put the road south of

Memphis in operation, for the plan was to move down the river as soon as a sufficient force could be collected. Land operations were to be restricted to minor blows, with troops supplied from the country as much as possible. The dispatch was not an unequivocal refusal of any additional locomotives, so Grant telegraphed to Parsons that he wanted six locomotives and two hundred cars. The dispatch is not in the records, but one Pride sent to Parsons the same day is. Grant, Pride said, wanted Parsons personally to visit roads in Indiana, Michigan, and the Northwest; the Northwest roads had not been much called upon and should do their duty. Perhaps a road here or a road there could not only give two locomotives but could alter them to 5-foot gauge in their own shops. And Parsons might keep his eye open for something else: "five good hand-cars for Memphis." [98]

Adroitly, Pride stated that Halleck had telegraphed that engines could not be procured in the East—a not unreasonable interpretation of what Halleck had said—but he made no reference to the General in Chief's statement that it was not "advisable" to put the road southward from Memphis in working order. In fact, he said additional locomotives were needed in order to open that road. Working through Allen's office was in no way by-passing Halleck, for the decision would go to him ultimately. The procedure was, in fact, proper, though it would have been wrong for Grant not to include in his frequent telegrams to Halleck direct statements about supply and equipment.

When Allen, who, like Grant, had gone to West Point from Georgetown, Ohio, and who was in his last year when Halleck was a plebe, saw the telegrams from La Grange, he must have thought of the vicissitudes of men's fortunes. He had been chief quartermaster in San Francisco when Grant stopped there on his way to New York after resigning from the army. While stories are contradictory, it seems certain that Allen, or his chief clerk, when he himself was out of the office, was helpful to Grant.[99] And now the man who had then needed assistance in getting home wanted six locomotives in order to prosecute a very difficult campaign!

Parsons was soon on his way to Chicago, telegraphing to Grant that the railroads terminating there had 10,000 cars. He wanted Grant to have his engines: "Would it not be better to make requisitions on them for 500 cars and 10 locomotives and take at once what you now require, and others as needed? Answer at Chicago."

Just what happened is not clear, though it looks as if Parsons saw Grant when the latter went to Columbus to see Sherman. Allen on his part dutifully reported to Halleck, asking him to please send the necessary telegraphic order to Parsons in Chicago. Halleck replied: "I have telegraphed to General Grant that it is not intended to use the railroads south of Memphis, and that only such cars and locomotives must be purchased as were necessary for the roads already in operation." [100]

In the end Grant did not want the Tennessee and Mississippi Railroad, though it is highly important to see how it had figured in his plans before he was given the use of the Mississippi River and authority to call for transports and gunboats. Nor did Halleck in the dispatch above—dated November 22—give an unexceptionable no as to locomotives; when Allen came back with the request on December 17 for six, Old Brains telegraphed, "Give General Grant the locomotives he requires." [101] The Georgetown team had won.

Grant had been conducting a fairly extensive correspondence with Pemberton that showed both Grant's kindness and his determination to accept no insinuations and unjust charges from an enemy commander. On November 19 Pemberton asked permission to send money and clothing to the sick and wounded Confederates at Iuka, as well as ambulances from time to time to bring back the convalescents. Generously he thanked Grant for the kind treatment the Confederate surgeon at Iuka reported was being given the Southern wounded. Grant's reply gave full permission for what was asked, and suggested a road, "This route will be left free for your ambulances while engaged in removing the sick and wounded." [102]

On December 5 Grant wrote to Pemberton, "I have now several hundred Confederate prisoners who by the Dix-Hill cartel will have to be sent to Vicksburg for exchange unless by agreement they will be received elsewhere." He proposed to deliver them at any point on the Mississippi Central Railroad that Pemberton might suggest, provided there would be an officer to receive and receipt for them. Or, if Pemberton preferred, Grant would parole and release the men at Oxford, sending certified rolls to Pemberton. In his reply the next day Pemberton loftily said, "The prisoners referred to I presume to be the sick who were necessarily left and stragglers from this army." He preferred to have the sick kept in a hospital until they could be sent for; because of the bad condition of the road and the destroyed railroad bridges he wished to have the stragglers sent to Vicksburg as "required by terms of the cartel." To that place he would send for exchange the some forty Federals who had been "taken in action."[103]

After receiving from Pemberton a sharp letter written on December 13 saying he understood that the benefits of exchange were not being given to Partisan Rangers, Grant two days later wrote that he would send them to Vicksburg for exchange "or set them loose." (Grant said the Rangers were a pest to the country where they operated, a view presently endorsed by the Confederate Secretary of War.) Then Grant wrote:

> I will state here that this is the third communication from you to General Sherman and myself since the present advance commenced that has been threatening in tone. One of your communications also implied a doubt of my veracity in the statement made by me as to prisoners taken as well as casting reflections upon the character of those prisoners.
>
> I will now state to you that the number of prisoners taken by my forces on this advance has been exclusive of sick and stragglers over 1,000. Most of this latter class have been persons who have become tired of the war and have been permitted to take the oath of allegiance and return to their homes.
>
> All communications heretofore received from officers of the Southern Army have been courteous and kind in spirit and have been replied to in the same tone. I regret the necessity for any other class of correspondence.[104]

Grant's dispatches to Halleck bear out what he had written to Washburne in June: he liked and respected Halleck. Doubtless, too, he comprehended the magnitude of Halleck's position and the difficulties caused by the intrigue and political atmosphere of Washington. Fiske's criticism of Halleck for not allowing Grant to abandon Corinth as he suggested in late October is very ill founded—an instance of the bricks thrown with gusto but no good basis at the general with the stern, forbidding visage.[105] Grant got excellent service out of Dodge's small force at Corinth. It protected his flank and he frequently appealed to Dodge to check on the recurring reports about Braxton Bragg. The importance of Corinth and of an officer like Dodge in that location will be quite obvious in the later phases of the Vicksburg story.

In connection with Grant's short service at Ironton in August, 1861, it was stated that some writers have exaggerated Grant's debt to

Rawlins, especially in the matter of operations. On the 15th of the December we are considering, Grant said in a letter to Halleck, "Colonel Rawlins I regard as the ablest and most reliable man in his department of the volunteer service, and with but few equals in the regular Army." [106] The temperament of the Galena lawyer was such that he sometimes expressed himself—and that very vehemently—about matters of no proper concern to an adjutant. Rawlins's quiet-spoken chief let him talk and swear—for such was Grant's kind and considerate nature—but it was he who did the careful thinking and painstaking planning that were revealed day after day in excellent dispatches.

CHAPTER VII

HOLLY SPRINGS AND CHICKASAW BLUFFS

I fear this has been a hard day for you.
Porter to Sherman

MORE disturbing than the Confederates in Grant's rear was a tele-gram from Halleck that arrived late in the night of December 18, the upshot doubtless of McClernand's messages to Washington the day before:

> The troops in your department, including those from Curtis' command which join down-river expedition, will be divided into four army corps. It is the wish of the President that General McClernand's corps shall con-stitute a part of the river expedition and that he shall have the immediate command under your direction.

A War Department order of the same day gave to McClernand, Sherman, Hurlbut, and McPherson, respectively, the Thirteenth, Fifteenth, Sixteenth, and Seventeenth Army Corps. Though it is un-certain when Grant received the designations of his corps and their assigned commanders, he could see from Halleck's telegram that he was to have a stronger and better organized force than he had had since October 24, when all the troops in his department were desig-nated the Thirteenth Corps.[1] In the future his new command would bear the proud name Army of the Tennessee.

Seniority of course placed McClernand over Sherman, unless the President specifically directed otherwise. Though mounting confidence in Grant was revealed by the increase of his command and the definite subordination of McClernand to him, Lincoln nonetheless ignored Grant's warning that the Vicksburg enterprise would be safer under Sherman than under McClernand. It is hard to believe that the President did not see that statement to Halleck or that the latter did not add full concurrence. Only Grant's personal presence could deprive McClernand of the command, and an explicit order for Grant to remain behind so that the Springfield general could unquestionably direct operations might have raised an issue that Lincoln would not have cared to face.

Soon, if he had not already received it, Halleck would be reading a long personal letter Grant wrote on the 14th, caused by a "private letter" from Washburne, reporting a conversation with Halleck, in which the latter had expressed confidence in Grant. (Elihu as well as brother Cadwallader could do timely things.) Grant expressed appreciation, and, laying aside some of his customary reserve, said he had heard that there was doubt of confirmation of recent promotions. "There are many of them I have no interest in," he continued, "but in the case of McPherson I am deeply interested. He is now second in command with the army in the field, and should his name be brought up and rejected I would feel the loss more than taking a division from me." As commander of a wing, McPherson was "worth more than a division," and should Grant lose him in that capacity he would have to look after that wing directly, in addition to his "duties with the whole." After expressing the hope that no officers would be sent to him who ranked those he had, Grant said, "I am sorry to say it, but I would regard it as particularly unfortunate to have either McClernand or Wallace sent to me. The latter I could manage if he had less rank, but the former is unmanageable and incompetent." [2]

Not a moment, however, was lost by Grant in writing to McClernand. After explaining the new division of his command, he said, "written and verbal instructions have been given General Sherman, which will be turned over to you on your arrival in Memphis. I hope you will find all the preliminary preparations accomplished on your arrival and the expedition ready to move. I will co-operate with the river expedition from here, commanding this portion of the army in person." It was desirable that there be no delay in starting, but if unforeseen obstacles arose Grant wished to be informed by messenger to Columbus, and telegraph from there; he closed by asking for a strength return of the river expedition.[3] It could not have been pleasant to feel that his expressed view as to the safety of the expedition had been rejected, but Grant did not modify instructions. McClernand, suspicious though he was, could not rightfully say that orders had been purposely drawn to limit him because he was not a West Pointer.

To Davies at Columbus, for forwarding to Sherman, Grant sent a copy of Halleck's telegram, and instructions to tell Sherman that his corps would consist of Steele's and Morgan Smith's divisions, while McClernand's would comprise those of A. J. Smith and George Morgan; the two corps to "descend the river." [4]

When on the night of the 18th Forrest sent a regiment to the north of Jackson "to tear up the railroad track and destroy the telegraph wires," and another force to the south, he could not have dreamed that he was in fact preventing the substitution of McClernand for Sherman. In a dispatch to McPherson the next day Grant said he was out of communication with Jackson, told of the replacement of Sherman by McClernand, and said, "I was in hopes the expedition would be off by this time, and it may be that they are about starting." [5]

To the question, Did Grant make his first move to get the expedition started under Sherman after he definitely knew that McClernand was to command it? the answer is an unqualified No. It was on December 7 that Halleck directed him to move his troops as he deemed best "to accomplish the great object in view," and told him to ask for all the steamers he wanted and to get in touch with Porter. In issuing the order to Sherman the next day, Grant was merely acting with customary promptness. It was not until the 9th that Halleck intimated that the President might insist on designating a separate commander, and it was on the 9th also that Grant received some sort of communication from McClernand. As Sherman did not leave Oxford until that day, it is probable that Grant apprised him of the new possibility; it was his duty to do so. But the order written the day before had told him to move down the river "as soon as possible." Grant would have been open to severe criticism if he had issued any sort of a delaying order after receiving Halleck's telegram of the 9th.

With a blackout of news about the enemy force in his rear and uncertainty as to the river expedition, a lesser commander might have been disturbed. Grant, confronted with discrepancies about Forrest's strength in reports from Sullivan and Dodge, stopped further advance, but said to McPherson: "We must be prepared for any move. I think, however, it will not be a retrograde one." Presently there came to headquarters an important telegram from Colonel Mizner at Water Valley: Scouts had brought word that a heavy enemy cavalry force had passed from Grenada toward Pontotoc, where it was rumored there was a part of Bragg's army. Jeff Davis had been in Grenada on the 14th, accompanied, it was said, by Joe Johnston. Apprehensively Mizner queried, "Do you hear from Colonel Dickey?" [6]

Grant had to reply that he had heard nothing from Dickey, though the cooperating force from Corinth had returned to that place. He would send two brigades of infantry to Pontotoc with five days' rations, and Mizner was told to attach at least one cavalry regiment. A second dispatch from Mizner indicated that the hostile column was commanded by Colonel W. H. Jackson; he thought it numbered only half the 7,000 that reports were giving it.[7]

Apprehension about Dickey disappeared when that generous, gracious, and popular—as well as able—officer, who had led Grant's advance against Fort Donelson, rode into Oxford as night was falling, with a report of a highly successful operation of his own, and alarming news of the enemy. When a few miles east of Pontotoc at noon on the 18th, he had learned of a strong enemy force at that place, presumably to intercept him. He turned to the right, thinking to pass around the Confederates, only to discover they were headed straight northward on the Ripley road. He then turned southward, and, passing through Pontotoc shortly after the last of the enemy had gone, veered northward again. Being now on the safe side of the much superior force, he demonstrated against it until dark, when he headed toward Oxford and camped for the night, but not without dispatching couriers to Grant. These troopers, however, got lost, and morning found them farther from Oxford than when they started. They did not arrive in fact until the morning of the 20th. Thus Dickey himself gave the news he had sought to speed to his chief.[8]

The objective of the enemy column was only too apparent, and Mizner was told to start in pursuit with all the cavalry available. Grant ordered: "When you get on Jackson's trail follow him until he is caught or dispersed. Jackson must be prevented from getting to the railroad in our rear if possible." Grierson, back from Helena some days since, was being sent to join him, but Mizner must "proceed without delay as per order." To the commanding officers at Holly

Springs, Davis's Mill, Grand Junction, La Grange, and Bolivar there sped the warning:

> Jackson's cavalry has gone north with the intention, probably, of striking the railroad north of this place and cutting off our communication. Keep a sharp lookout and defend the road, if attacked, at all hazards. A heavy cavalry force will be in pursuit of him from here.

A special message to Dodge put the enemy at about 3,000.[9]

Even though it intrudes at a time when the situation is tense, a digression is necessary to complete the picture of events in Grant's active theater.

Reports that Joe Johnston was in over-all command in the West and that he and the Confederate President were in the region were indeed true. Johnston—just recovered from the wound he had received in front of Richmond on May 31, 1862—had been placed over both Bragg and Pemberton on November 24, with Chattanooga designated as headquarters, though not unalterably, and with no restriction on his personal movements. To halt Grant's advance and save Vicksburg constituted his chief problem. "Should the enemy get possession of Vicksburg we cannot dislodge him," had been the new commander's warning to Cooper from Chattanooga on December 4. More troops were needed for Vicksburg, and Johnston wanted to levy heavily on Holmes in Arkansas, but that general objected because of the Federal advance from southwest Missouri. Suggestions, appeals, misrepresentations, orders, and counterorders featured the dispute—which had begun before Johnston's appointment. Finally, on the day after Holmes had had a large part of his command badly damaged at Prairie Grove (December 7), he handed Richmond a solemn warning about the unhappy political consequences of stripping Arkansas of troops; this proved effective. Time was also involved, for it was 300 miles from Little Rock to Vicksburg, and Holmes claimed the 6,000 men he might send could not arrive in less than thirty days.[10]

On December 6 Johnston was with Bragg at Murfreesboro, and must have learned that on November 29 Bragg had sent a strong brigade to Meridian, Mississippi, from where it could support either Mobile or Vicksburg, while a thousand additional men were on the way to join Pemberton. Though Rosecrans was quiescent at the time and a move from Nashville did not look imminent, Johnston did not want to weaken Bragg's infantry any further. He did, however, give approval to cavalry raids. As early as November 21 Bragg had telegraphed to Pemberton that he would have Forrest operate on Grant's rear, and Johnston, in reporting to Richmond, said that 2,000 cavalry would be sent to break up the Louisville and Nashville Railroad, while 4,000 would be launched into western Tennessee and northern Mississippi. He promised only moderately: "The latter may delay General Grant." [11]

The general picture that Bragg gave Johnston could not have been very cheering, for on November 24 Bragg had said in a long letter to Davis:

I hear bad accounts from our friends (citizens) in North Mississippi. Many declare their preference for Yankee military rule to the terrors of the mob now around them; they plead for discipline, and beg for men who will shoot marauders, if necessary, in their protection.[12]

A first-hand account of the situation went to Davis on December 9 from James Phelan, Confederate Senator from Mississippi, who lived at Aberdeen, not far to the east of the railroad that Dickey soon tore up. Inefficient enforcement of conscription, exemption of slaveowners, the possibility of furnishing substitutes, straggling troops that filled the countryside and said they would not return until put under competent officers—such were the ills that Phelan recounted. The retreat from Abbeville, where the army had worked hard preparing defenses, had, he feared, "put the finishing touches to its inefficiency," and the Senator declared, "Enthusiasm has expired to a cold pile of damp ashes."

Pemberton, Phelan said, had not impressed himself upon the army, and the Federal flank movement from Friar's Point, by which he had been forced to retreat, had "dealt a staggering blow upon those who desired to brace him with the public confidence." Few seemed to know that Pemberton was top commander in the state, people still speaking of "Van Dorn's Army"—but not proudly. Of Van Dorn, the Senator said, "He is regarded as the source of all our woes, and disaster, it is prophesied, will attend us so long as he is connected with this army. The atmosphere is dense with horrid narratives of his negligence, whoring, and drunkenness, for the truth of which I cannot vouch; but it is so fastened in the public belief that an acquittal by a court-martial of angels would not relieve him of the charge." [13]

Little did Phelan apparently dream of a spectacular exploit which would soon evoke loud cheers for his fellow Mississippian.

Another very unhappy person was Sterling Price. Both he and his Missourians had crossed to the east of the Mississippi very reluctantly, cheered only with the understanding that they would be returned as soon as possible. In mid-November Price urged that the time had come. His original 10,000 men had been worn down to 4,000, but he thought that from them excellent organizers and recruiters could be sent into Missouri, once they were beyond the great river. When a month had slipped away with the homesick Missourians still in Mississippi, a spirit of revolt began to appear, and in a long general order Price turned on a little of the rhetoric that had crackled in his proclamation of a year before: "Be then patient for awhile. Every effort is being made to accomplish your wishes and to take you back to your homes. Thwart not those efforts by mutinous behavior or dastardly desertion." [14] His son's defection did not make the general's position easier.

Phelan had pleaded with Davis to come to Mississippi, suggesting that he would evoke such an outburst of popular enthusiasm that the invaders would quail. Even as he wrote, the President was on the way, perhaps conferring with Johnston before visiting Bragg. From Murfreesboro he returned with spirits elevated by John Morgan's recent spectacular capture of the Federal force at Hartsville, Tennessee, in an operation that will be presently described. Without delay he informed Johnston that he had directed Bragg to send Stevenson to Pemberton with 9,000 men, and to his new Secretary of War, James A. Seddon, he reported: "Enemy is kept close in to Nashville, and indicate only defensive purposes." [15]

Dickey's raid took the Confederates by surprise and occasioned much alarm. The commanding officer at Columbus, Mississippi, where one of the Confederacy's most important ordnance works was, feared the Federals might go all the way to Meridian. Someone—perhaps a Union-loving Mississippian with a taste for practical jokes—stole a locomotive at West Point, news which must have further depressed the spirits of the Senator at nearby Aberdeen. Learning of the railroad attack, Johnston telegraphed to Bragg from Montgomery, "Hurry your cavalry operations and hasten the troops this way" (which looks as if he might have been glad of Davis's order). The next day—December 18—Bragg ordered Stevenson's division to entrain for Mississippi, by way of Mobile, and on the 19th Johnston informed the command-ing officer at Vicksburg that he and President Davis were coming that evening by train from Jackson. It was a time to unfurl the flags and drape the bunting: six staff officers were in the party.[16]

Before returning to Oxford and Grant we must take a glimpse at Memphis, and also the lower Mississippi.

"General Sherman is a trump, and makes things move. I like his business mode of doing things, his promptness and decision." Such was the ending of a dispatch that Parsons sent to Halleck from Memphis on the evening of the 20th. One division (10 boats) was just leaving; a second (13 boats) would follow in an hour; the third (13 boats), delayed by having a poor loading place, would follow early in the morning; Steele's division (15 boats) would join at Helena. Parsons thought he had sufficient fuel to reach Vicksburg, but 66,000 bushels of coal were on the way from Cairo, and several hundred axes were aboard for emergency wood cutting. There had never been such a troop movement; perhaps there has never since been a much smoother embarkation. Well could Parsons feel that they had done well "to load in a single day," especially since some of the boats had not arrived until the 20th. But he regretted that they were two days behind Grant's requested date of departure, and he pleaded the delay in Grant's order to St. Louis and the "extreme scarcity of fuel." Trump though Sherman might be, Quartermaster Parsons knew the general would have plenty to think about when he reached his destination; he himself would go along to get boats unloaded promptly and sent back.[17] The river had been stripped of bottoms, and it was a long way upstream to the great depots in St. Louis.

In New Orleans there was a new Federal commander. He was Nathaniel Banks, previously seen retreating precipitately down the Shenandoah Valley after Stonewall Jackson had stealthily seized Front Royal on May 23, then rebuffing Jackson sharply on August 9 at Cedar Mountain. Banks reached New Orleans with a considerable force of new troops on December 14. Butler promptly took leave of his men in an order that recounted their notable achievements, com-mended them to their new commander, and ended, "Farewell, my comrades! Again, Farewell!" [18]

Banks's mission was clearly set forth in a long directive Halleck wrote on November 9. He was to open the Mississippi and reduce Fort

Morgan or secure Mobile, "in order to control that bay and harbor"; naval forces were to act in cooperation. A military and naval expedition was being organized to move down the Mississippi from Memphis to cooperate with him against Vicksburg and other points. No doubt was left as to his seniority:

> As the ranking general in the Southwest, you are authorized to assume control of any military forces from the Upper Mississippi which may come within your command. The line of division between your department and that of Major-General Grant is therefore left undecided for the present, and you will exercise superior authority as far north as you may ascend the river.

"The President," Halleck said, "regards the opening of the Mississippi River as the first and most important of all our military and naval operations, and it is hoped that you will not lose a moment in accomplishing it." Specifically, Halleck did not wish to hamper Banks's operations in any way, leaving full judgment to him, urging only that he keep in mind the primary object—opening the river. Just what Halleck's personal opinion of Banks was, it is impossible to say, but he closed by assuring him that the Government had "unlimited confidence" not only in his judgment and discretion, but also in his energy and military promptness.[19]

And promptness Banks showed, for an order of the 15th directed that the transports, without disembarking any but the sick, proceed up the river to Baton Rouge. "Every exertion will be made to get under way this evening," was the injunction. Two days later the state capital was reoccupied by the division of Brigadier Cuvier Grover, a high-ranking West Point graduate of 1850. Writing to Halleck on the 18th, Banks said he hoped soon to move against Port Hudson, commanding the entrance to Red River. An enemy captain, known and regarded in New Orleans as reliable, had come in only the day before, and had given considerable information about topography and the new fortifications at Port Hudson, where he said there were 23,000 men (a great exaggeration), mostly conscripts from the surrounding country. (In his directive of November 9 Halleck had said nothing about Port Hudson, and he probably first learned of the enemy works at that important point from a report Butler wrote on the 29th.) Farragut was present, his earnestness, enthusiasm, and frankness being a delight to Banks. From up the river there was no news, though it was "reported from rebel sources that Commodore Porter has assaulted the rebel works at Vicksburg." [20]

Strange indeed had been the outcome of the summer operations in front of Washington. Pope had been sent to the inconsequential north end of the Mississippi, while Banks, his subordinate, got the south end and a command of the greatest importance. Banks—a Republican—had actually been Speaker of the House; Democrat McClernand, who would soon be steaming down the river with a multitudinous staff, had only been a twice-unsuccessful candidate.

If Grant had any thoughts on December 20 about the river expedition, they were surely fleeting ones, for it was a day of disaster in his rear, of conflicting reports, of new decisions, of many orders.

Before daylight he received this telegram from Colonel Robert C. Murphy, commanding at Holly Springs:

> Contraband just in reports Van Dorn only 14 miles from here with 5,000 cavalry, intending to destroy stores here, and then dash on Grand Junction. He is on the Ripley road and expected to reach here by daylight. Have ordered out my cavalry, but my force is only a handful.

Soon there arrived a second dispatch. Murphy had sent trains to bring troops from the north and south; in addition to the cavalry, which had been ordered to the east, he had less than 500 men. Paroled prisoners had reported the Holly Springs situation the day before to Van Dorn.[21]

The unknown Negro, hastening through the night with one of the most valuable commodities in war—crucial information of the enemy—had played a hero's part, but Grant must have doubted how well Murphy would play his. It was Murphy who had mismanaged the evacuation of stores from Iuka in September and had failed to destroy those that were left. For this Rosecrans had wanted him tried and punished, but Grant had interposed, excusing Murphy "on the ground of inexperience in military matters." Now the messages from Murphy foretold a greater catastrophe, for they said nothing of preparations in response to Grant's clear alert of the evening before. Several infantry regiments were at Murphy's disposal to protect the supply depot that had been opened on December 3, when the one at La Grange was closed. But the small infantry camp at the northeast corner of the town was not informed of danger, and Major John J.

Mudd of the Second Illinois Cavalry wrote a few days later that he knew no attack was expected until shortly before the infantry camp was captured.[22]

The six companies of Illinois troopers fought gallantly, boldly advancing to meet the enemy, breaking his lines, driving him in places, recapturing their own camp, where they freed some of their men, then riding to Coldwater and joining an infantry regiment. But soon Van Dorn—and it was he, not Jackson, who was in command of the Confederates—had the town and some thousand prisoners, who were paroled. Fires were kindled in the great warehouses, and stores to the value of $400,000 according to Grant, $1,500,000 according to Van Dorn, were destroyed. In vain did Surgeon Horace R. Wirtz plead for the saving of a great hospital—a former six-unit Confederate arsenal —that had just been made ready for 2,000 sick.[23]

"My fate is most mortifying," wrote Murphy at 7:00 P.M. "I have wished a hundred times to-day that I had been killed. I have done all in my power—in truth, my force was inadequate." But Major Mudd wrote, "I cannot doubt but that the place could have been successfully defended by even half the force here had suitable precautions been taken and the infantry been concentrated, their officers in camp with them and prepared to fight." This had not been done, for the infantry was scattered in four or five places about town, "their officers quietly sleeping at the houses of rebel citizens"—according to the angered major of horse, whose outfit had been camped at the fairgrounds.[24]

When Mudd rode into the town the next morning, a Sabbath's quiet rested on the smoldering ruins. At ten o'clock Colonel C. Carrol Marsh arrived from Waterford with some infantry. Marsh had first reported to Grant from the north side of the Tallahatchie that the enemy had seized Waterford as well as Holly Springs, but that he was pushing forward cautiously. Presently he held Waterford and could send word from a scout who had been in contact with enemy pickets. Information also came to headquarters from Mizner, who reached Abbeville at 6:30 P.M., after a rest in Oxford. The cavalryman put the enemy force at 4,000 and said Jackson and Armstrong were with Van Dorn. In telling Marsh that 2,000 cavalry would join him during the night, Grant said, "I want those fellows caught, if possible." Marsh was to give infantry and artillery support. "Shall be in Holly Springs or be whipped to-morrow morning," had been Marsh's reply. Highly displeased when he learned that Mizner had gone into camp on the

Tallahatchie, Grant repeated his order for him to proceed, so that Marsh would not "be cut up by piece-meal." To Marsh he also sent directions to arrest Mizner and turn over the command to the next in rank, if Mizner "shows any reluctance in the pursuit." And that was just what happened on the morning of the 21st, command passing to the aggressive Grierson.[25]

Though Grant telegraphed to Marsh on the 21st, "The enemy should be pursued," and said infantry and artillery thrown out laterally might cut routes of return, there was miscarriage somewhere, and Grant's aide Colonel Hillyer wired to him from Holly Springs the next day: "Grierson impatient to pursue enemy; has been after me several times to telegraph to you on the subject. He has been ready to pursue ever since yesterday noon." "Let Grierson, Lee, and Fifth Ohio Cavalry push after enemy until they find him," was Grant's reply.[26] A precious day had been lost.

Where had the enemy gone? Marsh must have been flooded with rumors, guesses, and varied fragments of overheard conversations on the afternoon of the 21st. Finally he wired to Grant that scouts were in from Lamar: nothing in that direction. Then he said, "All information leads to the belief that after going a short distance north they took a southeasterly course toward Rocky Ford." This would indicate that, satisfied with his accomplishment, the enemy was headed for home. But such was far from being the case. In a message written from Holly Springs informing Pemberton of his great success, Van Dorn had said, "I move on to Davis' Mill at once." [27] He must have practiced good deception or Marsh's scout was poor, for Davis's Mill was ten miles northeast of Lamar and a trestle over Wolf River made it a sensitive point. Doubtless Van Dorn was expecting another easy triumph, knowing he could throw a large number of men upon a small defending force.

At the mill there were only six companies of the Twenty-fourth Indiana Infantry and fifty men from two companies of the Fifth Ohio Cavalry. But Colonel William H. Morgan was equal to the occasion, and his 250 men were of the best. Upon receiving Grant's warning, Morgan set to work turning the sawmill into a blockhouse with railroad ties and cotton bales, while about the base of a mound he dug an intrenchment; the two works were so situated as to protect the trestle and give a cross fire on a bridge over the creek. About noon on Sunday Morgan's pickets were driven in and a part of Van Dorn's force, dismounted, moved to the attack with a loud cheer. When abruptly halted by sharp fire they were reenforced, only again to be stopped, and again be strengthened and again fail. After a conflict of three hours Van Dorn withdrew, but not without sending a mes-

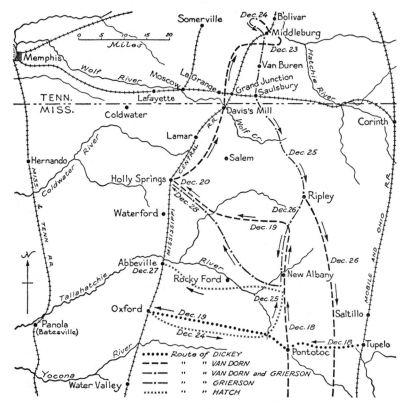

VAN DORN'S RAID, DECEMBER 18–26, 1862

Dickey observed Van Dorn's column and reported it to Grant at Oxford on the evening of the 19th. Warnings were sent northward, but Holly Springs was taken and supply depots were destroyed on the 20th. Grierson, moving in pursuit, reached Bolivar late on the 23rd. On the night of the 25th Van Dorn eluded Grierson and Hatch, who had moved to intercept him.

senger under a flag of truce to inquire if Morgan were contemplating surrender. To the courteous and thoughtful query the Federal replied with a "decided negative," whereupon the Confederates rode away, leaving 22 dead and 60 wounded. In addition, Morgan, who had only three men slightly wounded, secured 20 prisoners, bold men who had either crossed the bridge only to be driven beneath it, or had sought to ignite the trestle but had been pinned down by a shower of bullets. In his report the proud Morgan—who estimated the enemy at 6,000—requested that "along with the names of Donelson, Shiloh, and Metamora, Davis' Mill may be inscribed upon our banner." [28]

Rebuffed, and taking a goodly number of slightly wounded with him, Van Dorn continued northward. To Colonel John McDermott at Grand Junction, Grant telegraphed that a force from Holly Springs should reach him in the morning; if McDermott had cotton bales, he should barricade with them. Inspired by Morgan's example, McDermott wired to Sullivan at Jackson: "The enemy expected every moment. I am good for Van Dorn and all his imps in way of cavalry. I have a good position and will hold it." Presently Colonel Mason Brayman at Bolivar telegraphed to Sullivan that the enemy had passed to the west of Grand Junction and, supposedly 4,000 strong, was twelve miles away. But the 23rd passed with no attack; and at 11:00 P.M. Grierson rode into Bolivar and bivouacked his weary troopers and their mounts. To the southeast of the town and some six miles from it he had distinctly seen the enemy camp fires. Near daylight the Confederates, after making a wide circuit, attacked from the west. Said Grierson in his report: "I immediately moved out upon them on the Brownsville road, skirmishing and driving them for 2 miles. They not heretofore knowing of our presence at Bolivar became somewhat confused." [29]

When the enemy broke contact, Grierson showed his military judgment by retiring to Bolivar with his main force, while two companies pressed for information. In due time the blue troopers had it; Van Dorn was moving southeast; so Grierson started in pursuit with his whole command. At Middleburg he again gained touch, just after the raiders had been well rebuffed by the Twelfth Michigan Infantry; then Grierson pressed them in the direction of Van Buren. [30]

As ordered by Grant on the 23rd, Grierson was telegraphing whenever he could. Dispatches he sent from Middleburg and Van Buren were acknowledged by Rawlins with new information: Infantry and artillery were being sent east from Salem to try to block the road; Colonel Hatch was being dispatched from the Tallahatchie with cavalry in hopes of heading Van Dorn off. "Make every possible exertion to harass and destroy," was Rawlins's injunction. That same evening—December 24—the message reached Grierson at Saulsbury and a reply was sent at once: Grierson was encamped without fires within two and a half miles of the enemy. At 2:00 A.M. of Christmas day scouts "reported the enemy to have left after feeding," and two hours later Grierson's 1,800 troopers were again in the saddle following the 3,500 men of Earl Van Dorn.[31]

Mizner, reinstated to command on the 24th, joined the column and took over at 8:00 A.M. of the 25th. From Ripley he reported in midafternoon that he believed the enemy was then six miles south on the Pontotoc road. If Hatch could block the route he thought they might get a fight out of Van Dorn, who was making for Grenada or below as fast as he could travel. Hatch, to whom Grierson's dispatches had gone from Grant through McPherson, had, with 800 troopers, after a march made difficult by destroyed bridges, reached a point ten miles north of Pontotoc on the Ripley road on the morning of the 25th. Told by enemy prisoners that Van Dorn was making a stand against Federal cavalry at Ripley, Hatch moved northward. There had indeed been a clash south of Ripley in the fading light of Christmas day, in which, according to Grierson, Van Dorn commanded in person and had the rear of his column badly scattered, with a lieutenant and ten men left in Federal hands. But on reaching New Albany, Hatch learned that Van Dorn had turned eastward, whereupon he went into camp with a command that had covered 62 miles in 32 hours, including considerable time lost for various reasons.[32]

Thus Van Dorn escaped with trifling loss compared with the destruction of Grant's base. A brief telegram to Pemberton from Grenada announced his arrival there at four in the afternoon of the 28th, just twenty-four hours after Mizner's command, which had abandoned the pursuit between New Albany and Pontotoc, had gone into camp fifteen miles southwest of Holly Springs.[33]

Van Dorn's paroling of the Holly Springs prisoners was contrary to the Dix-Hill cartel. Though the cartel was being generally violated at the time in the matter of paroling, we have seen that Pemberton only two weeks before had declined to allow Grant to deliver captured Confederates elsewhere than at Vicksburg for exchange or parole (if there were not sufficient Federal prisoners to match them). Van Dorn could not have extricated his prisoners from the Federal lines for exchange or parole at Vicksburg, and one cannot but wonder how Pemberton reconciled what Van Dorn did with the position he himself had so recently taken.

During the week just described there were other things for Department Headquarters to do besides keeping track of Van Dorn and endeavoring to bring converging columns upon him.

While the thought may have come quickly to Grant that his advance would have to be halted, there was no precipitancy in orders, and it is interesting that McPherson wrote to Grant at length on the 20th an appraisal of the situation, with suggestions—and this certainly before he had learned of the Holly Springs raid—that might have led to the voluntary adoption of the course that Van Dorn brought about. McPherson was on the Yocknapatalfa River (now called the Yocona), and it was his view that the expedition down the Mississippi should be strengthened, so as greatly to outnumber the enemy at Vicksburg, where he was certain Pemberton was concentrating. Furthermore, it would take a long time to put the hundred-mile rail line from Grenada to Memphis in operating condition, and with that to Columbus already cut by Forrest and likely to be cut again, it would be difficult to advance beyond Grenada. Rebuild the rail line from Grand Junction to Memphis, said McPherson, covering it with strong posts as far to the south as Holly Springs and Hernando; then add the bulk of the army to that on the river. This recommendation, McPherson said, was being made as a result of a note at the bottom of a letter from Grant; the note unfortunately does not appear in the records. After referring to the fact that Washington orders had placed McClernand in command of the river expedition, McPherson said that, were he in Grant's place, he would take command in person, adding, "It is the great feature of the campaign and its execution rightfully belongs to you." Though ready to do anything assigned him, McPherson said he would like to go down the river with Grant, taking the divisions of Lauman and Logan.[34]

Before his letter had been read, McPherson may have received Grant's dispatch directing him to fall back behind the Tallahatchie with his three divisions. The cavalry, Grant said, would be instructed to move toward Grenada so as to give the idea of continued advance. A new note now entered. McPherson was to take all cattle fit for beef that he could find and all corn meal from the mills, which, as well as bridges, were to be destroyed after he had finished using them.

It was at 9:00 P.M. that the order went to Hatch to break up all cavalry camps, sending equipment to Oxford, and then advance with all his effective force as far toward Grenada as he could without serious resistance. In returning to Oxford, Hatch too was to destroy mills and bridges.[35]

As Grant's wagons began to bring in provisions from the country, the Secessionists who had smiled when they heard of Van Dorn's achievement began to realize that the first empty stomachs might be their own. Yet the Federals soon found their rations lacked articles they valued, and a soldier of the One Hundredth Indiana, who was having his first experience in campaigning, put down some of his meditations, seasoned with original spelling. Coffee was a soldier's "main stay"; it not only rained continuously but it was "an awful wet rain too." It was Murphy and his men, however, who made the Hoosier really unhappy: "Van Dorn paroled them in his hast[e], but we need the 'hard tack' and 's.b.' [sow belly] oh so much. It has left an aching void nigger beans can never fill." [36]

Rumors about Bragg were still coming in, and on the 21st Grant sent two of Hamilton's three divisions toward Corinth, informing McPherson that if Bragg advanced, "our whole force will be required for its defense." Otherwise it was his intention to take two divisions to Memphis to join the river expedition "if allowed," sending the remaining two to Bolivar. (Dodge again quieted the Bragg rumors.) And what about Washington? The message informing Halleck of what had happened was turned over to Marsh to send northward with a cavalry company—to be replaced by fresh units as needed—until an office was found that had communication to Columbus. The dispatch ended: "I would like to send two divisions more to Memphis and join the river expedition with them. This would make it necessary to fall back to Bolivar. The enemy are falling back from Grenada." [37]

Strange as it may seem, Grant's alert against Van Dorn had gone through to Halleck distorted into an actuality. In reporting on the 20th about Forrest's raid, Davies at Columbus said there had been no communication by rail or wire with Grant for two days, but added, "We have information that Holly Springs, Miss., fell into the hands of the enemy yesterday." So Halleck may not have been too surprised when Grant's dispatch came through six days later. But Grant's sister Mary could hardly have been prepared for the news, for Ulysses had written to her on December 15, "My plans are all complete for weeks to come and I hope to have them all work out just as planned." [38]

Where, one asks, was General McClernand? On the 23rd Grant wrote to the "Commanding Officer Expedition down Mississippi," an address that showed his uncertainty as to whether Sherman or Mc-Clernand was in command. He reported his own recent experiences and passed on reports from the south that Vicksburg had fallen to an attack by Butler and Farragut, the reports not having sufficient credibility, however, to warrant a change in plans. Perhaps at the same time McClernand was wiring from Springfield to Stanton a copy of a telegram he had received only the day before from Halleck, quoting the dispatch sent to Grant on the 18th. "Yet I am not relieved from duty here," said the distressed general, "so that I may go forward to receive orders from General Grant. Please order me forward." The Secretary promptly sped back a release.[39]

Not until the 26th did Grant's order to the expedition commander start to Memphis, in the custody of a heavily escorted train of three hundred wagons that also carried Grant's report to Halleck on Holly Springs. To Hurlbut he wrote about the order that had come from Halleck just as Forrest was starting his raid, and of the one he had at once written for McClernand, but which could not be sent because of broken communications. More rumors must have been received from the south, for Grant now thought it probable that Vicksburg was already in Federal possession. He would be glad, he said, if Hurlbut would let him know when the river expedition had sailed and any other news he might "have to communicate." One little tidbit Hurlbut did not know. Fifty-one-year-old McClernand was that day leaving Cairo with a brand-new bride.[40]

Two other minor matters are important for a rounded story before returning to Sherman and his fleet of transports.

The day before Christmas Thomas Davies, previously calm, went into a small panic over the safety of Columbus. On the 20th he had reported to Halleck that the enemy had taken Trenton and was moving on Kenton. He was withdrawing his fifty men at Union City and two companies north thereof, but there was confidence in his "I shall hold Columbus." As the depots bulged with $13,000,000 worth of supplies and equipment, it was important that he should. Halleck replied that Curtis and the commanding officer at Cairo had been ordered to reenforce him quickly, and enjoined him to do everything possible to reopen and protect the railroad. Optimistically, the General in Chief said that Porter would probably prevent the enemy from recrossing the Tennessee, and for good measure tossed in the question, "What is the enemy's force?" [41]

Although at the moment Davies did not have a tally of the raiders, he gave it to Halleck late on the 23rd, nicely broken down into nine units, as supplied by a paroled officer. In all, the invading force totaled 3,400 men and 8 guns. Furthermore, all information indicated that most of the Confederates were "unreliable men," though some were "picked." (Forrest did in fact have a great many recruits.) This must have looked reassuring in Washington, where presently there arrived another message from Columbus: Nothing had been heard of the enemy since he had left Rutherford; Davies was starting a construction train in the morning, carrying four bridges and 1,500 feet of prepared trestle work; within four or five days he hoped the enemy could be cleared out and communication restored; no news from below Trenton; nothing from Grant; Davies was trying to reach him by way of Memphis. [42]

All this could hardly have prepared Halleck for a dispatch Davies put on the wire at 8:00 A.M. of the 24th:

I am informed General Cheatham has crossed the Tennessee with 40,000 men and is marching north. I cannot hold Columbus against that force. The information had reached me before that he had crossed but I did not credit it till now. [43]

Such was the power of repeated, though fantastic, rumor. Beset as he was with troubles resulting from Burnside's defeat at Fredericksburg, Halleck could have had little time for the Columbus situation and is not to be blamed for wiring to Curtis, "Columbus is reported as in danger of an attack," and ordering prompt reenforcement. Davies, who had 5,000 men, proceeded to load all commissary supplies and small articles on boats, doubting the necessity, but still convincing himself that it was only "prudent." [44]

"Safely arrived. We can hold the post against the entire Confederacy, but not strong enough to go out and whip the rascals," said brave Brigadier Clinton B. Fisk in a telegram to Curtis on the 26th. The next day he wrote, "I fear General Davies is easily frightened," and tabulated indicting facts. Judging from the ending of his letter, the young Missourian, whose stars were only a month old, was really enjoying himself: "I am using for my headquarters the best secesh house in town, formerly occupied by the Right Rev. Maj. Gen. Bishop Polk, C.S. Army." [45]

Davies's fear for Columbus had subsided by the 29th when he reported that reliable information indicated that the enemy's real objectives were Island No. 10 and New Madrid. Already he had withdrawn the small garrison from Hickman, had rendered Island No. 10 useless, and would abandon New Madrid that night, after destroying its heavy armament. The next day he must have felt foolish when an officer from Grant's staff and some others came in. There was no enemy west of the railroad, he wired to Washington, and he thought it probable the Confederates had all departed. Telegraph, as well as rails, were working south of Dyer, said Davies. Simultaneously Fisk, who was not only particular about his headquarters but knew how to please a superior, was closing a letter to Curtis, "Your boys are all in fine spirits and very desirous to get back under your immediate direction." [46]

As Christmas neared, Memphis Secessionists grew hopeful of liberation. For a fort constructed for 8,000 men, Hurlbut had, he said in a dispatch to Halleck on the 24th, four regiments of raw infantry, 200 cavalry, and 27 artillerymen. Within five miles of the city there were approximately 1,300 Partisan Rangers, while reports put Van Dorn at Somerville, only forty-five miles away. Said Hurlbut, "I hold city by terror of heavy guns bearing upon it and the belief that an attack would cause its destruction." A report on the situation went to Curtis from his chief of staff, Colonel N. P. Chipman, en route for Helena:

> There is a general stampede here; several hundred cavalry hover around the city, threatening to enter. They saucily sent in [a] flag of truce yesterday to reconnoiter the position of things. Great fear among foreign traders and loyal citizens and equally strong hope among the rebels prevail, making the excitement intense.

After speaking of the great calamity that would follow the seizure of Columbus or Memphis, both left with small garrisons, Chipman said loftily, "Such risks are perilous." [47]

"You may calculate on our being at Vicksburg by Christmas. River has risen some feet, and all is now good navigation. Gunboats are at mouth of Yazoo now, and there will be no difficulty in effecting a landing up Yazoo within 12 miles of Vicksburg." Such was Sherman's promise in a letter to Rawlins on the 19th. Gorman was intending to send the balance of his forces—except a small garrison at Helena—to the mouth of the Arkansas River; they could then either reenforce at Vicksburg or move up the Arkansas. The conclusion of the letter stressed another contingent point of the plan: "At Vicksburg we will act so as to accomplish the original purpose, and will calculate to send you rations up the Yazoo. Yazoo City is the best point and can be reached after the reduction of the battery at Haynes' Bluff." Though the letter did not get through because of Forrest's raid, it shows how Sherman on the eve of departure sought to put in his chief's hands the latest and fullest information.[48]

In a dispatch from Helena on the 21st, Sherman put Steele's division at 12,500 (more than half the 20,000 of the other three divisions). Then he continued, "General Morgan L. Smith reported to me this a.m. in passing that some men, 25 in number, had come into Memphis after I left, reporting that Holly Springs had been captured by the enemy and that they were the sole survivors." Presumably the men were mounted, but even at that they had done no loitering. To say the least, the news was disconcerting, and Sherman's statement to Rawlins reveals how constancy struggled to maintain itself: "I hardly know what faith to put in such a report, but suppose whatever may be the case you will attend to it." [49]

No uncertainty lurked in a note from Porter, also at Helena. Steamboat captains were helping themselves to navy coal. If Porter had fuel to spare, it would, he assured, give him pleasure to part with some. But he had only enough to reach the mouth of the Yazoo; every bushel on his barges was "worth its weight in gold." The sailor probably had an eye cocked upon his coal piles, for on the 6th, when ordering Commander Gwin down the river in the *Benton,* he had written, "Take charge of coal barges and see them safely moored, and prevent the troops, if you can, from stealing our coal." [50] Porter liked soldiers well enough; but it was just as well to watch them.

The Acting Rear Admiral, upon whom so much depended, certainly had plenty of difficulties. Principal among them was lack of personnel. Although the Navy had now taken over the Army's rams, after scorning them when Ellet first proposed their construction, the Department seemed deaf to Porter's requests for seamen. On the 5th he had written to Assistant Secretary Gustavus Fox that, after sending away 600 sick, his vessels were only half-manned; as fast as they were put in shape he was sending them south, even if they had men for only one gun; a draft recently sent him from New York was "all boys and very ordinary landsmen"; his old sailors were mostly broken down. Six days later he wrote to Sherman that the Department had not supplied him with men, provisions, medicines, or clothing. Some of his crews were short fifty men, and he had ten light-draft vessels ready for service, but not a man for them. Bitterly he said, "I expected that the Government would send men from the East, but not a man will they send or notice my complaints, so we will have to go with what we have." [51]

After casting off from Helena, there was nothing more Sherman could tell Grant, but he had plenty to say to his division commanders in a letter dated the 23rd, with which went a map. He sketched the general military situation and threw in a comment on the principles of war. Banks was brought into the picture as well as the Navy, and Sherman said, "General Grant, with the Thirteenth Army Corps, of which we compose the right wing, is moving southward." The gunboats were holding the Yazoo for a distance of twenty-three miles, to the place where the enemy had a fort on Haynes Bluff. The first item on the agenda was demolition of the railroad running from opposite Vicksburg to Monroe, Louisiana, "to cut off that fruitful avenue of supply." Then the expedition would proceed to the Yazoo's mouth, "and, after possessing ourselves of the latest and most authentic information from naval officers now there," the whole force would land and move to the intersection of the Vicksburg–Jackson railroad and the Big Black River. Before attacking the city, "doubtless very strongly fortified both against the river and land approaches," it might be necessary to reduce the battery at Haynes Bluff so that lighter gunboats and transports could ascend the Yazoo and communicate with Grant. Wagons, provisions, axes, and intrenching tools were to be made ready; his letter could be read to regimental commanders and copies given to commanders of brigades; as many copies of the map as possible were to be made, with special care in copying names. This letter—saturated with Sherman's unique personality—ended by pointing out two places of strategic importance and the injunction that they "be well studied." [52] It is important to note that not a word in it suggested that seizure of the point east of Vicksburg depended on Grant's arrival and cooperation.

Those twenty-three miles of the Yazoo that Sherman said the Navy held were not free of problems. On December 13 Captain Henry Walke, commanding a few vessels at the mouth of the river, and who, like his boat the *Carondelet,* has been often mentioned before, reported on a reconnaissance made the day before. The *Marmora* and the *Signal*—two of the new light-draft "tin-clads," each carrying four howitzers—had gone upstream twenty miles and had found numerous mines, one of which had exploded near the *Signal,* while riflemen aboard the *Marmora* had set off another whose head was visible above water.[53]

It was easy to locate the mines (they were then called torpedoes) by the floats to which they were attached. Removing them was something else, for they were protected by sharpshooters on the shores. But the commanders of *Marmora* and *Signal* being optimistic, Walke (who had himself been sick with intermittent fever), sent them back next day to clear the channel, while the gunboats *Baron de Kalb, Cairo,* and *Pittsburg* shelled the river banks to keep down the fire upon men working in small boats. At the request of her commander the ram *Queen of the West,* star performer in the June naval battle at Memphis, went along. At 5:00 P.M. the expedition was back, "minus the *Cairo,*" as Walke put it in his report. Much was written as to what took place, but the *Marmora*'s log put it thus: "In endeavoring to dislodge one of the machines the *Cairo* had run over another, which, exploding with fearful violence, tore her bottom completely out of her. The sad catastrophe occurred at 11:55, and at 12:03 the *Cairo* was no more." Under perfect discipline the crew remained at their stations until ordered away, and not a life was lost. Ten mines were destroyed after the big blowup. For some distance below the fort, however, the river was still infested.[54]

Nor was that all. Remembering the *Arkansas* and how she had suddenly emerged from the Yazoo on July 15 to cause them so much humiliation during her brief career, Federal sailors naturally wondered if the river held more such threats. Navy officers had certainly heard stories such as Halleck had passed on to Grant about new vessels building up the Yazoo. On December 8 Walke got contradictory reports. A contraband from Yazoo City said there were no rams or gunboats up the river, building or complete, though there was a timber barricade at the fort twenty-three miles upstream, which he said mounted ten guns. A white man professing he had come aboard to escape conscription stated, however, that two or three ram gunboats were being built at Yazoo City. Materials had been shipped from Richmond, and the vessels were "to be ready at Christmas." [55]

The truth lay between. The very day after Walke heard these conflicting stories, able Commander Isaac Brown wrote to Pemberton from Yazoo City that the Confederate Navy Department had instructed him to discontinue work on the gunboats if the batteries and the barrier in the Yazoo would keep out the Federals. He described the armament of the forts: nine guns plus field artillery. Of the guns, he thought only the two rifled pieces could damage armor-plated vessels, and—being a stickler for thoroughness—he wanted a 10-incher so that enemy vessels halted by the raft "may be there destroyed." Brown believed the barrier impassable to ships if the enemy could be prevented from landing.[56] The letter could well have given Pemberton a feeling of comfort.

On Christmas Day, while Grierson was pressing Van Dorn, and Grant was issuing the order for the wagon train and writing his report on Holly Springs, and Davies was fearful about Columbus, and Hurlbut was keeping Memphis cowed by big guns, Sherman was tied up at Milliken's Bend, on the west shore of the Mississippi a few miles above the Yazoo's mouth. He was not taking the day off for his men to feast and doze, though most of them had a holiday while Sherman carried out an item on his agenda which can surely be questioned for its priority. Brigadier General Stephen G. Burbridge's six-regiment brigade of A. J. Smith's division, plus two companies of horse and a gun section, were ashore early, at Milliken's Bend, to destroy the railroad to Monroe. As he proceeded with his wrecking, Burbridge was mindful of "400 cavalry and four pieces of artillery fluttering" on his left flank; but he still could keep an eye open for items useful to the Union. Within a few hours a company was marching back to the river with a number of horses and 196 beef cattle, plus a few prisoners, who may or may not have been less hard to come by.[57]

It had been easy for the Confederates to learn of Sherman's embarkation and departure, and Major General Martin Smith, commanding at Vicksburg, at 2:00 A.M. on the 25th wired Pemberton,

"Sixty-four of enemy's boats have passed Lake Providence to-night. Send at once what re-enforcements you intend." Another report stated the boats were running without lights at eighteen miles an hour. Never had there been anything like that on Ol' Man River. The Yankees were really putting on a show. After day had broken, Smith received a message from the commander at Tallulah, twenty-five miles to the west: 6,000 Federals were ashore at Milliken's Bend; they had come at midnight, "a moment after I left the pickets." [58]

The warning started Pemberton for Vicksburg from Grenada, 150 rail miles away, but not fast ones. Already the previous day he had sent John Gregg's brigade forward and while en route had called up a regiment from Columbus. After he arrived at Vicksburg at noon of the 26th he telegraphed to General Maury at Vaughan—on the railroad east of Yazoo City—to bring his division as quickly as possible, leaving behind only Hébert's brigade.[59] With Grant's advance checked by Van Dorn's exploit, the Confederate commander was to have an unusual and historic opportunity to concentrate at a single threatened point, one whose great natural strength had been increased many times by trenches and batteries.

At eight o'clock on the morning of the 26th Sherman headed for the Yazoo. Leading the column was a light gunboat, then an ironclad, then Porter's flagship, then twenty transports, then another heavy gunboat, followed by twenty more transports, and so on. Upon every transport two companies were at stations with loaded rifles to return fire from the shore. The debarkation point was Johnson's farm,* some ten miles up the river, Sherman's order specifying an immediate unloading of "all things necessary for five days' operation." A. J. Smith was waiting at Milliken's Bend for Burbridge's return, but the other three divisions debarked, each pushing a brigade out a mile or so toward forbidding Walnut Hills (or Chickasaw Bluffs) beyond the soft wooded land cut by bayous and queer, elongated lakes. Enemy eyes saw everything, and Pemberton telegraphed to his adjutant at Jackson: "Push forward the troops as rapidly as possible. The enemy is landing." [60]

The order that Sherman wrote for the next day's operations was, to say the least, optimistic. Morgan, Steele, and M. L. Smith were to get their divisions—each less a regiment guarding boats—across the bayous and secure the County Road that came from Vicksburg and

* For map, see p. 214.

followed the base of Walnut Hills to Drumgould's and Haynes Bluffs, where the enemy batteries frowned upon the river just below the great barrier. A. J. Smith, maintaining contact with troops upon his left, was to follow a road running directly to Vicksburg, remove obstacles, and attract the attention of the enemy battery on the first hill north of town. When the high ground beyond the County Road had been reached, commanders would be at liberty to send back for wagons and provisions; "but," said Sherman, "we cannot be encumbered with a train for some days." A. J. Smith did not arrive; but rain did, and very heavily. So at 4:00 A.M. Sherman wrote to Porter that a change of plans must be made: Steele would reembark two of his three brigades and move them further up the river.[61]

The statement in Sherman's report, "All the heads of columns met the enemy's pickets and drove them toward Vicksburg," suffices to show that the actual objectives for the 27th were not attained. Hoping a move toward the batteries up the river might draw enemy troops in that direction and thus soften resistance to the army, Porter sent gunboats toward Drumgould's Bluff, dragging the river with various contrivances to remove the mines. At 2:30 the Confederates opened briskly with eight guns, Gwin in the *Benton* bearing the brunt. "We have been unfortunate to-day," was Porter's report to Sherman. The *Benton* had been cut up badly by the enemy rifled pieces, and Gwin, Porter feared, was mortally wounded. The fine sailor had refused to go into the shot-proof pilothouse because "a captain's place was on the quarter-deck." [62]

A heavy fog made movements difficult on the morning of the 28th, but in the course of the day De Courcy's brigade made progress until stopped by a strong abatis in front of a major bayou. The serious wounding of Morgan Smith took from Sherman an able subordinate. After command was exercised for a few hours by Brigadier David Stuart, Sherman annexed the two brigades of the division to those of A. J. Smith, who after debarking the afternoon before had gained contact with the right of the army on the morning of the 28th. Along with this setback on the right, there was a worse one on the left, where Steele floundered around for a second day in bayous and lagoons, to reembark at night for Johnson's farm.[63]

Then Sherman faced the first great decision of his career as a responsible commander. Nothing had been heard from Banks, nothing from Grant, except a dubious report. Although Sherman apparently was unaware that the Mississippi was effectively blocked at Port Hudson, he had no right to expect that Banks could be doing more than keep some enemy forces out of Vicksburg. As he had no way to get word through to Banks about his own expedition, so he had no grounds for looking for any message from the south. Doubtless he hoped to hear heavy guns proclaim that Farragut was close below, but he could not in justice feel that Banks had not kept a rendezvous. As to Grant, he wrote according to the record when he said in his *Memoirs:*

> Neither my orders to General Sherman, nor the correspondence between us or between General Halleck and myself, contemplated at the time my going further south then the Yallabusha.

It was indeed his intention, Grant continued, and so understood by Sherman, that if the enemy fell back, he would "follow him even to the gates of Vicksburg." [64] But no time could have been set for arrival; and Sherman could not have been kept posted as to Grant's progress.

Assuredly Sherman felt much alone that night on the Yazoo, with his army among the dismal bayous. If he believed that he ought to have heard from Grant or Banks, he did not collapse because he had not. Completely on his own, he took the first step toward becoming a real general. At Shiloh he had met a hard test well. Though unable to hold all his new troops in line, his fine personal bearing and leadership unquestionably kept other regiments at their work, and the enemy reports bore witness to the ferocity of the battle on the Union right. Yet on that Sunday morning he was just a subordinate; the army commander had come to him, and talked almost casually; had left with him a priceless word of approval for what he had done. But on the Yazoo it was different; he was the top commander; he had to make the decisions for tomorrow. When made, no one would quietly nod approval.

Time was everything, Sherman wrote in his report. He determined therefore to assault the enemy lines the next day, after forcing columns over the few passages across the bayou waters. He recorded nothing of the known approach of McClernand, but Parsons, writing to Halleck on the 27th, said: "The news came yesterday that General McClernand was soon to arrive and take command. Of course General Sherman must have felt unpleasantly, but he does not show it in

the least and bears it like the true soldier he is." [65] If the news of
the 26th helped shape the decision of the 28th, it is hard to be critical.

The written order that was issued suggests that Sherman may have
been poorly oriented. He specified that the three attacking divisions

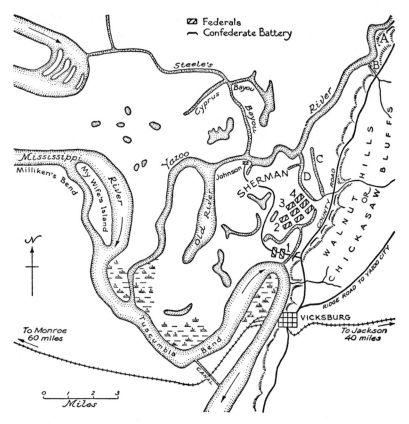

ATTACK ON CHICKASAW BLUFFS, DECEMBER 29, 1862

A, Haynes Bluff; B, Drumgould's Bluff; C, Thompson's Lake; D, Chickasaw
Bayou. Just above the heavy battery at Haynes Bluff the Yazoo was obstructed
by a heavy raft. Sherman's divisions were: 1, A. J. Smith; 2, M. L. Smith;
3, Morgan; 4, Steele. Four Confederate brigades occupied prepared positions
along the County Road.

were to face east, the whole line then to "move as nearly east as
possible as the ground will admit." Such a movement would, however,

have exposed his whole right, and the attack was generally in a south-easterly direction. There were moments of success, but the end was complete failure. Sherman would later have many battles to watch and appraise. Of this, his first attack, he wrote, simply, frankly:

> The assault was made and a lodgment effected on the hard table-land near the county road, and the heads of the assaulting columns reached different points of the enemy's works, but there met so withering a fire from the rifle-pits and cross-fire of grape and canister from the batteries that the column faltered, and finally fell back to the point of starting, leaving many dead, wounded, and prisoners in the hands of the enemy.[66]

For a "perfect understanding" of what had transpired, Sherman optimistically referred to the reports of subordinates. From them some details can be made out, but a reader is bewildered as to locations and engulfed in lakes and bayous. Leadership and cooperation were difficult, delay and blunders almost unavoidable. Some were the result of poor orders or carelessness. The pontoons had been attached to Morgan's division, and on the night of the 28th he directed the engineer captain to throw a bridge over the advanced bayou in front of the enemy's position. But "by a fatal mistake"—according to Morgan—the engineer "bridged a rear bayou." Brigadier John Thayer, veteran of Donelson and Shiloh, started at the head of a strong column and, when close to the enemy rifle pits and batteries, looked back from the vantage point of a rail fence, only to find a single regiment behind him instead of five. Someone had deflected the others. Someone had blundered.[67]

The Confederate reports make clear the excessive difficulty of the terrain. There were only four possible approaches to the County Road over dry ground, and the debouches from them were of course well covered with fire. The road itself gave means for rapid shifting of troops, and in addition to rifle pits there were levee banks to protect defending riflemen.

In the three days of operations Sherman suffered 1,776 casualties in 39 regiments; but of the 208 killed in 25 regiments, 156 were in the six regiments which really made the assault of the 29th. The total Confederate casualties were 187, the killed numbering 56. If Southern losses were small, it was because of the protection of their positions or poor marksmanship, not because their adversaries were chary of ammunition. One battery commander reported he fired 2,380 rounds, while another expended 335 rounds per gun in two days, retiring at noon on the 29th because his stock was gone. At 4:00 P.M. of the 29th Sherman wrote to Porter, "Spite of all I can do our men and officers waste too much ammunition." He had brought all the available stock from Memphis, but believing that 6,000,000 rounds of small-arms ammunition ordered for him by Grant's ordnance officer had probably since arrived, he asked that it be sent for. "The *Rattler* started for Memphis for your ammunition ten minutes after I received your letter," said the admiral in reply, after he had consolingly remarked, "I fear this has been a hard day for you." [68] If Sherman had requested a whole bushel of coal that evening he probably would have got it.

As he cogitated that night, did Sherman ever think of the wasted 25th? Evidently the destruction of the railroad to Monroe could have waited; if he got Vicksburg it would be of minor value to the enemy at best. It was not until daylight on Christmas that the Vicksburg troops, some ten regiments, were ordered into the intrenchments, under the direct command of Brigadier Stephen D. Lee. Had Sherman been able to debark on the 25th and advance with strength upon the 26th, he might have had success. The brigades of Barton, Gregg, and Vaughn did not reach Vicksburg until the afternoon and night of the 26th, but they were in position by morning of the 27th, "enabling the exposed points to be held in force and the whole front to be watched by skirmishers"—according to Martin Smith, who had planned the defenses of the city and knew every foot of the tricky area where Sherman was trapped.[69]

After a dark and rainy night the sky cleared. Sherman made a personal reconnaissance and reported to Porter that a second effort to cross the bayou by narrow paths would be fatal to a large part of his command. (Highly important was his statement that if his troops had "been a little more experienced" he was satisfied they could have carried a hill that appeared to be strongly connected with the ridge leading to Vicksburg.) On the right, his pickets extended to the Mississippi and could see the forts and the court house, but the intervening space was "one mingled web of fallen timber of great size, filled with sharpshooters." Sherman wrote Vicksburg off and turned to Haynes Bluff. Surely there must be some disembarkation point from which the battery could be "stormed without the exposure that marks all the crossing places here." If Porter would permit his ironclads to ascend and engage the battery, Sherman would order 10,000 of his best troops to embark by night. "Haynes' Bluff in our possession, we have a firm footing on terra firma, which we have not here," said the general.[70]

Porter was willing. Furthermore, he would prepare a ram to clear the river of remaining mines. As if recalling that the rams had been brought into the world by Edwin Stanton, the sailor said, "I propose to send her ahead and explode them; if we lose her, it does not matter much." He described means for keeping the transports from being seen. Having once said, "I can think of nothing else," his mind flashed again: "The defense of hay in front of the boilers should be 2 feet deep and as high as the first deck." Colonel Charles Rivers Ellet did not take to the idea of a sacrificial ram and proposed the construction on the night of the 30th of a strong framework protruding forty-five feet in front of the ram *Lioness,* carrying hooks with which to fish for the cords by which the mines were fired. Porter consented but stipulated that the *Lioness* carry "torpedoes" to place on the river barrier, and have a boat ready to pick up anyone left on the barrier to ignite the fuses. Now he was not so casual: "No man must undertake this job who is not cool and anxious to do it." [71]

Steele's division and Stuart's brigade were embarked on the night of the 31st; the gunboats were in position; at midnight Sherman left the admiral and went to his camp to get all officers to posts for a diverting attack when the sound of guns at Haynes Bluff was heard at 4:00 A.M. Instead of the noise of cannon there came a note from Steele saying Porter had found the fog so dense that the boats could not proceed. Then the moon moved thoughtlessly into the picture, Porter sending Sherman a note that said: "What next? The moon does not set to-morrow until twenty-five minutes past 5; that makes the landing a daylight affair, which is, in my opinion, too hazardous to try." [72]

After this frustration, Sherman, believing that Grant had been compelled to fall back behind the Tallahatchie, and knowing what a heavy rain would do to oozy bayou land, "saw no good reason for remaining in so unenviable a position any longer." When the entire expedition was aboard the transports and about to move to Milliken's Bend on the morning of January 2, McClernand appeared off the Yazoo's mouth. Not until he had consulted with McClernand and secured his approval did Sherman move. The next day—the day the suffering William Gwin died—Sherman wrote his report of his adventures and told Grant that the entire command was at Milliken's Bend, while the transports were returning northward. "I attribute our failure to the strength of the enemy's position, both natural and artificial," he said, "and not to his superior fighting; but as we must all in the future have ample opportunities to test this quality it is foolish to discuss it."[73]

McClernand, writing at length to Stanton, after pronouncing Sherman a brave and meritorious officer, said, "He has probably done all in the present case that any one could have done, and I would not detract anything from him, but give him all credit for good purposes, which unfortunately failed in execution." After verifying the condition of the army, he would, he said, assume command of it.[74]

The wagon trains carrying Grant's second order to McClernand had not reached Memphis when McClernand arrived on Sunday the 28th. He at once dispatched two staff officers to Holly Springs with a letter and four enclosures. The first was a copy of Stanton's order of October 21 with the omission of the final paragraph, but carrying Lincoln's indorsement previously quoted. The second was a copy of Halleck's telegram to Grant of the 18th, included, McClernand explained, lest the original had failed to arrive. The third was his release from duty at Springfield, and the fourth was a communication from Stanton about the importance of the river project and Banks's part in it. "I have the honor," said McClernand to Grant, "to ask your instruction in the premises, and that you will be kind enough to afford me every proper facility in reaching my command."[75]

The next day found McClernand writing at length to Lincoln about a "gentleman of the first respectability" who had come in from Grenada with a story of the possibility of making peace. Said the general, "If you should determine to act in the premises and should think that I could speak for you advantageously, either upon your or my responsibility, I am willing to do so." The letter, which was sent forward by a major of McClernand's staff, carried a postscript noting that no order had been sent him at Springfield until after Sherman had left Memphis. "Either accident or intention," McClernand said, "has conspired to thwart the authority of yourself and the Secretary of War and to betray me, but with your support I shall not despair of overcoming both." In his letter to Stanton from Milliken's Bend he named the villain: the General in Chief.[76]

In spite of everything, Grant finished the year with cheerful thoughts. From Lafayette a dispatch came on December 31 from his aide Major T. S. Bowers, just arrived there from Memphis. All reports, he said, confirmed the taking of Vicksburg by Sherman, though no particulars could be obtained. There was more good news than that. The railroad to Memphis was not badly damaged, and Bowers believed so little wire was missing that the telegraph could be repaired in a day. Guerrillas were so plentiful, however, that it would be necessary to keep the line well protected. Doubtless the major smiled as he wrote: "General McClernand and his 49 staff officers chartered the steamer Tigress and started for Vicksburg yesterday. Hurlbut thinks the enemy have erected batteries on the river that will prevent Mack from getting down." In passing the news to McPherson at Abbeville, Grant added an item of his own: "There has been a great deal of cannonading to-day east of Henderson Station. Hope Sullivan has Forrest in a tight place." [77]

After evading Federal troops for two weeks, Forrest was indeed in a tight place. Catching him with infantry was more than difficult, and the suggestion that came to Sullivan on December 19 from Nashville, "General Rosecrans advises that you mount your infantry and chase Forrest out of the country," was hardly one to be quickly put into effect. A week later Sullivan reported to Grant that he had been able to mount only 1,000 infantry. Though Forrest had destroyed extensively and had caused much alarm, he sent Bragg a letter on December 24th that contained sentences as inaccurate as the false news of the fall of Vicksburg that reached Grant:

Reports that are reliable show that the Federals are rapidly sending up troops from Memphis. One hundred and twenty-five transports passed down a few days ago within ten hours, and daily they are passing up loaded with troops. General Grant must either be in a very critical condition or else affairs in Kentucky require the movement.[78]

On the 27th Sullivan had information that Forrest had camped the night before at Dresden with 2,000 men and six guns, and at 11:30 A.M. he telegraphed to Grant from Trenton that the elusive raider was headed for the Tennessee River, reportedly to cross at Reynolds-burg; he himself was pursuing on the Huntingdon road. After commenting that the river had risen two feet since the 21st, Sullivan said, "I will not leave him until he is out of the district." [79]

THE REGION OF FORREST'S RAID, DECEMBER 18, 1862–
JANUARY 2, 1863

The cannonading that Grant hopefully spoke of took place a hundred miles from Holly Springs at a crossroads ten miles north of Lexington. It was a peculiar action in which Forrest was completely taken by surprise by Colonel Fuller's brigade of Sullivan's force while engaged with that of Colonel Cyrus L. Dunham of the Fiftieth Indiana. Dunham had three infantry regiments, 65 mounted men, and 3 guns—in all, 1,554 rank and file—while Fuller had two infantry regiments and some guns. Forrest probably had about 2,000 men, but Sullivan accepted a larger figure based apparently upon what one of Forrest's foraging parties had said. Dunham sent the figure to Sullivan at 2:00 A.M. of the 31st, along with Forrest's supposed position and the assurance that he would "try to coax or force a fight out of him in the morning."

Dunham denied that Forrest had things going well—as Forrest claimed—and that he was himself in difficulty when Fuller struck. He had, he said, stoutly refused a demand for surrender, and had just recaptured his train as well as several enemy officers—among them Forrest's aide (a colonel) and his adjutant (a major)—when he saw Fuller's guns taking position. In a dispatch to Grant at six o'clock in the evening, Sullivan reported a "glorious victory" over Forrest's 6,000 (a figure that Grant must have discounted considerably). For booty Sullivan enumerated 3 guns, over 200 prisoners, more than 350 horses, a large number of wagons and teams, and many small arms. Said Grant in reply on January 2: "You have done a fine job—retrieved all lost at Trenton and north of you. . . . Dodge is now out after Forrest's band." The "band" successfully crossed the river that afternoon and night.[80]

Four days before this engagement at Red Mound or Parker's Crossroads, Davies had sent a gloomy report to Halleck about the damage done to the railroad. It was not the destruction of trestles that he lamented, but the injury to rails by fires that made them buckle and break for mile after mile. He would not, he said, start rebuilding unless so directed by Halleck or Grant; he thought it might be necessary to change base to Memphis or below. Within ten days he was to write in a report to Grant, "A heavy construction train was set to work as early as possible, and the road will be in running order probably by January 15." [81]

The following May, Lieutenant Colonel James A. L. Fremantle, of Her Majesty's Coldstream Guards, visited Bragg and his army in Middle Tennessee to record his findings in his famous diary. John Morgan and Forrest went down as "the renowned guerrillas." [82]

Though the Britisher was a great admirer of the Southern army, which he was confident would win independence for the Confederacy, and made much of Federal depredations, he used the favorite Yankee name for the Western raiders, and this in spite of the fact that he had not yet been in the North.

CHAPTER VIII

HUMILIATION ON SUNDAY, DECEMBER 7

> The citizens living upon the border must aid in their own pro-
> tection. *Wright to Thomas Ewing*

Presumably Rosecrans had already done well by a traditionally
ample breakfast at one of Louisville's best hotels when he began a
telegram to Halleck at 8:00 A.M. on November 1: "Go to Bowling
Green this morning. Troops there and at Glasgow." Night was closing
in when he reported his arrival. The latest news from Nashville was
that 10,000 of Breckinridge's men were at Murfreesboro, but that
none of Bragg's old army was ordered there. "Joe Johnston to command. Bragg gone east," were other items that Rosecrans communicated without comment as to their credibility. He could hardly have
suspected that Bragg had gone to Richmond voluntarily, largely for
the purpose of laying the failure of his Kentucky campaign at the
door of General Polk, and would soon be back in Knoxville with new
plans; the statement about Johnston was decidedly premature. The
railroad, Rosecrans said, was open to within forty miles of Nashville,
and as fast as supplies could be obtained he would move toward
Gallatin and Nashville.[1]

As Rosecrans was riding southward a telegram passed him from
Colonel Sanders D. Bruce, commanding at Bowling Green. It contained these sentences: "Morgan was at Springfield yesterday with
fully 3,000. His object is, doubtless, to annoy our army as we move
down, or cut off the wagon train." John Morgan was, of course, not
averse to such purposes, and he had talent and experience in exe-

cuting them. Thus the new commander of the old Army of the Ohio, now officially the Fourteenth Army Corps, would early have contact with one of the Confederacy's leading troublemakers. On the 3rd Rosecrans ordered Colonel John Kennett, commanding his two-brigade cavalry division—smaller certainly than it should have been, though it was supplemented by several cavalry regiments with infantry divisions—to start at five the next morning with five days' rations, on three roads, to cover the advance of the army, "and to ascertain the position and whereabouts of the rebel cavalry, with a view, if possible, of striking a blow." [2]

The telegram that Rosecrans had sent to Halleck on October 30 asking for the assignment of Stanley as cavalry commander suggested that Buell's cavalry had not been aggressively led. But it may not have been until he reached Bowling Green that he learned that in addition to an adequate commander, it lacked arms. Though there may have been exaggeration in his statement to Halleck on the evening of the 4th, "Our cavalry are not half armed," the situation must have been bad. Bad too was Rosecrans's comment, "The arms are an indispensable necessity, you know," a sentence that certainly contained a dispensable word, in addition to being impertinent. Nor was the concluding statement an altogether happy one: "My cavalry are the eyes and feet of my army, and will be its providers." Even at that moment, quartermasters and commissaries were working hard to get supplies shipped on the railroad. In fact, Rosecrans's boast looks almost like a slap in the face for Halleck, who two days before had telegraphed, "When the Cumberland River becomes navigable, you can get a large part of your supplies from Saint Louis." [3] Rosecrans was certainly talking as if he intended to live largely on the country. If that is not what he meant, his statement was bombast.

While in Louisville, Rosecrans had naturally heard all sorts of reports about his predecessor's campaign. A previously quoted statement that he made to Grant shows he did not think well of Buell, and apparently he believed that the officers of the army as a whole needed some strong admonition. Inasmuch as Buell had the reputation of being a tight disciplinarian, Rosecrans could well have proceeded with tact, for unless discipline is notoriously weak, a new commander is ill-advised to begin by trying to frighten subordinates. But on November 3 Rosecrans published an order which contained a threat. On that day he telegraphed to Stanton for authority to deal summarily

without courts-martial—impossible, he said, "in a moving army"—
and before the date had changed he had received and published the

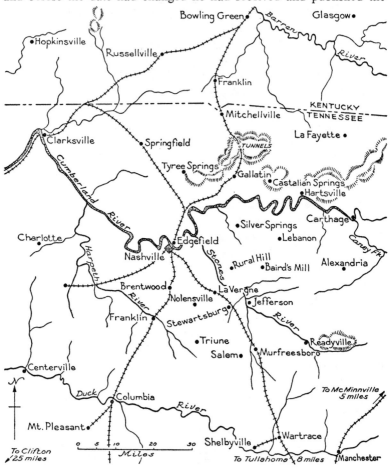

THE REGION OF ROSECRANS'S OPERATIONS

Secretary's reply that gave him a high degree of discretionary power:

The authority you ask, promptly to muster-out or dismiss from the
service officers, for flagrant misdemeanor and crimes, such as pillaging,
drunkenness, and misbehavior before the enemy or on guard duty, is
essential to discipline, and you are authorized to exercise it. Report of
the facts in each case should be immediately forwarded to the Department, in order to prevent improvident restoration.

In the concluding statement of the order Rosecrans said he was determined to exercise the authority given him.[4]

It may be recalled that the extraordinary power of summary dismissal had been given by Congress on July 29 solely to the President. The Washington order that followed Grant's dismissal of Colonel Murphy by just two days would begin significantly with the words: "By direction of the President." Thus Stanton was overstepping when he directed that Rosecrans report on cashiered officers for the purpose of preventing their "improvident restoration." No officer was lawfully out of the service until an order had been issued similar to that in the Murphy case. Unless an officer was out, there could be no question of restoration.

It was a remarkable coincidence that on the very day that Stanton was telegraphing to Rosecrans, Halleck was answering a letter from Butler in a way that shows that he would probably have handled Rosecrans differently than did the Secretary. Said the General in Chief: "A general can nominate, but he cannot appoint, 'subject to the approval of the President of the United States,' and the persons so appointed by you can exercise no legal authority. These illegal appointments will be regarded as recommendations to the President and their names submitted for appointments." [5] That was just as it should be, and had Stanton ended by telling Rosecrans to forward the facts at once, so that appropriate final action could be taken, so much sting would have been taken out of his dispatch that Rosecrans might not have published it.

Colonel James B. Fry, chief of staff under Buell, had quite naturally departed with the general, and Rosecrans's acting chief of staff was Lieutenant Colonel Arthur B. Ducat. At the Battle of Corinth, Ducat had written a good dispatch as to how matters were on the Federal right on the afternoon of the first day; at Chickamauga, also, he was to send some clear and discerning messages. In his new position he was a busy dispatch writer, but he sometimes seemed to forget that the army in which he now had a very important position was largely experienced. Though Kennett was doubtless inadequate as a cavalry division commander, it was hardly necessary to add as a postscript to a long message addressed to him: "Work secretly and quietly. Do not let the enemy know of your movements." [6] Just what did it mean? Was Ducat saying, "Do not talk publicly about your intended movements," or did he merely mean, "Keep John Morgan's scouts from watching you." After the experiences of the summer, the admonition could have made Kennett smile.

The War Department's unhappy label "corps" for Rosecrans's large command forced him to abolish that title for the three major subdivisions into which Buell had handily divided his army before he left Louisville—though it would still appear in correspondence. So, just as Grant was doing, he adopted the designations of wings and center, a poor expedient in all cases. Alexander McD. McCook got the Right Wing and Crittenden the Left. Thomas was given the Center, probably a more satisfying position than that of second in command— in which he had served in the Perryville campaign—especially since he was given five divisions, two of them being with Negley at Nashville. Rousseau's division was switched from McCook to Thomas, while one brigade of Jackson's division went to Thomas, the other staying in Kentucky. In replacement of the two divisions that he lost, McCook got Mitchell and Sheridan from Gilbert's old corps. (Daniel McCook's brigade went from Sheridan to Thomas, but was replaced by one from Palmer's division that Grant had sent to Buell.) Crittenden's command alone remained as it had been. Gilbert found himself in Kentucky in command of a brigade.[7]

Rumors and reports flowed into Bowling Green in a steady stream, and near midnight of the 6th Rosecrans reported to Halleck that it was said there would be 100,000 of the enemy in Murfreesboro within ten days. But he gave the assurance that he was advancing rapidly on Nashville, ending with the statement: "McCook will enter there to-morrow night. Crittenden will probably be at Gallatin by to-morrow night." His unfortunate habit of speaking in a tone of authority quickly revealed itself. The General in Chief was told that the Confederates could not live anywhere except in Middle Tennessee, with this addition, "They ought to abandon Mississippi, except a few points, and come here." He doubted the wisdom of sending any troops from Kentucky to help with the Vicksburg enterprise, and unabashedly told his superior: "Take troops from Illinois, Iowa, and Minnesota. You will want all you have in Ohio and Kentucky on this line." After giving some advice to Wright at Cincinnati, he closed a dispatch, "See how soon the work can be accomplished," and he ended one to Grant asking for the prompt release of Stanley to take command of his cavalry, with the lofty sentence, "You will do a most necessary thing for the service." [8]

Perhaps Rosecrans's midnight apprehension that the enemy would effect a heavy concentration against him was occasioned by a report that had arrived a few hours before from Colonel A. A. Stevens, commanding at Mitchellville, Tennessee. Along with the good news that a paroled Federal put Morgan's command at but six regiments and four howitzers, with personnel numbering only 2,400—which was about as accurate as a strength return by Morgan himself—there was a report that was a little disturbing. The First Michigan Engineers, who were working to the southward on the railroad, had heard firing in the direction of Nashville the previous day.[9]

There had indeed been an action on the 5th in the vicinity of the Tennessee capital. It involved not only Morgan but Forrest, who since the rout of some of his new units at La Vergne on October 7 had restricted himself to training his command and harassing on every occasion possible Negley's foraging operations. But Breckinridge, a week after taking over command at Murfreesboro, conceived a more ambitious idea. At Edgefield, across the river from Nashville, was a congregation of cars and locomotives, idle since Morgan's breaking of the railroad in the summer. With the road about to be reopened, these should be destroyed; and it would be fitting and just to have their end wrought by the man who had caused them to be so conveniently assembled. There was Morgan not far to the north of Nashville, quite as if destiny had brought him there to play the final act. So the demolition task was assigned to him, while Forrest was ordered to distract the Federals by attacking Nashville from the southeast and south. Though Forrest was not to expose his troops to a reverse, there was sparkle in Breckinridge's words: "Open at daybreak."

Of that day's adventures Morgan made no report. But years later Basil Duke, who served Morgan well in the saddle and with the pen, did. Morgan's command rode all night from Gallatin, and as day was breaking they heard the guns replying to Forrest's attack, quite as they expected. A half-mile from their quarry they struck a Union picket, and from behind a little house forty or fifty men in blue suddenly ran out and poured a volley into the Second Kentucky Cavalry that led the column. "I never saw men fight better than these fellows did," said Duke. "They turned and fought at every step. At least eight or ten were killed, and only three captured." He was wrong in speaking of the number of killed, for there were none, but it would seem that the pickets from the Sixteenth Illinois Infantry did their duty in textbook style.

The report that Negley wrote that same day from Nashville must have been satisfying reading for Rosecrans, and the concluding sentence of the covering note made a good introduction: "My command is in fine spirits and the transportation in excellent condition." Forrest had attacked, said Negley, at two in the morning with 3,000 cavalry and four guns. The pickets on the Murfreesboro road had gradually withdrawn so as to bring the enemy under the guns of Fort Negley, two of which opened and drove them back. Along the Franklin road there was action of a varying nature, which each side could interpret as it chose, depending on what it overlooked. As to Edgefield, the matter was undebatable. Negley put Morgan at 2,500 men and one gun, said he left a stand of colors, 5 killed, 19 wounded, and 2 captured artillery captains. He conceded only the destruction of an old railroad building; Duke claimed that a few cars were burned. Negley's total casualties were, according to himself, 26 wounded and 19 missing, though Forrest in a long report said, "Loss of Abolitionists, 15 killed, 20 prisoners, and supposed 20 wounded." What Negley called "a small affair" Bragg termed "a brisk skirmish" in a report to Richmond from Knoxville. He said, "Destroyed a large number of cars, engines, water-tanks, and bridges on Nashville and Louisville road." [10] What had been his expectation, he evidently reported as accomplishment.

The evening after the Nashville affair, McCook sent a message to Ducat, the new chief of staff, from Edgefield Junction, ten miles north of Edgefield. The divisions of Sill and Sheridan were there; Wood was at Tyree Springs. McCook set down an impressive schedule for the rations he could haul daily from Mitchellville, beginning with 200,000 on the 8th, 300,000 on the 9th, then dropping by steps to 100,000 on the 12th and remaining at that figure as long as desired. He was anxious about roads; heavy expected rains would make the stretch between the Springs and Mitchellville almost impassable—hardly a compliment for a supposedly good turnpike. The closing sentence showed that the commander of the Right Wing was planning to a nicety: "I will assume command of Nashville at 10 a.m. tomorrow." [11]

Actually, McCook rode into town at 8:00 A.M., and reported everything in good shape: "The troops are in excellent fighting order, and ready; want nothing but sugar and coffee, shoes and blankets. The sugar and coffee they will have to-night." The enemy, McCook said, was building up at Murfreesboro and at Tullahoma; Union sentiment in Nashville was deteriorating with each day; the inhabitants were bitter. A train of 250 wagons had started to Mitchellville, and McCook promised, "Feed Mitchellville Station well, and I will deliver all in Nashville promptly." The tone of his dispatches indicated he was glad to have a new army commander, and, after Perryville, it was no wonder. On the morning of the 10th he was saying: "We are all well and happy here. Supplies are arriving rapidly." He expected to have the railroad operating to Gallatin by the 15th; there were 300 cars and 15 good engines, thanks to the sturdy Sixteenth Illinois.[12]

That evening Rosecrans arrived, and at noon the next day he reported to Halleck a sufficiency of wagons to haul subsistence from Mitchellville until the railroad was opened, which might be in ten days. It would be interesting to know how Halleck appraised the statement that the enemy was retiring and destroying bridges. Rosecrans went even further than that: "Things now look like a withdrawal beyond the Tennessee, and probably sending off everything available toward Richmond. Will press them up solidly." He had the means to do so, for he telegraphed his strength that night: "Thomas, 26,000; McCook, 22,000; Crittenden, 22,000; cavalry, 4,000; in all, 74,000." [13]

It was a good-sized army and a toughened one. Even the new regiments with which Buell had left Louisville were now well road-broken, while some of them had seen hard fighting at Perryville. And the old regiments had marched to Nashville in February; then to Savannah to fight in the second day at Shiloh; had then been in the advance on Corinth; then marched almost to Chattanooga; then to Nashville and on to Louisville; then to Perryville, and once again to Nashville! They were indeed regiments with which one could press the enemy "solidly."

Before the day was over new information made Rosecrans completely change his mind. Now he believed the enemy intended to retire only to a position near Tullahoma. He could not be certain of their subsistence possibilities but told Halleck they ought to fight for Middle Tennessee. He hoped they would, "as in that case we shall be able to crush them by a decisive battle." He came near to thanking the General in Chief for new cavalry sent him; still his horsemen were not properly armed, and he entreated, "Please do all you can for us." [14]

On the 15th Thomas, who reached Gallatin on the 12th, sent Rosecrans a report based on what he had learned indirectly from a scout sent out by Crittenden. The enemy would not fight at Murfreesboro but at McMinnville or Chattanooga; they were in fact busily engaged in removing stores from Murfreesboro and would be for some days to come. The prospect elated Thomas: "We could take Murfreesboro, and march at once on McMinnville." If the enemy stood at that place, he could not only be beaten; he could be dispersed into the mountains. Thomas knew that region, he explained, and in addition he had an excellent map, "made from actual observation." [15]

A dispatch to Halleck the next night indicated that Rosecrans might be intending to act in conformity with Thomas's tip, for he said, "I wait the opening of the railroad, which will be on Thursday next [the 20th], before moving." Then followed sentences that began to mark him: "We move from, and they toward, supplies. Rain threatens." Twenty-four hours later—on the evening of the 17th—Rosecrans confirmed the view that the enemy intended to fight "on the table-lands near Tullahoma." Then he said:

I am trying to lull them into security, that I do not intend soon to move, until I can get the road fully opened and throw in a couple of millions of rations here. Should the present rain raise the river, it will be of the highest importance to have some gunboats for the Tennessee, for, in that case, I shall throw myself on their right flank and endeavor to make an end of them. Let me entreat you to give us cavalry arms.[16]

John Codman Ropes may be responsible for the common belief that Rosecrans told Halleck that he did not intend to advance until he had accumulated 2,000,000 rations.[17] The message above, which Ropes cites without quoting, may mean that. Or, was Rosecrans trying to deceive by spreading rumors of delay to amass rations? The reference to gunboats is quite baffling. None could ascend above Muscle Shoals even if the river rose. And if Rosecrans thought he could get so far on the Confederate right as to force them westward toward Savannah and the river, he was talking nonsense.

To the most disquieting features of Rosecrans's dispatches it would have been hard to reply briefly, and Halleck did not attempt to. But on the subject of cavalry arms he telegraphed:

Two thousand five hundred cavalry arms were sent to Louisville for your army. All revolving rifles that can be spared will also be sent. Each army receives its proportion of each kind of arms as fast as they can be procured. This rule must be followed, for we cannot "rob Peter to pay Paul."

Stanton, who had overstepped in granting one request, was becoming annoyed, and a telegram telling Rosecrans that 1,600 revolving rifles had gone to Louisville "at passenger-train speed" ended, "No effort shall be spared to supply what you ask for, but something is expected from you." Blunt though this was, it probably made no more impression on Rosecrans than the subtler appeal of Halleck, to whom on the same day he gave new advice: It would be well to send him the First Kanawha division "to place us in security in case of the loss of a battle." [18]

When Rosecrans so wrote, he had certainly already read a dispatch from Thomas of the day before—the 17th—predicting that the railroad would be in operation on the 20th, and outlining a plan of operations, conditioned on the hypothesis that the enemy was in McMinnville.[19] Actually, Rosecrans had the day before told Halleck that McMinnville was occupied by the enemy in addition to Murfreesboro and Tullahoma. In submitting the plan, Thomas was undoubtedly transgressing, unless Rosecrans had opened the way for suggestions. And while his proposal indicates that as a subordinate he thought it was time to advance, one cannot be entirely certain what he would have done if he had been the responsible commander.

It would seem certain, however, that a chance was missed when a substantial advance was not quickly made toward Murfreesboro. Both surprise and relief appear to lurk in Bragg's statement in a dispatch to Cooper on the 14th from Tullahoma, "The enemy keeps closely within his lines at Nashville." Six days later he telegraphed to Breckinridge at Murfreesboro: "Commence the works. Movement of troops commences to-morrow. Our Secretary Randolph has resigned; no loss." On the same day he issued an order changing the name of his command to the Army of Tennessee, and sending Polk's corps to Murfreesboro, Smith's to the front of Manchester, and Hardee's to the vicinity of Shelbyville. In a letter to Cooper on the 22nd he attributed the slowness of his movement from Knoxville to the condition of the railroad, but gave the assurance that there was an immense supply of subsistence, and considerable amounts of clothing, leather, and so forth, in the region he was occupying. In addition he said, "The people, with few exceptions, are loyal and true, having once felt the yoke of Abolition despotism, and are joining our ranks in large numbers." [20]

If Randolph was no loss, Rosecrans's inactivity was a positive gain to the Confederates, and Basil Duke comments upon the opportunity that had been open to the Federal commander. Though written years after the event, what he says conforms to what Thomas urged at the time: "We could take Murfreesboro." Five days before Thomas wrote, McCook had reported to Rosecrans, "I have made no movements to the front, Crittenden has moved so slowly." Yet Crittenden appears to have moved in conformity to orders. When instructing him near midnight of the 7th to proceed through Gallatin and cross the Cumberland, Ducat cautioned: "Do not demonstrate too boldly when you cross over. Let them come into your net." [21]

On the evening of the 11th Crittenden reached Silver Springs, eighteen miles northeast of Nashville, his wagons arriving during the night with five days' rations. A brigade he had sent by way of Lebanon had made some captures of men, mules, flour, and bacon, while Kennett had picked up some prisoners and a hundred mules at Hartsville. Hearing on the 14th from two sources, "deemed reliable," that Morgan had gone to Lebanon, Crittenden sent Wood's division there the next day. Instead of 6,000 Confederate cavalrymen, they found 300. After destroying the mill and some wheat and flour to pay him for his pains, Wood marched back to Silver Springs. A brigade that Crittenden had put at Rural Hill on Rosecrans's order was attacked by Morgan on the 18th, with slight losses on both sides. The next day Crittenden called in the brigade as well as Kennett at Hartsville and proceeded to Nashville. The weather was "very threatening," and he had already informed Rosecrans that, situated between Stones River and the Cumberland, he would, if the rivers should rise, be in "an ugly position." [22]

On the day of the affair at Rural Hill, Military Governor Andrew

Johnson said in a dispatch to Lincoln, "I feel in strong hopes that things will go well in a few days, as we have a man at the head of this army who will fight." It looked as if Rosecrans would have to do just that, for the next day, the day when Crittenden moved to Nashville, Rosecrans said in a dispatch to Wright, "I find the rebels concentrating to oppose this army." [23]

At first thought it would appear that in one important particular Rosecrans was not as favorably situated as was Grant. The latter was in command of the whole region through which ran the railroad back to Columbus; thus he could dispose of guards as he thought best. But most of the line that connected Rosecrans with Louisville was situated in Wright's Department of the Ohio, making the security of his communications depend upon another commander. Wright, however, was conscientious and desired to cooperate to the fullest extent, and Rosecrans was not to suffer from inability to command him.

On November 17 Wright, whose headquarters were still in Cincinnati, issued an order dividing the part of Kentucky in his department—the portion of the state east of the Tennessee River—into a western, a central, and an eastern district. They were to be commanded respectively by Brigadier Jeremiah Boyle, with headquarters at Louisville; Major General Gordon Granger, with headquarters at Lexington; and Colonel Jonathan Cranor, of the Fortieth Ohio Infantry, with headquarters in the field. The colonel's region consisted of only nine counties close to what is now West Virginia and a short stretch of the Ohio River; the generals received large slices of the state. Boundaries were not to be rigid; troops would operate "wherever required, without regard to district lines." [24]

A letter to Boyle bearing the same date as the order assigned the location of troops within his district, those along the railroad or close thereto being as follows: at Munfordville, a brigade of infantry, a regiment of cavalry, and a battery; at Bowling Green and at Columbia, the same; at Lebanon, a regiment of infantry and one of cavalry.[25] The force looks imposing; but it was all substantially in the south, evidently on the plausible theory that there could be no strong enemy penetration to the vicinity of Louisville. While two great trestles north of Elizabethtown would actually be protected by sizable garrisons, there was no reserve in Louisville.

Of course, it was confidently expected that Rosecrans would soon have the Cumberland River as an additional supply route, a route with no trestles or tunnels—and not often frozen. But the stream still contained obstructions about fifty miles from Smithland, placed there by the Confederates. These could, Wright informed Rosecrans on the 18th, be easily removed because of low water, and after querying whether this was being planned, he said, "If not, I will order Colonel Bruce to do it, as it is nearest his post." "Please order Bruce as you propose," was Rosecrans's prompt and cooperative response, to which Wright answered the next day, "Bruce has been ordered." Before long, Bruce could report to Rosecrans that a battalion was at work removing the obstructions so that Rosecrans could "get supplies by way of the river upon the slightest rise." [26]

In the western part of Boyle's domain there were hot secession spots—not quiet cells but demonstrative communities. At Hopkinsville, John Morgan had been warmly received on his way back to Tennessee, Duke recording that the people "were nearly all friendly." During their three days as guests of T. G. Woodward's regiment of irregulars, there were brought to them wagonloads of genuine Kentucky cooked hams, turkeys, and saddles of mutton, upon which Duke seemed almost to be feasting again as he wrote. Naturally, Wright's instructions to Boyle not only covered security of the railroad, but dealt with protection from guerrillas in the land to the west. Small forces had to be placed along the Ohio, at Smithland, Caseyville, Henderson, and Owensboro. In Tennessee, the town of Gallatin, near the tunnels whose timber linings Morgan had burned in the summer, was one that required careful watching. As their reopening neared, Rosecrans directed Thomas, "If public service would be benefited thereby, blot out Gallatin, or dispose of the secesh inhabitants in any way you think consistent with justice and public interests." In a report to Rosecrans as to how things stood at Russellville, Bruce said that active sympathizers and aiders of guerrillas were "being made to feel the power of the Government, and indemnify Union men for the property stolen or destroyed by paying for the same in cash." [27]

Gordon Granger had no secession centers to worry about in the southeastern part of his district; the people there remained strongly Unionist, enduring austerity in good spirit. But as early as the 21st Boyle got the report that the enemy was coming back through Cumberland Gap, 3,000 cavalry supported by infantry being said to be in

Barbourville. Correctly he passed the word to both Granger and Wright. The latter anxiously prodded Granger: "What do you know about it? You must see that they don't pass you toward the railroad. Answer." The reply was: "I have no information of rebels being this side of Cumberland Gap, but will endeavor to give the best reception we can afford in case they come. Have no confidence in the report." It was entirely proper for the department commander to be sensitive to that famous gap, and the next day he reminded Granger that if the enemy did come through in force, he would have to march to the Bluegrass at once; otherwise he would not eat. Thus Granger would have to keep forces dispersed to hold down guerrillas, but well enough in hand to concentrate rapidly.[28]

The best way to prevent a real intrusion through the Gap was a good foray into East Tennessee, and on November 25 Wright asked Colonel John Dils, Jr., commanding the Thirty-ninth Kentucky Cavalry in Pike County, if he could not make a dash through one of the upper gaps and seriously break the railroad by burning bridges. Wright understood that Humphrey Marshall had left Abingdon, and he thought that Dils, who had had some successful encounters with the enemy, might accomplish something handsome with his "hardy men"—"excellent material and good fighters," he called them in a letter to Cranor. But Dils did not want to venture out of the state until his regiment was properly mustered into Federal service and had good arms.[29]

All the many gaps were coming under Wright's purview, and as November ended he sent Rosecrans a report on those in Tennessee brought to him at Lexington by a "reliable scout." At Cumberland Gap, a regiment of sickly Mississippians and a little cavalry; at Baptist Gap, nothing; at Wood's and Roger's Gaps, a little cavalry; at Big Creek Gap—through which Kirby Smith had passed in August —a raw regiment of North Carolinians, reportedly conscripts, and some cavalry. But the whereabouts of Smith himself had balked the scout.[30] On his kind of business one had to be discreet, and though he doubtless had friends who kept eyes and ears open and reported gladly, a single question could betray him. He and many others like him, all with unrecorded names, show how inadequate is the picture of intelligence work if one considers only the better known and spectacular spies and agents.

Not only were there girls in Granger's bluegrass country who had smiled on Smith's men; there were persons who had wined and dined the general and his officers, and had aided him in recruiting and by hauling supplies. What to do about them was a vexatious matter, especially when their cases were pleaded by those whose protestations of strong Unionism were open to question. A disagreeable problem from many standpoints, it had its humorous side. Western Unionists had recently visited Washington to urge Wright's removal because, they said, he had revoked a tough order by Buell. Yet only ten days before this surprising charge was forwarded to Wright by Halleck, Rosecrans was reading a long intelligence report by a lieutenant of the Fifth U.S. Cavalry, recently paroled after two months' captivity, in which was the sentence, "General Breckinridge told me that General Buell hurt the South more than the armies of the United States, by his lenient policy." [31] The lieutenant evidently thought that Breckinridge was sincere and not trying to deceive. The situation was certainly confused.

Had Buell at the last actually grown hard? And what had Wright done that started the irate delegation for Washington, and what was Halleck's position in this difficult matter—not one with the drama of a battlefield, but essential, if we wish to glimpse even partially all the problems that commanders had to face in the great war of the sixties?

On October 26 Buell had issued an order specifying that all persons who had actively aided or abetted in the invasion of Kentucky should be immediately arrested and sent to Vicksburg, with return to Kentucky forbidden. Exempted from the order were those under indictment or held by civil authorities for trial; nor was anyone to be arrested on mere suspicion or insufficient evidence. Upon Boyle was placed the duty of executing the order; four days later he was enjoined by Buell to proceed "with caution and discretion." On November 1 Wright, at the time in Louisville where he had discussed the matter with Boyle, gave him a modification of Buell's order. Aiders and abettors of the invasion would in general not be sent to Vicksburg, but to Camp Chase, Ohio, as political prisoners—they might not be accepted by Vicksburg, and even if they should be accepted Wright did not want them to engage in mischief at a new location.[32]

In addition to the charge of leniency against Wright, there was naturally the opposite one of excessive severity. To Stanton he wrote that he had released some persons because of insufficiency of evidence, while in other cases, where he had been accused of inadequate proof, he had sound basis for his acts. It was Boyle who summed up the matter for Wright:

Complaints have been made by over-zealous Union men that the marshals did not do their duty in arresting the domestic traitors, etc., and the weak-back Union men, looking for rebel protection when the rebels should be in the ascendant, complained that they arrested too many, and indiscriminately. I believe they did their duty as well as any men who could have been selected.[33]

In his letter to Wright, Halleck said, "Domestic traitors, who seek the overthrow of our Government, are not entitled to its protection, and should be made to feel its power." Such had been his policy in Missouri, and it had brought results: "The hands of Union men were strengthened, and secessionists became Union men from interest, which, after all, is the very strongest lever to apply to them." The advice he gave was on the hard side: "Don't be influenced by those old political grannies, who are only half way Union men, and who are ever ready to shield and apologize for traitors." In his reply Wright stressed an important fact. Kentucky was as much under a recognized state government as was Ohio; it was equally the duty of civil authorities to act in all cases amenable to civil law in the one state as in the other. There was plenty of military power to give protection to civil authorities; no call had been made for it in vain. "The rights of the government and the people should be respected," and, according to Wright, martial law would not be justified.[34]

While Wright would thus clearly have preferred to let the civil authorities do the cleaning up after the invasion, he was not soft. When he learned that Bruce had returned to a Confederate Congressman a hotel in Russellville that had been used for a Federal hospital, he directed Boyle to have the restoration countermanded, while Bruce was to send an explanation of his act. (The seizure definitely came under the July Confiscation Act.) When Thomas Ewing, Sherman's foster father and father-in-law, distinguished lawyer, once Secretary of the Treasury and afterward of the Interior, grew fearful that hostile bands would cross the Ohio, Wright wrote to him at his Lancaster home, carefully explaining that, if all the military forces were spread along the river, they could not guarantee security against inroads by small parties, while they could better cope with large forces in the positions they occupied. Bluntly he said, "The citizens living upon the border must aid in their own protection." [35]

On November 13 Lieutenant Colonel Julius P. Garesché, fresh from the Adjutant General's office in Washington, was made Rosecrans's chief of staff, Ducat becoming inspector general. On the 24th General Stanley, relieved by Grant on the 11th, reported and was appointed chief of cavalry. No fewer than ten general orders, some rather long, appeared, regulating matters of wide variety. Surrender to the enemy for the purpose of being paroled was branded by Rosecrans as "even more base and cowardly than desertion," for desertion, being punishable by death, had "a semblance of courage when contrasted with voluntary capture." Strict regulations were established for foraging, as well as for the troublesome question of relations with civilians, while provost marshals were enjoined against arrests on insufficient grounds. Clamps were put on sutlers, sometimes a doubtful blessing for the Union army. In an order stating that he had received several applications from Kentuckians who had tired of secession and wanted to go home, and that he understood there were many such, Rosecrans sought to accommodate them without onerous conditions. They would merely have to "take the non-combatant's parole, and give proper security that they would keep it." So long as they kept faith they would not be molested by his army, but if they aided the enemy in any way they would "be summarily dealt with, as spies or perjured traitors, with the utmost rigor allowed by the laws of war." [36]

Washington found the new department commander a little difficult to deal with, though different agencies wished to be helpful, as shown by the question of a pontoon train. This Rosecrans threw at the Chief of Engineers in a telegram on November 22: "Can I have an iron pontoon train long enough to cross the Tennessee, say 700 yards?" No pontoons of any kind were available, said Brigadier General Joseph G. Totten in reply. A wooden bridge of the specified length would take a month to build; an iron one decidedly longer. Then he queried, "What do you say?" Wooden pontoons habitually got leaky, said Rosecrans. They could never be repaired for use in a reasonable time; iron ones were much better—if properly made. Then, quite as if he would be at the Tennessee almost any day, Rosecrans concluded, "We should have the train at once."

The engineer department referred the matter to Halleck for decision, explaining that either kind of bridge could be made in Cincinnati, a wooden one in six weeks, an iron one in four weeks longer; but the department had no models for iron boats. What had become of Buell's train, and why was another required, were the questions asked Rosecrans by George Washington Cullum, Halleck's chief of staff, who said a new train could not be made and forwarded in less than six or eight weeks. Buell's train had been destroyed so that the enemy could not get it, replied Rosecrans. Besides, the boats were leaky and were useless "without a very large amount of calking." (It would seem certain that the Confederates had Buell's train in use at the time.) Obviously he should have a train, said the Nashville general; and once he got moving he did not "want to stop and tinker."

A week later Wright informed Rosecrans that his engineer had been instructed to build a pontoon bridge "with all possible dispatch," and that he would get a progress report tomorrow. Rosecrans, who evidently had an antipathy for wood, began to talk about canvas boats. He could make them, said Wright, but he gave some good arguments against canvas, and weighty ones for wooden boats, if the lumber were well seasoned. "Buell's pontoons were made of green lumber," explained the Cincinnati general, who still, however, was willing to appease his colleague if he really wanted canvas.[37]

In addition to telling Stanton that he had only about a third of the artillery he should have, Rosecrans submitted a request for some special light guns, resembling mountain howitzers, but different. Chief of Ordnance Brigadier General James W. Ripley balked, but said that mountain howitzers, known to be reliable and effective, would be furnished on requisition. For Rosecrans's enlightenment he sent a copy of a letter he had submitted to Halleck on August 27, almost imploring the General in Chief to standardize artillery weapons and reduce varieties of ammunition. In the case of small arms, the evil had been brought under control, but not so in the case of artillery. Ripley said that to meet all calls it was necessary to have "not less than six hundred kinds of cannon ammunition." [38]

Even in the laudable effort to obtain overdue pay for his men, Rosecrans managed to bring a reproof upon himself. Two dispatches that he sent to Stanton made forthright statements, without the touch of dictation he often used. But one was addressed to an official in the paymaster department, and it requested that a certain paymaster be sent to Nashville with forty assistants. This was too much for Stanton, who had been strongly opposed to Rosecrans's appointment in the first place. Halleck was given the assignment of putting the Nashville general in his place, which Halleck sought to do in a dispatch that ended crisply, "This is not the first time I have been directed to call your attention to similar improprieties." But it merely brought to Halleck the retort that if he would get Rosecrans's views as to paymasters adopted it "would be a measure worthy of your administration." [39]

Before November had ended, Rosecrans was engaged in epistolary encounters with Bragg, who established headquarters at Murfreesboro about the 25th. The Confederate led off with a note about one W. H. Hawkins, acting adjutant of a battalion of Partisan Rangers, who had presented himself to a Federal post with a flag of truce, only to end up an unhappy prisoner at Alton, Illinois. This, Bragg said, must be the result of error or ignorance. Confidently he expected the man's prompt and unconditional release, with an explanation of the unusual procedure. In a reply on the same day, Rosecrans stated he was forwarding the letter to Wright, to whom the troops belonged who were alleged to have disregarded the flag. There were, however, things Rosecrans did not like, and the recent use of a flag of truce to communicate with his outposts induced him to ask Bragg to give proper instruction in such matters. Said the Federal general, "The flag must come from the senior officer commanding, and follow the most direct route."

Now just two weeks before this date Rosecrans had issued a long order to his command about the reception of flags of truce, but overlooked giving instructions about sending them. And as luck would have it, on the very day he laid down the law to Bragg, McCook addressed a note to the latter and dispatched it down the Franklin pike, while the next day Negley sent one, which Bragg, in a politely written letter to Rosecrans, said was objectionable and had been returned. Bragg also cited an item in a Nashville paper which revealed that two of McCook's staff officers had picked up valuable information while within the Confederate lines under a flag of truce as escort for a Nashville lady. Not an exploit to boast about, said Bragg, Number Five Man in the West Point class of 1837, to Rosecrans, Number Five in that of 1842. Nonetheless, he would be glad to accept Rosecrans's suggestion as to procedure with white flags as long as they held "present positions and relations." [40]

Exchanges on all manner of subjects followed, with advantage lying sometimes with one, sometimes with the other of the two commanders. In discussing the question of intelligence received from citizens expelled from Nashville, Bragg said, "If those sent give information, it is for you to check, not me. I assure you, however, I have no need for them on that score. The fact that you have penetrated a country so unanimously hostile to you and your Government should sufficiently account for the facility with which I can obtain information, without the necessity of devising means to procure it." "Hostile!" Rosecrans might have retorted. "Look at that flag flying over the statehouse! It belonged to a Nashvillian, who brought it reverently out of hiding when Buell marched in last February!" [41]

The first warning was gentle enough, and it came to Rosecrans in the last sentence of a dispatch Halleck sent on November 27: "If you remain long at Nashville you will disappoint the wishes of the Government." Six days later Rosecrans reported that McCook and Crittenden were from three to six miles "in front"; that Thomas was "closing down"; that he was five days ahead on rations; that cavalry arms were coming slowly, and were indispensable for an effectual and steady advance, the only kind that would net "anything worth the cost." If Rosecrans expected approval, he was disillusioned at what came the next day from Washington:

The President is very impatient at your long stay in Nashville. The favorable season for your campaign will soon be over. You give Bragg time to supply himself by plundering the country your army should have occupied. From all information received here, it is believed that he is carrying large quantities of stores into Alabama, and preparing to fall back partly on Chattanooga and partly on Columbus, Miss. Twice have I been asked to designate some one else to command your army. If you remain one more week at Nashville, I cannot prevent your removal. As I wrote you when you took the command, the Government demands action, and if you cannot respond to that demand some one else will be tried. [42]

Halleck wrote almost as if he had read a letter that Bragg had written to Cooper on November 22, in which was the sentence, "Supplies will go back rapidly, and we hope not only to feed our forces, but to spare largely for other localities." In face of this it is futile to argue that Rosecrans could not have advanced promptly on Murfreesboro because of subsistence. Nor did Rosecrans unduly stress supply in his message of explanations, which completely ignored the possibility of an advance before Bragg had occupied Murfreesboro in force, and which showed clearly that he was apprehensive about disaster in battle. A general who is haunted by that fear will look diligently for some sort of shortage. Rosecrans asserted that he had many soldiers who were barefoot and many who were without tents or blankets, and cavalry without horses—apparently a new discovery. No figures for the number of cases were set down, and without them one must be skeptical. Furthermore, when Rosecrans at last did march, he took but 50 per cent of his men into the field, and he knew that he was leaving behind a considerable garrison that would not be subjected to heavy duty. The general who had spoken about not wanting to stop and tinker ended grandiloquently: "To threats of removal or the like I must be permitted to say that I am insensible." [43]

"My telegram was not a threat, but merely a statement of facts," Halleck said in reply. He was not certain as to the precise cause of Lincoln's "great anxiety," but thought it was because the British Parliament would convene in January, when "the political pressure of the starving operatives [workers from closed cotton mills] may force the Government to join France in an intervention." Pointing to the fact that the summer gains by the Confederates had been erased except in Middle Tennessee, and that in some places there had been new Federal advances, Halleck said, "Tennessee is the only State which can be used as an argument in favor of intervention by England." "Why don't he move?" "Can't you make him move?"—such were the daily comments of members of the Cabinet. Nor did the General in Chief even hint that the Government was unreasonable. He concurred: impatience and dissatisfaction were justified "under the circumstances of the case." At the end there were very simple, yet very telling sentences: "No one doubted that General Buell would eventually have succeeded, but he was too slow to be in time. It was believed that you would move more rapidly. Hence the change." [44]

The letter came at an inopportune time. In addition to old problems Rosecrans had a new one, for the opening of the railroad had not proved an unmixed blessing. While it eliminated a long wagon haul and so allowed tired animals to be rested for an advance, it brought a deluge of civilians. On the very day that Halleck wrote, Rosecrans appealed to Boyle to hold them back. Not only were they using transportation the army needed; they were injuring discipline and causing inconvenience. Doubtless Boyle was happy to wave them goodbye, and either by way of answer or by coincidence, he telegraphed: "About 3,000 convalescents here. Can send 1,000 hale, hearty men belonging to your army if you will allow a train to be taken for the purpose. Can I take train and send the men? Anxious to do it." [45]

While the ladies and gentlemen arriving in Nashville may have been vexing, it is not in the record that they caused Rosecrans any humiliation, as John Morgan was soon to do.

Morgan had been much on the minds of Federal commanders; and, to their credit, they had not been thinking solely of defense; they had schemed to capture him. When Crittenden learned on the afternoon of November 7 that Morgan was presumably at Gallatin, he ordered Wood, who had already marched twenty miles that day, to start a picked brigade at two the next morning with instructions to capture any Confederates still in Gallatin. "This is hard on the men," he wrote, "but no chances are to be lost, and I count on you." [46] Well before the Federal column arrived, Morgan had left; and he had not gone to Lebanon in force, when Crittenden, as previously noted, sought to pin him down in that town. There is something pathetic in exhausting night—or even day—marching by infantry in the hope of catching cavalry. Nor was the frustration that it brought good for morale.

Both Wright and Rosecrans were short of cavalry. Of that there can be no doubt. The trouble was lack of equipment—twenty months after the beginning of the war. On December 3 Wright informed Rosecrans that he could not fit out the First Tennessee Cavalry, and the next day he amplified: "I cannot get arms or horse equipment for cavalry. If I could, I should have mounted troops enough and to spare." On the 6th Rosecrans appealed to Stanton for the Seventh Michigan Cavalry, "now armed and equipped at Detroit." Two days later Assistant Secretary of War Watson telegraphed that the regiment was ordered to the Army of the Potomac. (While one battalion went to Washington in late February, 1863, the balance of the regiment did not leave Michigan until May.) Then Watson quoted figures and asked questions that showed the department kept books and wanted cold facts from commanders. Replying the same night, Rosecrans said that the 3,600 carbines received during the day gave him a total of 6,096, leaving a deficit of 1,321, "supposing absentees return." Simultaneously Halleck told Wright to send Rosecrans any cavalry he could spare, and got the reply: "I have no cavalry to spare. There is a Tennessee regiment for General Rosecrans at Camp Dennison, waiting for arms and horse equipment, which I have been vainly endeavoring for a month to get. Some new Kentucky regiments are in same condition." [47]

The case looks bad for the Ordnance Department until one examines the reports showing the number of carbines, revolvers, sabers, and horse equipment which had been procured up to June 30, 1862, and to the same date a year later.[48] Many weapons must have been lost in the field; many must have been now in Confederate hands. Two weeks before Wright spoke of his inability to get equipment, Bragg said this to Cooper about Morgan: "He has raised his own command, and nearly armed and equipped it from the enemy's stores." But in all the cavalry force opposing Rosecrans—numbering 8,000 to 9,000 [49]—there surely were not 6,000 good carbines.

Washington had certainly not forgotten that on October 30 Rosecrans had telegraphed about eight cavalry regiments that could do wonders under an able chief, and had said, "Stanley will double our forces without any expense." As recently as December 4 the Nashville general, when informing Wright that he expected a battle with Bragg at Murfreesboro, had stated, "Should we defeat him, there will be little to fear from Morgan's men." But Rosecrans's delay and effort "to lull them into security" had left the initiative with Bragg. In the order of November 20 that reorganized and rechristened his army, Bragg withdrew from the army cavalry the commands of Morgan and Forrest for "special service." Forgetting that there were many ears friendly to the Federals in the region where he was, he spurred the raiders with high praise: "Much is expected by the army and its commander from the operations of these active and ever-successful leaders." [50]

When the Federal brigade was withdrawn from Rural Hill, Morgan had the chance to press a plan that Duke says he had been eager to carry out—an attack on the Federals at Hartsville. The raider was then at Baird's Mills, ten miles east of the hill, and to that place Bragg on December 1 sent an order for him to begin "with the least delay" operating on the enemy communication lines in the rear of Nashville. After listing tasteful specific items for Morgan's agenda, Bragg said, "In fine, harass him in every conceivable way in your power." [51] The Union force at Hartsville was an obstacle to an attack on the railroad, especially if there was a force holding the Cumberland at Carthage. That a brigade of Blue Coats would soon be on the march to secure the latter place Morgan could not know, but a move against Hartsville must have looked secure after the Federals obligingly fell back from Rural Hill, and seemed in general to be inactive.

At least, as a preliminary to an operation in Kentucky, Morgan set to work to plan a blow against the town near where, on August 21, he had defeated and captured Brigadier General Richard Johnson, as a sequel to his destruction of the Gallatin tunnels.

After his unhappy Edgefield experience it is not surprising that Morgan wanted some infantry, and he was given the Second and Ninth Kentucky regiments under the command of Colonel Thomas H. Hunt, Morgan's uncle, as well as a battery and two small howitzers. With these—totaling 695 officers and men—and 1,400 from his own command under Colonel Duke, plus his own two rifled guns, Morgan set out in mid-morning of December 6, a cold day with snow covering the ground. During the night he crossed the Cumberland below his objective, the infantry and artillery slowly and laboriously in two small boats that required constant bailing, the cavalry at a difficult ford six miles farther down, slowly and miserably. (The river had begun to rise.) Not all the cavalry was over when the two commands united, and with one regiment of horse sent to picket the roads that led to Hartsville, Morgan moved upon the Federal camp as day was breaking.

Again, as at Mill Springs and as at Shiloh, it was Sunday. Again everything had not gone perfectly with the attackers, Hunt writing in his report that his nephew's purpose "to surprise the enemy was defeated." When the Federal camp was sighted, Hunt saw the hostile "infantry already formed, occupying a very strong position on the crest of a hill, with a deep ravine in front and their artillery in battery." But the men in blue had not expected to hear the sound of reveille followed quickly by the "long roll," and Morgan still had many of the advantages of surprise. In addition, his infantry was seasoned, while the three Union regiments in line had been mustered during August and September.

Men from Ohio held the flanks of the Federal line, six companies of one regiment on the left, seven of another upon the right, some 400 in each case. In the center there were probably 700 men of the 104th Illinois. Two guns of an Indiana battery constituted the artillery observed by Hunt, and somewhere in the vicinity were 400 cavalrymen from Indiana and Kentucky regiments. The entire force was commanded by Colonel Absalom B. Moore of the Illinois regiment; it was his first fight and his last.

On the Confederate left Duke dismounted some 450 men of two new regiments and, deploying them so as to overreach the Federal right, pressed hard for the Union flank and rear. The 108th Ohio that was disadvantageously struck was under the command of a captain and had ammunition which did not fit their undependable Austrian rifles. After they had been forced well back, Hunt attacked the Union left and center, the result being that within an hour and a half of the beginning of the contest the Federals had been driven back to a cliff overlooking the river, where—according to Hunt—"they surrendered at discretion." There had been some sharp fighting, Hunt speaking of a "desperate struggle" at the crest of the hill, while Morgan spoke of the "great precision" with which the Federal guns were served. Some unknown gunner got a direct hit on a Confederate caisson, blowing it up, with heavy casualties.[52]

Nine miles westward at Castalian Springs were two Federal brigades under the command of Colonel John Marshall Harlan, his own, belonging to Speed S. Fry's division, and that of Colonel Abram O. Miller, from Dumont's division, of which Moore's had been a part. At 7:30 A.M. Harlan heard cannonading in the direction of Hartsville, and a courier he sent to investigate reported that the captain of a picket company thought he heard heavy musketry. At Harlan's direction, Miller soon had his brigade on the march, Harlan himself following with two of his own regiments and four guns, leaving two regiments and two guns to guard the camps. When some three miles from Hartsville, Harlan received a request from Miller to come forward and take command, as there was evidence there would be a fight.

On going forward, Harlan found Miller deployed, with his battery in position, a mile and a half from Hartsville. All firing had ceased, and the future Supreme Court Justice had a hard case to decide. Had the attack been repulsed, or had his friends been captured? Dense smoke arising from the known position of Moore's camp soon dispelled all doubt. Harlan then pressed on, his small cavalry detachment soon being at the river, and he himself arriving in time to see enemy cavalry riding away from the opposite bluff, each horse apparently carrying two men. Doubtless a pursuit was impossible, but it looks as if Miller could have arrived in time to destroy much of Morgan's command, or at least free many of the prisoners, if he had pressed forward resolutely and thrust aside the small force that Morgan had thrown across the road. Unfortunately, Harlan did not record his hour of arrival, nor did Morgan say when it was that the Federals appeared on the north bank.[53]

The Confederate commander must have been a very happy officer, and his successful crossing of the breast-high river, with all his command, 1,762 prisoners, and numerous wagons filled with captured arms, marked the conclusion of one of the boldest and most successfully executed minor operations in the war. Morgan, however, was lucky, not only in the absence of a good Federal commander at Hartsville, who would have had cavalry patroling beyond the river to alert both himself and Harlan, but in the timely presence at Murfreesboro of Joe Johnston. Johnston's Monday telegram to Cooper contained the sentence, "Morgan, the *partisan* [emphasis supplied], performed a brilliant feat yesterday, taking 1,800 prisoners—more than his own number. I recommend that he be appointed brigadier general immediately. He is indispensable." A few days later the town was visited by one of even higher rank than Johnston—Jefferson Davis. Beaming generals watched while Presidential hands received one of the three sets of Federal infantry colors that Morgan had brought home.[54]

Well before word had arrived of misfortune at Hartsville, Rosecrans was disturbed over the intentions of Forrest. On Saturday he had telegraphed to Boyle that the Confederate horseman was in Columbia the day before with six guns, preparing for a raid toward or through Clarksville, and he enjoined: "Bruce and McHenry must concentrate and whip him, and take his pieces." (Colonel John H. McHenry, Jr. was currently at Russellville with Bruce.) On Sunday the Nashville general sped a warning to Colonel Lowe at Fort Donelson: "Look out for Forrest. He was at Columbia yesterday and means business." After news had arrived about Hartsville, Rosecrans telegraphed to Wright: "Forrest was at Columbia yesterday with probably 5,000 men, and I think is bound for a raid in Lower Kentucky. I hope Bruce will fight, and not do as a green brigade of mine at Hartsville to-day, which, after a trifling stand for an hour and a quarter, surrendered to five regiments." Boyle passed word about the warning to Thomas, who, evidently skeptical about a raid into that part of Kentucky, asked Rosecrans, "Is this reliable?" [55]

Seemingly there was no reply, but the next day Thomas received the message: "Hire and keep spies out over the river in all directions. Get butternut clothing, if necessary." The sudden loss of one of his brigades did not unhinge Thomas. On the 7th he wrote out a new plan of campaign for Rosecrans's consideration. It contemplated that McCook and Crittenden advance southeastwardly, while he concentrated at Lebanon. After a ten-day supply of rations had been put down at Carthage by steamers, his corps could move on Sparta, "and thence to Crossville and Kingston, and from Kingston either on Loudon or Knoxville, or on both, as circumstances may justify." The program was certainly ambitious, and it would have pleased Lincoln if he could have seen it. Care of details shows that Thomas had considered matters carefully, for example, the statement, "There are two roads from Carthage to Knoxville, one by Sparta, good; the other by Montgomery, pretty good." At what hour on Sunday Thomas wrote, one cannot tell. Perhaps it was in the morning, and hence before the news arrived that he was short a brigade, with guns and cavalry. That he did not throw the plan away is shown by the ending of a message to Rosecrans on the 8th, "I will submit a plan of future operations by mail to-morrow for your consideration." [56]

In his reflections on Rosecrans's operations and of the part Thomas had in them, the reader should keep in mind that Thomas would probably have had the army if he had not shown weakness during the few hours he actually held command in September.

The next day found Rosecrans still thinking more surprises might be coming, and his chief of staff telegraphed to Thomas, "General desires you to cover your front with a constant cloud of scouts, so as to enable you to concentrate your forces and escape surprise." A message to McCook about adjusting his line because of enemy activity, contained the sentence, "Indications are that all this is a feint to cover attack on Fort Donelson, but it must be stopped." McCook's suppertime reply had a cheerful tone: "Will have all right. Corps in line in the morning. Have not heard from any reconnaissance save Sheridan's. No firing in front; all quiet." Not all of Rosecrans's thoughts were about near and present danger; and at some hour on the 9th he telegraphed to Wright: "You promised me about advancing into East Tennessee. Now is your time." [57]

On this December Tuesday Rosecrans received a short dispatch from Washington. Inasmuch as Brigadier General Richard Johnson, a regular cavalryman, had been badly used near Hartsville by Morgan on August 21 and was himself captured, news of a greater calamity at the place must have been a shock. The President, said Halleck, wanted to know why there was an isolated brigade at Hartsville, and by whose fault it had been surprised and captured. Rosecrans asked enlightenment from Thomas, and after prefacing Thomas's full statement about garrisons and the like with an essay of his own, he telegraphed the whole at 11:00 P.M. The next day Rosecrans had a reply: "The most important of the President's inquiries has not been answered. What officer or officers are chargeable with the surprise at Hartsville and deserve punishment?"

At midnight Rosecrans tried again, writing a very good account of what had happened, indicting the cavalry with the statement, "The behavior of the Second Indiana Cavalry seems to have been spiritless as their picketing," and closing, "No official reports yet in." When the reports were sent, they were returned by Halleck with the direction that Rosecrans "ascertain and report who are the guilty officers concerned in the surrender of Hartsville, Tenn." Now Rosecrans definitely pinned the blame on Colonel Moore's "ignorance or negligence." Having received this specific finding, Halleck recommended the colonel's dismissal "for neglect of duty, in not properly preparing for the enemy's attack." "Approved," wrote Stanton. But the President was cautious in using the extraordinary power reposed in him, and Moore, probably on the basis of the report he wrote on February 25, 1863, in Chicago, after he had been exchanged, was allowed to resign on account of disability.[58]

While Rosecrans was working on the telegram that Halleck said did not suffice, John Beatty was writing in his diary, "The whole army feels deeply mortified over the loss of the brigade at Hartsville. . . . I am glad Ohio does not have to bear the whole blame; two thirds is rather too much." How completely staggering the news had been was shown by the concluding and pleading sentence in Rosecrans's dispatch to Thomas at 11:00 P.M. on the 7th, "Are there none left?" [59]

When news arrived of the victory at Prairie Grove by Blunt and Herron, it would be seen that—even if the enemy attacked at dawn—Sunday, December 7, need not be a day of disaster for the arms of the United States.

A report from Colonel Lowe on the 10th was cheering. He had had many scouts out in all directions, as far as twenty-five miles—no contact. He was ready to move from Fort Henry to reenforce Donelson at a moment's notice, and he said: "What few troops I have are in grand fighting trim, and everything that can be done has been done. You shall have a good account of us, if attacked." Perhaps it was Lowe's report that gave Rosecrans the idea that Forrest might be intending to strike westward across the Tennessee; at least he warned Grant.[60]

From Thomas the news was mixed. He had not been able to get in touch with the brigade that was marching on Carthage when Hartsville was attacked; four sets of couriers had been sent to deflect it to Gallatin, but had not found it, so far as he then knew. Gallatin was believed to be the target of—of all persons—Kirby Smith. The Knoxville general had been reported on the 9th at Lebanon with 10,000 to 15,000 men, but Thomas had assured Rosecrans: "I think we can handle Smith here. I will make all dispositions at once." Cheerfully Gareschand wired to Boyle, "Hope soon to settle matters by a battle." Now on the 10th the news was a little different: Kirby Smith was not at Lebanon; he was merely expected. At midnight Rosecrans reported to Halleck that Henry and Donelson were "fully warned for a snap on them." Thomas was checking on Smith; Rosecrans hoped that the movements of the enemy would be such that he could strike him near Nashville, "which will virtually end the game." [61]

According to what he had professed to Halleck, Rosecrans should have been depressed by Thomas's report on the 14th; Smith was not at Lebanon; he had been seen at Manchester, fifty-five miles away. It is permissible, however, to think he was not. And it is hard to tell how he appraised militarily some news he next day put on the wire to Wright: "Morgan was married last night at Murfreesborough." If a wife kept the raider near home, it might be better for the Louisville and Nashville Railroad, but that would keep him from becoming

Wright's and Boyle's problem. Definitely good information came from Sullivan at Jackson. Forrest was crossing the Tennessee at Clifton; he would now be Grant's concern. In a second dispatch to Wright, Rosecrans gave an assignment and hinted at something impending: "Send expedition, with all possible dispatch, to destroy railroad bridge over Little Tennessee at Loudon. They watching me, will not suspect you." [62]

A message to Halleck stated that Jefferson Davis had attended the Morgan nuptials. When serenaded he had made a speech, in which he said that Lincoln's proclamation put black and white on an equality. He had urged the people of Middle Tennessee to hold at all hazards until Grant could be whipped. Three generals had protested and threatened to resign when Bragg had ordered that all Kentucky and Tennessee exiles should be conscripted. But "Jeff. took the matter in hand," Rosecrans explained, and then concluded, "Things will be ripe soon." In less than an hour Rosecrans telegraphed more information: ". . . rebel troops say they will fight us; Bragg to go to Mississippi; Johnston to stay; . . . Cumberland still very low; rain threatens; will be ready in a few days." [63]

CHAPTER IX

AN INDECISIVE BUT TIMELY VICTORY

*The general asked me if I could not do something to relieve
Colonel Beatty with my guns.   Captain John Mendenhall*

Eleven days later—December 26—Rosecrans's army was on the march. It was high time that he and Bragg tried to settle their differences by other means than letters. On the 16th Rosecrans had written to his opposite number:

You will see by the copies of reports to me, herewith inclosed, that another outrage of the grossest character has been perpetrated by your troops, in the presence of your own flag, commanded by a lieutenant colonel in your service, who but yesterday was courteously received. I cannot believe you had authorized, or will permit to go unpunished or without prompt reparation, such barbarous conduct, hardly paralleled by savages. You cannot restore life to my men who have been inhumanly murdered, but I shall leave to your own head and heart to devise such reparation as is demanded by your own honor and the honor of our common humanity.

What Rosecrans got from Bragg was a long letter dated the 23rd which contained the sentences, "With these facts before me, I consider myself justly entitled to apology and reparation for this unprecedented disrespect and outrage. To claim that a truce existed while my flag was forcibly detained by you is preposterous." [1]

Before Rosecrans had set forth, John Morgan had demonstrated that he had not been noticeably softened by matrimony. On the very day—December 19—that Grant sent warnings to his subordinates about Van Dorn, Rosecrans telegraphed to Robert Granger (still at Bowling Green) and Boyle that Morgan had just started from his camp below Lebanon with 5,000 to 6,000 cavalry, no infantry, and a few small batteries, to break the railroad. Though the message ended, "This news is positive," the larger figure was double the size of Morgan's command, and he did not break camp until the 22nd—as Rosecrans presently learned. Rosecrans on his part was definitely behind schedule, a dispatch to Halleck in late afternoon of the 24th stating that he was moving against the enemy at daylight. He had in Nashville, he explained, the essentials in ammunition and twenty days' rations; the departure of Forrest and Morgan would aid him materially. If the enemy met him, he would fight tomorrow; if the enemy waited on him, it would be the next day. To which statement he added: "If we beat them, I shall try to drive them to the wall." [2]

In addition to the gratifying intelligence that Morgan was well started into Kentucky and so was no longer his responsibility, Rosecrans knew that Wright had launched the requested demolition expedition into East Tennessee under Brigadier General Samuel P. Carter. This Tennessean, whose activities the previous year have already been described, was at the moment burdened with the displeasure of Andrew Johnson. In the letter to Lincoln in which he spoke so hopefully of Rosecrans, Johnson said that instead of making Carter a major general, as was being proposed, "it would be much better to send him back to his rank in the Navy." In place of going back to sea, Carter was setting out at the head of a thousand horsemen to cross the mountains east of Cumberland Gap and strike the railroad well up toward the Virginia line. To Rosecrans's statement that the announced expedition of 1,200 men, was "too slight and feeble," Wright replied that he was sending all he could spare; but, evidently thinking of compactness and mobility, he added that he was not sure he would make it stronger, if he could. With a touch of clairvoyance— it was the 19th—Wright said, "I have already weakened too much the cavalry on your line of communication." [3]

When Carter rendezvoused his force near Booneville on Goose Creek and totaled the strengths of his three battalions—from the Ninth Pennsylvania, Second Michigan, and Seventh Ohio cavalries— he found he had only about 980 men, a considerable portion of whom were in the field for the first time. That was on Christmas Day, and the next day, while Rosecrans was setting forth with hopes of driving Bragg to the wall, the little column of blue horsemen turned their faces toward the rugged mountains, to kindle fires in Bragg's rear.[4]

Already Morgan had struck the railroad above Munfordville, and some bridges were gone. Wright informed Boyle that Gordon Granger was receiving telegrams apparently sent by Morgan, and cautioned that everything to Granger must go in cipher. The Cincinnati general was disturbed: "We must open the railroad soon, or Rosecrans will starve." Presently more and larger bridges and trestles closer to Louisville would be in flames. But the night before—Christmas night—there was a present of heavy rain, and it continued through the 26th.[5] Now it was a question whether those twenty days of rations in Nashville warehouses would last till boats were at the landing. If they did, the laugh would be on Morgan.

The rain could not have been pleasant for the men in the long columns streaming out of Nashville, but for one thing they were surely grateful—firm macadamized roads.

Crittenden's corps,* covered by Colonel Minty's cavalry brigade, was on the Murfreesboro pike, John Palmer's division leading, followed by those of Thomas Wood and Horatio Van Cleve. McCook, who had on the 24th reported himself ready to move except for striking tents, was on the march toward Nolensville at 6:00 A.M., in accord with an order that had rattled out of his telegraph instrument at 4:30. He had the divisions of Jefferson C. Davis, Philip Sheridan, and recently exchanged Richard Johnson; he was protected by the reserve cavalry brigade under Stanley. Thomas, with Zahm's cavalry brigade, was on the Franklin pike, with orders to turn eastward at Brentwood. Less than half of his command was with Thomas, for two brigades of Speed S. Fry's division and the entire division of Joseph Reynolds were at Gallatin and other points on the railroad, while Robert Mitchell remained with his division and one brigade of Negley's as garrison for Nashville. Thus Thomas took the road with only the division of Rousseau, two brigades of Negley's, and Walker's brigade of Fry's division (less one regiment); but he said in his report that he had 13,395 effectives.[6]

All unconsciously, of course, Rosecrans was following the advice which had been constantly given his classmate John Pope by the

* This designation will be used in place of Wings and Center.

Negro cook who boasted of previous service with James Longstreet, another classmate: Advance in three columns. We cannot know where one would have found the staff of thirty officers enumerated in the order that Rosecrans had published on the 22nd for the information of his command. In those days, when there were no tables of organization for higher units and provisions for staffs were inadequate, it is not surprising to find Rosecrans augmenting his legal allowance by attaching ten officers from regiments.[7] These infantrymen, artillerymen, and cavalrymen would not feel frustrated by dripping skies. One may be sure that they thrilled when they glimpsed their outfits, spoke cheerily to close friends, and experienced perhaps a sense of guilt, though knowing they were part of the essential machinery of control of this large army.

It was known that contact would come very quickly: Wood wrote in his report that the enemy had been pressing up so closely with both cavalry and infantry that for some days "it had been necessary to fight for the greater part of the forage consumed by the animals." The Confederate cavalry screen consisted of the brigade of Georgia-born Joseph Wheeler, West Point graduate of 1859, whose subsequent long period of service in the House of Representatives covered Rosecrans's four-year congressional career, and who later served as a United States general in both Cuba and the Philippines, retiring finally as a brigadier general in the regular army. Now the young brigadier was Bragg's chief of cavalry, and in addition to his own brigade deployed on outpost duty he had Pegram's on the right and Wharton's on the left flank.[8]

In reporting on December 7 about the Hartsville affair, Rosecrans had said his own cavalry was "much cowed" because of inferior strength and want of weapons. By the time of the advance the Federal cavalry, though somewhat fewer in numbers, may have equaled the enemy's in fire power. In fact, on the 23rd Rosecrans seemed confident enough as to his mounted arm, for he sent a message to Stanley about 3,000 to 4,000 enemy horsemen southwest of Nashville with the cheerful ending, "You had better be prepared to bag them." [9] When he indicated to Halleck the next evening that if the enemy did not offer battle near at hand, he would be up to Murfreesboro on the second day, he was clearly implying the ability of his cavalry to handle rapidly their part in the advance. But the hostile cavalry that he wrote about on the 23rd was not bagged, and on the 26th and subsequent days they were very effective.

From a mile north of La Vergne, Crittenden reported, as the short winter day was ending, "I must camp here." Though he had been obstinately opposed by an enemy ready to take advantage of every opening, he had no reason to believe a heavy hostile force was near. He was moving a division early in the morning to try to save the bridge near Stewartsburg, "but with little hope." A later message said he was anxious for news from the right, where the firing for a time seemed heavy. Negley, leading Thomas's column, had also heard the action and, leaving his train under guard, had turned eastward to support Davis, whom he found hotly engaged with the enemy near Nolensville. But McCook, who had indeed been resisted throughout the day by cavalry and artillery, was cheerful when he reported himself in camp one mile south of the town. His casualties had been light, and he said: "The men in glorious spirits, and only want a chance. Negley is here with his division." The general who had borne the brunt at Perryville was alert to everything, and closed his dispatch, "Hardee had a dance given him at Triune last night." [10] Hardee being forty-seven and a bachelor, the event might have military significance. (He was married the next month.)

That evening Rosecrans personally directed McCook to attack Hardee at Triune in the morning. When the next day came, a fog cut visibility to objects close at hand, so McCook soon stopped his advance and sent a note to Garesché: "I will apprise you when I move forward. Can do nothing intelligently now." At 1:00 P.M. he was able to resume his advance and at 3:00 sent a dispatch from near Triune that reported Hardee had departed in one fog and had left another behind him: "Every prisoner I have taken has contradictory statements as to their destination." Whether Hardee was bound for Shelbyville or Murfreesboro, McCook could not say, but he promised, "I will know to-night." His message had a nice commendation for Federal horsemen—who had not been getting many—"My cavalry are all raw, but have done well to-day." [11]

Probably it was the fog that kept Crittenden from setting forth on his bridge-saving enterprise as early on the 27th as he had expected. It was not until nearly noon that he launched the brigade of Brigadier General Milo Hascall straight down the road to Murfreesboro and that of Colonel William B. Hazen down the pike to Jefferson. Both men were West Point graduates, Hascall having behind him some years in civil life that had done him no harm, Hazen some Indian wars that had left minor wounds. Both today saw their volunteers perform in excellent style. Hazen said he had a steeplechase, with the enemy horsemen outnumbering five to one the ninety troopers from the Fourth Michigan Cavalry who had been assigned him for his task. He won, and the bridge on that road was secured. Hascall had some fighting to do, for the Confederates held a good position in and beyond La Vergne. Here the situation was cleared by a bayonet charge which "left nothing to be desired." Then followed an advance over wet plowed fields, until the brigade was stopped by an enemy battery which with "fearful accuracy" knocked out the section of guns Hascall put in action. Upon sending to the rear, he was given a battery with better range, and soon he had the enemy's guns silenced. While this was going on, some of his skirmishers, concealed near the bank of Stewart's Creek, discovered that the bridge was loaded with rails which had been ignited. A call for volunteers to extinguish the fire brought a flood of responses. That bridge was also saved.[12]

The rain having rendered almost impassable the dirt crossroads that laced the pikes together, it was not until night that Rousseau reached Nolensville, whence Negley, who had been joined by his train, had set out in the morning and had hooked up with Crittenden near Stewartsburg. In order to have better roads, Walker, at Thomas's order, returned to Nashville and started all over again down the Nolensville pike.[13]

When morning came McCook still did not know whether Hardee had gone south or east, so he dispatched August Willich's brigade to find out. It was Willich who, on finding his men firing erratically when first engaged on the second day at Shiloh, had stopped his advance and steadied them by exercises in the manual of arms. Now a briga-dier's stars were on his shoulders. With some cavalry covering his advance, Willich went southward toward Shelbyville. Early in the afternoon a courier was back at McCook's headquarters with dis-patches. One from an aide stated they had reached the dirt road where the enemy had turned eastward—at least six brigades. General Willich, his mission performed, was returning. No enemy was visible; not even cavalry vedettes. So wrote Captain Horace Fisher. Then it was McCook's turn to write. In a message that described the ugly ter-rain he had encountered the day before and the blinding rain in which his infantry had fired into Stanley's cavalry, the Right Wing commander said to Rosecrans: "The following dispatch has just been received (*verbatim et literatim*) from General Willich, who is 7 miles in advance on the Shelbyville pike: 'The enemy is no more here; all gone to Murfreesboro.'" [14] Evidently McCook thought German-born Willich should be exercised in English.

In an evening dispatch, written at army headquarters on the Nashville-Murfreesboro pike, Garesché directed McCook to shift eastward. At 10:45 McCook replied that inasmuch as his column would threaten the enemy communications, he expected to be heavily resisted. But he added: "Will do everything mortal man can do to gain my position. It is 16 miles from here to Murfreesborough, and 2¼ miles of the road tolerably bad, but can make it." After explaining how he was handling his train so as to keep it safe, he ended on an alarming note: "The cavalry of the center has not a round of ammunition, and General Stanley reports that there is none in Nashville for these arms." [15]

Crittenden had stood fast during the day, Wood explaining, "Sunday, the 28th ultimo, we remained in camp, waiting for the troops of the Right Wing and Center to get in position." After night had closed in, Rousseau joined Negley near Stewartsburg, giving Thomas his entire command, save Walker, who was on the road to Nolensville. About the somewhat confusing shifts that were being made to bring Thomas from the right to the center, Garesché kept Mitchell at Nashville well posted. A message at high noon contained a sentence that switched from a tone of warning to a note of joy: "You are aware that our prospect of bringing the enemy to battle near Murfreesborough is becoming more and more bright." The ending, however, was grim enough: "The hospital and ambulance train can come up to-morrow." [16]

At four on Monday afternoon Crittenden reported himself three-fourths of a mile from Stone's River with the enemy in plain view. To his query "Shall I advance farther?" Garesché replied, "If you see good chance, open on them with artillery." The first sentence of a two-sentence dispatch that soon followed may have been quite unexpected by Crittenden: "Occupy Murfreesborough, if you can, with one division. Encamp main body of troops on this side, as before directed." To Crittenden's reply that Palmer and Wood were protesting against a night move, that a citizen had said there would be

trouble with the ford even if the enemy did not oppose, that a prisoner reported Breckinridge's division in position only a few hundred
yards in front, and that he was suspending the execution of the
order, Garesché replied at 9:00 P.M. "The order to occupy Murfreesborough was based on information received from General Palmer
that the enemy was running. You did right not to attempt its execution. . . . Try and open signal communication with McCook, who
is only 3 miles off." But before the order had been received, Harker's
brigade of Wood's division "had crossed Stone's River under a galling
fire, driven in the enemy's outposts, and seized a strong position,
which it held until nearly 10 o'clock that evening," when it was withdrawn.[17]

As he struggled through the mud, McCook was doubtless pleased
to receive a message from Garesché saying that Stanley was wrong
about ammunition; if he was out it was his fault; he must get some
without delay. But the Right Wing commander was a little disturbed
when at 4:25 P.M. he began a dispatch to Crittenden: "Dear Tom:
I am up and ready for work. My cavalry, I hear, have just made an
unfortunate dash on some rebel infantry, on the right of the Wilkinson pike." He had heard nothing of Thomas, Rousseau, or Negley;
nor had Rosecrans told him what to do. Though he supposed he
would receive instructions during the night, he thought a conference
would be a good thing. After saying he had had "a miserable road,"
McCook ended, "Was sick yesterday, but am well to-day. Would be
glad to see you." Before the general could have signed his name, Rosecrans's senior aide was writing some adequate instructions for him.
Five hours later McCook replied with full information about his position, the message containing the important sentence, "My right is
retired, and, I think, safe," and the priceless one, "The cars are very
busy, running in and out of Murfreesborough, to what effect none
but a rebel knows." [18]

It was not necessary for Rosecrans to ruin McCook's chance for
sleep by summoning him to headquarters at 1:00 A.M. of the 30th to
order him to advance in the morning and connect with the right of
Negley's division, which was under orders to take a position on
Crittenden's right. An early move was not specified, and it was 9:30
before Sheridan led the advance down the Wilkinson pike. Stout resistance soon compelled deployment, but the heavy Federal line drove

the enemy sharpshooters and skirmishers—supported by a battery—back upon their main positions. It cost Sheridan seventy-five casualties, but when night fell he had connected with Negley.[19]

Considering their strained relations, Braxton Bragg did not do too badly by William Rosecrans when he telegraphed to Samuel Cooper that evening: "Artillery firing at intervals and heavy skirmishing of light troops all day. Enemy very cautious, and decline a general engagement. Armies are in line of battle within sight." [20]

Had he known the facts, Bragg would surely have reported the havoc which Joe Wheeler had wrought that day among Federal trains, in a circuit which began when he struck at dawn near Jefferson and did not end until he had passed through La Vergne with the fury of a cyclone and dealt a final blow at Nolensville before starting for the Confederate left. Of this humiliating matter Rosecrans said not a word in his official report, while Stanley wrote, "On the 30th the entire cavalry force was engaged in guarding the flanks of the army, in position. Some small cavalry skirmishing occurred, but nothing of importance." Actually, though he was short of cavalry, the Federal general had two battalions forming a straggler line to pick up erring infantrymen. Included in the catastrophe at La Vergne was a company of the Second Indiana Cavalry that had escaped capture at Hartsville. When its captain—who got away—listed what he had lost, he included an item that would have brought a groan from Stanton: "11 Colt's revolving rifles." [21]

In a message informing Rosecrans of the capture of the wagon train which he had dispatched from Nashville the morning before, Mitchell said, "The telegraph wires are cut, and our messengers all taken or driven in." The duty at the base was heavy; but it would be endured cheerfully if it could "accomplish any good result." The enemy had been within a mile of his pickets that evening, though only in small numbers, and Mitchell said, "I think they will not find us asleep." Northward, however, there was real trouble: "Everything looks blue in Kentucky." As a matter of fact, Boyle, intent as he was on inflicting damage on Morgan, had not forgotten the advancing army, and he put on the wire a dispatch that would comfort Rosecrans: "I have ordered large amount of stores up Green River to Bowling Green; also up the Cumberland. I got General Wright to order 1,000,000 rations up the Cumberland from Cairo." [22]

In East Tennessee telegraph wires were humming, but there the Confederates were on the receiving end of a daring raid. At daylight Carter with his thousand men had surprised the town of Blountville, made some captures, and had then moved on Union, fifteen miles from part-Tennessee, part-Virginia Bristol. There he burned the 600-foot bridge over the Holston and made more extensive captures. In his report he wrote:

The prisoners were paroled, and a large number of them were that afternoon on their way to the mountains of North Carolina, swearing they would never be exchanged. Their joy at being captured seemed to be unbounded.[23]

Night had come before Carter kindled the 300-foot bridge over the Wautauga River. A captured locomotive was run into the river, destroying in its passage one of the piers of the bridge, while many arms and valuable stores were burned. Then Carter started homeward, just as Morgan, finding his position "sufficiently hazardous," was doing on this same day. Already some forty-five dispatches had passed in an effort to converge forces on Carter's men—thirty-five of them being impressively set down in the twenty-three large printed pages of explanations that Humphrey Marshall addressed to the new Confederate Secretary of War, James A. Seddon.[24]

On that night—December 30—Crittenden stood astride the Nash-ville–Murfreesboro pike and the railroad, Wood on the left, not far from Stones River, Palmer on the right, Van Cleve in reserve to the left and rear. Negley was next to Palmer. Then came Sheridan, then Davis, then Kirk's brigade of Johnson's division, its right covering the Franklin road. On Kirk's right was Willich's brigade, also of Johnson's division, with three regiments facing southward, one to the west, and one in reserve. All three of Davis's brigades were in the front line, but Sheridan had one in support behind his center, and Baldwin's brigade of Johnson's division was posted half a mile from the division center. With little of his corps in division reserve and nothing in corps reserve, McCook seemed to be depending largely on terrain, and he wrote, "My line was a strong one, open ground in front for a short distance." [25]

During the night Thomas ordered Rousseau—who was along the Nashville pike behind Palmer—to move by 6:00 A.M. to a position

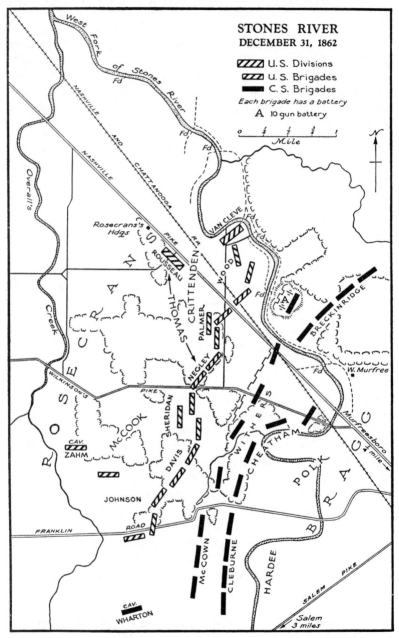

STONES RIVER
DECEMBER 31, 1862

U.S. Divisions
U.S. Brigades
C.S. Brigades

Each brigade has a battery

A   10 gun battery

0   ¼   ½   ¾   1
Mile

N

West Fork of Stones River

Fd

Fd

Fd

Fd

Overall's

Creek

NASHVILLE AND CHATTANOOGA

NASHVILLE PIKE

Rosecrans's Hdqs

ROUSSEAU

THOMAS

CRITTENDEN

VAN CLEVE

WOOD

Fd

A

BRECKINRIDGE

PALMER

NEGLEY

W. Murfree

Fd

R   O   S   E   C   R   A   N   S

WILKINSON'S PIKE

McCOOK

SHERIDAN

CAV. ZAHM

DAVIS

WITHERS

CHEATHAM

POLK

B   R   A   G   G

Murfreesboro   ¼ mile

JOHNSON

FRANKLIN   ROAD

McCOWN

CLEBURNE

HARDEE

SALEM PIKE

CAV. WHARTON

Salem 3 miles

[262]

behind Negley, and Walker—who was at Stewartsburg—to march when relieved by Stanley. Rousseau's division seems to have been the army reserve; in addition there was the pioneer brigade, consisting of 1,700 men and a battery, while six companies of the Fourth U.S. Cavalry were near headquarters. (This was little enough for a battle line more than three miles long.) Near midnight Stanley would move with two regiments of cavalry to La Vergne, near where Minty was camped with a regiment and a battalion that had been involved with Wheeler. The rest of Minty's command appears to have been on straggler and courier duty; but Zahm's brigade, with the remaining regiment of Stanley's reserve attached, was on the right.[26]

Bragg's army was astride Stones River, a position that could be embarrassing if the river should rise. Rather strangely, the bridge on the Nashville pike had never been rebuilt, though the Confederates had been in occupancy since September. When Bragg took up a defensive position on the 28th, only Polk's corps of two divisions— those of Withers and Cheatham—was west of the river, part of it in prepared intrenchments. Hardee, with the divisions of Breckinridge and Cleburne, and the attached division of McCown, was east of the river, to the north of Murfreesboro. On the 29th McCown was moved to the west bank and placed on the left of Withers; late the next day Hardee was directed to follow with the division of Cleburne and take personal command on the extreme left flank. The night was hardly a pleasant one for Cleburne or his men, and the words of the Irish-born soldier are eloquent:

It was dark when staff officers were sent to order me forward and show me my position. The passage of the river in the night was attended with many difficulties, and my whole division was not in position before midnight. As well as I could judge from the camp-fires, my line was a prolongation to the left of Cheatham's line, and was 400 or 500 yards in rear of McCown's division.

The northern front thus remained in the custody of Breckinridge's five-brigade division (one of them a temporary attachment). But his position was strong, the left being anchored to a dominating hill on which there were ten partially protected guns, the officer in support being enjoined that the eminence was "the key to the battle-field." [27]

In infantry the forces were: Rosecrans, 25 brigades, 104 regiments; Bragg, 20 brigades, 102 regiments. In the Federal army the artillery was divisional, though a battery was attached to each infantry brigade; in the Confederate command, a battery was organic to each brigade. Counting all arms, Rosecrans had about 44,000 "effectives," while Bragg had 37,713 "present for duty." It is not clear why Rosecrans's effectives should have numbered just a little under half of the aggregate present that he reported for December 20 in a return that did not include any of his men at Bowling Green or elsewhere in Kentucky.[28]

In his report Rosecrans said that he called a meeting of corps commanders for the evening of the 30th. Thomas came early, received instructions and left. Crittenden's chief of staff reported that the general was much fatigued and was asleep. Since Rosecrans had talked with him that afternoon, Crittenden was excused. McCook and Stanley arrived about nine o'clock and were given full explanations of the intended attack the next day. So wrote Rosecrans officially on February 12. Less than a month later he tried to inveigle McCook into saying that there had been an actual meeting of all corps commanders at his headquarters and that the battle plan had been fully explained. This, McCook denied; he had not been summoned; he had gone to headquarters from a sense of duty to report, and Stanley had gone with him. No general officers were present except Rosecrans and themselves. Furthermore, McCook denied the accuracy with which Rosecrans had put down their conversation in his report, and said he had not known the details of the latter's plan until he read his report in a Cincinnati newspaper.[29]

To Rosecrans's query whether instructions had been given to him at "my headquarters," Thomas answered no. The plan for the next day had been explained while they were riding from Thomas's headquarters toward those of Rosecrans; he had not gone to the latter's tent that night; he had gone the next morning. Stanley wrote essentially supporting McCook; no instructions whatever had been addressed to him while at headquarters, for he was already under orders to go to La Vergne to guard trains.[30]

It is McCook's report that is the important one. He said that at about 6:30 P.M. on the 30th he received this directive:

Take a strong position; if the enemy attacks you, fall back slowly, refusing your right, contesting the ground inch by inch. If the enemy does not attack you, you will attack him, not vigorously, but warmly; the time of attack by you to be designated by the general commanding.

McCook likewise stated that he was informed that simultaneously with his attack, Crittenden would move into Murfreesboro. His statement that he promptly gave instructions in writing to his division commanders is authenticated by the one to Davis, which happily is in the records. Faithfully McCook spoke therein of "inch by inch" resistance in case of attack, illustrating by adding, "and fight as well as the rebels fought you to-day." The contingent instructions for an offensive were carefully passed on: "If they do not attack you, you will attack warmly, not vigorously." Very important for the record was the sentence, "General Crittenden's corps will cross the river and take Murfreesborough, and attack any force in rear that falls in front of him, and try and work on the line in your front." The closing sentence, "I will go over to see General Rosecrans to-night," looks indeed as if the visit were voluntary.[31]

The details of Rosecrans's plan, that McCook said he learned of subsequently from a newspaper, were extra touches that Rosecrans inserted in his report. After Van Cleve and Wood had crossed the river, Rosecrans intended to advance Palmer and Thomas. Then the first two would turn westward, driving the enemy toward Salem with the prospect of "cutting off their retreat and probably destroying their army." If Rosecrans did so intend, it absolves him from a plan that would merely drive Bragg back on his line of communications if the attack by the Federal left succeeded. (One must recall, however, how quickly Rosecrans forgot that he intended to cut Price's route of retreat from Iuka, though it was in his plan.) To make the Confederate commander believe that the chief stroke would come against his left, McCook was ordered about 6:00 P.M. to build fires beyond his right. This, he said, was done.[32]

Though they may have been expecting orders, Van Cleve and Wood did not actually receive directions to cross the river until the morning of the 31st, Van Cleve at seven o'clock, Wood sometime after dawn—upon going to Crittenden's headquarters for instructions. Van Cleve crossed two brigades and his batteries, but Wood was only engaged in preparations when messengers, "riding in hot haste," confirmed what the "fierce roar and rattle of musketry" had already announced; Bragg had beaten Rosecrans to the attack, and was smashing the Federal right. It could hardly have surprised Wood, for sometime after midnight Colonel George Wagner, commanding one of

Wood's brigades, had sent word that "the enemy seemed to be moving large bodies of troops from his right to his left." Dutifully, Wood had passed the word to Crittenden's headquarters.[33]

The fraudulent campfires had frightened no one, and during the night Bragg had ordered Hardee to attack the Federal right with his corps and Wharton's cavalry brigade, the blow to fall at dawn. Wharton moved rapidly so as to get in the Federal rear with his some 2,000 horsemen, while the 10,000 infantry and artillery went forward—according to Hardee—"with animation."[34] None of the 16,000 men in McCook's corps would have challenged the words.

Johnson wrote that it was at 6:22 when the outposts of Kirk's and Willich's brigades were driven onto the main lines—where the men were apparently preparing breakfast. Nevertheless McCown recorded that a galling fire was poured into his flank from a cedar brake while infantry and artillery opened on him in front. But the two brigades soon "crumbled to pieces"—Rosecrans's words—and were driven back, leaving one battery and part of another in enemy hands. Kirk was severely wounded; Willich was wounded and taken prisoner.[35]

Stragglers from the brigades of Kirk and Willich informed Baldwin of the crushing attack. Johnson, after Baldwin had promptly formed his brigade in the edge of some timber, ordered some changes, which had hardly been effected when the Confederates were on him. Before Baldwin's musketry and gunfire, the dense mass recoiled, but the attacking line so far overlapped him that he was compelled to fall back, eventually to the railroad, after he had made some short but ineffective stands. It was there—three miles from the place where his brigades had prepared their tardy breakfasts—that Johnson reorganized his command.[36]

In spite of the quick victory over Johnson, matters were not to be simple for the attackers. McCown wrote that resistance in his front prevented him from swinging his left around as early as Hardee had ordered, and the thrusts against his flank caused him to say, "The moment was critical." Cleburne, following behind McCown, found that the latter had "unaccountably disappeared" from his front, as he swung around and was unexpectedly taken under fire. A great deal of crowding and opening took place in the center of Cleburne's line, and he recorded that it was only three-fourths of a mile from where he had bivouacked that he encountered the first solid Union line. But

Hardee was on the field, watching for every opening, and his generalship was undoubtedly of the greatest moment that day.[37]

Davis, against whose right flank Kirk had rested, swung his right brigade under Post around so as to meet the envelopment, while Carlin and Woodruff met attacks in their fronts, the conflict there being "fierce in the extreme on both sides." Losses were heavy, and according to Davis's observations it was the best contested point of the day—though this must be questioned—and would have been held had not the flank been so severely threatened. How far the enemy had advanced into the original Union rear was shown by Wharton's capture of part of one of Post's regiments. After Davis had retired toward the Nashville pike, he for some time had little success in reforming his thinned regiments, and he spoke of men who skulked in dense woods that he passed.[38]

Having been informed at three o'clock by General Sill that there was much activity by the enemy in his front, Sheridan sent to Sill's brigade—the right one in his line—two regiments from the division reserve, and at four o'clock he had his whole command under arms with "the cannoneers at their pieces." It was Withers's division of Polk's corps which attacked Sheridan, and Polk wrote that Withers found him "fully prepared" and in a strong position. The destruction wrought by Sill's fire on the close enemy mass—several regiments deep—was terrible. When they broke and fled, Joshua Sill—classmate of Sheridan and third man in his class—ordered a charge. The order, Sheridan said, was well responded to, the enemy being driven across the valley and into his intrenchments. Sill was killed. Though the brigade rallied and was reformed, the situation on Sheridan's right presently caused him to retire. After forming one line facing southward, he was ordered by McCook to take position on Negley's right, facing south and east, which he did, every regiment "remaining unbroken." [39]

What had Rosecrans been doing to get some measure of control of the battle, or at least to save his army? Unfortunately, as in all battles of the Civil War, exact times are often uncertain, for no journals were then kept at headquarters. But—according to Rosecrans—within an hour of the opening of the battle one of McCook's staff officers brought word that the right needed help, and he was sent back with the reply that McCook must dispose of his troops to the best advantage and "hold his ground obstinately." Hot upon the heels of the first messenger there came a second with word that "the right wing was being driven." Then—and this should have been by eight o'clock—Rosecrans immediately sent Thomas to put Rousseau into the cedar brakes to the right and rear of Sheridan. Van Cleve was ordered to suspend his crossing and, leaving one brigade to guard the ford, to move with the other two toward the railroad to become a reserve. Wood was ordered to stop his preparations for crossing.[40]

It was—said Rousseau—at nine o'clock that Thomas ordered him to take position "so as to resist the pressure on McCook." He moved into the dense cedars, on the right and rear of Sheridan, facing west—according to Thomas—"so as to support Sheridan, should he be able to hold his ground, or to cover him, should he be compelled to fall back." Already against the center of the Federal line—held by Negley and Sheridan—Polk was waging an attack of stern ferocity, for it was the purpose of the Confederates to throw the Union center back in front of McCown and Cleburne, now advancing northward, squarely across the original rear of Rosecrans's army.[41]

On the field of Perryville, Sheridan's star had risen. Here, near the banks of Stones River, it burned with much brilliance. Assault after assault was launched at the brigade of Colonel George Roberts, which formed Sheridan's left. Roberts threw back Coltart's brigade of Withers's division—this is from Polk's report—then Vaughan's from Cheatham's, then, probably with the help of Negley, the brigade of Manigault. Then Vaughan and Coltart, uniting forces, tried again. Before the heavy musketry and the close gunfire of the Federals, one-third of Vaughan's command went down. But Roberts was dead. His men—said Sheridan—gave no sign of faltering, but cried for more ammunition. Cartridges, however, were nearly gone, because wagons had been driven to safety from Wharton's eager horsemen. Schaefer's brigade had already expended its last round. Now Sheridan told it to fix bayonets and await the enemy. Leaving behind one battery and part of another because of the density of the woods, Sheridan withdrew. Schaefer's regiments, their ammunition replenished, supported by four guns that had been saved, were afterward in action on the Federal left. Roberts's men, emerging from the woods unbroken but with only a few rounds of ammunition, were met by McCook, taken to the west, and thrown into a timely charge. They drove back the enemy from too near the crucial pike, took some prisoners, and recaptured two guns.[42]

It was about eleven o'clock when Sheridan told Thomas that ammunition shortage was compelling him to withdraw. This made the retirement of Rousseau necessary, for the enemy began pressing into his rear. In falling back, the brigade of regular battalions—a perfect model of steadiness—came under a murderous fire that raised its casualties to more than a third of its numbers. A good position was found on high ground south of the pike, and there the three brigades took post, supported by two batteries of artillery. The withdrawal of Sheridan compelled the withdrawal of Negley, whose division had early been taken under heavy converging fire that passed over the attacking Confederate infantry. Negley's three batteries and two of Sheridan's had replied and had also poured destructive volleys into the advancing columns, which Negley said were "maddened to desperation by the determined resistance." In retiring, Negley had to drive the enemy from his path at the same time that he held back a column pressing his rear. But it was all done successfully, and Negley reported with his two brigades—less some guns left behind—to Thomas, who now had his command together.[43]

As Rosecrans formed his new battle line along the turnpike, at right angle to the position in the morning, it was imperative that its left should hold. If that gave way, all was lost. To the south of the pike was Palmer's division, Hazen's and Cruft's brigades in the front line, Grose's in support. Connecting with Hazen's left, at a point 500 yards northeast of the sharp crossing of the turnpike and railroad, was Wagner's brigade of Wood's division. By ten o'clock some of the enemy had worked around Negley's left, so that Grose had to be faced to the rear. Almost simultaneously Chalmers's brigade, supported by Donelson's, which were on Polk's extreme right reaching to the river, moved to the attack, coming over the crest in Hazen's front "at double-quick." Hazen knew how vital his position was. So did John M. Palmer—lawyer friend of Lincoln and a future governor of Illinois. To one battery commander Palmer gave a simple order, but adequate: "Fight where you can do the most good." By early afternoon two assaults had been repelled and the crucial left was still holding, though Cruft—who had done so well with green men at Richmond, Kentucky, had been forced to retire. But Grose, commanding Jacob Ammen's old brigade, was still in place. In defending Hazen's flank, Grose was to suffer more than twice Hazen's loss in killed. [44]

What about the rest of Crittenden's corps? Why could it not make the left certain beyond all doubt?

We have seen that one brigade of Van Cleve's division remained at the ford, while the other two were ordered to form a reserve, to be soon, however, placed upon the right. While inspecting the situation upon the left, Rosecrans gave orders directly to Harker and Hascall to move their brigades of Wood's division to the right. Harker made the move, though with much difficulty because of retreating columns and disorganized groups of men; Hascall was blocked. An aide from Palmer brought him word that unless help came, he would be compelled to give way. After consulting with Crittenden, Hascall sent the Third Kentucky. Soon his adjutant came back to say the regiment was already badly cut up and its colonel killed. It was one of those moments for a general. Hascall's decision was prompt and right: "I therefore moved at once, with the other three regiments of my command, to their relief." [45]

Upon Hascall's return, Wood placed him next to Hazen, which strengthened not only Hazen but Wagner, whose left reached toward the river. The fact that divisions came together at a very vital point was not to be a cause of weakness, for Hascall, a brigadier, gave unity by virtually taking control over Hazen and Grose, both colonels.[46] It was another decision which seems to have been of much importance.

Near the road leading out of aristocratic and warmly secessionist Murfreesboro, named in honor of a colonel in the Revolutionary War and onetime capital of the state, on whose streets carriages could be seen as fine as those in larger cities, were the headquarters of both Bragg and Polk, one just east of the river, the other a little to the west. Rosecrans's headquarters were also near the road, and only a mile northwest of where the fight for the left was taking place; and it was to that general region that the brigades from the right had retired. Thereabout trains had also sought safety, especially from Wharton's cavalry. Something like order had developed. In spite of spots of confusion along the road, Davis and Johnson got their divisions re-formed in fair manner along the road on the extreme right. Then came Harker's brigade, then Van Cleve's two brigades, then the pioneer brigade. In the interval between the pioneers and Palmer and Wood were Rousseau's division and some of Negley's. While Schaefer's brigade of Sheridan's division was with Palmer, the other two were on the right. Colonel Luther Bradley, commanding Sheridan's third brigade after Colonel Roberts and then Colonel Harrington had been killed, said it was about 1:00 P.M. when he stacked arms and supplied his men—four Illinois regiments—with ammunition, and that this was after he had helped Harker repel an attack.[47] The time may have been later, but surely there were yet usable hours of afternoon.

What of the cavalry?

Zahm's brigade—First, Third, and Fourth Ohio, reenforced by the Second East Tennessee from Stanley's reserve—had formed line of battle at daylight near where it had camped, not far, it would seem, to the west of Johnson's division. Learning of the catastrophe to the right, Zahm retired before Wharton's brigade and, being informed that all of McCook's ammunition train was near at hand, took the saving of it as his special task, while Wharton eyed it covetously. Zahm's own words have a quality rare in battle reports, and merit quoting:

At this juncture the First and Fourth retired pretty fast, the enemy in close pursuit after them, the Second East Tennessee having the lead of them all. Matters looked pretty blue now; the ammunition train was supposed to be gone up, when the Third charged upon the enemy, driving him back, capturing several prisoners, and recapturing a good many of our men, and saved the train. I was with the three regiments that skedaddled, and among the last to leave the field. Tried hard to rally them, but the panic was so great I could not do it.

Beyond Overall's Creek horses apparently tired and riders calmed. At last Zahm got his regiments under control, brought them back across the stream, joined the valiant Third, and repulsed several charges.[48]

When day broke, Stanley, chief of cavalry, was fifteen miles away, commanding a small brigade. Word came from Rosecrans at 9:30 to hasten to the right, while Minty, with the little force he had near La Vergne, also received orders from the army commander to report to Stanley. Kennett, commander of the cavalry division, was directed by Rosecrans in person to do what he could for the right flank with the odds and ends at his disposal. Captain Otis, commanding the unattached Fourth U.S. Cavalry, had, however, to content himself with an order from the chief of staff.

Stanley and Minty, ultimately joined by Kennett, fought with Wheeler's brigade not far from Overall's Creek, an engagement in which, according to Minty's report—the best from the Federals—the Confederates were ultimately bested. Wheeler denied this. On one occasion the chief of cavalry led a charge by three companies and captured a stand of colors. Otis in a charge by his six companies—in line of columns of fours—routed a sizable fraction of Wharton's brigade sometime in the morning. Then an order from Rosecrans sent him to the pike, the captain writing in his report, "have since thought that the general did not know my position, or he would have allowed me to follow up the enemy." [49] Certainly it was a strange day in cavalry command.

Bragg wrote that by two o'clock there was such a concentration of force in front of Hardee that he could advance no farther. The hour harmonizes fairly well with what Colonel Bradley set down, and also with Hardee's statement, if one understands that Hardee referred— as he naturally would—to a time subsequent to the last assaults that were roughly thrown back, mainly by Harker and Van Cleve. The extreme left of the Confederate line was now held by Cleburne, who had pushed the hardest over the difficult terrain; McCown had moved over to fill the space between him and Polk. Cleburne said that his men, who had had no rest the night before, who had been fighting since dawn without relief, food or water, and who had had very heavy casualties in their successive fights, were met by a fresh line of battle, "supported by a heavier and closer artillery fire" than he had yet encountered. That was precisely the situation. Not only were Cleburne and McCown held—they were pushed back beyond the high tide of their historic advance.[50]

But on the Federal left, it was Bragg who had fresh brigades—the five of Breckinridge. Hours had passed before they were put in action, largely because of Van Cleve's crossing of the river. Though not a diversionary move, but the initial step in Rosecrans's planned attack, it had worked well. Breckinridge said that Pegram, whose cavalry brigade covered the Confederate right, reported the Federals had crossed and were moving on his position in line of battle. Bragg stated that at about ten o'clock the report reached him that a heavy Federal force was advancing from the north on the Lebanon road, was only five miles away, and that he sent Pegram to develop what it was.

"These unfortunate misapprehensions"—wrote the Confederate commander—caused him to hold out of battle Breckinridge's division until Rosecrans had checked him on the left.[51] In contemplating how a couple of brigades of Breckinridge's division would have aided Hardee, one must recall that Rosecrans also kept the five regiments of one of Van Cleve's brigades as nothing but watchers over fords, merely because Breckinridge lay beyond that part of the river.

At length four brigades from Breckinridge's division were assigned to Polk to crush the defiant Federal left or, failing that, to compel Rosecrans to bring troops from the right, allowing Hardee to resume his advance upon the coveted road to Nashville.[52] But the successive attacks—furious though they were—were broken by troops already there, under superb tactical handling, good musketry, and grand artillery work. There were two main assaults, and it has been claimed that the action failed because it was piecemeal. Actually, however, there seems to have been room for no more than a two-brigade front, and how close one assault can follow another must always be a matter of dispute. A long interval favors the defender, but a short one can cause the second assault to become disorganized by men from the one that has failed.

Here is what Hazen wrote:

At about 4 p.m. the enemy again advanced upon my front in two lines. The battle had hushed, and the dreadful splendor of this advance can only be conceived, as all description must fall vastly short. His right was even with my left, and his left was lost in the distance. He advanced steadily, and, as it seemed, certainly to victory. I sent back all my remaining staff successively to ask for support, and braced up my own lines as perfectly as possible.

It must have been very comforting to learn that one of Sheridan's brigades was "but a few hundred yards in rear, replenishing their boxes." [53]

Rosecrans personally saw the breaking of the last assault upon the left. Garesché was killed by a cannonball while close beside him; and Colonel Frederick Schaefer—the last of the three brigade commanders with whom Sheridan had begun the day—was also killed. But the little "Round Forest," so earnestly desired by the enemy, was still in Federal hands, and Hazen could proudly say that his brigade "rested where it had fought, not a stone's throw from where it was posted in the morning." [54]

If the defense was heroic, so also was the attack, and some of the losses suffered in the vain efforts to secure the historic little woods were staggering. Prior to the final two attacks by Breckinridge, and after the initial one by Chalmers's brigade of Mississippians, Donelson had attacked with his five regiments of Tennesseans. Half of the men in the Sixteenth Tennessee were killed or wounded, while the toll in the Eighth was 306 men and officers out of 424. In addition to the fire of the batteries of the attacking brigade, the Federals had been pounded by the 10-gun battery advantageously placed on the hill beyond the river. But Federal guns countered them, leading Captain Robert Cobb to write: "During this day's engagement I had the misfortune to lose Corpl. J. F. Hawes, who had distinguished himself throughout by his courage and the great accuracy of his fire. He fell, while watching the effect of his shot." [55]

So rapid had been the enemy success upon Rosecrans's right, and so threatening the envelopment, that it is not strange that he became absorbed solely in arresting it. Unquestionably he did right in quickly stopping his own advance with the left; but one must ask whether there was not an opportunity for a heavy counterstroke upon the right, for as Hardee made his great swing and advanced northward, he badly exposed his left flank, and he had not so much as a single fresh regiment with which to protect it. Whether a general in a critical situation is able to think of giving blows as well as warding them off, is acknowledged to be one of the differences between a fair commander and one of distinction.

Although McCook's brigades had suffered losses, they had been successfully disengaged, and it would seem safe to say that eight of them were on the right by two o'clock. In addition, Walker's brigade of Thomas's corps arrived from Stewartsburg, was assigned to McCook, and was placed by him upon his left, at one o'clock.[56] While Rosecrans had nothing like a modern staff to canvass possibilities at once, he did have McCook. Few officers should ever have been more eager to make a counterstroke. At Perryville he had been broken when on the left; today he had been driven when on the right. Richard Johnson likewise now had a second disaster in his record; while Davis's retreat would hardly quiet criticism for his previously mentioned shooting of William Nelson. Sheridan had not started the day with a black mark against him, but he had been buffeted enough since morning to put him in fine fettle. Four regular officers these were—four men who were soldiers by profession.

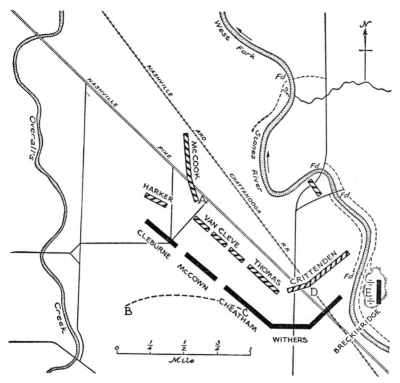

BATTLE OF STONES RIVER, DECEMBER 31, 1862, EVENING

Short troop symbols represent brigades. One of McCook's brigades was with Crittenden, but Harker's brigade belonged to Crittenden's corps, as did Van Cleve's division. A represents Rosecrans's headquarters; BC, the line to which the Confederates retired and fortified during the night; D, the Round Forest; E, a strong Confederate battery.

All that should have been necessary on Rosecrans's part would have been an order to McCook to reorganize his corps, not for defense but for attack, with directions to reconnoiter the enemy left for an opening and, if he found one, to strike. There is, however, no evidence that Rosecrans ever entertained such a thought or that McCook pressed him for a chance. The forward moves that Harker made, as well as Cleburne's report, seem to indicate that the chance was there.

That the enemy must be having difficulty with ammunition supply in a battle in which they had fought so much and advanced so far, over terrain where wagons would have trouble in following, should have been apparent.

Unquestionably Rosecrans's presence on the field was inspiring to many soldiers. Negley commended it in his report; Sheridan recalled it years later in his memoirs and spoke of Rosecrans's calmness. But Crittenden had a different story to tell the Buell Court of Inquiry. At Perryville he had not seen Buell, but he had since heard him both criticized and defended. On December 31 he had, however, frequently seen Rosecrans galloping about in "many directions," and he had since heard him "censured by a great many officers for his impetuosity," and for his great excitement during the battle. More telling perhaps was the statement, "I have heard him censured by commanders because they said they could not turn their backs on their commands without his ordering portions of them away." [57]

There are serious contradictions in the postwar statements about the conference or council of war that Rosecrans held that night, and it is impossible to say how strong was his impulse to retire, if indeed he seriously considered such a move, and how much he needed to be bolstered by his corps commanders. All that seems certain is that an order for the night said lines were to be pushed forward a mile if possible. Troops in the second line could have fires in the rear, and they were to rotate with those in the line of battle. It is doubtful if the order could be generally carried out because of the woods; before morning, Crittenden actually retired his line 500 yards. Troops were reunited, Harker to Wood, Schaefer's old brigade to the other two of Sheridan. Even before the issuance of Rosecrans's order at 7:00 P.M., Starkweather's brigade, which had been at Jefferson, had joined Rousseau, bringing back to the army an accumulation of stragglers.[58]

Though the road to Nashville was congested, Rosecrans should soon be receiving, if he had not already done so, an interesting message the Nashville chief of police had written the day before. One C. H. Hall and a Miss Collins, whom he had sent on the 26th to Murfreesboro by way of Lebanon, had just come back by way of Shelbyville. Bragg was claiming 60,000 men, well armed and clothed, the message said, but Major McConnico, "in personal conversation," had put the Confederate strength at only 40,000.[59] Miss Collins must have had the proper approach for the rebel major.

At three the next morning Colonel Samuel Beatty, who had succeeded to the command of Van Cleve's division because of the wounding of that officer (as Hascall had to that of Wood), was ordered to cross the river and hold the hill overlooking the ford, a move that was promptly carried out without enemy interference. On his part, Polk took over the Round Forest and its dead; except for pickets, it had been abandoned when Crittenden retired his lines, and the bishop-general could truthfully say "the opening of the new year found us masters of the field." Emboldened perhaps by this easy success, the Confederates repeatedly tried to advance on Thomas's front during the morning hours, but were driven back before emerging from the woods, the fresh brigade of Starkweather taking part in the rebuffs. A brigade that charged Sheridan's line about three o'clock in the afternoon was "handsomely repulsed." But in spite of such sallies and angry exchanges of artillery fire, the day was quiet, both sides being content to rest and eat whatever was available. The Confederates did some policing of the field, burned some wagons, and paroled many of the numerous prisoners they had taken, principally from McCook. Bragg's ever busy cavalry brought word that pleased that grim-visaged man: movements of well guarded trains indicated the Unionists had had enough and were retiring.[60]

In the terrific fighting of the 31st John Beatty had commanded a brigade in Rousseau's division. The region was not new to him, for he had been at Murfreesboro with Ormsby Mitchel's division the preceding spring. Some of his idle hours had then been spent musing about military life:

The army, for a temperate, cleanly, cheerful man, is, I have no doubt, the healthiest place in the world. The coarse fare provided by the government is the most wholesome that can be furnished. The boys oftenest on the sick list are those who are constantly running to the sutler's for gingerbread, sweetmeats; raisins, and nuts. They eat enormous quantities of this unwholesome stuff and lose appetite for more substantial food.

In his picture of the first night of 1863 Beatty complained of no appetites wrecked by a sutler's dainties. The thousands of men lying beside their guns were hungry. For himself there was a piece of raw pork and a few crackers in his pocket; and no food had ever tasted sweeter. Spirits were rising; all gloried in the obstinacy with which Rosecrans had clung to his position. Innumerable campfires began to glimmer; a few mounted men galloped up; from the picket line came occasional shots. Said Beatty, one of the many volunteer colonels now at the head of brigades, "The gloom has lifted, and I wrap myself in my blanket and lie down contentedly for the night." [61]

When day came Wheeler and Wharton, back only a few hours from heavy work, still insisted that the Federals were retiring. But Bragg saw no indications of it on his front, and at an unrecorded hour he summoned Breckinridge, who had reconnoitered Samuel Beatty's position east of the river, and directed him to drive the Federals back. Beatty commanded and enfiladed the right of Polk's new line, making his expulsion or the withdrawal of Polk a necessity—such was Bragg's explanation of his catastrophic order.[62]

During the morning Grose's brigade crossed to strengthen Beatty—it had been with him the day before but had gone back during the evening—and as Beatty saw enemy batteries and infantry moving into attack positions, he duly reported to Crittenden, and more troops were sent across the river. It was about four o'clock when Breckinridge launched his assault, with two brigades in the front line under Gideon Pillow (who had just reported for duty), and two in support—about 4,500 men in all. Soon the attacking line was under artillery fire that Breckinridge called "heavy, accurate, and destructive." But just as Pillow had had initial success in his effort to escape from Fort Donelson by throwing back Grant's right, so here he carried everything before him, driving Beatty across the river. Hazen, who presently arrived with his brigade, reported the situation under control, thanks to Grose and a part of Negley's division, with the help of artillery fire from Cruft's position west of the river. Hazen had been the amused witness of a double retreat: "It was difficult to say which was running away the more rapidly, the division of Van Cleve [Beatty] to the rear, or the enemy in the opposite direction." [63]

More should be said about the artillery fire than either Hazen or Breckinridge recorded, though the latter said there were enough guns "to sweep the whole position from the front, the left, and the right, and to render it wholly untenable." How they came to be where they were is an important part of the story, and it was told by Hoosier-born Captain John Mendenhall, eleven years out of West Point, and Crittenden's chief of artillery. At about four o'clock he and the general were riding along the pike, when heavy artillery and infantry

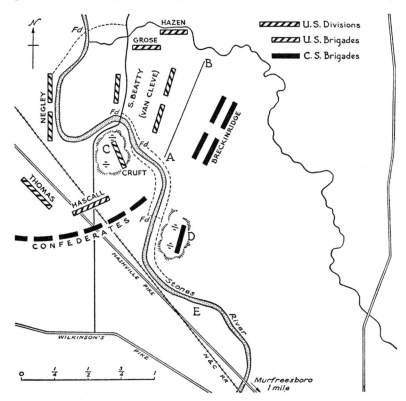

BATTLE OF STONES RIVER, JANUARY 2, 1863, AFTERNOON

Grose and Negley intervened when Breckinridge drove Beatty's division across the river, and the 58 guns that Mendenhall concentrated at C swept the field. Hazen arrived as the Confederates were retiring with heavy loss, and the divisions of Davis and Hascall took position along line AB about dark. D marks the position of a strong Confederate battery and E the headquarters of Polk and Bragg.

fire broke out to the left. Galloping quickly to the hill near the ford, they beheld the Federal infantry retiring. In these simple words Mendenhall described that crisis in the battle: "The general asked me if

I could not do something to relieve Colonel Beatty with my guns." [64]

One battery was already in action at the point. Others were not far off; they were quickly shifted; some, more remote, were called up. No one who has not known horse-drawn artillery can imagine what that hill was like in the waning hours of the winter afternoon. The guns that were too many for Breckinridge to count finally numbered 37 upon the hill, while near-by batteries raised the count to 58. Of course, the massive array of metal was a magnet for all enemy guns that could reach it. Cruft, whose men were in support, said that perhaps there had been no greater exhibition of "cool moral courage" in the war than that exhibited by his brigade as it lay quietly behind frail works, "with the shot and shell of the enemy coming from three directions and bursting above, in front of it, and all around it, while our own massed batteries were belching out their contents in front of and over it." Having expended his rhetoric, Charles Cruft wrote simply, "The roar of artillery was terrific." [65]

After an action of about an hour Mendenhall quieted his guns; it was almost dark, and friendly infantry was moving across the river. Samuel Beatty was happy to record that the colors of three of his discomfited regiments went back ahead of Davis's division, which Rosecrans had ordered over soon after the attack began. In their haste the Confederates abandoned three or four guns, and a new line they formed quickly withdrew when taken under fire by one of Davis's batteries. Night had closed in when Hascall formed on the left of Davis, firm masters of the field.[66] Two swift hours had brought a dramatic change and had shown that it is well for a general to keep a good artilleryman near his side.

Though the guns had swept the field, they could not hold it. It took the rifles and bayonets of the regiments of Davis and Hascall to do that. Crittenden wrote that Davis had sent a brigade to his assistance without orders and had requested permission of Rosecrans to follow with the rest of his division. Here was the desire to atone for retirement on the morning of the 31st that might have been utilized in the afternoon of that day. Johnson too was able to deal some blows, for his reserve brigade attacked effectively about five o'clock upon Palmer's request, after the withdrawal of Hascall had left an opening on the right of Cruft. Farther to the right Sheridan at 7:30 in the evening threw out Walker's brigade, which had been put under his command, on a reconnaissance which carried it a quarter of a mile to the front, where a half-hour brisk skirmish closed the day's activities.[67]

Bragg certainly blundered when he ordered Breckinridge to attack without considering the possibility of a concentration of enemy guns. At Shiloh he had seen Ruggles's great battery pound the hard-fighting Federals in the Hornets' Nest until 2,200 of them surrendered. He knew full well that the mighty array of guns that Grant assembled just beyond Dill's Branch had broken the attacks of Chalmers and Jackson by which he had hoped to gain the crucial Landing. And only two days before he gave the fateful order to Breckinridge he had seen the devastating power of Federal batteries. Infantryman John Beatty wrote in his diary that it was really the Union artillery that broke the last efforts of the Confederates to gain the road to Nashville in the final hours of Wednesday afternoon.[68]

Bragg should have known better. Bragg had himself been a proud U.S. artilleryman. When he threw in with the Confederacy the Union was not stripped of able gunners.

At three the next morning it began to rain heavily. Two hours later a welcome train of 303 wagons loaded with "commissary stores"— in plain words, food—arrived. It had left Nashville late the afternoon before under the protection of a reenforced brigade commanded by Brigadier General James G. Spears. Spears had headed one of George Morgan's brigades at Cumberland Gap, and two of his four regiments were the First and Second East Tennessee infantries. To the men who had made the very hard September march to Greenup on the Ohio, the advance toward Murfreesboro must have seemed a trifling matter. The brigade was turned over to McCook, who put it in line of battle on the right wing; the enemy being quiet, Spears's men "stacked arms and took refreshment." [69]

In a dispatch late on the 2nd a *New York Tribune* correspondent said: "To-morrow morning, however, the battle will be resumed. We now feel confident of ultimate victory." But the battle was not resumed; Rosecrans said that he did not advance because of nonarrival of ammunition. Skirmishing there was, however, Spears's newly arrived brigade being sufficiently involved for three of its regiments to report casualties, while Polk recaptured the Round Forest, from which his men had been driven late the afternoon before. Within less than ten miles of Nashville, the ammunition and hospital stores train which was being convoyed by a brigade under Colonel Daniel McCook was attacked by the persistent Wheeler, who on the 1st had struck unsuccessfully at empty wagons returning to the base. For a while the horseman thought he would be successful in his bid for a richer prize, and he reported he had actually captured the train when some blue infantry arrived, whereupon he was "obliged to retire." Zahm, who was present with the Third Ohio and two companies of the Fourth, was roundly praised by McCook "for his good judgment and dashing bravery during the fight." [70]

The long dispatch to Halleck that Rosecrans wrote at the close of the day and which concluded, "Further report by letter as soon as I can get an opportunity," was soon in print in the North. The story that it told of the battle could raise hopes for something decisive; but there was also in it a sentence that might erase them, "To-morrow, being Sunday, we shall probably not fight, unless attacked." [71]

Knowing from newspaper dispatches that a crucial battle was being fought, there was grave concern in the White House, in the Secretary's office, and at Army Headquarters. Nor was tension lessened by a telegram that had come to Stanton the day before from Governor Morton, which spoke of "great signs of trouble" in Indiana, such as he could not telegraph. He would use a letter. But on the 3rd the worried governor trusted his secret to the wires:

I am advised that it is contemplated when the Legislature meets in this State to pass a joint resolution acknowledging the Southern Confederacy, and urging the States of the Northwest to dissolve all constitutional relations with the New England States. The same thing is on foot in Illinois.

As Indiana had gone against the Republicans in the fall elections and had many disloyal cells, Morton was by no means merely imagining danger. From Springfield, Illinois, McClernand had, as early as November 10, written to Stanton of disaffection and had warned of the likelihood of "demagogical appeals designed to array the people of the West against the people of the East." [72]

On the night of the 3rd, while the ammunition train was arriving safely and Rosecrans was withdrawing his men through the cold waters of the rising river lest they be cut off, Bragg was retreating. About seven o'clock on the 4th Rosecrans learned the enemy had disappeared, and sometime during the day he directed Thomas to prepare his command "to pursue the enemy, starting at 7 o'clock in the morning." The railroad bridge had been saved, a dispatch to Halleck announced, and two brigades were just west of the river. Then caution appeared: "Will not, probably, be prudent to advance the army very far until communication shall be open to Nashville." [73] When a long wagon train had just covered the thirty miles, communication with Nashville was already open.

At 6:00 P.M. that day Wharton wrote to Cheatham from ten miles below Murfreesboro a dispatch that could hardly have raised hopeful expectations if it had been seen in Washington: "At 2:30 o'clock this afternoon the enemy were advancing upon Murfreesboro very slowly and with great caution. . . . You need feel no uneasiness, and your command can rest in perfect security. Your rear is well guarded. . . . I will advise you promptly of any movement of the enemy." Then the canny cavalryman said, "The above in regard to the enemy's advance on Murfreesborough is reported to me, but I don't believe it." [74]

The 5th was a day of many telegrams. Samuel Cooper queried Colonel Benjamin Ewell in Chattanooga where he got the news that Bragg had retreated, which he had sent the day before in cipher. From many sources, the colonel answered; besides, Bragg now had it on the wire himself. "God bless you, and all with you!" was one of three sentences Lincoln sent to Rosecrans. "The country is filled with admiration of the gallantry and heroic achievement of yourself and the officers and troops under your command, and we are anxiously waiting for further intelligence," was the ending of a message from Stanton. Good news came from Boyle: "I can send you from ten to fifteen regiments and two batteries. How shall I send them?" Three boats had reached Bowling Green with provisions. (No damage had been done to the railroad between there and Nashville.) "I can feed your army for a year, if necessary," said the happy Louisville general. "What glorious fighting you have done!" [75]

Graciously Rosecrans said in reply to Boyle the next day, "I thank you for prompt care of me and mine." A dispatch to Wright congratulated him on "the Carter expedition, and the final expulsion of John H. Morgan." After stating that captured officers put the Confederate loss at from 13,000 to 15,000, Rosecrans said: "I now wish to push them to the wall, but the pursuit will be heavy work. Send me what force you can spare, and take care of the railroad." A message to Halleck on the 8th reported the railroad would be completed into Murfreesboro within a few days and ended, "The Cumberland River is now navigable." Apparently the General in Chief had wanted to read Southern newspapers before fully believing Rosecrans's claims, his congratulatory message on the 9th beginning, "Rebel accounts fully confirm your telegrams from the battle-field." [76]

And Halleck would certainly have seen the full meaning of the dispatch that Bragg had sent to Cooper from Decherd on the 7th: "We shall hold line of Duck River, if possible. Our losses will reach 9,000; the enemy has not advanced from Murfreesborough." [77]

In the rocky meadows, the mucky fields where crops had grown, the woods and tangled thickets, thousands of men had fallen. The numbers engaged had been close to those in the first day at Shiloh, with Rosecrans's 1,730 killed exceeding Grant's by 200, while Bragg's 1,294 were only slightly more than two-thirds of the 1,730 Confederates who lost their lives upon the other field. There were 7,802 Federals wounded and 7,945 Confederates; in captured and missing the figures were 3,717 and about 2,500, respectively.[78] Total casualties on each side were thus close to 12,000, nearly one-third of those engaged. In few battles have there been losses of such relative magnitude.

Militarily the battle was indecisive, and it is probably true that Rosecrans had merely won by costly fighting a position he could have easily secured if he had moved resolutely from Nashville soon after McCook arrived on November 7. But the North was desperately in need of a victory after Burnside's tragedy at Fredericksburg, and when the news of Sherman's sharp repulse at Chickasaw Bluffs tardily arrived, it would fall less heavily because there had just been a success of arms.

There is something more. Rosecrans's army came largely from Ohio, Indiana, and Illinois, the three states where the Copperheads were most industrious. With sorrow widely spread and the determination of those who meant to see the war through mounting, the plotters for a time became more cautious. On the last day of January, Rosecrans published to his army a resolution of thanks passed by the general assembly of Ohio "for the glorious victory resulting in the capture of Murfreesborough and the defeat of the rebel forces in that place." Over the line in Indiana, Morton was having plenty of trouble with a hostile legislature; insolently the House returned his message and passed a resolution adopting that of the Democrat Governor of

New York. But with Mendenhall, Cruft, Grose, and others acclaimed even by those who mourned, it was not a time to be seditious. On February 15 Rosecrans was able to publish a resolution of the Indiana legislature that made the Ohio document look mild; the names of each fallen and surviving patriot soldier would be remembered "to the latest generation, as among the brightest jewels of an undivided republic." [79]

At the end of the next August, when Lincoln was highly dissatisfied with Rosecrans, he concluded a letter to him:

> I can never forget, while I remember anything, that at about the end of last year, and beginning of this, you gave us a hard victory which, had there been a defeat instead, the nation could scarely have lived over. Neither can I forget the check you so opportunely gave to a dangerous sentiment which was spreading in the North.[80]

If Jefferson Davis, against the advice of Joseph Johnston, had not sent Stevenson's division to Mississippi, while Bragg, with Johnston's hearty approbation, dispatched Forrest and Morgan on raids that really netted nothing,[81] the battle could not have been won by Rosecrans, and he probably would have been nearly destroyed the first day. But if Bragg had not been so depleted, it is doubtful if Rosecrans would have advanced upon him, and what would have happened is beyond conjecture.

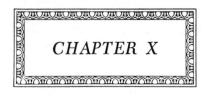

CHAPTER X

MEMPHIS INTERLUDE

> The work of taking Vicksburg will take time and men, but
> it can be accomplished.   *Grant to Halleck*

F OR A while there would be a respite from great battles. The papers
for the first month of 1863 were nonetheless heavily loaded with important war news. The story of Murfreesboro was soon received and
raised hopes in the North after Burnside's heavy defeat at Fredericksburg. Everyone could hail Bragg's retirement to Tullahoma as auspi-
cious and join in expecting that Rosecrans would press forward, even
as dispute went on over the Proclamation of Emancipation which
greeted 1863 as an actuality. But neither events in Tennessee and
elsewhere, nor political controversy, could keep thoughts away from
northern Mississippi and the great silent river below Memphis.

The first reports were that Sherman had been victorious, and the
cheering started by Rosecrans was revitalized. "Murfreesboro—Victory . . ." was the heading for a fresh account in the left column of
Henry Raymond's *New York Times* on Tuesday, January 6, while
the right column blazed forth: "Vicksburg—Victory . . ." Greeley's
Tribune and Bennett's *Herald,* as well as papers elsewhere, also announced a Federal success.

The headlines were built upon a sentence in a dispatch that Grant
had sent to Halleck from Holly Springs in early afternoon of January
4: "From rebel sources I learn that the *Grenada Appeal* says that
Yankees have got possession of Vicksburg." If an enemy paper near
the scene of action admitted defeat, it must be true, even though it
conflicted with a telegram that Pemberton had sent to his government

on December 30, claiming that Sherman had been heavily repulsed the day before, and which—reprinted from Richmond papers—had appeared in the North on January 5. Three days later the *Herald* suggested that possibly a false report had been put in the Grenada paper to keep Grant from sending reenforcements while more defenders were rushed into Vicksburg. The next day—January 9—Northern papers had Pemberton's conclusive dispatch of the 2nd. Still there was nothing directly from Sherman! A dispatch out of Cairo on the 8th gave the reason: a steamer just arrived had reported that a Confederate battery was preventing communication up the river.

Not until January 12 were dwindling hopes and specious reasoning finally crushed by a message from Cairo on the 11th: "An arrival to-night from the mouth of the Yazoo brings authentic accounts from Vicksburg. Gen. Sherman's repulse was complete." The troops, the dispatch continued, had been reembarked by the recently arrived McClernand and were on the way to Napoleon, at the mouth of the Arkansas. There was no effort to minimize the price of failure: 600 killed; 1,500 wounded; 1,000 missing—more than double the true count.

Bad news did not come singly. Simultaneously with the conclusive report of Sherman's failure, word was published of the Confederate recapture of Galveston on January 1. This would be associated in the public mind with the chances against Vicksburg, for one of Banks's first acts upon his arrival at New Orleans had been to send to Galveston—upon the urging of Farragut and Butler—part of a regiment (the rest of which, with a battery, was to follow) to make secure the position the navy had taken on October 5, 1862. The small force had landed on Christmas Day and had barricaded a wharf. When the three companies were captured a week later, it did not look as if Banks were beginning auspiciously, even though the real disgrace rested on the navy.[1]

Furthermore, January 11 had seen the appearance of a New Orleans story about the great strength of Port Hudson, on the Mississippi between New Orleans and Vicksburg. Thus when the news of Sherman's defeat arrived, it was known that Banks could probably only indirectly contribute to the taking of Vicksburg by compelling a division of enemy forces. On the 13th Bennett cheered his readers with the statement that a new Vicksburg attack had been decided upon; the precise spot had even been picked—"but its publicity has been strictly forbidden." Such an announcement, however, had to be weighed against Pemberton's dispatch of the 8th, copied at the same time from Richmond papers, which ended on a note of quiet yet firm determination: "Vicksburg is daily growing stronger. We intend to hold it." [2]

Missouri was also back on the front pages. This must have been both surprising and discouraging to many readers after the victory at Prairie Grove and the recent report that the aggressive Blunt-Herron team had executed a swift move over intervening mountains—where twelve horses had been needed on a gun while fifteen men pulled with drag ropes—to capture on December 28 the town of Van Buren, situated on the Arkansas River close to Indian Territory. Before returning to Prairie Grove the Federals destroyed four steamers, a ferry, and considerable scarce corn that Hindman had collected.[3]

But the "tricky rebel" who Herron said had been bearded in his den had on December 31 launched a cavalry stroke to destroy the Federal base at Springfield. The first reports of the blow struck on January 8 by Brigadier General John Sappington Marmaduke—Missouri-born and West Point graduate of 1857—were black. Better news soon followed, and on the 13th Greeley announced: "Springfield Not Lost—The Rebels Repulsed." A telegram from Curtis to Halleck on the 11th—which was promptly released to the press—ended, "The troops, including the enrolled militia, behaved nobly." A simultaneously published press dispatch sent from St. Louis on the 12th indicated that Marmaduke had afterward moved to strike Hartville—forty-five miles east of Springfield—but Curtis's statement that he had three columns heading for the enemy was sufficient to allay fears. Soon it would be learned that Marmaduke had started back to Arkansas and had been caught in rain that turned to snow.[4] Once again it looked as if operations against Vicksburg might proceed without distractions by the Confederates west of the Mississippi.

By the time that danger from Marmaduke had passed, Grant had been in Memphis for three days, after a week which had begun with uncertainty and ended with quick movements. The sentence in his dispatch that had brought the headlines that Vicksburg had been taken had actually been followed by a sentence indicating some doubt. Optimism, however, had conquered him before his telegram to Halleck the next day—January 5. Grant had had no news directly from

Sherman, but he had received word relayed by Gorman at Helena covering events through December 29. Sherman had had a terrible fight and, though he had achieved a measure of success, he had ultimately been forced to retire. But Grant did not accept this as final, for Gorman had said that before the boat bearing the news had left the Yazoo a fleet had been seen coming up the river. It must be Banks, and Grant said, "I am firm in the belief that news from the south that Vicksburg has fallen is correct." [5]

Two days later—January 7—Halleck had put on the wire a dispatch beginning: "Richmond papers of the 5th and 6th say that Sherman has been defeated and repulsed from Vicksburg." In a two-sentence reply that Grant sent at 3:00 A.M. of the 6th, he said, "I have had no reports to confirm statements of the Richmond papers." He would, however, send reenforcements to Sherman without delay. Halleck had said that every effort must be made to strengthen the river expedition, ending with the statement, "We must not fail in this if within human power to accomplish it."

Washington was not, Halleck explained, in communication with Banks, but his instructions were to lose no time in cooperating against Vicksburg. Already Curtis had been told to do all he could, and Grant must use everything possible from Tennessee. The 9th brought Grant a dispatch from Halleck that Wright was sending Ewing's brigade to Memphis—it had been intended for Rosecrans. Grant's answering telegram from La Grange at 9:00 P.M., that told how many men Sherman had and what he could send, ended, "I am on my way to Memphis to attend to all wants of the expedition." [6]

The move to Memphis would relieve the subsistence problem, which had been difficult since Van Dorn's raid. Shortage of rolling stock reduced the reopened railroad from Memphis to low efficiency, and cars could not be brought from Columbus until the damage done to the Mobile and Ohio Railroad by Forrest had been repaired. In a letter to Hurlbut at Memphis, Grant had said he meant to operate the railroad if he had to remove every family and every species of personal property between the Hatchie and Coldwater rivers to do it. Hurlbut was directed to announce that for every raid or attempted raid on the railroad by guerrillas, ten families of the most noted Secessionists would be sent south. There would be no such reprisals if the enemy attacked "with his regularly-organized forces." But guerrillas were being both encouraged and assisted by secessionist families, and the latter would pay heavily for sabotage. Grant's policy was clear: "I will make it the interest of the citizens to leave our lines of communications unmolested." [7]

Quinby, whose division had already moved over toward Memphis, had received similar instructions. This New Jersey-born classmate of Grant and former artilleryman, who had come back to the army after teaching for eight years at the University of Rochester (to which he would soon return for twenty more years of service after resigning because of illness), had reported another disturbing problem. Coming from Mississippi over the "Pigeon Roost road" was a continuous stream of wagons loaded with cotton, whose loads on their return trips contained all manner of supplies, in spite of the fact that their owners acknowledged disloyalty. Even a onetime professor of mathematics could see that that was wrong, and with a flourish of academic freedom Quinby had put a stop to it. [8]

It was Sullivan who had reported from Jackson on the 6th the news of Rosecrans's victory. In passing it on to Hamilton at La Grange, Grant had said that Van Dorn was probably going to Murfreesboro. In this he was anticipating, for a week passed before Van Dorn received a preparatory order about joining Bragg. Grant's feeling that Van Dorn would move eastward would lessen his concern about Corinth, where Dodge was to remain. A few days previously, a scout from Pontotoc had told him that Van Dorn had moved eastward, gathering up all the cavalry and Partisan Rangers. Thinking at that time that Corinth was the target, Grant had warned Dodge, "He evidently means mischief." Now Rosecrans's move, which had been expected earlier, might be expected to divide the enemy's attention. Furthermore, the rise in the Tennessee made it less likely that the Confederates would again cross the river, as Sullivan had actually reported they were doing. [9]

During the withdrawal the management of the southern front was in the capable hands of McPherson. Grierson was conducting the cavalry screen, and on the 7th McPherson sent him his final instructions from Holly Springs. Except for two battalions that were to search westward for enemy cavalry, which McPherson did not believe was in the strength reported, and patrols to the Tallahatchie, Grierson was to fall back to the Springs. The message ended, "Send one of your staff officers in advance and I will show him where you will camp." [10] That may look like a very minor matter. But it was a host of little things that made Grant value McPherson so highly, and a multitude of minor acts as well as his superb character that made McPherson's officers and men revere and trust him. The past four months had started him on his way to distinction, though he was yet to be tried by heavy battle.

Along with the army went a host of contrabands—men, women, children. On the 6th Grant had asked Halleck, "What will I do with surplus negroes?" As usual, he was trying to work out a solution himself, and he stated that he had authorized an Ohio philanthropist to take all the contrabands at Columbus, Kentucky, to Ohio at government expense. This statement he followed with a hint: he would like to dispose of some more in the same way. Though colonization by emancipated slaves had once been favored by Lincoln, he had not had in mind sending them in large numbers to any Northern state. So, just as Grant had been ordered to revoke his order expelling Jews, he was soon told to cancel his arrangement with the philanthropist, and no substitute scheme was given him. Later John Eaton would describe how he moved his army of contrabands first to Memphis and then to a camp below the city. Fearful that they would be left behind, the refugees crowded into cars and crouched upon roofs. The suffering that was inevitable because of lack of clothing was intensified by a fall of snow and delay in completion of the camp.[11]

Dodge's responsibilities were rounded out by the continuance of a refugee camp at Corinth.

Grant had arrived in Memphis on the morning of January 10. A letter to McClernand with that date began, "Since General Sherman left here I have been unable to learn anything official from the expedition which you now command. Your wants and requirements can only be guessed at." Reenforcements could be sent at once, but Grant wished to know what had been accomplished, and what had to be contended with, with an estimate of needs. At a time when rumors were probably plentiful and when exaggerated stories were afloat, he said with customary calm, "I would like to have a full report immediately for my guidance as to what is to be done." Dealing as he was with an insubordinate officer, one could almost wish that Grant had omitted the first word in a sentence in a later short dispatch. After explaining that no gunboats could be obtained from Cairo to convoy reenforcements, this message said, "Please request Admiral Porter, if practicable, to detach boats from his fleet for that purpose." [12]

With the letter to McClernand there went one to Porter. Grant was sending Colonel Bissell to make a survey to determine the practicability of reopening the canal across the tongue of land opposite Vicksburg that General Williams had futilely constructed the summer before. Bissell's Engineer Regiment of the West has been previously seen sawing trees below the surface of the water to allow light-draft steamers to bypass Confederate guns at Island No. 10, a feat which contributed much to Pope's operations against that very strong position. Although he had not yet had a personal look at Vicksburg, Grant was well posted about the peculiarities of the position and meant to lose no time in exploiting all possibilities. To the energetic admiral he said, "Any suggestions from you I would be most happy to receive." A look at a friendly, newsy letter that Porter had written to Admiral Foote on the 3rd would have been interesting to Grant. In it were the sentences: "McClernand has just arrived and will take command. Sherman, though, will have all the brains." [13]

The bearer of Grant's dispatches was Clinton B. Fisk, the brigadier who had slept in the old bed of Leonidas Polk at Columbus, when he had been sent there near the end of December to bolster Davies. The future held a distinguished career for Fisk; among other things he would be founder of a university and Prohibition candidate for President. But today he was merely an enthusiastic young general eager for glory. He had arrived the night before with a brigade from St. Louis, where he had been acquainted with Grant before the war. On this January 10 he had a long conference with Grant, according to a letter he wrote to Curtis while waiting for the preparation of Grant's dispatches. Fisk's statements confirm what is clearly implied by Grant's letters to both McClernand and Porter. Grant did not at this time intend to take personal command of the expedition, doubtless because of Halleck's statement that it was the President's wish that McClernand "have the immediate command." Said Fisk: "General McClernand is to command the down stream force. This arrangement causes much bitterness among us generals, who are all ambitious of doing brave deeds in opening the Mississippi. I am quite discouraged." [14]

The silence which had rested so heavily over the great river was broken the next day by the arrival of a startling letter of the 8th from McClernand. He was on his way for the mouth of the White River, which he would enter, then take the cut-off into the Arkansas, and ascend that stream for the purpose of reducing Arkansas Post, a well fortified position by which the Confederates hoped to block the river that led to Little Rock. After listing six reasons for his expedition, McClernand said, "I expect, after completing any operations undertaken in Arkansas, unless otherwise directed, to return with my command to a point on the Mississippi River near Vicksburg." Item one on his program after that was the seizure of Monroe, seventy miles west of Vicksburg.[15]

Although there was a hint that McClernand might prolong his stay up the Arkansas River after unblocking it, Little Rock was not mentioned. That place, however, was definitely announced as a possible objective in a letter he wrote the same day to Curtis, the decision whether he would go there being left to "circumstances yet undeveloped." Furthermore, Little Rock was set down as McClernand's objective in a letter that Gorman wrote to Curtis on the 10th. Gorman had been down the river where he had had "a personal conference with General Sherman, etc." Before speaking of his own projected move against De Valls Bluff on the White River, Gorman said, "General McClernand designs to go entirely up to Little Rock." [16]

One is happy to note that in Grant's prompt reply to McClernand's letter, the word "please" does not appear. As the operation against Arkansas Post has been a subject of some dispute, Grant's letter is given in its entirety:

General: Unless absolutely necessary for the object of your expedition you will abstain from all moves not connected with it.

I do not approve of your move on the Post of Arkansas while the other is in abeyance. It will lead to the loss of men without a result. So long as Arkansas cannot re-enforce the enemy east of the river we have no present interest in troubling them. It might answer for some of the purposes you suggest, but certainly not as a military movement looking to the accomplishment of the one great result, the capture of Vicksburg.

Unless you are acting under authority not derived from me keep your command where it can soonest be assembled for the renewal of the attack on Vicksburg.

Major-General Banks has orders from Washington to co-operate in the reduction of Vicksburg, and if not already off that place may be daily expected. You will therefore keep your forces well in hand at some point on the Mississippi River, where you can communicate with General Banks on his arrival. Should you learn, before you have an opportunity of communicating with him, that he is making an attack on Vicksburg, move at once to his support. Every effort must be directed to the reduction of that place.

From the best information I have, Milliken's Bend is the proper place for you to be, and unless there is some great reason of which I am not advised you will immediately proceed to that point and await the arrival of re-enforcements and General Banks's expedition, keeping me advised of your movements.[17]

Much of Grant's military philosophy is here clearly set forth, so that the letter transcends the question of Arkansas Post. It was, of course, no single incident but Grant's whole career that led C. F. Atkinson, distinguished British soldier and military writer, to his high opinion of the American general. But the appraisal Grant addressed on January 11, 1863, to McClernand gives good support to Atkinson's statement that Grant—in addition to courage that rose higher with each obstacle—had "the clear judgment to distinguish the essential from the minor issues of war." [18]

Because of a shortage of boats the dispatch to McClernand was not sent until the 13th, but at 3:30 P.M. of the 11th this telegram went to Halleck: "General McClernand has fallen back to White River, and gone on a wild-goose chase to the Post of Arkansas. I am ready to re-enforce, but must await further information before knowing what to do." [19]

Swift indeed was the reaction in Washington, and the next day Halleck telegraphed to Grant: "You are hereby authorized to relieve General McClernand from command of the expedition against Vicksburg, giving it to the next in rank or taking it yourself." [20]

Of course, the decision had been Lincoln's, and it is unfortunate that we do not know what was said at the meeting which must have taken place—one of the most important in the war. Could it be that the letter McClernand had written from Memphis on December 29 had been so revealing that Lincoln was prepared for prompt action and was glad to take it? He certainly should have been disturbed by the way McClernand had gone up the Arkansas River after he had so stressed the importance of taking Vicksburg and had pleaded for the chance to do it.

Before the General in Chief's message had arrived, Grant had received an encouraging and thoughtful dispatch from Curtis, quoting one he had sent on the 11th to Gorman, bidding that officer to regard the Vicksburg operation as primary, other movements being delayed if necessary. Boats and men were to be furnished for the main object, subject only to the restriction that his base should not be weakened to the danger point. Grant passed the message to Gorman with the request that every available man be sent to McClernand, "keeping in view the safety of Helena." Five days before this, Grant had queried Halleck from Holly Springs as to whether Helena was in his department.[21] As matters were working out, it made little difference, though all doubts were presently removed by a definite order.

Good news also came to Grant from Sullivan, who had made the front pages of the great dailies because of the engagement his troops had fought with Forrest at Red Mound. Sullivan had driven Richardson—a colonel of Partisan Rangers—across the Hatchie and had captured some of his men. To Dodge the Jackson commander reported more fully and said, "I can hear of no band of guerrillas in my district." Then Sullivan showed how well imbued he was with the spirit of cooperation by telling Dodge that three regiments Grant had left with him could go to Corinth if needed. While awaiting his reply from Halleck, Grant could feel that the region behind him was in good hands. On the 11th he made a change of commanders at Columbus, replacing Davies by Alexander Asboth, recently on duty at Memphis and previously seen at the Battle of Pea Ridge.[22]

At Arkansas Post McClernand achieved success swiftly and decisively. Disembarkation began late in the afternoon of the 9th at a point some three miles below the position, and in spite of heavy rain during the night it was completed by noon the next day. The objective—Fort Hindman—was advantageously situated at a U-bend in the river near the village of Post Arkansas—founded by the French in 1685—and on ground high enough to be above flood waters. While its guns could fire effectively on vessels ascending the river and on any that had rounded the bend and passed above, there were only three heavy pieces, of 8-inch and 9-inch caliber, the balance of the armament consisting of four 3-inch rifled guns and four smooth-bore 6-pounders. A former naval officer of the United States, Colonel John W. Dunnington, was in command of the fort, while the mobile force—

about 5,000 strong—that was to garrison rifle pits and serve the six field pieces, were under Brigadier General Thomas J. Churchill. From McClernand's landing point a good road ran along the river, joining near the fort the road to Little Rock, 117 miles distant, the road crossing to the other side of the river at a ferry a few miles away. Swampy lands made impracticable a route that led to points above the fort, a fact that Steele's division learned the hard way on the afternoon of the 10th.[23]

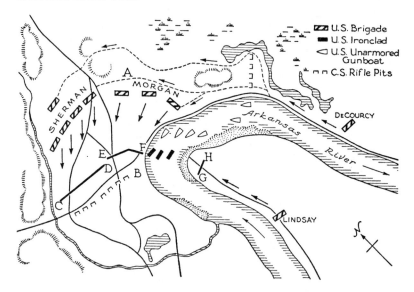

BATTLE OF ARKANSAS POST, JANUARY 11, 1862

A, Headquarters of McClernand, Federal commander; B, Fort Hindman, Confederate; CD, EF, and GH, positions to which the Federals had advanced at the time of the Confederate capitulation. Naval fire had driven the Confederates from the eastern rifle pits on the 10th. Cantonments of log huts were in the region where Sherman deployed.

As the army started forward, Porter sent the *Louisville, De Kalb,* and *Cincinnati* to engage the fort. In describing the action, Mahan said, "The vessels fought bows on, three guns each; the odds being thus three guns afloat to one in casemate on shore, leaving the advantage by the old calculation, four to one, rather with the fort, without counting the light field pieces in the latter." The hostile guns, however, were situated relatively low, as at Fort Henry, where the gunboats won, not high, as at Donelson, where they lost. Being able to reach their targets, the Federal guns were very effective. With the engagement well under way at a range of four hundred yards, Porter brought up his light boats, *Black Hawk*—flying his flag—*Lexington,* and *Rattler,* to throw shrapnel and light shell. After the enemy fire had slackened and the *Rattler* had driven some infantry from their rifle pits, she was sent past the fort to do some enfilading, suffering considerably in the passage and finally becoming so entangled with snags that she returned below and spent the night with the rest of the fleet.[24]

While the sailors were comfortable as they waited for another day, the soldiers were not, Sherman noting that those of his troops who had reached their positions "bivouacked without fires through that bitter night," listening to the busy axes of the enemy and the crash of falling trees intended to bar their advance. When the moon rose at 1:00 A.M. Sherman went on a reconnaissance and showed Stuart where to put a battery and observed Steele's division, back from its futile struggles in the swamp, moving to its position on the right of Stuart. On Sherman's left, reaching to the river, was George Morgan with his two-division corps, which with Sherman's composed what McClernand had christened the Army of the Mississippi. De Courcy's brigade—which had suffered badly in the assault of December 29—was guarding boats, while that of Colonel Daniel Lindsey had been put ashore on the right bank with the mission of harassing the enemy from a position across from the fort.[25]

At noon on the 11th McClernand notified Porter that the army was ready to push an attack; thereupon the ironclads steamed back to engage the fort. In the second attack, the ram *Monarch,* Colonel Charles Rivers Ellet commanding, followed the gunboats "with instructions to take the lead if a rebel ram appeared." (Since their experience with the *Arkansas,* the Federal sailors looked on all rivers with suspicion.) At 4:00 P.M. the guns of the fort fell silent and the *Monarch* was sent up the river to cut off the retreat of the enemy. Being equipped with guns—which the first rams did not carry—she shelled the woods and at several points drove groups of Confederates from the riverbanks. Twelve miles up, after grounding four times, she found the water too shallow to continue. Upon her return the *Glide* went upstream and destroyed the ferry.[26]

When the gunboat fire was heard about 1:00 P.M., Sherman's and

Morgan's guns joined the cannonade, as those of Lindsey soon did from a position that enfiladed the Confederate infantry. A Wisconsin battery commander in Lindsey's force reported that "every shell burst, and just at the right point." While supervising the advance of his own men, Sherman's ear—that of a onetime field artilleryman—was tuned to the navy guns, whose fire he said was at first slow and steady, then increasing in rapidity as the fort was approached. Though relatively few in numbers compared with the attackers, the Confederates were in trenches and their fire was so sharp that on the request of one of Sherman's staff officers, Morgan sent Sherman three regiments.

In his report Morgan wrote, "Several times, at different parts of the field, unauthorized white flags were run up and torn down again by the enemy." Finally, after Sherman had advanced his line to within 100 yards of the enemy and had the Confederate left enveloped, and the fort had ceased its fire, and Porter's flag could be seen directly beneath it, Sherman saw a large white flag at the point where the main road ran into the Confederate works. This was official. In his report Sherman wrote: "The enemy resisted well and manfully to [on] our front, but his resistance was idle after the reduction of the fort, in the face of our greatly superior numbers. Of course, immediately on the display of the white flag our lines and columns poured into the works with cheers and hallooing." To his brother he indicated that after the navy had done its work, the task of the army was easy.[27]

Porter was well satisfied, claiming the victory for the navy in a message to Pennock that ended, "This was a most beautiful fight." With a touch of pride for the service which he graced as an eminent student of his profession, Mahan stated: "It was impossible that the work of the navy could be done more thoroughly than in this instance." [28]

McClernand's casualties numbered 1,032 (134 killed and 898 wounded) while those of the sheltered Confederates amounted to but 109. Some 30 gunboatmen were killed or wounded. Fruits of victory were considerable: ordnance, stores of various kinds, 4,701 prisoners. Though now himself a land-fighter, Dunnington still had a preference for seafaring men, and requested Porter to come ashore so that he could surrender to a sailor; with him went 36 men of the Confederate Navy. To Gideon Welles, Porter wrote that captured Confederates had told him, "You can't expect men to stand up against the fire of those gunboats"; he also proudly reported: "The *Cincinnati* was

MAJOR GENERAL GEORGE H. THOMAS

MAJOR GENERAL ALEXANDER McD. McCOOK

MAJOR GENERAL WILLIAM S. ROSECRANS

BRIGADIER GENERAL JOHN A. RAWLINS

Courtesy Library of Congress

BRIGADIER GENERAL BENJAMIN H. GRIERSON

struck eight times on her pilot house with IX-inch shells, which glanced off like peas against glass." [29]

Far more modest than the force with which McClernand had engulfed the enemy had been the 6,000 infantry and 2,000 cavalry with which Hovey had left Helena in November for the purpose of taking Arkansas Post. Stopped by low water in the White River, he was preparing to move overland when a dispatch arrived bidding him return because other uses for his men were contemplated. In his report he said, "I deeply regret that we could not have been permitted to consummate our plans, as I feel confident that we should have captured the Post, with a large number of prisoners and stores." While not the responsible commander on January 11, Hovey was present with his six-regiment brigade, and Sherman stated that he did some of the most stubborn fighting, and that his "difficulties were increased by the blind character of the ground, every foot of which he had to study as he advanced under a galling fire." Though wounded in the arm by a shell, Hovey did not relinquish command, and was still directing his brigade when the admiring Sherman wrote his report on the 13th.[30] All this gives some color to the belief that Hovey had not written idly on November 22.

Why, one can ask, did not Churchill abandon the position and save his command when he saw the Federals had an overwhelming force? The answer is that he had a specific order to stay, having received on the night of the 10th, when evacuation was still possible, a telegraphic order from Holmes "to hold out till help arrived or until all dead." In his indorsement on Churchill's report, Holmes characterized his own order as hasty and approved of the capitulation. Then he fired a well-aimed shot: "It never occurred to me when the order was issued that such an overpowering command would be devoted to an end so trivial." [31]

On the day of his success McClernand reported briefly to Grant, giving Porter his full share of credit for the victory. Received by Grant on the 13th, the dispatch was forwarded at once to Washington. During the short interval since he had written to McClernand, some knowledge about the great strength of Port Hudson must have reached Grant, for in replying to McClernand's message of the 11th he alluded to it when referring to Banks, and added, "Should he get past that place, however, it is our duty to be prepared to cooperate." An additional brigade, Grant stated, was going down the river simultaneously with his dispatch; two divisions could follow as soon as there was transportation. That Halleck's dispatch of the 12th had arrived was indicated by the first sentence in a telegram to McPherson—sent before receipt of McClernand's victory message—"It is my present intention to command the expedition down the river in person." [32]

Midnight had just passed when Grant telegraphed to Halleck that a special messenger sent to the fleet had reported it would be fifteen days before they could act efficiently again. He had hoped to get off early the next week—which would begin on the 18th—but would have to delay while preparations were made. In the interim he would go down the river to take a look for himself. McClernand, he thought, was moving on De Valls Bluff. But orders had been sent him to concentrate on the Mississippi to cooperate with any force coming up the river.[33]

Grant was incorrect in thinking that McClernand was considering a stroke against strategic De Valls Bluff, whence a railroad ran from the White River to Little Rock. But he was right in believing that McClernand had been wishing for easy additional conquests before returning to the Mississippi, for later on January 14 McClernand would say in a dispatch to him, "I would sail from here to Little Rock and reduce that place but for want of sufficient water in the channel of the Arkansas River." Within a matter of hours Grant's dispatch of the 10th—the one which had asked merely for information—was in his hands, and in answering McClernand said he would return immediately to the Mississippi and with as little delay as possible go to Milliken's Bend, unless otherwise ordered. In a dispatch to Gorman on the 14th he stated, however, that he would delay a day or two in executing Grant's order "in order to threaten Little Rock and Pine Bluff as a diversion in your favor." Of course, McClernand did not know that two days previously Grant had forwarded to Gorman, Curtis's order to stop his projected operation. That directive had not arrived in time, and Gorman actually ascended the White River 217 miles to Des Arc, making a capture of men and some new British Enfield rifles, as well as destroying equipment and facilities. Grant, on his part, when contemplating what McClernand might do, did not know that in the preceding June, McClernand had earnestly besought Lincoln to give him an independent command not only in the part of

Arkansas south of the river of that name, but in western Louisiana and Texas.[34]

When Grant's dispatches of the 11th and 13th reached McClernand on the 16th, he reacted violently. In his letter to Grant there was a hit at Sherman in the statement that if Port Hudson was strong, Banks would be some time in reaching Vicksburg to cooperate with the Mississippi expedition "unless he should prove more successful than the latter." When he said he would consider that he had been guilty of a great crime if he had remained idle at Milliken's Bend, he forgot that he had listed several projects he would undertake when he got back to that place. A copy of the letter went to Lincoln and in his covering communication McClernand said, "I believe my success here is gall and wormwood to the clique of West Pointers who have been persecuting me for months." He asked the President not to let him "be clandestinely destroyed, or, what is worse, dishonored without a hearing." After inquiring how Grant could intelligently command the army when 400 miles away, he answered his own question, then advised and mildly admonished the President: "He cannot do it. It should be made an independent command, as both you and the Secretary of War, as I believe, originally intended." [35] It would seem that the President had no right to change his mind, if, instead of having been merely ambiguous, he had actually meant to make McClernand free of all control.

From La Grange, McPherson was writing very differently to Grant than the angered conqueror of Post Arkansas. As soon as he got Logan's division on the march, he would leave. Roads were horrible, but Logan and his men were keen to reach Memphis and go down the river. Word had come to McPherson that he too was going, and he said to his chief, "I cannot express to you the gratification it gives me, and I shall most assuredly do my utmost to merit your confidence." [36]

The next day another soldier sent Grant a letter—Sherman. He wrote "direct, semi-officially," almost as a pupil to a teacher. He defended the move against Arkansas Post, having judged from a remark made by McClernand that Grant had disapproved of it. Sherman stressed the claim that its capture would prevent the recurrence of an incident like the capture of the *Red Wing,* which had been bringing him artillery ammunition, driving home the point with the statement, "I assure you when next at Vicksburg I will feel much less uneasiness about our communications." Of course, Sherman was not aware that Hurlbut believed that the *Red Wing* had been deliberately surrendered, and it is not clear how a fort fifty miles up the Arkansas threatened anything. After saying that he wished Grant would come and look matters over, Sherman added, "I only fear that McClernand may attempt impossibilities." Federal soldiers received a criticism when Sherman followed his statement about bringing picks, axes, and spades with the explanation: "We built batteries at Yazoo and up at the Post, and you know how details of our careless men neglect tools." Much was packed in the last sentence, which must have touched Grant: "An attack on Vicksburg will surely draw thither the Grenada force, so that I think you might safely join us and direct our movements." [37]

The letter made Grant feel differently about the Arkansas Post operation, though Sherman did not tell him that it had been he who had suggested it to Porter as a useful activity while they waited for Banks.[38] Quite aside from whether it really made the operation against Vicksburg more secure, was the good effect it had on Northern morale after the defeat at Chickasaw Bluffs. The capture of 5,000 men was a cheering matter.

Even while Sherman was urging him to come and take a look Grant was planning to do so. At 4:30 in the afternoon of the same day—January 17—he telegraphed to Halleck: "I start immediately to the fleet." Affairs at the great base would not lag during his short absence; reenforcements would "be forwarded with all dispatch." [39]

As companions on his visit Grant took Rawlins and James H. Wilson, the latter being the only regular officer then on his staff. Years later Wilson would write that on the trip everything in connection with the operation was fully discussed, including the fundamental topic of the policy of the government for this theater of war. "Grant," he said, "without the slightest show of reserve, took the lead in the conversation and showed an active interest in all that was said. Without showing the slightest reserve he treated Rawlins and myself as equals, and encouraged us to express ourselves with the utmost freedom." [40] The boat ride must have been a relaxation; not for months had Grant been in a place where at any moment some disturbing news might not arrive that required quick decision.

On this occasion, however, Grant did not see the spires of Vicksburg, the hills with guns immune from effective naval fire, or the waters coming out of the baffling, tricky Yazoo. He went only to Napoleon, the small town which had been badly damaged on the 17th by a fire that caused Sherman to write that he was "free to admit we all deserve to be killed unless we can produce a state of discipline when such disgraceful acts cannot be committed unpunished." After conferring with McClernand, Sherman, and Porter, Grant was back in Memphis on the night of the 19th, even before the forwarding from there of a short dispatch to Halleck that he had written while off Napoleon on the 18th. In view of what lay ahead, the last of its three sentences is important: "What may be necessary to reduce the place [Vicksburg] I do not yet know, but since the late rains think our troops must get below the city to be used effectively." [41]

In the long report to Halleck that Grant wrote on the 20th he spoke of the "intolerable rains" which had so filled swamps and bayous that they would not dry up during the winter. Were it not for that, roads might be constructed through to the Yazoo above the raft that blocked the stream under the guns at Haynes Bluff. If this could be done the enemy could be "compelled to come out and give us an open field fight, or submit to having all his communications cut and be left to starve out." Grant was intending to dig a canal so as to get below the city, but not where it had been started the preceding summer, for the mouth of that one was in an eddy; the river would not accommodatingly wash it into a good channel. Besides, the canal's lower end was under gunfire.

Grant took up a question for which Wilson afterward claimed credit, introducing it by saying he would not make unrequested suggestions if Halleck were present to see matters for himself. A demonstration by the enemy into his old district of West Tennessee might force him to withdraw a large part of his Vicksburg force; therefore he respectfully asked if it would not be policy to combine the four departments in the West (those of Banks, Rosecrans, Curtis, and himself) under a single commander. Forgetting that Banks had been made a major general nine months before himself, Grant said, "As I am senior department commander in the West, I will state that I have no desire whatever for such combined command, but would prefer the command I now have to any other that can be given."

What Grant said concerning McClernand should be seen precisely as he wrote it:

I regard it as my duty to state that I found there was not sufficient confidence felt in General McClernand as a commander, either by the Army or Navy, to insure him success. Of course, all would co-operate to the best of their ability, but still with a distrust. This is a matter I made no inquiries about, but it was forced upon me. As it is my intention to command in person, unless otherwise directed, there is no special necessity of mentioning this matter; but I want you to know that others besides myself agree in the necessity of the course I had already determined upon pursuing. Admiral Porter told me that he had written freely to the Secretary of the Navy, with the request that what he said might be shown to the Secretary of War.[42]

Essential matters were condensed into a telegram. The expedition had been started down the river from the mouth of the Arkansas. A canal would be at once surveyed and begun, but the weather was unfavorable and rivers were rising. Gorman, with needed transportation, was not yet back from up the White River. Two sentences there were for the High Command to ponder, one tucked into the middle of the message: "The work of reducing Vicksburg will take time and men, but can be accomplished," and the final one, which merely repeated what Grant—unknown to Wilson—had said two months before: "Both banks of the Mississippi should be under one commander, at least during present operations." [43]

The response to the last sentence was immediate, and a telegram that Halleck put on the wire the next day began, "The President has directed that so much of Arkansas as you may desire to control be temporarily attached to your department. This will give you control of both banks of the river." But the General in Chief now said not to count too much upon direct help from Banks; he might not be able to pass or reduce Port Hudson.[44]

On the 23rd Curtis wrote cordially, expressing his best wishes for Grant's success. He knew of course that Grant would take over Helena, and he had but one concern: "If Holmes and Hindman mass all their forces this side of the Arkansas River they may give me trouble, but I hope you will close out Vicksburg before they can do much and return to my command all the force necessary to clean out Arkansas." Gorman wrote about his accomplishments up the White River; he also brought Grant up to date on his old friend of Cairo days M. Jeff Thompson.[45]

Stanton, however, was muddying the water. Not until this day—

January 24—did he answer the long letter that McClernand had written to him on the 3rd. While most of what he said was guarded and evasive, the ending was, "I shall be happy to hear from you fully whenever it is convenient for you to write, and shall be glad to contribute to your success." [46]

Lincoln, too, emerged from the shadows and stepped clearly into the picture. Familiar as he was with the channel-changing habit of the Mississippi, he thought a little help might be all that was needed to cause the river itself to solve the Vicksburg problem, so Halleck telegraphed to Grant on the 25th: "Direct your attention particularly to the canal proposed across the point. The President attaches much importance to this." The message passed one from Grant that said, "I leave for the fleet at Vicksburg to-morrow." Work at the base, however, kept him in Memphis until the 27th, and a new dispatch began in a way that doubtless brought satisfaction in the White House: "News just received from Vicksburg says water in old canal, and rising rapidly." [47]

CHAPTER XI

WINTER IN THE BAYOUS

The eyes and hopes of the whole country are now directed to
your army.
Halleck to Grant

M<small>CCLERNAND</small> quickly challenged Grant's authority to take personal
command. A letter written on January 30 began by denouncing "as
an act of insubordination" a complaint which one of his officers had
made directly to Grant. Then, after lecturing Grant a little, he
launched into the more fundamental question with the words: "And,
having said this much, general, it is proper that I should add one or
two other words." Grant was, McClernand understood, giving orders
directly to corps commanders. Inasmuch as an order by the Secretary
of War, indorsed by the President, had put him in command of all
forces operating on the Mississippi River, all orders for those forces
should pass through his headquarters, or there would be confusion.
If Grant thought differently, the matter should be referred to Washington. "One thing is certain," McClernand concluded, "two generals
cannot command this army, issuing independent and direct orders to
subordinate officers, and the public service be promoted." [1]

The letter caused Grant to issue the same day a formal order
assuming command, and assigning to the "Thirteenth Army Corps,
Maj. Gen. J. A. McClernand commanding," the mission of garrisoning
Helena and points south thereof on the west bank of the river. Before
the 30th had ended Grant had received a long communication from
his irate subordinate, quoting the Washington instructions of October

21 and December 18, and complaining of the task assigned the Thirteenth Corps in the new order.

In his reply the next day Grant said that instead of weakening the Thirteenth Corps by the assignment he had given it, he was strengthening it by 7,000 men, not including the garrison at Helena. All forces and garrisons belonging to the corps would be under McClernand's orders, "subject, of course, to directions from these headquarters." After explaining that he would obey every order of the President, Grant informed McClernand of the dispatch he had received from Halleck subsequent to the orders upon which McClernand was resting his claim. He had not intended at first to publish an order taking command, but it had soon become apparent that it would be much more convenient to issue orders directly to corps commanders while he was present than have them go through someone else.

In an answer dated February 1 McClernand said he acquiesced to Grant's order "for the purpose of avoiding a conflict of authority in the presence of the enemy," but he still protested "against its competency and justice," and he asked that papers be forwarded to the General in Chief and through him to the Secretary of War and the President, concluding with the statement, "I request this, not only in respect for the President and Secretary, under whose express authority I claim the right to command the expedition, but in justice to myself as its author and actual promoter."

Also on February 1 Grant sent a copy of his order and the exchange of letters it had provoked to Halleck's chief of staff. In the accompanying letter he said that if Sherman had been left in command, he would not have thought his personal presence was necessary. But he did not believe McClernand's ability as a soldier was sufficient to conduct "an expedition of the magnitude of this one successfully." There was no doubt in his mind that the same opinion was held by a majority of the officers in the expedition, though he had "not questioned one of them on the subject." He respectfully submitted the entire matter to the General in Chief and the President with the assurance that he would obey cheerfully any decision "and give a hearty support." [2]

McClernand did not let the matter rest with a request that Grant forward the papers to Washington. On the day when Grant was writing to Halleck's chief of staff McClernand was writing to the President, and inclosing a copy of his second letter to Grant of the

30th. He said, "Please cause it to be signified to me whether Genl Grant or myself will have *immediate* command of the Miss. river Expedition." The old canal was a failure, and he doubted whether it could be made useful. After saying that nothing reliable had been heard from Banks, he outlined what his plan of operations would be. In a second letter to the President the next day, McClernand had a new idea, as set forth in one he had addressed to Grant on the 1st, a copy of which he inclosed. In this letter he predicted that the rising river would drive all forces to the transports, and he asked permission to make an extensive campaign with his corps into Arkansas. Among other things, if the expedition moved swiftly, it might be possible to capture some transports "said to be at Arkadelphia." Then he could sail down the Ouachita and Red Rivers to the Mississippi and join the forces of Banks. The body of the letter addressed to Lincoln was written by a clerk, but above the signature, in McClernand's hand, is the sentence, "Sickness, including small pox, prevails in the camp." [3]

If the Yazoo River was one of nature's curiosities, so was John McClernand. Apparently the President did not favor him with a reply. On his part, Grant treated McClernand's challenge only briefly in his *Memoirs,* but he put much into the statement that McClernand's correspondence "was more in the nature of a reprimand than a protest." Unequivocally he labeled it "highly insubordinate," adding that he overlooked it for what he believed to be the good of the service.[4] That McClernand would write directly to the President, after requesting him to refer the issue in the proper way, could hardly have occurred to Grant.

When McClernand steamed north on January 4 against Arkansas Post, Porter had left behind a small force, the senior officer being enjoined to "watch this river." Though the boats remaining served notice that the Federals might return, the Confederates had a good opportunity to take stock of men and supplies and to put matters in order. On the 6th Joe Johnston, still in Jackson, Mississippi, told Pemberton to send a messenger into Arkansas to learn if cooperative moves were being made in that state. He had written to Jefferson Davis on the 2nd that if Grant should join Sherman at Vicksburg, it would be very embarrassing. He felt certain that the 20,000 men that Davis had asked Holmes to send while Davis was on his Vicksburg visit would not be received, yet that number of men was required if he were to "make headway against both Grant and Sherman." He asked if Lee's great victory at Fredericksburg would not make it possible to spare some men from the East. If the Federal forces were respectably handled, the task assigned him would be above his ability. But Almighty God had "delivered" the Confederates in times of danger just as great. Believing Him on their side, Johnston assured the President he would not lose hope.[5]

In due time Johnston would receive a letter Holmes had written on the day of Sherman's final repulse at Chickasaw Bluffs, in answer to the appeal by Davis to send troops to Vicksburg. In spite of his repeated efforts, Holmes said the War Department seemed unable to correct erroneous beliefs as to his strength. At no time had there been over 22,000 effective men in Arkansas, including several Indian regiments upon which no reliance could be placed. Sickness, desertion, and battle had reduced his force to but little more than 16,000, exclusive of troops in fortifications. After the Confederate defeat at Prairie Grove he had been in hopes that the barren condition of the northwest section of the state would stay the Federal advance, but only the day before he had learned that the Blue Coats were moving on Van Buren and were only twenty miles from the Arkansas River (the Blunt–Herron operation previously mentioned). While Hindman's force, reduced by illness and battle to about 10,000, was safe on the south side of the Arkansas River, Holmes urged that it would not be prudent to strip the country "of its only means of defense, thereby allowing the enemy to overrun the State and win a wavering people from their loyalty to us by the seductive promises of peace and protection." In any case it was doubtful if men sent to Vicksburg would arrive in time. While this point had been invalidated to a large degree by Sherman's defeat, the loss of Arkansas Post would soon inject a new element into the situation. Not without reason could Holmes believe early in January that the Vicksburg garrison had proved its adequacy and that he himself had become the Federal target. If he had had a column marching to augment the 18,000 effectives in and about Vicksburg, he would probably have halted it.[6]

Matching Holmes's fear of the effect on a wavering population of Federal promises of peace and protection was Pemberton's concern about the morale of the people of Mississippi. When Davis had visited Vicksburg he had spoken to Pemberton of the harmful influence of government contracts with Southerners to obtain supplies from the

North. On the very day that Grant was at Napoleon giving instructions for a new operation against Vicksburg, Secretary of War Seddon was writing to Pemberton about the agreements which he said he disliked—made of course with Southerners, but with the government's full knowledge of where the goods would be secured.

Passing over any principle involved, Seddon said, "The contracts were of course made reluctantly, but under a strong conviction of the necessity of resorting to such means of obtaining adequate supplies, especially of shoes and blankets, for the army." Recent success in running the blockade made him hope the practice could be reduced and, since hearing of Pemberton's complaint, he had made no new contracts, though he much feared that agreements for supplying bacon and pork for the army from Northern sources would have to be made. (One recalls the stream of wagons coming out of Memphis that Quinby had stopped.) While Seddon conceded that the "moral influence may be injurious," if traders took to the Federal lines more cotton than they were supposed to (and thus put Northern dollars into their pockets), he thought that with proper watchfulness Pemberton could prevent abuse, and he closed by saying he would welcome suggestions for avoiding evil results if meat contracts became indispensable.[7]

While the Confederates had no reserves of men to call upon and no sources of supply comparable to those of the North, they had great allies: the line of hills from Warrenton to Haynes Bluff, where they pinched down to the Yazoo, and where well placed guns made high ground inaccessible by way of the river's mouth; the winter torrents in the Mississippi; the soft, oozy land of the great delta, cut by bayous, and shrouded by great forests, whose trees stood ready to knock down the smokestacks of steamers or waited for the ax to fell them across the water from bank to bank. These allies needed no orders to move them to the right place. They were there, twenty-four hours each day. No one can estimate their worth in batteries, in regiments, or in brigades. Yet there are those who would have us merely tally the numbers on each side as we appraise the struggle for the great fortress.[8]

"So here we are again, but not a word from Banks." Thus wrote Sherman to his brother on January 25. The rapidly rising river had already filled the old canal—only a narrow ditch, according to the general—but had so far shown no inclination to convert it into a navigable channel and "leave Vicksburg out in the cold." All of Sherman's men were engaged night and day in throwing up a levee along the right bank of the canal so as not to be washed away. His line extended down the river and he had guns in position to hinder enemy boats coming up to Vicksburg. Even if the river converted the canal into a good channel, he saw no hope: the enemy could shift guns to command the river below it. "They are as well supplied as we," said Sherman, "and have an abundance of the best cannon, arms and ammunition." He even claimed that the Confederates outnumbered the Federals.[9]

Two days later Porter cheerily ended a note to Sherman, "If this rain lasts much longer we will not need a canal. I think the whole point will disappear, troops and all, in which case the gunboats will have the field to themselves." In reporting to Welles on the 28th about the canal prospects, the admiral said, "General Grant is here now, and I hope for a better state of things."[10]

While the army went ahead with the canal and two other projects that Grant quickly initiated in the hope of mastering Vicksburg, the navy was left free to engage in its own spectacular action. Porter's plans may not have been fully formed when on February 1 he ordered Colonel Charles Rivers Ellet, son of the creator of the ram fleet and its present commander, to take the *Queen of the West* and destroy the enemy steamer *Vicksburg,* lying off the town, then go down the river to Sherman's batteries, tie up and report. Sending one of the Ellets on a mission in the *Queen* was almost certain to lead to high drama.

In the early light of the next morning Ellet started for his target. The same eddies and currents that had prevented his uncle, Alfred W. Ellet (now brigadier general in command of the anomalous Mississippi Marine Brigade), from striking the *Arkansas* a heavy blow the preceding summer, now saved the *Vicksburg.* Nevertheless a fire was started on the enemy craft by an incendiary shell, although the protective cotton bales upon the *Queen* were ignited by her own guns (originally she had had none) as well as those of the enemy. Enveloped in heavy smoke, Ellet dared not maneuver for another strike, and drew away. In reporting the effort to Welles, Porter said he could not speak too highly of Ellet's daring, Porter's only trouble being "to hold him in and keep him out of danger." Ellet would undertake anything "without asking questions." That was the kind of man Porter said he liked to command.[11]

Porter next turned Ellet into a commerce destroyer. After the colonel had returned from one successful trip because of exhaustion of fuel, a barge with 20,000 bushels of coal was set adrift, passed Vicksburg in the night without apparently being seen, and reached the waiting *Queen* within ten minutes of the appointed time. "This gives the ram nearly coal enough to last a month," Porter informed Welles, "in which time she can commit great havoc, if no accident happens to her." [12]

On the night of February 10, accompanied by the *De Soto,* a former enemy vessel which had been captured by the army and turned over to the navy, and his barge of coal, Ellet descended the river. To prevent supplies passing from the west bank, issuing largely from the mouth of the Red River, was Ellet's special mission. Aboard the *Queen* were no fewer than three reporters, equipped with the necessary implements of their calling and a great stock of words to put the cruise properly into history.

After destroying skiffs and flatboats on both banks, Ellet turned into the Red River and from it into the Atchafalaya, where some destructive work was carried on and First Master Thompson was wounded by fire from the shore. Upon resuming his course up the Red River, Ellet captured the well-loaded *Era No. 5,* then continued on in the hope of destroying three other vessels whose presence had been reported to him. Unfortunately, the *Queen*'s wheel on February 14 was not in the hand of Scott Long, who had handled her brilliantly in the attack upon the *Vicksburg.* Long being ill, his position had been taken by a substitute. At a sharp bend that was reached a little before dusk, Ellet ordered the pilot to proceed with great caution; as the *Queen* nosed around the point shots were poured into her from well placed guns. Instead of backing as Ellet instantly ordered, the pilot ran the boat aground. Exposed and helpless, her steam pipe was cut, making abandonment necessary, Ellet and most of the crew floating down the river on cotton bales. The *Queen*'s yawl having disappeared, Ellet had not been able to evacuate the wounded Thompson and burn the vessel. Two men were sent back for Thompson with the yawl of the *De Soto,* which had been left below. There also—as Mahan points out—Thompson should have been left when Ellet started into what he knew was a possible trap; but it is not strange that the nineteen-year-old fleet commander did not think of that.

One of the would-be rescuers escaped, but the other was captured by the Confederates who were jubilantly boarding the stranded ram. Also captured were Thompson and the *New York Herald* reporter. The *Chicago Tribune* correspondent and the one for the *Cincinnati Commercial* floated bravely to safety, and their dampening experience in no way lessened the fervor with which they told the world the story of the *Queen*'s adventure and capture.

The night was only beginning. In a fog that suddenly encompassed the river, the *De Soto* ran into the bank and lost her rudder. Drifting down to where he had left the *Era*, Ellet scuttled and burned the *De Soto*, transferred to the *Era*, which he lightened by throwing her cargo into the water, and proceeded to the Mississippi. There the pilot ran the *Era*—which drew only thirty inches of water—so hard aground that she was got off with difficulty. This second incident, together with some remarks the man had made, caused Ellet to place him in arrest.[13]

A short distance below Natchez, Ellet met the *Indianola*, a new ironclad which had just run the Vicksburg batteries with two barges of coal, and whose mission was to protect the *Queen* from the enemy's fast ram *Webb*. The *Indianola*'s captain, Lieutenant Commander George Brown, upon hearing of the *Queen*'s fate, decided to go at least as far as the Red River. Ellet turned back with him and presently they encountered the *Webb*, in hot pursuit of the *Era*. One look at the *Indianola* caused the *Webb*'s commander to turn and start back down the river, encouraged by two heavy shells from the *Indianola* that fell short, though the guns had all the elevation the ports would allow.[14]

Unable to find a Red River pilot—Porter had told him not to venture up the stream unless he did—Brown stayed to watch its mouth. Ellet returned north with the unarmed *Era* after taking aboard 170 bales of cotton for protection and making on the way a call at St. Joseph * to pick up Confederate mailbags. Though heavy fire from both shores was directed at the *Era* and Ellet had to stop to clean her furnaces, he arrived safely on the 20th. His note informing Porter that he had returned without the *Queen*, but with a good load of cotton on a captured vessel, ended in a manner befitting a colonel of those primi-

---

* This and some of the other places mentioned in this chapter are not on the map with the chapter, but are on the map on page 348.

tive days: "I shall report to you in person as soon as I can obtain a horse." [15]

Only a few days remained for the *Indianola*. Learning that the *Queen* and the *Webb*—which had sought sanctuary in the Red River —and some cotton-clad vessels with boarding parties were preparing to attack him, Brown prudently started north. Though the *Indianola*'s bunkers were full, Brown stubbornly held onto his precious barges— one lashed to either side of the ship—in spite of the great reduction of speed they caused, for he knew that if other vessels were sent down the river, Porter would expect him to coal them. As heavy darkness settled over the river on February 24, his pursuers overtook him, and after a hard fight in which Brown delivered considerable damage, especially to enemy personnel, the *Indianola* was sunk on the west bank, when she had almost reached a place of safety.[16]

It was not until the 27th, when an escaped seaman from the *Indianola* came aboard the flagship *Black Hawk,* that Porter learned of the fate of the gunboat he had sent below with the hope that she and the *Queen* would help the army by cutting off both Vicksburg and Port Hudson from an important source of supplies. In a dispatch that was sent the same day for telegraphing from Memphis, Porter said he did not know the particulars, but he prejudged the case by saying the loss could "be traced to a noncompliance with my instructions." He warned that if the *Indianola* had not been actually sunk, she might be used against the fleet in the lower part of the river. Thinking that Washington might not understand, he added, "It would be well to caution them." In replying, the Navy Secretary took a grave view of the possibilities but seemed quite helpless: "The Department has no means of notifying the fleet at New Orleans." [17]

Fears about the situation below were unnecessary, for the Confederates had obligingly already done heavy damage to the partially submerged *Indianola,* thanks to the fact that Porter had a bent for practical jokes. A dummy monitor which he had had constructed, and which had floated past the Vicksburg batteries in a hail of shells and had stuck on a mud bar, frightened salvagers away from the *Indianola.* In this final act the *Queen* played an important role and, as if unhappy with the colors she now flew, served her old side well. The *Queen* was coming up to Vicksburg with dispatches for General Stevenson, commanding at the place, and also to get pumps, to aid in emptying the

Indianola, when she saw Porter's monster resting on the mud bar. She promptly turned and fled, spreading the alarm that a gunboat was approaching.[18]

On the 28th the telegraph from Jackson carried to Richmond this dispatch from Pemberton: "Confederate fleet abandoned the *Indianola* on approach of what was supposed to be a turreted ironclad. I am not satisfied that it was a gunboat, but have no definite intelligence yet. *Indianola* was blown up, by order of General Stevenson on the night of the 26th. I approve." Pemberton was too modest: he had ordered the vessel's destruction.[19]

What Porter wrote to Welles on February 22 about the loss of the *Queen* was hardly as flowery as the account which Albert H. Bodman had just sent to the *Chicago Tribune.* But Porter could put more of the significant into a few words than could the journalist: "The intrinsic value of the *Queen of the West* is nothing. She paid for herself five times over by the destruction and capture of rebel property, only she has a national character." [20]

The *Queen* had indeed held a high place in Northern affections from the day of her spectacular performance in the Battle of Memphis, where her designer and commander, the father of the youth who had bravely taken her up the Red River, had received the apparently trifling wound from which he soon died. In October, 1863, six months after Federal guns had eagerly—yet with sorrow—destroyed the *Queen,* there would again be mourning over the death from typhoid of her last fearless and inspiring Federal commander—Charles Rivers Ellet.

The day after Ellet had returned for fuel and to report that the enemy now had three vigilant batteries at Warrenton, Assistant Secretary of the Navy Gustavus Fox wrote to Porter, tempering good advice with unbecoming remarks. After congratulating Porter on Arkansas Post, Fox said, "If you open the Father of Waters you will at once be made an admiral [Porter was an Acting Rear Admiral]; besides we will try for a ribboned star." General Frank Blair had written in a complimentary manner of the navy's work on January 11, but Fox hoped there would never be any reciprocity in the jealousy that Blair had said the army entertained for the navy. "Do your work up clean, as at Arkansas, and the public will never be in doubt as to who did it,"

Fox enjoined, then added: "The flaming army correspondence misleads nobody. Keep cool, be very modest under great success, as a contrast to the soldiers."

Fox thought the entire army should be put to work cutting a canal farther back "and let Vicksburg go." He doubted, in fact, if the army could take the place. When a canal was opened, a move could be made against Port Hudson, a position Banks alone could not take, according to the Assistant Navy Secretary. Fox warned against a long siege at Vicksburg: "The country can not stand it at home or abroad." This letter, in which modesty was recommended to Porter, ended, "The President is of my opinion, that you better cut through farther back and do it at once." [21]

One cannot blame the able Gustavus Fox for being pleased by Presidential approval or for wanting to be helpful, but matters were moving well without him. On January 29, eight days before Fox wrote to Porter, Grant had telegraphed to Halleck—the message having to go to Memphis by boat for transmission—that, though the water was rising in the old canal, there were no signs of its enlarging. Already Colonel Wilson had been sent to see if it would be possible to reach the Coldwater River by cutting the Mississippi levee at Yazoo Pass. Two days later Grant telegraphed again: he was pushing everything to bypass Vicksburg; prospects not being good by the old canal, other routes were being investigated while work went ahead on the old one.[22]

In a letter on February 4 to Colonel Kelton, Halleck's chief of staff, Grant explained everything fully. Though he had little faith in the old canal, it had a diversionary value, and the Confederates, seeing the Federals again busy at it, were giving much attention to fortifying Warrenton. There was, Grant said, a much better route by way of bayous that left the river at Milliken's Bend and joined it again at New Carthage, well below the hostile guns at Warrenton—though not below those at Grand Gulf. This much more practicable route could not now be developed because water was all over the country. Accordingly the old canal was being pushed, but with a new inlet and a new outlet, "so that the water will be received where the current strikes the shore." No word, Grant said, had been received from Wilson about the Coldwater River prospects, but he inclosed two encouraging reports about another alternative route.[23]

Both of the new projects, and still a third, were to end in failure. Work on them nevertheless did much to train and temper an army, while it enabled its commander to reveal his persistence and resourcefulness under difficulties and his poise under criticism. The Administration also had the chance to show its courage and steadfastness, and also the country, about which Fox was doubtful. That truthful reporting of the Vicksburg operations need not be expected had been proved, for a correspondent of the *New York Herald* had written an account of Sherman's December effort against Chickasaw Bluffs that was very damaging to Sherman, and whose falsity the reporter—Thomas W. Knox—soon admitted.

Sherman not having seen fit to lay his plans before Knox, the journalist wrote that attacks were made with "no common understanding among the various generals of divisions and brigades," and made other false and malicious statements. In a letter of apology dated February 1, Knox said to Sherman: "Yesterday I had the opportunity of listening to the reading of the orders, plans, and reports connected with those operations. For the first time I have the correct history of the proceedings. I find to my regret that I labored under repeated errors, and made in consequence several misstatements, which I now take pleasure in correcting." Though Knox ended by stating that he was now convinced of Sherman's "prompt, efficient, and judicious management of the troops" under his control from the commencement of the campaign, and deplored his errors and expressed the hope that no other journalist would be so unfortunate, his groveling did not save him. Four days later Sherman had him before a court-martial, which, to its great credit, ordered that he be sent beyond the lines of the army, not to return under penalty of imprisonment. "Findings and sentence approved, and will be carried into effect," was the indorsement presently written at Grant's order on the record of the trial.[24]

It would have been only a mild lesson at best, and it was probably soon known that Knox had appealed to Lincoln. Two months later he was back with a Presidential paper that reopened the case. From Sherman he got a withering and wholesome blast. Grant, with whom the ultimate decision rested, was no more diverted by Lincoln's note from doing full justice to a great subordinate than he was by nature's enmity from pressing the operations against Vicksburg. He reaffirmed Knox's banishment.[25]

Within Grant's own camp there was a correspondent who, after some inconspicuous postwar years, used his leisure as a sheep raiser to write in the mid-nineties an account of his experiences, only recently published. The man's name was Sylvanus Cadwallader and he represented the *Chicago Times,* a bitterly anti-Lincoln paper that was often called secessionist at the time and is still so labeled by historians. That the Confederates found the paper militarily useful is shown by the previously mentioned clipping from it that Holmes sent to Hindman. The editor of the *Times,* W. F. Story, is said to have instructed his reporters, "If there is no news, send rumors!"

"Furtive," was the description that a fellow correspondent applied to Cadwallader. To his manuscript Cadwallader gave the title *Four Years with Grant,* but the editor of the printed work changed it to *Three Years with Grant.* Inasmuch as Cadwallader spent only thirty months in the field with Grant, further pruning would not have been amiss. Upon examining the manuscript one soon finds that Cadwallader's inventiveness was not restricted to titles. He gave an explanation of Grant's "expulsion order" that is completely shattered by the chronology of events. Significantly, it is not found in the published work; but, fortunately, another writer—who had a typed copy of the manuscript—found the Cadwallader story so absorbing that he quoted nearly a page.[26]

We have it from Wilson, who himself reported to Grant soon after Cadwallader had presented his credentials in October, 1862, that from the first the journalist not only messed with the staff and was given shelter and transportation, but was treated in all respects as a commissioned officer.[27] This is in no way surprising; it was merely in harmony with Grant's usual considerateness and kindness. When over thirty years later Cadwallader set down his recollections, he showed himself deficient in some of the human qualities that helped make Grant a great general. One must suspect that his book was largely the effort of an obscure but artful man to turn himself into one of consequence.

Grant's winter before Vicksburg was one of the great testing periods of the war, and the story of the three futile efforts that he initiated—with much cooperation from Porter in the two which were pushed the hardest—is essential if one is to appreciate the final Vicksburg triumph. One should not worry about the discomfort of the soldiers; most of the time they had plenty of substantial food and did not over-exert themselves. They were the more content for being busy, though even then they got homesick, as soldiers always do. When not think-ing of home, many of them were doubtless longing for the sutler's sweetmeats and deadly pies. Their record would be much better if Sherman had not had to write to his brother: "Farms disappear, houses are burned and plundered, and every living animal killed and eaten. General officers make feeble efforts to stay the disorder, but it is idle." [28]

The army that emerged from the frustrating winter months Grant led into a bold operation with full confidence that his men did not intend to be defeated in battle. Whence came their determination? It did not come out of letters from home, nor from papers that they read. It came from Grant. Napoleon knew soldiers, knew how valorous they could be. Yet he said that in war it is "the man" who counts. The regiments in blue are there before Vicksburg, along the river and the bayous; the regiments in gray are there, on good solid ground, and not entirely disinclined to do some plundering of the home folks. It is in no way demeaning the men who carried Northern muskets to say: "Do not become engrossed with them. Watch the man who is calmly and resolutely directing the great drama." Note what Grant is telling Washington, what he writes to his subordinates. He cannot control the great flood of waters; he cannot make a different man of John McClernand; he cannot silence defamers. But in his mes-sages to Halleck he can reveal himself to the Administration and show that there is a cool mind and a steady hand in control. And he can inspire the army in blue. Vicksburg is Grant.

It was on the first day after his arrival at the mouth of the Yazoo that Grant gave Wilson instructions to return immediately to Helena to organize an expedition to open a route using the Yazoo Pass, Moon Lake, the Coldwater River, and the Tallahatchie, at length to reach the Yazoo above the place where it was blocked by the great raft and the batteries at Haynes Bluff. High land could then be gained and the batteries dislodged from the rear. The route was to start from a point on the east bank of the Mississippi a few miles below Helena, and General Gorman was to furnish men, boats, and tools. (Presently

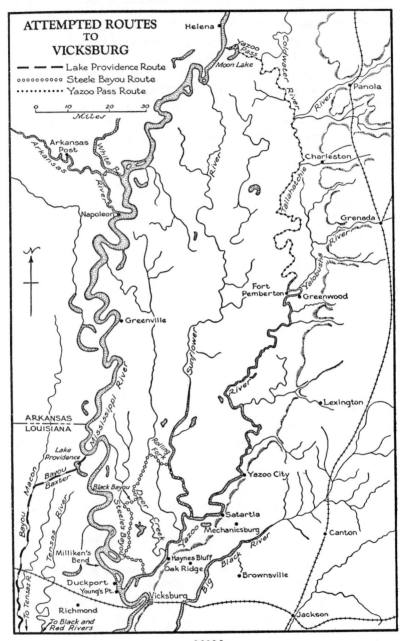

ATTEMPTED ROUTES
TO
VICKSBURG

— — — Lake Providence Route
ooooooooo Steele Bayou Route
·········· Yazoo Pass Route

0   10   20   30
Miles

General Prentiss, together with a new quartermaster and a new provost marshal, would be sent to Helena because of reports reaching Grant about Gorman's administration.) [29]

Wilson was only four days in getting to work, and at 2:00 P.M. on February 2 a detail of 400 men with shovels, axes, and picks began to cut the Mississippi levee. The next evening mines were exploded, and in a short time the entrance widened and water was pouring in like nothing Wilson had ever seen except Niagara. "Logs, trees, and great masses of earth were torn away with the greatest of ease." But it would be several days before boats could enter with safety, he reported to Grant. Then, according to a rebel general in Helena, they could easily reach the Yazoo with boats of medium size.[30]

The second route that Grant sketched to Kelton was to the west of the Mississippi. It started at Lake Providence, whence a network of waterways led to the Red River. A report dated the 3rd by Colonel George W. Deitzler, commanding a brigade of McArthur's division of McPherson's corps, spoke enthusiastically about the prospects. After Lake Providence had been connected with the Mississippi and the water level had risen, entrance could be had to Baxter Bayou; then by cutting trees "so as not to interfere with chimneys," it would be possible to reach Bayou Macon. "Once in Bayou Macon, we shall have a clear coast to Red River," was the way Deitzler put it.[31] And this was quite true, though the colonel simplified matters by neglecting to say that Bayou Macon led into the Tensas River, and it into the Black, which reached the Red River about thirty miles above where it emptied into the Mississippi.

Grant himself visited Lake Providence on the 5th and wrote to McPherson, waiting at Memphis with his two remaining divisions. McPherson was told to come forward with one division with as little delay as possible, leaving the other in readiness to follow. "This bids fair to be the most practicable route for turning Vicksburg," Grant said, adding that Lake Providence could be connected with the Mississippi with a quarter of the digging that had been done across the point opposite Vicksburg. Grant would send the balance of McArthur's division up to Lake Providence as soon as he got below and would return in a few days to see McPherson. "Our marching orders have come, and it is for us to respond with promptness and alacrity," was the beginning of the order that McPherson soon issued to his troops.[32]

That Grant still considered the rapacious traders a handicap to operations is shown by the ending of his letter to McPherson: "Cotton speculators will follow you in spite of every effort to prevent it. Make orders excluding all citizens from coming within your lines, so that if any of these fellows get outside they can be kept out." Having been directed to revoke his unhappy expulsion order of December, Grant was proceeding with tact. There was little danger of being denounced in Congress if sentinels turned back *citizens* from lines as close to Vicksburg as Lake Providence. About the time when McPherson was starting for Memphis, Grant was reading a letter from Hamilton that indicated that "the trade business" at Memphis and Corinth was giving him "enough to do." The letter also had a sentence on another delicate matter: "Both Hurlbut and myself have prohibited circulation of *Chicago Times* in our commands." [33]

In a letter on the 13th from Lake Providence to Hurlbut—the senior officer at Memphis—Grant made it very clear that trade was not opened below Helena. He also took up the question of the *Chicago Times*. He doubted the "propriety" of excluding the paper from a single command, for it "would still find its way into the hands of the enemy, through other channels, and do all the mischief it is now doing." What Grant referred to was of course the carrying of helpful information to the enemy, a concern that was much on Sherman's mind a few days later when he wrote his brother about the "agents of the press" revealing "prematurely all our plans and designs." Grant, however, had more than negative reasons for directing that Hurlbut's order be revoked; the order would "give the paper a notoriety evidently sought, and which probably would increase the sale of it." Thirty years afterward Cadwallader claimed the credit for Grant's revocation of Hurlbut's order. It may indeed have been the reporter who showed Grant the copy of the order he had seen, though it should be noted that on February 9 Hamilton had written Grant that both he and Hurlbut had forbidden the circulation of the *Times* within their commands. Certainly the incident was most fortunate; it caused Grant to put into the record his unequivocal opinion of the paper for which Cadwallader was writing: "There is no doubt but that paper, and several others in the North, should have been suppressed long since by authority from Washington." [34]

Stephen Hurlbut is too often a forgotten general in the great campaign. He led no troops on a hard march as he had done to cut Van

Dorn's avenue of escape from Corinth; he commanded subordinately in none of the battles; he held no sector in the final encircling line at Vicksburg. But he played a very vital part from the first day of the campaign to the last. When a river town of size becomes a base for soldiers, sailors, smugglers, and spies, and has within its confines enterprising men looking for cotton and friendly women eager for some of the meager pay of servicemen and a share of the copious dollars of the speculators, and has houses from which messages are sent to guerrilla bands, as well as a vital telegraph office with wires running through uncertain country and ultimately back to a far-away capital, and in addition to all this has on its border a great camp for refugees recently slaves—it will not be easy to keep order. Hurlbut minced no words: "The city of Memphis has more iniquity in it than any place since Sodom." But he assured Rawlins and through him Grant that certain examples were being made which might "do good." [35]

As he watched what was going on in the streets, with awareness of what was transpiring under cover in his iniquitous base, Hurlbut also kept an eye on Van Dorn. On the day that Grant directed him to revoke his order about the *Times,* Hurlbut—in response to information Dodge had sent from Corinth—requested navy Captain Pennock at Cairo to send a gunboat to Florence or Eastport, if possible, explaining, "Van Dorn is moving on the point, but has been delayed by our cavalry." Of course, if Van Dorn should cross the Tennessee, it would relieve Grant, but it was not in Grant's nature or in Hurlbut's to help Van Dorn in a move that would take him into Rosecrans's field of operations. Hurlbut warned Rosecrans and informed Halleck, while to Grant he wrote that if Van Dorn should come back, he would concentrate and whip him. At present the roads were horrible.[36]

The smuggling problem was one of the hardest, and on the 22nd Grant told Hurlbut he did not know what to suggest; Hurlbut would have to use his own judgment. But Hurlbut's problems were lessened a little when Grant gave him permission to abandon the railroad north of Jackson as soon as all the rolling stock had been brought away from Columbus. It also bettered his situation when Grant directed that the six 8-inch howitzers and the ammunition for them should be sent to Dodge instead of down the river. The surrendering of territory north of Jackson would have an effect on communications with Washington. From time to time wires would be broken and telegraph instruments would fall silent. Then repairmen would have to be sent out, while messages coming up the river to Memphis continued on by boat to Cairo for telegraphing.[37]

In general, the long, broad Mississippi was a secure communication line. Yet field guns hidden opportunely on the banks could do damage to steamers. On the 13th, while Grant was at Lake Providence, Porter informed McClernand, next in command, that the Confederates had sent two regiments and some guns up the Sunflower River to Greenville to interrupt traffic. Without delay McClernand dispatched a reenforced brigade to drive them out.[38]

Such occasional functioning as over-all commander during Grant's absence did not, however, satisfy McClernand, and he still wanted to make an independent operation in Arkansas. On the 15th he requested permission to take a force of 20,000 infantry, including all that were at Helena, together with the proper complement of artillery, and move against the enemy at Pine Bluff, reported to be 10,000 strong. In replying, Grant said the one objection he had was that the project would retard progress on "the one great object, that of opening the Mississippi." He did not, however, entirely shut the door, but said it might be possible to send such an expedition after the return to Helena of Ross's division—which was standing by to help Wilson— and the brigade McClernand had sent to Greenville. That Grant was not discriminating against the general who had challenged his right to command was shown by the fact that he presently told Hurlbut that McClernand's corps was deficient in artillery, and he wanted a heavy battery sent to him.[39]

So unrelenting had been the rise of the great river that the army had difficulty keeping its camps out of the water, and work on the canal had accordingly slowed down. Such was Grant's statement in a telegram to Halleck on February 9. He was hoping to be able to say something precise in a day or so about the practicability of the Yazoo Pass route. The time ran on beyond that, but at noon on the 15th Grant could send something definite and also encouraging: "Steamboats through Yazoo Pass have gone to within 6 miles of Coldwater. Express no fear but that they will reach it and the Yazoo." [40]

A general progress report was contained in a letter of the 18th. Considering that most of the time that the troops could be out had had to be spent keeping water out of their camps, progress on the canal had been satisfactory. With five good working days it could be completed to a width of sixty feet and to a depth that would admit any vessel present. Judging, however, from the past, it would require ten or twelve days to yield the five good ones. Then an extra three days should perhaps be allowed, because the work of soldiers, even under the most favorable circumstances, did not come up to the calculations of the engineers. McPherson's corps was still prosecuting the work at Lake Providence, and Grant had sent Ross's division from Helena to join Wilson, whose last report had already been sent to Halleck. If successful, they would capture or destroy all the enemy transports in the Yazoo and its tributaries.

With his three enterprises disposed of, Grant concluded with a paragraph whose restraint was eloquent and in sharp contrast with the way other generals sometimes wrote:

The health of this command is not what is represented in the public journals. It is as good as any previous calculation could have prognosticated. I believe, too, that there is the best of feeling and greatest confidence of success among them. The greatest drawback to the spirits of the troops has been the great delay in paying them. Many of them have families at home who are, no doubt, in a suffering condition for want of the amount due them, and they are bound for their support.[41]

Instead of being made more careful by the punishment of Knox, the correspondents may have been resentful that one of the fraternity had been expelled. At least, Grant's statement about the health of his men definitely indicted the truthfulness of the reporters. While the failure of the soldiers to receive their pay was now new, that fact did not lessen the hardship that would result.

March began with prospects fairly good, but there was a touch of grimness in the ending of a telegram that Grant sent Halleck on the 6th (the message clearing Cairo on the 12th): "The canal is near completion. Troops expected from Saint Louis not yet heard from. I will have Vicksburg this month, or fail in the attempt." In the eyes of Porter the Yazoo Pass project was likewise encouraging, and on the 2nd he had ended a letter to Secretary Welles:

Our expedition across to the Tallahatchie, through Yazoo Pass, is succeeding, and we have 10 vessels, at last accounts, within a short distance of the Tallahatchie. Officers and men, assisted by the troops, working with a determination that nothing can conquer, and driving the enemy before them. There are but few troops in Vicksburg at this moment, and matters look prosperous.[42]

But the next day—March 7—the changes began steadily to dwindle. The waters were still rising, and an order by Sherman stated: "Our camps being threatened with overflow, preparation must be made to meet such an event. The only safe ground will be the levee in front of our camps till the troops can be embarked." While no unit was to move for the present, all must be ready to take designated positions. Furthermore, during the night a mishap had befallen the canal. One of the dams at the upper end had given way and water had rushed into the place where men had just been at work removing stumps. In reporting the occurrence to Halleck, Grant said that it would have been necessary to suspend all work until the water fell three feet, if it had not been for the excellent dredges that Colonel Pride had selected and brought from the north. These had worked like a charm.

Grant had, however, to report that the Lake Providence route, which a month before had seemed so promising, was a failure. If it could have been begun earlier, it unquestionably would have succeeded, but now Bayou Baxter was lost in the cypress swamp connecting the lake with Bayou Macon. The water was so high that it was impossible to cut the timber and dig a channel. McPherson would be withdrawn and added to the Yazoo Pass expedition, which seemed on the verge of success. There had been an agreement that the gunboats would fire when they neared Haynes Bluff, and Grant stated, "Last night, about twelve o'clock, Admiral Porter sent me word that the signal agreed upon had been heard." [43]

Unhappily, the admiral's ears were unaccustomed to the capriciousness of land-borne sounds, and before long it was known that the Yazoo Pass project was a failure. Wilson had been writing full progress reports, addressed to Rawlins, but with the knowledge that they would be read by the army commander. After great labor in clearing the channel of trees that had been felled to block boats, Wilson wrote on March 15 from within five miles north of Greenwood, where Fort Pemberton had been constructed to prevent entrance into the Yazoo. The entire country being practically under water, land operations against the fort were impossible and no effective landing could be made until the fort's guns were silenced. Unless two or three good ironclads were sent very soon, "the game is blocked on us here as well as below." Such was Wilson's view. [44]

Three days later Wilson wrote that operations were at an end. The naval officer in charge was leaving because of illness, after expressing the opinion that the *Chillicothe* and *De Kalb* could not destroy the two enemy guns opposing them; his successor had insisted on withdrawing. A deserter from the enemy who had just come in stated that in the attack made on the fort on the 16th, the Confederate 6.4 rifle had been silenced for want of ammunition. In that fight the *Chillicothe* had withdrawn early, according to Wilson, while the *De Kalb* had not been allowed to press the contest. On the following night a small amount of ammunition, according to the deserter, had been received at the fort, so that the effective rifle was again supplied. Wilson also reported that the deserter had said a force of a thousand men was working constantly to complete a great raft to block the river near Yazoo City; but that, except for a gunboat that would not be finished for two years because of lack of materials, there was no war vessel on the river.

A magnificent chance had been lost, said Wilson, first by the naval commander's culpable and inexcusable slowness and then by his timidity and caution. It was indeed a fact that the hostile guns had only recently been put in position, and this was not Wilson's first report about the slowness of the gunboats, for on the 13th he had written: "Ross has done all in his power to urge this thing forward. If what he suggested had been adopted, the ironclads would have been here fifteen days ago and found no battery of importance. So much for speed." Yet even on the 18th there was still a chance, and before he closed his report on that day with the statement, "I can't begin to give you an idea of my disgust," Wilson said:

> If Admiral Porter can send three good iron-clads, well supplied with ammunition, say, 400 rounds for each gun, and a good man to fight them, they can yet capture the place. If he can't do so, it is childish folly to keep the present force here, thereby causing the enemy to strengthen his position and allowing him an opportunity to bag our entire force.[45]

Was Wilson engaging in easy criticism? Might he not also have faltered if he had been the responsible officer? The answer seems simple. A little over a year later Grant would pick Wilson for the responsible and delicate task of leading the advance across the Rapidan, and the young general subsequently distinguished himself for determination and boldness as an independent commander. Wilson, however, probably did not take sufficiently into account the difficulties of gunboats when fighting downstream. Yet Mahan in a way supports Wilson when he says the range was never lowered below 800 yards; he supports him still more when he says there is reason to believe that "had a little more feverish energy been displayed the vessels might have got possession of Fort Pemberton before its guns were mounted." [46]

With a touch of exuberance the Confederate commander at Fort Pemberton, Major General William W. Loring, reported to General Pemberton on March 20 that the Federals had commenced a precipitate retreat up the Tallahatchie, and that he had ordered a pursuit on their flank and rear. A confirmatory message in late afternoon said the enemy was in full run as fast as steam could carry him. In it was the important statement, "This place capable of very strong defense; should be made perfect, and I have given orders to have it so."

Believing the Federal project a closed affair, Loring two days later wrote a long report, with a day-by-day account from the appearance of the gunboats on March 11 to the morning of the 20th. The story ended with an impressive touch: "Thus was conducted the battle of the Tallahatchie." Correctly Loring began his final paragraph, "I would here remark that this expedition was the prominent one of a great plan for the attack of Vicksburg in rear." But he was a little premature when he predicted—after an allusion to the "ignominious retreat" of the Federals—that there would be no further effort of "invasion of the State of Mississippi by the way of the Tallahatchie and Yazoo Rivers." In fact, at 4:30 the next afternoon—March 23— Loring found it necessary to telegraph to Pemberton, "The enemy in force with their gunboats have again made their appearance, opening fire at 2.15 and immediately ceasing fire."

While retiring because he thought the fate of the operation had already been decided, Ross had met Quinby's division, and at Quinby's desire the whole expedition had returned. A touch of alarm was in some of the dispatches that Loring sent in the first days of April, that of the 2nd reading: "The enemy are sending their boats to the Pass for re-enforcements. They are receiving heavy guns. Can any heavy guns be sent here?" To this Pemberton replied, "I am expecting more heavy guns, but have none now to lend you." On April 6 Loring could report that the enemy was again moving up the Tallahatchie toward the mouth of the Coldwater, with the probable intention of continuing to the Mississippi. But on this occasion he waited a longer time before writing a final report. In it he stated that during the Federal absence he had greatly strengthened his line.[47]

Well before Ross's first retreat from in front of Fort Pemberton, efforts were under way to reach the Yazoo River above Haynes Bluff by another water route. While Wilson was witnessing the feeble attack by the *Chillicothe* and the *De Kalb,* Grant and Porter were reconnoitering thirty miles up Steele's Bayou and Deer Creek in the hope of reaching the Yazoo below Yazoo City by the Sunflower River. Already Sherman was working on an expedition over this route, and on the same day he wrote, "The iron-clads push their way along unharmed, but the trees and overhanging limbs tear the wooden boats all to pieces." The loyal and vigorous lieutenant did everything possible to make the operation succeed and sent long reports that gave his appreciative chief a full picture of everything. Finally, on March 27, Grant had to tell Halleck that the enemy had "got wind of the movement" in time to move troops to meet the threat, while Porter had been "forced to desist from further efforts to proceed when within a few hundred yards of clear sailing in the Yazoo." Then it was that Grant also sent the final order to liquidate the effort through Yazoo Pass. He was not as hard on the navy for failure at Fort Pemberton as was Wilson, saying to the General in Chief: "From information I have, other and great difficulties would be found in navigating the Yazoo below Greenwood. Considerable preparation has been made to receive our forces coming by that route." Vicksburg papers were reaching Grant regularly and deserters were telling much; but he could draw no "definite conclusion" as to the size of the enemy force.[48]

The same letter informed Washington that the canal would be of no use, except to send light-draft boats through to be employed below; dredging operations had had to be completely abandoned because of enemy gunfire.

Four projects now had failed: the canal, the Lake Providence project to reach bayous and rivers leading to Red River, the attempt through Yazoo Pass to reach the Yazoo above Haynes Bluff, and that by Steele's Bayou for the same purpose. But there was one item that held a little cheer. Farragut was holding the river above Fort Hudson, though Grant did not know the details of the hard fight on the night of the 13th, when the heavily gunned flagship *Hartford* and the six-gun *Albatross* passed through the heavy barrage hurled by the Confederate batteries, while five other vessels failed to pass. Two Ellet rams had made a daylight dash on the 25th to join the ships below; one, a fine vessel, had been successful, though frequently hit by the Vicksburg guns; the other, a poor craft, had disintegrated upon taking a single shot. Said the general who habitually looked on the bright side: "It is almost certain that had she made one *ram* into another vessel she would have *closed up* like a *spy-glass,* encompassing all on board." But Farragut was unhappy, remarking in a letter to Grant, "I blame myself very much for not insisting on General Ellet's waiting for a dark night. I was so much afraid of their impetuosity that it deprived me of sleep all night, but I never for a moment supposed he would come down in the daytime." [49]

Being under fire apparently had a fascination for the Ellets.

In mid-February, Grant had issued an order saying "the enticing of negroes to leave their homes to come within the lines of the army is positively forbidden." Those already present were not to be turned out, but in the future, no person, "white or black," was to be permitted to pass the line of sentinels, either to enter or to leave camps, without proper authorization. The order was only partially designed to prevent an inundation of contrabands; it also had security purposes. Specifically it said, "No flag of truce will hereafter be allowed to pass our outposts." [50]

No order, however, could protect Grant from erroneous reports by correspondents or from enemies within his midst. On March 15 McClernand addressed to "His Excellency, A. Lincoln, Prest," a short note: "Permit me to present to you Capt. Kountz, an honest and reliable gentleman. I would add more but he must embark." At Pittsburgh, Kountz added over his own signature a statement showing the nature of his errand. He had been informed, he said, that Grant had been "gloriously drunk" on March 13 and sick in bed all the next day. If Lincoln were averse to such behavior by his generals, Kountz could give the names of officers of high standing to substantiate his statement. Fortunately, a report about the former steamboat captain whom McClernand so warmly endorsed had already been put into the record, and by Grant himself. In January 1862, while Grant was carrying out Halleck's order for a demonstration against Columbus, Kountz had so interfered that Grant had put him in arrest, saying in an explanatory letter to Kelton that Kountz seemed to have desired duty in Cairo "for no other purpose than to wreak his revenge upon some river men whom he dislikes, and to get into the service of Government a boat in which he has an interest, either as owner or a former proprietorship, not yet settled for." [51] McClernand of course knew that his confidential courier was not disinterested, but, like himself, was eager to have Grant removed.

On the day that Kountz was embarking with his little note to Lincoln, Sherman was writing vigorously to Colonel R. C. Wood, Assistant Surgeon General, who had come to investigate reports that had reached Washington. Praise of the highest sort was given by Sherman to the surgeon who had made provision for the wounded at Chickasaw Bluffs and at Arkansas Post. In no other battle had he seen such good system and care. While there had probably been exceptions, Sherman said, "The man who would enlarge on a single case of exception, and publish it to the world as a sample of the whole, is to be pitied as a miserable wretch, beneath the notice of a Government." Matters were not easy for some of the finest commanders that ever lived, in that hard theater of war before Vicksburg, and one can dwell upon the concluding paragraph written by the commander of the Fifteenth Army Corps:

Our army is admirably supplied in all respects, and no one deplores more than I do the spirit of falsehood and calumny that harrows the minds of our people at home, and has led to your visit to our camps. In war we must expect sickness and death, but so far as your department is concerned, I feel assured all has been done and will continue to be done which skill, science, and foresight can accomplish. Our soldiers need far more the respect and confidence of their fellow-countrymen at home than they do increased supplies of medicines and hospital stores.[52]

Grant would later write that both Lincoln and Halleck stood firmly behind him in the entire campaign, and the records give substantiation. In a letter of March 20 Halleck said to Grant, "The eyes and hopes of the whole country are now directed to your army." The statement did not even hint at the charges and criticisms against Grant. The General in Chief went further and wrote these fine words: "In my opinion, the opening of the Mississippi River will be to us of more advantage than the capture of forty Richmonds. We shall omit nothing which we can do to assist you." [53]

Halleck's letter followed by nearly three weeks a telegram for which he has been much criticized: "There is a vacant major-generalcy in the Regular Army, and I am authorized to say that it will be given to the general in the field who first wins an important and decisive victory." Grant took no notice of the unusual dispatch, but Rosecrans—wintering comfortably in Murfreesboro—who received a similar message, flared into outraged denunciation: promotions should not be auctioned off. Where lay the responsibility for the unwise appeal, which, however, went little beyond what Fox had told Porter would be his for the opening of the Mississippi? It is significant that Halleck used the word "authorized," not the word "directed," that occurs in some of his dispatches. It is difficult, however, to believe that the thought was his, and one military writer puts the responsibility on Stanton, though without a bit of evidence.[54] Inasmuch as Lincoln was the one who would have to recommend to the Senate a commission in the regular army, it seems certain that the telegram was at least sanctioned by him.

No criticism should be made of Halleck because in his letter to Grant on March 20 he cautioned against dispersal and stressed the importance of concentration. Nor should exception be taken to the fact that he began a telegram on the 24th with the sentence, "I must again call your attention to the importance of your not retaining so many steamers in the Mississippi." Boats were badly needed elsewhere, and detaining transportation that has been given them is not uncommon on the part of commanders. The boat incident actually reveals the understanding that Halleck was now showing Grant, who had been prompt in replying to Halleck's telegram. He had, Grant said, given reiterated orders to McClernand about the necessity of returning boats without delay, but had found when he himself arrived below that the river was "rising so rapidly that there was no telling what moment all hands might be driven to the boats." Then, after the danger had passed, he had released so many boats that he could have moved only a small force at a time. Promptly on receiving Grant's letter the General in Chief began one in reply, "Your explanation in regard to sending back steamers is satisfactory." [55]

At last April came; the high waters began to recede; land languidly threw off its wet covering. On the very day—the 2nd—when Halleck wrote Grant that the President seemed "to be rather impatient about matters in Mississippi," and was repeating his question as to whether cooperation with Banks were not possible, Grant was writing a letter to Porter and a telegram to Halleck which gave a new look to everything.

On the 1st he had reconnoitered Haynes Bluff with Porter and Sherman. After telling the admiral that an attack there "would be attended with immense sacrifice of life, if not defeat," he said, "This, then closes out the last hope of turning the enemy by the right." Already a new way of working around the Confederate left was under way, one that Grant had told Halleck about in his letter of February 4. Some troops were already at New Carthage, and bayous were being opened to get a route to that place through Richmond. Grant had sent to St. Louis and Chicago for barges and tugs, and had ordered the barges already present to be fitted up to move troops and artillery, hoping to be able to transport 20,000 men at one time. After getting below Vicksburg he would eventually have to cross the Mississippi, his plan for that move being indicated by the statement, "To-morrow I shall have work commenced to prepare at least six steamers to run the blockade." Grant felt certain that two gunboats and one army corps could take and hold Grand Gulf, on the east bank forty-five river miles below Vicksburg, until the rest of the army was brought down and provision was made for supplying it. In order to deceive the enemy, a division was being left along Deer Creek connecting westward with the Mississippi and getting supplies from a rich region. He hoped to entice the Confederates into further strengthening of the locality, and said, "My force had as well be there as here until I want to use them."[56]

Porter had been a little shaken by his futile effort to reach the Yazoo by the Steele's Bayou, Deer Creek, and Sunflower River route, although because of his perseverance the attempt had nearly succeeded. The old gunboats, of which he had recently spoken disparagingly to Welles, had won his affection for the way they could knock down trees, tear them up by their roots, and demolish bridges. The shortage of small boats and the inability of the towering steamers to navigate beneath overhanging branches had made it impractical for the army to give Porter protection from enemy sharpshooters and guns. When at last he had been forced to give up after he had almost reached the Sunflower, and, after unshipping his rudders, had started to return by bounding "from tree to tree," he might have been captured by forces blocking the channel, but for a rescue operation by Sherman. The general also had had his difficulties and told in his report of forcing his way at night through a thick canebrake with the aid of lighted candles. It was a historic operation that gave correspondents the opportunity to use their powers of description and artists the chance to draw amazing pictures for the illustrated weeklies. No one, however, was more surprised than the inhabitants of that bayou land. Porter put it thus: "Never did those people expect to see ironclads floating where the keel of a flat boat never passed."

In the confidential part of his report Porter said that there "never yet had been two men who would labor harder than Generals Grant and Sherman to forward an expedition for the overthrow of Vicksburg." But discouragement lay in the words: "There is but one thing now to be done, and that is to start an army of 150,000 men from Memphis, via Grenada, and let them go supplied with everything required to take Vicksburg." [57]

A note that Porter received from Grant on the 29th had shown that the determined general had no idea of going back but was thinking of advancing and operating below the coveted city. The very same day Porter replied with an expression of readiness to do his essential part,[58] and doubtless he was his usual buoyant and talkative self when, along with Sherman, he accompanied Grant on April 1 for the final conclusive look at the dreary region below Chickasaw Bluffs, at whose base ran the road lined with trenches and the batteries whose guns covered the few passages through the bayous that led to firm land. It must have been an experience to listen to the vigorous language that the general so gifted with eloquence directed at the one with the rarer gift of attentive, reflective silence. With a feeling that there would be ready assent and perfect cooperation, Grant could write on this April 2: "I would, admiral, therefore renew my request to prepare for running the blockade at as early a day as possible."

Fewer words were needed in the dispatch that would go to Washington through the Cairo telegrapher:

In two weeks I expect to be able to collect all my forces and turn the enemy's left. With present high water the extent of ground upon which troops could land at Haynes' Bluff is so limited that the place is impregnable. I reconnoitered the place yesterday with Porter and Sherman.[59]

A long letter of the 4th began by giving Halleck information that pointed to an attack on Rosecrans and related what was being done to strengthen Dodge at Corinth and prevent a simultaneous raid into western Tennessee. Then, after saying that hostile guns kept the canal from being of much use, Grant explained that the dredges were busily at work connecting bayous and streams from Milliken's Bend through Richmond to New Carthage. He told of his call on Allen at St. Louis for more barges and six tugs. One should, however, read Grant's own words about the only plan he now saw as practicable, and which he hoped the General in Chief would approve. The words are simple, but the proposal is audacious:

My expectation is for a portion of the naval fleet to run the batteries of Vicksburg, whilst the army moves through by this route. Once there, I will move either to Warrenton or Grand Gulf; most probably the latter. From either of these points there are good roads to Vicksburg, and from Grand Gulf there is a good road to Jackson and the Black River Bridge without crossing the Black River.[60]

Jackson! Why should Grant be talking about a road to Jackson when his objective was Vicksburg? Although it cannot be said with certainty that at this time he definitely intended to strike at Jackson before he turned on Vicksburg, the possibility of a move in the direction of the state capital was certainly in his mind. The reference is also important because it is repeatedly claimed that Grant kept his plans a secret from Halleck until it was too late for the General in Chief to interfere.

After quoting from the letter to Porter, the soldier-historian Francis Greene says:

Grant was now at the turning-point, not only of this campaign but of his whole career. He had not then the world-renowned fame with which we have so long been accustomed to associate his name; at that time he occupied a position in popular estimation similar to that held by Hooker, Rosecrans, and Banks, who then commanded the other principal armies, and like them he was on trial.[61]

Though it is impossible to achieve the state of mind of those who had watched through months of failure, to whom the story of the great weeks ahead would come slowly and imperfectly, piece by piece, defying belief and sometimes raising fears, one should try.

A Very Important Person was to view the speed and confidence with which the new plan moved forward, no other indeed than a special investigator and reporter for the Secretary of War. He was

Charles A. Dana, who had been managing editor of the *New York Tribune* for thirteen years, but had finally resigned upon Greeley's request because of differences in their views. Grant had met Dana while in Memphis prior to coming down the river to assume command. At that time Dana was making a special investigation about cotton buying, and as a result of his report Lincoln issued on April 2 a proclamation declaring unlawful all commercial intercourse with the insurrectionary states, except when carried on in accordance with regulations prescribed by the Secretary of the Treasury.[62]

Dana had little more than settled himself again in New York when he was called back to Washington and on March 12 accepted a new assignment. The identical letters that he was to present to Generals Sumner, Grant, and Rosecrans stated that he was commissioned to investigate and report about the condition of the pay service in the Western armies. (Sumner died on March 21 while en route to take command of the Department of the Missouri.) Years later Dana recorded that, at least in the case of Grant, the introduction he presented had been a mere blind. His real mission had been to report on military proceedings and give such information as would enable Lincoln and Stanton to settle their minds about Grant and the reports and complaints about him.[63]

In a dispatch written at Memphis on April 1 Dana said, "I have no doubt that General Grant is about to move the bulk of his army back up the river." This view was happily corrected the next day by the arrival of Brigadier General Joseph Webster, to whom Grant had just given the task of rebuilding the railroad from Grand Junction to Corinth. Webster was posted on the new program, and in his dispatch of the 2nd Dana sketched it for Stanton, who should have been receiving it about the time that it reached Halleck directly from Grant.[64]

When he stopped at Helena on the 5th, Dana learned that McClernand's corps should already be at New Carthage, but he could hear nothing about the return of the troops that had been operating against Fort Pemberton. The next day he reached Milliken's Bend and from then on sent dispatches that constitute one of the best accounts of the campaign. "Everything is going on cheeringly," was the beginning of the message on the 6th. Even small matters were not overlooked by the former newspaper man, who seemed a little concerned about comfort, to judge from the statements: "Weather continues cool here. Neither mosquitoes nor gnats have yet troubled men or animals." On the 10th Dana was saying that Sherman had thought Grant's plan precarious—as a letter to Rawlins on the 8th confirming Sherman's verbal protest to Grant had clearly recorded—but seemed to be changing his mind. Grant was firm in his determination, and Porter cordially supported the plan. It was not certain, Dana said, whether the enemy was aware of the new program. Parts of it had been published in Northern papers; but the Confederates probably would believe them a mere blind; they seemed to be making preparations to defend the bluffs.[65]

Dana's report of the 12th about a change of plans was a little inaccurate. A letter received from Halleck on the 10th had, he said, made Grant decide not to move up the Big Black toward Jackson and the bridge in the rear of Vicksburg, but to send the "main force" against Port Hudson. The letter referred to was probably the one Halleck had written on the 2nd, that what was most desired was cooperation of Grant's force and that of Banks "as early as possible." Halleck asked if Grant could not "get troops down to help" Banks at Port Hudson, if Banks could get none up the river to aid him at Vicksburg. He added that he knew Grant could judge better than he, and he was merely repeating a question the President had several times put to him. The letter called for no major change such as Dana indicated, and in a telegram to Halleck on the 11th, Grant had said, "Grand Gulf is the point at which I expect to strike, and send an army corps to Port Hudson to co-operate with General Banks." [66]

Anxiously the watch was kept to see if the Confederates had discerned the new plan. They still had not on the 14th, according to Dana's dispatch, but seemed to be expecting an assault on Haynes Bluff or on Vicksburg itself. And there was more good news than that: "Health and spirits of troops excellent. Weather cool and somewhat rainy, but not enough to spoil the roads." [67]

Pemberton was not only unaware of what was transpiring; he actually believed that because of Grant's double frustration above the city, Vicksburg was now in little danger. A telegram he had sent to Joe Johnston at Tullahoma on the 11th had ended, "Part of Grant's army reported to be going to Corinth and down the Mobile and Ohio Railroad; the balance to re-enforce Rosecrans." One the next day read: "I will forward troops to you as fast as transportation can be furnished—about 8,000 men. Am satisfied Rosecrans will be re-enforced from Grant's army. Shall I order troops to Tullahoma?"

Not until the 16th did he realize how completely in error he had been ever since the Federals had for the second time retired from in front of Fort Pemberton. Now he surprised Johnston with the message: "I can send you only two brigades. The latest information induces the belief that no large part of Grant's army will be removed." Still there was no indication that he had divined where the new stroke would be made. Troops already dispatched to strengthen Bragg, some of which had reached Chattanooga, were soon halted and returned to Mississippi.[68]

On the night of the 17th seven gunboats and three transports with boilers protected by bales of cotton and hay, and bearing loads of commissary stores, ran the Vicksburg batteries. Naval casualties were trifling, but the crew of one transport took to yawls when a shell exploded in the vessel, and she was lost. Dana counted 525 discharges from the Vicksburg batteries, which were aided by light from great fires upon the shore. On the 21st Grant told Halleck, "If I do not underestimate the enemy, my force is abundant, with a foothold once obtained, to do the work." The next night six transports, prepared like those on the test run, but for the most part manned by select crews from a host of competing volunteers from the army, ran past the hostile guns. All were struck and damaged in the blast of shells, but only the *Tigress*—Grant's headquarters boat in Shiloh days—was sunk, though the entire crew was saved. "Little extras" for wounded men that she carried, were, however, lost. Half of the twelve barges loaded with forage and rations that were in tow got through with cargoes fit for use. "I look upon this as a great success," Grant commented in a dispatch to Washington. The next afternoon—the 24th— Dana reported from New Carthage: "General Grant arrived here last night, and has gone with Admiral Porter to reconnoiter Grand Gulf. . . . The weather is hot, but the troops are in high spirits at the prospects of fighting." [69]

The White House and the War Office were getting the answers to any lingering doubts from the able pen of the special investigator.

As dawn was breaking on the day that Porter's gunboats tied up after their successful run, Colonel Grierson was riding out of La Grange, Tennessee, at the head of 1,700 troopers and a six-gun battery on one of the most remarkable raids of the war. It was an integral part of the Vicksburg operation, its aim being the distraction and confusion of the enemy and the interruption of supplies. As early as February 13 Grant had said in a dispatch to Hurlbut:

> It seems to me that Grierson, with about 500 picked men, might succeed in making his way south, and cut the railroad east of Jackson, Miss. The undertaking would be a hazardous one, but would pay well if carried out. I do not direct that this shall be done, but leave it for a volunteer enterprise.

Suggestions were made by Hurlbut, to whom Dickey a month later brought a message saying Grant wanted "the available cavalry put in as good condition as possible in the next few weeks for heavy service." In the operation that Grant sketched, no vehicles were to go except ambulances, and these were each to have an extra pair of horses. The message ended: "I look upon Grierson as being much better qualified to command this expedition than either Lee or Mizner. I do not dictate, however, who shall be sent. The date when the expedition should start will depend upon movements here. You will be informed of the exact time for them to start."

Although Grant's plans were subsequently changed, a cavalry operation into Mississippi from Tennessee remained a part of the program. On the day that Grierson rode away at the head of the Sixth and Seventh Illinois cavalries and the Second Iowa, and Battery K, First Illinois Artillery, Hurlbut wrote to Rawlins about his efforts to distract the enemy's attention and allow Grierson to get a fair start; then he said: "God speed him, for he has started gallantly on a long and perilous ride. I shall anxiously await intelligence of the result." [70]

The good news that the diversionary blow from La Grange had been launched and was in the best of hands may have arrived in time to lessen a new disappointment. "Owing to the limited number of transports below Vicksburg," Grant wrote in his report, "it was found necessary to extend our line of land travel to Hard Times, La., which, by the circuitous route it was necessary to take, increased the distance to about 70 miles from Milliken's Bend, our starting point." McClernand's corps, which had had to bridge numerous bayous in order to reach Perkins's plantation, five miles below New Carthage, and had had some desultory fighting with hostile cavalry, was, however, able to make the trip in steamboats. In reporting to Sherman on the reconnaissance that he had made with Porter, Grant said, "I foresee great difficulties in our present position, but it will not do to let these retard any movements." The letter ended: "It may possibly happen that the enemy may so weaken his forces about Vicksburg and Haynes' Bluff as to make the latter vulnerable, particularly with a fall of water to give an extended landing. I leave the management of affairs at your end of the line to you. I shall send Surgeon Hewitt to the Bend tomorrow, to consult with the medical director about the best policy to pursue for our sick and wounded." [71]

Charles Dana was not the only Very Important Person surveying operations. Lorenzo Thomas, Adjutant General of the Army, was also in front of Vicksburg. He had had many years of army life, having graduated from West Point in 1823, the year after David Hunter, but, unlike Hunter, he had served without a break. On March 25, thirteen days after he had sent Dana westward, Stanton ordered Thomas to the Mississippi Valley to make a general inspection and inaugurate the raising of Negro troops. The same Indiana soldier who had complained of the "aching void" caused by Van Dorn's destruction of hardtack and sowbelly recorded that he had never seen such a gorgeous uniform as Thomas wore when the Hoosier's brigade was paraded somewhere between Grand Junction and Memphis. After hearing Thomas read the order, Theodore Upson saw him draw "his splendid sword" and proclaim the order in effect. But to his diary Upson confided that none of the men in his regiment liked the idea of arming Negroes: it was a white man's war. [72]

Both David Dixon Porter and Sylvanus Cadwallader surpassed Upson in putting Thomas's visit into the record. In Porter's chatty, unreliable recollections, Thomas appears along with Governor Yates of Illinois and Congressman Elihu Washburne as a delegation to observe Grant, Thomas having in his satchel authority to remove Grant and name his successor. It is hardly complimentary to Lincoln to say that he sent three men to check on Dana; and there is the added difficulty of a cordial invitation to visit the army sent by Grant to Washburne on March 10. Cadwallader on his part states that Dana was ordered to carry out the mission of observing Grant, which had previously been given Thomas, but which the latter was neglecting. According to Cadwallader, it was feared that Thomas would not reach Grant's headquarters until midsummer, and Dana was dispatched. [73] Again chronology destroys a Cadwallader story. Thomas did not precede Dana; he followed Dana to the West.

Hurlbut informed Grant on April 5 that Thomas was in Memphis, and on the 11th Grant said in a letter to Fred Steele, "General L. Thomas is now here, with authority to make ample provision for the negro." In a dispatch to Stanton on the 12th, telling what had been done and what was to follow, Thomas said, "This army is in very fine condition, unusually healthy, and in good heart." [74] In that sentence alone Thomas earned a year's pay.

Five days later, when Pemberton was unhappily reporting to the Confederate Adjutant General about the running of the Vicksburg batteries, Thomas was writing to Stanton of what he had personally witnessed the night before when the first run was made over the fire-lighted river. Sherman, Thomas said, had taken position below the city in a small skiff and had boarded the *Benton* and seen the admiral. Again he waited in his skiff, a full half-hour, for the second boat, "and to the general's hail the answer was 'All well.' " On the 23rd Thomas wrote of the passage of the six steamers and the barges through the barrage of five hundred shells. Once more Sherman was there, this time with surgeons who boarded the boats to attend the wounded. Thomas named the officer in command of the transports—Colonel Lagow of Grant's staff, who had been in the lead on the ill-fated *Tigress*.[75]

Thomas probably did not know that a twelve-year-old boy had made the dangerous trip—Grant's oldest son, Frederick Dent Grant. Though the captain of the boat had sought to keep him below, the general's son wanted to witness the spectacle and managed to get on deck, where a coil of ship's cable gave him a measure of protection.[76]

Even after he had seen the first part of the hazardous operation succeed, Sherman was still gripped by doubts and fears. Nor did he realize that it was Grant's inner drive, the unconquerable spirit of never turning back, that was urging him on. To his brother, Sherman wrote that Grant was being impelled by clamor in the rear, clamor by "the same old damned cowardly herd, who disgrace our nation," and who remained in Ohio and other remote places, raising a hue and cry that made it necessary to "disregard all sense and wisdom to risk the impossibilities." Suspicion of the important Washington observer lurked in a sentence of a previous letter: "Mr. Dana is here I suppose to watch us all." (When it was all over Dana would say of Sherman in a letter to Stanton: "What a splendid soldier he is!") [77]

Lorenzo Thomas did not confine himself to the spectacular. A letter to Quartermaster General Montgomery Meigs had an ending that showed the tightening of matters in his department: "Colonel Reynolds has been relieved from duty here as chief quartermaster, by General Grant, and I have ordered him to report in person to you." [78]

Grant's reconnaissance of Grand Gulf on the 24th caused him to believe that the position was not as strong as Porter had deduced from a look at it on the 22nd. By replying to the gunboat fire on that day the Confederates had disclosed their batteries: four distinct works on the heights, with three guns in each. In addition, there were intrenchments for riflemen; Porter had put the garrison at 12,000. This picture of the situation had gone to Stanton from Dana, who had also reported that Adjutant General Thomas was making bad speeches to the troops, but that officers would nonetheless obey orders on the subject of Negro troops. Dana had also cautioned the Secretary on another point. A very trustworthy spy of Grant's had brought the information that in Mississippi there were agents of secret organizations in southern Indiana and Illinois, "who report that they are armed and ready for insurrection." [79] Though eventually this might concern Grant, his interest at the moment was in the Grand Gulf guns.

McClernand's corps having had the lead, it had been marked to gain the foothold on the east bank. Dana's report of the 25th noted that there was apparent confusion in the command, especially in McClernand's staff and headquarters. While Dana stated that the attack would be made the next day or the day after, the thought with which he closed was not of guns: "Though it is ordered that officers' horses and tents must be left behind, McClernand carries his bride along with him." In explaining two days later why the attack had not been made, Dana said one boat had made but a single trip to Hard Times instead of the two that Grant had ordered, partly because it had been "delayed by carrying General McClernand's wife, with her servants and baggage." McClernand had also, Dana said, taken time to review a brigade of Illinois troops in honor of Governor Yates, with cannons firing a salute "notwithstanding that positive orders had repeatedly been given to use no ammunition for any purpose except against the enemy." McPherson had now arrived with one division, and General Thomas had told Dana that his corps could probably be embarked before McClernand's.[80]

It was hardly a time to antagonize still more a close friend of the Illinois governor and, so far as Grant could then see, a favorite of the President. But a directive Grant gave McClernand on the 27th began quite bluntly: "Commence immediately the embarkation of your corps, or so much of it as there is transportation for." Now Grant foresaw that the enemy might occupy positions safe from the guns of the fleet, making it desirable to pass Grand Gulf and land ten miles below at Rodney. As it would be necessary in that case to land the troops for another march while the transports and gunboats ran the batteries, several signals had to be arranged. At the end the order switched to food: "If not already directed, require your men to keep three days' rations in their haversacks, not to be touched until a movement commences." [81]

Gallantly the navy attacked the Grand Gulf batteries at eight on the morning of the 29th and for five hours kept up a furious bombardment. To Grant, observing the battle from a tug, it seemed that Porter had his vessels within pistol shot of the hostile guns. The next day a Confederate would write that the firing had exceeded anything he had ever heard, adding: "I believe, too they gave us rather the worst of it. We did not sink a single boat, while they silenced one of our batteries, dismounted 4 pieces, killed Colonel Wade, commanding artillery, and one of his staff, and some 5 or 6 men." But the attackers took heavier punishment, the *Benton,* flying Porter's flag, being struck 47 times, and having 7 killed and 19 wounded, including 4 officers. The *Pittsburg* and the *Tuscumbia* also had killed and wounded, while the *Lafayette* was badly damaged. "At 12:25 rounded out and stood upstream to communicate with General Grant, who was on a tug. While going up used our stern guns," wrote the *Benton*'s captain, Lieutenant Commander James A. Greer.[82]

The gunboats being unable to silence the batteries, and it being clear to Grant that the Confederates were prepared to move field batteries to positions to oppose landings, the *Benton* broke out the signal, "Transports cannot pass." The troops were put ashore again at Hard Times and marched to a position opposite Bruinsburg, while the transports, under an evening shelling of the batteries by the gunboats, passed below to join them, Porter following in their rear. During the night a bit of luck made its appearance in the form of a Negro. There was, he said, a good road from Bruinsburg to Port Gibson; Grant, having faith in him, decided to land there rather than at Rodney.[83]

A letter to Sherman, who had been demonstrating against Haynes Bluff, began: "We have had terrific cannonading all day, without silencing the enemy's guns. Finding the position too strong, late in the day I decided to again run the blockade, which has been successfully done." Grant was landing the next day on the east bank with McClernand's corps and Logan's division of McPherson's; another of McPherson's could follow a day later. Because Sherman might worry about food, Grant said: "Under the directions sent a few days ago, between Macfeely and Bingham [the new chief quartermaster], the public teams and barges, rations ought to get along to supply the army. The cavalry can collect beef-cattle and grain for some little time." [84]

Halleck, who would appreciate the problem of supply as well as the boldness of the move, and the President must have found it hard to wait patiently for the next dispatch after they had read this:

The gunboats engaged Grand Gulf batteries from 8 a.m. until 1 p.m., and from dusk until 10 p.m. The army and transports are now below Grand Gulf. A landing will be effected on the east bank of the river to-morrow. I feel that the battle is now more than half won.[85]

"The casualties on the fleet to-day have been 22 killed and 55 wounded," was the ending of the dispatch that Dana sent just before midnight. He was doubtful if McClernand's corps would all be embarked before daylight, though Grant had given the most urgent orders. Not until early evening on May 8 would the message be in Washington.[86]

"Tomorrow"—Thursday, April 30, 1863—was the day which Lincoln, upon request of the Senate, had designated in a proclamation just a month before, "as a day of national humiliation, fasting, and prayer." It was an inspired selection, for two great operations were in a critical state upon that day. After a brilliant turning movement, part of Hooker's army had crossed the Rapidan and was in position behind Lee at Chancellorsville. But his success caused Hooker to issue a boastful and vainglorious order to his troops on the day the President had set aside for prayer.[87] Catastrophe followed swiftly. While Grant was clearly pleased and confident when the 29th had finally ended, there was no relaxing. Darkness had only caused "most urgent orders."

On the 29th Pemberton, still in Jackson, had much business for his telegrapher, and messages eastward went on wires recently repaired after Grierson's demolitions. On the 24th the raider had damaged the railroad and telegraph line to Meridian, and had captured and destroyed two trains, one loaded with railroad ties, the other with commissary stores and ammunition, including several thousand loaded shells. Now on the 29th in a message to Cooper, that began by reporting the heavy attack on Grand Gulf, Pemberton stated:

> The telegraph wires are down. The enemy has, therefore, either landed on this side of Mississippi River, or they have been cut by Grierson's cavalry, which had reached Union Church, on road from Hazelhurst to Natchez. All the cavalry I can raise is close on their rear. Skirmishing with them yesterday evening.

Grant could not have given orders more to his purpose than those which sent all Pemberton's cavalry after the raider. In a letter to Johnston of this date, Pemberton stated that Grierson had studiously avoided meeting infantry and presumably was en route to join Banks at Baton Rouge.[88]

Grierson was perhaps unglamorous, being only a former music teacher with a strong dislike for horses caused by a kick implanted on his face when he was a boy, which had left a lasting scar. But on April 29, 1863, and for weeks to come his name was on many tongues in Mississippi, some even voicing praise for the good discipline of his command. He was operating very coolly and very skillfully. On April 20 he had sent 175 men and one gun back to La Grange as a convoy for captured men and property. The next day he had sent Hatch with the Iowa regiment and one gun in the direction of Columbus in order to confuse the Confederates. Thus his force was now reduced to the thousand men of the two Illinois regiments and four guns.[89] Grierson's ride can be studied profitably even in these mechanical days when there are no columns of men on horseback with booted carbines and awesome sabers.

CHAPTER XII

THREE BATTLE-STUDDED WEEKS

The road to Vicksburg is open. All we want now are men, ammunition, and hard bread. *Grant to Sherman*

Upon one occasion you made two days' rations last seven. We may have to do the same thing again. *Grant to McPherson*

At early daylight on April 30 McClernand's Thirteenth Corps began to cross the Mississippi, gunboats lending aid to the few available steamers. The movement and the issuance of three days' rations consumed most of the day, and it was four o'clock before the regiments and batteries took the road to Port Gibson, eleven miles from Bruinsburg. Grant was eager to get firm high ground under his feet before he met resistance. But he also had to think about supply. A note to Quartermaster Bingham instructed that officer to prepare at once two tugs to run the blockade, each to tow two barges loaded with rations and some protective oats and hay. Bingham was to start the expedition within two days if possible. "Time is of immense importance. Should their crews decline coming through, call on the commanding officer for volunteers, and discharge the crews." [1]

McClernand's wagons and even his cavalry had been left on the west bank of the river until the combat elements of McPherson's Seventeenth Corps joined the advance. In a steamboat collision in the early hours of May 1, one of McPherson's batteries had been sunk with the transport conveying them, though only a few horses and three men were lost. The accident, however, delayed the passage of one brigade and some guns, while two brigades of Logan's division of McPherson's corps, and a battery, were hurried eastward, whence had come the sound of heavy and rapid gunfire. Though the heat was intense, the men moved with alacrity, for they were eager to have a part in the first battle, after their months of marching, idle waiting, or vain toil. Sherman, who had demonstrated against Chickasaw Bluffs on the 29th and 30th with Blair's division—gunboats cooperating energetically to make it look like a real attack—now put those of Steele and Tuttle on the march to Hard Times. Writing to Blair from the *Black Hawk,* Sherman instructed him to leave the Yazoo at eight o'clock and "let out for home"—Milliken's Bend, where Blair was temporarily to cover the army's rear. There was, however, a program for the afternoon, Sherman saying: "I will hammer away this p.m., because Major Rowley, now here, says that our division [diversion?] has had perfect success, great activity being seen in Vicksburg, and troops pushing up this way. By prolonging the effort, we give Grant more chance." To Grant there went a full report that contained the sentence, "We will be there as soon as possible." [2]

McClernand's advance had been met by light infantry fire and some artillery discharges about one o'clock in the morning of May 1, at a point some four miles from Port Gibson. Line of battle was formed and the fire was returned, but was stopped when the enemy guns became silent. Prudently McClernand waited for daylight before venturing farther. When day came he found himself at a fork in the road; what might have been a puzzling question was resolved when a Negro informed him that both roads led to Port Gibson. Brigadier General Peter J. Osterhaus (formerly seen at the Battle of Pea Ridge) was ordered to advance on the left road, as a diversion in favor of a heavy move down the road to the right—where the enemy was supposed to be the strongest—by the divisions of A. J. Smith, Hovey, and Eugene Carr (also seen at Pea Ridge). Each of McClernand's divisions had but two brigades of infantry, and an average of two batteries. [3]

When Grant arrived in person during the morning he found the first battle of the campaign in progress in country which he would describe to Halleck two days later as the most broken terrain he had ever seen. Irregular wooded ridges along which the roads mainly ran were separated from each other by deep ravines where timber was

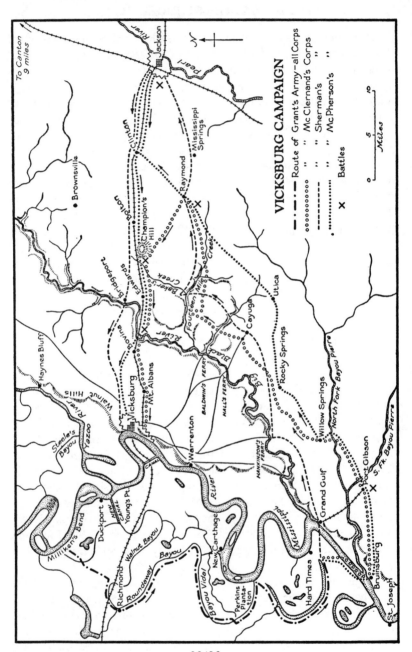

VICKSBURG CAMPAIGN

—·—·— Route of Grant's Army—all Corps
—·—·— " " McClernand's Corps
∘∘∘∘∘∘ " " Sherman's "
– – – – " " McPherson's "
∙∙∙∙∙∙ Battles
✕ Battles

Miles

interwoven with heavy undergrowth. It was a perfect region for the delaying of a superior force by a small one, and the 5,164 men with whom General Bowen had moved to Port Gibson from Grand Gulf were ably handled and fought subbornly. Repeated calls were made by McClernand for assistance, but though a personal inspection had made him think no more men could be used advantageously on the right, Grant had John D. Stevenson's brigade of Logan's division advance down the right-hand road. Bowen reported that an attempt he had made to turn the Federal position on that road routed one battle line, caused another to waver, but was stopped by a third line that stood firm. His statement that he was forced to fall back late in the afternoon only after a long and desperate struggle is confirmed by McClernand's report.[4]

Logan had personally gone with the brigade to the right, while McPherson took that of John E. Smith down the left road. There it worked over to the left of Osterhaus, and by making a vigorous charge as Osterhaus pressed forward, Smith—a man of Belmont, Donelson, and Shiloh—drove the enemy from a strong position. The Confederates were then pressed steadily back to near Port Gibson, where, as darkness fell, they rallied, causing the Federals to lie upon their arms and await the morning.[5]

In a later afternoon message Bowen informed Pemberton, now at Vicksburg, that he would "retire under cover of night to the other side of Bayou Pierre, and await re-enforcements." There was a happy ending: "The bacon is all removed out of Port Gibson. They will not get it." Pemberton's reply at 7:30 had begun hopefully: "Is it not probable that the enemy will himself retire to-night?" Pemberton felt it was very important for Bowen to hold his present position, if possible. To this statement he added, "You must, however, of course be guided by your own judgment. You and your men have done nobly. The account of the bacon is very gratifying." [6]

Signs of confusion were beginning to appear. In a later message to Bowen, Pemberton spoke of the great importance of driving the enemy back and keeping open communications with Grand Gulf and Port Gibson, then indicated displeasure: "You said this evening you would fight him on the other side of Bayou Pierre. Why have you changed your mind? You have now about 9,000 men, and ought to attack before he can greatly increase his strength." No fewer than six telegrams went to General Tilghman at Edwards about moving two regiments to the support of Bowen. Numerous messages passed between Pemberton and Loring at Jackson, one from the latter containing the sentences: "Your telegram says via Vicksburg, but does not say where we are to go. Please state also if wagons are to go." The cavalry that had been pursuing Grierson was ordered toward Port Gibson, and a telegram to President Davis informing him of the furious battle that had been in progress since daylight ended: "Am hurrying all re-enforcements I possibly can to Bowen. Enemy's success in passing our batteries has completely changed character of defense." [7]

Although Pemberton had telegraphed to Davis about the fight at Port Gibson, he also passed the news to the Confederate Adjutant General, with the expression of his confidence in Bowen's judgment. Cooper could cheer the President with two statements that did not go directly to Davis. The bacon had been moved to Grand Gulf—an assertion that went beyond what Bowen had said—and there had been no further demonstration at Chickasaw Bayou—which did not accord with Hébert's subsequent report to Pemberton about a "terrific bombardment" by the Federals from 3:00 until 7:30 P.M. To Johnston, Pemberton wired that he could not send the heavy reenforcements which Daniel Ruggles, at Columbus, Mississippi, was demanding, if it were true that the enemy was crossing the Tallahatchie at New Albany. Then, doubtless remembering Grierson's raiders, Pemberton said, "If these raids from Tennessee are not prevented, I cannot keep up railroad communication." [8]

Top Confederates were not unresponsive to the Vicksburg general on his unhappy May Day. Jefferson Davis wired that he had telegraphed Johnston about more cavalry and would try to obtain some from southern Alabama. Secretary Seddon acknowledged receipt of Pemberton's dispatch to Davis—there were two—and said, "Heavy re-enforcements will be sent from General Beauregard's command." From Tullahoma, where Davis had ordered him to go on January 22 to bolster Bragg, Joe Johnston sent advice: "If Grant's army lands on this side of the river, the safety of Mississippi depends on beating it. For that object you should unite your whole force." [9]

McClernand and McPherson were in motion early on the 2nd and soon discovered that Port Gibson had been vacated by the enemy.

Quick pursuit, however, was impossible, for the bridge on the rail-road to Grand Gulf and the near-by suspension bridge over the north fork of Bayou Pierre had been burned. So also had the suspension bridge over the south fork on the road leading northeast. Colonel Wilson was present with Grant and was assigned the task of building a bridge over the south fork with the aid of men from McClernand's corps, while the brigades of Smith and Elias A. Dennis—the remaining brigade of Logan's division, which had arrived late the day before—went three miles upstream under the guidance of a Negro and crossed at a ford. On moving to a position opposite the town, they encountered some of the now famous bacon. As there is a strong possibility that it was part Yankee, having been cured with northern salt that had come through the Memphis gateway, it was fitting that it be liberated.[10]

Meanwhile Wilson, who above all else believed in speed, had to wait three hours for the brigade which McClernand had early promised, and for which renewed requests, under Grant's order, were sent. It finally appeared at noon. Then things really moved. Some men went to work tearing down buildings, while others carried the materials to the stream, and yet others worked on the approaches. At 4:30 P.M. the division of Marcellus Crocker (replacement for the sick Quinby) of McPherson's corps was in "full motion" over "a continuous raft 166 feet long, 12 feet wide, with three rows of large mill-beams lying across the current, and the intervals between them closely filled by buoyant timber; the whole firmly tied together by a cross-floor or deck of 2-inch stuff." To make movement easier for the batteries and the wagons that eventually would follow, a roadway of timbers was laid parallel to the axis of the bridge; to keep men and animals out of the five feet of water upon which the raft floated strong side rails were added. The approaches being over quicksand, they were corduroyed, then covered with earth. Abutments had also been necessary; they were "formed by building a slight crib-work, and filling in with rails covered by sand."[11]

This was doubtless the finest structure that Grant had yet seen spring into being under the direction of tough-minded James Wilson, his inspector general.

For over a month McClernand had had the advance. But today his corps remained at Port Gibson while McPherson pushed on eight miles with the divisions of Crocker and Logan to Grindstone Ford over the north fork of Bayou Pierre (south of Willow Springs), where they extinguished a fire that had practically destroyed a fine suspension bridge. The bridge having been repaired under Wilson's direction during the night, the corps was on the move at daylight, Logan leading. As they neared Willow Springs, about three miles beyond the stream, deployment became necessary when artillery fire greeted the column. Though the hostile force was not large, it was advantageously placed; when dislodged it retreated northward toward Hankinson's Ferry. At the crossroads in Willow Springs, Grant turned westward toward Grand Gulf with one brigade of Logan's division, while the balance of the division with that of Crocker pushed northward after the retreating Confederates.[12]

On the 2nd Pemberton telegraphed to Governor Pettus that he thought it likely that Grant would move on Jackson. He recommended that the state archives be removed, and he ordered his own subordinates to send records and machinery eastward, while all possible ordnance and ammunition were sent to Vicksburg. As to himself, Pemberton said, "I am moving all my forces to relieve Bowen." [13]

That Pemberton strengthened Bowen so as to block a Federal move directly from Port Gibson to Grand Gulf was indicated in a dispatch that McClernand sent to Grant on the 3rd. But the thrust toward Willow Springs had, McClernand said, caused the retreat of the Confederates, his statement being based upon a reconnaissance made by men Carr had thrown across the bayou on the ruins of the railroad bridge. In a second message from near Willow Springs informing Grant that his corps was close upon McPherson's train, McClernand cautioned, "Had you not better be careful lest you may personally fall in with the enemy on your way to Grand Gulf?" Grant, however, was anxious to reach that place, and upon learning from contrabands and prisoners that the last of the enemy had passed, he left the infantry brigade and covered the remaining seven miles with an escort of about twenty cavalrymen.[14]

Pemberton received some cheering news from Johnston on the 2nd. Referring doubtless to threats by Rosecrans's troops, Johnston said, "Enemy reported falling back." Already he had Forrest moving toward the west, while cavalry had been instructed to operate in Mississippi. Carefully refraining from using the word Vicksburg, he hinted in the concluding sentences that even that place might best be abandoned: "If Grant crosses, unite all your troops to beat him.

Success will give back what was abandoned to win it." This and previous messages caused Pemberton to put a note of temperate optimism into a dispatch of the 3rd to Davis that he would concentrate west of the Big Black: "With cavalry in Northern Mississippi and re-enforcements promised, think we will be all right." [15]

Porter could not have been happy at his failure to silence the Grand Gulf guns, and on the morning of May 3 he returned with four gunboats to make a new attack. The enemy had already left, after spiking his large pieces, burying or taking with him his smaller ones, and blowing up his ammunition. In a letter to Welles, Porter said, "We had a hard fight for these forts, and it is with great pleasure that I report that the Navy holds the door to Vicksburg." Actually, Porter had done nothing that really counted in gaining the position except to repair promptly and efficiently transports badly damaged in running the Vicksburg batteries, protect them, and help ferry troops across the river. His fire, he reported to the Navy Secretary, had literally torn the forts to pieces, leaving everything so covered with earth that it was hard to tell at a glance what was there. He was much impressed by the position, saying: "Grand Gulf is the strongest place on the Mississippi. Had the enemy succeeded in finishing the fortifications no fleet could have taken them." Porter thought that Grant would move against Grand Gulf, for he said, "I hear nothing of our army as yet; was expecting to hear their guns as we advanced on the forts." [16]

Before Porter departed for Red River, as he said he would do within the hour, the army appeared: Grant and his twenty troopers. The general tells us in his *Memoirs* that he at once got a bath, borrowed some fresh underclothing from one of the naval officers, and had a good meal on the flagship.[17] In the minds of the flagship officers it must have augured well when Grant went ashore in fresh navy underwear.

Though there is some contradiction in the record, it was probably at Grand Gulf that Grant received a letter from Farragut, written on May 1 in the famous *Hartford,* off Red River. It transmitted a letter from Banks to Grant dated April 10 at Brashear City (present Morgan City), seventy miles west of New Orleans, and fifteen miles from the mouth of the Atchafalaya River.[18] Before telling what Banks had to say and the additional and important news which Farragut imparted, something should be said to explain why Banks was in this position so remote from Port Hudson, where lay the great Confederate fort that had kept him from carrying out his instructions to ascend the Mississippi and cooperate with Grant, orders, it will be recalled, which were issued before the great strength of this enemy position was

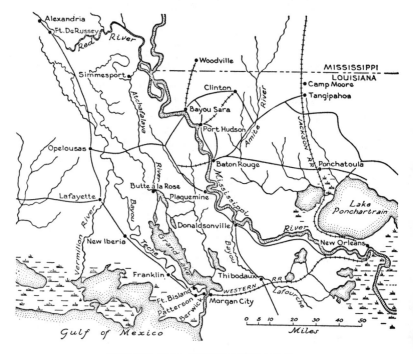

REGION OF BANKS'S OPERATIONS

known in Washington. As it is customary to look condescendingly upon Banks or to belittle him, his operations will be noticed briefly. The occasion seems propitious, because the corps of McClernand and McPherson will remain comparatively inactive for a few days, while Grant makes important decisions and awaits supplies and the eager red-haired Sherman.

The total force that Banks had in his department numbered 30,000, but of his fifty-six regiments twenty-two had been enlisted for only nine months, with the first enlistments expiring in May, others in July, and the balance in August. After providing for the many places he was compelled to garrison along the Gulf, and for Baton Rouge, Banks had only from 12,000 to 14,000 men available for an operation against Port Hudson. He moved most of his mobile force to the rear of that place on March 13 to make a demonstration to assist Farragut in his only partially successful passage of the batteries. If Banks over-estimated the enemy force in the works, he was no more guilty than Sherman had been when in front of Vicksburg in the last days of December, and there is no reason to think he could have easily carried the position. Though he returned to Baton Rouge on the 15th, he presently carried out a successful passage of a point of land across from Port Hudson, but failed to make contact with Farragut, who had moved to the mouth of the Red River. Then, on the 25th, he transferred his main operations to the west, where Brigadier General Godfrey Weitzel was in position to operate on the Teche (a river-like bayou that joined the Atchafalaya near Morgan City and reached up to the vicinity of Opelousas), as well as on the Atchafalaya. Four light gunboats were present to assist him.[19]

If it seems that Banks was launched upon a circuitous approach to his assigned target, it is to be noted that Grant, when he read Banks's dispatch, was likewise far from Oxford where his headquarters had been when Van Dorn destroyed his supplies at Holly Springs. Banks's move was to have a very valuable diversionary effect upon the Confederates in Louisiana. They were under the immediate command of Major General Richard Taylor, but Edmund Kirby Smith had recently taken control of all forces west of the Mississippi with headquarters at Shreveport. (Holmes had dropped down to command of the District of Arkansas; Hindman had disappeared from the Arkansas scene; Sterling Price had reappeared, leaving, however, his homesick regiments east of the Mississippi.) [20]

In his April 10 dispatch Banks told Grant that Farragut's secretary had just called and imparted the substance of the message that Grant had written on March 22 in answer to the letter Banks had given Farragut on the 13th to take up the river. The secretary had also reported on the contents of a letter that Grant had written the admiral on March 23 with the request that what he had said should be communicated to Banks. The papers had been too important to trust to the skiff in which the secretary had passed the Port Hudson guns, and by relying on verbal transmission a serious error was committed. Grant's statement in the letter to Farragut that he could send 20,000 men to help Banks at Port Hudson *if* he could obtain boats able to go through the Lake Providence route was transmitted without the vital proviso. Accordingly, Banks said that after completing a move on Opelousas which would start the next day, he would hasten back to Baton Rouge with his 15,000 men and be ready to cooperate with Grant by May 10. But this he did not do, partly perhaps because of the stimulation of success he had achieved in routing Taylor's force, and partly because the arrival at Opelousas on April 21 of the actual messages Grant had written revealed the false idea that had been given him by Farragut's secretary.[21]

The long letter that Banks wrote on April 23 explaining what had taken place, and in which he said his advance was thirty miles beyond Opelousas on the road to Alexandria, had not reached Farragut when, on May 1, the admiral forwarded to Grant the one brought back by his secretary. In his covering letter Farragut could, however, inform Grant that Banks had defeated Taylor and captured 2,000 prisoners— which the able and highly polished presidential son vigorously denied. But the sailor's statement that the gunboats operating with Banks had destroyed the *Queen of the West* was solid truth. Her end had come in a fight that began at dawn while she was convoying two transports, one filled with troops, on Grand Lake, a little above Morgan City. Under date of April 14 a member of the crew of the *Calhoun,* that fired the fatal shell at extreme range, wrote: ". . . I did not see the shot, but I heard it fired, heard its flight, and its landing on the *Queen,* its explosion and the rush of steam that followed. . . . The engineers were driven from the casemate and no pump could be started; in a few moments the *Queen of the West* was in a blaze. . . . The boats of our fleet took off her crew, and in about two hours (7:40) her magazine exploded and she was no more. . . . This was a remarkable battle. . . ."

From the pocket of one of the *Queen's* officers there was taken a letter from Taylor which revealed that Taylor had planned an attack upon Morgan City the day before Banks had attacked one of Taylor's forts and compelled its abandonment. Previous to this, Banks had destroyed the enemy gunboat *Diana,* another vessel that had been captured from the Federals.[22]

While Banks was pressing on toward Opelousas, Pemberton was hoping for aid from west of the Mississippi. An appeal of April 17 to "Lieutenant-General Smith or Major-General Taylor" was followed by this on the 18th: "The enemy are cutting a passage from near Young's Point to Bayou Vidal, to reach the Mississippi River near New Carthage. Without co-operation it is impossible to oppose him. Inform me what action you intend to take." Smith on his part, however, was on the eve of earnestly soliciting help from Pemberton. Taylor, he wrote, was being compelled to retire before overwhelming forces. An effort would be made to hold Opelousas, but unless reenforcements came swiftly, it would be impossible to keep Banks out of Alexandria. Could not help be sent to Taylor from Port Hudson? Such was Smith's query on April 19. Of course, Pemberton was not so improvident as to send any troops beyond the great river. How they would have crossed is not clear; and because of time and distance, nothing but a sizable drop of paratroopers could have bolstered Taylor. It was in fact the day after Smith made his appeal that Banks entered Opelousas—where Governor Moore had set up operations after Ben Butler had driven him out of Baton Rouge—the enemy, according to Banks, "retreating toward Alexandria in disorder, and destroying the bridges in his flight." [23] The onetime governor of Massachusetts and former Speaker of the House, who less than a year before had made a historic descent of the Shenandoah Valley to find sanctuary beyond the Potomac from Stonewall Jackson, can surely be pardoned if he warmed with pleasure at being on the persuading end of a pursuit.

After observing that it had taken forty days for Grant to receive a reply to his letter to Banks of March 22—and at that not a reply based on actual reading of the letter—Greene aptly says, "It was hopeless to effect any co-operation between two armies with such delay in communicating intelligence." Grant saw this clearly, and quickly discarded his intention of cooperating with Banks against Port Hudson in accordance with the strong wish of the President. It had been his plan to use Grand Gulf as a base and send McClernand to aid Banks, expecting that after the reduction of Port Hudson, Banks would join him with his own and McClernand's corps. But the delay that would be involved, and the unexpected smallness of Banks's force, which would be further reduced by operations and the necessity of holding positions on the long stretch of river between Grand Gulf and Port Hudson, made this program simply out of the question. In casting it aside Grant could feel that he was not acting contrary to the judgment of the General in Chief, for Halleck had clearly implied that he raised the question about the possibility of moving to aid Banks solely because of Lincoln's impatience and repeated questioning. Some doubt about such a move certainly lurked in Halleck's statement, "I know that you can judge of these matters there much better than I can here." [24]

Grant probably estimated the force in Vicksburg at about 23,000, an imposing number for a position naturally strong and elaborately intrenched. There were, furthermore, other forces available to Pemberton, his return for March showing no fewer than 61,495 men present.[25] This total would exceed the number of men Grant would have with him for some weeks. While he could only guess at the forces that Pemberton might concentrate, he knew of their existence; he also knew that over the railroad from the east reenforcements would come to Jackson. To wait for Banks could find Grant relatively weaker than he was at the moment. It was essential that he operate with the force he had. But how?

In appraising the situation Liddell Hart says, "Grant's bold move had succeeded thus far, but the worst risk was still ahead." Fuller is still more emphatic: "Grant was now faced by a problem unique in the history of war," and he adds that "it would be almost impossible to devise a more desperate one." [26]

Supply of his army on conventional lines was impossible, even though the gaining of Grand Gulf had cut a few miles from the route traveled by McClernand and McPherson. The Vicksburg guns would exact a toll of all boats and barges that followed the direct river route; hostile cavalry could interrupt the circuitous road and canal-bayou routes to the west, and forces left to guard them would deplete Grant's striking power. Bayous and swampy regions beyond gave some protection, but land was drying, and Grant was neither intimately familiar with the region nor did he know what cavalry and guerrilla bands might be able to strike columns of vulnerable wagons. If Banks had withdrawn his force after a move on Opelousas, as he had said he would do, and was already en route to Port Hudson by the way he had advanced, Taylor's forces had been freed of any pressure and could strike at Grant's installations and communication line in Louisiana.

On this day, while Grant was weighing and deciding, Hooker would struggle to save the army he had led to Chancellorsville and would personally become a casualty. Three days later his bewildered subordinates would lead the Army of the Potomac back across the Rappahannock, though half of its units had been unengaged in the fighting. Just how or when Grant first learned of all this one cannot say; and it is of no importance. But the government in Washington knew about it and the North knew about it. This fact should be recalled, if one chooses to reflect upon the reaction in Washington to the news that belatedly came from below Vicksburg while the dust was still settling along the Rappahannock.

The first unimpeachable documents in the case are the dispatches Grant wrote at Grand Gulf on May 3. Unfortunately, hours are not shown, but the first message must have been a short one to Halleck. After stating—certainly not for the purpose of having an excuse on file—"The country is the most broken and difficult to operate in I ever saw," Grant continued, "Our victory has been most complete, and the enemy thoroughly demoralized." In a letter that went into detail, Grant wrote: "General Bowen's (the rebel commander) defense was a very bold one and well carried out. My force, however, was too heavy for him, and composed of well-disciplined and hardy men, who know no defeat, and are not willing to learn what it is."

The *Memoirs* seem to imply that Grant's decision to cut loose from his base and live entirely on the country was made on the 3rd. It must have been made after the letter to Halleck, for in this he said, "The country will supply all the forage required for anything like an active campaign, and the necessary fresh beef. Other supplies will have to be drawn from Milliken's Bend. This is a long and precarious route, but I have every confidence in succeeding in doing it." Living on the Southerners would be entirely in line with what Halleck said when replying to Grant after Corinth: "Why not re-enforce Rosecrans and pursue the enemy into Mississippi, *supporting your army on the country*?" (Italics supplied.) Again, when outlining Washington plans on November 15, he had spoken of "feeding as far as possible on the country." [27]

To General Sullivan, who had been brought from Jackson and was in command of troops along the supply route, Grant sent directions to shorten the line and, as soon as the river had fallen sufficiently, to build a road from Young's Point to a landing just below Warrenton. A dispatch to Sherman indicated another stage in the evolution of logistics on this day. Sherman was to collect 120 wagons, load them with 100,000 pounds of bacon, then fill up with coffee, sugar, salt, and hard bread. On advancing from Grand Gulf, he was to load his own regimental wagons with five days' rations; he was also reminded of the "overwhelming importance" of "celerity" in his movements. After explaining what had been accomplished, and asserting that the enemy had been badly beaten and was demoralized, Grant closed in a manner to make Sherman still more eager to be with the striking force: "The road to Vicksburg is open. All we want now are men, ammunition, and hard bread. We can subsist our horses on the country, and obtain considerable supplies for our troops." [28]

In his letter to Halleck, Grant noted that Porter had left in the morning for the mouth of the Red River. Comment about Banks was equally brief: a letter from Farragut said he had defeated Taylor and captured 2,000 prisoners. While it is strange that Grant did not mention the three-weeks-old letter from Banks that had been responsible for Farragut's letter, the fact that cooperation with Banks had been dismissed was revealed as clearly as if spelled out explicitly: "I shall not bring my troops into this place, but immediately follow the enemy, and, if all promises as favorable hereafter as it does now, not stop until Vicksburg is in our possession." When Halleck read that, he would see that Grant was certainly fulfilling the last words of the letter he had written him on April 2, quoted from above: "I hope you will push matters with all possible dispatch."

The concluding paragraph of Grant's letter was devoted to Grierson, whose raid Grant pronounced "the most successful thing of the kind" since the beginning of the war. "The Southern papers and Southern people regard it," Grant said, "as one of the most daring exploits of the war. I am told the whole State is filled with men paroled by Grierson." Happy indeed would the warmhearted general have been if he could have known that while he was sprucing up on the gunboat, Grierson's troopers were spending the Sunday resting and improving their appearance in a magnolia grove near Baton Rouge. They had arrived there the day before and many were soon too fast asleep to be aroused to eat the food brought by squads of the Thirty-eighth Massachusetts and One Hundred and Sixteenth New York Infantry regiments.[29]

Grant had also made a contribution to a very bold but ill-fated raid that Colonel Abel D. Streight was then making into Alabama at the instance of General Rosecrans. A dispatch from Hurlbut on May 3 told Grant that, in accordance with instructions, Dodge had furnished 500 horses for the expedition, which had ascended the Tennessee in boats. Before he made his Grand Gulf decisions, Grant probably had received a message Hurlbut had written on April 28, reporting that he had sent some of Grant's troops into Missouri. Marmaduke was on another raid and had attacked Cape Girardeau. On learning of this from Asboth at Columbus, Hurlbut had promptly ordered that two regiments, a squadron of cavalry, and two guns should be sent, with instructions to return when reenforcements arrived from St. Louis.[30] Grant would surely indorse such action, for aiding a threatened command was one of his basic tenets, and Curtis—under whom Asboth had previously served—had been depleted to strengthen the Vicksburg thrust. Here is evidence that department lines were not the inflexible barriers sometimes represented. Washington had directed that Grant make a contribution to the department commander to the east; one of Grant's subordinates took the responsibility in the case of the one to the west.

Grant did not tarry at Grand Gulf; midnight found him riding to join his army.[31] At some place on the road he must have encountered Federal pickets, and it would have been interesting to hear the challenge and the answer. If it was his voice, and not that of the commander of the escort, that made the response, it was probably recognized. The men in the advance knew him well. And he knew them—he had this day testified to that in what he had said to Halleck.

The 5th found Grant at Hankinson's Ferry on the Big Black River, where Crocker's division of McPherson's corps had arrived on the 3rd after pushing back a stubborn enemy over equally stubborn terrain. Upon the appearance of Logan's division in a manner that threatened their right, the Confederates retreated in haste toward the ferry. Dennis's brigade of the division—four regiments of Fort Donelson and Shiloh men—were in time to capture some pioneer tools and save the bridge. One of the regiments—the Twentieth Ohio—was commanded by Manning Force, previously seen both as a troop commander and as a historian of the war. In his report he said that continuous forced marching for nine days, with loss of sleep and sore feet, while others fought, had had an effect upon his men by the 3rd. Then he added, "But as soon as word was given that an enemy was in front, and the firing of skirmishers was heard, every eye lighted up." [32]

While McPherson on the 5th was vigorously reconnoitering beyond the Big Black in the direction of Warrenton and Vicksburg, Grant was writing several important messages. Captain D. E. Owen, of the Navy (Porter, it will be recalled, had left for the Red River), was asked to place his flagship in the mouth of the Big Black to block that stream, and to leave another vessel at Grand Gulf to protect stores and convoy any steamer that might require it. The remaining ironclads Grant wanted sent to Warrenton to prevent the Confederates crossing the river to break his delicate line back to Milliken's Bend and Young's Point. Prentiss at Helena was directed to send all his cavalry except two regiments to Memphis because of threats from east of the Tennessee. Too often it has been forgotten that while Grant was facing great logistical problems south of Vicksburg he still had to give earnest thoughts to western Tennessee. A letter to Hurlbut told him to send Lauman's division to Milliken's Bend with full equipment, and apprised him of the cavalry being sent him by Prentiss. As soon as the railroad was operating all the way to Corinth, Hurlbut could abandon everything north of the line, but he was to throw into Corinth a sixty-day supply of rations and forage. His cavalry force was to wage a pretty tough war, crippling "the rebellion in every way, without insulting women and children or taking their clothing, jewelry, etc." [33]

A dispatch to Colonel Hillyer at Grand Gulf began, "We will risk no more rations to run the Vicksburg batteries." After giving full directions about the troops that were still to come forward, Grant ended, "All other forces are to return to Young's Point." Another staff member, Major T. S. Bowers, still at Milliken's Bend, was growing fearful about how the army would live. Supplies had to be wagoned forty-four miles before steamers could pick them up. Because of limited transportation and the lengthening line as Grant moved inland, Bowers feared it would be "impossible to keep the army from suffering." So he took it upon himself to appeal to Hurlbut for more vehicles.[34]

Sherman likewise was anxious. A dispatch at 7:00 A.M. from Perkins's plantation to Blair began, "I received your letter last night, telling of the sinking of one tug, and the two burning barges floating by tell the rest of the tale." Blair was now to come forward, turning over command to Sullivan; though he was to hurry, he was to arrive with his men "in good shape." Steele was informed by Sherman that he had only twenty miles to march before he could cross. Tuttle, commanding Sherman's remaining division, was told of the two burning barges that had ominously floated past. In addition, Grant had directed Sherman to make three days' rations last five. Regimental commanders must therefore save every ounce of food. Eagerness, pride, and wisdom were in Sherman's concluding sentence: "There are now six divisions of our men across and operating east of Grand Gulf. Let us catch up as quickly as possible consistent with bringing our men there in good fighting condition." [35]

In an informative dispatch from Grand Gulf on the 4th, Dana had spelled out for Stanton in clear fashion the plan as it then stood:

General Grant intends to lose no time in pushing his army toward the Big Black and Jackson, threatening both and striking at either, as is most convenient. As soon as Sherman comes up and the rations on the way arrive, he will disregard his base and depend on the country for meat and even for bread. Beef-cattle and corn are both abundant everywhere.[36]

Dana's previous dispatches had brought conviction to the White House and the War Office. While Sherman was hurrying Steele, Tuttle, and Blair forward, Stanton was sending Dana a message, perfect in the sweep of its thought and flawless in its language:

General Grant has full and absolute authority to enforce his own commands, and to remove any person who, by ignorance, inaction, or any cause, interferes with or delays his operations. He has the full confidence of the Government, is expected to enforce his authority, and will be firmly and heartily supported; but he will be responsible for any failure to exert his powers. You may communicate this to him.[37]

On the 6th Grant and Sherman wrote characteristic messages. Into a few lines to Hurlbut, Grant packed much. The Memphis general was to report directly to Halleck how many of his troops Grant had called forward. In the future he would do as he saw fit, referring important matters to Washington, but letting Grant know what was transpiring. Realizing how eager Hurlbut would be for news, Grant said, "Everything here looks highly favorable at present." He had had troops to within seven miles of Warrenton; he commanded the next crossing over the Big Black, which was fifteen miles up the stream, whence a road led directly to Vicksburg. Knowing that Sherman would not fail him, Grant could say, "Rations now are our only delay." [38]

Not a dull line was in the long letter that Sherman sent to Frank Blair at noon from opposite Grand Gulf. It was sixty-three miles from Milliken's Bend; the road could not be mistaken; it was better at the end than at the beginning. While Sherman grieved at the loss of the tug, he said the barges had been picked up and some of the provisions would be saved; "but none of the reporters 'floated.' " He offered an explanation and some reflections about the missing newsmen: "They were so deeply laden with weighty matter that they must have sunk. In the language of our Dutch captain, 'What a pity for religion in this war!' but in our affliction we can console ourselves with the pious reflection that there are plenty more left of the same sort." (The correspondents had not sunk but were safely in Confederate hands.) Because of the delay in getting wagons over the river, Blair was told he need not force his men; he must, however, do his best in bringing salt, coffee, sugar, and bread. Not many soldiers have been privileged to receive such a letter. The ending was:

I shall begin to look for you on the third day from this, unless we move far inland. Grant is now 18 miles northeast of Grand Gulf.

I shall keep in mind where you are, and await your junction with great anxiety.

With great respect, your friend,

W. T. SHERMAN [39]

On the day that Grant cut Hurlbut loose from him, he hinted strongly to Halleck as to how he would operate, though not as explicitly as Dana had explained the plan to Stanton. As soon as he had three days' supply of rations he would move, sending wagons back to Grand Gulf for more. From information communicated by Southerners, he was led to believe that the enemy was bringing reenforcements from Tullahoma. His own experience with the Federal commander at Murfreesboro makes it likely that he was not optimistic when he queried, "Should not General Rosecrans at least make a demonstration of advancing?" [40]

Only the orders and messages in the *Official Records* tell the story adequately and reveal the feelings of the chief participants in the campaign. One must read the well-timed order in which Grant spoke to his troops on the 7th; his directives; his dispatch to Bowers on the 9th, explaining precisely what he wanted impressed upon the generals still on the Louisiana side; the full reports to him from McClernand; the terse messages from McPherson to his division commanders (one to Crocker has a postscript that reveals the fewness of the maps: "Colonel Boomer has the map showing the road to Utica, etc."); the vibrant letters of Sherman. Even the letter that the quartermaster at Milliken's Bend sent Grant on the 8th is eloquent with figures: the supplies that had gone by wagon; the 2,000,000 complete rations at the base; the half-million en route; the assurance that a stock of 3,000,000 would be kept on hand. It all meant planning and hard work by countless people, reaching back to the houses and fields in the states whence came the men to whom Grant said: "More difficulties and privations are before us. Let us endure them manfully. Other battles are to be fought. Let us fight them bravely." [41]

Nor should one overlook the masterful reporting that Charles Dana was doing, which did much to build confidence in Washington. He detailed troop movements and threw in touches sometimes lacking elsewhere. On the 8th he said that Colonel Prime had sent word that the shorter wagon route from Milliken's Bend, for which Grant had been earnestly hoping, could not be achieved. There was an intervening crevasse that could not be conquered. As if to suggest that the many miles were not too wearisome, he said, "The weather is cool and splendid." [42]

The 8th found Sherman arriving at Hankinson's Ferry with the divisions of Steele and Tuttle. Crocker's division, which had been holding a bridgehead suggestive of a direct advance on Vicksburg, was relieved and hastened to join McPherson at Rocky Springs, where Grant also had his headquarters. In between, along the road from Willow Springs, lay McClernand's corps. At four the next morning Sherman wrote to Grant of his anxiety over the congestion at Grand Gulf. Hillyer, he said, was doing his best to control traffic, but division and brigade commanders were all trying to get their vehicles across the river. Sherman wanted an order issued at once that would regulate matters, to be sent to corps, division, and brigade commanders, and which Hillyer could enforce. As if in despair, Sherman said: "Stop all troops till your army is partially supplied with wagons, and then act as quickly as possible, for this road will be jammed as sure as life if you attempt to supply 50,000 men by one single road." [43]

The answer that Sherman received began: "I do not calculate upon the possibility of supplying the army with full rations from Grand Gulf. I know it will be impossible without constructing additional roads. What I expect, however, is to get up what rations of hard bread, coffee, and salt we can, and make the country furnish the balance." Grant had left Bruinsburg with an average of only two days' rations, but had found "some corn meal, bacon, and vegetables" and an abundance of beef and mutton. If Sherman found provisions scarce at Hankinson's, it was because troops had lived in that vicinity. As new soil was reached food was more plentiful, especially corn and cattle.[44]

In his *Memoirs* Grant explained that every plantation "had a run of stone, propelled by mule power, to grind corn for the owners and their slaves. All these were kept running while we were stopping, day and night, and when we were marching, during the night, at all plantations covered by the troops." All men, however, would not get meal, for there was not sufficient to go around.[45]

Men might fight without bread; but they could not do so without ammunition. Yet Grant had started his troops eastward from Bruinsburg to certain combat before any wagons had crossed the river. To make good the cartridges that would be fired, he had ordered immediately on landing upon the east bank that all animals—horses, mules, and oxen—as well as vehicles, be collected. The first train to reach him was a motley aggregation of vehicles from fine carriages to plantation wagons, all loaded with boxes of ammunition.[46] The makeshift served initial requirements well but every rifle cartridge, every artillery round for the campaign had to come from Milliken's Bend, cross the river, and go forward either with the combat troops or in wagons adequately guarded.

A talk with Grant did not entirely convince Sherman, for on the 9th he began a letter to Blair: "I rode forward 6 miles to-day to Rocky Springs, and found all the army moving. Also General Grant, with whom I had a full conversation. He is satisfied that he will succeed in his plan, and, of course, we must do our full share." The next day the bridge would be broken, Sherman said, and the march started for Jackson. There was some, though not too much danger, that Blair might be attacked, as he brought up the army rear, but Sherman cautioned him about letting his wagons be filled with "trash." He feared the "want of salt, bread, sugar, and coffee." [47]

In spite of what Sherman said, a direct march on Jackson did not start at once. The 10th found Grant still at Rocky Springs, replying to a message Banks had written only four days before at Opelousas, remarkable for its brevity: "By the 25th, probably, by the 1st certainly, we will be there" (meaning, of course, Port Hudson). Equally discreet was Grant in his reply which explained why he had not turned southward toward Port Hudson: "For fear of this accidentally falling into the hands of the enemy, I will not communicate to you my force." But the important sentence was the one that asked cooperation from Banks against Vicksburg. Grant thought the battle for Vicksburg would start soon, and it was impossible to predict how long it would last. "Urgently," he requested Banks to join him or send all the force he could "spare to co-operate in the great struggle for opening the Mississippi River." [48]

Entirely in harmony with Grant's request was a dispatch that Halleck sent him the next day, May 11, the pertinent part of which was:

If possible, the forces of yourself and of General Banks should be united between Vicksburg and Port Hudson, so as to attack these places separately with the combined forces. The same thing has been urged upon General Banks.

This message, which we shall see apparently reached Grant about the time new letters came from Banks, may have been the basis for the claim soon to be made that Grant was able to carry through his movement against Vicksburg only by neglecting a direct order from Halleck that reached him in the field. The qualifying words at the start are not to be overlooked. On the 15th, and thus well before he could have received Halleck's message, Grant informed the General in Chief that on the 10th he had asked Banks to join him "as soon as possible." [49]

Greene says in his discerning book, "On the night of the 11th Grant had his army well in hand." The line, as Grant explained it in a message to Halleck, was generally east and west, with the left—McClernand—near the Big Black, the line as far advanced toward Fourteen Mile Creek as possible "without bringing on a general engagement." Storing up food was the concern of the moment, Grant saying in a directive to McPherson, who was on the right (Sherman was in the center at Auburn, five miles northeast of Cayuga):

Move your command to-night to the next cross-roads if there is water, and to-morrow with all activity into Raymond. At the latter place you will use your utmost exertions to secure all the subsistence stores that may be there, as well as in the vicinity. We must fight the enemy before our rations fail, and we are equally bound to make our rations last as long as possible. Upon one occasion you made two days' rations last seven. We may have to do the same thing again.[50]

At 3:30 on the morning of the 12th, McPherson marched from a position northeast of Utica, his leading division being that of Logan, "gallant and irrepressible"—according to Dana and Wilson, who wrote soon after the war when men and events were still fresh in their memories. Because of enemy vedettes, it was soon necessary to deploy a regiment on either side of the road and advance with skirmishers in front of a battle line, while the cavalry, called in from the front, explored the flanks. At about eleven o'clock, when within two miles of Raymond, an enemy force was encountered which McPherson estimated at from 4,000 to 5,000, not a bad figure for the seven-regiment brigade of Brigadier General John Gregg, which was "judiciously posted, with two batteries of artillery so placed as to sweep the road and a bridge over which it was necessary to pass." Gregg had taken position only the day before, upon direct orders from Pemberton. Having been informed by his superior that the Federals were moving on Edwards, Gregg inferred that the column was only "a brigade on a marauding excursion." His erroneous view was strengthened by the reports of his scouts that the force they had seen amounted to some 2,500 to 3,000 men.

Without delay McPherson ordered wagons out of the road so that Crocker could get forward, Logan in the meantime pushing the attack with two brigades and a battery, to be joined presently by his third brigade. Though the battle was a small one, there was fury in the contest that broke out when the Confederates were found massed under cover of woods in a ravine from which Gregg had hoped to capture the Federals. An effort to seize Logan's battery was broken by heavy fire of grape and canister, the attacking unit leaving the field in disorder. Even before Crocker's division could enter action, Gregg had discovered his error and had retired, aided by six companies of cavalry that had arrived opportunely. At five o'clock McPherson marched into Raymond. Gregg continued his retreat toward Jackson, but halted after he had been joined by Brigadier General W. H. T.

Walker, who was marching to his aid with about a thousand men just arrived from South Carolina.[51]

The Thirteenth and Fifteenth corps had also felt the enemy, but more lightly.

Taking the road at 4:00 A.M., as the advance of McClernand's corps upon the left, Hovey had found that the route lay through rugged country with little or no water. The only way to quench thirst caused by the dust and the heat of the warm day was to drive the enemy beyond Fourteen Mile Creek, held as a covering position for the hostile force at Edwards. This was done, Hovey writing, "Our men enjoyed both the skirmish and the water." Sherman likewise met opposition at Fourteen Mile Creek, coming, he later learned, from Wirt Adams's cavalry. A hundred dismounted troopers were unable to clear the situation with their carbines. Soon the old field artillery-man was himself at the head of the column and, seeing puffs of smoke coming from dense bushes, was not long in having a battery throwing into them "a few quick rounds of canister." Thereupon the hostile cavalrymen withdrew to the north side of the stream. A brigade of Steele's division was soon across the creek, pushing the enemy back so that Sherman's pioneer company could replace the burned bridge. In all, three hours had been lost, and Sherman, under Grant's personal direction, went into camp not far beyond with Steele's division, that of Tuttle being thrown to the right.[52]

When news of McPherson's fight at Raymond reached Grant, he immediately decided to settle matters in that direction by throwing his whole strength swiftly upon Jackson, orders marked 9:15 P.M. going to his three corps commanders. That to McPherson, headed "Dillon's Plantation," whose location it must be assumed McPherson knew or could learn from the courier, read:

> Move on to Clinton and Jackson at daylight in the morning. Sherman will leave here at 4 a.m. to follow and support you. McClernand will also follow from his position, which is about 4 miles northwest of here.[53]

The orders can be taken as initiating the four days that Colonel Whitton, the British military historian, has said "form a brilliant vindication of the tactical maxim to hit hard, hit often, and keep on hitting." [54]

Probably the courier riding eastward through the warm May night passed one bearing a message that McPherson wrote at 11:00 P.M., stating it was rumored that heavy reenforcements were moving that night from Jackson, the enemy intending to fight a new battle at Raymond in the morning. How true the reports were McPherson did not know, but he assured his chief that he would "try and be prepared for them," should they come.[55] It is to be noted that no new order went to McPherson. Knowing Grant as well as he did by this time, he may have expected none, but the direct road to Jackson through Mississippi Springs would be well reconnoitered before he made a flank march to Clinton across the enemy's front.

It would be difficult to imagine a situation where it was harder to sift error from fact in reports about the enemy. In a dispatch to Grant on the 9th, with which he sent a sketch of his camp and a Vicksburg paper of the 6th, McPherson had said, "Some of the citizens in the vicinity of Utica say Beauregard is at or near Jackson." The Fort Sumter general was of course safe in Charleston, and the rumor of his presence must have grown out of the fact that he had dispatched troops to aid at Vicksburg—two strong brigades according to Joe Johnston; 5,000 men with 4,000 more to follow, according to Secretary Seddon. While there was no truth in the report that reenforcements were marching from Jackson toward Raymond, stout assistance was about to arrive in Mississippi's capital in addition to troops from the east and from Port Hudson. On the 9th Seddon had ordered Johnston to proceed from Tullahoma "at once to Mississippi and take chief command of the forces, giving to those in the field, as far as practicable, the encouragement and benefit of your personal direction." He was to have "3,000 good troops" from Bragg's army follow him, they in turn to be replaced by men captured at Arkansas Post, who had been exchanged and were currently on the way to Pemberton.[56]

Johnston replied forthwith that he would go at once, although unfit for field service. Two days previously, matters at Tullahoma had been upset by the assassination of Van Dorn, then in command of Bragg's cavalry corps. In the person of Nathan Bedford Forrest an able successor was available, and Johnston and Bragg joined in recommending him. From Montgomery, while en route to Jackson, Johnston wired to General Ruggles, who seemed still disturbed by Grierson's raid, that he knew of no Federal advance on Columbus, Mississippi, and cheered him with the news that Forrest was coming into the state from the direction of Tuscumbia. Though considerable cavalry was to come westward, Forrest himself was detained.[57]

Johnston was apparently optimistic while he rode westward, for on the 8th, in reply to a message from Pemberton, the part of which pertaining to Port Hudson he had been unable to decipher, he reported, "Disposition of troops, as far as understood, judicious; can be readily concentrated against Grant's army." But what he learned after his train reached Jackson on the 13th apparently took the heart out of him and he made haste to wire to Seddon: "I arrived this evening, finding the enemy's force between this place and General Pemberton, cutting off the communication. I am too late." Greene comments: "He seemed to foresee disaster, and desired to clear himself in advance of any responsibility for it, rather than to bend his whole energy to avert it." While assigning Johnston a place well above Pemberton as a general, Greene does not credit him with "that divine fire that gains battles." [58]

On that day blue columns of confident men were marching eastward. Riding probably with the still uncertain Sherman was the general, who after four months of frustrated efforts and of unjust criticism by his countrymen had his fine army in tight control. But the enemy must be beaten quickly and before he could unite, or all might be lost.

With cavalry well out to the flanks, McPherson had entered Clinton about 2:00 P.M. Captain Andrew Hickenlooper, seen at Shiloh as a skillful battery commander, now corps engineer (though still on the roster of the Fifth Ohio Battery), was sent with a regiment to wreck the railroad to the west, and instructions to follow eastward on the same work the next day. Sherman had reached Raymond before McPherson's column had entirely cleared it. During the night the two advanced on Jackson, McPherson on the north road, Sherman to the south, keeping contact as best they could in a torrential rain that quickly turned the dusty roads into heavy mud and caused streams to overflow. At about ten o'clock on the 14th, when three miles from Jackson, Sherman heard McPherson's guns.

So hard was the rain that McPherson had delayed attacking lest water fill the cartridge boxes of his men as they reached for their paper-wrapped ammunition. When it slackened at eleven o'clock he pushed forward a battle line from Crocker's division—Logan was in reserve that day—well covered with skirmishers. The Confederate skirmishers were driven back on their main line, and when McPherson's skirmishers were stopped by heavy fire they were called back to their regiments and a charge by the battle line was ordered. It moved forward in good order and with cheers drove the enemy from his position, McPherson pressing forward for over a mile until he was within range of any artillery that might be in the prepared defenses of Jackson. Lines disorganized by the advance were reformed, batteries were put into position, and skirmishers were again thrown out, while officers reconnoitered the enemy's position and works. Presently it was reported that the Confederate lines had been evacuated. Without delay they were occupied by McPherson's men while the flag of the Forty-ninth Indiana was sent to be raised above the dome of the capitol. But a brigade sent toward the Canton road in the hope of cutting off the enemy's retreat northward was not successful.[59]

The force that had opposed McPherson was Gregg's brigade (commanded that day by Colonel R. Farquharson), that part of the brigade of Brigadier General S. R. Gist that had arrived from Charleston, and a major portion of Walker's men. The force was a sizable one, and its original position had been very advantageously chosen. In comparison, not much more than a token force had held the Raymond road against Sherman. Well-placed riflemen and a battery, however, had to be driven away, and a stream with precipitous banks that could be crossed only at a bridge—which the Confederates failed to destroy —delayed the advance. The bridge having been crossed, Mower's brigade was formed on the left of the road and that of Matthies on the right; two batteries were in the center and Buckland's brigade was held in reserve. The sequel Sherman pictured clearly:

As we emerged from the woods, to our front and as far to the left as we could see, appeared a line of intrenchments, and the enemy kept up a pretty brisk fire with artillery from the points that enfiladed our road. In order to ascertain the nature of the flanks of this line of intrenchments, I directed Captain Pitzman, acting engineer, to take a regiment of the reserve, namely, the Ninety-fifth Ohio, and make a detour to the right to see what was there. While he was gone, Steele's division closed up. About 1 p.m. Captain Pitzman returned, reporting that he had found the enemy's intrenchments abandoned at the point where they crossed the railroad, and he had left the Ninety-fifth Ohio there in possession.[60]

The divisions of Steele and Tuttle were soon in the outskirts of the town. While the enemy had made good the escape of their train, they had been compelled to abandon seventeen guns. Grant had been with the regiment that explored to the right, and soon an order summoned Sherman to the hotel near the State House, where he found the army commander and McPherson.[61]

On the day that Jackson fell, Stanton's telegram telling Dana that Grant had the full confidence of the government and unrestricted power to remove any officer reached Dana and was "communicated" to Grant. It was worth more than the seventeen guns that had been captured, and it offset the discovery that Johnston was present with the enemy. The guns were also less valuable than a copy of the message that Johnston had sent the night before to Pemberton. The dispatch reached Grant not by luck but because Hurlbut had shrewdly expelled from Memphis with considerable publicity a man who had been induced to denounce the Federals and all their works, but who Hurlbut knew was a trustworthy Union man. How it happened that this counteragent was one of three messengers selected to take Johnston's first dispatch through to Pemberton is a missing part of the story, but selected he was. He may have known McPherson; at least it was to McPherson, conveniently situated that night on the road to Vicksburg, that the message was delivered. This is what Grant read when it was passed to him:

I have lately arrived, and learn that Major General Sherman is between us, with four divisions, at Clinton. It is important to re-establish communications, that you may be re-enforced. If practicable, come up in his rear at once. To beat such a detachment would be of immense value. The troops here could co-operate. All the strength you can quickly assemble should be brought. Time is all important.[62]

Time was likewise all-important for Grant. An army had to be reversed, its rear becoming its advance in a movement westward. Roads had to be freed from trains to make way for infantry and guns. While Sherman was set to work destroying railroads, and the Jackson arsenal, gun factory, and manufactories capable of making munitions, Grant sent McClernand, who had reached Raymond, word of the victory and an explanation of the need for speed: "The enemy retreated north toward Canton; Johnston in command. It is evidently the design of the enemy to get north of us, and cross the Big Black and beat us into Vicksburg." McClernand was to concentrate at Bolton. A note also went to Blair, for whom A. J. Smith had waited in the vicinity of Auburn so that his riflemen and guns could give added security to the army train Blair was convoying. Those two generals were also to move on Bolton, by parallel roads if practicable. With the arrival of Blair, Grant's force was raised to something like 45,000 men, with an eloquent Congressman in each corps.[63] For Logan and Blair he was to form a very high regard as generals, both being able and obedient.

An actual concentration at Bolton was not carried out, and the evening of the 15th found the army headed westward on three roads that converged a little to the east of Edwards (two of them uniting before they met the third as a single road). On the direct Jackson-Vicksburg road was Hovey's division, which in its move eastward on the 13th had fairly brushed past Confederate encampments. On the 14th Hovey had passed through Raymond, with pioneers draining the road in places so that wagons could pass, to encamp finally not far from Clinton. The 15th saw him leading the westward advance on the northern road, his division in combat order without having tangled troops and wagons by reversing the column. At four o'clock McPherson's corps, Logan leading, came up to where Hovey had camped not far from Bolton. Osterhaus was on the middle road, while Carr's division was on the southern, or direct road from Raymond, from which the middle road was but an offshoot. Smith was not far from Carr, and Blair was at Raymond.[64]

McClernand's troops thus had the advance on all the roads. On the 14th he had noted in a letter to Grant that his command was more scattered than the others, forgetting that he had as many divisions as McPherson and Sherman together in the move on Jackson. But before the month was over, McClernand would inform Lincoln in a "private" letter how he had marched upon three converging roads toward Edwards, saying boastfully, "My corps, again, led the advance." Today— May 15—he showed his vanity in the ending of a dispatch to Blair: "I have suggested to General Grant to move McPherson on the north side of the railroad, to cut off the escape of the enemy, if we should engage and beat him." [65] Blair, who already knew that Sherman had managed the Arkansas Post operation, was not likely to need reassur-

ance from McClernand. And the morrow would give the latter an
opportunity to show just how well he could play the role he claimed
he had suggested for McPherson.

Grant naturally expected Pemberton to act in accordance with
Johnston's instructions and move eastward; because he knew
hostile troops were already east of the Big Black, he expected
contact soon. Pemberton would later say in a letter to Johnston
on May 27, "I greatly regret that I felt compelled to make the
advance beyond the Big Black, which has proved so disastrous in
its results," but he already had a major portion of his command in
the vicinity of Edwards. As early as the 11th he had in fact telegraphed
to the quartermaster at Jackson, "If the enemy moves on Jackson,
I will advance to meet them, and must have subsistence provided at
Jackson." One of the copies of Johnston's message was received by
Pemberton between nine and ten in the morning of the 14th at Bovina,
not far west of the Big Black, and in his reply he said, "I move at
once with whole available force (about 16,000) from Edwards
Depot." Other troops mentioned by Pemberton totaled 10,500, including 7,500 "effective men," left to guard works extending from
Haynes Bluff to Warrenton. That Pemberton was already on the move
was indicated by the statement, "The men have been marching several
days, are much fatigued, and I fear will straggle very much." This
looks like an excuse for future failure, while the ending hardly harmonized with what he had said to the Jackson quartermaster on the
11th: "In directing this move, I do not think you fully comprehend
the position that Vicksburg will be left in, but I comply at once with
your order." [66]

According to McClernand, Smith's division, which had relieved
Carr's on the southern road so that the latter could move in support
of Osterhaus on the middle road, encountered the enemy's skirmishers
about 7:30 A.M. of the 16th. They were dislodged with no trouble,
and a battery presently uncovered was silenced, but McClernand,
fearing his left would be turned, seems to have had Smith, supported
by Blair, do nothing but cover himself with a strong skirmish line,
while Osterhaus drove in a screen of skirmishers and ultimately "discovered the enemy in strong force." The hostile position was also very
strong, and Pemberton was in it partly by accident, a washed-out
bridge having delayed his projected move toward Raymond to cut

Grant's non-existent supply line. Subsequently his chief engineer officer wrote that instead of attacking Grant in rear while Johnston attacked him in front, Pemberton "encountered Grant's victorious army returning, exultant and eager for more prizes, from the capture of Jackson." [67]

We leave McClernand and view the battle from the road on the right where Grant saw it and sought to bring all his forces into effective action and destroy the enemy.

Hovey's advance guard came from the brigade of Brigadier General George F. McGinnis, to which a part of Hovey's personal cavalry escort had been attached. Upon arriving at Champion's Hill about ten o'clock, McGinnis "discovered the enemy posted on the crest of the hill, with a battery of four guns in the woods near the road, and on the highest point for many miles around." Hovey, riding between his two brigades so as to be in a favorable position if there were a flank attack, found, upon arriving at the front, three regiments already in line of battle with skirmishers in front. The other brigade was soon deployed, and messengers were sent to get in touch with Osterhaus. Before they had returned with a report of no success, Grant and McPherson had arrived. Timely additional information as to what was in front had been brought to Grant at five o'clock at Clinton, where he had spent the night, by two employees of the Vicksburg–Jackson railroad. They had passed through Pemberton's lines the preceding night and reported his force—eighty regiments, they said—at about 25,000 men with ten batteries. After sending instructions to Sherman to terminate his demolitions and advance without delay, and a staff officer to bring McClernand up to date, Grant had set out for the front, clearing Hovey's wagons from the road so that McPherson's men and guns could get forward. Foreseeing that there would be an intermingling of corps, McPherson had at 6:00 A.M. sent to Grant the message, "I think it advisable for you to come to the front as soon as you can."

Grant found Hovey in a position where he "could have brought on an engagement at any moment," but confronted by a difficult terrain situation. The road at that point made a sharp left turn and ascended a narrow ridge, whose top, as well as the precipitous hillside to the left, was covered by dense forest and undergrowth. To the right, the slope was gentler, with timber giving way to cultivated fields. It was along the narrow ridge that Pemberton had posted his divisions in the order, left to right, Stevenson, Bowen, Loring. Logan's division was put on the Federal right in a position looking down the rear of the enemy line; but Grant held back an attack pending word from Mc-Clernand. When this arrived, it revealed that the route of communication was two and a half miles long.

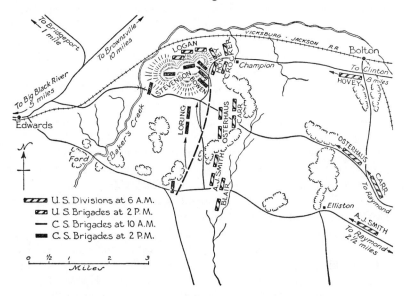

BATTLE OF CHAMPION'S HILL, MAY 16, 1863

The over-all commanders were Grant and Pemberton. Smith's, Osterhaus's, Carr's, and Hovey's divisions formed McClernand's corps, to which Blair's division of Sherman's corps was attached. Logan's and Crocker's divisions were from McPherson's corps and were east of Bolton at 6:00 A.M. Grant personally directed the battle for the hill; McClernand was relatively inactive on the middle and south roads.

Then Hovey, whose skirmishing had become very bitter, was launched in an attack against the formidable position, while Logan worked toward the rear of the hostile line. Pemberton's situation would have quickly become desperate were it not that McClernand's failure to advance vigorously allowed Pemberton to shift troops and change front, Bowen bringing aid of the most valuable sort. Hovey was compelled to yield ground, and it appeared that the Confederates were countering the thrust against their left by making one against what was actually the left of the Federal fighting line. When Crocker came up, his leading brigade—Boomer's—was sent to support Hovey, the next one—that of Sanborn, who had borne the brunt at Iuka—being sent to the right, largely to support Logan's batteries.

In his report Crocker speaks of the continued and furious assaults against Hovey and Boomer; and in a postwar article Sanborn states that he informed Grant of the bad situation on the left and has Grant say: " 'Hovey's division and Boomer's brigade are good troops, and if the enemy has driven them, he is not in good plight himself. If we can go in again here and make a little showing, I think he will give way.' " The fire from three batteries had already checked the Confederate counterstroke, and now Sanborn was sent with an order to Colonel S. A. Holmes, who was approaching the field with two regiments of his brigade of Crocker's division. They were thrown into an assault, and, reanimated by them, the Federal left swept to victory, driving the enemy over ground already twice contested, and retaking guns that the enemy had once recaptured. Holmes put the number of prisoners that he captured at not less than 300.

To Logan it had looked as though Leggett's brigade on the right of Hovey had been chosen as a target by the enemy "for a grand attack." With the aid of well placed batteries it stood firm and the Confederates were driven back. Another of Logan's brigades farther to the right, after working through an almost impassable hollow, made a charge that drove the enemy and netted a five-gun battery. Upon riding forward—at perhaps four o'clock—with the expectation of finding a new hostile line, Grant discovered that the Confederates were in retreat. When he reached the Raymond road, he saw a column of troops approaching from the left; it was Carr's division; with it was McClernand. A short time afterward Osterhaus appeared "with his skirmishers well in advance." These two divisions were sent in pursuit of the enemy in the hope of cutting off his retreat. Already, however, Logan had a brigade, weary though it was from heavy combat, moving at the double-quick after the Confederates hastening toward the Big Black, the accompanying Federal battery giving encouragement by some salvos. Carr pushed his advance until dark and was rewarded by capturing a burning train loaded with ordnance and commissary stores as well as other property, which were partially saved.

If it had been known that the road turned westward again after a southerly course of about a mile, the brigade of Logan's division that had been very effective on the right might have pushed still farther and increased the handsome total of prisoners that were taken. In his *Memoirs* Grant wrote, "Had McClernand come up with reasonable promptness, or had I known the ground as I did afterwards, I cannot see how Pemberton could have escaped with any organized force." Not only had McClernand been within hearing of the battle by noon; Grant had sent staff officers to him competent to explain the situation. By following the route taken by them, McClernand could, Grant said, have turned the flank of the relatively small force that was in his front in a good position beyond a ravine.

Loring stated in his report that when he reached his final position after steadily shifting to the left to keep closed on Bowen as the latter moved, he found things had gone to pieces. The brigade of Lloyd Tilghman, who was killed, was heavily engaged, and Loring wrote, "The bold stand of this brigade under the lamented hero saved a large portion of the army." A written communication informed him that Bowen, after being outflanked, had been compelled to retire precipitately, and bade him do his best to save his own division. This he did under the direction of local guides; but, unable to cross Baker's Creek and reach the Big Black, he extricated himself by moving in the direction of Utica, minus his train, which had started to Vicksburg.[68]

The Battle of Champion's Hill—or Baker's Creek—has been called by some the decisive battle of the war. Livermore puts Grant's available effectives at 29,373 and Pemberton's at about 20,000. He counters Grant's statement that he had only 15,000 men actually engaged by saying that the other Federal divisions, though suffering small loss, materially influenced the Confederate disposition of force. Initially this was true, but as noted above, even a part of Loring's division moved away from in front of McClernand, and in addition to those of Stevenson and Bowen, was in action against the three divisions of Grant's army that really were engaged.

According to Sanborn, Champion's Hill was won because Grant did not withdraw to form a new line when the situation looked desperate, but threw in his rear guard "to make a little showing." "It was Gen. Grant who won the battle."

The Federal casualties numbered 2,441; those of the Confederates totaled 3,851—and eleven guns. Hovey's losses were nearly a third of his strength and about half of the Federal total. "I cannot think of this bloody hill without sadness and pride," was his comment a few days later. With regard to Tilghman, struck down by a cannonball, Loring wrote, "A brigade swept over the dying hero; alike beautiful as it was touching." [69]

At about the hour when Confederate riflemen opened on the head of Smith's column, Johnston was writing a letter to Secretary Seddon from Calhoun, telling of his movement from that place and saying that "a dispatch from Lieutenant-General Pemberton, received yesterday, informed me that he would march on the 15th from Edwards Station to a point 7½ miles west of Raymond." Even without the record of the 16th to change the prospects, it did not look as if cooperation was promising because of the diverging movements of Johnston and Pemberton, and on the letter the Confederate President recorded his perplexity:

Read and returned to the Secretary of War. Do not perceive why a junction was not attempted, which would have made our force equal in number to the estimated strength of the enemy, and might have resulted in his total defeat under circumstances which rendered retreat or re-enforcement to him scarcely practicable.[70]

At daylight on the 17th the pursuit was resumed with McClernand's corps again in advance, Carr leading, Osterhaus following closely. It was only six miles to the Big Black where the enemy was found with a strongly intrenched bridgehead on the east of the river, while other troops occupied the top of the sharply rising bluffs on the west. Pemberton had not planned a defense east of the river but had held the position to make possible the crossing of Loring, who was expected throughout the night with the Federals pressing hard upon him. The position, however, was a very strong one because level, cultivated ground extending eastward for a mile gave guns and riflemen in the bridgehead trenches, as well as those on the commanding west bank, an excellent field of fire, while a bayou formed a natural protective ditch for the trenches.[71]

Carr took position to the right of the road and Osterhaus to the left. Because of a bend in the river, the brigade of Brigadier General Michael K. Lawler, consisting of three Iowa regiments and one from Wisconsin, which was on the extreme right, touched the Big Black, though a detached enemy work sought to give security to that part of the bridgehead. Along the road not far to the east the division of Logan was resting, together with the brigade of Brigadier General

Thomas Ransom, of McArthur's division, which had arrived late the day before. At the river's edge to the north was the division which had been led so well throughout the campaign by Marcellus Crocker, but which was this morning taken over by Quinby, who had been ill, and who had arrived the day before. Sherman, who had spent the night with his two divisions near Bolton, was coming swiftly forward, to swing off, in accordance with an order from Grant, to Bridgeport, where he arrived about noon, finding Blair waiting for him with a pontoon train.[72]

The description in Grant's report of what happened at the bridge-head cannot be improved on:

After a few hours' skirmishing, Lawler discovered that by moving a portion of his brigade under cover of the river bank he could get a position from which that place could be successfully assaulted, and ordered a charge accordingly. Notwithstanding the level ground over which a portion of his troops had to pass without cover, and the great obstacle of the ditch in front of the enemy's works, the charge was gallantly and successfully made, and in a few minutes the entire garrison, with seventeen pieces of artillery were the trophies of this brilliant and daring movement. The enemy on the west bank of the river immediately set fire to the railroad bridge and retreated, thus cutting off all chance of escape for any portion of his forces remaining on the east bank.[73]

From Lawler's report we learn that when late afternoon had come without his being able to advance, Colonel William H. Kinsman of the Twenty-third Iowa proposed a charge by his regiment. Lawler promptly consented "to his daring proposition" and arranged to give full support by his entire command. Before Kinsman, who had had the honor of giving the word "forward" to the leading regiments, had advanced half the intervening distance, he fell badly wounded. He got to his feet, took a few steps onward as he cheered his men, then, struck by a second and a fatal ball, he fell again. After the line had advanced "under a wasting fire" and broken the enemy's center, Lawler threw two supporting Indiana regiments forward on his left and two regiments of his own brigade against the enemy strong point on his right. Of the outcome on the right he wrote, "The rebels broke and fled before the Twenty-second Iowa and fell an easy prey into the hands of the Eleventh Wisconsin Volunteers." [74]

In a letter to Stanton in which Dana assessed Grant's subordinates, Lawler was put down as a first-rate soldier and a good disciplinarian;

he had once summarily hanged a man for murdering a comrade. Dana commented, "Grant has two or three times gently reprimanded him for indiscretions, but is pretty sure to go and thank him after a battle." [75]

When Pemberton wrote his report he spoke with bitterness of the behavior of his troops at the Big Black River, though his leadership may have had much to do with their loss of the will to fight. Without reservation he said "a strong position, with an ample force of infantry and artillery to hold it, was shamefully abandoned almost without resistance." [76] While Lawler reported that he had captured more men than he had had in the charge, he added, "but this brilliant success was not accomplished without considerable loss; 14 killed and 185 wounded in the space of three minutes, the time occupied in reaching the enemy's works, attest the severity of the fire to which my men were subjected."

One must question Grant's statement in his *Memoirs* that just before Lawler's charge an officer of Banks's staff presented him with a letter from Halleck dated May 11, sent by way of New Orleans for Banks to forward, ordering Grant to return to Grand Gulf and cooperate with Banks against Port Hudson, taking care of Vicksburg later.[77] The message in the *Official Records* dated May 11 from Halleck to Grant—the only one Halleck sent Grant during May—was given complete on page 367 except for an irrelevant sentence quoted in the notes. Grant's statement describes it poorly, and even if the dispatch were not marked "via Memphis" it would be impossible to believe it was sent to Grant through Banks, for that officer was in Alexandria, and far more than six days would have been required for transmission. (New York was six days by steamer from New Orleans.) Furthermore, we shall presently see Halleck trying to communicate with Banks through Grant and telling the latter that he had sent "dispatch after dispatch" for Banks to join the Vicksburg operation.

There can be no doubt, however, that a staff officer from Banks arrived—perhaps three of them. On May 12 Banks, replying to Grant's letter of the 10th, regretted that it was impossible for him to join Grant in time and in sufficient strength to be of service at Vicksburg. He had neither the requisite water nor land transportation; the most he could do would be to ferry his infantry and artillery across the Mississippi for the purpose of operating with Grant against Port

Hudson. Then Banks changed his mind and the next day began a second message: "More complete investigation of the country on the Red and Mississippi Rivers leads me to believe it is possible for me to join you." He would, he now stated, sacrifice and hazard everything to reach Grand Gulf, hoping he could do so within ten or twelve days, and with about 12,000 men. But the matter did not rest there. A second letter of the 12th said, "I have sent, subsequent to the dispatch of yesterday, transmitted by Captain Gibbs, a note of this date, informing you of my determination to join you at all hazards with as little delay as possible." Now, however, Banks had swung back something more than halfway to his position of the day before; he thought Grant's first suggestion of sending a force to help him take Port Hudson was best. Nevertheless, Banks said that if Grant could not assist him, he would as soon as possible join Grant. Inclosed with the letter was a memorandum listing six benefits that would result from reducing Port Hudson before Vicksburg.[78]

Grant's subsequent linking of Halleck's dispatch—which may have arrived from Grand Gulf simultaneously with one of Banks's couriers —with the messages from Alexandria was not unnatural. The crumbling of the enemy bridgehead on that May 17 was perhaps the most dramatic moment of the campaign. A telegram from Washington and messengers from Banks could hardly compete with the word that came from Lawler—the brigadier who sometimes had to be admonished. It was Lawler's day of greatness; never could Grant have felt a greater desire to give him thanks.

The river that separated it from its goal was not an obstacle to daunt the hard-marching army, flushed with victory, its parts moving in smooth coordination. While ingenious officers and men of McPherson's and McClernand's corps went to work to build bridges out of any materials at hand, Sherman, properly equipped, was not held in leash. A note from Grant said: "Our bridges here will not be ready to cross before daylight in the morning. Secure a commanding position on the west bank of Black River as soon as you can." Sherman was in fact told that, if, after crossing the river, he could gain information which he thought warranted it, he should advance immediately into Vicksburg. In any event, Grant intended to move rapidly and take advantage of the demoralization he believed the enemy felt from the defeats of that day and the day before. If roads could be found, he intended to advance in three columns "and either have Vicksburg or Haynes' Bluff tomorrow night." [79]

It was entirely in conformity with Grant's method of command that he should go to Sherman in person even though written directions had been clear; it was one of the historic nights of the war when he may have desired to be with the greatest of his lieutenants. It is from Sherman's *Memoirs* that we learn how the two sat together on a log as fires of pitch pine illuminated the scene: "the bridge swayed to and fro under the passing feet, and made a fine war-picture." [80] Perhaps Sherman was in one of his rare, quiet, musing moods; probably he was still a little doubtful of the final success of the unprecedented campaign. But one may be certain that the darkness into which his men were vanishing beyond the lighted bridge held no fears that would hold him back in the rapidly approaching final hours. And Grant? There can be no doubt that he was thinking of the next day. It was still thirteen miles both to the defenses of Vicksburg and to Haynes Bluff, and they were rugged, uncertain miles, whose poorly mapped roads had never been trod by men of his command. There might be confusing crossroads and road junctions, and answers to questions would need to be viewed with skepticism. But Grant could know his advance guards and skirmishers would be bold. It may not be too much to say that no army has ever been more infused—"electrified" is the word Fuller uses—with the energy and spirit of its commander.

By 9:30 the next morning the head of Sherman's column had reached a road that he knew gave him control of the Yazoo and that interposed his command between Vicksburg and the forts that had made necessary the march of so many miles. After resting long enough for his men to close up, he moved to a road fork, threw out covering forces, unlimbered a battery, and "awaited General Grant's arrival." He knew he had the situation under control by his strategic position and, with no desire for personal accomplishment, he wanted the army commander entirely unhampered. One can do no better than quote Sherman's report. The reference being to Grant, he says:

He came up very soon, and directed me to operate on the right, McPherson on the center, and McClernand on the left. Leaving a sufficient force on the main road to hold it till McPherson came up, I pushed the head of my column on this road till the skirmishers were within musket-range of the defenses of Vicksburg. Here I disposed Blair's division to the front, Tuttle's in support, and ordered Steele to follow a blind road to the right till he reached the Mississippi.[81]

While McPherson had swung northward to the Bridgeport-Vicksburg road, McClernand had moved straight ahead on the road from Jackson, veering over to the left so as to gain control of the road to Baldwin's Ferry over the Big Black. After describing the moves, Grant says in his report:

By this disposition the three army corps covered all the ground their strength would admit of, and by the morning of the 19th the investment of Vicksburg was made as complete as could be by the forces at my command.

Though the forts at Haynes Bluff had not been taken, they had been abandoned and lay awaiting a new occupant.

Grant's chief concern was to secure a base of supplies on the Yazoo. While skirmishing was still going on with enemy detachments on the right, he rode with Sherman to Walnut Hills. That, too, was a historic moment. To a man of Sherman's nature it must have been almost overpowering to look down on the swampy, bayou country where nearly five months before he had made his unsuccessful attack. With his matchless honesty he told Grant that until that moment he had not been certain that the operation would succeed, but that it had been a successful campaign even if they never took Vicksburg.[82]

The next morning Sherman sent the Fourth Iowa Cavalry to Haynes Bluff. The troopers took possession of the batteries, then, seeing a gunboat in the Yazoo—the *De Kalb*—they made contact with it and turned the once defiant guns together with a full magazine over to the navy. Believing that a prompt assault might win the town, Grant ordered an attack at 2:00 P.M. Though repulsed, the effort allowed some units to gain better positions than those they had held.[83]

At 6:00 A.M. of the 20th Dana, whose last dispatch had been written on the 10th, was again at work with his reportorial pen:

General Grant has won a great and momentous victory over the rebels under Pemberton, on the Jackson and Vicksburg road, at Baker's Creek, on the 16th instant. Pemberton had a most formidable position on the crest of a wooded hill, over which the road passes longitudinally. He had about 25,000 men. The battle began at about 11 a.m. and was gained at

4 p.m. Its brunt was borne by Hovey's division of McClernand's corps, and by Logan's and Crocker's of McPherson's.

This was excellent reporting, as was also the statement about the manner in which Logan had operated on the right and rear of the enemy. It would delight not only the Secretary of War but the public. Hovey, however, was justifiably angered when he read in a newspaper that, after losing 1,600 men, his division had been "succeeded" by two brigades of Crocker's division, not merely reenforced by them, and that Crocker's men had ended the conflict "in that part of the field."

Dana put the prisoners captured at 2,000, told of Lawler's fine charge at the river, of the guns taken, and added:

> Building four bridges over the Big Black, General Grant arrived before the town on the evening of the 18th, and now holds it closely [closely though only partially, would have been better] invested. He has opened a line of supplies via Chickasaw Bayou, having cut the enemy off from Haynes' Bluff, which is abandoned by the enemy, and which General Grant will occupy. There was sharp fighting, through the day yesterday. Steele won, and holds the upper bluffs and the enemy's upper water batteries, and gets water from the Mississippi.
>
> Sherman's corps lost yesterday 500 killed and wounded. McPherson, who holds the center, lost little, as did McClernand, who holds the left.[84]

Dana had evidently been getting around successfully, though he and Grant's son had started the campaign on very unpromising horses. When Grant left Bruinsburg, Fred was asleep on a gunboat; upon awakening he started to join his father, his guide being the gunfire at Port Gibson; Dana, likewise afoot, caught up with him, and after foraging as best they could, they found army headquarters the next day in the captured town, the boy being greeted by his father with the words, "So, there you are!" As Grant had no mess facilities at the time, Fred and Dana, like himself, had to pick up what they could from troops. However they may have started, the pair had not arrived on foot, Grant later saying "they were mounted on two enormous horses, grown white from age, each equipped with dilapidated saddles and bridles." Dana's situation was, however, improved a few days later when a well-mounted Confederate officer was captured. Though the officer insisted that his horse was personal property and hoped it would be returned to him, Grant informed him that he himself had four or five first-rate horses wandering about somewhere in the Confederacy. The captured man was given any one of those horses that he might find, but the animal he had been riding seemed "just about the horse Mr. Dana needs." [85]

The War Department representative heard plenty of gunfire and musketry during the memorable eighteen days; so had Fred Grant, who had something to prove it: a wound in the leg. One must praise Dana for putting into his dispatch of the 20th a little touch that would gratify Gideon Welles; but he revealed his reportorial genius by not stopping after relating a fact: "The gunboats kept the enemy alert during the night, and probably the town will be carried to-day."

On the 18th President Davis telegraphed to Governor Pettus: "Get the people in Mississippi to join Johnston and attack the enemy in rear. Do not let him get to the river or effect a junction with his reserve." In the speed with which they could communicate the Confederates had an advantage; and Pettus, when dispossessed of his capital, had set up in a town whose name seemed chosen for the occasion, as Davis would see from the date line of his reply: "Enterprise, May 19, 1863." The first sentence fitted excellently: "Orders issued. All available troops to aid General Johnston. Companies organizing in every county." The arms and ammunition that Pettus said he must have, the Confederacy now possessed in abundance, though lack of rolling stock as well as carelessness confused the situation. Davis could derive encouragement from Pettus's statement that Loring had "cut his way out" and was moving to Jackson, where provisions would await him. But the ending, "Re-enforcements prompt and heavy are necessary," served notice on him that he too must show some real initiative. [86]

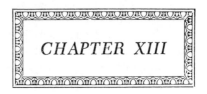

CHAPTER XIII

UNRELENTING SIEGE AND FINAL VICTORY

The enemy surrendered this morning.—Grant to Halleck

THE ATTACK that Dana had expected on May 20 did not take place; nor was there one on the 21st. Both days were spent opening roads to a supply base on the Yazoo. For three weeks most of the troops had been marching and fighting on but five days' rations. While they had not suffered for food, their diet had been largely meat, and even chickens and other fowls that on occasion would have been relished, though breaking the monotony of beef, had been a poor substitute for the eagerly desired bread. By the evening of the 21st there were wagonloads of bread, and Grant would not again hear the words "Hardtack," first faintly uttered by a single soldier, then taken up by many voices in the investing line.[1]

In comparison with his recent situation, Grant's supplies were assured, but large stocks on hand were necessary, for the long supply line reached back hundreds of miles, with only Lake Providence, Helena, Memphis, New Madrid, and Columbus points of actual Federal occupation. The energetic and resourceful enemy would neglect no chance to hamper the flow of men and provisions. Even field batteries might sink or damage steamers before they could be driven away by gunboat fire, or be attacked by the Marine Brigade of General Alfred W. Ellet, habitually kept on boats for just such special missions.[2]

On the 21st orders were issued for an assault the next day at 10:00 A.M. Several factors led to Grant's decision. In the first place, he believed the assault would be successful; his men held better positions from which to launch an attack, and there would be more time for preparation and coordination than in the assault of the 19th. If Vicksburg were carried promptly, Grant could turn on Johnston before the latter's strength had been increased and before the excessive heat of summer closed in. In addition, there was the temper of his men. Flushed with victory, they were eager for the prize, and in no mood to settle down to the tedium of a siege with its digging and vigils: trenches and camps in front of Vicksburg would hardly be a summer resort. Even a timid commander should be slow to hold such men in leash. And Grant was far from timid. Every soldier knew he had great personal courage, and every soldier knew that in addition to being modest, considerate, and thoughtful of them, his courage as a commander who had to make the hard decisions knew no limit. They were not only ready to assault; they "were eager" to, according to engineer captain Frederick Prime.[3]

During the Civil War attacks were usually launched by a signal gun. But at Vicksburg on May 22 eyes were fixed on the hands of watches. Those of corps commanders had been synchronized with Grant's; perhaps it was the first time that this was ever done.

It is hardly necessary to say that the assault was bravely made. But it failed, though Porter had hammered the enemy batteries for two hours after playing upon them all night. Fuller states it might well have succeeded if a better technique had been used. Livermore puts the number of men Grant had engaged at 34,446, and Pemberton, 22,301. The superiority was far from being as pronounced as it is often stated that it should be for a successful attack on well-prepared defenses. Grant may have overestimated the enemy's demoralization and underestimated his numbers. While in his dispatch on the morning after the assault of the 19th, Dana had put the enemy force in Vicksburg at 15,000 to 20,000, he added, "Pemberton fights with the greater obstinacy, because his people believe he has sold their cause."[4] (He was, it may be recalled, a Pennsylvanian by birth.)

The toll in killed and wounded was 3,052, while 147 were listed as captured or missing. Federal flags had been placed upon the parapets in several points, and a message that McClernand sent to Grant indicating success led Grant to send Quinby's division to the support of McClernand and to order Sherman and McPherson to renew their attacks as a diversion to aid the left. Later Grant said this resulted in an increase of casualties by 50 per cent and challenged the accuracy of the dispatch he had received. McClernand would retort by calling into question what Grant said.[5]

In a message at 8:30 that evening, Grant wrote to Porter: "Our troops succeeded in gaining positions close up to the enemy's batteries, which we yet hold, and, in one or two instances, getting into them. I now find the position of the enemy so strong that I shall be compelled to regularly besiege the city. I would request, therefore, that you give me all the assistance you can with the mortars and gunboats." A long postscript was probably based on a dispatch from Sherman that began, "We have had a hard day's work, and all are exhausted." In the postscript Grant said, "If the gunboats could come up and silence the upper water battery and clear the southern slope of the second range of hills from the Yazoo Bottom, it would enable Sherman to carry that position, and virtually give us the city." [6]

The next day Porter answered: "I do not think it possible to get the gunboats up to the point you speak of without sacrificing every vessel and man on board, but I am feeling my way along with the mortars, and drop them down a little every day." After stating he thought a chance of getting into a fort on the left had been missed on the 22nd, the admiral said, "Hope you will soon finish up this Vicksburg business, or these people may get relief." In that he put his finger on the crux of the matter; knowing how busy Grant was—he was never idle himself—he reported, "I wrote to General Hurlbut four days ago, telling him that I thought you would thank him for every man he or any one else could send you." Then he blighted any hope Grant might have been entertaining for help from the south: "General Banks is not coming here with his men. He is going to occupy the attention of Port Hudson, and has landed at Bayou Sara, using your transports for the purpose." [7] This may have been merely factual reporting; if the admiral was intentionally criticizing, he was doing so without weighing certain considerations that Banks could not overlook.

Grant's reply—which made no reference to Banks—began: "Your note of this date is just received. I am satisfied that you are doing all that can be done in aid of the reduction of Vicksburg. There is no doubt of the fall of this place ultimately, but how long it will be is a matter of doubt. I intend to lose no more men, but to force the enemy from one position to another without exposing my troops." He reported that a hostile force was collecting at Yazoo City; already it numbered 2,000 men; if Porter thought it endangered his boats in the Yazoo, Grant would send Lauman's division—recently arrived from Memphis—to disperse it, though he did not like to detach troops until the Vicksburg job was "closed out." As he wrote, Grant grew more determined; having begun by putting the capture of the city in the indefinite future, he ended, "One week is as long as I think the enemy can possibly hold out." [8]

Inasmuch as the McClernand case presently burst before the public, the reader should see what Dana was sending to Washington. In his message of the 23rd, reporting the failure of the assault of the preceding day, he said:

At 2 p.m. McClernand reported that he was in possession of two forts of the rebel line, was hard pressed, and in great need of re-enforcements. Not doubting that he had really succeeding in taking and holding the works he pretended to hold, General Grant ordered J. G. Lauman's [Quinby's] division, of McPherson's corps, to his support, and at the same time McPherson and Sherman both made new attacks. McClernand's report was false, as he held not a single fort, and the result was disastrous. Lauman's [Quinby's] division was pushed by McClernand to his front and suffered heavily, Col. G. H. Boomer, Twenty-sixth Missouri, among the killed.

The next day Dana reported that Grant had determined to relieve McClernand, but had reconsidered, thinking it better to let him serve through the siege and persuade him afterward to request a leave of absence. In the meantime, however, Grant would supervise McClernand's operations and put no reliance on his reports "unless otherwise corroborated." (Without meaning to do so, Dana was laying a foundation for a correct appraisal of the boastful "private" letter that McClernand soon wrote Lincoln, claiming credit for most of the campaign, including the Battle of Champion's Hill, because of Hovey's part in it.) Dana had his own opinion of the Springfield general, and for good measure tossed it in: "My own judgment is that McClernand has not the qualities necessary for a good commander, even of a regiment." [9]

Because of the remoteness of the operation, Washington relied for some of its first reports on Richmond papers, and how carefully

Lincoln was reading and weighing these was revealed by a dispatch he sent to Hurlbut on the 22nd:

We have news here in the Richmond papers of the 20th and 21st, including a dispatch from General Joe Johnston himself, that on 15th or 16th—a little confusion as to the day—Grant beat Pemberton and Loring near Edwards Station, at the end of a nine hours' fight, driving Pemberton over the Big Black, and cutting Loring off and driving him south to Crystal Springs, 25 miles below Jackson. Joe Johnston telegraphed all this, except about Loring, from his camp between Brownsville and Lexington, on the 18th. Another dispatch indicates that Grant was moving against Johnston on the 18th.[10]

Evidently Lincoln had ignored a Mobile dispatch of the 18th that appeared in the *Richmond Enquirer* of the 21st, that said the Federals had been whipped badly at Baker's Creek, and that Pemberton put their loss at thrice his own 3,000. Lincoln also probably paid little heed to a headline in Greeley's *Tribune* on the 21st: "Copperhead Meeting in Indiana." Democrats had gathered in Indianapolis to denounce the war acts of the Administration, especially the recent arrest in Ohio of Clement Vallandigham, Hoosier oratory being reenforced by that of two critics from the President's home state. Soldiers had patrolled the streets, particularly in the vicinity of the convention hall; and there had been arrests because of carrying of concealed weapons and shouts for Jeff Davis.[11]

On the 24th Lincoln would have—and the press would have it on the 25th—Hurlbut's reply. He quoted a short synopsis of the campaign which Rawlins had written on the 20th and which said Vicksburg had been closely invested on the 18th with the right of the army resting on the Mississippi. Quickly on the heels of Hurlbut's message came one that Porter had sent Selfridge at Cairo on the 20th, portraying things heard, seen, and done upon the great river. Nothing ever suffered in the telling by the pen of David Dixon Porter, and men and women in the North would complete the picture according to their own imagination and depth of feeling:

On the 18th, at meridian, firing was heard in the rear of Vicksburg, which assured me that Gen. Grant was approaching the city. The cannonading was kept up furiously for some time, when, by the aid of glasses, I discovered a company of our artillery advancing and driving the enemy before them.[12]

The engineers took over their task promptly, Hickenlooper writing in his day-by-day diary as the entry for May 23: "Orders issued for

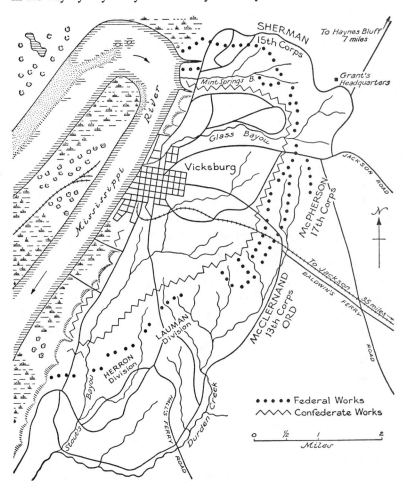

SIEGE OF VICKSBURG, MAY 18–JULY 4, 1863

The high bluff on which the city is located is cut into deep ravines. The Federal approaches are incompletely shown.

construction of regular approaches." Direction of all work fell on Captain Frederick Prime, top man in the West Point class of 1850, who said in his report, "Thirty officers of engineers would have found full employment. When the siege commenced there were with the army two engineer officers doing engineer duty." Apparently Grant made no appeal for more; he knew the shortage that existed and trusted his superior to do the best he could. Of course, all West Point graduates had received some instruction in siege work, and there were civilians like Hickenlooper with great aptitude, while resourcefulness was an attribute of the Army of the Tennessee.[13]

The pioneer companies of the command supplemented the battalion of the Engineer Regiment of the West, the only army engineering unit that Grant's roster shows. Though some Negroes were hired at $10 a month, infantrymen and artillerymen would do much digging of approaches and make other constructions. Soldiers whose engineering experience had been limited to digging farm ditches, building fences, and excavating potatoes would soon be talking about progress on their saps and boasting of their sap rollers; those who had cut wood only for stoves would be speaking fluently of gabions and fascines; men who had patiently smoothed earth so that radishes might grow better would be talking affectionately of terrepleins for guns. Prime paid full credit to all who were employed, but added, "Without the stimulus of danger or pecuniary reward, troops of the line will not work efficiently, especially at night, after the novelty has worn off."

No fewer than nine approaches were run, with appropriate parallels, to enable an assault to be made with certainty of success and small cost in lives. Time was essential because of the danger of an attack by Johnston, and to Prime, unable to give attention and direction at all points, wasted effort caused by faulty locations must have been exasperating. According to his estimate, the time required could have been greatly cut—perhaps almost in half—if there had been sufficient engineer officers "to see that every shovelful of earth thrown brought us nearer to the end, and personally to push and constantly supervise the special works to which they were assigned." Headed, "Officers and men had to learn to be engineers while the siege was going on."

In certain ways the very rugged nature of the terrain, where "the sides of the smaller and newer ravines were often so steep that their ascent was difficult to a footman unless he aided himself with his hands," made siege work easier. In his order Grant had said, "Every advantage will be taken of the natural inequalities of the ground to gain positions from which to start mines, trenches, or advance batteries." Yet it was not always easy to locate approaches so that they did not run down the exposed side of a ridge; when they did that, they had to be "blinded."

Having had full leisure to prepare against the day of investment, the enemy line was well placed. Leaving the river on the north side of the city where the bluff crowded close to the water, it followed commanding ridges until it reached the bluff two miles below Vicksburg, at a place where the high ground stood back a mile from the river's edge. In two places the line dipped into the valleys of small streams, one above the city and one below. At commanding places there were small works of "weak profile," all open at the gorge, except one redoubt thirty yards square. These strong points, varying from 75 to 500 yards from one another, were laced together with trenches and rifle pits. To the professional eye of Frederick Prime, Vicksburg was "rather an intrenched camp than a fortified place, owing much of its strength to the difficult ground, obstructed by fallen trees in its front, which rendered rapidity of movement and *ensemble* in an assault impossible."

Though younger than Prime, the chief engineer for the defense, Major Samuel N. Lockett, from whose postwar article a quotation has already been taken, stood up to him in ability. In his record of the siege, Lockett said under date of May 29 that "Whistling Dick"—an 18-pounder rifled gun—had been put in position and a new battery position had been started, but that Federal sharpshooters had driven off the working party and the project was stopped.

How frequently the 18-pounder fired Lockett did not say, but in general the Federals were surprised at the small amount of hostile artillery fire with which they were harassed. Scarcity of ammunition was a natural inference, and some Confederate officers afterward assigned that as a reason; but 40,000 rounds of artillery ammunition were to be taken in the city. Lieutenant Peter C. Hains, a onetime artilleryman who, like Hickenlooper, had switched from guns and caissons to shovels and axes, and was engineer officer for McClernand, wrote under date of June 19: "Very little firing to-day. They gave a few rounds from a gun in a new work they have thrown up behind their main line. All our batteries opened on it, and in a few minutes it was silenced." Prime wrote that if the enemy had concentrated a dozen or so guns instead of firing with one or two which invited a deluge of Federal shells, they might have seriously delayed the work of the besiegers. It appeared to him as if the Confederates were waiting for the final assault, "losing in the mean time as few men as possible." Then he commented, "This indifference to our approach became in some points almost ludicrous."

Once, according to Prime, Southern hospitality was really at its best. When the pickets covering a night-time working party of the Thirteenth Corps became mixed up with their opposite numbers, the Confederates did not even hurl the ugly word "aggressors" at the Yankees. Instead, the officers of the two groups met and agreed on boundary lines so as to give a buffer zone, that in some places was only ten yards wide. Not everywhere, however, was the enemy "so courteous." In places he made sharp, vigorous sorties that inflicted casualties and retarded work.[14]

Even before the engineers had selected their routes of approach, signal corps men were busy tying command posts together. Of course, this was not the first time they had had important parts in the campaign. Different headquarters had been kept in contact as the army advanced from Milliken's Bend through Richmond, and a signal officer was aboard the *Benton* when she passed the Grand Gulf batteries. Eight signal officers had joined Grant between Bruinsburg and Port Gibson. Two of them he sent back to Bruinsburg to open communication across the river and to Hard Times, the line being kept open for several days. Signal officers were with Grant when he went to Grand Gulf and within ten minutes were in communication with Hard Times. During his brief stay the commanding general made much use of this line, and it remained in operation while the wagon train and Sherman's corps were crossing the river.

But, once the army had left the Mississippi, the country was so wooded and so lacking in commanding elevations from which signals could be flashed that the signalmen were employed almost solely on reconnoitering. May 18 brought an end to such limited work, and from then on the detachment sought to keep at army headquarters an up-to-date picture of all that was transpiring. One group of signalmen remained with Grant at the position he had selected for himself, close behind the investing line, near the interval between Sherman on the right and McPherson in the center, where he would not be far from his base on the Yazoo. Groups of signalmen were also at each corps headquarters, reconnoitering during the day and reporting to the corps commanders. In the evening their accumulated information was picked up by an officer from army headquarters and taken back to Grant.

While the telegraph was used, much reliance had to be placed on flags. The best officers were on the stations connecting Grant with Haynes Bluff, where presently there would be a force watching for a possible crossing of the upper Black River by Johnston. "It works to a charm," was a report about that vital line. Medical, commissary, quartermaster, and ordnance officers were to keep the line busy that reached to the base rapidly developed on the Yazoo. A station across the Mississippi at Young's Point tied the army in with the navy, a proud signal captain writing, "Admiral Porter is highly pleased with the corps." [15]

In addition to the letter that told of the commendation of the admiral, soldiers in the lines about the invested city would also be writing of visits from the commanding general, one of the greatest experiences a soldier can have. Sherman, in a letter to his brother on April 3, in which he castigated Knox and other reporters for their misrepresentations, said: "It is absurd to say these correspondents relieve the anxiety of parents, friends, &c. My soldiers write constantly and receive immense numbers of letters." This, he added, was right. While there had been some good reporting of the campaign behind Vicksburg, nothing any correspondent wrote of the battles or the siege could equal the letters from the trenches. A reporter might tell that Grant had slept at Jackson in a bed occupied the night before by Joe Johnston. Though the fact was amusing, it was unimportant. But not unimportant was a letter which told that Grant had talked with a son, a brother, or a husband.[16]

As he settled down to a siege Grant's chief concern came from the inadequacy of his force. He needed more men to close the ring tightly about Vicksburg while holding part of his command as a mobile force to meet Johnston, whose growing strength he could not know with accuracy. On the day that Grant was arriving before the town, Pemberton was reading a message that Johnston had sent the day before. It told him that if Haynes Bluff could not be held, Vicksburg was untenable and if besieged he would ultimately have to surrender. It was a question of saving troops, and Johnston said, "If it is not too late, evacuate Vicksburg and its dependencies, and march to the northeast." Though Pemberton might have circled and joined Johnston after his defeat at Champion's Hill, such a move was now definitely too late; Grant had foreseen that possibility and had thrown his army into a position to make it impossible.[17]

In a long letter to Halleck on the 24th Grant said: "I hear a great deal of the enemy bringing a large force from the east to effect a raising of the siege. They may attempt something of the kind, but I do not see how they can do it." Reports of Johnston's relieving force continued to mount, and the next day Grant reported, "I can manage the force in Vicksburg and an attacking force on the rear of 30,000, but may have more to contend against." He could increase by 10,000 men from his own command the effective 50,000 men that he had on hand. Another message of the same day reported the capture of eight men with 200,000 percussion caps which they were trying to smuggle into Vicksburg. More important was a cipher message from Johnston to Pemberton, also dated the 25th, that Grant could not read and sent forward. When unraveled it said: "Bragg is sending a division. When it joins I will come to you. Which do you think the best route? How and where is the enemy operating? What is your force?" [18]

On the same day General Gist—whom we have seen in the operation against Jackson—was writing at length to Beauregard from near Canton. Hard things, he reported, were being said about Pemberton, but he had repulsed Grant's assaults, had enough provisions, and, if troops were sent in time, Vicksburg could still be saved. Then he said: "We will move as soon as we are strong enough to be effective. Officers, men, and citizens have unbounded confidence in Johnston." The 25th also was the day scheduled for the fulfillment of Pettus's telegram to Johnston from Meridian: "Will be in Jackson in two days. Have ordered mounted militia there." Bragg telegraphed that cavalry would press in the direction of Corinth immediately, and said, "We are in great suspense, but hopeful." [19]

A dispatch that Grant sent Halleck on the 29th of May, reporting that if Banks did not bring assistance he would have to be reenforced from elsewhere, was in Washington on June 2 and brought quick action. Lincoln telegraphed:

Are you in communication with General Banks? Is he coming toward you or going farther off? Is there or has there been anything to hinder his coming directly to you by water from Alexandria? [20]

Much more agreeable than a Presidential questioning about another commander was a sentence in Halleck's dispatch of the 2nd: "I will do all I can to assist you." It is hard to believe that any General in Chief could have acted more effectively. To Schofield, now commanding the Department of the Missouri, there went an order to send Grant any troops he could possibly spare. A message to Burnside, who had replaced Wright in the Department of the Ohio, with head-quarters still at Cincinnati, contained the sentences: "It is important to re-enforce General Grant. What troops you have, not necessary to hold your positions, should be sent to him." The ending was a flat question: "How many can you spare?" Nor did Halleck overlook the chance to prod Rosecrans, who, with spring all but gone, was still in Murfreesboro:

> All accounts concur that Johnston is collecting a large force against General Grant, a part of which comes from Bragg's army. If you can do nothing yourself, a portion of your troops must be sent to Grant's relief.

The lengthy telegram in which Rosecrans justified his peculiar method of campaigning ended, "The time appears now nearly ripe, and we have begun a movement, which, with God's blessing, will give us some good results." But Rosecrans would have to get along without more than good wishes from Ambrose Burnside, who was on the eve of a move into East Tennessee. Halleck had bluntly told the Cincinnati general to stop his operation and send 8,000 men down the Mississippi. A second telegram said: "If you cannot hire river boats, you must impress them. Telegrams from Memphis say that Bragg is sending large re-enforcements to Johnston." Schofield had been instantly ready to aid, and almost within hours swift-moving Francis Herron had eight regiments and three batteries on the road, some for St. Genevieve where they would embark, others for Rolla, whence trains would carry them to St. Louis and waiting steamers.[21]

In informing Hurlbut that 8,000 men were going to Grant from Kentucky and 5,000 from Missouri, Halleck warned: "Keep your forces well in hand, and watch Johnston closely. He may make a sudden movement north, if unable to raise the siege of Vicksburg." Hurlbut was directed to keep Grant posted on Halleck's instructions to him. He was also empowered to hold some of the reenforcements going to Grant if Memphis were seriously threatened. At about the time that Halleck's message arrived over the uncertain telegraph wire, Hurlbut should have had a dispatch from Grant that said: "Every day pushes us a little nearer the enemy. Joe Johnston is still threatening us on the other side of the Big Black. What his force is now is hard to tell, but all the loose characters in the country seem to be joining his standard, besides troops coming over the railroad daily. I have a strong position front and rear, and expect to worry him out, if he should come." [22]

Grant's news of Johnston rested largely on a report that Frank Blair had made on May 31 after a strong reconnaissance northeasterly from Haynes Bluff. Congressmen are good at learning what is happening in the precincts, and Blair wrote: "Every man I picked up was going to Canton to join him. The negroes told me their masters had joined him there, and those who were too old to go, or who could escape on any other pretext, told me the same story." [23]

Concurrently with Blair's reconnaissance to Mechanicsburg, gunboats under Lieutenant Commander John G. Walker had ascended the Yazoo to within fifteen miles of Fort Pemberton, where the river had been blocked by the sinking of four fine steamers. Lacking means of raising the steamers, Walker fired them, and after waiting to see them well consumed, and driving away an attacking force, and burning a large sawmill, returned to Yazoo City. From the Confederate navy yard at that place—where the famous *Arkansas* had been built— Walker took a large quantity of iron, and reached the mouth of the Yazoo on June 1, after having made a side trip up the Sunflower, which Porter had striven so desperately to reach through Steele's Bayou and Deer Creek. A cutter that had been abandoned in that earlier effort was repossessed.[24]

With the Yazoo opened but with the situation in the vicinity of Mechanicsburg uncertain or insecure, Grant on June 2 ordered Brigadier General Joseph Mower to move his brigade and 1,200 cavalry up the river to Satartia and thence to Mechanicsburg. Gunboats escorted the transports, and the next day Brigadier General Nathan Kimball was sent with more troops to take command of the strategically located force. Kimball was clearly instructed what was wanted: "The object of placing troops at Mechanicsburg is to watch the movements of the enemy, who are said to be collecting a large force in the vicinity of Canton." He was to observe all ferries over the Big Black north of Bridgeport; obstruct in every possible way all roads leading westward that he himself did not need. Forage, cattle, and provisions were to be collected from the country; what Kimball could not use was to be destroyed to keep it out of Johnston's hands. Wagons, horses, and mules were also to be gathered up to deny mobility to the Confederates at Canton. Finally, Kimball was instructed to collect all possible information about hostile movements and send it promptly to Grant. Authority was given him to employ spies, his orders on the subject being sent to the quartermaster, who would make payments upon the approval of army headquarters.[25]

On the morning of the 4th new information about Johnston had reached Grant, and he again wrote to Kimball. Some of the Confederates had gone to Yazoo City. Any cavalry Kimball sent northward might be cut off. The position and number of the enemy must be well ascertained before Kimball advanced much beyond Mechanicsburg, and Grant concluded: "I do not want to run any great risk of having any portion of the army cut off or defeated. If, therefore, your judgment is against reaching Big Black River Bridge with security, and getting back again, you need not attempt it." [26]

Kimball reached Satartia a little before noon on the 4th, and promptly moved forward with Mower, driving the enemy to Mechanicsburg, where he found them drawn up in line of battle. An attack with a brigade dispersed the Confederates, and the Federal cavalry started in pursuit. More important than the ending of Kimball's message, "General Mower behaved with gallantry," was the postscript: "Send me more artillery. Johnston is massing considerable force at Canton. Please send my remaining infantry forward. We hold Mechanicsburg. I will report as soon as possible." [27]

Kimball's reports the next day were full of alarm. One said the enemy was in force at Yazoo City and had 8,000 men on the river only six miles north of Satartia, with 20,000 men and 25 guns along the Big Black, and a rumored 60,000 at Canton. An advance by the Confederates seemed probable, and the message ended, "Should I not be able to beat or repulse them, I shall hold to the very last." A later dispatch stated that 15,000 Confederates were between the Yazoo and Big Black rivers, but cut the Canton force to 40,000. Extending considerably the discretion Grant had given him on the 4th, Kimball said, "I leave to-day for Haynes' Bluff." [28]

Dana's dispatch to Stanton on the 6th shows that Grant must have sensed something amiss in the postscript to Kimball's message of the 4th. After stating that Kimball had driven the enemy out of Mechanicsburg and that the cavalry was pursuing, Dana said: "General Grant has just started for the place, deeming it necessary to examine the situation there himself. I go with him." Grant himself wrote to his three corps commanders: "I am going up to Mechanicsburg. Cannot be back before to-morrow night. Make all advance possible in approaches during my absence. Communications signaled to Haynes' Bluff will reach me." [29]

Although the records thus clearly show that on June 6 Grant revealed fine qualities as a commander, a recent writer makes the day the occasion for a derogatory charge, apparently to supply a basis for a sensational story by Cadwallader. Grant, according to the writer, was suffering from moodiness, tinged with melancholy. His legs grew itchy, and accordingly he one day "disappeared." [30]

Perhaps it was while Grant and Dana were riding with a cavalry escort to embark at Haynes Bluff on a small steamer kept there for Grant's use that Kimball was writing to Rawlins from Satartia:

There is in front of me a large force, of which I cannot ascertain the exact amount, but which is not less than 15,000; and in view of the fact that the river is falling rapidly, and gunboats will soon be unable to recross the bar below, I shall to-day move toward Haynes' Bluff, starting as soon as I can get ready.[31]

Dana's message to Stanton on the 7th, written at Haynes Bluff began:

On approaching to within 2 miles of Satartia last evening, we found that N. Kimball had retreated to Oak Ridge Post-Office, sending the commissary stores and baggage by the river to this place. The gunboats were also coming down, and General Grant returned here with them.

It was, Dana explained, the extraordinary fall of the river that had caused Kimball's move. But he added that a deserter had reported eight Confederate brigades were at Yazoo City, while Johnston was advancing from Canton to the Big Black with a large force. Being short of officers, Grant asked Dana to go to the vicinity of Mechanicsburg with a party of cavalry in order to obtain more information. The assignment kept Dana away all night, and it was not until 10:00 A.M. of the 8th that he was back at the headquarters camp with the information that there were no signs of any considerable force of the enemy, though Kimball had retreated on the 6th in a semipanic.[32]

Lincoln's telegram with the query about Banks probably arrived on the 7th, and it was definitely on that day that a member of Grant's staff returned with a letter from Port Hudson. It gave Banks's reason for not coming to Vicksburg. If he came with all his force, the enemy at Port Hudson could join with forces at Brashear City (Morgan City) and Mobile for an attack on New Orleans. If he sent part of his command to New Orleans to make that place secure, the contribution he could bring to Grant would be offset by the Confederates at Port Hudson joining Johnston—which was what Johnston had urged before Banks had shut them in. On the 7th Hurlbut wrote to Rawlins that he was sending his most effective spy to pass through the entire enemy line. If he arrived, reliance could be put on what he said about enemy forces, for he was "a man of sharp observation and of capital judgment, and about as effective a scamp as the Nineteenth Illinois ever had on their rolls." [33]

The next day Grant telegraphed to Lincoln: "I send by mail letter from General Banks, of June 4. I am in communication with him. He has Port Hudson closely invested." The President's specific question went unanswered; he could decide for himself when Banks's letter came whether that general had done all he could to cooperate against Vicksburg. Grant would not appraise a fellow department commander if he could avoid it. But while Grant was giving the President the means of deciding as to Banks, and Halleck was telegraphing to Hurlbut, "Please keep me advised on the progress of re-enforcements to General Grant," General Blair took it upon himself to give advice and pass judgment on Banks. To his brother, the Postmaster General, he sent the dispatch: "Tell the President to re-enforce this army, as there is great peril. General Banks declines to co-operate with General Grant." [34]

Uncertainty lay not only to the eastward. On the 3rd, Porter warned Grant: "A deserter just came in; says they talk of cutting their way out." That night men slept upon their arms, took position at two the next morning, and so remained "until after sunrise." Until the arrival of more troops so as to extend and strengthen the line on the left, something in the way of a sortie might have been partially effective, even though Lauman's division of the Sixteenth Corps had on May 28 been ordered into position on McClernand's left. More indicative of the future, however, was a warning that had come the day before from Sullivan at Milliken's Bend: "Rumors of an attack on this place." [35]

The first indication that hostile forces might be gathering for a blow against Grant's holdings west of the Mississippi had come in a long letter that Brigadier General Hugh T. Reid had written at Lake Providence on May 12. He had received the report that 10,000 Confederates had moved from Little Rock to Monroe with Alexandria as their destination. Upon learning that Banks was retiring, they had halted. "If this be true," said Reid, "it may be expected that an attempt will be made to operate upon your line of communication from Duckport to Carthage." [36]

Reid was more than a little shrewd. Kirby Smith had ordered that the force from Arkansas—John G. Walker's division—should join Richard Taylor in an attack on New Carthage, an attack which Smith hoped would complete the destruction of Grant's army. Incredible as it seems, reports at Shreveport as late as June 5 not only had Grant defeated, but probably captured. Taylor doubtless knew better, but there was still a surprise in store for him when he reached Richmond on the 5th. The once vulnerable Federal line west of the Mississippi was no longer of importance, while nearly all of Grant's stores had been removed to the new base on the Yazoo. Nevertheless the energetic Taylor went ahead with what he believed was a faultlessly planned operation and struck on the morning of the 7th, a day when even Southerners complained of the intensity of the heat—95° in the shade. The brigade of Walker's division that attacked Milliken's Bend, where there were some ill-trained Negro troops supported by a detachment of the Tenth Illinois Cavalry, had considerable success until gunboats intervened. A sentence in Taylor's report had an unpleasant implication: "A very large number of the negroes were killed and wounded, and, unfortunately, some 50, with 2 of their white officers, captured."

The brigade that was to attack Young's Point found embarrassing gunboats on hand, and its commander lost heart when he thought he saw Federal regiments arriving. He marched back to Richmond, to have his action later called into question in Richmond, Virginia. Taylor reported that Walker had for weeks been pressing Kirby Smith for some such exploit as had been attempted, and, indulging his proneness to criticize others, said, "Unfortunately I discovered too late that the officers and men of this division were possessed of a dread of gunboats such as pervaded our people at the commencement of the war." He candidly admitted that the results obtained were not commensurate with the force that had been employed.[37]

The short dispatch which Porter sent Grant on the 7th about the Milliken's Bend affair was hardly accurate, but the last sentence had a pleasing ring: "The *Choctaw* and *Lexington* were there." A second message that recommended the removal of everything from Young's Point also contained one of the apt statements for which the sailor had a gift: "They got nothing but hard knocks." [38]

Grant promptly reenforced the troops across the river with Mower's brigade, telling Dennis, who was in over-all command, that the enemy should be driven from the vicinity of Richmond and beyond the Tensas River, with Federal troops going as far as Monroe. He wanted information of the enemy strength, which he did not believe was large, for "No such blind move could be made by an intelligent foe as to send more than a force for a raid into such a pocket" as the peninsula across from Vicksburg. Grant nonetheless had to keep close attention on the region where the forces of Kirby Smith were operating, and on the 11th he wrote Halleck, "I now fear trouble on the opposite side of the river, between Lake Providence and Milliken's Bend." The problem was not purely military, for in that region the government was operating some leased plantations. Grant had urged that the experiment be conducted north of the White River; though he had not been heeded he still had to give protection to the fields and workers. Washington, however, would surely pay attention to the excellent intelligence summary that Grant sent on this June 11:

I have reliable information from the entire interior of the South. Johnston has been re-enforced by 3,000 troops from Mobile and other parts of Georgia [Alabama?]; by McCown's and Breckinridge's divisions (9,000 men), and 4,000 of Forrest's cavalry, from Bragg's army; 9,000 men from Charleston, and 2,200 from Port Hudson. Orders were sent the very day General Banks invested Port Hudson, to evacuate it. Garrison there now 8,000. Lee's army has not been reduced; Bragg's force now 46,000 infantry and artillery and 15,000 cavalry. Everything not required for daily use has been removed to Atlanta, Ga. His army can fall back to Bristol or Chattanooga at a moment's notice, which places, it is thought, he can hold, and spare 25,000 troops. Mobile and Savannah are now almost entirely without garrisons further than those to manage large guns. No troops are left in the interior to send to any place. All further re-enforcements will have to come from one of the great armies. There are about 32,000 men west of the Mississippi, exclusive of the troops in Texas. Orders were sent them one week ago by Johnston. The purport of the order not known. Herron has arrived here, and troops from Burnside looked for to-morrow.[39]

It mattered not whether every statement was accurate. The High Command had here a report that could be checked with others. "Lee's army has not been reduced," would be a helpful confirmation at a time when the Army of Northern Virginia was on the move toward the Shenandoah from its position near Fredericksburg.

While Grant may have started the day's work with the intention of sending Halleck a general intelligence summary, he could have had no idea that he would write Lincoln a highly important letter. John Eaton occasioned it and afterward described the incident. He had come from Memphis with a report on the contraband question— thirty-four foolscap pages covered on both sides. Upon his arrival at Yazoo, Dr. Warriner of the Sanitary Commission told him he would find Grant with new wrinkles in his face and looking like half a dozen men condensed into one. The heat of the summer was on, Eaton recalled, and there was much sputter and rattle of musketry with the angrier noise of guns and bursting shells. As he passed Grant's tent on his way to that of the adjutant, the general hailed him, and upon going to greet him, Eaton noted a record of the campaign that Warriner had not mentioned: holes in the general's trousers rubbed through by his bootstraps.

When Eaton spoke of the report he was taking to Rawlins, Grant said he would like to hear it. It was too long, Eaton replied, but, like his earlier protest when Grant first gave him the Negro problem, the objection was of no avail. With Grant's assurance that if necessary he would tell him to stop, Eaton sat down and commenced reading. Every word was read and attentively listened to. After pronouncing the report a very important one, Grant said Eaton must take it to the President, and he immediately wrote a letter that described the problem leading to Eaton's appointment and gave his own evaluation of Eaton's work. He commended the young officer's report to Lincoln's "favorable notice, and especially that portion of it which would suggest orders regulating the subject of providing for the government of the contraband subject, which a Department Commander is not competent to issue." [40]

Though it lacks the drama of the running of the batteries and the march and battles behind Vicksburg, Grant's handling of the Negro problem had likewise required courage, imagination, and judgment, because of possible political repercussions. Now Lincoln was to have a fine report with a respectful suggestion that action was necessary in Washington.

The next day Halleck sent Grant the only dispatch of the siege that savored of admonition. The eyes of the capital were upon Lee's mysterious shift toward the Shenandoah and Hooker's moves to cover Washington. But the General in Chief could not think solely of Virginia and Vicksburg, and near noon on June 12 he telegraphed:

> I hope you fully appreciate the importance of time in the reduction of Vicksburg. The large re-enforcements sent to you have opened Missouri and Kentucky to rebel raids. The siege should be pushed night and day with all possible dispatch.[41]

This too was courteous and unexceptionable.

Herron, twenty-five years old, but with two stars on each shoulder, and the youngest Federal to wear them, was put on the extreme left of the line, between Lauman and the river. Dana would later recall Herron as the only consummate dandy he had ever seen in the army. Though Herron might not go into battle with a lace handkerchief, he would at least have a clean white one. His fastidiousness extended into military matters, and Dana reported to Stanton that Herron's troops were superior in discipline and organization to others in the Western army. Yet Herron needed watching, and Grant did not succeed in getting him properly to picket the bottom between the bluff and the river until he gave him a peremptory order.[42]

Before a week had passed, Porter received a note from Lieutenant Commander James Shirk of the *Lexington* that showed that the navy had become acquainted with the new commander on the army's left. Shirk will be remembered as the lieutenant in command of the *Lexington* when she and the *Tyler* hurled timely shells at Shiloh. Now he wrote Porter that Herron wanted to borrow some guns to take care of "Whistling Dick," the offensive Confederate piece having knocked one of Herron's "10-pound Parrotts some ten rods to the rear this morning."[43]

Herron's messages at times had sparkle like his handkerchiefs, even if written very early in the morning:

HERRON'S, June 23, 1863—2 a.m.

Have just taken another rifle-pit and 13 prisoners in moving up my right line of skirmishers. Will be ready for your final orders to move. I believe I can go into the enemy's works from this position to-morrow night.

HERRON,

MAJOR-GENERAL GRANT [44]   *Major-General*

Burnside's men, consisting of two divisions of the Ninth Corps, under Major General John G. Parke, were sent to Haynes Bluff. The three brigades of the division of Brigadier General Robert S. Potter were composed of regiments from New Hampshire, Rhode Island, Massachusetts, New York, and Pennsylvania; the two constituting the division of Brigadier General Thomas Welsh had four regiments of Eastern men mixed with five from Michigan. Almost without exception the regiments brought by Parke were composed of veterans, and a list of battle names upon their colors would have been a veritable roster of the battles in the East through 1862: First Bull Run, Winchester, Fair Oaks, the Seven Days, Cedar Mountain, Groveton, Second Bull Run, Chantilly, South Mountain, Antietam, Fredericksburg, as well as operations on the coasts of North and South Carolina.

The new corps, which would give Vicksburg greater meaning to the people in the East, together with one division from Sherman's corps and one from McPherson's, constituted the chief force with which Grant intended to keep Johnston away while the siege progressed. In late May, Osterhaus's division of McClernand's corps had been withdrawn from the investing line and placed at the Big Black River Railroad bridge. Osterhaus heard much of reenforcements going to Johnston in the vicinity of Canton, and on June 8 commented in a report to Rawlins, "The people are undoubtedly fed upon that hopeful prospect." [45]

The watchful eye of Frank Blair had an important part in the disappearance of McClernand from the Vicksburg scene. On the evening of June 16 he called Sherman's attention to a congratulatory order McClernand had issued to his corps, as printed in the *Memphis Evening Bulletin* of the 13th. In a letter to Grant dated the 17th and inclosing the clipping, Sherman said, "It certainly gives me no pleasure or satisfaction to notice such a catalogue of nonsense—such an effusion of vain-glory and hypocrisy; nor can I believe General

McClernand ever published such an order officially to his corps." If not a forgery, the order was, said Sherman, obviously "addressed not to an army, but to a constituency in Illinois," and he cited a War Department order of 1862 "which actually forbids the publication of all official letters and reports, and requires the name of the writer to be laid before the President of the United States for dismissal." Not often did Sherman seek vainly for words, and he certainly did not when he described what McClernand had said: "It perverts the truth to the ends of flattery and self-glorification, and contains many untruths, among which is one of monstrous falsehood. It substantially accuses General McPherson and myself with disobeying the orders of General Grant in not assaulting on May 19 and 22, and allowing on the latter day the enemy to mass his forces against the Thirteenth Army Corps alone."

Before the day was over a dispatch had gone from Grant to McClernand:

> Inclosed I send you what purports to be your congratulatory address to the Thirteenth Army Corps. I would respectfully ask if it is a true copy. If it is not a correct copy, furnish me one by bearer, as required both by regulations and existing orders of the Department.

When the message arrived, McClernand was not at his headquarters, but under date of June 18 he wrote to Grant: "I have just returned. The newspaper slip is a correct copy of my congratulatory order, No. 72. I am prepared to maintain its statements. I regret that my adjutant did not send you a copy promptly as he ought, and I thought he had." By now McPherson had also written to Grant, inclosing a copy of the order as published in the *Missouri Democrat* on the 10th. Before the night was over, McClernand had been removed, his place being taken by a soldier, Edward Ord, seen previously receiving a wound at Davis's Bridge over the Hatchie. Quite as if the emergency had been foreseen, a Washington order of May 25 had directed Ord to report to Grant in person, and in his telegram of the 17th Dana had informed Stanton: "General Ord is expected to-day. He will command both Herron's and Lauman's divisions." A change in assignment was a simple matter.

In reporting McClernand's removal to Halleck, Grant said, "I should have relieved him long since for general unfitness for his position." Dana, aware of the deposed general's political power, made haste to make a full report to Stanton, even sending by telegram from Memphis the correspondence between Grant and McClernand. Included was McClernand's letter questioning Grant's authority to remove him since he had been placed in command of his corps by the President. He forebore, he said, actually challenging it "at present." Lincoln was well posted on the case when he received the telegram McClernand sent him from Cairo: "I have been relieved for an omission of my adjutant. Hear me." [46]

The sappers got closer and the days got hotter, though in mid-June Dana was reporting that nights were cool; showers also had laid the dust. When streams in the ravines went dry, wells were dug, or water was hauled. Soon Dana was saying, "Weather is hot; thermometer at 95 degrees," with no reference to relief at night. The well water turned bad, the newspaperman explaining that the lime in it came from decayed shells.[47] Men thirsty from hours of digging would have found the water no better for such an explanation, while wondering probably how the shells got there.

Tension mounted not only at Vicksburg but all along the great river valley as the Confederates sought by every means to bring direct or indirect aid to the men and the many guns shut within the tightening lines of Blue. As early as June 3 Ellet, after a reconnaissance down the Atchafalaya in the *Switzerland,* that took him as far as Simmesport, had reported that he had been fired upon by five guns and a regiment of infantry. On the 16th Porter closed a letter to Grant, "Hearing that Price was advancing on Helena, I sent a force of gunboats there." Though Superintendent of Telegraphs Anson Stager had closed a dispatch to Stanton from Cairo reporting that the wire from Memphis was again operating, with the sentence, "Weather hot and interesting items scarce," messages between the generals were bursting with them. One which Porter sent Welles on the 14th had an ending that did not suggest quiet and repose: "I think the town cannot hold out longer than 22d of June. The gunboats and mortars keep up a continual fire." [48]

Just below Cairo, at Columbus, situated like Vicksburg on high bluffs, fear seemed to be habitual. Quite as Davies had panicked when Forrest was nearby in Tennessee, so Asboth now became alarmed. On the 20th Hurlbut cautioned: "I particularly wish that you should exercise extreme care in the dispatches you forward to General

Halleck. Nothing is more serious offense with him than exaggerated reports. A few days earlier Schofield had said incredulously in a reply to a message from Asboth, "Is Columbus itself in danger?" Halleck had told Asboth he did not believe anything threatened him except guerrillas, though Burnside would be directed to be ready to lend aid. Simultaneously Stager was telegraphing to Stanton that he thought Asboth was stampeding. This may have been read by Halleck; at least a week later he telegraphed to the Columbus general:

> The tone of your dispatches is not satisfactory. They have too much the character of a stampede. If you fight half as well as the enemy, you can readily hold your posts against any force with which the rebels can attack you. If you have not confidence in yourself or in your command, you should ask to be relieved.[49]

All along the line from Memphis, where Veatch was in local command, through La Grange, where Richard Oglesby presided, to Corinth, still under Dodge, there were threats. None of the generals grew alarmed, though Veatch—strong Shiloh fighter—sent a message to Hurlbut that began, "I am glad to hear the gunboats are here," and Oglesby sent one that ended: "Could not hear from Dodge. The line was down last night." It was not necessary to explain why the line had fallen. All positions between Memphis and Corinth—Jackson, Tennessee, it will be recalled, had been given up—were subject to attack by concentrations of the enemy. On the 22nd Oglesby suggested sending his sick to Memphis so as to be better prepared for eventualities. Two days later Hurlbut ended a message to Oglesby, "Anything more of the force in your front? Keep me advised as long as the telegraph lasts." [50]

Though removed from the river, Corinth was still very important, for from there Dodge was sending his well trained agents into the areas behind both Vicksburg and Tullahoma. Grant never had any doubt about the man who would later carry the rails of the Union Pacific Railroad across the mountains to Ogden. He was reliable and his talents were many.[51]

On June 22 it appeared to Grant that an attack by Johnston was imminent. Sherman was sent with additional troops to join Parke while other units in the investing line were alerted to be ready to follow. A letter of explanation to Sherman said, "You will go and command the entire force," and one to Parke ended, "We want to whip Johnston at least 15 miles off, if possible." A long report on the 28th from Hurlbut gave the pleasant information that a rise in the Tennessee and Rosecrans's advance—long overdue—had caused enemy detachments west of the Tennessee to be called in. Its ending revealed that Hurlbut's agents were alert: "I learn from spies that a heavy force, under General Sherman, moved out to look for Johnston, but hear of no results." [52]

Sherman now had an army with a special mission, and Grant assured Hurlbut that if Johnston moved off from his present position he would be followed, "whether it be to East or West Tennessee." And of course if Johnston had started southward to attack Banks, Sherman would have been upon his heels. A message Grant sent Sherman on the 25th told of interesting letters taken from a captured courier out of Vicksburg. They gave details about short rations, and Grant said: "Strong faith is expressed by some in Johnston's coming to their relief. Withers, particularly, cannot believe they have been so wicked as for Providence to allow the loss of their stronghold of Vicksburg. Their principal faith seems to be in Providence and Joe Johnston." [53]

Rumors of course abounded, and Grant said it was not true that Port Hudson had fallen. In fact, Porter had informed him that Banks had lost severely in assaults, and that Kirby Smith was trying to relieve the Confederates in Port Hudson from the opposite side of the river. McPherson would spring two mines that afternoon and would try to secure a place in the fort in his front. Dana, Grant stated, would probably come out to see Sherman in the evening, bringing later news. Sherman knew by this time that Dana shared his own confidence in the commanding general.

From Sherman to the northeast, and McPherson and his mines in the center, Grant's mind this day went to Herron on the left, and toward evening he sent to Ord, to whose corps Lauman's division had been attached, the dispatch: "The operator at General Herron's headquarters reports that the rebels have driven in Herron's pickets. Notify General Lauman to be in readiness all night to afford any assistance necessary." The second of the two sentences that Ord addressed to Lauman as an indorsement of what Grant said was: "At least half your force not in the trenches should sleep on their arms, ready to move at a moment's notice." [54]

Sherman wrote long and careful orders for his army-in-readiness, and on the 29th Grant complimented: "The dispositions you made are excellent. It will be impossible for Johnston to cross the Big Black north of the railroad, without being discovered and your troops ready for him." Grant's only apprehension was that Johnston would move southward and make a quick thrust across the Big Black from that point of the compass. But Ord's cavalry was watching ferries; they had seen hostile horsemen east of the river, but no indications of a crossing. Grant reported that a scout he had sent out, as well as a deserter, had said no troops had been moved south of the railroad, adding the comment, "In the mean time Johnston may have changed his plans and the position of his troops half a dozen times." [55]

On the 27th Dodge sent a long intelligence summary to Oglesby. One of Dodge's scouts reported that people in Mississippi had been expecting the Vicksburg garrison to escape across the river. Boats were believed to have been built, and if such an attempt were not made Pemberton might try to supply himself from the west shore. That he was in constant communication with outside forces was known, for skiffs could easily cross or go down the river, and some land messengers could get through southward. Porter had picked up a courier floating in a canoe, who had thrown a package overboard and would not talk, beyond saying that the town had supplies for sixty days and no damage had been done by the bombardment. "They have signals going on all around here," Porter commented. He also stated, "With the boats, flats, and coal barges they have they can transport their whole force to this side from Vicksburg in six hours," and if a Confederate force simultaneously seized Young's Point, such a move, the admiral thought, could not be prevented. In reporting to Porter that a deserter had said boats were being made out of materials from wrecked houses, Grant suggested, "If possible, fix up material to light and illuminate the river, should a large number of boats attempt to cross." [56]

Before he had left for Alexandria after his fruitless attack at Milliken's Bend, Taylor had actually directed that beef-cattle be collected to swim the Mississippi.[57] If cows and steers were expected to make so great an exertion merely to be slaughtered, the enemy needed watching everywhere.

On the 24th, the day when it became certain that Lee's army was definitely headed for Pennsylvania, Halleck had time to think a little of Sterling Price. It may be recalled that in his early days at St. Louis, Halleck had written to Price about what was and what was not the proper way to strike at the enemy's rear with demolitions, and what was and what was not the proper etiquette for flags of truce. Now Price's activities were giving concern to Hurlbut and more especially to Prentiss at Helena. To Schofield, Halleck telegraphed: "Move the troops as you deem most advantageous, with the view of keeping Price's troops away from the Mississippi River till Grant gets through with Vicksburg." [58]

At last July came. "Militia collecting at Jackson, Johnston vibrating between Jackson and Canton," was the ending of a message to Grant from Sherman. One from McPherson began: "The mine on Logan's front is ready, and the enemy appear to be digging toward it. Shall I explode it?" The reply was:

> Explode the mine as soon as ready. Notify Ord the hour so that he may be ready to make a demonstration should the enemy attempt to move toward you. You need not do more than have rifle-pits filled with sharpshooters. Take all advantage you can, after the explosion, of the breach made, either to advance guns or your sharpshooters.

Hickenlooper, McPherson's engineer, had been sick in his tent since June 28, but he still was keeping a record, and after putting down that the mine under the left curtain of Fort Hill had been fired at 1:00 P.M. of July 1, he commented, "Perfect success, blowing some 7 or 8 rebels, who were engaged in countermining, within our lines." One was alive.[59]

It looked, however, as if Johnston might at last be coming, for Ord on the same day sent word that a hostile force was reported to have crossed the Big Black at Hankinson's Ferry. If so, they should be met, was Grant's reply, but he would "telegraph General Herron to ascertain more fully." The young general from Iowa replied: "I do not place any confidence in the report of the infantry being at Hankinson's Ferry, but think it probable a scout of their cavalry crossed. I have telegraphed fully to General Ord." A query to Sherman brought this reply the next day:

> I do not believe Johnston will come in by Hankinson's, but will be ready to move in that direction on short notice. My scout to Auburn will develop the truth, and I had him make speed.[60]

The really arresting message of July 2 came from the pen of Cyrus B. Comstock, young captain of engineers, who had taken over the duties of the sick Captain Prime. His sentences, addressed to Grant's classmate, Frederick Steele, now commanding Sherman's corps, were without a trace of feeling, and the better they were because of that; it was a time for cool, calm, calculating thought. In Grant's name Comstock gave directions as a surgeon might lay out instruments.

The three approaches in front of the Fifteenth Corps were to be put in condition for men to move swiftly in columns of fours. For sixty feet back from the ends next the enemy they were to be cut in "gentle steps, so that troops can leave the trenches rapidly and in order." Preparations were to be made for crossing ditches. Planks should be on hand, as well as sandbags, stuffed tightly with cotton, to throw into ditches. Enough men were to be used on the work to insure its completion in three days—by July 5. From different vantage points careful study should be made of the ground in the rear of the enemy works, and all possible information about it should be obtained "for the use of generals commanding divisions and corps." [61]

It was not a comfortable day for digging; it was not a comfortable day even for a high War Department observer. Dana began his dispatch of the 2nd with the mostly timely military news: no positive information about Joe Johnston. But he ended meteorologically: "The weather is hot; thermometer at noon above 100 degrees."

Jefferson Davis showed his discomfort over Vicksburg by telegraphing to Johnston—who had actually advanced and was reconnoitering for an opening north of the railroad—"I have this day sent a dispatch to General E. K. Smith, and to your care. Please send copies of the dispatch to General Smith by several reliable couriers, going at different times, so as to insure its speedy delivery."

The President's appeal to Smith may have been the response to a telegram from Johnston that there was no longer hope "of the purchase of Helena." He might, however, be able to destroy Federal transports. Agents had already been dispatched. Funds were ample; Johnston would "probably not require a tenth part of the money" he had.[62]

Time was running out. On June 28 Porter had informed Grant that two deserters had reported that there remained in Vicksburg quarter-rations for only six days; after firing a salute the town would surrender on July 4. Six deserters to Herron the same day gave confirmation. Likewise on June 28 a soldier wrote to Pemberton:

. . . If you can't feed us, you had better surrender us, horrible as the idea is, than suffer this noble army to disgrace themselves by desertion. I tell you plainly, men are not going to lie here and perish, if they do love their country dearly. Self-preservation is the first law of nature, and hunger will compel a man to do almost anything.

You had better heed a warning voice, though it is the voice of a private soldier.

This army is now ripe for mutiny, unless it can be fed.

Just think of one small biscuit and one or two mouthfuls of bacon per day. General, please direct your inquiries in the proper channel, and see if I have not stated stubborn facts, which had better be heeded before we are disgraced.

That night Pemberton also knew that Grant knew his ration situation. A Confederate signalman had read Porter's message to Grant as it flashed across the river.[63]

Reliance, however, was not being put upon hunger. If it did not capitulate, Vicksburg was to be taken by assault as day broke on July 6. That was the meaning of Comstock's directive.[64]

To aid the attacking infantry, there were, close behind the twelve miles of trenches, 89 batteries with 220 guns. There were also the gunboats and the mortars. In a brief note on the 2nd informing Porter that Hovey had reported the mortar fire was very accurate, Grant said: "One shell fell into the large fort, and several along the lines of the rifle pits. Please have them continue firing in the same direction and elevation." [65] It was not an army operations officer appealing to his opposite number on a warship. It was the top soldier talking to the top sailor.

The 3rd found Sherman three miles from the end of the telegraph, where there waited a "swift messenger." He was making preparations to be off after Johnston the moment the city fell. A dispatch from Grant told him that Pemberton had just asked him "to appoint three commissioners to arrange terms of capitulation, to save effusion of blood, etc." He had replied, he said, that that was not necessary because Pemberton could put an end to it by surrendering, when he would "be treated with all the respect due prisoners of war." Grant was thinking not only of making an end of Pemberton and of striking Johnston; he was also thinking of helping to take the enemy holding the other fortress that blocked the river. After assuring Sherman that he could have more men, Grant's message ended, "I must have some troops to send to Banks, to use against Port Hudson." [66]

Presently Sherman queried Parke, "If Vicksburg is going to surrender to-night what does that firing mean?" Parke wired Grant, "General Sherman desires me to ask what means the heavy firing at Vicksburg." The reply, signed "U.S.G.," was brief: "Flag of truce only covered bearer of dispatches; firing was continued by balance of the line." Still Sherman was perplexed, and a note explaining to Parke how he expected to move against Johnston began, "I have received your note and Grant's dispatch, which in a measure explains the strange firing after the news of the proposition to surrender." Nothing was being taken for granted by the Federal commander. Finally a note from Ord, whose subordinate A. J. Smith had made the preliminary arrangements with General Bowen, an old and respected Missouri neighbor of Grant's, informed Grant where a white flag might be expected in front of McPherson's line at 3:00 P.M. Ord was watching details, and informed Grant that "rebel time" was forty-eight minutes faster than his. He was sending his watch to Grant.[67]

Many have written of the historic meeting between Grant and Pemberton that grew out of the verbal message Grant had sent back with his note refusing to appoint commissioners, and there has been pointless argument as to just who said what. A dispatch to Porter from Grant said the enemy had requested an armistice to arrange terms of capitulation, and asked Porter to cease firing until notified otherwise, or heard Grant's guns. The message ended, "I shall fire a national salute into the city at daylight if they do not surrender." Another dispatch had the brevity and simplicity of great drama: "There is a cessation of hostilities. You will please cease firing till you hear from me." Still another told Porter that Grant had felt opposed to Pemberton's offer of paroling officers and men, but his own subordinates thought the advantage gained in having forces and transports available for other use more than counterbalanced the effect of not sending prisoners north. No thought of anything but pressing the campaign was in Grant's message to Sherman:

There is but little doubt but the enemy will surrender to-night or in the morning; make your calculations to attack Johnston; destroy the road north of Jackson. The country from Baldwin's to Hankinson's is picketed and patrolled every day by Ord's force.[68]

Rain had fallen; Sherman told Parke it favored him, "provided always Vicksburg has surrendered." The news was so good he could hardly realize it, though he had "wished for it now fully six months." The soldier who had been impressed by Lorenzo Thomas's gorgeous uniform and who had recently arrived at Haynes Bluff was also recording happy thoughts: "We have been paid today and most of the boys have sent thier [sic] money home by an express agt who has been here to look after it. We have no use for money here but I have kept 50 dollars and sewed it up in the watch pocket of my pants." [69]

Notes over Rawlins's signature directed McPherson, Ord, and Herron to allow "discreet persons" to inform the Confederates that Grant had offered to parole them. But Herron also received a warning: "Direct your pickets to watch closely the enemy to-night, lest he may attempt to get out by your front. Permit no person to pass your lines from Vicksburg." McPherson directed Logan to have his men spruce up, but to keep all of those not on duty well in hand. Presently McPherson called off the salute that had been ordered for 5:00 A.M. of the Fourth—a gun for each of the thirty-four states that Lincoln insisted made the Union.[70]

A half-hour after the time appointed for the canceled national salute, Grant wrote to Porter: "The enemy has accepted in the main my terms of capitulation, and will surrender the city, works, and garrison at 10 a.m. The firing now going on arises from misapprehension." A circular that Wilson wrote was amazingly brief:

Should white flags be displayed upon the enemy's works at 10 o'clock this morning, it will be to signify the acceptance of the terms of capitulation.

The enemy will be permitted to move to the front of his works, and, after stacking flags and arms, will return to their camps.

The works will be occupied only by such troops as may hereafter be selected. Those troops not designated for the purpose will not occupy the enemy's line, but remain in their present camps.[71]

A half-hour after the stipulated hour Grant sent Halleck a brief dispatch that opened with the simple and eloquent sentence, "The enemy surrendered this morning." An assistant engineer officer who was digging another mine wrote in his report: "Here I worked day and night, with six-hour reliefs, up to 10.30 a.m., July 4, the miners suffering much from the extreme heat and want of air, when I received verbal orders from Maj. Gen. U. S. Grant to stop all work, the place having surrendered." When the telegraph brought the news to Sherman he could "hardly contain" himself, and he bubbled over in a message to his chief that sounded a warning:

Did I not know the honesty, modesty, and purity of your nature, I would be tempted to follow the examples of my standard enemies of the press in indulging in wanton flattery; but as a man and soldier, and ardent friend of yours, I warn you against the incense of flattery that will fill our land from one extreme to the other. Be natural and yourself, and this glittering flattery will be as the passing breeze of the sea on a warm summer day. To me the delicacy with which you have treated a brave but deluded enemy is more eloquent than the most gorgeous oratory of an Everett.

The letter ended: "I did want rest, but I ask nothing until the Mississippi River is ours, and Sunday and 4th of July are as nothing to Americans till the river of our greatness is free as God made it. Though in the background, as I ever wish to be in civil war, I feel that I have labored some to secure this glorious result." But Sherman wrote this only after he had said, "Already are my orders out to give one big huzza and sling knapsacks for new fields." [72]

Sherman was not the only one who would have no rest; Grant was writing to him that Ord and Steele would start that evening to join him. He burdened Sherman with no detailed order, saying only: "I want you to drive Johnston out in your own way, and inflict on the enemy all the punishment you can. I will support you to the last man that can be spared." [73]

Thus Vicksburg fell with Grant writing of the future. Dana likewise was busy with his pen. Toward the end of his long dispatch to Stanton he said: "All preparations for occupying the town are completed. In an hour it will be in our possession." Logan's division, which had approached nearest the enemy works, had the honor to be the first to march into the city, the flag of one of its regiments soon replacing the Confederate emblem over the court house. The army which had taken what it wanted and which contained many men who had pillaged or wantonly destroyed did not engage in exultation. Grant afterward spoke of this with pride, while Major Lockett concluded his postwar article about the defense of the city with the statement: "General Grant says there was no cheering by the Federal troops. My recollection is that on our right a hearty cheer was given by one Federal division 'for the gallant defenders of Vicksburg!' " Such a salute quite harmonized with Grant's statement, "The men of the two armies fraternized as if they had been fighting for the same cause." [74]

The captured totaled 2,166 officers, 27,230 enlisted men, and 115 civilian employees. All were paroled except the one officer and 708 men who preferred to go North as prisoners. In addition, there was a rich harvest of ordnance: 172 pieces of artillery, and between 50,000 and 60,000 muskets and rifles. So good were most of the Confederate arms that Grant had some of his regiments exchange their weapons for those the enemy had stacked. The amount of good ammunition was amazing. In his report Pemberton said that it was the exhaustion of his men from continuous duty, not the shortage of provisions, that had compelled him to surrender. Yet the rations he enumerated as still existing were a meager supply for 30,000 men, and they had been laid aside for use in case he should attempt to cut his way out. Many civilians emerged from caves to resume life in badly damaged homes. Dana, who rode into the city with Grant and later recalled Pemberton's discourteous behavior, found the damage less than he had expected. A reporter, however, recorded that nearly every house had suffered and that a whole pane of glass was not to be found.[75]

The Federal casualties for the campaign, from the Battle of Port Gibson on May 1 to the surrender, amounted to 1,514 killed, 7,395 wounded, and 453 captured or missing, giving a total of 9,362. Of these, more than half—5,640—were entered against Champion's Hill and the assault on May 22. The killed exceeded by just one man the number for the Army of the Tennessee in the two-days' battle at Shiloh, but the total casualties were well under those of Grant and Buell on that bloody field in western Tennessee. They were not half of those just suffered by the Army of the Potomac in the three days at Gettysburg.[76]

Waiting to carry dispatches to a telegraph instrument was the fast steamer *V. F. Wilson*. The message to Welles from Porter was a single sentence: "I have the honor to inform you that Vicksburg has surrendered to the U.S. forces on this 4th of July." Grant's longer message to Halleck went in the care of Lieutenant V. M. Dunn of General Sullivan's staff. At Memphis it would seem that Dunn was put ashore to use the telegraph if it were working, while the *V. F. Wilson* sped toward Cairo where there was sure to be an open wire. She arrived about noon on Tuesday the 7th, and Porter's message was in Washington at 12:40, a little too late for a Cabinet meeting. After hurrying back to the White House, Welles handed it to Lincoln, who was at a map explaining some of Grant's moves to Secretary Chase and others. The line out of Memphis had been dead, and Dunn reached Cairo aboard the *Niagara* on the 8th. Soon Halleck had Grant's dispatch. But already on the 7th he had telegraphed: "It gives me great pleasure to inform you that you have been appointed a major-general in the Regular Army, to rank from July 4, the date of your capture of Vicksburg." [77] The slight ambiguity in Porter's words "U.S. forces" did not cause Halleck to say "the" instead of "your."

A word should be said about Joe Johnston. His reconnaissance north of the railroad having proved discouraging, he moved to the south, "although the consequences of defeat might be more disastrous." On the night of July 3 he sent a messenger to Pemberton saying that he hoped to attack the enemy about the 7th. On the 4th he telegraphed to Davis, "Your dispatch of the 2nd instant received, but none of it can be deciphered." The next day word of the surrender reached him, but it was not until the 7th that he telegraphed to Secretary Seddon: "Vicksburg capitulated on the 4th instant. . . . In consequence, I am falling back from the Big Black River to Jackson." [78]

One turns reluctantly from the messages and orders of July 4 and the stories that came from the pens of journalists. In comparison with that record, the many tablets and monuments in the great Vicksburg National Military Park, with its impressive valleys and ridges, must of necessity be mute. Even markers to heroism in the final weeks can give no indication of the greatness of the campaign that ended at the famous river city.

No one could have put more feeling or more truth into what he said than Sherman did when on May 18 he looked down with Grant into the valley of the Yazoo from Walnut Hills and remarked that until that moment he had had doubts, but that the campaign had been a great one even if they never took the city. Unaware of what Sherman had said when he saw the rear of the trenches and batteries that a few months before had burst into flame against his attacking columns, Lincoln, eight days later, in the quiet of his White House study, wrote to a fellow Illinoisan, Congressmen Isaac N. Arnold:

And now my good friend, let me turn your eyes upon another point. Whether Gen. Grant shall or shall not consummate the capture of Vicksburg, his campaign from the beginning of the month up to the twenty-second day of it, is one of the most brilliant in the world.[79]

Nine days after the surrender Porter wrote eloquently to Secretary Welles. On the 4th he had been prompt to congratulate Grant "in getting Vicksburg on any honorable terms," and had indicated approval of paroling prisoners rather than of transporting "so many men." In what Porter said on July 13, his first duty was of course to give full credit to the officers and men of his own command, who had run batteries, engaged heavy shore guns at close range, and carried on ceaseless vigils in stifling ships in the same undaunted spirit which he himself had shown in the unlimited and matchless cooperation he had given Grant. But the admiral, who was never overmodest about his own accomplishments, said that it was to the army that there was due "immediate thanks for the capture of Vicksburg," and that its investment and capture would "be characterized as one of the greatest military achievements ever known." The conception, he said, belonged entirely to Grant, who had "adopted a course in which great labor was performed, great battles were fought, and great risks were run." A single blunder, Porter stated, would have caused great difficulty, "but so well were all the plans matured, so well were all the movements timed, and so rapid were the evolutions performed that not a mistake" had occurred after the fleet passed Vicksburg. After saying that he had had such confidence in Grant's ability to carry out his plans that he had dropped below the city without hesitation, Porter summed up: "The work was hard, the fighting severe, but the blows struck were constant." [80]

On the day that Porter was writing, Lincoln was sending Grant the well known letter which began: "I do not remember that you and I ever met personally. I write this now as a grateful acknowledgment for the almost inestimable service you have done the country." After commenting on the fruitless efforts in the bayous, the President said:

When you got below and took Port Gibson, Grand Gulf, and vicinity, I thought you should go down the river and join General Banks; and when you turned northward, east of the Big Black, I feared it was a mistake. I now wish to make the personal acknowledgment that you were right and I was wrong.

Grant's reply was carried to Washington by Rawlins, with reports of the campaign, as well as rolls and paroles of prisoners. The ending of Grant's letter rivaled that of Lincoln's:

I would be pleased if you could give Colonel Rawlins an interview, and I know in asking this you will feel relieved when I tell you he has not a favor to ask for himself or any other living being. Even in my position it is a great luxury to meet a gentleman who has no ax to grind, and I can appreciate it is infinitely more so in yours.[81]

Rawlins was invited to a meeting of the Cabinet, and Welles left a record of the favorable impression he made.[82] When Rawlins had finished his story, all felt better acquainted with the general who had been severely criticized, but who in the end had taken 172 guns and sent forward the paroles of 30,000 men. As Lincoln listened to the fervid, eloquent Rawlins, he must have been grateful for those stanch believers who had stoutly denied the calumnies against Grant when he, as Commander in Chief and President, had need of such denials. Of Grant's supporters none had been more constant than Elihu Washburne and none could have taken greater satisfaction in the capture of Vicksburg as a personal vindication of his faith. Never again need Washburne fear receiving from the office of the *Chicago Tribune* a letter signed "J. M." such as had been written on May 24, 1862, after Shiloh, and which had ended: "I admire your pertinacity and steadfastness in behalf of your friend, but I fear he is played out. The soldiers are down on him." [83]

Halleck, who had sent no commendations after Grant's previous successes, but whose messages for months had revealed his confidence in him, at last unbent. Before Rawlins's arrival he was already well posted on the main aspects of the campaign, but he lost no time in reading the most important of the papers Grant's courier had brought, and at 9:45 of the morning of August 1 he sent this dispatch to Grant:

Your report, dated July 6, of your campaign in Mississippi, ending in the capitulation of Vicksburg, was received last evening. Your narrative of the campaign, like the operations themselves, is brief, soldierly, and in every respect creditable and satisfactory. In boldness of plan, rapidity of execution, and brilliancy of results, these operations will compare most favorably with those of Napoleon about Ulm. You and your army have well deserved the gratitude of your country, and it will be the boast of your children that their fathers were of the heroic army which reopened the Mississippi River.[84]

Nor was the General in Chief's praise limited to that midsummer day; when he wrote his report for the year, he said:

When we consider the character of the country in which this army operated, the formidable obstacles to be overcome, the number of the enemy's forces, and the strength of his works, we cannot fail to admire the courage and endurance of the troops and the skill and daring of their commander. No more brilliant exploit can be found in military history.

Because Halleck knew military history perhaps better than any man on the continent, he was making no valueless guess. The General in Chief also branded as untrue the allegation, "widely circulated by the press," that Grant in conducting his campaign had "positively disobeyed the instructions of his superiors." Grant had, Halleck stated, not only obeyed orders; he had carried out "to the best of his ability, every wish or suggestion made to him by the Government." In going even beyond that, Halleck put into the record on November 15, 1863, one of the characteristics of Grant, which none could have appreciated so fully as Lincoln, Stanton, and himself: "Moreover, he has never complained that the Government did not furnish him all the means and assistance in its power to facilitate the execution of any plan which he saw fit to adopt." [85]

Fuller has understood the uniqueness and greatness of the Vicksburg campaign as clearly as anyone and has made notable comments of his own. Though he wrote years after Francis Greene, with extensive knowledge of intervening wars and the advantage of participation in several of them, this distinguished British general found himself unwilling to dissent from and unable to improve upon the broad characterization by the gifted young American military engineer: "We must go back to the campaigns of Napoleon to find equally brilliant results accomplished in the same space of time with such small loss." [86]

What was the grand result? With the prompt fall of Port Hudson inevitable, the reopening of the Mississippi River was at hand. No longer could the Confederate states east of the river easily draw supplies in large amounts from the productive region to the west. Liddell Hart points to something else: "Loss of hope is worse than loss of men and land. It was the moral effect, above all, which made Vicksburg the great turning point of the war." [87] But it was not to be lastingly a turning point for the North. While there was a raising of hope and a lifting of spirit for some months, morale sank again and reached its lowest points over a year later, when one of the great political parties virtually pronounced the war a failure and formally demanded that it be ended. But militarily, when viewed in retrospect, Vicksburg was decisive.

During the siege Grant scrutinized his masterpiece, as he examined all his operations, to see if he had made mistakes. In a letter to his father on June 15, he said he had no doubt of the fall of Vicksburg but regretted the failure of the assault of May 22, for if he had taken the city then, there would have been time for a new campaign before the season was so far advanced that it would "be difficult to find water for a marching army," while heat and dust increased discomfort. After stating that the fall of the city would open the Mississippi and cause demoralization to the enemy, Grant concluded: "I intended more from it. I did my best, however, and looking back can see no blunder committed." [88]

That best was very, very good. And if there was a blunder, it still is undetected.

APPENDIX

I. BUTLER'S NEW ORLEANS RÉGIME

Butler's military government in New Orleans caused denunciation from the South because of harshness, from foreign countries because of seizures of money and goods belonging to their citizens, and from people in the North because of financial transactions in which it was thought he had gained. The protests of foreign countries were noted in the text in connection with the investigation by Reverdy Johnson. The other two matters will be treated briefly.

Much was made in the South of Butler's hanging, in early June, 1862, of William B. Mumford because he had pulled the United States flag down from the mint on Apr. 27 and had then dragged it through the streets. In the long proclamation on Dec. 23 in which he declared Butler a felon and directed that he "be immediately executed by hanging" if captured, President Davis said it had not been even alleged that Mumford had committed any offense after the capture of the city. Recently Coulter has stated that the flag torn down had been raised above the mint "prematurely." [1]

In a letter of April 25, addressed to the "Common Council" of the city, the major, John T. Monroe, said that at 1:30 P.M. he "was waited on by Captain Bailey, second in command of the Federal fleet now lying in front of the city, bearing a demand from Flag-Officer Farragut for the unconditional surrender of the city of New Orleans and the hoisting of the United States flag on the custom-house, post-office, and mint." After receiving a written demand from Farragut the next day, the mayor sent the latter a letter—also dated the 26th—in which he said he did not know how to surrender an undefended city (the garrison had departed), adding: "To surrender such a place were an idle and unmeaning ceremony. The city is yours by the power of brutal force and not by any choice or consent of its inhabitants. It is for you to determine what shall be the fate that awaits her." If this does not say that the city was Farragut's, language means nothing. Two days later Monroe sought to repudiate what he had said on the 26th, and spoke in a letter to Farragut of the U.S. flag above the mint having been raised "while the negotiations for a surrender between you and the city authorities were still pending." [2] If this was for the purpose of evading some punishment for Mumford's act, it was crude enough, and could not have deceived Farragut.

It has also been claimed that the flag which Mumford tore down had not been raised by Farragut's order. On the 26th Farragut wrote to Capt. Morris of the *Pensacola:* "The United States mint, now in possession of the rebels, lies under the cover of your guns. You will therefore send your marine officer with a strong guard on shore and seize it, with all its treasure, and also the dies for coining money, and hoist the flag of the United States upon the building." In a letter to the mayor on the 28th, Farragut said, ". . . and the flag which had been hoisted by my orders on the mint was pulled down and dragged through the streets." [3]

In a well-known work written soon after the war, the distinguished author James Parton tried to justify Butler for all, or practically all, that he did. While one must be careful not to be beguiled by Parton's smooth writing and reasoning, it must be said that he certainly appreciated the difficulty of governing a generally hostile and turbulent city of 168,000— by far the largest in the Confederacy—by a small force, much better than many of Butler's critics. Not without logic did Parton say that Butler's reprieve of six Confederates who had been condemned to death by a Military Commission for violation of their paroles made the saving of Mumford impossible. "Mumford hanged, the mob was subdued. Mumford spared, the mob remained to be quelled by final grape and canister." [4]

In his previously cited proclamation, Gov. Moore—who, it may be recalled, said Butler held New Orleans by a force "insignificant in numbers"—stated that at the scaffold Mumford was offered "his life on the condition that he would abjure his country and swear allegiance to her foe." Then Moore added, "He spurned the offer." This must have been said in the hope of making Mumford a martyr and a hero, but the claim lacks substantiation. Butler's order for Mumford's execution was unconditional, and any mitigation is inconsistent with what he wrote to Stanton. The *N.Y. Tribune* published on June 19 a long account of the execution copied from the *New Orleans Delta* of the 8th, which cannot be reconciled with Moore's claim.

The famous "woman-order" that Butler issued on May 15 was even denounced in the British Parliament. It stated that any "female" who would "by word, gesture, or movement," insult or show contempt for an officer or soldier of the United States would be "held liable to be treated as a woman of the town, plying her avocation." Though one might discount subsequent statements about conduct which led to the order, one cannot easily dismiss what was written before. In a letter from New Orleans dated May 12, the correspondent of the *N.Y. Herald* described at some length provocative acts on the part of the women, saying they "would insure six months' hard labor at the forts to a man guilty of like actions." Satire alone had been used against them up to the moment, but, said the correspondent, "unless they mend their manners soon, they will find that their sex will not protect them from a proper punishment." [5]

In his remarkable diary, Capt. John De Forest, who was camped outside the city, made an interesting entry on May 23: "Officers who have visited New Orleans report that the citizens have dropped their surly air, and show a willingness to talk civilly if not cordially. For the present General Butler is rather popular with them than otherwise." Doubtless De Forest was misinformed about Butler's popularity, but his failure to mention the famous order is hard to fit into a picture of violent and immediate reaction against it.[6]

The woman who President Davis charged had been confined on an island of barren sand, fed loathsome rations, and exposed to the vilest insults was undoubtedly Mrs. Philip Philips, who Butler stated had once been arrested for training her children to spit at Federal officers and had been released after apologizing. She was taken into custody a second time for laughing at the funeral of a Federal officer, and Butler pronounced her a "bad, and dangerous woman, stirring up strife and inciting to riot." He directed that she be confined on Ship Island with a female servant, be given a hospital house for quarters, and a soldier's rations with the means to cook them. In a lengthy letter to Davis of Sept. 13, 1862, Alexander Walker, another of Butler's fifty prisoners on Ship Island, stated that Mrs. Philips's sole offense had been a smile discerned by a Federal officer as the funeral procession passed beneath her balcony. When taken before Butler she had "refused to make any concessions or apologies to the vulgar tyrant." Mrs. Philips was, Walker said, "a delicate woman of the highest refinement, the mother of nine children." [7]

It was not the first time that Mrs. Philips—wife of a Washington lawyer and former Congressman from Alabama—had found herself in trouble. Her Washington home had been taken over by Federal agents in the summer of 1861 and her papers searched after she, her two daughters, and her sister were put in arrest in the house of Mrs. Rose Greenhow, soon after that clever and aristocratic spy was put in arrest. Mrs. Philips and her entourage were sent South, but not until her flirtations with men in high places in Washington were noted in Mary Chesnut's *A Diary from Dixie*, where, however, she was put down as nothing worse than a "mad, bad woman." [8]

That Butler was harsh not only toward Secessionists but toward his own men when he felt they had shirked was shown by the bitter denunciation he made of the behavior of the 7th Vermont at the Battle of Baton Rouge, after he had praised the colonel of the regiment, who was killed while trying to rally it. The governor of Vermont protested strongly to Washington, and the findings of a Court of Inquiry indicated that Butler had pronounced judgment without full information. [9]

Early in 1863 Butler appeared before the Committee on the Conduct of the War. He stressed the means he had taken to feed the people of New Orleans, where the situation soon became grave because the city had depended on supplies from up the Red River. He also emphasized measures promptly taken for the health of the population, which at the same time gave employment to many workers:

All the drainage of the city is done by means of canals, and we cleaned out between ten and eleven miles of canals, some of which had not been cleaned for twelve or fifteen years. The consequence was that we had comparatively no sickness in the city of New Orleans. I had a regiment, a thousand strong, in the city during the months of July and August, and it buried but one man.

Butler also claimed that because of the strict quarantine—complained of by foreign powers—there had been but one case of yellow fever.

In connection with the enlistment of Negroes—for which Gen. Phelps had been proscribed by Davis—Butler said: "They are already disciplined. They have already learned to do exactly as they are told, and that is a thing we never can teach our white soldiers." [10] He may have had in mind depredations committed by some of his troops.

The most serious charge against Butler was probably that he was a silent partner in lucrative commercial enterprises engaged in by his brother. With regard to Parton's claim that Butler did not profit, Flower states: "In his anxiety to do justice to this man whom he considered greatly maligned, Parton sometimes failed to exercise his keen perception of affairs and high moral judgment. To the impartial historian it seems clear that both the General and his brother profited personally from the spoils of war, but Parton implicitly trusted Butler's own statements concerning cotton and sugar." Certainly Butler's representations are open to doubt, but the words "seems clear" reveal that there is no unquestionable proof of Butler's gain. After a discussion of the case, Howard Johnson says Parton's statement cannot be disproved because of lack of evidence to the contrary, and states:

In conclusion, then, it can only be said that, whatever his intention, General Butler acted indiscreetly or impulsively enough to bring suspicion on himself; and, in allowing his brother to carry on his operations so close at hand, despite warnings from Mrs. Butler and Secretary Chase, he acted unwisely.[11]

In a letter that Butler wrote to Lincoln in November, 1862, he spoke of himself as the senior major general. He should have known better at the time, yet he continued to hold to the error and a recent biographer defends him in it.[12]

II. THE CASE OF JOHN McCLERNAND

It was noted in the text that on the very day—January 30, 1863—when McClernand sent Lincoln a copy of the letter to Grant which the latter called "more in the nature of a reprimand than a protest," he complained to Grant because one of his own officers had bypassed him and gone directly to Grant. The matter involved was the location of a camp, and McClernand said: "I denounce his complaint as an act of insubordination. Please advise me who made the complaint." [13] To McClernand subordination was something to be followed by his subordinates, but freely ignored by himself in his dealings with his superiors.

The *affaire McClernand* is an excellent example of what can happen when correct procedures are not followed, and Lincoln cannot be absolved of initial responsibility. Though in the end he stood firmly behind Grant, it is hard to see how anyone can read the McClernand letters to Lincoln that are in the Robert Todd Lincoln collection of his father's papers and not experience a sense of exasperation that no adequate reproof was ever given to the intriguer. Lincoln could reprimand in a masterful way, but he had received from McClernand so many letters without reproof that, when the matter came to a climax, he was so much a party to what had taken place that he could not censure without admitting his own fault. That, however, was something he on occasion unhesitatingly did.

In the conversation that certainly preceded the writing of McClernand's long document of Sept. 28, 1862, soliciting command of a Vicksburg expedition, Lincoln could easily have told the general that as he expected his subordinates to follow proper military procedure, it was incumbent upon him to do the same. If Lincoln wished to compliment or appease his fellow townsman by receiving the plan himself, he should have made it very clear that it would be thoroughly canvassed with Halleck before any decision was made. Had that been done, the records would not contain that strange document: a letter from McClernand to the General in

Chief apprising the latter of a program that had been worked out with the Secretary of War! [14]

That Halleck had already tried to put an end to McClernand's irregular procedures is proved by a letter of Aug. 20. McClernand's recent direct application to Lincoln for a leave of absence had, he said, been referred to him. After stating that the War Department had directed that no leaves be granted "except in extraordinary cases," and that he could not make an exception in the present instance, Halleck plainly told McClernand that his letter to the President was a violation of Army Regulations. Nor was it the first time that he had had to remind McClernand of prescribed procedures. After stating that a young officer had been tried by a court-martial a few weeks previously and sentenced to dismissal for doing what McClernand had done, Halleck concluded by asking, "Are Major Genls less bound by the law & Regulations than their subordinates?" [15]

Inasmuch as Halleck specifically refused a leave of absence to McClernand and five days later ordered him to Springfield to "assist the Governor in raising volunteers," the question arises as to how McClernand happened to be in Washington in the latter part of September. Governor Yates was a close friend of McClernand's, and on Sept. 22 accommodated him with the note: "You will please repair to Washington City, without delay, to assist me in regard to matters affecting the organization of the new levies of troops in this State." [16] As McClernand was in Federal service, Yates had no authority whatever to order him away from the place where competent authority had assigned him. There seems to be no evidence that McClernand did anything whatever while in Washington toward furthering the weak pretext the governor had trumped up.

Lincoln's high character and an appreciation of the military and political problems in the fall of 1862 have led Lincoln scholars not unnaturally to be generous to him in the McClernand case. Sandburg used the more than questionable story of David Porter, who, before going to Cairo to take command of the gunboats, had an interview with the President about Western operations. Lincoln listened to Porter's statement that an army expedition against Vicksburg should be commanded by Grant or Sherman, and then surprised him by announcing that the project was to be given to McClernand because of his ability to raise the required troops. Sandburg clearly believed that McClernand raised an entire army corps *after* leaving Washington in late October.[17] Assuredly that would have been "an able piece of recruiting work." But McClernand accomplished nothing resembling such a feat.

In response to Lincoln's call for 300,000 men on July 2, 1862, Illinois furnished 58,589, more than doubling its quota, and making a record no other state equaled, though some, notably Ohio and Indiana, went well over their allotments. Because Halleck's telegram ordering McClernand, then at Jackson, Tenn., to go to Illinois to assist the governor, was dated Aug. 25, McClernand could have had little, if any, influence in raising the 34 new Illinois infantry regiments mustered in by Sept. 6, 1862. Because McClernand left for Washington on Sept. 22 and did not leave that city until Oct. 22, little credit should be given him for the 28 regiments mustered between Sept. 6 and Nov. 13. Only four regiments were mustered in after he reached Springfield on Oct. 25, and they must have been nearing readiness before that date.[18]

The mustering-in strengths of the various regiments could of course be ascertained, but they hardly seem important. Subsequent enlistments were sought up to the time regiments were sent forward, but these could not have been extensive. On Oct. 30 Stanton informed McClernand that bounty money was dwindling so that he would have to depend upon personal influence. If he was personally responsible for enlistments in the 128th Infantry, mustered in at Springfield on Nov. 4, he should have felt considerable chagrin when Grant ordered it disbanded on Apr. 1, 1863, after it had lost 700 men, principally by desertion, a record worse even than that of the 109th of Holly Springs fame, mustered in on Sept. 11 and disbanded on Apr. 10, 1863, except for a company-size residue of reliable men.[19]

Actually, McClernand wrote to Stanton and Halleck on Nov. 10 about the tardiness of enlistments, which he ascribed partly to the scarcity of labor after the summer's recruiting and partly to the recent elections. More helpful than a keg of bounty money or than his personal influence was a telegram that Stanton sent him on Nov. 16: "All the Indiana troops taken at Richmond [Kentucky] have been exchanged. This will increase the force for your expedition about eight thousand." [20]

The *primary* duty given McClernand in the confidential order of Oct. 21 was not recruiting, but the forwarding to Cairo and Memphis of regiments already raised in Indiana, Illinois, and Iowa. That work could have been done perfectly well without him. To meet the threat of Bragg's invasion of Kentucky, the regular military authorities of Illinois had sent forward some twenty-five new regiments without McClernand's assistance, while Indiana and Ohio had likewise done nicely. (It may be recalled here that Lew Wallace had helped stimulate enlistments in Indiana during part of August.) Sherman perhaps was unfair when he wrote to his brother on Nov. 24, "McClernand is announced as forming a grand army to sweep the Mississippi, when, the truth is, he is in Springfield, Ill., trying to be elected to the U.S. Senate." But it is not unfair to challenge McClernand's value as "Superintendent Mustering Service"—as he signed one report to Stanton.[21]

From the first, McClernand had moments of uncertainty about the Mississippi expedition. In a letter to Stanton on Nov. 10, protesting much, asking pardon for overboldness and forgiveness if he had said too much, McClernand raised the question of the possible collapse of the enterprise. In that case he wished to go back to duty with Grant—if he "might be allowed a discretion." Three days later, in a telegram reporting the departure of five Indiana regiments for Memphis, he revealed a suspicion: "I infer that General Grant claims the right to change their destination, and to control all the troops sent to Columbus." Information as to the orders under which Grant was operating, which McClernand seemed to be fishing for, was not forthcoming, and Stanton brushed him off in the first sentence of a telegram dated Nov. 15: "Your several telegrams have been received, and, so far as answer is required, will be answered by the general-in-chief, to whom they have been referred." [22]

Here was a clear hint for McClernand to conduct business properly, but on Dec. 1 he sent something like a final report directly to Stanton. He had forwarded infantry regiments as follows: from Indiana, 12; from Illinois, 16; from Iowa, 12; leaving in those states, respectively, 8, 4, and 7 regiments that should soon follow. Information about cavalry and artillery was also given.

"Under the circumstances," McClernand continued, "I trust it will meet with your views to order me forward to Memphis, or such other rendezvous as you may think preferable, in order that I may enter upon the more advanced work of organizing, drilling, and disciplining my command, preparatory to an early and successful movement, having for its object the important end of liberating the navigation of the Mississippi River."

Then followed a paragraph of typical protestations of assiduity and zealousness, a sly indication of gubernatorial and popular approval of himself, and a final plea for the continued encouragement by the honorable Secretary of War's "sympathy and support." Eventually the letter concluded, "I await your orders in the premises." [23]

In view of the indication that Stanton had given two weeks previously that orders would come from Halleck, this letter could well have irritated the Secretary of War, and the more so because he had sent McClernand warm and more than adequately encouraging dispatches when he first went to Springfield. What happened to this letter is not certain. But McClernand continued to await orders in Springfield.

Days passed, and on the 12th McClernand telegraphed to Lincoln a brief report—49 regiments of infantry and two batteries forwarded, aggregating 40,000 men. The message ended, "May I not ask therefore to be sent forward immediately?" A dispatch the same day to Stanton concluded, "I am anxiously awaiting your order sending me forward for duty in connection with the Mississippi expedition." "I had supposed that you had received your orders from the General-in-Chief. I will see him and have the matter attended to without delay," was Stanton's reply on the 15th. But without waiting to hear, McClernand the next day—Dec. 16—did what he should have done in the first place. He wired to Halleck. And he got everything needed into one sentence that ended, "I beg to be sent forward in accordance with the order of the Secretary of War of the 21st of October giving me command of the Mississippi expedition." [24]

When a copy of Halleck's telegram to Grant of Dec. 18 about McClernand having immediate command of the Vicksburg expedition, "under your direction," arrived in Springfield on the 22nd, it was not accompanied by a release, and Stanton's reply to McClernand's telegram pointing this out read:

It has not been my understanding that you should remain at Springfield a single hour beyond your own pleasure and judgment of the necessity of collecting and forwarding the troops. You are relieved of duty at Springfield, and will report to General Grant for the purpose specified in the order of the General-in-Chief.[25]

That the contention in the first sentence did not harmonize with Stanton's telegram of the 15th was certainly apparent to McClernand. An order relieving him from duty as "Superintendent Mustering Service" would certainly seem to have been called for, even though he had pinned the impressive title on himself. Since it had been an order by Stanton that had sent McClernand back to Springfield, Halleck was justified in leaving his release to the Secretary. By appealing to Lincoln, Stanton, and Halleck, McClernand had confused the whole matter and made it easy to shift responsibility. Even his trip down the Mississippi with his new wife and the assumption of command of the Vicksburg expedition on Jan. 4, 1863, did not lessen McClernand's wrath against Halleck, and on the 7th he wrote Lincoln a bitter letter in which he said, "I charge Maj. Genl Henry W. Halleck for wilful contempt of superior authority, and utter incompetency for the extraordinary and vital functions with which he is charged as Genl-in-Chief." Immediately upon the receipt of the letter on the 23rd, Lincoln replied, but whatever there was of reproof in the statement, "The charges, in their nature, are such that I must know as much about the facts involved, as you can," was lost in what followed, and the net result of McClernand's insubordination was praise: "Your success upon the Arkansas, was both brilliant and valuable, and is fully appreciated by the country and government." [26]

Matching his resentful denunciation of Halleck was McClernand's effort to arrogate to himself credit for the success of the campaign behind Vicksburg in the letter to Lincoln of May 29, mentioned in the text.[27] He set something of a record for presumptuousness when he claimed credit for Champion's Hill, where, according to Liddell Hart's trenchant statement, Pemberton would almost certainly have been overwhelmed but for McClernand's inertia in keeping four divisions out of the battle. In speaking of the fine performance of Hovey, McClernand did not state that that general fought under the personal direction of Grant, well removed from where he personally was. Nor did he say anything about Hovey's fighting in close cooperation with the two divisions of McPherson. All this showed not only lack of integrity; it revealed a great deficiency of intelligence. McClernand knew that Dana was present and must have supposed he was making full reports to Stanton. While it would be too much to say that McClernand would have been deflated by the White House indorsement on the envelope containing his letter, he might have thought there was some irony: "Maj. Gen. J. A. McClernand claims the glory of the Vicksburg campaign thus far and denounces those who, as he says, are trying to injure him and his command. Gives an account of the manner in which he won several battles and captured a portion of the fortifications of Vicksburg."

In a letter to Stanton from Springfield, Ill., dated June 27, 1863, McClernand charged Grant had "assumed power" both to relieve him and to banish him from the department, and he asked for an investigation of Grant's and his own conduct as officers since Belmont to the Vicksburg assault of May 22. (McClernand again showed lack of intelligence in assuming that Grant had not been given the explicit power over all subordinates that any army commander should have when conducting an operation such as that at Vicksburg.) Three days later Governor Yates wrote to Lincoln that McClernand had been received with the greatest demonstrations of respect, and he said all regretted that McClernand was not in the field. Yates suggested that if McClernand was put in command in Pennsylvania, and was given some Western troops, it would inspire great hope and confidence in the Northwest "and perhaps throughout the country"—which was about as foolish a proposal as could be made. On Aug. 6 the governor and two other state officials sent by private hands a letter to Lincoln which included the sentences: "The popular verdict is irreversibly in his [McClernand's] favor as a general, unless by some future act he should himself reverse it. Since his return, although taunted by the opponents of the war at his misfortune, he has borne himself with admirable equanimity." [28]

Lincoln's reply of Aug. 12 was addressed directly to McClernand. He now stood firm and wrote notable sentences:

. . . All there is, so far as I have heard, is General Grant's statement of his reasons for relieving you. And even this I have not seen or sought to see, because it is a case, as appears to me, in which I could do nothing without doing harm. General Grant and yourself have been conspicuous in our most important successes, and for me to interfere and thus magnify a breach between you could not but be of evil effect. Better leave it where the law of the case has placed it. For me to force you back upon General Grant would be forcing him to resign. I cannot give you a new command, because I have no forces except such as already have commanders.

I am constantly pressed by those who scold before they think, or without thinking at all, to give commands respectively to Frémont, McClellan, Butler, Sigel, Curtis, Hunter, Hooker, and perhaps others, when all else out of the way, I have no commands to give them. This is now your case, which as I have said, pains me not less than it does you. . . .[29]

It is difficult to believe that Lincoln had not been told Grant's basis for removing McClernand, though he may not have actually read Grant's note to Halleck or the letter and documents that Dana had sent to Stanton. Lincoln may have done little more than accept the statements of Halleck and Stanton that the action had been fully warranted. But it is impossible to believe he had not read McClernand's telegram directed to him personally, which said his removal was because of an omission by his adjutant. One cannot help wishing that Lincoln's letter of Aug. 12 had made some tactful reference to McClernand's boastful letter of May 29, which had been filed away with an indorsement indicating it had not been accepted as fully truthful.

The case was indeed strange. Grant had removed McClernand for insubordination, and Lincoln had in his possession evidence of insubordination greater than Grant had. McClernand of course knew this, but his egotism was such that he could not properly appraise the case. The President's failure to turn everything upside down because of what had happened, but to let the matter lie where the law put it, should have been a great shock to McClernand's vanity.

McClernand's reply of Aug. 24 asked for "an impartial court," and took exception to Grant's report on the Vicksburg campaign, which had now been published. Not having heard from Stanton, he wrote to him again on the same day. When advised by the Secretary that Lincoln declined to order a court of inquiry, McClernand made a notable retreat on Sept. 5. He no longer asked that Grant's part in the operation be investigated; he would be satisfied with an inquiry into his own. On the 14th Stanton replied that the President had directed him to say the investigation of any subjects mentioned in McClernand's letter of the 5th would necessarily withdraw from the field many officers whose presence with their command was absolutely indispensable.[30]

Already McClernand had written to some seven officers who had been at Vicksburg, but who for one reason or another were not now in the field, for statements in support of his case, and on Sept. 25, he addressed a long document to Halleck. A covering note to Lincoln said that, having failed to receive a new command or a court of inquiry, "no other mode of self-vindication is left for me than an official and responsible statement by myself of my own case." He asked the President to peruse the paper, and even pronounced it a "matter rightfully claiming" Lincoln's attention. Most of the nineteen printed pages—a large part of which is small print—deal with a few statements in Grant's report and with the assault of May 22. It is inconceivable that Lincoln, Stanton, or Halleck, all of whom received copies, ever read it. Halleck probably accepted Grant's appraisal of McClernand as "unmanageable and incompetent," and Stanton had Dana's statement that he would not make a good regimental commander. But if Lincoln even looked at it, his eye must have fallen on the first sentence of the second paragraph, which read: "How far General Grant is indebted to the forbearance of officers under his command for his retention in the public service so long, I will not undertake to state unless he should challenge it." [31] When he spoke thus, McClernand was really putting himself in the President's chair, and the man who sat there must have recalled that McClernand had not forborne, but not long before had slyly sent a bearer of tales to him in the hope of dislodging Grant.

The forbearance had been on Grant's side, as James Wilson, who had known McClernand from youth, later made clear. He put McClernand down as a man of hasty and violent temper, with whom it was hard to get along smoothly, even for one of Grant's self-control. If Wilson's story of an outburst in which McClernand indulged when Wilson brought him a verbal order from Grant is accurate, McClernand would have fared badly before a court when Wilson was put on the stand. That Wilson would have appeared is certain, for McClernand's language and statements had been so startling that Wilson said he had felt it his duty to communicate what had transpired to Rawlins, who in turn had informed Grant. While one can question Wilson's recollection of an incident many years old, no such doubt can be entertained about his judgment when he wrote: "Grant had already shown himself to be a patient and prudent man, of unusual reserve and self-possession, with whom a more impulsive man was always at a disadvantage." [32]

Both Butler and McClernand had prima donna traits. While both are now off the stage, both will return. Grant will see Butler fail as a field commander in Virginia, just as he saw McClernand fail on May 16, 1863, at Champion's Hill. McClernand will have only a minor and brief command, and that far away from Grant's presence. The exposure of Grant which he threatened to publish he lived to see in the pages of the *Official Records,* where it did no harm to Grant and no good to his own record.[33]

III. THE CADWALLADER STORY OF JUNE 6 AND 7, 1863

In an address that Douglas Southall Freeman delivered only a year before his death, and which fittingly was used as the first article in the first number of *Civil War History,* there is a warning against "records of events made after a prolonged interval." Freeman cautioned particularly about the man who had become a public lecturer, for he may have given his story new adornment with each telling.[34] It is surely also necessary to be on special guard in the case of a wartime newspaper correspondent who had subsequently been completely forgotten and in his declining years wrote recollections which make him generally important and on one occasion a hero.

As he cut away "dross" and material of which Sylvanus Cadwallader obviously had no personal knowledge, the editor of Cadwallader's memoirs, Benjamin P. Thomas, must have been aware that questions could be raised about the reliability of what remained. He was, however, willing to accept another's guarantee of a manuscript that had remained unpublished for sixty years, and he says in the Introduction, "General James H. Wilson read it, made a few minor suggestions, and vouched for its accuracy."[35]

The manner in which Wilson's indorsement may have been made is of no importance, for it is not to be believed that he checked Cadwallader's work against official records, and he read it at a time when his own memory may have been inaccurate. In any event, Wilson had no first-hand knowledge of many of the things that Cadwallader described. In particular, he saw none of the incidents that formed Cadwallader's most sensational story, and it will be seen that his own writing about the matter was most inaccurate. For the first half of the last year of the war, Wilson, though a cavalry commander in the Army of the Potomac, was not habitually at Grant's headquarters; during the last half of the year he was in a theater of war remote from Grant. Wilson has been seen in the Vicksburg campaign as an officer of exceptional ability. But he must be dismissed as an acceptable underwriter for Cadwallader.

Though Thomas's statement about Wilson carries no weight, one he makes on the next page is of much importance. After noting that Cadwallader had given his work the title *Four Years with Grant,* he states, "I have subtracted one year for the sake of accuracy." This surely admits that there was something deceptive in the title that Cadwallader gave his manuscript. As noted previously, he was in the field with Grant for only thirty months, so the title even as amended includes six months of indefinite Washington contact with the general.

The first page of the book contains what looks like a spurious letter. It is dated August 8th, 1862, and is from Grant to Sherman. It speaks of inclosing an article "false in fact and mischievous in character," credited to the Memphis correspondent of the *Chicago Times,* and it directs Sherman to arrest the author and send him to the Alton penitentiary. The message is not in the *Official Records*—as are none from Grant to subordinates during August—and search elsewhere has failed to reveal it. The absence of the place of sending the dispatch is highly suspicious, for an examination of the some 330 telegrams and letters over Grant's signature which cover the period from June 19, 1862, to Jan. 20, 1863, shows that Grant was very particular about proper headings for communications.[36]

Nothing like the address "Major General W. T. Sherman, commanding United States forces, Memphis, Tennessee," and the formal ending, "I am respectfully Your Obedient Servant, U. S. Grant, Major General, etc.," is to be found in any of Grant's ten letters to Sherman for the period in question, that are in the *Official Records,* except in the long one of Nov. 6. In all but one of the letters—that of Dec. 8—Sherman's first name is given in full; in all of them the rank is abbreviated in the address.[37]

The probability that in one and the same letter to Sherman, Grant would omit the place of writing, use a formal address and ending, spell out Sherman's rank but abbreviate his first name to an initial, is very small. It falls to a still smaller figure if one includes the chance that Grant would also spell out Tennessee, put the date line below the address, and end with "etc."

That Grant directed Sherman to arrest a correspondent is shown by Sherman's letter to Grant of Aug. 17, replying to one from Grant of the 4th (not in the records), which had not been received until the 16th. In his letter Sherman says, "Your order of arrest of newspaper correspondent is executed, and he will be sent to Alton by the first opportunity." An Alton record that gives Aug. 15 as the date of the man's arrest—if not incorrect—precludes the possibility that Grant's order was given in his letter of the 4th. Sherman's journal of communications received, which notes the receipt of the latter letter as well as a long explanation from the offending correspondent—W. P. Isham—does not mention a letter from Grant of Aug. 8.[38]

How, one must also ask, would a letter from Grant have come into the possession of Isham, or of Cadwallader, after the latter became the *Times* correspondent two months later? And how did it happen that Cadwallader in the mid-nineties had a Grant-to-Sherman letter when he himself says he had lost *all* his correspondence in the great Chicago fire?[39]

Unless the original of the letter given by Cadwallader is located, or a trustworthy copy of it is found, the verdict would seem to be this: Cadwallader knew that Grant had directed the arrest and confinement of his predecessor, but was not satisfied with that simple fact. A letter would be more impressive, and so Cadwallader composed one (and misapplied the description "Special Order"). Because he did not know the location of Grant's headquarters—Corinth at the time—the place of writing was omitted; because he was not familiar with Grant's style, he also betrayed himself in other ways.

Before considering Cadwallader's account of June 6 and 7, 1863, we recall three black marks against him because of his stories of previous incidents. His explanation of Grant's "expulsion order"—strangely omitted from *Three Years*—has a touch of sensationalism but is completely disproved by chronology. His blaming the destruction of Holly Springs on Col. Dickey as much as on Col. Murphy reveals confused thinking, differs from Grant's official appraisal, and includes a derogatory statement about Dickey factually incorrect. What Cadwallader says about the sending of Lorenzo Thomas and Charles Dana to the West is so far from the truth that it looks like pure invention. It also has a touch of the sensational and in addition implies that the Adjutant General of the Army could be remiss in carrying out an order.[40]

Cadwallader states that Satartia was about a hundred miles up the Yazoo and that he was coming down the river on the *Diligence* after an unsuccessful expedition in search of news when they met a boat flying Grant's flag. Actually, it was only about fifty miles to Satartia from the Yazoo's mouth, and there was no steamer *Diligence* in the region, though there was a *Diligent*. Cadwallader does not fix the exact date (nor does his editor), but it will be recalled that it was on June 6, 1863, that Grant went up the river with Dana in order to look at the situation in the vicinity of Mechanicsburg (five miles east of Satartia), where Kimball's division had been sent.[41]

Cadwallader's account places him at Satartia on June 5, the day after Kimball had had a clash with the enemy at Mechanicsburg, and the day after the Confederates, supported by some 500 cavalry, had put two guns in position and shelled the transports at Satartia, until driven away by the gunboats. Back in Satartia on the 5th, Kimball reported to Rawlins that the enemy was in force at Yazoo City and had 8,000 men only six miles away.[42] But Cadwallader states that there were no Confederate troops in the vicinity of Satartia.

According to Cadwallader, Grant transferred to the *"Diligence"* presumably because it was the faster boat. He asserts that Grant had been drinking heavily and that the general made several trips to the bar of the *"Diligence."* Cadwallader then took the situation in hand, and succeeded in getting Grant into a stateroom, got his coat, vest, and boots off, and fanned him to sleep.

Cadwallader has the *"Diligence"* actually reach Satartia, and he asserts that Grant insisted on going ashore. This Cadwallader, after considerable effort, persuaded him not to do, and he got Grant back into his cabin, where the general again went to sleep. It is certain that in his advanced years on his isolated California sheep ranch, forgotten by the world, Cadwallader wished to be regarded as having saved Grant—and perhaps the Union—for he wrote: "I have never doubted but he would have ridden off into the enemy lines that night if he had been allowed to do so." (The day before there had been no enemy in the vicinity; where they had suddenly come from is not explained.)

A previously quoted dispatch that Dana sent Stanton the next morning—June 7—shows that the gunboats were met coming down the river two miles below Satartia (a sudden fall in the river made it likely that they might not be able to cross a mud bar) and that Grant returned with them to Haynes Bluff, where Dana wrote his message. In his *Recollections of the Civil War* Dana confirms this, and it is important to see exactly what he wrote. After repeating essentially what he had said in his dispatch to Stanton on June 6, 1863, about Grant's desire to inspect the situation in the vicinity of Satartia, Dana states that at breakfast Grant said, "Mr. Dana, I am going to Satartia to-day; would you like to go along?" His narrative continues as follows:

I said I would, and we were soon on horseback, riding with a cavalry guard to Haynes's Bluff, where we took a small steamer reserved for Grant's use and carrying his flag. Grant was ill and went to bed soon after he started.

It is to be observed that Dana did not say that Grant became ill *after* they had embarked. Dana's next sentences are:

We had gone up the river to within two miles of Satartia, when we met two gunboats coming down. Seeing the general's flag, the officers in charge of the gunboats came aboard our steamer and asked where the general was going. I told them to Satartia.

The naval officers said it would not be safe to proceed; Kimball was retreating and the enemy was probably already in the town. Dana explained that Grant was sick and asleep and he did not want to waken him. The officers insisted that it was "unsafe to go on," and Dana called Grant. After observing that Grant was too sick to decide, Dana states, " 'I will leave it with you,' he said. I immediately said we would go back to Haynes's Bluff, which we did." In view of what the gunboat officers had said, it was not a hard decision, and Dana did not cast himself in a hero's role.[43]

An editorial note in *Three Years* makes no reference to the official dispatch that Dana sent to Stanton the next morning, and says that Dana reported "tactfully" on the trip in his *Recollections*. Inaccurately it states: "Dana says that *when the boat reached Satartia,* he knocked on Grant's door." (Emphasis supplied.) The unquoted part of the sentence adds that Dana knocked to report that Satartia was infested with guerrillas and to ask if they should turn back. How Dana learned of the infestation is not explained, and it was not a case of guerrillas: the troops of Brig. Gen. W. H. Jackson had advanced after Kimball's retreat.[44]

It is impossible to harmonize Dana's story and that of Cadwallader, not only with regard to reaching Satartia but with regard to a change of boats by Grant. Thomas does not challenge Dana's account; he merely asserts that Dana says something very different from what he actually states. In his *Bohemian Brigade,* Louis M. Starr (who had used the Cadwallader manuscript) avoids the change of boats by having Grant *embark* on the *"Diligence."* Cadwallader is thus rescued by ignoring his story up to the moment when he perceived that Grant had been drinking. (His presence on the boat is not explained.) Like Thomas, Starr says nothing about meeting the gunboats and has Dana knock on Grant's door when the boat reached Satartia; he also has Satartia infested with guerrillas.[45]

In his *The Web of Victory* Miers devotes five pages to Cadwallader's account, but he makes no reference to Dana's *Recollections,* a work which he cites, however, on other occasions. Miers's assignment of "itchy" legs to Grant, apparently as motivation for his trip up the Yazoo, was noted in the text. Also given was the dispatch that Grant sent to his three corps commanders before starting, telling them where he was going, when he would be back, and how he could be reached. Anyone who has difficulty believing that Cadwallader could have made up his story out of nothing might reflect on the paragraph that Miers wrote that climaxes with the "itchy" legs, and on the next single-sentence paragraph, "And so one day Grant disappeared." [46]

Cadwallader's statement that it was soon apparent that Grant had been drinking heavily must have seemed loose and inadequate to Miers. He states that Grant's condition was obvious from a dozen yards. It is gratifying to have exactness in such matters. Since Miers says nothing about Dana, we shall probably never know at what distance it could be told that the high War Department observer was 100 per cent sober.

After seeing the efforts to save Cadwallader, it is not surprising to find Starr stating that there is a perceptible tongue in Dana's cheek when he wrote that the "next morning Grant came out to breakfast fresh as a rose, clean shirt and all, quite himself," and said, "I suppose we are at Satartia now."

We recall that just about a month before—May 3—Grant had gone aboard Porter's flagship and had come off "fresh as a rose," bathed and wearing borrowed underwear.[47]

The question whether Dana had special meaning when he said that Grant was ill will be deferred, in order to consider Cadwallader's account of June 7. His claim about June 6 being repudiated by the fact that Grant did not reach Satartia, what he says about June 7 is—to put it mildly —not acceptable. Of the two stories, it must have been that of the 6th that Cadwallader cherished most. While he had entertainment and excitement on the 7th, his heroism that day is hardly to be compared with his achievement the day before. He did, however, give a story with an amusing ending when he said he took Grant back to camp in an ambulance from which Grant alighted and walked to his tent as steadily as he ever walked in his life; but an artful ending is hardly a guarantee of accuracy.

A strange letter that Rawlins wrote to Grant has been made to appear as supporting the Cadwallader story, when in fact it challenges it. The letter was given by Wilson in his life of Rawlins and it bears the heading "June 6th, 1863, 1 a.m." Thus it was written a few hours before Grant and Dana left for Satartia. Rawlins said that he had heard that Dr. McMillan at Sherman's headquarters had recently induced Grant to drink a glass of wine, which violated a pledge Grant had given him. Furthermore, Rawlins had on the 5th found a box of wine in front of Grant's tent, which he had had removed. Worse than that, Rawlins had in the evening found Grant "where the wine bottle had just been emptied, in company with those who drink and urge you to do likewise." The letter ends with a plea by Rawlins for Grant not "to touch a single drop of any kind of liquor, no matter by whom asked or under what circumstances." If Grant did not wish to make such a pledge, then Rawlins wished to be immediately relieved from duty in Grant's department.[48]

Though there is impressive earnestness and sincerity in the letter, it makes Rawlins appear foolish for making much out of little. In what looks like an effort to free Rawlins from the dubious position in which his letter places him, Wilson mixes the letter up with the Satartia trip. He makes a correct page reference to Dana's *Recollections*, but though Dana specifically states that it was on the morning of June 6 that Grant invited him to go to Satartia, and has Grant eat breakfast at Haynes Bluff the next morning, Wilson states that Rawlins wrote to Grant near midnight of the day on which he had left. In cutting the trip to one day Wilson is poor support for Cadwallader's story of the 7th. In the preface of the book Wilson speaks of having had "access" to the Cadwallader manuscript, and in another connection he actually quotes from it; but Cadwallader's name is not mentioned in connection with Grant's Satartia trip.[49]

In comments following the Rawlins letter, Wilson says:

It appears from an endorsement which Rawlins placed on his retained copy of the letter, in the possession of his family, that his admonitions were not resented, but were heeded for a season. This was certainly the case till after the capture of Vicksburg, but it is well known that his apprehensions were never entirely dismissed.

Here Wilson has Rawlins merely continue to entertain his fears; he does not say that any incident ever gave strong support for them. One must recall also that Rawlins's extreme attitude toward drinking antedated his acquaintance with Grant, and came from the fact that liquor had been the ruination of his father, and he himself had lived in fear that the least indulgence might start him on a fatal downward path.

There is obvious difficulty in fitting the Rawlins letter in with the Cadwallader story. If Grant had read the letter before leaving for Satartia on the 6th and had then done some drinking, Rawlins's endorsement was a mammoth falsehood. It cannot be believed that he would have written untruthfully. Thus Grant must have departed without having read the letter. If Rawlins had on the evening of the 7th received a call from Cadwallader to send an ambulance to bring Grant to camp, Rawlins surely would have repossessed the letter. It would have needed a postscript.

In a long letter that Dana wrote to Stanton on July 13, 1863, from Cairo, he described various members of Grant's staff. He stated that Rawlins was a very industrious and conscientious man, who never lost a moment and never gave himself any "indulgence except swearing and scolding." He did not believe Rawlins was as good an adjutant as Grant considered him; Rawlins could not write the English language correctly without great difficulty. Dana stated that Rawlins watched over Grant day and night, and whenever he committed "the folly of touching liquor" made haste to remind him of his pledge.[50] One may interpret this as one wishes, but inasmuch as Wilson says Rawlins told both him and Dana about the letter he had written, it looks like a reference to that.

Although Starr has Grant start for Satartia on June 6, he has Rawlins write his letter about an hour after Grant's return.[51] As he accepts Cadwallader's story, this would have had Rawlins write two days later than the date that stands out clearly on his letter. Certainly the editor of the Cadwallader manuscript had an unusual opportunity to point out the confusion that was in Wilson's mind and correct the error that Starr had made. But having supported Cadwallader by an inaccurate statement as to what Dana had said, Thomas again follows Starr, and states in a note that the Rawlins letter was written the morning after the return to the headquarters camp, when Cadwallader portrays himself as fearing he would be summoned into Grant's presence.[52] Like Starr, Thomas gives the first sentence of the Rawlins letter—a rather awesome one in which Rawlins speaks of his solicitude for the safety of the army prompting him to raise again the subject of Grant's drinking. In the very next sentence Rawlins said he might be doing Grant an injustice by "unfounded suspicion," a possibility to which he returned in the last paragraph of his letter. The reader of *Three Years* will naturally believe that Rawlins reproached Grant, not for some suspicions about wine drinking, but because of the incidents that Cadwallader asserts he had related. It is understatement to say that the note is mischievous.

In an attempt to bolster what he had written, Cadwallader flatly contradicts a previous statement about Grant's drinking that can probably be accepted. He states that the first time he ever saw Grant use spirituous liquor was on the night of May 12, 1863, when he came into Col. Duff's tent and asked for some whisky, and it looks as if he had not heard reliably of any previous occasions. May 12 had been a crucial day in the Vicksburg campaign, and Grant's desiring a stimulant is entirely in conformity with Horace Porter's statement, in *Campaigning with Grant* (that covers the last year of the war), that after a hard day's ride the general occasionally joined other members of his staff in a whisky toddy.

Cadwallader says that Grant's stay in Duff's tent did not exceed twenty or thirty minutes and that he then left. After he had told the Satartia story he said that Grant could not drink "moderately." If he took just one glass, he "invariably" drank to excess unless someone led him away from temptation. Cadwallader had forgotten that neither he nor Duff had had to lead Grant out of Duff's tent.[53]

If anything such as Cadwallader describes for either June 6 or 7 (especially the latter) had occurred, it would have soon been known to the entire army. In particular, Theodore Upson, whose regiment arrived at Haynes Bluff about June 11, would have learned of it. Troops in that vicinity were not particularly busy; a chief activity must have been gossiping. About a year later, after Grant had gone to the East, Upson put into the record a very important statement. What he wrote on Apr. 3, 1864, was not casual comment, but was in answer to specific queries in "several letters from home people" and his foster father's anxious remark that he hoped Theodore was not becoming a drunkard, as he heard many soldiers were doing.

Though not under oath, Upson was addressing the woman he called "mother" and who had shown as much devotion to him as to an actual son. He was sorry to say that there was drinking among the men, but it was the exception. While some officers indulged in "social glasses," few drank to excess, and Theodore thought the number was decreasing. They knew that men distrusted officers who were intemperate, and made fun of them; then their usefulness was over. After saying that he knew what he was talking about because he had been around headquarters enough to learn the habits of the generals, Upson wrote, "Grant does not drink at all; Sherman but little, if any; I dont think any. Howard never; McPherson, I think, never; Logan is no tippler; and in our Division and Brigade officers all, or nearly all, are total abstainers." [54]

Upson's statement has the ring of honesty, and though he was incorrect in saying that Grant never drank, no one who has had experience with soldiers and the army will think Upson's statement can be easily reconciled with the Cadwallader story of June 7. ("The Army is as prone to gossip as a New England sewing-society," was the judgment of the founder of the *Army and Navy Journal*.) [55]

It has already been noted that Dana's statement "Grant was ill," clearly applies to the time he embarked at Haynes Bluff. Do those who think that Dana was speaking euphemistically wish us to believe that Grant did some drinking before leaving camp or while riding with the cavalry escort, or that Dana was so unskillful with verbs that he has *A* happen before *B*, when *B* really happened before *A*?

John Eaton relates that at Memphis (probably in January, 1863) he corrected the wrong judgment of a young dentist by telling him that Grant had suffered the night before from one of the severe headaches to which he was subject, and had not been drinking. Eaton had himself witnessed Grant's illness and had seen his wife apply poultices to his neck and feet in an effort to bring relief.[56] Two later attacks of the same sort will be mentioned. Though the last of them takes us to incidents that one would prefer to postpone, it gives another instance of Cadwallader's unreliability.

On May 28, 1864, Theodore Lyman, aide to General Meade, said in a letter to his wife:

I discovered to-day that the Lieutenant-General [Grant] has sick-headaches periodically—one now, for example, for which he put some chloroform on his head.

On Apr. 8, 1865, the day before Lee's surrender, Lyman wrote that Grant's and Meade's staffs had halted for the night at Stute's house, and as Grant's wagons had not arrived, Meade and his staff had fed Grant and his officers and loaned them blankets. He continued:

Grant has one of his sick headaches, which are rare, but cause him fearful pain, such as almost overcomes even his iron stoicism. To show how really amiable he is, he let the officers drum on the family piano a long while before he even would hint he didn't like it.[57]

In Horace Porter's work there is a statement about Grant's illness:

General Grant had been suffering all the afternoon from a severe headache, the result of fatigue, anxiety, scant fare, and loss of sleep, and by night he grew much worse. He was induced to bathe his feet in hot water and mustard, and apply mustard-plasters to his wrists and the back of his neck; but these remedies afforded little relief.

Cadwallader's description of the night is much different from Porter's. He has Grant upstairs in bed with Rawlins when an important message arrived from Lee; Porter has him on a sofa in a downstairs room. Porter's statement as to what Grant said to him and Rawlins after reading Lee's message—he would have to wait until morning before he could reply— is much different from what Cadwallader claims he heard Grant say in mild reproof of Rawlins's denunciation of Lee. (Through the open parlor door Cadwallader had heard Rawlins read Lee's dispatch aloud and then had heard the talk between him and Grant—all upstairs.)

Cadwallader says not a word about Grant's illness. According to both Porter and Grant's *Memoirs*, the illness lasted into the next morning, and Porter says that after drinking some coffee at Meade's camp Grant felt better and was able to write to Lee. The only way to free Cadwallader from the charge of not having been in the house that night is to say that he did not know what was important and what was trivial. He tells that when sleeping on the floor, a corner is preferable to a spot in front of the door, and he informs us that he had selected the best place for himself and his head was pillowed on his field glasses when he was aroused by the arrival of Lee's message. The challenge of the sentinel, the clinking spurs, and the clanking saber are there, and also the impressive call, "Dispatches for General Grant." But there is no mention of the fact that Grant that night was in great agony.[58]

While Cadwallader painted good military background for the night of Apr. 8, his description of the next afternoon contains a phrase that suggests failing memory. He states that after Grant had gone into the McLean house to meet Lee, the staff all remained on their horses. No officer would have remained mounted when the General in Chief of the Armies of the United States dismounted. Furthermore, mounted men habitually dismounted whenever they could, to rest themselves and more particularly their horses. Porter does not fail to say that the staff "dismounted."

Cadwallader also forgot, if he ever knew, that Col. Babcock of Grant's staff was waiting in the famous little parlor with Lee and his military secretary, Col. Charles Marshall. According to Porter—who never mentions Cadwallader in his book—Babcock, who had been watching at the window, opened the door of the room for Grant to enter. According to Cadwallader, Lee opened the front door of the house, greeted Grant and, after exchanging saluations, conducted him into the front room on the left of the hall. Porter states that in a few moments Babcock came to the front door and beckoned the others to come in; Cadwallader says it was Grant who called them in—including Cadwallader.[59]

Just as Cadwallader's account of the night of the 8th omits the important fact of Grant's illness, so his description of what transpired in the McLean house passes over the high point of the great drama. It was Grant—the man who had been so sick just a few hours before, but who now seemed to be "fresh as a rose"—who put the surrender terms on paper, got up and carried them across the room to Lee. In that there was greatness. But Cadwallader does not mention it.

Although there appears to be no list of persons who were in the surrender room that can be confidently regarded as all-inclusive, one must question whether Cadwallader was present. What he put down in later years while reflecting on his early and more stirring days is not in good agreement with the dispatch that he wrote at 6:00 P.M. on April 9, 1865, and which was published in the *New York Herald* on the 14th. After speaking of Lee's going to the McLean house on receiving a message from Grant, he continues: "General Grant arrived about fifteen minutes later, and entered the parlor where General Lee was awaiting him. The meeting was very nearly a private one at the outset. After a few moments' conversation General Grant's staff officers were called in and formally presented. The conversation was sober and confined solely to business, excepting a few allusions to the past between Lee and General Seth Williams and perhaps one or two others. The terms of surrender were soon agreed upon, reduced to writing and signed, after which Lee soon departed to within his own army. . . ."

Quite as one should expect, Lee's meeting Grant at the threshold and Grant himself coming to the door to beckon "to us to come in," were adornments of passing years. Cadwallader was certainly not a staff officer and so is not explicitly included in his description, and he said nothing that could not have been told him by someone else. Actually, if Cadwallader witnessed what took place, he was a very poor reporter when he wrote in a manner to cause a reader to believe that a document was drawn up which both Grant and Lee signed, rather than that the surrender was accomplished by an exchange of letters.

In his book, Cadwallader contradicts himself. On one page he says that the time occupied in making duplicates of the "letters" gave an excellent opportunity for studying the two principal actors in the great drama; on the next page he asserts that while the writing was going on within the house, he went outside to make a sketch of it. Cadwallader also undermines what he had previously said when he states that in the afternoon he rode to the headquarters of the Fifth Corps to put its *Herald* correspondent, John A. Brady, in possession of all the facts he had *gathered* concerning the events of the day so that Brady could commence his dispatch. The word "gathered" hardly suggests that Cadwallader had witnessed a great event.

As a matter of fact, the *Herald* correspondent with the Fifth Corps was not John A. Brady, but Leonard A. Hendricks. On the 8th Brady had sent a dispatch from the Twenty-fourth Corps, and at midnight on the 9th he wrote a very long dispatch at the headquarters of the Army of the James, which was commanded by General Ord, and to which the Twenty-fourth Corps belonged.

Cadwallader uses a page to relate how, while lying on the ground and briefing Brady, he became involved in a sharp dispute with General Griffin, commander of the Fifth Corps. After Cadwallader had put the general in his place, Griffin had to be led away by his staff lest there be a personal encounter. This and the subsequent encounter in which Cadwallader claimed he declined Griffin's outstretched hand should not be taken seriously. Cadwallader's statement about giving information to Brady so that Brady could "commence" his dispatch is pure boastful nonsense.

Most of Brady's three columns are concerned with events of the day and night before and with the many stirring incidents of the morning of the 9th, which he had witnessed but Cadwallader *had not*. Brady says only a little about the surrender, and that must be pronounced inaccurate, unless one is interested solely in whether the McLean parlor tables were up to date or reflected an earlier period: "The minutes were drawn up on a small table, and immediately made out in proper form, and signed by the two generals on a marble topped centre table of somewhat antique fashion." If Cadwallader's admirers wish to give him credit for that, no one should object.

Because of Cadwallader's sensational Yazoo story, it was due to Grant that all serious errors and questionable material in Cadwallader's *complete* book be clearly and fully pointed out, so that a reader could form a judgment of his credibility. Dana's important official dispatch to Stanton of June 7, 1863, should have been given in part, and a careful and adequate quotation should have been made from his *Recollections*. The Rawlins letter to Grant should have been properly described, with emphasis on the fact that not only the date on the letter, but its contents, show that it was not the result of anything that had occurred on Grant's trip up the Yazoo. That it presents a sharp challenge to the Cadwallader story, particularly because of the indorsement that Rawlins put on his retained copy, should have been noted. Finally, it was due to Grant to give pertinent facts so that the reader could decide for himself what Dana meant when he said, "Grant was ill and went to bed soon after he started."

"Flawlessly the gentleman," were words Freeman used at the dedication of the Appomattox Court House National Historical Monument, when he described Grant's conduct.[60] The military career that Grant ended on that day is inspiring, not only because of his great genius as a soldier, but because of his never-failing courtesy and consideration for others, which at Appomattox were by no means confined to the scene in the McLean parlor. If the kindness that Grant habitually displayed during four hard years of war is not a precious part of the American heritage, we have lost all sense of values. No special pleading for Grant was needed in publishing Cadwallader's recollections; but simple justice to the man to whom so much is owed, and who was the embodiment of thoughtfulness for others, required that Cadwallader's book be thoroughly and accurately annotated.

IV. SIDE LIGHTS ON VICKSBURG

Having dispatched some thousands of men to Johnston, it was not strange that the imaginative Beauregard, not overly occupied at Charleston, should have had ideas as to how they might best be used. On May 16, 1863, he sent Johnston some "general views of the coming summer campaign." If Johnston thought well of them, he might, Beauregard suggested, send them to the War Department—provided Johnston himself had not thought of them and done exactly that. Johnston, according to Beauregard, should stand on the defensive in Mississippi. Then, after 25,000 or 30,000 men had been added to those in Tennessee, Rosecrans could be suddenly attacked and destroyed. This done, at least 10,000 more men could be raised in Tennessee; in Kentucky, probably 20,000. A blow could next be struck toward the Mississippi, in the vicinity of Columbus or Fort Pillow. After Grant's army had been obliterated, a sufficient force could be thrown across the Mississippi to enable Kirby Smith to liberate Louisiana, while another contingent went to Price to carry freedom to Missouri. Any unneeded force could go to Virginia, if perchance there was danger there—hardly likely, in view of the "terrible lesson" the Federals had been given at Chancellorsville.[61]

When a letter from Johnston failed to refer to his proposals, Beauregard was not cast down or disquieted. He remained calm and sent Johnston a duplicate of the first letter, with some added meditations of June 21 as to what might have already been accomplished. The date being July 1 led Beauregard to remark, "I fear, though, it is now too late to undertake it." There still remained, however, less comprehensive things that might be done. Why did not Johnston send a sufficient force to make an end of Banks? Then Gardner's men could be added to Johnston's. Of course, the Charleston general was a little handicapped—he did not know of Sherman's mobile army of observation. But he knew Johnston faced a difficult situation, and there was not too much cheer in his comment, "I hope everything will yet turn out well, although I do not exactly see how." [62]

In his memoirs James Longstreet wrote that on his way to join Lee after the Battle of Chancellorsville (he had been south of the James River with two divisions aggregating about 12,000 men), he saw both President Davis and Secretary Seddon (on May 6), and suggested to Seddon that Johnston take his men to reenforce Bragg for an attack on Rosecrans and thus take pressure off Pemberton, a proposal he made a few days later to Lee. That the Secretary favored a direct reenforcement of Pemberton is proved by a telegram and a letter that Lee sent Seddon on the 10th. The wire said:

Your dispatch could not be deciphered till noon to-day. The adoption of your proposition is hazardous, and it becomes a question between Virginia and the Mississippi. The distance and the uncertainty of the employment of the troops are unfavorable. But, if necessary, order Pickett at once.

The amplifying letter contained an amazing appraisal: "If you determine to send Pickett's division to General Pemberton, presume it could not reach him until the last of this month. If anything is done in that quarter, it will be over by that time, as the climate will force the enemy to retire."

The question was settled by an indorsement that Davis wrote on Lee's telegram: "The answer of General Lee was such as I should have anticipated, and in which I concur." [63]

Davis being unable to come to Fredericksburg so that Lee might consult him, Lee went to Richmond, where he remained from May 14 to 17. The entire war situation was canvassed and Lee's advice about Mississippi was clearly indicated by a sentence in a long letter Davis wrote to him on May 31: "General Johnston did not, as you thought advisable, attack Grant promptly, and I fear the result is what you anticipated, if time was given." Lee's suggestion had naturally been predicated upon the exaggerated idea as to Johnston's strength which Davis then held, and without knowledge of logistical difficulties—lack of wagons. "The last intelligence," Davis continued, "indicates that Grant's army is concentrating on the Yazoo, where he connects with his gunboats and river transportation, and threatens the line of communication between Jackson and Vicksburg." To this Lee replied on June 2, "The enemy may be drawing to the Yazoo for the purpose of reaching their transports and retiring from the contest, which I hope is the case." [64]

One might explain Lee's statement on May 10 that the climate would compel Grant to give up his Vicksburg effort after June 1 by saying he was upset by the news of Jackson's death, which arrived on that Sunday. But there is no explaining his statement of June 2. Grant's persistence during the winter and his brilliant campaign behind Vicksburg had taught Lee nothing about the character of the soldier he would a year later have to face.

Although Lee had recommended that Johnston attack Grant promptly, he was uncertain on June 2 whether he would himself be able to move toward the Shenandoah Valley and Pennsylvania. In Beauregard's eyes Lee's venture northward was pure folly, and he spoke plainly in his letter to Johnston on July 1:

> An effort was lately made to deplete me still more of my forces, but it could only be done at the imminent risk of losing Charleston and Savannah. Whereas of what earthly use is that "raid" of Lee's army into Maryland, in violation of all the principles of war? Is it going to end the struggle, take Washington, or save the Mississippi Valley? Why not have kept on the defensive in Virginia, sent Longstreet's 20,000 men (who were not in the battle of Chancellorsville) to re-enforce Bragg, who with the 10,000 I sent you, could have crushed Rosecrans, and then sent about 50,000 men to Memphis and Fort Pillow and then to your assistance.[65]

If reenforcements had not gone to Johnston from Bragg and Beauregard, it would not have been necessary to send Grant the two divisions from Burnside's corps and Herron's division from Missouri. They would have been available to reenforce Rosecrans. Nor was Beauregard any better posted about the situation in Virginia than he was as to the number of men of Longstreet's corps not present at Chancellorsville—or the correct count of the number of effectives he had himself sent to Johnston. That the Army of the Potomac was still to be reckoned with was shown by a statement Lee made to Davis in a letter of May 30: "I have for nearly a month been endeavoring to get this army in a condition to move—to anticipate a blow from the enemy. I fear I shall have to receive it here at a disadvantage, or to retreat." [66]

In his well-known book of the early eighties, Davis in a single sentence put full responsibility for everything on Johnston: "When he reached Jackson, learning that the enemy was between that place and the position occupied by General Pemberton's forces, about thirty miles distant, he halted there and opened correspondence with Pemberton, from which a confusion with consequent disaster resulted, which might have been avoided had he, with or without his reënforcements, proceeded to Pemberton's headquarters in the field." [67]

There was great inconsiderateness here, for, as Johnston pointed out, Davis knew that he, Johnston, was sick when he left Tullahoma, and in no condition for a long ride immediately after a hard train trip of several days. Furthermore, the contention did not harmonize with the previously quoted indorsement that Davis put on the telegram in which Johnston reported his arrival in Jackson to Seddon and described the situation as he knew it early on the morning of May 16. What Davis said was of course an instance of after-knowledge, and is even then not convincing. With the situation as Johnston knew it on the night of May 13, a prompt ride to join Pemberton might have been the worst thing he could have done, even if he had been physically equal to it. He sent an order which he expected would be obeyed.

In the article in which he replied to Davis,[68] Johnston put complete blame for everything upon the former President. Proper use of available forces would, he asserted, have averted the great catastrophe. He would have had Grant's command defeated in the summer of 1862, by uniting all the Confederate forces in Mississippi under Bragg. We have seen that Bragg *was* placed in command of all troops in Mississippi, and that it was he—not Davis—who made the decision to move eastward to meet the threat of Buell against Chattanooga, which Johnston ignored. He speaks of Bragg as being *sent* on a wild expedition into Kentucky, which is a very inaccurate description of what had taken place. Bragg could have directed his operation against Nashville if he had wished to, and for a while considered doing so.

Johnston claimed that the situation could have been saved even in 1863 if the Confederates west of the Mississippi had been united with those to the east. This would have meant the voluntary surrender of Arkansas in addition to Louisiana and have cut off resources from beyond the river. Eventually, exactly that happened, but it is not strange that the Confederate government did not make the decision in 1863—a protest of the strongest sort would have been raised. Johnston also failed to consider that a change in Confederate operations would have caused an alteration in those of the Federals, and he was a little naïve when he spoke as if Grant would have crossed the river with 43,000 men in the face of a combined force of 70,000.

Finally, Johnston contended that the reenforcements that were sent to Mississippi in late May could just as well have been sent in early April, "and then, without bad generalship on our part, the chance of success would have been in our favor, decidedly." But up through March it looked as if Pemberton were the master of the situation, and it was noted in the text that in mid-April, Pemberton, believing that the threat to Vicksburg had passed, reported to Johnston that he was sending troops to Bragg, and that some of them actually reached Chattanooga. With the passage of years, Johnston had forgotten a good deal—but probably not the long presidential letter to which he had to reply because Davis insisted on being falsely held guiltless in a misunderstanding that had really done no harm.[69]

If we dismiss the postwar feud between Davis and Johnston, we still have the question whether Johnston could have broken Grant's investment of Vicksburg. Pemberton's grandson has stated that Johnston was an officer who shrank from attacking, and has added McClellan to Grant and Sherman as an opponent with whom Johnston never took a strong line of action. Are we to forget Fair Oaks, where Johnston boldly concentrated 23 of his 27 brigades to attack the part of McClellan's army that was south of the Chickahominy, while the remaining four watched the heavy Federal force north of the river? The grandson quotes from a letter written him by Col. Matthew Steele to the effect that Johnston was of practically no aid to his grandfather. But he does not quote a concluding statement about the Confederate commander that Steele put in his *American Campaigns:* "Then later, when Johnston, who saw that all hope of saving Vicksburg was lost, ordered Pemberton to evacuate the place, Pemberton by vigorous movement might have still saved the remnant of his army, if he had obeyed Johnston's order. Instead of doing so Pemberton remained in Vicksburg, and lost his army as well as the town." [70]

After describing Johnston's probings of Sherman's front on the first days of July, Liddell Hart states, "However desperate the need of Vicksburg, Johnston was too intelligent a commander to risk the inevitable result of a direct assault on Sherman's entrenchments, realizing that it was useless to sacrifice two armies for an illusory hope of saving one." [71]

If one wishes to criticize Johnston for being late in his move against Grant,[72] he should recall that on May 30, 1863, just four days before Lee started the march that led to Gettysburg, he said in a letter to Davis, "I fear the time has passed when I could have taken the offensive with advantage." [73] On July 5, when Lee was retreating toward the Potomac with a badly shattered army after an adventure which his own words tend to condemn, Johnston was falling back to Jackson with the entire force with which he had marched. He also still had the respect not only of the people and Confederate soldiers in Mississippi,[74] but of William Tecumseh Sherman and U. S. Grant.

V. ANNA ELLA CARROLL AND VICKSBURG

Although Sydney and Marjorie Barstow Greenbie in their *Anna Ella Carroll and Abraham Lincoln* put forward Miss Carroll as the real planner of the final successful Vicksburg campaign, the claim is so strained that nothing more than some lines in a note would have been given to it, if it were not desired to complete in important ways the previous discussion of the Carroll Tennessee River claim.[75]

It was noted that there is a significant difference in the versions of the letter that Thomas A. Scott, former Assistant Secretary of War, wrote on June 24, 1870, to Sen. J. M. Howard, in support of Miss Carroll, as the letter is found in various congressional documents. It was not observed, however, that a letter to Sen. Howard that Scott had written nine days previously is given in the documents completely altered from the form in which it is found in Miss Carroll's handwriting among her papers in the Maryland Historical Society Library. (It is marked "Copy.") With permission I quote in full from a photostat:

I learn from Miss Carroll that she has a claim before Congress for services rendered in the year 1861, in aid of the government and she desires me to say what I know in relation to the matter.

Miss Carroll presented to me as Assistant Secretary of War some papers written and published by herself, that I think were valuable at that time and served a good purpose. I recommended them and I believe now that the government ought to reward her liberally for the efforts she made in its behalf, to rouse the people against the rebellious actions of the South.

I hope you will be able to pass some measure that will give Miss Carroll what she is certainly entitled to.

Thus Scott recalled only Miss Carroll's political writings, and nothing whatever about any military plan that she had proposed. This letter would obviously have been of no use to her; it would in fact have been fatal to the claim she was pressing. In the congressional documents the letter appears as follows:

I learn from Miss Carroll that she has a claim before Congress for services rendered in the year 1861 in aid of the government. I believe the government ought now to reward her liberally for the efforts she made in its behalf. I hope you will be able to pass some measure that will give Miss Carroll what she is most certainly entitled to.[76]

Only one word (*now*) had its position changed; only one new word (*most*) was inserted; but by skillful deletions a damaging letter was changed into one that gave general support. After quoting the letter as found in the congressional documents—without alluding to the letter in the Baltimore collection of papers to which they elsewhere make reference—the Greenbies state that the letter was not specific enough with regard to the services rendered—an amusing remark in view of the very definite character of the actual letter—so on June 24 Scott again wrote to Howard.[77] (Had Scott's letter of the 15th really been what the Greenbies give, he might of his own accord have written a second letter; the letter being what in fact it was, that hardly looks likely. Something seems missing.)

As formerly pointed out, Scott's second letter of June, 1870, and the letter he wrote on May 1, 1872 are—as given in the congressional documents—completely contradicted by the letters he wrote to Stanton in the winter of 1862, while he was in the West. It may not, however, have been merely a case of poor memory, for the distortion that was made in his first letter renders it possible that we do not have correct copies of his other two letters. A search in the National Archives failed to reveal either of them. (If some of Miss Carroll's papers had not been destroyed, we might have had reliable copies of the letters.)

The new edition of Lincoln's collected works gives a short note that he wrote to Miss Carroll on Aug. 19, 1862, which puts an end to all doubt as to whether Miss Carroll had misquoted Lincoln in the angry letter she had written to him a few days previously. In the note Lincoln spoke in a complimentary manner of an address to Maryland which Miss Carroll had sent him, but he did not say that she had misquoted or misrepresented him in her recent letter.[78] Nor did he apologize. Thus the harsh words that Miss Carroll recorded that Lincoln had used to characterize a proposal she had made must be accepted.

The Greenbie claim for Vicksburg as a Carroll achievement is built largely upon a sentence in Grant's memoirs, in which he speaks of Stanton's having had the telegraph wires occasionally cleared at night so that they could hold conversations. In the Greenbie book these conversations are described as taking place in the winter of 1863, and Stanton talked to Grant in order to pass on suggestions Miss Carroll had made about the correct approach to Vicksburg. The sentence that precedes the one the Greenbies quote from Grant states clearly that the conversations occurred in 1862 and while Grant was in Tennessee.[79] They probably were in the summer and were concerned with the rather hazardous position in which Grant was then placed. At any rate, they were before Dec. 1—for during the last month of 1862 Grant was in northern Mississippi—and well in advance of Grant's winter operations against Vicksburg. It would appear that the Greenbies believed a wire connected Washington with Grant's headquarters after he went down the Mississippi near the end of January, 1863.

We are informed in the Greenbie book that in eighteen days Grant won five victories with a force of 5,000 men, destroying or capturing more than 12,000 of the enemy.[80] The Confederate casualties for the period were probably about 7,000,[81] but the figure for Grant's force differs greatly from the truth. Perhaps it was magnanimity that caused Mr. and Mrs. Greenbie to make Grant a terrific fighter, one fit to be the instrument of Miss Carroll's brains.[82]

NOTES

References to the *Official Records* are given in such a way as to show the number of dispatches supporting a paragraph, as well as their proper order. Thus, *O.R., 7,* 562–563, indicates a single message running from p. 562 to p. 563, while *O.R., 7,* 562, 562–563, 563, indicates additional dispatches on pp. 562 and 563. The repetition of a page number may also appear, as in *O.R., 8,* 530, 532, 540, 532.

NOTES TO CHAPTER I

1. Grant, *Memoirs,* I, 395 (Long, ed., p. 205); Sherman to Halleck and reply, *O.R., 25,* 79, 83. As to trackage in operating order and statement about locomotives, see Halleck to Stanton, July 1, with inclosure from McPherson, dated June 29. Because of difference in gauge, Northern rolling stock could not be used until altered. McPherson said he had heard that 25 locomotives had been ordered by the Mobile and Ohio from a Paterson, N.J., manufacturer, and that half of them had been built but not delivered when the war broke out. Halleck told Stanton he had asked the quartermaster general to buy them; it must have proved to be a false report (*O.R., 25,* 78; *23,* 151).

It was stated *supra,* III, 437, that Grant rode back to Corinth from Memphis. A dispatch of July 15 from Corinth to the *N.Y. Tribune,* published on the 22nd, said, "Gen. Grant most unexpectedly emerged out of last night's train from Columbus." Though Grant remained only a district commander after Halleck's departure, he reported directly to the latter in Washington.

2. *O.R., 25,* 100, 102–103, 106.

3. *Ibid.,* pp. 29–30, 109, 111.

4. *Ibid.,* pp. 83, 114, 143, 144 (strength returns and rosters for July 31).

5. *Ibid.,* p. 648.

6. *O.R., 21,* 758, 768.

7. *Ibid.,* pp. 26–28, 769–770.

8. *O.R., 25,* 624; *21,* 771, 778, 792, 770.

9. *O.R., 25,* 640–642; *21,* 783–784. Jordan enclosed a newspaper clipping by a correspondent who had been "expelled" by Beauregard "as a letter-writer," describing the "lost opportunity" at Shiloh. He said the reporter was well acquainted with the officer he suspected "of starting the under-current." Jordan also made an interesting comment about what Prentiss had said of the assured presence of Buell on Apr. 7 (second day of Shiloh).

10. *O.R., 21,* 753–754.

11. *Ibid.,* pp. 502–510. Butler stated that prominent men in New Orleans had expressed disapproval of guerrilla warfare and would do all they could to discourage it. Though willing to take an oath of allegiance to the United States, they thought it better not to, because it would prevent communication with the Partisan Rangers. The oath had been taken by Solomon Benjamin, brother of the recent Secretary of War and the new Secretary of State. Butler described at length the problem of feeding the people of New Orleans and what he was doing to solve it.

12. *Ibid.,* pp. 760, 779. There was considerable correspondence between Moore and Richmond on the subject of arms. On June 25 the governor wrote to Randolph (*ibid.,* p. 766): "My guns have been seized again by General Van Dorn. Am I never to get even my own property? . . . The Confederacy has never sent me a musket. Let it not take what I have paid for. . . ."

13. On Jan. 10 the Confederate Secretary of War apparently intruded on A. S. Johnston as commander of the Western Department by creating the Trans-Mississippi District and assigning Van Dorn to it. On May 26 the Trans-Mississippi Department—Missouri, Arkansas, Indian Territory, Texas, and the part of Louisiana west of the Mississippi—was created. After some talk of putting Maj. Gen. J. B. Magruder in command, the department was given to Maj. Gen. Theophilus H. Holmes. Holmes issued an order taking command at Vicksburg on July 30, and one at Little Rock on Aug. 20 dividing his department into three districts. Bragg was informed about the new department and the assignment of Holmes on July 25. (*O.R., 19,* 830, 829, 845, 855, 860, 877; *25,* 655.)

14. *O.R., 21,* 780–782, 779.

15. *O.R., 25,* 74; *24,* 17–20; *25,* 75, 83. Sheridan put the attacking force at eight or ten regiments; Rosecrans, in his highly laudatory order the next day, put it at eight. See also Sheridan, *Memoirs,* I, 156–164.

In his dispatch to Granger on the 5th, Sheridan said it was his impression that the Confederates had thrown out a column to cover their movement eastward and "possibly to make an attack on the railroad to cut off Buell from Corinth."

16. *O.R., 25,* 103, 114.

17. *Ibid.,* pp. 130, 131–132, 130–131.

18. *Ibid.,* pp. 139, 76.

19. *O.R., 110,* 330; *25,* 655–656. In a dispatch to Davis on the 22nd (*O.R., 110,* 330), Bragg specifically spoke of danger to Chattanooga as a reason for his "change of base." His movement order dated July 21 is in *O.R., 25,* 656–657.

In a dispatch to Cooper on July 10 Bragg said, "A long and disastrous drought, threatening destruction to the grain crop, continues here, and renders any move impracticable for want of water." In a letter two days later he reverted to the subject, saying the Federals as well as his own command relied entirely on wells. He reported a marked improvement in organization, discipline, and instruction, and also in the health and general tone of his command. (*O.R., 25,* 644, 644–646.)

20. *Ibid.,* pp. 651–652.

21. *O.R., 110,* 330–331. The letters of Western officers only occasionally refer to events in the East, but in his letter to Beauregard, Bragg made the interesting comment: "We can congratulate ourselves that McClellan was satisfied with changing his base, for it occurs to my obtuse mind that a bold stroke at Richmond, while we were hunting for him, would have ruined us."

22. *O.R., 23,* 734–735. The Richmond order of June 25 that gave Bragg territory south of the 33rd parallel extended his eastern boundary "to the line of railroad from Chattanooga via Atlanta to West Point, on the Chattahoochee River, and thence down the Chattahoochee and Apalachicola Rivers to the Gulf of Mexico." A letter informed Bragg of his acquisition. The order of July 18 took the Georgia bulge away from Bragg and gave it to Smith, but Bragg certainly began his move under the belief that he was still responsible for a vital part of Georgia. (*O.R., 25,* 624, 627; *21,* 784; *23,* 729.)

On July 14 Smith wrote to President Davis that McCown had arrived on the 3rd and that he himself had just returned to duty from an attack of typhoid fever. On the 21st he reported to Cooper that the Federals had arrived in front of Chattanooga, and the next day he wrote that his own army had been greatly reenforced. (*O.R., 23,* 726–727, 730–731, 733.)

23. *O.R., 21,* 25–26, 27–28, 31–33.

24. *Supra,* III, 440; *O.R. Navies,* Ser. I, XIX, 44–45. When the *Arkansas* made her run to Vicksburg on July 15, Farragut's fleet was above the city with Davis's gunboat flotilla. That night he dropped down the river, hoping to destroy the ram by gunfire, but it was a dark night and the craft was not seen. (Lewis, *Farragut,* II, 113–119, for this and actions prior to the attack on July 22.)

25. Davis to Farragut, July 21, predicting success, *O.R. Navies,* Ser. I, XIX, 16; reports of Ellet, Porter, and Farragut, *ibid.,* pp. 45–47, 60–62, 96–98; subsequent account by Lieut. George W. Gift, of the *Arkansas,* in Gosnell, *Guns on the Western Waters.*

The armored ram *Sumter,* below the city with Farragut, was supposed to take part in the attack but did not, for some unexplained reason. Ellet said the position of the *Arkansas* made it impossible for him to hit her most vulnerable side without reducing speed. The *N.Y. Tribune*'s account of Aug. 6 said that the *Essex* was supposed to grapple the *Arkansas* and pull her out from the bank for the *Queen* to ram; if the latter failed, the *Sumter* was to act. This seems to have been merely a reporter's invention.

26. *O.R. Navies,* Ser. I, XIX, 74–75, 47–48; *O.R., 25,* 148–149.

27. *O.R. Navies,* Ser. I, XIX, 19, 53, 36; *O.R., 21,* 33.

28. Reports by Van Dorn, Breckinridge, Lieut. Godfrey Weitzel (Butler's engineer officer), and Col. Thomas W. Cahill (successor to Williams's com-

mand), *O.R., 21,* 15–19, 76–81, 51–53, 54–58; reports by Porter and Lieut. F. A. Roe (commanding the *Katahdin*), *O.R. Navies,* Ser. I, XIX, 117, 118–119.

29. For Farragut's passing of the forts, see Mahan, *The Gulf and Inland Waters;* Lewis, *David Glasgow Farragut,* II, Chap. VII; David D. Porter, "The Opening of the Lower Mississippi," *B. and L.,* III, 22–54; John R. Russell, "The 'Brooklyn' at the Passage of the Forts," *ibid.,* pp. 56–69; Beverly Kennon, "Fighting Farragut Below New Orleans," *ibid.,* pp. 76–89.

Accounts of the surrender and occupation of New Orleans are in *B. and L.,* II, 91–99, with a particularly moving page, p. 21, in an article by George Washington Cabell. A dramatic description of the debarkation of troops is in De Forest, *A Volunteer's Adventures,* pp. 18–19.

Farragut arrived at the city on Apr. 25, and the log of the *Brooklyn* for that day says: "While steaming up the lower part of the river we were cheered by the crowd assembled on the levee. Immediately there was a volley of musketry discharged among them by some soldiers standing near. A number were seen to fall, and the crowd dispersed in all directions." The diary of Commander James Alden, of the *Richmond,* states for the same date: "The *Mississippi* ran in close to the wharf, and their band struck up 'The Star-Spangled Banner.' When the people heard that glorious old air once more they cheered and waved their hats and handkerchiefs at the *Mississippi.* At the same moment a troop of horsemen came riding up one of the streets and fired a volley into the men, women, and children. If it had not been for the innocent people who would have been destroyed we would have fired a whole broadside of grape into them." (*O.R. Navies,* Ser. I, XVIII, 760, 740.)

30. *O.R., 21,* 51, 40, 93, 80. The *N.Y. Tribune* on Aug. 21 noted that Mrs. Lincoln's brother had been killed. Phisterer gives (*Statistical Record,* pp. 318–320) a list of 38 general officers killed in action, followed by one of those who died of wounds. He omitted the name of Gen. Nathaniel Lyon, killed Aug. 10, 1861, at Wilson's Creek.

31. Breckinridge's report, *O.R., 21,* 76–81; paper by Acting Mate John A. Wilson, of the *Arkansas, O.R. Navies,* Ser. I, XIX, 132–136; account by Lieut. Clift, in Gosnell, *op. cit.,* pp. 132–135. (Wilson also gives a graphic account of the ghastly condition of the *Arkansas* after she had run through the Federal fleets on July 15.) The vessel was destroyed on the right bank of the river. The claim that Porter made in connection with her destruction brought him a letter of censure from Secretary Welles, while Farragut directed that a court of inquiry look into the matter; the inquiry, however, was never held. (*O.R. Navies,* Ser. I, XIX, 130–131, 122–123, 126–130.) But for strong praise of Porter, see Welles, *Diary,* I, 88–89, quoted by West, *Gideon Welles,* p. 192. West speaks (p. 199) of Porter's "destruction of the ram," words which might imply it had been done by the guns of the *Essex.*

William D. Porter was the elder brother of David Dixon Porter, who commanded the mortars which were used in attacking the forts below New Orleans and which came up to Vicksburg with Farragut. He will be seen later commanding the gunboat fleet above Vicksburg. It was William Porter, not David, who should have been referred to *supra,* III, 183, 199. (*O.R., 7,* index, erroneously attributes the dispatch on p. 561 from Grant to "Captain Porter" as to D. D. Porter.) The two men were foster brothers of Farragut and sons of Capt. David Porter, a distinguished naval officer of the War of 1812. While both were able, both had traits that made them somewhat unpopular; not without reason William carried the nickname "Dirty Bill."

32. In a letter to Stanton from Cairo dated Sept. 28 (*O.R.*, *25*, 241–242), Ellet said in reference to the *Arkansas:* "Recent developments seem to show conclusively that the final destruction was partially, at least, owing to the severe shock she received from the *Queen of the West*, which disarranged her engine and caused her machinery to break down."

33. Butler believed the Confederates were preparing to attack New Orleans. (The statement Van Dorn made in his report was, "The recapture of New Orleans has been made easier to our army.") Plans were actually drawn up, for on Sept. 11 Brig. Gen. Daniel Ruggles wired to Cooper from Jackson, Miss., "I recommend an immediate movement against New Orleans. I send proposed plan by messenger." A letter that accompanied the plan the same day ended, "The combined operations of a force of 20,000 men within from four to six weeks would probably prove adequate to the great object in view." (*O.R.*, *21*, 806–807.)

34. *Ibid.*, p. 471.

35. Johnson's report, Senate Exec. Doc. No. 16, 37th Cong., 3rd Sess.

36. Butler, *Butler's Book*, p. 522. This work contains much malice and enough errors to make one very cautious in using it.

37. Butler to Stanton with inclosures, *O.R.*, *21*, 485–491.

38. *O.R.*, *111*, 528–529. George F. Shepley of Maine, who had commanded one of Butler's regiments, was made military governor of Louisiana in June. About a month later he was raised to the rank of brigadier general.

39. *O.R.*, *21*, 542–543. See also Butler to Stanton with inclosures, Aug. 2, *ibid.*, pp. 534–537.

40. War Department G.O. 181, 1862; *O.R.*, *20*, 599.

41. *O.R.*, *19*, 541, 447, 541, 519–520, 457, 524–525. For actions by Pike, whose resignation was not accepted until Nov. 5, see *ibid.*, pp. 841–874; *111*, 820–822.

42. *N.Y. Tribune*, Aug. 6, 1862; *O.R.*, *19*, 524–525, 552–553.

43. *O.R.*, *19*, 571, 546.

44. Schofield's report, *ibid.*, pp. 7–21.

45. Browning to Lincoln, *ibid.*, pp. 533–534.

46. Schofield to Halleck, Aug. 5, *ibid.*, p. 535; Schofield's report. A dispatch from St. Louis in the *N.Y. Tribune* for Aug. 21 spoke of the discovery of guerrilla camps within a few miles of the city. As a result Schofield had ordered all houses in the suburbs to be searched for arms. This led to the arrest of a brother of Gen. J. E. Johnston and his wife because Mrs. Johnston had been abusive of the officers making a search. The dispatch said the organization of the militia in country districts was going better than had been expected.

47. *O.R.*, *19*, 108–109; *O.R. Navies*, Ser. I, XIX, 130–131. Because of illness (Gosnell, *op. cit.*, p. 131), Brown was not in the *Arkansas* at the time of her destruction, but the next day he wrote to Breckinridge from near Clinton (30

miles northeast of Baton Rouge) reporting what he had learned from the vessel's chief pilot, whom he had just met. After stating that a camp of guerrillas stampeded when some of his men—who had succeeded in crossing the river—approached it in search of food and protection, the angry sailor urged that "all such running heroes" be added to the conscript rolls.

Coulter says (*The Confederate States of America*, p. 338) that there was some sentiment toward authorization of guerrillas but that the Confederate authorities never countenanced such warfare. He does not state that efforts were made to suppress such bands or that they did not exist. He refers to the rangers as "soldiers" and notes that having been authorized in April, 1862, they were abolished in February, 1864, because they were troublesome to loyal Confederates. That is about what Col. Fitch predicted. Van Dorn recommended to the Secretary of War, on Sept. 12, 1862, that the Partisan Rangers be disbanded (*O.R., 25,* 701).

48. *N.Y. Tribune,* Aug. 11, 1862—a dispatch from Headquarters on Wolf Creek, Cherokee Nation, dated July 22; *O.R., 19,* 430–431, 445. In speaking of sickness, Weer wrote on June 23, "There is an utter destitution of salt and medical supplies in this part of the command."

On July 21 Blunt sent to Secretary Stanton a letter about the Cherokees, inclosing with it a number of communications dealing with their support of the Confederacy (*O.R., 19,* 486–505). The chief of the Cherokees was a remarkable man named John Ross, whose father was Scotch and whose mother was also Scotch with one-fourth Cherokee. He was born near Chattanooga, was well educated, and a leader in his tribe before and after its removal to Indian Territory. The letters he wrote seeking to maintain the neutrality of the Cherokees are able and interesting papers. The Cherokees were slaveholders, Ross himself having a large plantation cultivated by slaves.

49. *O.R., 19,* 459–461, 3, 181–184; Dyer, *Compendium,* p. 986; *O.R., 19,* 482–483, 484–485, 476–477, 511–512, 531–532, 551–552, 595.

Salomon reported that he was bringing back the Ross family and also the "treasury of the Cherokee Nation, and the valuables of Ross." On Aug. 13 Blunt wrote a letter to Lincoln (*ibid.,* pp. 565–566), to be presented by "John Ross, Chief of the Cherokee Nation," who was going to Washington at his suggestion. Blunt said, "I have no doubt as to the loyalty of the Ross family and three-fourths of the Cherokee people." He commended Ross as "a man of candor and frankness" upon whose representations the President could rely.

50. *N.Y. Tribune,* May 10, 1862; Nicolay and Hay, *Lincoln,* VI, 90–95, 98, 102–103.

51. *N.Y. Tribune,* Aug. 12, 20; Greeley, *The American Conflict,* II, 250; Nicolay and Hay, *op. cit.,* pp. 125–130. There are not only incompletenesses but there are inconsistencies in statements about the Cabinet meeting of July 22 when Lincoln read his first draft of an emancipation proclamation.

52. Russell, *My Diary North and South* (Fletcher Pratt, ed.), pp. 160, 171.

53. *N.Y. Tribune,* Aug. 6. Military government had of course been instituted in Memphis by Grant during his three weeks there. On July 10 he telegraphed to Halleck: "There are a great many families of officers in the rebel army here who are very violent. Will you approve of sending them all south of our

lines?" The reply the same day was, "Yes, if you deem it expedient." (*O.R.*, *25*, 88.) As a result, there was a vacancy of houses; but Richardson complained that the homes of Unionists who had gone north for the summer were being used by the Federals, quite as well as those of Secessionists. On Aug. 7 Sherman wrote a letter (*ibid.*, pp. 156–157) to the assistant quartermaster at Memphis, answering thirteen questions the latter had asked with regard to the administration of property. His reply to the query concerning unoccupied houses owned by loyal citizens was, "Such should not be disturbed, but it would be well to advise them to have some servant at the house to occupy it."

A correspondent other than Richardson wrote on Aug. 8 (*N.Y. Tribune*, Aug. 15) about the excellent orders of Grant and Hovey and condemned modifications made by Sherman, saying, "This leap toward a mild rule has already produced a discouraging effect on Union men, while Rebels are again becoming insolent and bold."

How badly-informed and unjust the correspondents were to Sherman is shown by the letter he wrote on Aug. 11 to Treasury Secretary S. P. Chase as a result of the order to pay gold, silver, and treasury notes for cotton. He said: ". . . Also, gold will purchase arms and ammunition at Nassau, in the Bahamas, and you know that one vessel out of three can run the blockade. . . . I had so arranged that cotton could be had for currency, Tennessee and other bank notes good here but not elsewhere. The whole South is now up, and all they want is arms and provisions. Salt at Grenada is worth $100 a barrel, and if trade be opened Memphis is better to our enemy than before it was taken." (*O.R.*, *123*, 349).

Sherman was not a man who would divulge orders he had received from a superior, and some of the correspondents probably never imagined that he might be acting in accordance with instructions.

For Sherman's correspondence with his brother Sen. John Sherman about his Memphis régime, see Thorndike, ed., *The Sherman Letters*, pp. 156–158.

54. *O.R.*, *25*, 178–179 (Sherman to Grant, Aug. 17); *109*, 275–276. On the subject of the arrest of the *Chicago Times* correspondent, see Appendix III.

NOTES TO CHAPTER II

1. *O.R.*, *23*, 315–316, 333; *25*, 173; *23*, 726–727.

2. *O.R.*, *25*, 175, 177, 176, 179, 182–183, 183, 182. For the surrender of Clarksville and action against responsible officers, see *O.R.*, *22*, 862–869.

3. *O.R.*, *23*, 8; *10*, 671. For the first dispatches between Lincoln and Halleck with regard to a move toward Chattanooga, see *supra*, III, 535–536.

4. *Supra*, III, 434–435; *O.R.*, *23*, 75.

5. *O.R.*, *23*, 9. For Buell's subsequent statement that the initial order was verbal and for his comments, see *O.R.*, *22*, 409, 419.

6. *O.R.*, *23*, 5–7; *supra*, III, Chap. XV. Almost immediately after Beauregard's evacuation of Corinth, Halleck began to plan a move toward Chattanooga. On June 3 Buell appointed Brig. Gen. W. Sooy Smith—who after

resigning from the army in 1854 had been a successful railroad engineer—to have general supervision of the repair of the railroad. The next day Halleck told Buell that not a moment should be lost in opening communications with Mitchel. Because of Pope's illness, Buell was on the 5th given direction of the pursuit of Beauregard, but this did not prevent Halleck from telling him on the 7th that he was dissatisfied with the progress being made by Wood and the engineers in rebuilding the bridge over Bear Creek, the largest structure that had to be replaced. The final order starting Buell eastward was issued the day the pursuit of Beauregard was stopped.

In his dispatch about the Bear Creek bridge, Halleck pointed out some expedients that were being used in other places. In doing this he was acting in a field of special competence, for he had been an engineer officer (Smith had been an artilleryman), and after his resignation from the army—in 1854, as were those of Smith and Grant—had demonstrated ability at bold and unusual construction. (*O.R.*, *11*, 628, 629, 267–268, 268, 280–281; *supra,* III, 104–105.)

7. The record of the Buell Commission is in *O.R.*, *22*, 6–726. Maj. Gen. Lew Wallace was president and Maj. Donn Piatt was judge advocate and recorder. The original proceedings were lost, but Congress, on June 5, 1872, authorized the reporter, Benn Pitman, to furnish a new transcript from his stenographic notes, which was done. It is sometimes suggested (e.g., by McKee, *"Ben-Hur" Wallace,* p. 64) that the record was "lost" by Halleck because it contained some criticism of him. From November, 1861, Halleck had shown that he was not disturbed even by virulent criticism, and it is to be noted that in a letter of Apr. 13, 1872, to the House of Representatives, Secretary of War William W. Belknap said a "copy of the original opinion of the Commission" and a copy of a long paper given the Commission by Buell at the end of the hearings were on file, as well as a copy of the unsigned communication reviewing the proceedings (probably written by Piatt, and which was very critical of Buell.) Thus the actual findings of the Commission and Buell's statement about the campaign had not been lost. The testimony is interesting, important, at times very conflicting, and laborious to work through. It seems unlikely that anyone who has suggested that Halleck was responsible for the disappearance of this part of the record has ever taken the trouble to go through it, to point out what it was that Halleck was desirous to have lost.

The appointing order spoke of the investigating group as a Military Commission. The proceedings frequently use the expression "The court was closed," and the act of Congress authorizing a new transcript spoke of the Court of Inquiry. The investigating body is here referred to both as a Commission and as a Court.

In his *Victory Rode the Rails,* Turner goes far beyond the customary charge about Halleck being responsible for delays in Buell's march, and states (p. 179) that Halleck ordered Buell to base his operation on Memphis, and that if Buell had been left to his own discretion he would have used Nashville. The charge is sufficiently answered by the concluding sentence of a dispatch Halleck sent to Buell on June 9: "Give such orders about supplies for your troops going east as you may deem proper" (*O.R.*, *11*, 281).

It will appear presently that Buell did base on Nashville, except at the start and for some subsequent use of his depot at Eastport, and that when Nashville failed him he even sought to get supplies from Memphis, though, as has been seen, the railroad thence from Corinth was not in operation (a strange fact to find overlooked in a book devoted to the railroads).

8. *O.R., 23,* 18 (Fry to McCook, June 12, about his own and Crittenden's move to Florence), 49 (Buell to Nelson, June 22), 57–58 (Fry to Wood, June 24), 17 (Buell to Mitchel), 20 (Fry to Boyle).

9. *Ibid.,* pp. 16, 48, 56–57 (Buell to Halleck, June 12, 22, 24, respectively). In the dispatch of the 12th Buell said he expected the road to be completed to Decatur on the 23rd—four days later than he set in the telegram the same day to Mitchel. The message (*ibid.,* p. 14) from Halleck to Stanton stating that Buell's "advance will probably reach Decatur to-morrow night" certainly should be dated the 19th instead of the 12th. It contains a reference to the reported Confederate evacuation of Cumberland Gap, which occurred on the 18th.

It would seem that Buell should not have crossed at Florence but at Eastport, to where he moved his supplies from his old depot just above Pittsburg Landing, and from where an army train hauled subsistence to replenish field trains as they passed Iuka. Another refilling point was set up at South Florence, but because of the shoals great difficulty was experienced in getting supplies up the river. (Three shoals pilots were seized at night and paroled under penalty of death if they ran away; three steamers were seriously injured and threats had to be made against crews.) Boats drawing over 16 inches of water could not carry more than 30 or 40 tons, and on June 20 Buell wrote to Halleck from Florence, "The river between here and Eastport is fast falling, and troops here are already dependent on the railroad for supplies."

Capt. James Morton, who built the ferry at Florence from a steamer and two barges taken up from Eastport, and timber from wrecked warehouses in Florence, was on June 22 ordered to build a ferry at Eastport, and it was there that the army train and Nelson's division train crossed. (*O.R., 23,* 3–4; *22,* 602–603; *23,* 40; *22,* 721–722; *23,* 54–55, 57, 54.)

It was practically the same distance from Iuka to Florence by way of Eastport and the north bank of the river as it was by Tuscumbia. If the Eastport route had been used, it would not have been necessary to haul rations to Iuka.

10. *O.R., 23,* 67–68, 68–69, 38–39, 37; *22,* 603 (Lieut. Col. Darr's statement that the wagon haul was 40 miles.) On June 20 Mitchel informed Buell that a wagon train had passed through a tunnel that he had had planked, thereby reducing the haul to 23 miles. Darr made no mention of the expedient, but on July 9 Fry directed Nelson to send a regiment to put the tunnel "in order for wagons," saying the work could be done in a day if the regiment applied itself "diligently." (*O.R., 23,* 41–42, 37, 111–112.)

11. *O.R., 23,* 39 (explanatory telegram, Buell to Mitchel, June 19), 68, 68–69, 70, 73, 71, 11–12.

12. *O.R., 23,* 76–77; *22,* 31 (in Buell's statement to the Commission).

13. *O.R., 23,* 77, 15.

14. *O.R., 23,* 23, 155; *11,* 628; *23,* 14, 31.

15. *O.R., 23,* 17, 33, 33–34, 43–44. Buell also said that the exposure of

the road made it "extremely objectionable." Halleck replied that a small enemy force might strike it if it were not sufficiently guarded, but that he did not think there was serious risk of a flank attack in force from Fulton because Beauregard's lack of transportation kept him from operating far from the railroad to Mobile.

It will be seen that once the road was repaired Buell was very eager to keep it open.

16. *Ibid.,* pp. 58–59, 61, 64.

17. *Ibid.,* pp. 73, 74, 77, 76, 78–79.

18. In response to a query by Thomas, Buell said on June 24, "I do not intend to use Eastport for a depot longer than is necessary to draw about fifteen days' supply of forage from it." Taken alone, this would mean forage for the entire army. But the next sentence was, "If you should be detained on this line, which I should be very sorry for, it may be convenient for you to use it." Forage for fifteen days for five divisions—forgetting Mitchel—would have lasted Thomas seventy-five days, and no detention like that was contemplated. Fry's message to Thomas on the 29th suggests an entirely uncontemplated procedure. See also Fry's dispatch to Capt. O. D. Greene, adjutant at Nashville, about supply arrangements, both as to the initial stocks at Athens and subsequently, which do not seem to have been modified (*ibid.,* p. 23).

19. *Ibid.,* pp. 82, 84.

20. *Supra,* III, 409. As noted *ibid.,* p. 536, Halleck called the destruction of the bridge foolish, but he did not have sufficient knowledge of Mitchel's situation to make an acceptable judgment. It will be recalled that having initially saved the long bridge at Decatur from flames kindled by the Confederates, Mitchel had destroyed it for security reasons when he withdrew his troops from the north bank. Henceforth he contented himself with keeping the railroad open from the gap north of Athens, while he reached eastward toward Chattanooga as far as he could.

21. *O.R., 23,* 84, 89–90. On June 7 Mitchel informed Buell that he had been ordered by Halleck to transfer a locomotive to Decatur, but that it could not be done until the enemy was driven away. On the 9th Buell told Mitchel that it was of the "greatest importance" that cars and locomotives be carried over "with all possible dispatch," Mitchel replying the next day, "Our boat to cross locomotives will be ready on Friday" [June 13]. Obviously no boat was built, and Buell must have forgotten about previous dispatches when he told Halleck on July 2 that he had not known "that the transfer of engines had been ordered." In replying the next day Halleck said that Mitchel had promised to cross some, and in a dispatch to Stanton about the locomotive shortage he said Mitchel should be required to explain why he had not done so. (*O.R., 11,* 271, 283, 288; *23,* 89–90, 93, 92–93.)

Mitchel had an excellent reason for not actually crossing any equipment; his failure to have a boat made is another matter.

22. *O.R., 23,* 96, 93–94, 116, 104. The date July 9, supplied by the editors to Streight's dispatch, may be in error. Swords replied to Buell that the Louisville depot was crowded but that the railroad could not handle the business until it got its "original equipment." Turner states (*op. cit.,* pp. 248–249) that

15 engines and 400 freight cars had been brought from Ohio and altered to the gauge of the L. & N.

23. *O.R.*, *22*, 605; *23*, 85, 117. Capt. H. C. Symonds, commissary officer at Louisville, put the gross weight of a single ration at about 3¼ pounds (*O.R.*, *22*, 340). The ration components were set by Army Regulations, the 1861 revision carrying a footnote on p. 243 authorizing certain increases "during the rebellion in the Southern States."

24. Halleck, *Elements of Military Art and Science*, pp. 94–96. Halleck could not have had in mind the great revolution that railroads would produce in supplying an army. But their demonstrated vulnerability when one had advanced deeply into enemy territory caused much that he said still to be valid. A footnote Halleck appended to the word "foraging" revealed his penchant for precision: "This term is sometimes, though improperly, applied to the operation of forcibly collecting food for the troops."

25. *O.R.*, *23*, 165, 179–180, 198; *22*, 400; *supra*, pp. 241–242.

26. *O.R.*, *22*, 339; *23*, 127; *22*, 31, 485–486 (Buell's comment about, and Yates's description of, the Decatur ferry).

27. *O.R.*, *23*, 10, 16–17, 17 (important dispatch, Mitchel to Buell, and reply). The force repairing the Decatur road north of the break was under the direction of J. B. Anderson, superintendent of railroads for Buell, who disagreed with Mitchel as to which road could be repaired first. Buell clearly accepted Mitchel's judgment.

In a dispatch to Halleck on July 1, Buell indicated that the Nashville–Stevenson road still had priority; an order to the engineers the next day suggests a shift; a dispatch to Halleck on the 4th seems to confirm it. In his long statement to the Commission in response to a question by Buell, Darr indicated in the clearest and most emphatic manner that, beginning early in July, every effort was made to complete the Decatur line first. The testimony of Col. W. P. Innes, of the engineers, gave general support to Darr, and Buell did not challenge the statements of either. There was certainly place for more expert labor on the Stevenson line, for on July 8 an infantry brigade was sent northward from Stevenson not only to protect it but to expedite the work. (*O.R.*, *23*, 83, 90, 93–94; *22*, 603–604, 247–248, 249; *23*, 109–110).

On July 1 Thomas was ordered to build stockades for the guards at all bridges and trestles between Iuka and Decatur. A dispatch to Fry on the 11th from Capt. W. H. Wade, commanding at Decatur, gave information about damage to the telegraph and the burning of water tanks and some bridges by a small body of enemy cavalry or citizens. At that time the *Sam Cruse* had not returned with the trainload of forage. Wade had received on the 9th the report that the train had come to Courtland—twenty miles west of Decatur—where the cars had been left while the engine went back because it was out of order. If Thomas had made an effort to carry out the order given him on June 24 about protecting the road, he certainly had not been successful. Wade said that if he "had a full company of cavalry and permission to operate on the offensive," he could protect railroad and telegraph for ten miles. (*O.R.*, *23*, 85–86, 125.)

28. Yates's testimony, *O.R.*, *22*, 485–492. On cross-examination, Gen. Daniel

Tyler asked, "Would not a single company or half a company guarantee these mills from incursions by guerrillas?" Yates answered, "It would have needed as much as one company, and that company would have needed stockades for protection." There was abundant material, and stockades were built at bridges and trestles.

Morton stated in his testimony—a deposition for the defense—that it was about July 6 when he drew up plans and specifications for a pontoon bridge to be thrown near Bridgeport. One of the baffling points in the bridge matter is the query that Buell put on June 22 to J. B. Anderson, "Have you such facilities that you can in ten days build 100 boats similar to those you made at Louisville?" The reply seems missing; if none in the negative was made, the question must have been dropped. But Buell's query merely raises another. What about the boats built in Louisville to which he referred? It will be recalled that the bridge and small steamer to take it up the Tennessee which Buell had purchased for $12,000 had arrived at Savannah a short time before he arrived there on April 5. In his dispatch to Halleck on June 17, Buell asked to have this bridge thrown at Eastport, saying that although parts had been used in bridging small creeks, they could be quickly replaced. Halleck replied that he saw no reason for a floating bridge at Eastport—a reply justified by his knowledge that Buell was crossing at Florence. Actually, Morton had looked at the pontoons on June 13 with a view to utilizing them at Florence, but had found them "unfit for use." Buell apparently did not know this when he made his query of Halleck, so he had never contemplated taking his old pontoons with him in his advance on Chattanooga for the purpose of crossing the river near Bridgeport. It will be seen that in November, Halleck's chief of staff was of the opinion that Buell had crossed at Florence with those pontoons and had then taken them eastward. (*O.R., 22, 722; 23,* 49; *supra,* III, 326, 352; *O.R., 23, 33, 33–34; 22,* 722; *infra,* p. 529, n. 37.)

29. *O.R., 23,* 17–18, 30, 45–46.

30. *Ibid.,* pp. 51, 48–49.

31. *Ibid.,* pp. 51, 55, 51, 58. On June 20 Mitchel told Buell the running time from Athens to Stevenson was about six hours, and he said he could transport 18 wagons with teams and 1,500 men at a trip (*ibid.,* pp. 41–42).

32. *Ibid.,* pp. 94, 109–110.

33. *Ibid.,* p. 104.

34. *Ibid.,* pp. 122, 122–123.

35. *Ibid.,* pp. 130, 128.

36. *Ibid.,* p. 131.

37. *Supra,* III, 437–438; *O.R., 23,* 137, 127; *22,* 517 (Crittenden's testimony about finding Hascall at Battle Creek).

Forrest's blow had fallen before Buell had received Halleck's dispatch of the 14th telling him to do all he could to put down Morgan's raid even if the Chattanooga expedition were delayed. Morgan of necessity had to be left to Boyle, though on the 14th Buell telegraphed him that he was moving troops toward Kentucky as rapidly as possible. (*O.R., 23,* 143; *22,* 739.)

38. *O.R., 23,* 146, 147, 147–148, 148, 157 (Thomas to Halleck, saying: "General Buell directs me to hurry on supplies. His men are on half rations

since the break in the railroad at Murfreesborough"), 155 (Fry to Swords and reply). A message from Bingham (*ibid.*, p. 153) said: "No supplies have been received from Louisville for several days until yesterday, when 11 car loads of forage came. This I forward to-day to Reynolds. A large portion of the 50,000 rations of forage forwarded to Murfreesborough by Captain Nigh has been captured or burned. Mr. Anderson saved one train on Sunday. Colonel Swords answers my requisitions for supplies that they will be sent as soon as transportation can be furnished at Louisville."

Darr stated in his testimony that about the middle of July Buell sent him to Thomas to urge the latter to bring forward all the supplies he could, including beef cattle, and to learn from Halleck's commissary officer "if supplies could not be brought by rail from Memphis and by river to Eastport." His assertion that Thomas said he could hardly supply himself does not harmonize with Thomas's statement to Halleck, in which, in addition to the sentences already quoted about supplying Buell, he stated, "There should be a train devoted to that business." Nor does it fit with Fry's statement of June 24 that there were 1,000,000 rations at Eastport, or with the statement of Gen. Robert Allen, Halleck's chief quartermaster, to Buell on June 28, "The 100 wagons of General Thomas cannot transport to Iuka all the stores at Eastport in less than a month." So far as obtaining anything by the river was concerned, Halleck had told Buell on June 22, "The Tennessee is falling so fast that nearly all the boats are leaving." (*O.R., 23,* 71, 48–49.)

39. *O.R., 23,* 154, 151. In a dispatch on the 15th Halleck informed Buell of his reluctant departure for Washington, saying that while he was abandoning the line to Memphis (meaning from Grand Junction), he would keep the one open to Decatur as long as *Buell wished it.* On the same day Halleck told Thomas to push forward supplies and prepare to join Buell, the dispatch ending, "You will be replaced by a division from here." (*Ibid.*, pp. 151, 157.)

In the paper given to the Commission, Buell spoke of Thomas's division having been detained a "month longer" guarding the railroad (meaning through July), and he stressed how few supplies were drawn over it. He said nothing, however, about his eagerness to have it kept open for communication purposes only. Nor did he mention the telegram he sent to Halleck on July 26, that spoke of the "disgraceful and serious results" from attacks by the enemy's cavalry the day before, notably at Courtland (between Tuscumbia and Decatur). That message ended, "I have requested General Grant to open the road again, for it is important to both of us." (*O.R., 22,* 819–820.) It is difficult to believe that Buell did not know the line was of no use to Grant, but merely a burden.

40. Beatty, *Memoirs of a Volunteer,* pp. 112, 119, 118; *O.R., 23,* 216; *22,* 674. Brownlow stated that the Confederates had shown quite the reverse of an "amiable policy" toward Unionists in East Tennessee, and when asked if the latter would approve a policy of stripping the country by the regular supply departments of the army, in case the Federals should enter the region, he replied, "It would meet with the hearty approbation of the whole Union population and would be doing just what they would expect" (*ibid.*, pp. 675, 680).

41. *O.R., 23,* 230–231 (Buell to Thomas, July 30, saying trains had come

through from Nashville on the Chattanooga road "yesterday"); *22*, 609 (Darr's testimony about rations, and saying first train had passed on July 28); *23*, 186–188 (Thomas's march order), 196 (Thomas to Buell, July 21, indicating one brigade had left for Decatur), 218 (Thomas to Buell, Florence, July 27, saying the attack at Courtland had delayed him a day, but that he would start for Athens "to-morrow"), 227 (Buell to Nelson, July 17, about his own moves and those of Wood); *22*, 517 (Crittenden's statement about arrival of McCook at Battle Creek); *23*, 226 (Nelson to Buell, Murfreesboro, July 29, and reply about position at McMinnville), 227 (McCook to Fry, Battle Creek, July 29).

It is hardly necessary to comment on Turner's statement (*op. cit.*, p. 180) about Buell having worked his way slowly along the Memphis and Charleston Railroad to where he encountered the heavy damage done by Mitchel, clearly meaning the vicinity of Stevenson, or on his statement that at that point Buell assumed the responsibility of changing the procedure by switching to Nashville as a supply base. But it will be noted that the bridge in Stevenson and the one a few miles to the west that Mitchel replaced in June had definitely been destroyed by the Confederates (Mitchel to Buell, Apr. 20, *O.R., 11*, 618–619).

42. *O.R., 23*, 188, 221, 237. Grant's statement in his *Memoirs*, I, 401 (Long, ed., pp. 208–209) that Buell could have reached Chattanooga in "eighteen days at the outside," if he had not been required to repair the railroad, and that he would have anticipated the Confederates, may be responsible for a good deal of the misconception about Buell's move. A more difficult error to understand is the statement (*ibid.*, p. 414; Long, ed., p. 214) that Thomas was ordered to Buell on Sept. 19. This made Grant stronger and Buell weaker for two months than was actually the case.

43. *Supra*, III, 254; *O.R., 23*, 236.

44. *O.R., 23*, 265, 258, 266.

45. *Ibid.*, p. 266.

46. *Ibid.*, p. 279.

47. *O.R., 23*, 302; *22*, 248, 490.

48. *O.R., 23*, 312, 311; *supra*, III, 438.

49. Various reports and statements, *O.R., 22*, 843–857.

50. *Ibid.*, p. 857.

51. *O.R., 23*, 752–753, 354, 352, 344, 354, 344. On the 15th Bragg was in one of his buoyant moods, saying to Smith, "Everything is ripe for success. The country is aroused and expecting us. Buell's forces are much scattered, and from all accounts much demoralized. By rapid movements and vigorous blows we may beat him in detail, or by gaining his rear very much increase his demoralization and break him up." (*Ibid.*, pp. 758–759.)

52. *Ibid.*, p. 357; Beatty, *op. cit.*, p. 131; *O.R., 25*, 239.

53. *O.R., 23*, 369, 394, 359, 351, 353, 359–360, 361.

54. *Ibid.*, pp. 360, 360–361. On Aug. 12 Halleck had confidentially informed Buell that there was talk of replacing him. Although Buell put the blame for shortage of cavalry on the War Department, he seems to have been partly to blame himself. On June 12 he indicated to Swords that only 1,000 cavalry horses were needed; if Swords did not have that number he was to buy up to the figure. Not until the 30th did Buell give an explicit order for Swords to

start buying immediately to the number of 5,000. (*Ibid.,* pp. 314–315, 19, 77.)

55. *Ibid.,* pp. 361–362. See also pp. 208 and 212 for earlier orders to Johnson.

56. Various reports, *O.R., 22,* 871–882.

57. *O.R., 23,* 286; War Department G.O. 107, 1862.

58. *O.R., 22,* 839.

59. *O.R., 23,* 281, 389, 758–759.

60. *Ibid.,* pp. 388, 365, 350, 392.

61. *Ibid.,* pp. 399–400, 386, 392–393, 398, 397.

62. *Ibid.,* pp. 419, 420–421, 425–426. Some of Buell's messages could not have left a good impression on Thomas. To the one directing him to go from Decherd to McMinnville and take command of all troops that might arrive, he had had to reply, "Am I to go with any of my division or only with a guard?" On the other hand, in a message of the 22nd (dated the 23rd, but clearly erroneously, because of the reference to McCook's dispatch), telling Thomas to be ready to march to Altamont, Buell had asked, "Are you provided with ammunition?" The subsequent dispatch ordering the move stated that in the mountain region one battery per division would suffice. Because McCook and Crittenden would have six, Thomas was told, "Leave all of yours therefore; at least don't take more than one." A message the next day read, "Take two batteries instead of one; and if you think it will not retard your progress take three if you think best." (*Ibid.,* pp. 350, 400, 399–400, 400.)

63. *O.R., 22,* 134; *23,* 429, 445–446, 443.

64. *O.R., 23,* 444; Beatty, *op. cit.,* pp. 132–133.

65. *O.R., 23,* 452–453, 454–455.

66. *Ibid.,* pp. 775, 451.

67. *Ibid.,* p. 439.

68. *Ibid.,* pp. 406–407, 420–421, 438, 439. In a dispatch to Halleck on the 29th Buell said he could not concentrate more than 30,000 men east of Murfreesboro, and stated definitely that he was preparing to concentrate at that place (*ibid.,* pp. 441–442).

69. *Ibid.,* pp. 424, 357. Macfeely was a government witness before the Commission, and he stated that he had bought 8,000 to 10,000 barrels of flour in the open market. When the judge advocate asked him if he did not know that officers in charge of foraging had complained of being "embarrassed by safeguards distributed over the country," Macfeely replied negatively; but he added that, in addition to the order to seize subsistence stores in and about Nashville that he had received late in August, he had received an order from Buell "stating that all safeguards heretofore given by him would not be considered as protecting provisions and forage." After some objection, Buell succeeded in getting into the record a statement by Macfeely that it had been necessary for him to depend upon reports by others as to availability of supplies in the country adjoining Nashville and that his duties would have suffered if he had made a personal survey. It is not apparent how this helped Buell, for it was not developed that any reliable, energetic officer was detailed to make an investigation and report. (*O.R., 22,* 333–338.)

Bingham on the other hand appeared as a defense witness. His figures for the amount of forage available in two counties not far from Nashville are fairly impressive, and he purchased about 36,000 bushels of corn, and said the quartermaster at Columbia had bought hay. In some areas the people were afraid to sell because of possible guerrilla retaliation, and Bingham failed to obtain sellers even when he sent disguised agents. Under cross-examination by the judge advocate, Bingham replied affirmatively to the question as to whether the country about Nashville was very productive. He also stated that up to Aug. 22 he had paid cash, but that after that—because of the Confiscation Act and the resulting War Department order—he had given "accounts bearing the conditions for payments, to be settled hereafter as the Government may direct." At another point in the hearings Buell spoke of the order requiring receipts to be given to persons from whom supplies had been received, the condition of payment upon the certificates being that "the claimant shall prove his loyalty." (*Ibid.*, pp. 627–631, 680.)

It was stated in the text that Buell should have modified his views as a result of the killing of Robert McCook and the hard circumstances in which he found himself in the matter of supplies, but there is no record of his indorsement of the Confiscation Act, whose passage Beatty approvingly noted on July 24. Beatty was in no way a harsh man, nor was George Thomas. Yet on July 12, before the passage of the act, Thomas wrote to Fry that he thought that many of the citizens living along the railroad between Tuscumbia and Decatur should be arrested and have their property seized, because they seemed to be involved in sabotaging the road. (Beatty, *op. cit.*, p. 122; *O.R., 23,* 132.)

On Feb. 23, 1863, Judge G. W. Lane, of Huntsville, appeared before the Commission as a defense witness. He soon found it necessary to state that Buell had sought to make the words "conciliatory policy" mean just the opposite of what he had intended. To Buell's question whether he would take property of Secessionists without compensation, Lane replied, "I should be governed entirely by what I considered military necessity required, and at the same time I should be opposed to any wanton destruction of property or any illegal or unconstitutional use of it. These are my present views, and not the views that I entertained at the time General Mitchel and yourself entered Tennessee with the Federal army. My views were then very different."

During the cross-examination of Lane, Buell strove unsuccessfully to have Lane answer a question by the judge advocate "as a lawyer," apparently believing that on that basis Lane would contend that the constitutional protection of property extended to persons in rebellion or at least to those who were aiding them. In his reply, however, Lane recognized the "law of military necessity," and said he supposed a commander "would have the right to levy contributions upon the enemy to the amount of what was necessary for his present and pressing necessities." The judge disagreed with Brownlow in the matter of how the people of the South had viewed a mild policy, saying they had regarded it "not as an evidence of weakness, but as an extreme disposition to conciliate." In answer to the question whether the Confederate government had been in the habit of prosecuting Unionists "to the furthest extent of their power," he replied, "Of that fact I have no personal knowledge, but from reliable information I believe they have." (*O.R., 22,* 479–480, 480, 483–484.)

Though Lane admitted a great alteration in opinion, Buell apparently had not changed his views when Bingham appeared a month later on Mar. 27. He asked whether the new type of receipts Bingham had begun to issue in late August had "facilitated or embarrassed him in procuring supplies." In barring an answer, the Commission decided soundly: Buell's campaign, not the wisdom of acts of Congress, was the subject of investigation.

NOTES TO CHAPTER III

1. Various reports, *O.R., 22,* 907–952. Federal casualties were: killed, 206; wounded, 844; missing, 4,303; total, 5,353. Confederate losses were: killed, 78; wounded, 372; missing, 1; total, 451.

In a letter to Bragg on Aug. 24, Smith had said he would have about 12,000 effective men, but his entire force was not in action, though some of the unused part must have been relatively near at hand. Livermore puts the number of Confederates engaged at 6,850 as against 6,500 for the Federals. (*O.R., 23,* 775–776; Livermore, *Numbers and Losses,* p. 89.)

Parks gives (*General Kirby Smith, C.S.A.,* pp. 213–217) a fairly complete account of the battle from the Confederate standpoint. Though he quotes Nelson's derogatory statement that in the last position his men stood about three volleys and then broke, he does not note that Churchill called the artillery fire of the Federals "most terrible," while Smith referred to "murderous fire." Smith also said, "Owing to the open character of the country our loss in the last fight was quite heavy, including some valuable regimental officers." If there was a battle in the war in which green men fighting against well-hardened divisions should be given their due, it was this one.

Parks states that Smith was probably correct in believing that the Federals were surprised, and that Manson may have thought he was opposed by a small force that had come to forage. This claim is inconsistent with Manson's report. After speaking of a reported advance by 4,000 or 5,000 Confederates, Manson said, "The only question for me now to determine was whether I should allow the enemy to attack me in my camp or whether I should advance and meet him." That was on Aug. 29. Manson advanced to get a favorable position, and after some action that afternoon had his command in line at 4:00 A.M. of the 30th, while details from each company made coffee and filled canteens with fresh water. Cruft, still near Richmond, had his men in line of battle at 3:00 A.M. Later he breakfasted his command, formed line again and, on hearing heavy firing, advanced to join Manson, who had again moved forward upon learning that the enemy was advancing upon him.

Both Manson and Cruft had been sent from Buell's army to assist Nelson (*O.R., 22,* 348, 357).

2. Nelson's report.

3. *O.R., 23,* 464, 465, 466. Boyle's reference to the 18th Kentucky as not being a new regiment was misleading. While it had been mustered into service on Feb. 8, it had only been doing duty guarding railroads, etc., and Cruft

said in his report that it "had seen no field service, very little drill, and was now, for the first time since its formation, collected as a regiment."

4. *O.R., 23,* 464. The "route" had technical reference to procedure in encoding.

5. *Ibid.,* pp. 767–768, 768–769, 775–776; *22,* 936. In a letter to Cooper on Sept. 6, Smith reported entering Lexington on the 2nd, spoke of forces at Frankfort and Cynthiana, and said, "At both Louisville and Cincinnati the troops are said to be collecting in large numbers" (*ibid.,* p. 933).

6. Dyer, *Compendium,* gives service records of the various regiments.

7. *O.R., 23,* 468–469, 471. Smith reported that a good many of Bragg's men had shotguns. Thomas's dispatch of the 2nd was one of the best in the entire campaign.

8. *Ibid.,* pp. 470–471, 784 (Bragg's strength return for Aug. 27). Bragg had 27,816 officers and men present for duty out of a total present of 31,884. The 431 cavalrymen shown fall far short of the two brigades of horse he soon had; the eight regiments must have totaled upward of 3,000 men. Bragg had four divisions, two under Polk, two under Hardee.

More should be said about the maturing of Confederate plans. On Aug. 8 Bragg wrote to Smith about being embarrassed at receiving a copy of the War Department order of July 18 that had so recast departments that Chattanooga and the northwest part of Georgia had passed to Smith. He would, he said, feel that he had been guilty of "an unjustifiable intrusion but for your letter of the 24th ultimo, received by me at Montgomery, inviting me to make the move I was then executing." The letter ended: "Neither of us has any other object than the success of our cause. I am satisfied no misunderstanding can occur from the necessary union of our troops." Bragg had already shown his desire to cooperate by sending the brigades of Cleburne and Preston Smith to Knoxville, and presently McCown's division. These moves were reported to Buell in exaggerated form that beclouded Confederate intentions. (*Ibid.,* pp. 745–746, 280, 307.)

In acknowledging McCown's arrival, Smith suggested a change of plans. He understood that George Morgan was well supplied and could not be easily ousted from Cumberland Gap, but he said a move on Lexington would blockade Morgan and would be attended with "other most brilliant results." In replying on Aug. 10 Bragg said he did not credit the report about Morgan's supplies but had confidence in his "timidity." Information that he hoped soon to receive would, he stated, determine whether his own route would lead to Nashville or to Lexington, though his momentary inclination was for the latter place. When Bragg's protestations of the 8th arrived, Smith matched them: "I deem it almost superfluous to say that I will make no movement that your judgment does not sanction." Finally, in his letter of Aug. 20 announcing his departure from Barbourville, he said, "I still cordially invite you to make this the line of your operations, so that you may act with our forces concentrated." (*Ibid.,* pp. 748, 748–749, 751, 766–767.)

Even before reading Smith's reference to the superfluous, Bragg must have received Jefferson Davis's letter of the 5th telling him that Smith was "one of our ablest and purest officers," whose promotion, like Bragg's, had been unsought. The President expressed confidence in the "cordial co-operation" of the two generals, and extended to Bragg a compliment that was a little unusual: "You have the misfortune of being regarded as my personal friend, and are pursued, therefore, with malignant censure by men regardless of truth, and whose want of principle to guide their conduct renders them incapable of conceiving that you are trusted because of your known fitness for command and not because of friendly regard." (*O.R., 110, 334–336.*)

The clear warning that bitter criticism might follow failure did not cause Bragg's rhetoric to weaken when he composed the final sentence in his order to his troops on Aug. 25: "Soldiers, the enemy is before you and your banners are free. It is for you to decide whether our brothers and sisters of Tennessee and Kentucky shall remain bondmen and bondwomen of the Abolition tyrant or be restored to the freedom inherited from their fathers." Two days later he began a dispatch to Breckinridge: "We leave for your beloved home. Would that you were with us." The ending was conclusive as to route, and continued the beguiling touch: "We go by way of Sparta and Burkeville into the heart of Kentucky." (*O.R., 23, 779, 996.*)

9. *O.R., 23,* 471. The date Sept. 7 on the copy of Halleck's telegram in *O.R., 22,* 18, is evidently incorrect.

10. *O.R., 22,* 658, 653, 9. Davis's division from Grant's army, now under Robert B. Mitchell, was met at Murfreesboro, having marched there from Columbia (*ibid.,* p. 92).

The Buell Commission asked many questions about the possibility of intercepting Bragg at Sparta. Thomas, a government witness, in one instance sought to shield Buell by answering, "I believe that General Buell thought so." When Brig. Gen. H. J. T. Dana pressed him by saying, "I am not asking that; I am asking your judgment," Thomas replied, "I have said already that I desired to concentrate the army and meet Bragg at Sparta and fight him, because I thought we had supplies enough to enable us to do it." Dana persisted: "How am I to understand your answer, general?" to which Thomas answered, "According to my judgment there was not a sufficient reason for falling back from Murfreesborough to Nashviile." Thomas stuck to his position under Buell's cross-examination, stating that he thought Bragg could have been brought to battle at Sparta and that 24,000 men would have been sufficient to keep him out of Tennessee [Kentucky], because he did not think Bragg could have brought more than 30,000 into an engagement. To effect this result, Thomas thought twenty days' supplies would have sufficed, after which it would have been necessary to live on the country, which he thought—not from positive knowledge, but from reliable information—could have been done for another ten days. Buell did not challenge Thomas's implication that there would have been twenty days' supplies for the four divisions he spoke of as being sufficient at Sparta, but confined himself to possible action after that, if Bragg had not in the meantime been brought to battle. (*Ibid.,* 202–203.)

11. *O.R., 22,* 151; *23,* 493, 799–800, 497, 498.

12. *O.R., 22,* 44; *23,* 501. On the 6th Buell had telegraphed to Col. S. D. Bruce, commanding at Bowling Green, about preparations to resist an attack in order to protect supplies (*ibid.,* p. 490).

13. *O.R., 23,* 501–502.

14. *Ibid.,* p. 509. On Sept. 7th Lincoln had wired to Boyle: "Where is General Bragg? What do you know on the subject?" Of Wright he asked: "Do you know to any certainty where General Bragg is? May he not be in Virginia?" Wright replied that while there was no certainty, all rumors indicated Bragg had crossed the Tennessee. Boyle's reply of 8:00 P.M. began, "I think there is no doubt that General Bragg is moving along General Buell's right." At eleven o'clock the next morning Boyle repudiated his good dispatch by telegraphing to Lincoln: "Intelligent persons who left Nashville on 6th instant say that nothing is known of Bragg's army in Tennessee. There is some conjecture that Bragg may have joined the forces near Washington. My view of their plans is likely all wrong." This probably was what caused the President to telegraph to Buell at 7:20 P.M. of the 8th, "What degree of certainty have you that Bragg with his command is not now in the valley of the Shenandoah, Virginia?" It was not until noon on the 10th that Buell began a reply, "Bragg is certainly this side of the Cumberland Mountains with his whole force, except what is in Kentucky under Smith." The message ended: "Cut off effectually from supplies, it is impossible for me to operate in force where I am; but I shall endeavor to hold Nashville, and at the same time drive Smith out of Kentucky and hold my communications." (*Ibid.,* pp. 495, 496, 497, 500.)

15. *Ibid.,* pp. 508–509. Stager had been prominent in the development of the telegraph industry, and was made general superintendent of the Western Union upon its formation in 1856, with offices in Cleveland. He had been promoted from captain to colonel on Feb. 26, 1862 (*D.A.B.*).

16. *O.R., 22,* 654; *23,* 512–513.

17. *O.R., 22,* 123; *23,* 511–512. At the inquiry, Buell's adjutant, Maj. J. M. Wright, mentioned only Rousseau's and Wood's divisions as being at Bowling Green when Buell arrived at 6:00 A.M. of the 14th. But Crittenden had been moving with Rousseau, and McCook placed him in Bowling Green.

18. McKee, *"Ben-Hur" Wallace,* p. 58; *O.R., 109,* 273, 274, 274–275, 277–278 (Wallace's proclamation of martial law); *23,* 492 (order of Sept. 6 by Wright about resumption of business, etc., and assigning Wallace to duty in Covington), 499–500, 495. On the 5th Wright sent a copy of Wallace's proclamation to the adjutant general of the Army, asking that it be approved by the Secretary of War. He said it had been issued after consultation with the governors of Indiana and Kentucky, who had given approval. The order applied to Cincinnati, Covington, and Newport.

19. *O.R., 23,* 504, Tod to Stanton, 11:00 A.M., Sept. 10, beginning, "At 2.30 a.m. I received orders from Major-General Wright to send forward to Cincinnati all the armed men of the State."

20. *Ibid.,* pp. 504, 505, 502.

21. *Ibid.,* pp. 504 (Tod to Stanton), 506–507, 505–506, 509. Robinson told Halleck that there were 45,000 troops at Cincinnati and only 25,000 at Louisville. On the 8th Wright wrote to Wallace, "The force of regularly organized troops is accumulating so rapidly that I trust you will shortly be able to return to their homes the unorganized forces now under your command. . . . Several regiments are reported to arrive to-night." (*Ibid.,* p. 499.)

Tod said to Stanton: "It is proper to add that General Wright commands my fullest confidence. I have reason to fear, however, that he has some difficulty with our Indiana friends." Since Morton had furnished six of the regiments that had fought at Richmond, while Tod had sent one, it was a rather ungracious remark. It was natural that the governor of Indiana should feel more concern about Louisville than over Cincinnati.

22. *Ibid.*, pp. 482–483.

23. *Ibid.*, p. 510. On Sept. 1 Wright appointed Capt. C. C. Gilbert a major general of volunteers, subject to the President's approval. On the 9th Halleck assigned him as a brigadier general to Wright. (*Ibid.*, pp. 987, 530.)

24. *Ibid.*, pp. 510, 511.

25. *Ibid.*, pp. 513, 517. Wright told the President he had no intention of abandoning Louisville and that only two regiments had been withdrawn, leaving there about 30 regiments and more than 30 guns.

26. *Ibid.*, p. 514.

27. Cramer, ed., *Letters of Grant*, p. 85.

28. *O.R.*, *23*, 514.

29. *Ibid.*, p. 524.

30. *Ibid.*, p. 515.

31. *O.R.*, *22*, 1090.

32. Chalmers's report, *ibid.*, pp. 971–980.

33. Chalmers's report; Wilder's and Dunham's reports, *O.R.*, *22*, 959–963, 963–967. Although several cars were completely wrecked, all of Col. Dunham's men escaped injury, a fact which he said seemed to inspire them "with even greater confidence, as of feeling themselves under the special protection of an overruling Providence." Knapsacks and blankets were hidden in a thicket, while Unionists in the vicinity of the wreck removed and concealed the ammunition, which was brought into town on the 15th with the aid of citizens of Munfordville.

34. *Ibid.*, pp. 972, 980.

35. Bragg's report, *ibid.*, p. 1090; Wilder's and Dunham's reports; Wilder's testimony and notes exchanged with Bragg, *ibid.*, pp. 1090, 209–210, 968–971; Bragg's order of 1:00 A.M., Sept. 17, covering the surrender, *O.R.*, *23*, 842. In his testimony before the Buell Commission, Wilder spoke of the council of officers meeting at four o'clock of the 16th, but his report makes it clear that they met after receipt of the surrender demand. The report, dated Sept. 18, stated that the paroled officers and men were "about to start for the Ohio River." They were, however, sent to Buell.

Though Dunham was senior to Wilder, he declined to take command until the morning of the 15th. In spite of investment on the north, the telegraph line was put in operation on the 16th, and in the afternoon Dunham reported to Gilbert that they had held the enemy at bay, but that it remained to be seen whether they could stand against the increasing hostile force. In answer, Gilbert ordered Dunham to turn over the command to Wilder, which he did after the meeting of officers, Wilder saying he received it at 7:00 P.M. In reporting his action to Gilbert, Dunham stated he would go into the trenches with a musket. While cordial relations existed between him and Wilder, he considered Gilbert's order not only unjust but an insinuation of weakness, and he did not wish to fight as an officer under a junior. (Actually, the 62nd Article of War reserved to the President the power to have an officer serve under one to whom he was senior.) Thereupon Gilbert directed him, "to report to Colonel Wilder under arrest," which he did. When he finally reached Louisville, Dunham learned that Gilbert had within a few moments sent a dispatch releasing him from arrest and restoring him to command; but telegraphic communication had been broken.

36. *O.R.*, *22*, 968. For the entire Munfordville operation the Federal killed numbered 15; wounded, 57; captured or missing, 4,076. The Confederates lost 35 killed (including an able colonel) and 250 wounded. (*Ibid.*, pp. 967, 982.)

37. *O.R.*, *23*, 518. The account given here of the Munfordville surrender is quite different from that by Horn in *The Army of Tennessee*, pp. 168–169, which makes reference to an article by Basil W. Duke in the *Southern Bivouac*. There seems no reason for accepting what was written years after the event by a Confederate officer who was not present, and rejecting Wilder's and Dunham's reports and Wilder's sworn testimony before the Buell Commission. Horn has Wilder, whom he represents as militarily naïve, going to Buckner for advice. It is true that Buckner was one of the best living authorities on the subject of surrendering. But Wilder, who was, as Horn states, an Indiana industrialist—and later a Tennessee industrialist of distinction—was by this time a seasoned soldier. His regiment, the 17th Indiana, went to West Virginia in July, 1861, and was transferred to Louisville on Nov. 19. It was in the advance to Nashville and reached Pittsburg Landing on Apr. 7. In his report on the move against Corinth, Gen. Wood singled out Wilder and another officer as "zealous at any and all times in performance of every duty, whether it appropriately belonged to them or not" (*O.R.*, *10*, 709).

In the summer of 1862 Wilder had been in Indiana recruiting for his regiment and was on the way to join Buell with 214 men when he was caught at Munfordville. Wright apparently ordered both Brig. Gen. W. T. Ward and Col. Dunham away from the vicinity to give command to Wilder (*O.R.*, *22*, 211–212).

The regiments and separate recruits at Munfordville were green; but Wilder was not.

38. *Ibid.*, p. 214. Gen. Tyler concluded the government's examination of Wilder by asking, "Why did you not leave the position?" to which Wilder replied, "I had been ordered to hold out as long as possible and telegraphed the whole statement of facts to General Gilbert, expecting him to order me to get away if I could, which he did not."

There had been telegraphic discussion between Wright and Boyle about the desirability of evacuating both Bowling Green and Munfordville. See *O.R.*, *23*, 484, 494, 487.

39. *O.R.*, *22*, 207–208, 212, 45–46, 105, 208. McCook said he had thought Bragg's "march would be by Columbia." Buell described three better routes for Bragg to join Smith than the one through Munfordville.

40. *O.R.*, *22*, 48; *23*, 527. Buell's message was sent from Dripping Springs, about halfway from Bowling Green to Munfordville.

On Sept. 5 Buell's cavalry was organized into a division under Col. John Kennett. The first brigade, under Col. Edward M. McCook, consisted of four regiments and a battalion; the second brigade, under Col. Lewis Zahm, had three regiments. It is not clear what patroling the cavalry did or where its main body was on the 15th, but a dispatch on the 16th directed Kennett to be ready to march at 2:00 P.M. (*Ibid.*, pp. 484, 521.)

41. Don Carlos Buell, "East Tennessee and the Campaign of Perryville," *B. and L.*, III, 31–51, especially p. 42; *O.R., 22*, 849. When Buell gave 40,000 as Bragg's maximum strength, he certainly meant aggregate present, not "effectives."

At his headquarters near Cave City, Buell received a second report from J. T. Pratt, a schoolteacher of La Grange, Tenn., who had seen Bragg's army at Tupelo, then at Chattanooga, then in the Sequatchie Valley, whence he rode to Nashville and told Buell that it numbered from 22,000 to 25,000 men. From Nashville, Pratt went to Glasgow and saw what he "considered the bulk" of the Confederate force. After Bragg had left, Pratt went again to Buell; though he gave no over-all figure, so far as his later testimony before the Commission showed, he imparted considerable information. During the late evening of the 18th Wilder reached Buell's headquarters with his paroled men. He put the enemy at from 35,000 to 40,000 and said they did not have provisions to sustain them for three days. In his testimony, Wilder paid tribute to the discipline of the Confederates, but he also said, "They were terribly ragged and dirty and apparently tired out." Doubtless he told the same thing to Buell, and Steedman testified that he had heard much discussion of Bragg's strength when at Cave City, officers generally putting it at about 25,000. (*O.R., 22*, 82–86, 208, 131.)

42. *O.R., 23*, 849, 856, 859.

43. Buell, *loc. cit.; O.R., 23*, 533, 542, 541, 540. Wilder testified: "I was present with General Buell when the information reached him that the enemy had reached [left] Munfordville. That was on Sunday 21st, then about 7 miles from Munfordville. We were then moving forward in line of battle apparently." Wilder also testified that the bridge over Salt River—at West Point—had been destroyed by guerrillas on or about Sept. 7. (*O.R., 22*, 208, 204.)

44. *O.R., 22*, 135, 134. Steedman stated that the army had originally been enthusiastic for Buell, cheering upon his appearance. But, at least so far as his own command was concerned, there had been a change after the retreat began, when Buell became "decidedly unpopular." When pressed by the Commission for names of officers who had impugned Buell's loyalty, Steedman gave three, including that of Gen. Schoepf, a member of the Commission, and added, "I am unable to recollect all the officers by name." Three months later—Mar. 9, 1863—Buell virtually challenged Schoepf's fitness to serve (poor health had taken him from the field and made him available), and an application by Schoepf for permission to withdraw was sent to Halleck. On the 13th he was relieved from duty with the Commission, Gen. Ord being relieved at the same time, but solely for a new assignment. (*O.R., 22*, 133, 591–592; *23*, 676–677.)

Buell appeared ready to concede that there had been demoralization in his army, but to wish to attribute it in part to living on the country, in the case of the men, and to lack of knowledge, in the case of officers. In the important matter of Bragg's strength, it was, of course, those who put it at about 30,000 who were eventually correct.

45. *O.R., 23,* 461; *25,* 194, 198, 199.

46. *O.R., 25,* 192, 194, 197, 204, 204–205, 206. In accordance with Halleck's instructions to Grant on June 30, Memphis had been well fortified on the land side (*ibid.,* pp. 56, 217–218).

47. *Ibid.,* p. 220.

48. *Ibid.,* pp. 220, 222.

49. *Ibid.,* p. 223.

50. *Ibid.,* pp. 223–224, 224.

51. Cramer, ed., *op. cit.,* pp. 90–92.

52. *O.R., 25,* 224.

53. *O.R., 25,* 698, 897; *110,* 350. On July 25 Bragg telegraphed to Van Dorn from Meridian, Miss., telling him to act in conjunction with Price, the message ending, "You have the fullest confidence of all." (*O.R., 25,* 897.)

54. *O.R., 25,* 700, 702. For dispatches from Bragg to Price on Aug. 29 and Sept. 6 directing him to move on Nashville, see *ibid.,* pp. 690, 694. The prevention of a union of Rosecrans and Buell being Bragg's basic desire, Price was certainly justified in giving up his intention of moving toward Nashville when he discovered that Rosecrans had moved to Corinth. In his final report on the Kentucky campaign (*O.R., 22,* 1088–1094), Bragg did not even mention Price. Inasmuch as he never hesitated to complain of subordinates, this would indicate that he thought Price had made the correct decision.

55. *O.R., 24,* 118; *25,* 225.

56. *O.R., 25,* 705–706. In a dispatch on Sept. 16, Secretary Randolph gave Van Dorn much latitude, but said the Department wanted cooperation between him and Price, the message ending, "You are the senior officer, and, subject to General Bragg's instructions, can exercise your own discretion" (*ibid.,* p. 704). This did not take away from Price the responsibility in interpreting orders he had received directly from Bragg.

NOTES TO CHAPTER IV

1. Grant, *Memoirs,* I, 408 (Long, ed., p. 212); C. S. Hamilton, "The Battle of Iuka," *B. and L.,* II, 734–736.

2. *O.R., 25,* 224; Grant's and Ord's reports, *ibid., 24,* 64–69, 117–119.

3. *Ibid., 25,* 223, 227; Grant's and Ord's reports; Hurlbut to Rawlins, *O.R., 25,* 226.

4. Grant's and Ord's reports.

5. *O.R., 25,* 229–230.

6. *Ibid., 24,* 121–122; *25,* 230.

7. Reports by Rosecrans, Surgeon Archibald B. Campbell, Hamilton, Willcox, Col. John K. Mizner (commanding cavalry), Col. Charles L. Matthies (5th Iowa), Lieut. Col. John H. Holman (26th Missouri), Col. John B. Sanborn

(commanding 1st brigade of Hamilton's division), *O.R., 24,* 69, 72–75, 79–80, 89–93, 115–117, 113–115, 99–100, 103–105, 94–97. Hamilton said four companies of the 5th Iowa were deployed; Matthies said three, and identified them. Rosecrans stated he had five batteries, but the roster in the casualty report lists six.

8. Reports of Hamilton, Price, Brig. Gen. Louis Hébert (who succeeded to command of Little's division), Stanley, *ibid.,* pp. 89–93, 119–124, 124–126, 81–82. It is difficult to tell with certainty how many Confederate regiments were in line when fire was opened upon the Federal skirmishers. Hamilton spoke of the enemy being "drawn up in great force and occupying a strong position along a deep ravine running transversely with the main road and behind the crest of the hill." Sanborn said the enemy was "drawn up in line of battle, in strong force (about 18,000 infantry, with cavalry and artillery)." On the other hand Hébert spoke of *meeting* the Federals three-fourths of a mile from town "and quickly forming line of battle." Col. J. W. Whitefield, commanding the 1st Texas Legion, said (*ibid.,* p. 128), "On the afternoon of Friday, September 19, we formed line of battle about 1 mile south of the town, on the Bay Springs road, the enemy approaching in large force." (Bay Springs was about 20 miles south of Iuka.) This suggests the Confederates were deployed and waiting. In his subsequent *B. and L.* article Hamilton indicates that two Confederate brigades—ten regiments—were in line of battle concealed in woods, while two more had arrived on the field. In his report he said that the enemy fire drove the skirmish line back on the head of the column, but Col. George B. Boomer (26th Missouri) said (*O.R., 24,* 102) that the skirmishers under Lieut. Col. Holman "continued to drive the enemy's line till they came upon his main body, from which they received a volley, causing considerable loss. They remained in position till the column came up. . . ." Thus even in simple matters relative to the beginning of the battle there are notable contradictions in the record.

Badeau relates (*Military History of Ulysses S. Grant,* I, 114–115) a story that came to Ord from a brother-in-law, who was a colonel in the Confederate army, to the effect that Price learned of Rosecrans's march from a doctor serving Rosecrans as a scout and spy, but who left the Federal column and "hurried into town" and reported to Price. This does not agree with Price's statement (*O.R., 24,* 122): "During the early part of the afternoon of the same day [Sept. 19] my pickets on the Jacinto road were driven in. About 2:30 o'clock they reported that the enemy were advancing on that road in force."

9. Reports previously mentioned; Federal casualty report, *O.R., 24,* 77–78. There is great contradiction as to Confederate losses. Hébert's report gives 86 killed and 408 wounded. On the other hand Capt. W. M. Miles, provost marshal for Rosecrans, reported, "Number killed, found upon the field and buried by our men, 265, number died of wounds since battle, 120." On the 21st Rosecrans wrote to Grant that the enemy "had collected 162 for burial 200 yards in rear of their little hospital, where they were found yesterday covered with tarpaulins." Referring to another group he said, "My count was 99. These with the 162 make 261 rebels killed." (*Ibid.,* pp. 80, 72.) Did Miles and Rosecrans do any counting personally? If not, their reports were misleading; if they did, their care seems suspect. The editors of *B. and L.* (II, 736) virtually accept

Hébert's figure, putting the Confederate killed at 85 without comment. Grant naturally passed Rosecrans's report on to Washington and incorrectly said the Federal killed would be less than 100 (*O.R., 24*, 64).

10. *O.R., 24*, 69, 67. In his 6:00 A.M. message Rosecrans said, "Hamilton will go up Fulton and Iuka road; Stanley up Jacinto road from Barnett's; when we get near will be governed by circumstances." At 12:40 P.M. he sent Grant a message from Barnett's (*ibid.*, p. 69). It reported skirmishing with an enemy picket but gave no indication of a change in plan of advance. In his *B. and L.* article Hamilton wrote that he had expected to march to the Fulton road from Barnett's, but at that point "was furnished a guide, and directed to continue his march on the Tuscumbia road without further instructions," and he observed that the change of plan made by Rosecrans "for reasons of his own" left "the Fulton road open." Rosecrans's failure to mention the change in his report is the more puzzling because he emphasized the fact that the original plan was his.

Rosecrans's comment about the country being "unknown" conflicts with a statement in Grant's *Memoirs* (*loc. cit.*). After noting that Rosecrans had at first had his headquarters at Iuka, Grant said, "While there he had a most excellent map prepared showing all the roads and streams in the surrounding country. He was also personally familiar with the ground, so that I deferred very much to him in my plans for the approach."

11. Ord's report. It would seem that Rosecrans's 12:40 P.M. message should have been received by Grant by the time he conferred with Ord. In the 6:00 A.M. message Rosecrans said, "Eighteen miles to Iuka, but think I shall make it by the time mentioned—2 o'clock p.m." He spoke as if, on the basis of his own optimism, Grant would have had Ord already attack Price so that he could come in and "finish him."

12. *O.R., 24*, 136.

13. Grant's and Ord's reports. In his 12:40 P.M. dispatch Rosecrans said, "Colonels Dickey and Lagow arrived here half an hour ago." It is hard to believe that they did not make it clear that there would be no attack from the north until cooperation was certain.

14. Stanley's report, Rosecrans to Grant, *O.R., 24*, 70. There was also a message at 7:00 A.M. that had to go around by the courier line to the rear and one at 8:45 by way of Iuka.

15. Ord closed his report, "Corinth still being threatened, you directed me to return with my whole force at once, leaving Crocker's brigade as a garrison in the town of Iuka, which I did."

16. Grant's report, *ibid.*, p. 68; *supra*, n. 10; Mizner's report. In speaking of the pursuit, Rosecrans said, "The cavalry advanced by the intermediate road between the Fulton and Jacinto roads." Though Grant was surprised when he learned the Fulton road was entirely open, he said in his report, "A partial examination of the country afterward convinced me, however, that troops moving in separate columns by the two routes suggested could not support each other until they arrived near Iuka." A mounted delaying force could have taken care of itself.

17. *O.R., 24,* 64. Though somewhat long, this report was sent by telegraph, for it was published in newspapers on Sept. 22.

Grant sent two telegrams to Halleck from Burnsville on the 19th (*O.R., 25,* 227–228, 228). In the first he said: "General Rosecrans is south of the enemy moving on him, while Ord attacks from the west. Corinth is well watched at a long distance out, and unless the approach of a large force on that place should call us back I think it will be impossible for Price to get into Tennessee. I will do all in my power to prevent such a catastrophe." In the second he described the demonstration Hurlbut was to make from Bolivar.

Accounts of the pursuit differ. Stanley, after speaking of dislodging the Confederate rear guard at Iuka, said, "No further sight of them was had that day, they being in full retreat on the Fulton road." On the other hand Maury, who had one brigade ahead of Price's train and two covering the retreat, wrote, "The enemy followed us feebly, with cavalry chiefly, which was held in check all the time by the cavalry, under General Armstrong, covering my rear." He said that at about 2:00 P.M., at a point eight miles from Iuka, the Federals were drawn into an ambuscade and "utterly routed." Col. Edward Hatch of the 2nd Iowa Cavalry admits the ambuscade but gives a different picture of what resulted. After describing the action he says, "Our infantry coming up rapidly, the enemy retreated." He claimed to have destroyed 300 to 400 arms and a wagon. (*O.R., 24,* 81, 137, 139–140.)

18. Thomas L. Snead, "With Price East of the Mississippi," *B. and L.,* II, 717–734; Price's report, *O.R., 24,* 122; *25,* 707. Snead stated that on the night of the 18th one of Van Dorn's staff officers brought Price a dispatch which said that "Van Dorn had been directed by the President to take command of Price and the Army of the West." It is a fact that on the 19th Price reported the arrival of two couriers with Van Dorn's dispatches of the 16th, the one in the records not fitting Snead's statement. That Van Dorn's message of the 17th was a telegram that arrived later on the 19th seems indicated by the reply, a sentence of which is quoted in the text. (*O.R., 25,* 708, 703–704, 705, 707.) Horn states, without citing authority, that while Price hesitated at Iuka, Price received orders placing him under Van Dorn and that the projected move to Nashville was automatically abandoned (*The Army of Tennessee,* p. 174). Neither Snead's nor Horn's statement accords with Price's report. After speaking of Bragg's erroneous belief about Rosecrans being the cause of his not crossing the Tennessee, Price said, "Early on the morning of September 19 I received dispatches from General Van Dorn, saying that he acceded to my proposition [to join in an attack on Corinth] and requesting me to move immediately to Rienzi" (*O.R., 24,* 121).

That Davis was trying not to intrude is shown by a telegram he sent Bragg on the 19th, in which he said: "No copy of your instructions in regard to operations in Tennessee has been received, and I am at a loss to know how to remedy evils without damaging your plans. If Van Dorn, Bragg, and Breckinridge each act for himself disaster for all must be the result." (*Ibid., 25,* 707.)

19. Conger's treatment of Iuka (*The Rise of U. S. Grant,* p. 279) is something less than adequate. He portrays Grant's attack as nothing more than

retaliation for Price's seizure of the town, though Grant made his reason clear enough. In calling the means of coordination relied upon totally inadequate he overlooks the fact that originally it was intended that the attacks by Rosecrans and Ord should be made virtually at the same clock time, Grant saying it was expected "that General Rosecrans would be near enough by the night of the 18th to make it safe for Ord to press forward on the morning of the 19th and bring on an engagement." It was only when Rosecrans fell behind schedule that the sound of gunfire was adopted as a coordinating medium.

20. *O.R.*, 24, 71.

21. Rosecrans evidently learned of his promotion upon reaching Jacinto. For his letter to Halleck complaining of being ranked by Buell and five others, and Halleck's reply, see *O.R.*, 25, 239, 251. The question of Rosecrans's promotion was discussed *supra*, III, 447–448, where it was noted that his commission eventually was dated back to Mar. 21, 1862, and he was put at the head of the eight officers made major generals of volunteers as of that date.

22. *O.R.*, 25, 231.

23. *Ibid.*, pp. 232–233, 900. In various Federal dispatches there is reference to Breckinridge's departure with three Kentucky regiments, which harmonized with Van Dorn's statement to Price on Sept. 18 that Breckinridge had been ordered to Chattanooga with "Kentucky regiments." Breckinridge's movement order, however, explicitly included the Tennessee brigade. Nor was the order changed, for on Sept. 29 Maj. Gen. Sam Jones, who was in command at Knoxville, telegraphed to Cooper that Breckinridge had wired from Mobile that he had only 2,000 of the exchanged prisoners and 3,000 of his own division. The latter number certainly indicates six regiments. On Oct. 11 Breckinridge telegraphed to Cooper about being ready to move "with 1,500 Kentuckians and 2,000 Tennesseans, some of them exchanged prisoners." (*Ibid.*, p. 706; *23*, 889, 933–934.)

24. *O.R.*, 25, 234.

25. *Ibid.*, p. 225.

26. *O.R.*, 19, 556, 605, 653. The new department consisted of Missouri, Arkansas, Kansas, "and the bordering Indian Territory." The old Department of the Missouri had been merged into that of the Mississippi on Mar. 11; then it was made into a military district and divided into divisions on June 5. (Dyer, *Compendium*, p. 540.)

27. *O.R.*, 25, 232, 234, 235. In a second dispatch to Halleck on the 22nd (*ibid.*, p. 232) Grant had "respectfully" requested that some of the new regiments being organized be sent to him, saying they could guard railroads and occupy posts; an unarmed regiment could be used at Memphis to man siege guns.

28. *O.R.*, 25, 238; *23*, 541. While in St. Louis, Grant received a telegram from Hurlbut about a strong enemy cavalry force with four days' rations moving toward Bethel or Purdy. He telegraphed to Ord to reenforce Hurlbut if necessary, informed the latter of his action, and told him, "Communicate with Ord until my return." (*O.R.*, 25, 238–239.)

29. *Ibid.*, pp. 244–245. Sherman began his letter of the 30th, "Yours of the 27th is this moment received." An editorial note indicates that Grant's letter

was not found. That he wrote from Columbus seems indicated by the fact that Rosecrans wired to him at that place on the 28th (*ibid.*, p. 241).

30. *Ibid.*, pp. 240, 242, 235.

31. *Ibid.*, pp. 243, 244–245. Sherman described how he could cooperate with Steele. In *Memoirs*, I, 415 (Long, ed., p. 215), Grant refers to the force at Helena, saying that if it had been under his command he could have ordered it across the river to break up the Mississippi Central Railroad to the south of Van Dorn. He makes no reference to his visit to St. Louis to Curtis and does not raise the question of enemy activity in Arkansas and Missouri.

32. *O.R.*, *25*, 250.

33. *Ibid.*, p. 717.

34. *O.R.*, *25*, 237 (Grant's reorganization order of Sept. 23); Grant's and Van Dorn's reports, *24*, 157–159, 376–382; strength return, *25*, 245–246; Grant's postbattle order, *24*, 159. In a letter to Price on Sept. 24 (*ibid.*, *25*, 711–712), Van Dorn said that Rosecrans and Hurlbut combined were stronger than he had supposed, and that it might be necessary to defer operations until some of the recently exchanged prisoners were received, of which he was to get 8,000 and Price 5,000.

35. *O.R.*, *25*, 251; Rosecrans's and Oliver's reports, *O.R.*, *24*, 166–170, 351–356.

36. Oliver's report.

37. Rosecrans's report.

38. McKean's, McArthur's, Baldwin's reports, *O.R.*, *24*, 335–341, 344–346, 289–290; Oliver's and Rosecrans's reports.

39. Davies's report, *ibid.*, pp. 251–262; McArthur's and Rosecrans's reports.

40. Davies's report; Charles S. Hamilton, "Hamilton's Division at Corinth," *B. and L.*, II, 757–758.

41. McKean's, McArthur's, and Baldwin's reports; Crocker's report, *O.R.*, *24*, 358–361. Crocker particularly praised Col. William W. Belknap of the 15th Iowa for great gallantry.

42. Hamilton's report with appended correspondence, *ibid.*, pp. 205–215. The ambiguous order was written by Rosecrans's chief of staff.

43. Hamilton's report; Sullivan's report, *ibid.*, pp. 226–229. At the end of Hamilton's report, Rosecrans wrote the indorsement, "I observe in reading your report you entirely omit to mention that you had express orders to make the movement on the enemy's left flank which you consider had such happy results, and that an aide explained to you the intention thereof and its bearing on the battle to be fought. The omission is grave and ought to be corrected." As printed, the report indicates that Hamilton prepared to attack the enemy's left flank "in order to carry out the instructions of the general commanding." Rosecrans's indorsement on the message Hamilton said he could not understand was, "Colonel Ducat has been sent to explain it."

On his part, Hamilton in his *B. and L.* note, gave the "If you see the chance . . ." order, and commented, "As a simple order to attack the enemy in flank could have reached me by courier from General Rosecrans, any time after 2 P.M., in 15 minutes, the verbosity of the above is apparent." He gave an order which he said reached him between eight and nine in the evening, leading to an interview with Rosecrans, and which caused the editors of *B. and L.* to comment, "The 'Official Records' do not contain this order or any allusion to the subject of it." Nor do the subsequently published supplementary volumes, though one of these volumes gives a note from Ducat to Rosecrans that indicates that Hamilton moved to attack at 3:30 P.M.; but it is wrongly dated Oct. 2 (*ibid., 109,* 286).

44. Van Dorn's report; Cabell's report, *O.R., 24,* 400–404. Livermore (*Numbers and Losses,* p. 94) accepts the statement of Van Dorn that he "had about 22,000." A field return of Price's command for Oct. 1 gives his effective strength as 14,363 and 44 guns. A return for Lovell's division seems missing, but on Sept. 16 Van Dorn wrote to Price that he could reach him in three days with 10,000 men; on the 24th he said, "I now have 7,000." In the letter of the 16th he spoke of attacking Corinth "from the west and southwest"—as Grant had expected; in the message of the 24th he said, "We are in fine spirits and in good health." (*O.R., 25,* 718–719, 703–704, 711–712.)

45. Davies's report; Rosecrans to Grant, *O.R., 24,* 160–161. Rosecrans's first message ended: "Our men did not act or fight well. I think we shall handle them. We are at the outer line of works."

46. *O.R., 25,* 253, 257, 258.

47. McPherson's report, *O.R., 24,* 367–370; *25,* 257 (Grant's order of Oct. 3 putting McPherson in command of the two-regiment brigades of Col. M. K. Lawler and Col. John D. Stevenson).

48. *O.R., 25,* 251, 255–256, 255; Grant's report.

49. Buford's report, *O.R., 24,* 216–217; Van Dorn's report.

50. Van Dorn's, Rosecrans's, and Davies's reports. The horses of two caissons and two limbers in a battery of the 2nd Division became unmanageable and ran away with their carriages, going through the 12th Illinois, commanded by Col. Augustus L. Chetlain, who was originally the captain of the Galena company which had been drilled by Grant (Chetlain's report, *ibid.,* pp. 284–285).

51. Fuller's and Stanley's reports, *ibid.,* pp. 183–187, 178–182. Stanley challenged a statement Rosecrans made in his *B. and L.* article relative to personal action connected with Robinett, saying, "The lapse of a quarter of a century has certainly made the memory of the worthy general treacherous" (*B. and L.,* II, 759).

52. Hamilton's and Van Dorn's reports; Cummins to Beauregard, *O.R., 24,* 395–397.

53. Stanley's and Hamilton's reports; casualty report, *ibid.,* p. 175; *B. and L.,* II, 748. Rosecrans said in his report, "Thus by noon ended the battle of October 4." On Oct. 23 Davies wrote to Rosecrans about his charge against the 2nd Division and received a reply in which the words "cowardly stampeding" occur. In his congratulatory order of Oct. 25 Rosecrans said, "I desire especially to offer my thanks to General Davies and his division, whose magnificent fighting on the 3rd more than atones for all that was lacking on the 4th." (*O.R., 24,* 267, 172–173.)

54. McPherson's report.

55. Hurlbut's report and order, *ibid.,* pp. 305–307, 308–309; *25,* 259. In

his *Memoirs,* I, 417, Grant indicated that he had notified Rosecrans that Hurlbut would have 4,000 men; in a dispatch to Halleck on Oct. 5 (*O.R., 24,* 155), he said Hurlbut had 5,000 to 6,000, the increase probably being due to the addition of a two-regiment brigade under Col. R. K. Scott.

56. *O.R., 25,* 259. The courier left McPherson's command for Corinth at 8:00 A.M., but before McPherson had personally joined with the two regiments that came from Jackson during the night.

57. Hurlbut's report; Ord's, Veatch's, and Lauman's reports, *O.R., 24,* 302–303, 321–324, 311–313.

58. *Ibid.,* pp. 301–303. Ord said two batteries had been captured.

59. Hurlbut's report; Maj. C. S. Hayes's report, *ibid.,* pp. 320–321.

60. *O.R., 25,* 259; McArthur's report.

61. Pursuit order, *O.R., 25,* 265–266; Hamilton's and Stanley's reports; Rosecrans to McKean, Stanley, and McPherson, *O.R., 25,* 263–265. Hamilton, the senior division commander, said he felt restrained by his instructions from assuming command "so long as the march was without resistance."

62. *O.R., 24,* 162, 161.

63. *Ibid.,* p. 155.

64. *O.R., 25,* 264.

65. McPherson's and Van Dorn's reports; Lawler's report, *O.R., 24,* 372–374.

66. *O.R., 24,* 375–376.

67. *Ibid.,* p. 164; *25,* 262. Referring to Hurlbut, Rosecrans said, "I have ordered rations sent to Cypress for him and have begged him not to return to Bolivar until I can communicate with Sherman; I want him to appear to threaten the enemy." In a dispatch apparently lost, Grant evidently protested Rosecrans's directly communicating with Sherman, which brought from Rosecrans the statement: "I sent word to Hurlbut wishing him to tell Sherman where we were and asking cooperation. I should not think of communicating with him in any official way except through you." In this he not only denied what he had plainly said but made an unchivalrous defense—he had merely tried to get Hurlbut to do what he would not do himself! He also sought to get Grant to adopt irregular procedure when he said in a dispatch at midnight on the 7th, "Appeal to the Governors of the States to rush down some twenty or thirty new regiments to hold our rear and we can make a triumph of our start." (*O.R., 24,* 164–165, 163–164.)

For messages from Rosecrans to Hurlbut, see *O.R., 109,* 287.

68. *O.R., 24,* 170, 163, 441. It is interesting that on Oct. 2 Hurlbut reported to Grant that the united Confederate force at Pocahontas was "probably 18,000 strong" (*O.R., 25,* 253). Grant's reasoning was revealed in his congratulatory order to his troops on Oct. 7, in which he said (*O.R., 24,* 159), "The enemy chose his own time and place of attack, and knowing the troops of the West as he does, and with great facilities for knowing their number, never would have made the attack except with a superior force numerically." The reasoning was correct, but Grant was in error in not knowing that Van Dorn believed he could strike and win at Corinth before all Federal troops in the vicinity could be concentrated.

69. *Ibid.*, pp. 306, 158, 156. Hurlbut reported his return to Bolivar at 9:30 P.M. of the 7th. He spoke of a message from Rosecrans urgently requesting him to proceed south, adding that the state of his command and Grant's "orders had determined the question." There was an interesting postscript: "My surgeons demand ice for the wounded, say for 200 men. Will you order it from Columbus at once?" (*O.R., 25,* 268.)

70. *O.R., 24,* 156. McPherson had four of the regiments drawn from guarding the railroad and Hurlbut had two (Grant's report).

71. Grant to Washburne, July 22, 1862. Quoted from "Grant's letters to Elihu B. Washburne," *Journal of the Illinois State Historical Society,* XLV (1952), 257–261. The letter is not in Wilson, ed., *Grant's Letters to a Friend,* doubtless because more than half of it was devoted to Grant's reply to Washburne's inquiry concerning Capt. Henry S. Fitch, a quartermaster at Memphis.

It was stated *supra,* III, 439, that there was no one better qualified than Halleck for the position of General in Chief at the time he was appointed. Grant's statement supports this position. It should be noted also that he clearly implied Halleck's proper place was not in the field.

72. *Supra,* II, 468; *O.R., 19,* 704, 715; *20,* 382, 383–384, 384–385.

73. Documents in War Records Office, National Archives. The volume of originals of telegrams received for July 19 through Aug. 27, 1862, contains 448 pages. Dates were selected to cover Halleck's first weeks in Washington. No roster of his staff for that period was found, and the one used was for February, 1863. His staff during his first weeks would presumably not have been larger, and might have been smaller.

74. *The Collected Works of Abraham Lincoln,* V, 347–419; *O.R., 24,* 159–160 (Grant's order publishing Lincoln's telegram). For the interval from July 29 to Sept. 12 there are some 170 letters, telegrams, or messages from Lincoln to Cabinet members or other persons in Washington, 37 of them being to Stanton, several of routine character.

75. Federal returns, *O.R., 24,* 173–176 (Corinth: killed, 355; wounded, 1,841; missing, 324), 304 (Hatchie: killed, 46; wounded, 493; missing, 31); Confederate returns, pp. 382–384 (Corinth and the Hatchie: killed, 505; wounded, 2,150; missing, 2,183). Livermore (*Numbers and Losses,* p. 94) accepts the Confederate totals and then makes deductions for the Hatchie. See also *B. and L.,* II, 760.

Rosecrans's medical officer reported (*O.R., 24,* 178), "The loss of the enemy, calculated from the best sources of information within my reach, was, 1,423 buried, 3,000 prisoners, including their wounded left in our hands, and 5,000 wounded taken away and dropped by the road-side; making 9,423 in all." In his report Rosecrans repeated the 1,423 for the enemy killed.

In replying on Oct. 8 to Lincoln's dispatch (*ibid.,* pp. 156–157), Grant greatly exaggerated the enemy loss and understated his own, except for Hurlbut's engagement at the Hatchie.

76. *B. and L.,* II, 755; *O.R., 25,* 276. Grant telegraphed to Halleck on the same day, Oct. 13: "General Rosecrans reports a rumor that Johnston, with 40,000 men, has arrived at Oxford. Should reports prove true I will concentrate my forces at Bolivar and be prepared to meet him." (*Ibid.*)

77. In his advance on Corinth, Van Dorn left Adams's two-regiment cavalry brigade at Davis's Bridge and Hawkins's infantry regiment and a battery on the Bone Yard road. In the retreat he spent the night of the 4th in the vicinity of Chewalla, with the intention of turning to the left through Bone Yard and Kossuth to Rienzi. With this in mind, he ordered Armstrong's and Jackson's brigades (probably four regiments in all) and a battery to Rienzi. He gave up his plan not because it exposed his flank to an attack from Corinth, but because Price represented his troops as somewhat disorganized and advised falling back to Ripley by the route they had used in their advance. His orders countermanding the move to Rienzi reached the cavalry at Kossuth. (*O.R., 24,* 378, 380, 384.)

78. Though Grant's actual instructions to Rosecrans are missing, he said in his report, "I had informed General Rosecrans where Generals Ord and Hurlbut would be, and directed him to follow up the enemy the moment he began to retreat; to follow him to Bolivar if he should fall upon Ord's command and drive it that far."

79. A recent U.S. Army staff manual, *F.M. 100–5,* "Field Service Regulations," states (paragraph 561): "The object of the pursuit is the annihilation of the hostile forces. This can seldom be accomplished by a straight pushing back of the hostile force on their lines of communication. Direct pressure against the retreating force must be combined with an enveloping or encircling maneuver to place troops across the enemy's lines of retreat."

80. Although one cannot tell what maps Rosecrans had, the existence of the road from Bone Yard to Davis's Bridge must have been known to him. Col. Mizner said in his report (*O.R., 24,* 242–245), "On October 1 a portion of the Third Michigan Cavalry, occupying a position near Kossuth, proceeding via Bone Yard to Davis' Bridge were attacked by the enemy's advancing column, and after a stout skirmish the enemy retired." In view of this cavalry operation, it would hardly be favoring Rosecrans to say he did not know that the road through Bone Yard gave a route of advance on Davis's Bridge, and one not much longer than that through Chewalla. Furthermore, Rosecrans said in a dispatch to Grant on Sept. 30 (*O.R., 25,* 243), "My reasons for proposing to put Stanley at or near Kossuth is that he would cover all the Hatchie crossings, except heavy forces as far as Pocahontas." This surely implies knowledge of the road in question.

I am indebted to Charles E. Shedd, Jr., historian of the Shiloh National Military Park, for a report on a personal reconnaissance of the Bone Yard–Davis's Bridge road as it exists today. His observations and inquiries indicate that the present road is about as it was in 1862. The map on p. 100 follows one furnished me by Mr. Shedd, who was able to locate the position of Davis's Bridge, though the structure no longer exists, because the present east-west highway does not follow the State Line road of Civil War days.

81. Since Van Dorn expected the Federals at Bolivar to move out and "dispute the passage of the Hatchie Bridge," one can ask whether he should not have decided to take the Bone Yard–Jonesboro road when he gave up the plan of going to Rienzi. The length of the route, and the fact that Davis's Bridge had already been rebuilt while that at Crum's Mill had not, probably

influenced his decision. One cannot say when he made his second change of plan. But it was 7:30 A.M. of the 5th when Hawkins was ordered to join Adams at the Hatchie (see n. 77) with his regiment and a section of guns, an hour later when he arrived, and three-fourths of an hour before he crossed the river and began to oppose the Federals. This suggests action to open the road and not merely to delay the enemy, and it is difficult to believe that Van Dorn decided to turn southward before the middle of the morning. All his command had been moved forward to oppose Hurlbut except Bowen's brigade, which was the rear guard and covered the crossing of wagons at the Tuscumbia. When Hurlbut stopped advancing—which he put at 3:30 P.M.—Price's two divisions and Rust's brigade of Lovell's division were withdrawn and started toward Bone Yard, Villepigue's brigade being left as "western front" rear guard. It was after sunset when the last wagons crossed the Tuscumbia, whereupon Bowen followed, destroyed the bridge, and joined his division three miles to the west. (*O.R., 24,* 380, 392–393, 380, 306, 388, 406, 413.)

On hearing the firing at Davis's Bridge, Armstrong and Jackson moved in that direction from Kossuth and advanced on the Ripley road to within one and a half miles of Pocahontas. Van Dorn spoke of ordering the cavalry to cover the train, but Jackson indicated no actual contact with it, though he said the move to near Pocahontas—where he reported some skirmishing (probably with the 5th Ohio Cavalry)—was "very favorable to saving the train of wagons." Capt. Cummins, Van Dorn's inspector general, said Armstrong "proved our salvation" by rebuilding the bridge at Crum's Mill. Cummins put Hurlbut's force at 12,000, and Van Dorn may have so appraised it. (*Ibid.,* pp. 384, 380, 321, 396.)

It seems doubtful if any wagons could have reached Bone Yard before afternoon of the 5th or troops in any number before early evening. At the Court of Inquiry into Van Dorn's actions, Bowen—who preferred the charges— said he marched eight miles on the 6th and bivouacked seven miles from Ripley. This would indicate he camped west of the Hatchie on the night of the 6th, as Green, commanding Hébert's division, said he did. It was possibly a picket that crossed the bridge a half-hour before McPherson arrived at noon on the 6th, but which he called the rear guard. (*Ibid.,* pp. 430, 423, 392, 368.)

82. In *Memoirs,* I, 418 (Long, ed., 217), Grant says, "Rosecrans did not start in pursuit till the morning of the 5th and then took the wrong road." Though it is not possible to tell just what road Grant thought Van Dorn used on his retreat, it is clear he did not think it was the direct one to Chewalla.

Mr. Shedd has called my attention to the fact that Badeau makes a statement similar to that of Grant (*Military History of Ulysses S. Grant,* I, 119). Badeau's map shows a road running from Corinth to Davis's Bridge that passes south of Chewalla but considerably north of Bone Yard, and it is probably the one that he and Grant thought Van Dorn used. (The start of the road is indicated on the map in Grant's *Memoirs,* I, 409.) Mr. Shedd could find no basis for the existence of such a road at the time of the battle. If it was there, it was certainly not used by Van Dorn, who definitely went through Chewalla.

NOTES TO CHAPTER V

1. *O.R., 22,* 1090; Joseph Wheeler, "Bragg's Invasion of Kentucky," *B. and L.,* III, 1–25; Horn, *The Army of Tennessee,* pp. 170–171; Henry, *"First With the Most" Forrest,* p. 100. Horn repeats Duke's statement (*Southern Bivouac,* 2nd Series, I, 300) that while Bragg was at Glasgow, Buell made a challenging gesture but Bragg did not take the dare. Neither in his report nor in his *B. and L.* article does Buell indicate he made any move against Glasgow until the afternoon of the 16th, when he found Bragg had left.

2. *O.R., 23,* 830. Smith ended his dispatch by saying he had accumulated sufficient stores "to subsist a large army for some time."

3. *Ibid.,* pp. 841–842, 843, 849. At 1:00 A.M. of the 19th Bragg wrote to Polk that reports from Cave City indicated it was more than probable that Buell was moving his entire force to that place in order to attack. He directed, "Please recall Cheatham's division and be ready to move upon the enemy." Where Cheatham was is not clear, but Polk at once ordered him to return. It must have been soon discovered that Buell's movements were not very serious, for a message to Chalmers from the division adjutant said, "The major-general commanding desires me to say that General Buckner has been ordered to move forward to Cave City and feel the enemy and make the necessary development of his strength, if it is only a small force covering the retreat of Buell's army." (*Ibid.,* pp. 843, 848, 849.)

General Polk's son, chief of artillery in his father's corps, wrote long after the event that Bragg's vacillation at Munfordville between attacking Buell and marching to join Smith was a shock to Bragg's subordinates. He stated that the arrival of Thomas's division on the 20th made Bragg decide not to fight (W. M. Polk, *Leonidas Polk,* II, 130–131). That this is incorrect is proved by the fact that orders were issued on the 19th for Polk's command to march at daylight the next day. The statement (p. 124) that Bragg intended to fight Buell "south of the Cumberland River if possible," is contradicted by Bragg's assertion to Breckinridge that he was headed straight for Kentucky (*supra,* p. 477). Though W. M. Polk could hardly have been biased in favor of Bragg, because of the blame the latter put on his father in connection with Perryville, it is to be noted that he did not criticize Bragg for not having ordered Smith to join him at Munfordville, and did not suggest that Bragg had Buell "in the hollow of his hand."

4. *O.R., 22,* 248, 250; *23,* 876. There is some conflict as to rations at Bowling Green. The commissary of subsistence at Louisville gave the Buell Court of Inquiry an itemized list of what reached Bowling Green after the interruption of the railroad between there and Nashville. It confirms fairly well the report Rousseau made that there were 1,200,000 rations except bread, though not uniformly as to all articles. Rousseau stated he had seized 100 barrels of salt and was sending back to Franklin for $17,000 worth of flour. Darr said that during the four or five days the army was at Bowling Green, it was necessary to bring in wheat to make flour, of which he made sufficient for

400,000 rations. Salt meat was in short supply, but there is no indication of great scarcity of cattle, and Rousseau stated he had ordered fresh beef to be used. Rousseau also indicated in his dispatch of the 13th that he would soon have the fortifications on College Hill repaired and fit for use. (*O.R., 22,* 340; *23,* 512–513; *22,* 606; *23,* 512.)

Bragg's statement in his letter to Cooper of Sept. 25, "Efforts were made to bring Buell to an engagement, but he declined, and it was reported to me he was moving by way of Brownsville to the nearest point on the Ohio," has some support in the message given in the last note that alludes to a possible retreat by Buell.

5. *O.R., 23,* 868.

6. George W. Morgan, "Cumberland Gap," *B. and L.,* III, 62–69; Morgan's report, *O.R., 22,* 992–996; *23,* 839–847. On Sept. 14 McCown wrote to Bragg, "The enemy have blockaded the Gaps through which General Smith passed into Kentucky" (*O.R., 23,* 820–821). See also *ibid.,* pp. 836, 846–847, 853.

Morgan had four brigades. In addition to the six Tennessee regiments (all organized in Kentucky, the 5th and 6th in the winter and spring of 1862) there were four from Kentucky, two from Indiana, and two from Ohio. The three batteries were from Michigan, Ohio, and Wisconsin. With regard to the evacuation Morgan said, "At 8 o'clock that night my command wheeled into column with the coolness and precision of troops on review; and without hurry, without confusion, with no loud commands, but with resolute confidence, the little army, surrounded by peril on every side, set out on its march of more than two hundred miles through the wilderness." (Dyer, *Compendium; O.R., 23,* 7; *B. and L.,* III, 68.)

7. *O.R., 22,* 1091.

8. *Ibid., 23,* 846.

9. *Ibid.,* pp. 845–846.

10. *Ibid.,* pp. 821, 839–840. In a message of the 19th McCown said to Bragg, "The convalescents, with ordnance and money train, left Clinton via Jamestown previous to the evacuation" (of Cumberland Gap). On the same day Jones informed McCown that Brig. Gen. S. B. Maxey was going from Chattanooga to Knoxville with all troops that could be spared for Kentucky and was taking all spare arms. (*Ibid.,* pp. 852–853, 854.)

11. *Ibid.,* pp. 850, 856. Horn states (*op. cit.,* p. 171) that Bragg received a supply train from Smith on the 19th. In his letter of the 19th Smith said he was sending 50 wagons, 30 of which would leave Danville on the 21st loaded with flour and hard bread. He made no reference to a previous train.

12. *Ibid.,* pp. 863–864, 859, 860. On the 21st Smith wrote to Bragg: "My force is now at Georgetown and Paris, and will join you by a rapid march if under existing circumstances you so direct. With the enemy advancing from Covington and the Gap, and Marshall not in supporting distance, a junction with you below Louisville both loses us the valuable stores and supplies captured here and checks the organization of the new levies now in fair progress." He spoke of having halted Cleburne. (*Ibid.,* p. 861.)

13. *Ibid.,* pp. 866, 864, 867.

14. *Ibid.,* pp. 867, 851, 866–867.

15. *Ibid.*, pp. 869–872. In all there are six messages by Smith on the 24th.

16. *Ibid.*, p. 873.

17. *B. and L.*, III, 66–68. Morgan said, "I fully expected to be met by the enemy in force at Proctor, where the deep and abrupt banks would have rendered the passage of the Kentucky River perilous and difficult if disputed." He moved to the river in two columns and got a brigade and a battery over so as to clear the situation if an enemy force were present. He said nothing about having more than his divisional artillery, so the report about thirty-six guns may have meant guns and caissons.

18. *O.R., 23*, 876. In a letter to his wife on the 27th Smith seemed as optimistic about George Morgan's destruction as he had been on the 25th in his message to Marshall, and he alluded to "our brilliant little campaign." Parks places upon Smith the responsibility for Morgan's escape, though he suggests that Bragg could have interfered if he did not wish Smith to make the effort. (Sparks, *General Edmund Kirby Smith, C.S.A.*, pp. 231, 232.)

19. *O.R., 23*, 891–892. On the 24th Smith had told Stevenson, "You will push on with all possible speed, as a big battle must be fought soon near Frankfort." In informing Bragg the next day that he had ordered his entire force to Mount Sterling to intercept Morgan, Smith said he was directing Stevenson to march on Harrodsburg and report to him (Bragg). The order to Stevenson was from Smith's adjutant, and stated that Bragg was menaced by a largely superior force, and that Smith had "this day moved to Mount Sterling." (*Ibid.*, pp. 871, 873, 875.)

20. *Ibid.*, pp. 780, 876, 875.

21. *Ibid.*, pp. 766 (indorsement by Randolph on letter from Marshall of Aug. 19), 868–869, 794–795.

22. *Ibid.*, pp. 836, 841.

23. *Ibid.*, pp. 851, 868–869. Randolph closed his dispatch to Jones, "Confer with Governor Harris, act in concert with him, and be on your guard in listening to the advice of persons exasperated by contact with the disaffected." Jones not only wrote to Harris a dispatch ending, "It will give me pleasure to co-operate with you in the execution of the law," but asked McCown to leave him a letter with his views "about the best way of carrying out conscription." Still believing there were eager, unarmed Kentuckians, he said, "Can any transportation be procured at Knoxville for arms ordered to Kentucky? We shall want all we can get." (*Ibid.*, pp. 862, 857–858.)

On Aug. 27, Jones—an academy classmate of Buell's—congratulated Maxey on the reoccupation of Bridgeport, and said: "Ascertain what has become of the boats which it is reported the enemy had constructed near Stevenson. If they have not been destroyed it is not improbable that they may have been sunk somewhere in the river near by." The next day, in a telegram from Atlanta, Jones informed Cooper that he could have the bridge over the Tennessee River rebuilt in a short time and on reasonable terms. He considered its reconstruction a military necessity and asked if he should have it ordered. An answering dispatch from Richmond on Sept. 2 directed, "Rebuild the bridge at Bridgeport and make arrangements, if possible, with the railroad company to share the cost." In a message to Bragg on the 6th Jones said

Maxey had secured the boats that Buell had had built. (*Ibid.*, pp. 783, 785–786, 794, 798.)

24. *Ibid.*, pp. 894–895, 756, 908–911. In August 1861 Horace Maynard and Nelson were elected over secessionist candidates for the Confederate Congress, but they claimed the election entitled them to sit in the United States Congress because they were elected by loyal men. While Maynard reached Washington and was given a seat in the 37th Congress, Nelson was arrested in Virginia and taken to Richmond, where, after a short imprisonment, he took the oath of allegiance to the Confederate Government and returned home. (Patton, *Unionism and Reconstruction in Tennessee, 1860–1869*, p. 28.)

25. *O.R., 23*, 658.

26. *O.R., 22*, 1009. The opening and only other sentence in Morgan's telegram of June 24 was, "Citizens of Virginia, Kentucky, and Tennessee come in by the dozen to take the oath of allegiance to the United States."

27. *O.R., 23*, 538, 539.

28. *Ibid.*, pp. 549, 554. McKibben ended his telegram, "I shall await orders before leaving." Halleck replied, "You will return to Washington" (*ibid.*, p. 554).

29. *Ibid.*, p. 557. The dispatch was signed by Brig. Gen. W. Scott Ketchum, of the regular army, who was on duty in Springfield.

30. *Ibid.*, p. 555.

31. *Ibid.*, pp. 555, 554. The order recasting the army was issued on Sept. 29, and it must have been an oversight that it did not make Thomas second in command, as was done the next day. In his testimony before the Court, Thomas said, "Whenever we met General Buell was always communicative, and after our arrival at Louisville I think that he explained to me his plan of the campaign as fully as was necessary." (*O.R., 23*, 558–559, 560; *22*, 189.)

In replying to the telegram Buell sent from Bowling Green on the 14th, Halleck made an inaccurate and very unfair statement. The message did not arrive until the 20th, and Halleck said the situation had unquestionably so changed as to make any instructions inapplicable, and that Buell's movement into Kentucky after Bragg had turned his flank was probably the best thing to do. But he feared that, as elsewhere, Buell moved too slowly and would permit the junction of Bragg and Smith before he opened the line to Louisville. Then he said: "The immobility of your army is most surprising. Bragg in the last two months has marched four times the distance you have." Buell replied in very good temper from Louisville on the 25th, the day after Halleck's message arrived, pointing out that his army had marched much farther than Bragg's.

32. *O.R., 23*, 557–558. Davis was a Senator; Crittenden, though distinguished for his service in the Senate, was now in the House.

Jefferson C. Davis was an Indianian who had remained in the army after the Mexican War. He had come to Louisville to take command of his division, which was under Mitchell when it joined Buell, Davis having turned over command in Mississippi because of illness. For some real or fancied neglect of duty that Nelson had assigned him, Davis was sharply reprimanded by that officer, was told to report to Wright, and threatened with arrest if he did not comply.

Upon the arrival of Buell's army at Louisville, Wright directed him to return, which he did by way of Indianapolis, where he was joined by Morton—according to Buell. Early on the 29th Davis accosted Nelson in the Galt House, demanding satisfaction. Nelson struck him in the face, whereupon Davis procured a pistol from some nearby person, followed Nelson, and shot him. According to Col. Fry—who said he had the story from Davis—Nelson first made an insulting reply to Davis's question about satisfaction, causing Davis to flip a crumpled visiting card into Nelson's face, after which there came the slap. (*B. and L.,* III, 43, 60–61.) In his *Annals of the Army of the Cumberland,* Fitch says (p. 169), "After a few days' arrest, he [Davis] was released, much to the gratification of the public, and ordered to report to Cincinnati for duty, where he was assigned to the temporary command of the forces around Newport and Covington."

33. *O.R., 23,* 555, 559.

34. *Ibid.,* p. 556.

35. *O.R., 23,* 547–548, 540, 526, 553; *22,* 1005. No dispatch from Morgan on which Wright could have based his statement seems to be in the record. In a message to Halleck on Aug. 19 (*O.R., 23,* 374) he said that he would not evacuate, but that it would be necessary to act at once to open a road to him, for his supplies were limited. One can understand Morgan's indignation over official and public criticism, but his letter to the Adjutant General of the Army on June 6, 1863, was not well advised. The documents on the evacuation question are *O.R., 22,* 990–1010. Phisterer (*Statistical Record,* p. 272) carries Morgan as resigning on June 8, 1863.

36. *O.R., 23,* 561, 562, 569; *B. and L.,* III, 69; *O.R., 22,* 995.

37. *O.R., 23,* 564, 566. On Oct. 2 Col. Zahm, whose cavalry brigade was convoying the great train that moved through Leitchfield, reported to Fry from the mouth of Salt River that the head of his column had arrived there at 7:30 A.M. and that the first of the three sections would reach Louisville that night. Though proud of the fact that they "had not lost a dollar's worth of property, with the exception of a few broken-down wagons," Zahm said, "I do not ask it as a favor to shoulder such a responsibility very soon again." With regard to an order for his brigade to move to Shepherdsville, he said, "As we are now we are in a poor condition to move against the enemy." (*Ibid.,* pp. 567–568.)

38. *B. and L.,* III, 30 (strength return); *O.R., 23,* 591–596 (roster). The editors of the *O.R.* noted that the strength return *ibid.,* pp. 562–564, while purportedly for Sept. 30, is probably for an earlier date and does not conform with the roster.

It is impossible to reconcile various strength figures. In a dispatch to Halleck on Sept. 27 from Louisville, Wright said he had collected 45,000 to 50,000 men at that place, and had left in Cincinnati "only about ten raw and indifferent regiments." According to Maj. J. M. Wright, Buell's adjutant, about 45,000 men arrived at Louisville from Nashville, giving a total at Louisville of 90,000 to 95,000. Taking the force that marched out on Oct. 2 at 60,000 (Maj. Wright said 58,000, including Sill), and Dumont's division at 15,000 (his strength seems nowhere mentioned, but his regiments being new it should have been large), a balance of 15,000 to 20,000 remains. But Boyle reported only

3,800 men left in Louisville after Dumont's departure. (*O.R., 23*, 550–551; *22*, 659, 660; *23*, 589.)

In his article "Bragg's Invasion of Kentucky" (*B. and L.*, III, 1–25) Wheeler gives the force at Cincinnati as 45,000 and at Louisville as 30,000 but probably has many men counted at both places. His figure of 54,000 for Buell's army as it arrived in Louisville, cannot be accepted. His total, including Morgan, of 137,282 is probably about 37,000 too large. It might be added that on Oct. 1 Wright informed Buell he had only 10,000 raw troops in Cincinnati with which to advance. (*O.R., 23*, 561.)

39. *O.R., 23*, 542–543. Wheeler states (*op. cit.*, p. 12) that Kirby Smith took 10,000 to Kentucky, though Smith reported he had "about 12,000 effective men," he puts Marshall at 2,160, while Smith put him at 3,000; he gives Stevenson 7,500, though Bragg gave him 8,000; he says John Morgan had 1,300, while Duke wrote in his article "Morgan's Cavalry During the Bragg Invasion" that Morgan returned to Tennessee nearly 2,000 strong. Wheeler completely omits Maxey, whom Smith put at 2,000 at the time that he placed other raw recruits at 1,200 (*O.R., 23*, 905). Taking Bragg's present-for-duty 31,884 at the time he crossed the Tennessee, we get a total of 60,084. It is impossible to estimate the number of men sick or the deserters, but they, as well as battle casualties, were probably more than offset by new enlistments. Wheeler's total of 48,776 is certainly to be rejected. W. M. Polk quotes Smith as saying that the Confederates could have put 60,000 veterans in line of battle (*op. cit.*, p. 164).

40. *O.R., 23*, 565; *22*, 143; Sheridan, *Memoirs*, I, 193; *O.R., 23*, 575.

41. Gilbert's and Mitchell's reports, *O.R., 22*, 1072–1074, 1076–1079; *23*, 578–579.

42. *O.R., 23*, 580–581.

43. *Ibid.*, p. 580.

44. *Ibid.*, pp. 587–588; McCook's report, *O.R., 22*, 1038–1044. The dispatch to McCook of Oct. 7, 8:00 P.M., though referred to by McCook, seems missing, but it is safe to assume it was similar to that sent to Crittenden; and McCook said (*ibid.*, p. 104) that it induced him to believe Buell meant to attack the enemy at Perryville.

45. *O.R., 23*, 587.

46. Livermore, *Numbers and Losses*, p. 95; *B. and L.*, III, 30.

47. *O.R., 23*, 840, 846, 895.

48. *O.R., 110*, 358–361, 363–365, 367–368.

49. *O.R., 23*, 897, 901, 903–904, 905.

50. *O.R., 23*, 915; *22*, 1095; W. M. Polk, *op. cit.*, p. 149.

51. *O.R., 23*, 919–924. A dispatch from Smith's chief of staff to Stevenson at Versailles said, "Have the country in your front immediately and thoroughly reconnoitered, with a view of fighting the enemy there."

Kirby Smith's dispatches bear the heading McCown's Ferry, but according to William R. Townsend, of Lexington, Ky., the pioneer family of Woodford County spelled the name McCoun.

52. *O.R., 22*, 1095–1096, 1099.

53. Gilbert's, Sheridan's, and Col. McCook's reports, *ibid.*, pp. 1072–1074,

1081–1082, 1083–1085; Gilbert's article "On the Field of Perryville," *B. and L.,* III, 52–59; Sheridan's *Memoirs,* I, 193–195; Mitchell's report. In his testimony before the Court, Gen. McCook said (*O.R., 22,* 114): "The bed of Chaplin River is a very deep one. It was dry with the exception of water standing in pools." Some of the reports indicate that the order to seize the pools in Doctor's Creek originated with Buell. According to Mitchell, it was 2 o'clock when he advanced to the position indicated by Gilbert.

54. Don Carlos Buell, "East Tennessee and the Campaign of Perryville," *B. and L.,* III, 31–35, especially p. 48; *O.R., 22,* 90, 275.

The Second Corps was certainly not pushed, for Crittenden said to the Court: "We marched at 7 with the First Division; at 9 the Second Division was marched; and at 11 General Wood's Division, which had been all night getting into camp, marched, being put in the rear again in order that the men might rest. We reached Perryville with the First Division about 10 or 11 o'clock." In his message at 3:00 A.M. Thomas gave no indication that troops were still on the road, though he said somewhat ambiguously, "Reached this place at 11 o'clock last night, but all the trains are not up yet."

Both in his reports and in his order congratulating his command, Wheeler said he charged the Federal cavalry covering the advance on the Lebanon-Perryville road, routing it, pursuing it, and driving it under cover of infantry. (*O.R., 22,* 897; *23,* 976–977.)

55. *O.R., 22,* 187, 276. Mack said, "While I was going to General Buell's headquarters and while I remained there I heard heavy firing, and I supposed there was an action going on until I reached his headquarters, and was there informed that it was the cavalry under Captain Gay and the rebels, with artillery on both sides."

The fact that the brigade of cavalry with Gilbert's corps was commanded by a captain was an anomalous arrangement. On Sept. 17 Wright directed Nelson, "Make Gay your chief of cavalry, and thus put him in control of that arm." The colonels of the three regiments seemed to acquiesce under the belief that he had been recommended for a brigadiership. (*O.R., 23,* 523; *22,* 661.) He was never so commissioned, and the *Register of Graduates* of West Point indicates that Ebenezer Gay of the class of 1855 was dismissed from the Army in 1869 when a major, was reappointed in 1870, and honorably resigned in 1871.

Col. McCook, in alluding to Gay's work on the morning of the 8th, called him "General Gay."

56. *O.R., 22,* 1022–1023. Thomas's statement (*ibid.,* p. 187) that Mack was back about noon cannot be accepted in view of the latter's more detailed testimony.

57. *Ibid.,* pp. 90, 1040; Polk's report, *ibid.,* 1109–1112. Because he knew he was greatly outnumbered, Polk had planned to fight a "defensive-offensive" battle, until Bragg arrived and gave explicit orders for an attack, leaving him, however, to conduct it. Accounts of the battle from the Confederate standpoint are given by Horn, *op. cit.,* pp. 183–185, and W. M. Polk, *op. cit.,* II, 153–158.

58. McCook's, Rousseau's, and Starkweather's reports, *O.R., 22,* 1038–1044, 1044–1049, 1155–1156.

59. Oldershaw's (adjutant of Jackson's division) report, *ibid.,* pp. 1059–

1062; Rousseau's report, Gooding's and Steedman's reports, *ibid.,* pp. 1079–1081, 1075–1076.

60. Sheridan's and Mitchell's reports. In his report Buell praised Carlin's exploit, but he did not mention it either in the paper he presented to the Court or in his *B. and L.* article. Carlin's success showed that the enemy was not in strength in the center, and Buell said in his article that it was supposed the entire enemy force was in front. Yet McCook testified, "I asked Colonel Fry who was down in Perryville. He replied Hardee was there with two divisions."

Carlin, a native of Illinois, had graduated from West Point in 1850, and had attained a captaincy when he accepted the colonelcy of the 38th Illinois on Aug. 15, 1861. He commanded at Ironton for some weeks that fall and had a brigade the next spring in Steele's advance into Arkansas (*supra,* III, 295). In May he was sent to Pope's army before Corinth. (Fitch, *Annals of the Army of the Potomac,* pp. 225–229.)

61. *O.R., 22,* 235–238. Wagner said, "Colonel Carlin took position on my left."

O.R., Atlas, Plate XXIV–2, gives a map of the Perryville battlefield, "surveyed and compiled" by Thomas's order. It is not dated but gives the new Mackville pike with the notation "constructed since the battle." It not only indicates heavy Confederate forces in front of Crittenden, but shows Van Cleve's division of Crittenden's corps as on the right of Carlin's brigade in the evening of the 8th. The Federal troop indications are clearly for brigades, and it can be assumed that the same was intended for the Confederates. Twenty Confederate brigades are shown, while only eleven infantry brigades and two small cavalry brigades were present. As to Van Cleve, it is to be noted that he made no report and did not testify before the Buell Commission. Nothing in the *O.R.* seems to justify the evening position assigned him.

The map in *B. and L.,* III, 24, is essentially a reproduction of the Thomas map, and is the basis for the map *supra* p. 131, except for the positions on the Federal right and the Confederate left, and the insertion of two brigades of Schoepf's division, which were not in action except for one regiment, and which would seem to have been somewhere behind Sheridan. The position of a Confederate brigade north of Perryville is doubtful. The map given by W. M. Polk, *op. cit.,* II, opposite p. 151, shows initial positions of all 11 Confederate brigades, but evening positions of only eight.

62. *O.R., 23,* 976–977; *22,* 464, 577. See also Wheeler's report, *ibid.,* p. 898.

Neither the judge advocate nor any member of the Commission appears to have asked Thomas, Crittenden, Wood, or Smith (Van Cleve, commander of the remaining division of the corps, did not testify) anything about reconnaissance during the day, or enemy activity in their front.

When queried as to how long he could have remained in line without advancing to get water, Crittenden replied: "My own forces had an abundant supply of water the night before. They had been ordered to supply themselves and fill their canteens. I do not think my own forces suffered particularly for want of water that day. I do not know how long we could have staid there without water; not a great while certainly." (*O.R., 22,* 556.)

63. *Ibid.,* pp. 656, 660, 51. Seitz (*Braxton Bragg,* pp. 200–201) increases the distance of Buell's headquarters from the action to five miles, and recalls that Grant when in front of Iuka did not know a battle was in progress "but seven miles away." The cases were entirely different. Grant did not even hear artillery fire; Buell did. Furthermore, Buell's entire army was easily accessible to him, while very difficult country and the enemy separated Grant from Rosecrans. Grant was compelled to rely on sound; Buell was not.

The Commission held that Buell was culpable for not being on the field in person or taking better precautions to assure transmission of information, and it held McCook equally blameworthy for not instantly reporting the heavy attack.

64. Merrill's and Wright's testimony, *O.R., 22,* 505–513, 655–656. See also J. Montgomery Wright, "Notes of a Staff-Officer at Perryville," *B. and L.,* III, 60–61, in which he makes the amazing statement, "At one bound my horse carried me from stillness into the uproar of battle." In both places he says that Fry did not tell him that McCook was in great difficulty when he sent him to Gilbert with instructions to send two brigades to McCook.

Col. Daniel McCook testified (*O.R., 22,* 240–241) that he was satisfied that at about 2:15 P.M. a dispatch reporting the attack went through the signal office at Rousseau's, and Merrill stated he had seen such an assertion "in what purported to be a letter written by Col. Dan McCook to his brother, in which he repeated this message."

Gilbert said in his report, "The officers of the signal corps rendered ready and useful service all day on the 7th and 8th," which supports the statement of Sheridan, though Merrill presented no messages between Sheridan and Gilbert.

65. Capt. Fitzhugh's testimony, *O.R., 22,* 667–670. In his article "Morgan's Cavalry During the Bragg Invasion," *B. and L.,* III, 26–28, Brig. Gen. Basil W. Duke not only noted the opportunity there was to destroy the Confederate forces attacking at Perryville, but the chance that would have been open on the 9th to deal with those to the north, saying that "nothing but disaster could have befallen the Confederates."

W. M. Polk said (*op. cit.,* II, 157) that if Sheridan had shown but half of the enterprise that characterized his subsequent behavior he could have blighted Polk's triumph almost before it began. While it is of course true that Sheridan had not reached his full development, it must be remembered that he was acting under orders from others. But the remark shows how vulnerable the Confederates were.

When speaking of the situation on the left, McCook said, "The moon came up, a bright moon, and they could have fought as well as by day" (*O.R., 22,* 99).

66. *O.R., 22,* 670. Both Thomas and Crittenden (who said Thomas was with him or in his sight until late in the day or night) tried to obtain from Gilbert an explanation of the heavy artillery fire, but got nothing indicating that McCook had been badly defeated. Crittenden stated (*ibid.,* p. 528) that at 4 o'clock he received a note from Gilbert saying, "The noise you hear on the left is from McCook," and that he added, "in a vein of pleasantry," "My

children are all quiet, and by sunset we will have them in bed and nicely tucked up, as we used to do in Corinth." Crittenden did not present the amazing dispatch, but said he had it "somewhere."

Fitzhugh stated that Thomas directed him "to tell General Buell that the enemy were in strong force right in his front, and that an advance of 100 yards on his part would bring on an engagement along the whole line." He also said Smith told him the enemy "had thirty pieces of artillery right on his front."

In commenting on Fitzhugh's testimony, Buell stressed that he did not criticize Thomas for not attacking at night. His 6:30 message, though apparently not in the *O.R.*, is in his *B. and L.* article.

67. *O.R., 22,* 1036, 1112; *23,* 574, 589. The low stage of the Ohio River was shown by Wright's saying to Morgan in a telegram on the 4th (*ibid.,* p. 573) that he could not send boats to bring him to Cincinnati because the river was too low.

68. *O.R., 23,* 589. Pressure to send the Kentucky and Tennessee regiments elsewhere continued, Congressman Maynard and ultimately Gov. Andrew Johnson intervening. When asked by Wright for a special report on those regiments, Morgan said the Kentucky units were all well commanded and would do good service wherever sent. He described the East Tennesseans as brave and anxious to learn, but clannish and given to imagining slights when none was intended. His statement, "All of these troops detest Western Virginia and prefer a campaign in Kentucky," was doubtless responsible for Wright's reporting it would be judicious to withdraw them, as was presently done. (*Ibid.,* pp. 604, 634–635, 651, 609–610, 635.)

69. *O.R., 22,* 536, 510. The message is given as Crittenden presented it to the Commission; as Merrill gave it, the words "advance division" occurred in place of "different divisions." In his *B. and L.* article Buell leaves the impression that the words "ready to" were due to Thomas, but it is impossible to believe they were not stipulated by Buell, for his 6:30 message used the words "prepared to attack," although no attack was ordered.

70. W. M. Polk, *op. cit.,* II, 159; *O.R., 23,* 927, 602. In his *B. and L.* article Buell stated that it was learned in Perryville that only three enemy divisions had been in the battle.

In his *The Army under Buell,* Fry wrote (p. 62), "Knowing that the rebel forces were concentrated at Harrodsburg, Buell waited until Sill's division joined him. . . ." Buell did not *know* the Confederates were concentrated; he merely feared they were, and gave them time to do so. Fry does not reveal that Buell was not on the field on Oct. 8 and knew nothing of the battle until 4:30; nor does he attempt an explanation as to why Crittenden was not engaged. His own record would have been better if he had not written his little book.

71. Polk, *op. cit.,* II, 163; Seitz, *op. cit.,* pp. 206–207.

72. *O.R., 23,* 887, 879, 605–606, 606, 608.

73. *O.R., 23,* 609; *22,* 12.

74. *O.R., 23,* 619, 623.

75. *Ibid.,* pp. 625, 621–622, 626–627.

76. *Ibid.*, pp. 627–628.

77. *O.R.*, 22, 1149. In addition to his own report, Cruft submitted one by a board of officers. The Confederates lost no time trying to get salt, Morgan writing to Fry on Aug. 24 (*O.R.*, 23, 411), "The enemy has sent 200 wagons to Goose Creek Salt-Works. Of that number 100 were captured between Cumberland Ford and London."

78. *O.R.*, 23, 634.

79. *Ibid.*, pp. 636–637. Death sentences for civil crimes were carried out without reference to Washington. George Morgan wrote (*B. and L.*, III, 68) that as the Gap was being evacuated, a soldier was shot for murdering a comrade in cold blood a day or so before.

80. *O.R.*, 23, 638.

81. *Ibid.*, p. 639.

82. *Ibid.*, p. 642.

83. *Ibid.*, pp. 650, 641–642, 642.

84. *Ibid.*, p. 652. Washington dispatches of the 24th told of the replacement of Buell by Rosecrans.

The *N.Y. Tribune* of Oct. 28 carried a dispatch of the 27th from Washington, reading, "If half the charges made against Gen. Buell which are made in private letters from his officers are true, he ought to be court-martialed at once." Gen. Steedman testified that some sort of a protest against Buell was sent to Lincoln after Perryville, signed by 21 or 31 regimental commanders (*O.R.*, 22, 135–136).

85. *O.R.*, 23, 655.

86. Holland, *Morgan and His Raiders*, pp. 154–158.

87. *O.R.*, 23, 640–641.

88. *O.R.*, 23, 634, 876–877; 22, 1020–1021; 23, 980–981, 976. See also Horn, *op. cit.*, p. 189 (saying Polk took the army by rail to Murfreesboro), W. M. Polk, *op. cit.*, II, 165 (saying Bragg made the transfer).

89. *Supra*, pp. 9–10. Bragg's subsequent effort to shift blame to Polk was very discreditable. See *O.R.*, 22, 1088–1107. Hardee forwarded a letter Bragg wrote to him on Apr. 13, 1863, to Polk with an indorsement that ended, "If you choose to rip up the Kentucky campaign you can tear Bragg to tatters" (*ibid.*, p. 1098). He certainly had in mind what happened subsequent to arrival at Bardstown, where, as previously noted, he spoke of affairs being "prosperous." Even in his note to Bragg on Oct. 7, he spoke of success as being certain if Bragg united his forces. See also Horn, *op. cit.*, pp. 190–191, and W. M. Polk, *op. cit.*, II, 165–167.

90. *O.R.*, 22, 525. Italics supplied.

91. In his *Indiana Politics During the Civil War*, Stampp says (p. 160), "Besides falling victim to civilian meddling and western discontent, Buell was something of a scapegoat for disappointed Union party politicians." In her *Veterans in Politics*, Mary A. Dearing states (p. 12) that the Committee on the Conduct of the War "caused Buell's dismissal."

NOTES TO CHAPTER VI

1. *O.R., 25,* 279, 291. The order forming the Department of the Tennessee and assigning Grant to command was dated Oct. 16, 1862. The department included Cairo, Forts Henry and Donelson, northern Mississippi, and the portions of Kentucky and Tennessee west of the Tennessee River. A copy of the order may not have reached Grant for some days, for his order taking command was not issued until the 25th. (*Ibid.,* pp. 278, 294.)

Grant's dispatch to Halleck (*ibid.,* p. 290) of 10:00 A.M., Oct. 23, reporting enemy reenforcements and ending, "Is it not probable that Bragg will come this way?" may have been sent after receipt of Rosecrans's message.

2. *Ibid.,* pp. 290, 283. Rosecrans ended his telegram of the 23rd, referring to Bragg, "Please answer my personal dispatch."

3. *Ibid.,* pp. 286–287.

4. *O.R., 109,* 295.

5. *Ibid.*

6. *O.R., 25,* 307–308, 858–859; Grant, *Memoirs,* I, 420 (Long, ed., p. 418). Sherman's statement that Hillyer and Lagow were in Memphis indicates that Hillyer must have been the bearer of his own letter. Sherman gave no indication of a discussion of the Rosecrans case.

7. *Supra,* III, 58, 90, 187, 465–466, 491, McClernand to Lincoln, June 20, 1862, Robert Todd Lincoln Collection, Vol. LXVII.

8. Horan and Swiggett, *The Pinkerton Story,* p. 120.

9. *O.R., 25,* 849–853. The original is in the Robert Todd Lincoln Collection and bears the indorsement, "Gen. McClernand's plan for putting down the rebellion." It ends with the statement that the views in the letter and the accompanying map were "deferentially and distrustfully submitted." As given in the *O.R.* the final adverb is omitted.

10. *O.R., 25,* 274–275. In a communication to Stanton on Oct. 15, McClernand put the infantry force desired at 24,000, with enough other troops to bring the expedition up to approximately 30,000. A message to Halleck the next day repeated this, and said he was writing "at the instance of the Secretary of War." He stated that he was advised that an expedition would be put on foot immediately upon the Mississippi but did not say he was to have any connection with it. (*Ibid.,* pp. 277–278, 852.)

11. *Ibid.,* p. 282.

12. *Ibid.,* p. 502.

13. For Grant to Washburne, July 22, 1862, see n. 71, Chap. IV; *O.R., 25,* 296, 296–297. In a dispatch of the 17th (*ibid.,* p. 279) Grant gave his effective strength as 48,000 with a breakdown at four locations.

14. *O.R., 25,* 900–901.

15. *O.R. Navies,* Ser. I, XXIII, 377, 380–381.

16. *O.R., 19,* 656, 667–668. The telegram of the 22nd revoking the leave was addressed to Keokuk, Iowa. Curtis was certainly in St. Louis when Grant was in the city on the 25th.

17. Phelps to Halleck, Sept. 28, *ibid.*, pp. 683–684; Thomas L. Snead, "The Conquest of Arkansas," *B. and L.*, III, 441–459, especially pp. 443–445; *O.R., 19,* 560–561, 557–558; *O.R. Navies,* Ser. I, XXIII, 580–581.

18. *O.R., 19,* 671.

19. *O.R., 19,* 670, 673; *8,* 69–70.

20. *O.R., 19,* 685.

21. *Ibid.*, pp. 698, 702. On Oct. 1 Curtis informed Schofield (*ibid.*, p. 695) that Phelps had telegraphed to him from Cairo, urging him to cancel the order for Steele's move, and said he was not countermanding it, but hoped Steele was "moving up so I can have more force for your army and that in the southeast of this State."

22. *Ibid.*, pp. 702, 632. The apprehension that existed is shown by dispatches on Sept. 29 and Oct. 2 from Brig. Gen. John W. Davidson at St. Louis to Col. Chester Harding, Jr., at Pilot Knob. They dealt with disbanding militia units and concentration of other forces. (*Ibid.*, pp. 689, 703.) That an effort was made to make administration efficient was shown by the attachment of Alton, Ill., to the Department of the Missouri. Prisoners were confined there.

23. Curtis to Schofield and Schofield to Curtis, *ibid.*, pp. 23, 25, 25–28, 932–933, 648–649, 650. On Sept. 17 Schofield said in a dispatch to Halleck, "If General Steele's force is not strong enough to move from Helena would it not be well to bring it up to Cape Girardeau and let it move from that point? This would enable me to take the aggressive immediately." (*Ibid.*, p. 646.)

24. Cooper's report, *O.R., 19,* 296–300; Snead, *op. cit.*, p. 446; Federal reports, *O.R., 19,* 287–296; *ibid.*, p. 18 (Schofield's statement that about 4,500 Federals were engaged), p. 299 (Cooper's statement that not over 4,000 Confederates were involved). Salomon put the Confederates at 7,000; Cooper said the Federals had 6,000 (*ibid.*, pp. 287, 299). For an account of the Newtonia engagement, see also O'Flaherty, *General Jo Shelby,* pp. 124–126. In Monaghan's *Civil War on the Western Border,* the backgrounds and characteristics of commanders are discussed as well as operations.

25. *O.R., 19,* 19, 710–711.

26. *Ibid.*, pp. 19–20, 754–755 (Schofield's operation order); Blunt's report, *ibid.*, pp. 325–328. Totten, a West Point graduate, was a brigadier general in the Missouri militia, and presumably had some militia regiments. Herron's command included the 7th Missouri Militia Cavalry, which Schofield complimented highly.

A vivid picture of conditions in Missouri was given by James B. Eads in a letter to Totten from Sedalia on June 17, in which he said, "No man's life is safe, and we are liable to be shot by the infuriated troops or bushwhackers at any time." He pleaded for disciplined troops. (*Ibid.*, pp. 435–437.)

27. *Ibid.*, pp. 891–892. One might temper his judgment on the way in which Curtis was deceived if he recalls that American operations in World War II were influenced by the purely fanciful belief that the Germans intended to retire into a Mountain Redoubt (Bradley, *A Soldier's Story,* pp. 536–537.)

28. *O.R., 25,* 285–286; *117,* 642–643 (Gov. Gamble to Curtis, Oct. 22); *25,* 279–280. Gamble praised Edwin Price for observing his parole, and said he had promised to return home and use his influence to keep people at peace

with the government. On Gamble's representation, Price was given a full pardon by Lincoln on Nov. 21 (*O.R., 117*, 742).

29. *O.R., 25*, 281, 668–669, 289–290; *24*, 461–463 (Grierson's report). The force that attacked Island No. 10 got close to the Federal camp at about 4:00 A.M. When a Union sentinel discharged his piece, the rear of the attacking column fired upon the front, whereupon the front, believing it was attacked by Federals in the rear, returned the compliment, and a general panic followed. Faulkner and some of the force were captured during a pursuit. (*O.R., 24*, 460–461.)

Halleck replied to Grant that he knew nothing of "Falkner" and left the case with him. Faulkner was sent to Alton, but escaped on Nov. 15 while being transferred to Johnson's Island in Lake Erie. There is a little confusion in the *O.R.* between the two partisans, and the case is complicated by the fact that in 1863, after Falkner had resigned, Faulkner went to Mississippi, and Falkner's son subsequently changed the spelling of his name to Faulkner. (*O.R., 25*, 283; *118*, 99; Andrew Brown, "The First Mississippi Partisan Rangers," *Civil War History*, I, 371–399, particularly, p. 388, n. 59.)

30. *O.R., 25*, 287–288. Sherman said that cannon and musket balls had been fired through steamers having women and children aboard. In a letter of Sept. 24 to Col. C. C. Walcutt he spoke of the packet *Eugene* being fired upon while carrying women, children, and merchandise. In his letter to Rawlins of Nov. 1 he said, "I shall enforce the banishment of the proscribed families, because if we must fight for the river we cannot afford to do it for the benefit of the families of men in open hostility. I have thrown the onus on them." In replying on Nov. 7 to a protest against the removal order by Mrs. Valeria Hurlbut of Memphis, he said lives had been taken of persons not engaged in the war, and made the strong statement, "The absolute destruction of Memphis, New Orleans, and every city, town, and hamlet of the South would not be too severe a punishment to a people for attempting to interfere with the navigation of the Mississippi." He called his removal measure mild. (*Ibid.*, pp. 235–236, 857–858, 860.)

31. *O.R., 19*, 747–748, 742–743. In his letter to Curtis Sherman named three boats fired upon from the Arkansas shore, the boats being engaged exclusively in private business, "in no way connected with the Government or the Army."

32. *O.R., 25*, 272–274.

33. *Ibid.*, pp. 288–289, 856, 856–857. On Oct. 25 Sherman issued a new order on military government that said, "The interest and laws of the United States must be paramount to all others, but so far as the laws, ordinances, and performances of the people of this community are consistent with those of the General Government they should be respected" (*ibid.*, pp. 294–296).

34. *Ibid.*, pp. 298, 307–308.

35. *Ibid.*, p. 300.

36. *O.R., 24*, 466–467; *25*, 312; *24*, 467; *19*, 761.

37. *O.R., 19*, 773, 773–774. A Sempronius H. Boyd was commanding and enrolling militia in the vicinity of Greenville, Mo. On Nov. 1 Curtis telegraphed to Steele at Ironton: "Boyd's movement must be supported. Go forward with

your command, except such as may be unfit for service." Steele promptly replied: "Please explain what you mean by Boyd's movement. The only movement of Boyd's that I know of is to get himself elected to Congress." (*Ibid.*, pp. 613, 773.)

38. *Ibid.*, pp. 768, 771. O'Flaherty states (*op. cit.*, pp. 121–122) that in early October the time was ripe for a Confederate thrust at Helena, and asserts that if Shelby had been a general—he was a colonel—such a move would have been made. There is no question that Shelby, who was under Hindman, was an extremely able officer. In the article previously cited, Snead refers to Shelby as "one of the best officers I have ever known," and his judgment is not to be in the least discounted. But O'Flaherty's discussion of a complex question is neither complete nor convincing. He does not state how strong or how well equipped a force could have moved against Helena. While he cites authority for a strength of 50,000 on the part of Holmes in three states, he gives nothing that will challenge Schofield's statement that the enemy's "large mass of conscripts had not yet received arms," and that his own command, though smaller, was "more formidable."

It would have taken a long time to cover the 250 miles from Newtonia, where O'Flaherty notes Shelby was on Sept. 28, to Helena. The logistical problem was simply ignored, as well as the fact that the Federal force at Helena did not remain at the 3,000 figure that O'Flaherty puts down. O'Flaherty states that if Helena had been gained, the Confederates might have been able to send 30,000 to 40,000 men to the east of the Mississippi, as Price had taken 5,000 to Corinth. (Van Dorn and Price took 15,000 to 20,000 men across the river.) This overlooks the Federal gunboats which controlled the Mississippi to the mouth of the Yazoo. (When Van Dorn crossed that was not the case, for a considerable Confederate fleet was based on Memphis. The naval battle at Memphis had greatly changed the situation.) Ascribing Curtis's attitude on Oct. 2 as in any way the result of the fact that he "was due for promotion soon and would be leaving anyway," ignores hard facts. Curtis had been made a major general on Mar. 21, was assigned to command of the Department of the Missouri on Sept. 19, 1862, assumed command on the 24th, and held it until May 24, 1863.

39. For references to sickness of the Helena command, see *O.R.*, *19*, 738–739, 746, 747, 752.

40. *O.R.*, *25*, 279–280; J. C. Pemberton, *Pemberton, Defender of Vicksburg*, pp. 29–32; *O.R.*, *25*, 716–717. The order establishing the new department and putting Pemberton in command was issued Oct. 1 (*ibid.*, p. 718).

41. *Ibid.*, pp. 285–286, 288–289, 290, 318, 327–328. (See also a 15-minute earlier dispatch from McPherson, *O.R.*, *24*, 486–487.) On Oct. 12 Rosecrans sent Stanton a map of Corinth and vicinity, speaking in his accompanying letter of the shortage of maps and topographical engineers. He said that after he had a map made he resorted to the services of an "improvised photographer, who, taking likenesses, was required to provide himself with the means of copying maps as the tax for the privilege of staying in camp." (*O.R.*, *25*, 286.)

42. *O.R.*, *25*, 328, 331, 380; J. C. Pemberton, *op. cit.*, p. 14. A dispatch

of Nov. 8 to Price from an aide of Pemberton's refers to the latter as a lieutenant general (*ibid.*, pp. 902–903).

43. Wilson, *The Life of John A. Rawlins*, pp. 99–101, 103; *O.R., 25*, 347–348. A number of dispatches from La Grange show that Grant was not in Memphis on Nov. 8 or near that date. A letter to Sherman on the 10th (*O.R., 25*, 335–336) proves that he had not seen Sherman recently.

44. The War Department order assigning Wilson to Grant's command is not in the *O.R.*, but it would seem that it was issued after McClernand's request of Oct. 15 for Wilson's assignment to him.

45. *O.R., 25*, 322–323, 327; *24*, 468.

46. *O.R., 24*, 468–469. On Oct. 30 Halleck had directed Wright at Cincinnati to send available troops to Grant at Columbus; after receiving Grant's dispatch he wired to Wright to send them to Memphis (*O.R., 23*, 656; *25*, 335).

47. *O.R., 25*, 902. For the near-capture incident, see *supra*, III, 432. The description of Jackson as a general but without initials was based on Grant's statement in his *Memoirs*. Grant met Jackson after the war and of course used the highest rank he attained. Jackson was a Tennessean and graduated from West Point in 1856.

48. Eaton, *Grant, Lincoln and the Freedmen*, p. 5. The preface of this book, which was written by Ethel Osgood Mason, daughter of a close friend of Eaton, gives a biography of Eaton that was drawn upon in this and the next paragraph.

49. Eaton, *op. cit.*, pp. 5, 9–11, 20–21, xix–xxii; *O.R., 109*, 301–302.

50. *O.R., 25*, 330, 315, 337.

51. *O.R., 25*, 140–141; *123*, 349; *19*, 552–553, 783–784. In a letter to the Adjutant General of the Army, dated Aug. 11, a copy of which was sent to Grant, Sherman said: "This cotton order is worse to us than a defeat. The country will swarm with dishonest Jews who will smuggle powder, pistols, percussion-caps, etc., in spite of all the guards and precautions we can give. Honest men can buy all the cotton accessible to us with Tennessee bank notes." (*O.R., 123*, 350.) The order which Sherman protested both to Secretary Chase and to the Adjutant General provided for payment for cotton with gold, silver, and Treasury notes. Tennessee bank notes would not have had much value abroad for the purchase of munitions.

52. *O.R., 25*, 326–327, 319–320, 335, 336. Grant's order of Nov. 7 stated that the acts of vandalism which he enumerated were punishable by death under the "articles of War and existing orders," and he said further, "They are calculated to destroy the efficiency of an army and to make open enemies of those who before, if not friends, were at least non-combatants." In an order two days later (*ibid.*, pp. 331–332) he directed that payment be assessed on divisions if a smaller unit or the guilty parties could not be identified. When offences could be traced to individuals, they were to be tried by a general court-martial and the severest penalties provided were to be "imposed and executed." The admonition ended: "This order will be read on dress-parades before each regiment or detachment for three successive evenings."

53. *O.R., 19*, 787.

54. *O.R., 25*, 347–348; Sherman, *Memoirs*, I, 270 (dispatch to Sherman

from La Grange on the 15th—doubtless telegraphed to Columbus and by boat from there—directing Sherman to meet him in Columbus "on Thursday next"— the 20th); Thorndike, ed., *The Sherman Letters,* p. 168 (letter from Sherman to his brother dated Memphis the 24th, saying he was just back from Columbus where he had gone to meet Grant); *O.R., 24,* 471 (Halleck to Grant and answer); *25,* 356 (Porter to Grant, Nov. 22).

In his postwar reminiscences Porter describes his first meeting with Grant at Cairo on the headquarters boat of Capt. McAllister, Cairo quartermaster, in the latter part of November. It must have been about the 21st, on the occasion of Grant's trip to Columbus to see Sherman. Porter states that Grant said he would immediately write to Sherman to have 30,000 men ready for a river movement against Vicksburg the moment Porter got to Memphis with gunboats, and that Grant said, "General Joe Johnston is near Vicksburg with forty thousand men, besides the garrison of the place under General Pemberton." (Porter, *Incidents and Anecdotes of the Civil War,* p. 125.) Grant of course never made such statements and Porter was ascribing to November later situations. In the case of Johnston he anticipated by six months. His book, though entertaining, is not trustworthy.

55. *O.R., 25,* 364, 337–338 (strength return, Sherman's, McPherson's, and Hamilton's forces); Sherman to his brother, Nov. 24 and Dec. 6 (his own expected strength and estimated enemy strength), Thorndike, ed., *op. cit.,* pp. 168, 170; *O.R., 25,* 366–367. There seem to be no Confederate strength returns, but in a dispatch to Bragg on Dec. 4 Pemberton spoke of having about 21,000 effectives with him (*ibid.,* p. 778).

56. *O.R., 24,* 471.

57. Reports by Steele, Hovey, and Washburn, *ibid.,* pp. 528–539. Cadwallader Washburn had been a Congressman from Wisconsin at the same time Elihu was representing the Galena, Ill., district, and a third brother, Israel, was representing one in Maine.

The movement from Helena toward Grenada was in part due to confusion and misunderstanding in Washington. In a letter of Nov. 27 Steele said to Curtis that it was made on the basis of a letter Sherman had written after an interview with Grant, as well as a communication from Curtis to Hovey. On Dec. 4 Halleck telegraphed to Curtis: "I regret very much that you have moved General Steele into Mississippi without authority. It seriously interferes with operations ordered by the President. . . ." Greatly surprised, Curtis wrote at length the same day, "I carefully planned at your suggestion a move on Grenada, and sent General Washburn with careful instructions as to how it should be executed if you sent me permission; also writing General Hovey. This was about the 8th of November, and I informed you, asking if the blow should be struck. You did not respond, and so the matter rested." (*O.R., 24,* 529; *25,* 382, 383–384.)

In a letter of the 12th Halleck told Curtis that his explanation was satisfactory and said the language of his own telegram of Nov. 3 was "perhaps a little ambiguous," but that it was not intended to authorize the sending of troops to Grenada. The first object of the concentration at Helena had been, Halleck said, the capture of Little Rock, continuously urged upon him for the last six months. If that were not possible, the troops might cooperate with Grant, but it was not intended that they be sent to Grenada, as "the President had directed that all available troops on the Mississippi be sent to another place." The unexpected move of troops toward Grenada had, Halleck said, put him in the position of not being able to "carry out the President's wishes either by moving the Helena forces on Little Rock or down the Mississippi River." (*O.R., 25,* 401–402.)

Halleck's dispatch of Nov. 3 read: "Let me know immediately what forces you send to Helena and when they will reach that point. If they cannot move on Little Rock they must co-operate with General Grant against Grenada. No troops not absolutely necessary will be kept in Missouri." It certainly would have been better if Curtis had not moved without a definite answer from Halleck to his dispatch of the 6th, which, without saying whether a move on Little Rock was or was not possible, asked, "Shall I destroy railroad at Grenada if I can?" A second message describing his plan indicated that he would do nothing without express approval. (*O.R., 19,* 778; *25,* 321, 322.)

Lincoln's ideas about Little Rock and the McClernand matter were probably not too clear, and in his letter to Curtis, Halleck explained another difficulty: "The movements on the Western rivers are frequently determined on by the joint action of the War and Navy Departments, and it sometimes happens that I can give no answer to the proposed plans of our generals in the West." Though this may have been in part an excuse, a difficulty certainly existed over which Halleck had no control. How the operations along the Mississippi would have been planned if there had been no intrusion by McClernand, it is impossible to say.

58. *O.R., 24,* 472, 505, 503.

59. *O.R., 24,* 472; *25,* 386. The telegraph superintendent J. C. Van Duzer was the subject of several telegrams to and from Washington. On Dec. 3 Grant sent a long letter to Col. Kelton of Halleck's staff, explaining why he had arrested and confined Van Duzer. The difficulty had begun on Nov. 26 when Grant learned that dispatches he had had delivered to the telegraph office in the morning were not sent until 10 o'clock at night. The wires had been down for about three hours, but the operator explained that "other offices were sending cotton-dispatches." Upon this Grant informed Van Duzer in writing that orders forbidding "the transmission of commercial or private dispatches over the telegraph lines" to Cairo, except before 10:00 A.M., were still in force and would be observed. Apparently by way of reprisal, Van Duzer removed the operator who had given the explanation to Grant, whereupon Grant told Van Duzer he would have no one about the office who would not let him know "when dispatches could not be sent and the reason why." On the 28th Col. Stager, the general superintendent of telegraphs, sent operators a message to take orders from Van Duzer and to obey no orders "from any other source." The usually mild general was aroused as he seldom was, and he telegraphed to Stager, "Your insolent dispatch to telegraph operators in this department just received. My orders must be obeyed and Mr. Van Duzer removed and some one else appointed to fill his place. I send Van Duzer out immediately." (*Ibid.,* pp. 377–379, 368.)

On Dec. 8 Sam Bruch at Louisville transmitted to Stager a telegram Van Duzer had sent him from St. Louis. He wanted to return but said he "must have safe-conduct of War Department or General Grant will shoot me" (*ibid.*, p. 394). Apparently the war ran along without "Van"—as Bruch called him—after that, though he reappeared later.

There was an exchange of dispatches on the subject between Grant and Assistant Secretary of War P. H. Watson on Nov. 14, and an operator named Schermerhorn reported on Dec. 5 that the telegraph men were dissatisfied and wanted to leave. (*Ibid.*, pp. 346, 347, 385–386.)

60. *O.R.*, 24, 473.

61. *Ibid.*, pp. 473–474, 474. Grant's order to Sherman (*ibid.*, p. 601) clearly set forth Sherman's mission. As soon as possible he was to proceed to the vicinity of Vicksburg and with the cooperation of Porter's gunboat fleet reduce the position in such manner as circumstances and Sherman's judgment might dictate.

Sherman gives (*op. cit.*, I, 281) a letter not in the *O.R.* that he received on the 8th from Grant, in which, after quoting Halleck's telegram, Grant said, "I wish you would come over this evening and stay to-night, or come in the morning. I would like to talk with you about this matter. . . ." Grant sketched two plans, the first being to send two divisions back to Memphis to operate down the river, and he said he favored it. His telegram to Halleck of 9:00 A.M. shows he soon made his decision. The order given Sherman was in accordance with the conclusions reached in the conference.

62. *O.R.*, 25, 392.

63. *Ibid.*, pp. 392–393.

64. *O.R.*, 24, 474, 475.

65. *O.R.*, 25, 396, 410, 406–407. In a letter to Halleck on Dec. 4, Curtis said, "I will send General Steele with the troops and place General Gorman in command at Helena, hoping he will make a better administrative officer than General Steele, and believing General Steele will prefer to go with troops." Steele indicated a personal desire for field duty, but ended, "All I ask is that I may not be prejudiced by *ex-parte* presentations on my acts and intentions." (*Ibid.*, p. 383.)

66. *Ibid.*, p. 395; reports on Battle of Prairie Grove, *O.R.*, 32, 68–158. See also Snead, *op. cit.*, pp. 449–450; O'Flaherty, *op. cit.*, pp. 134–146; Monaghan, *op. cit.*, pp. 265–271. On Nov. 28 Blunt had had an engagement with the enemy at Cane Hill, in which he reported success (*O.R.*, 32, 43–46). On Nov. 29 Herron's cavalry returned to Springfield after a 250-mile march of five days to and from Yellville, Ark., where an arsenal and storehouses were destroyed, 100 good horses seized, and the patients in a hospital paroled (*ibid.*, pp. 38–39). In all cases Curtis issued prompt congratulations to his commanders.

67. *O.R.*, 25, 390–391, 397, 407. None of the Tennessee regiments that had been with Morgan at Cumberland Gap were now with him, but he still had two Ohio, two Kentucky, and one Indiana regiment of his old division.

68. *Ibid.*, pp. 397, 399, 413–414.

69. *O.R.*, 24, 474, 473, 475; 25, 399, 400. With respect to his agents, Haynie said, "They are citizen scouts, but are reliable and active. I have furnished them

arms. They are away from home and need subsistence. May I issue to them?"

70. *O.R., 25,* 380–381, 405, 404. On Dec. 5 the commander at Humboldt wrote apprehensively about pretended deserters and others who took an oath of allegiance. He feared they were building up a band of guerrillas within Federal lines (*ibid.,* p. 388).

71. *Ibid.,* p. 405.

72. *Ibid.,* p. 411.

73. *Ibid.,* pp. 410, 411. Grant's instructions to Dodge said, "Your troops should be instructed to be back within six days, and to run no risk of being cut off" (*ibid.,* p. 411).

For the organization of the cavalry division, see Dickey's order of Nov. 25 (*ibid.,* pp. 363–364). See also Grant's previous instructions to Dickey (*ibid.,* pp. 388, 395, 399, 403). Dodge sent two regiments totaling 1,000 men, hauling them in wagons (*ibid.,* pp. 403–404).

74. *O.R., 24,* 600–601; *25,* 412. Sherman reported he had reached Memphis at noon on the 12th, the day he wrote.

75. *O.R., 25,* 414, 415. While Grant said it was to be hoped that there would be no trouble in getting possession of the Helena troops, Sherman was to "be prepared to act positively if necessary." In a dispatch to Rawlins on the 13th Sherman had expressed doubt as to whether Halleck's order covered the Helena troops inasmuch as they had returned to that place. On the 12th Sherman sent an aide to Helena to bring back full information (*ibid.,* pp. 408, 402–403).

76. *O.R., 24,* 476.

77. *O.R., 25,* 420.

78. *Ibid.,* p. 421.

79. *Ibid.,* p. 423.

80. *Ibid.,* pp. 421, 423–424.

81. *Ibid.,* p. 423.

82. *Ibid.,* p. 422.

83. *Ibid.,* pp. 422–423, 423.

84. Eaton, *op. cit.,* pp. 26–27. The order is not in the *O.R.,* nor was it found in Grant's headquarters records in the Manuscripts Division of the Library of Congress, but there would seem to be no question about its issuance. What Eaton gives on pp. 20 and 21 as special orders are essentially paragraphs in special orders found in the headquarters records.

85. *O.R., 25,* 424, 421–422. The order appears with Holly Springs as place of issue, but as found in the headquarters records it carries the heading Oxford, as do all of Grant's dispatches on the 17th. The number on the order in the headquarters records is 12, not 11, as it is in the *O.R.* The difference is accounted for by the fact that G.O. 9 was not issued. It had been drawn up at La Grange on Nov. 23, but the headquarters records carry the statement "Recalled—will not be issued." There are also some textual differences between the expulsion order as given in the *O.R.* and in the headquarters records, the chief one being in the sentence in which the 24-hour limit appears. Renumbering on account of the unissued order and inserting the Eaton order gives fourteen general orders for Grant for the year as department commander. This harmonizes with the last one which is given in *O.R., 17,* 461.

86. *O.R., 25,* 506 (D. Wolff & Bros., C. F. Kaswell, and J. W. Kaswell to Lincoln, Paducah, Dec. 29, 1862); Korn, *American Jewry and the Civil War,* pp. 140–144, 146; Jesse R. Grant to Elihu Washburne, Covington, Ky., Jan. 20, 1863, Washburne Papers, Vol. XXIX.

Jesse Grant's letter begins, "I went down to Dixie about the 13th of Dec. & staid until the 5th inst." This does not fix the date of arrival or departure from Oxford, but a letter U. S. Grant wrote to his sister from that place on Dec. 15 said he had learned by telegraph that their father was at Holly Springs, and he spoke of his wife also being there. As he expected the railroad to be completed to Oxford "by tomorrow," he looked for them to come down. Eaton states that the general's father and wife left Oxford on the same train with him after Van Dorn's Holly Springs raid of Dec. 20. He states that Jesse Grant stopped with him at his headquarters at Grand Junction, but does not say how long. Korn implies that Jesse Grant was at Oxford from Dec. 15 to Jan. 5, and specifically says that the expulsion order had already been revoked on the latter date. Halleck's telegram directing that it be rescinded was sent on Jan. 4, and Grant's order doing so was issued on the 7th, so it appears certain that Jesse Grant heard no talk at headquarters occasioned by Halleck's dispatch. (Cramer, ed., *Letters of Grant,* pp. 95–96; Eaton, *op. cit.,* pp. 28–29; Korn, *op. cit.,* pp. 141, 280; *O.R., 25,* 530, 544.)

Jesse Grant's comment in his letter to Washburne about the expulsion order was casual. After a rather full discussion of matters in his son's department (he emphasized the extent to which Grant was living on the country), he said, "That Jew order so much harped on in congress was issued on express instructions from Washington." He did not cite his son as authority, and when speaking of his son's intentions, Jesse Grant once used the words, "I then thought," and at another time, "I think it probable," which suggest that there had been reticence on the general's part. It is highly improbable that Jesse Grant knew anything about the message that had been sent to Webster on Nov. 10.

The quotation that Korn gives from a letter to the *Cincinnati Commercial* by a writer who signed himself merely "Gentile," and who said he had heard Grant read a telegram from Washington on the evening of Dec. 17 directing the issuance of an order, must be regarded as highly suspect. It would have been out of character for Grant to read official telegrams from Washington aloud in the presence of civilians. Grant's order, furthermore, went beyond what the person said he had heard read—there was to be expulsion beyond Grant's "lines" (not department), and only Jews who could not give satisfactory evidence of their honesty of intentions were to be evicted. If such a directive had been sent to Grant, it would in all likelihood also have been sent to Curtis because of the Helena situation, but Curtis issued no order on the subject. Korn quotes from a newspaper letter that Rawlins wrote six years later that has Grant impelled to the issuance of the order by mail he received from Washington on Dec. 17. This is far different than saying there had been a specific telegraphic directive. The explanation that Sylvanus Cadwallader gave years afterward will be noted later.

87. The Wolff-Kaswell telegram to Lincoln was vigorous and ended, "We respectfully ask for immediate instructions to be sent to the commander of this post."

I think that Korn is not justified in saying that the letter to Wolcott proves that Grant was "eager" to use any means of ridding himself of the Jews. Unquestionably the letter was outspoken, but the concluding sentence pronounced *all traders* a curse, and indicated that Grant would have liked to get rid of *every one* of them. In his discussion of the expulsion order Korn makes no reference to the contraband order, though they both dealt with the same large problem.

88. *O.R., 25,* 363, 352. Sherman said he was constructing a kind of pontoon train for Hovey and one for himself.

89. *O.R., 25,* 428; *24,* 551. In an earlier dispatch Sullivan had said his preparations for defense were good, that he could hold Jackson against 10,000, and meet and whip the enemy if he were 5,000 strong. Replying to Grant's dispatch, he said in a telegram at 5:00 P.M., "Want of information from Colonel Ingersoll as to direction the enemy are marching keeps me still." (*O.R., 25,* 430.)

90. *O.R., 24,* 568 (Fuller's report); *25,* 426.

91. *O.R., 25,* 428.

92. *Ibid.,* p. 327.

93. *Ibid.,* pp. 372, 365.

94. *Ibid.,* pp. 342, 343.

95. *Ibid.,* pp. 343, 343–344.

96. *Ibid.,* p. 380.

97. Wilson, ed., *Grant's Letters to a Friend,* pp. 18–22; *O.R., 24,* 469–470, 470. The letter to Washburne refers to Lincoln's close friend Leonard Swett, with whom Grant had had unhappy relations while at Cairo because of Swett's connections with contractors and speculators. The editor added an interesting note.

98. *O.R., 24,* 470; *25,* 352–353.

99. Lewis, *Captain Sam Grant,* pp. 336–337. In a letter to his sister from Cairo on Sept. 25, 1861, Grant spoke of Allen being chief quartermaster in St. Louis and said: "Father remembers his father well. He is a son of old Irish Jimmy, as he used to be called about Georgetown to distinguish him from the other two Jimmy Allens. He is a friend of mine also." (Cramer, ed., *Letters of Grant,* pp. 59–63.)

100. *O.R., 25,* 355–356, 355.

101. *Ibid.,* p. 433.

102. *O.R., 117,* 731, 747. The cartel on the exchange and parole of prisoners (*ibid.,* pp. 266–268) had been signed on July 22, 1862, at Haxall's Landing on the James River, Maj. Gen. John A. Dix being the representative for the United States and Maj. Gen. D. H. Hill the representative for the Confederacy. It was published to the army on Sept. 24 as General Order 139 for 1862.

103. *O.R., 118,* 27, 32. The two places for the exchange or parole of prisoners named in Article 7 of the cartel were Dutch Gap on the James (replaced presently by City Point) and Vicksburg. The last sentence of the article read, "But nothing in this article contained shall prevent the commanders of two opposing armies from exchanging prisoners or releasing them on parole from other points mutually agreed on by said commanders." (The word "contained" seems misplaced but appears as given in both the *O.R.* and the G.O.)

The article did not allow battlefield paroling, but the practice was carried on by both sides. Even the statement "No paroling on the battle-field" in U.S. War Department G.O. 49, of Feb. 28, 1863 (*O.R., 118,* 306–307) was not effective, and the subject was to be dealt with more strictly in G.O. 307 of July 3 (*O.R., 119,* 78–79).

104. *O.R., 118,* 83–84. Grant evidently had not received a copy of the circular issued by the Federal agent for exchange on Nov. 20 that specifically stated that the Confederate Partisan Rangers would be exchanged when captured (*O.R., 117,* 739).

In his report to President Davis on Jan. 3, 1863, Secretary Seddon said with regard to the Partisan Rangers, "They have not unfrequently excited more odium and done more damage with friends than enemies" (*O.R., 123,* 289).

105. Fiske, *The Mississippi Valley in the Civil War,* p. 188. I find no dispatch from Halleck specifically answering Grant's message of Oct. 26 about completely giving up Corinth; Fiske perhaps inferred one into existence. Grant may have himself decided to hold the place; he certainly used most of the garrison in his advance—three divisions, according to his telegram to Halleck on Nov. 2. As early as Nov. 18 Grant was calling on Dodge for reports about the enemy, a dispatch of that day reading, "Can you get information from the East, say as far as Florence? I want to hear from along the Tennessee from Tuscumbia eastward to know if any rebel troops are crossing there." On Dec. 14 Dodge sent Grant the report of a reconnaissance that had penetrated Alabama a distance of 100 miles and had "ascertained that none of Bragg's army had gone to either Columbus or Meridian by way of the east road." The message ended, "The scout was a very daring and successful one, and settles the flying reports from that quarter." Grant considered it so important that he forwarded it to Halleck. (*O.R., 25,* 353; *24,* 475–476.)

106. *O.R., 109,* 313–314.

NOTES TO CHAPTER VII

1. *O.R., 24,* 476; *25,* 432–433; *23,* 641–642. General Order No. 14 (*O.R., 25,* 461), dated Holly Springs, Dec. 22, carried out the division of Grant's command into the four corps with the commanders mentioned in the War Department order of the 18th. As communications were broken on the 19th, the Washington order must have come by telegraph. The perplexing thing is that all of Grant's special orders and special field orders for the remainder of 1862, as well as Special Field Order No. 2, Jan. 2, 1863 (*ibid.,* p. 523), carried the designation Hdqrs. 13th A.C., Dept. of the Tenn., a strange heading to use after the issuance of G.O. 14.

2. *O.R., 109,* 313–314. Wallace had been assigned to Grant on Oct. 30 (*O.R., 25,* 308) but was reassigned to the Buell Commission.

3. *O.R., 25,* 425.

4. *Ibid.* The War Department order numbering corps and assigning commanders could not have yet been received, or Grant would surely have told Sherman that he was to have the 15th Corps and McClernand the 13th.

5. *O.R.*, *24*, 593 (Forrest's report); *25*, 435–436. In a message to McPherson on the 19th Grant spoke of Halleck's telegram being received "late last night" (*ibid.*, pp. 435–436). Gen. Fuller speaks of Forrest "fortunately" cutting the telegraph (*The Generalship of Ulysses S. Grant*, p. 128).

6. *O.R.*, *25*, 437.

7. *Ibid.*, pp. 437, 439. The Jackson referred to had been made Van Dorn's chief of cavalry on Oct. 16. The order referred to him as a colonel, but Sherman spoke of him as a general on Oct. 29, and Joseph E. Johnston explicitly stated he was a brigadier on Jan. 2, 1863 (*ibid.*, pp. 729, 854, 820).

8. *D.A.B.* (for characterization of Dickey); Dickey's report, *O.R.*, *24*, 496–499. Dickey said, "In six days we marched about 200 miles, worked two days at the railroad, captured about 150 prisoners, destroyed 34 miles of important railroad, and a large amount of public stores of the enemy, and returned passing around an enemy of nine to our one [he put the Confederate strength at 6,000 or 7,000], and reached camp without having a man killed, wounded, or captured."

The couriers who got lost constituted Dickey's second effort to inform Grant about the hostile column, the first having been made at Pontotoc; but when he went into camp he found to his surprise "that the escort and couriers by a fatal misapprehension" of his orders had not left the column.

W. H. L. Wallace spoke of the good work of Dickey and the 4th Illinois Cavalry in the advance on Fort Donelson (*O.R.*, *7*, 192). For an interesting incident of Dickey's connection with Lincoln in 1854, see the opening paragraph in Monaghan's *Civil War on the Western Border*.

9. *O.R.*, *25*, 439, 436. In his report Dickey said he arrived at 5:30 P.M. of the 19th and that notice of the large enemy force "was at once telegraphed to every point on the railroad north of us." The report was dated Dec. 20.

10. *Ibid.*, pp. 757–758, 787–788. Johnston was in Richmond when the order was issued that placed him in command in the West, and on the same day he wrote Cooper a letter saying that Holmes had in the Trans-Mississippi Department a force "very much larger than that of the United States," while the two Confederate armies east of the Mississippi were not only separated by the Tennessee but by Grant's army, "larger probably than either of them." (The statement about the Federal force west of the Mississippi could have been little more than a conjecture, and Holmes would certainly have disputed it.) Johnston wanted Holmes to unite with Pemberton and fall upon Grant, with some help from Bragg "if practicable." With Grant disposed of, Holmes could return and "move into Missouri." (*Ibid.*, p. 758.)

On Nov. 19 Cooper had informed Holmes that Vicksburg was in danger, and had asked, "Can you send troops from your command—say 10,000—to operate either opposite to Vicksburg or to cross the river?" On the same day Cooper misrepresented what he had done by telling Bragg that he had "requested" Holmes to send 10,000, while he told Pemberton he had "ordered" him to do so. On the 26th Cooper had a reply from Holmes saying he could not reach Vicksburg in two weeks, that there was nothing to subsist on en route, and that the Federal force at Helena would take Little Rock. After repeating on the 28th to Holmes his "proposal" about aid to Vicksburg, Cooper did the next day send through Pemberton an actual order to Holmes, adding, "The case is urgent and will not admit of delay." (*Ibid.*, pp. 753, 752, 753, 758, 765–766, 768.)

On Dec. 8 Richmond received a telegram from Holmes dated the 5th saying that two-thirds of his force was in northwest Arkansas and that he expected a fight daily. He further insisted that not a Federal soldier had left Helena though the force there had been raised to 25,000. In a long letter of the 5th Holmes went into details. In a telegram of the 8th that reached Richmond the next day, he spoke of a Federal demonstration against the Post of Arkansas that had failed, and said he was preparing to send a force of 6,000 men to Vicksburg under H. E. McCulloch, though it would not arrive for 30 days. To the warning, "Then the enemy has us at his discretion," he added, "Solemnly, under the circumstances, I regard the movement as equivalent to abandoning Arkansas." On the 11th Cooper told Holmes to use his discretion, but said that if he could give aid to Vicksburg, it was "hoped" he "would do so." (*Ibid.*, pp. 782–783, 783–784, 787–788, 793.)

11. *O.R.*, 25, 769, 755; 30, 441. That the 1,000 men that Bragg spoke of were in addition to the brigade is shown by his statement in a letter to Davis on Nov. 24, "I have ordered about 1,000 men from here to fill Pemberton's Tennessee regiments. . . ." (*ibid.*, p. 423). The brigade sent was Vaughn's (*O.R.*, 25, 773, Forney to Pemberton).

12. *O.R.*, 30, 421–423.

13. *O.R.*, 25, 788–792.

14. *O.R.*, 25, 759–761, 794–796. The homesickness of Price's Missourians was partly relieved by home letters brought by Absolom Grimes, a voluntary and resourceful mail agent. In 1910–1911 Grimes dictated an account of his experiences to his daughter, basing it upon a sort of shorthand notes he had kept. Subsequent to his death the narrative was edited by M. M. Quaife and published under the title *Absolom Grimes, Confederate Mail Runner*. It is very interesting, but in addition to being probably harmlessly embellished, it is not free of revealing errors. Grimes recounts (pp. 50–51) how he left St. Louis with his second mail on May 1, 1862, and in the course of his efforts to reach Fort Pillow observed the Federal operations against Island No. 10, which he categorically says was then in Confederate hands. The island had been captured by Pope on Apr. 8 (*supra*, III, 396–400). The error could not have been in the time of Grimes's second trip, for he states that he had started northward from Rienzi, Miss., on Apr. 15, with a consignment of letters from Price's men.

15. *O.R.*, 30, 449–450. Davis concluded his dispatch, "The feeling in East Tennessee and North Alabama is far from what we desire. There is some hostility, and much want of confidence in our strength."

Johnston's statement, in his *Narrative of Military Operations* (pp. 151–152), that Davis specified that Stevenson's division and a brigade of McCown's should be sent to Mississippi is not in strict agreement with the order he issued on Dec. 15. This said that under the President's instructions, four brigades of Kirby Smith's corps, then some ten miles east of Murfreesboro, should be detached under the command of Stevenson "to re-enforce temporarily the army in Mississippi." Then followed the sentence, "The brigades will be designated by Lieutenant-General Smith." (*O.R., 110,* 397.)

16. *O.R., 25,* 798, 800.

17. *Ibid.,* p. 441.

18. *O.R., 21,* 613–614, 610. From newspapers Butler had learned that Banks was coming, but he believed that he himself was to remain in command of the department, with Banks assigned a special project. The prospect did not please him, and on Nov. 29 he wrote a long letter to Lincoln (*O.R., 111,* 543–544), not as "Chief Magistrate and Commander-in-Chief, but as both friend and just man." He recounted his achievements, said he had eaten what had been set before him without complaint and did not now complain. He declared he had the kindest feelings for Banks, who had been his friend for years, but said the department should be under one head. For a refutation of Butler's claim that he was the senior general in the service, see n. 12 of the Appendix.

19. *O.R., 21,* 590–591.

20. *Ibid.,* pp. 609, 613–614. In his letter to Halleck (*ibid.,* pp. 602–603), Butler said the enemy had "concentrated a large force, not less probably than 10,000 men—some excellent authorities stating the numbers as high as 15,000—at Port Hudson. The position is naturally a strong one, stronger even, it is believed, than Vicksburg. The design of the enemy is to fight the great battle for the possession of the Mississippi at that point. For the want of a sufficient land force—the Navy says they must have 10,000 at least—I have been compelled to postpone a projected attack upon the position. It might have been taken by five regiments four weeks since had I had troops sufficient to hold it."

In a dispatch to Price on Aug. 11 Van Dorn (then at Jackson and in command in Mississippi) said: "Very important to secure mouth of Red River. Can you not, therefore, send Breckinridge a brigade to make sure?" In a message to President Davis the same day, he said: "Hope to establish batteries at Port Hudson. Can you order me more heavy guns?" On Aug. 18 Brig. Gen. John S. Bowen was assigned to command; on Aug. 31 there were present a staff, two infantry regiments, 6 artillery companies, and two Partisan Rangers companies, with a total of 1,175; on Oct. 24 there were 2,412 (including a regiment and a battalion of heavy artillery and some light artillery); on Dec. 3 Pemberton reported to Bragg the number of effectives as 4,500. (*O.R., 25,* 675; *110,* 340; *21,* 801, 804, 841; *25,* 778.) Negroes were of course used extensively in constructing the works.

21. *O.R., 25,* 444.

22. Grant, *Memoirs,* I, 434 (Long, ed., p. 226); Mudd's report, *O.R., 24,* 512–514. As to supply depots, see Rawlins to Quartermaster Reynolds (*O.R., 25,* 380).

23. Mudd's report; Wirtz's report, *O.R., 24,* 510–511. Wirtz stated that the destruction of the hospital was in direct violation of a promise given by Van Dorn's adjutant. He also said that an attempt was made to destroy the general hospital, located on the main square, which contained over 500 sick.

24. Murphy's report, *O.R., 24,* 508–509; Mudd's report. On Dec. 23 Grant issued at Holly Springs an order that condemned the surrender of the town

and referred to the warning that had been "given of the advance of the enemy northward the evening previous." He characterized the conduct of officers and men who accepted parole as "highly reprehensible and, to say the least, thoughtless." He praised the 2nd Illinois Cavalry. In a letter to Kelton on the 25th he spoke of the information brought by Dickey, saying he at once sent out a warning. He stated that Holly Springs was taken while the "troops were quietly in bed," Murphy not having notified a single officer of approaching danger. (*Ibid.*, pp. 515–516, 477–478.) That Murphy was himself not captured in bed is proved by the telegrams he sent that morning before the attack.

On Jan. 8, 1863, Grant issued an order discharging Murphy, giving an impressive list of specifications against him, and saying circumstances made a court martial impractical. A War Department order followed two days later. (*Ibid.*, p. 516.)

On Jan. 2 a Court of Inquiry was ordered to investigate the behavior of the 109th Illinois Infantry at Holly Springs. An order of Feb. 1 exonerated "the regiment, as a regiment, from all suspicion of disloyalty," but dismissed eight officers. The findings were too favorable, for the regiment was disbanded on Apr. 10, 1863, after having lost 347 men by desertion. Company K, which had competent officers, was transferred to the 11th Illinois. The *Chicago Tribune* referred to the 109th as virtually a branch of the Knights of the Golden Circle. (*O.R., 25,* 523, 586–587, 590–591; Horan, *Confederate Agent,* p. 18.)

That Murphy's previous action at Iuka had occasioned considerable talk was shown by Davies's statement in a telegraphic report to Halleck on the Holly Springs affair on Dec. 25: "Murphy, of Iuka fame, was in command" (*O.R., 25,* 479).

In his report Murphy spoke of a telegram received from Rawlins the night before. Presumably *after* Grant had sent the general warning, he wired to Murphy to send out cavalry and watch Jackson's movements, saying Jackson would probably camp that night (Dec. 19) at Rocky Ford. Murphy replied that he did not know where Rocky Ford was. Grant then described its location and said, "In the morning will be early enough for your cavalry to start, and then go due east from Holly Springs to watch the enemy." (*O.R., 25,* 439–440.) This message in no way relieved Murphy of the duty of preparing to defend his position "at all hazards."

In 1901 J. C. Deupree, one of Van Dorn's men, published an article, "The Capture of Holly Springs, Miss., Dec. 20, 1862," in the *Publications of the Mississippi Historical Society* (VI, 49–51). He states that Mrs. Grant was in the town at the time of the raid but that she was not disturbed. Out of gratitude, Grant, according to Deupree, directed that the house should be held inviolate throughout the war. The order was respected, and hard-pressed Confederates often found sanctuary there. It is a good story, but it must be rejected.

Gen. U. S. Grant, 3rd, has told me that he had heard his grandmother tell that she had gone with her four-year-old son Jesse from Holly Springs to Oxford on the afternoon of Dec. 19. She was accompanied by Mrs. Hillyer, wife of Grant's aide, and they reached Oxford late in the afternoon, about the time that Col. Dickey brought warning of Van Dorn's column. Mrs. Grant's carriage at Holly Springs was burned and her horses were taken, but the woman with whom she had been staying protected her personal baggage. The later recollections of Jesse Root Grant seem to have been inaccurate as to the hour of departure from Holly Springs, but confirm the fact that he and his mother were not in the town at the time of the raid (*In the Days of My Father,* p. 14).

It should be noted that in his letter of Dec. 15, 1862, to his sister, in which he said he expected his wife to come to Oxford the next day (*supra,* p. 513), Grant spoke with concern about the railroad that formed his line of supply running for 190 miles through enemy country, or at least through territory occupied by embittered and hostile people.

25. *O.R., 25,* 443, 448, 442, 443; *24,* 518 (Grierson's report). In replying to Mizner's explanation of his march, Grant said he would feel insecure with Mizner in command, because of his reluctance to leave Oxford and his lack of alacrity in obeying orders (*O.R., 25,* 448).

26. *O.R., 25,* 449, 457.

27. *O.R., 25,* 449; *24,* 503.

28. Morgan's report, *O.R., 24,* 521–523. Morgan's regiment had been in the Ord-Hurlbut column that won the fight for the bridge over the Hatchie River on Oct. 5. The report of Maj. Hayes of the 6th Ohio Cavalry spoke of "the small village of Metamora, situated on the river above Davis's Bridge," and Hurlbut spoke of the "field of Metamora" in his congratulatory order (*ibid.,* pp. 320, 308).

29. *O.R., 25,* 459, 458; *24,* 518–520 (Grierson's report).

30. Grierson's report. In a telegram to Sullivan on the 24th Brayman said: "Better still. The 12th Michigan beat them off before the cavalry arrived, killing a dozen and wounding more. The rebels fled toward Saulsbury and the Jay-hawkers are after them." On the 22nd Marsh reported to Grant from Grand Junction that the 12th Michigan had repulsed Van Dorn that morning, taking some prisoners (*O.R., 25,* 476, 454).

31. *O.R., 25,* 465, 474–475, 475, 814 (Pemberton's strength return for Dec. 31, which gives the cavalry 3,853 men present for duty). On the 24th Brayman wired to Sullivan from Bolivar: "Colonels Grierson and Lee are here with 1,500 cavalry and will pursue until they overtake the enemy. I join the pursuit." In a second dispatch from Saulsbury, Grierson informed Grant that scouts had brought word an hour before that the enemy had departed and that he would follow in an hour. (*Ibid.,* p. 475.)

32. *O.R., 25,* 484; *24,* 502–503 (Hatch's report). In his dispatch Mizner said Van Dorn had left his camp two miles south of Saulsbury at 8:00 P.M. of the 24th and that he had not been able to get close enough to engage him. Grierson complained in his report that Lee held back on the 24th, taking time to reconnoiter ground over which he himself "had passed with all due caution two hours previously." He also said that Mizner "with some hesitation" gave him permission to take the lead on the 25th with the 6th Illinois, when the horses of the 3rd Michigan showed fatigue. At Ripley he met a detachment of the 2nd Illinois, under Maj. Mudd, that had come directly from Holly Springs.

33. *O.R., 25,* 808 (Loring to Pemberton), 498–499 (Mizner to Grant). The heading "Jackson" on Loring's one-sentence telegram announcing the

arrival of Van Dorn and his command at 4 o'clock, is clearly an error. On p. 807 there is a dispatch from Loring on the 28th headed "Grenada."

34. *O.R.*, 25, 446.

35. *Ibid.*, pp. 445, 442–443.

36. Grant, *Memoirs*, I, 435–436 (Long, ed., pp. 226–227); Winther, ed., *With Sherman to the Sea* (letters and diaries of Theodore F. Upson), p. 40.

37. *O.R.*, 25, 451; 451–452; 24, 477. On the 25th Dodge reported, "I heard from Bragg's army; scout seven days on the road; everything was in same position as I last reported, except one brigade at Shelbyville has been mounted." Dodge expected more news the next day. (*O.R.*, 25, 482–483.)

On the 16th Sherman said in a letter to Adj. Gen. Alonzo Thomas that a gentleman who had previously given valuable information had arrived from the Yazoo, with a report based on talk current in Jackson, heard by a planter friend during a recent visit in the Mississippi capital. Grant was to be allowed to advance and the Mississippi River expedition to move on Vicksburg. Then, while Rosecrans was amused with feigned attacks, the bulk of Bragg's army would be returned by rail to the vicinity of Tupelo and Baldwyn, to strike later for the Mississippi above Memphis, while Holmes moved from Little Rock for the same purpose. (*O.R.*, 24, 602–603.) Though fantastically grandiose, Sherman still thought he should pass the report to Washington.

There was only a brief interruption of communications with Jackson, Tenn., and on the 22nd Grant queried Sullivan, "Are the road and wires right north of you?" (*O.R.*, 25, 458).

38. *O.R.*, 25, 441–442; Cramer, ed., *Letters of Grant*, p. 96.

39. *O.R.*, 25, 463, 461–462, 462. For further discussion of the McClernand case, see the Appendix.

40. *O.R.*, 25, 480–481; Lewis, *Sherman*, p. 258. Rawlins wrote a dispatch addressed to "Commanding Officer Memphis," which began, "Inclosed find communication for General J. A. McClernand, which you will deliver to him if he be at Memphis. If he has gone down the river you will forward it to him." Rawlins said the "original letter" had been sent to the commanding officer at Cairo for delivery to McClernand, but had probably not reached him because of the cutting of communications. This is a variant of Grant's statement that communications were cut before his order to McClernand "got off." An editorial note identifies the communication inclosed by Rawlins as probably that of Grant to the expedition commander. (*O.R.*, 25, 480.)

Grant's report about Holly Springs specifically said it was being carried by "a large wagon train to Memphis after supplies," and that the train afforded the first opportunity of communicating for over a week. The train was composed of fifty wagons from each division, escorted by Quinby's division, the order for the train, like the letters, being dated the 25th, with the departure time for the train set for the afternoon of the 26th. (*O.R.*, 24, 477–478; 25, 485.)

41. *O.R.*, 25, 441–442, 453–454, 447.

42. *Ibid.*, pp. 462, 462–463.

43. *Ibid.*, p. 470.

44. *Ibid.*, pp. 471, 470.

45. *Ibid.*, pp. 486, 494–495.

46. *Ibid.*, pp. 500, 505, 504–505. In his report of Jan. 9, 1863 (*O.R., 24,* 548–549), Davies said that his evacuation of New Madrid was based on the report that Jeff Thompson and W. L. Jeffers were operating in that vicinity, and he stated that Fisk and Gen. Tuttle agreed in thinking the move wise.

47. *O.R., 25,* 470–471, 471–472. On Dec. 28 Curtis sent a dispatch to Hurlbut that began, "I am sending some force to re-enforce your point, regarding it as rather weak and of utmost importance to the whole country." He hoped his men would be returned as soon as possible and that there would be reciprocation if danger appeared on his side of "the common artery of the West." Halleck had telegraphed the day before, not ordering, but asking if Curtis could give Hurlbut some reenforcement for a short time. (*Ibid.*, pp. 499–500, 493.)

48. *O.R., 24,* 603–604.

49. *Ibid.*, pp. 604–606.

50. *O.R. Navies,* Ser. I, XXIII, 561, 527.

51. *Ibid.*, pp. 535, 540–541. On Oct. 20 Stanton telegraphed to Col. Alfred W. Ellet, commanding the ram fleet, at Mound City, Ill., that the rams were not included in the transfer of the gunboats to the Navy Department, their disposition to be left for further consideration, Ellet in the meantime remaining in command. On Nov. 7 Lincoln issued an order for Ellet, a brigadier since Nov. 1, to report to Porter. On Dec. 11 Halleck telegraphed to Ellet that Grant had been ordered to assign Co. K, 18th Illinois, to the ram fleet, telling him to communicate with Grant as to where the company was and when it would join him. On the 13th Ellet sent a dispatch to Halleck saying that recruiting for the Mississippi Marine Brigade was progressing slowly. He suggested that convalescents be taken from hospitals: it would relieve the hospitals; service on the rams was not as heavy as in the field; it would give him trained men without depleting other units. (*O.R., 25,* 282, 323, 398, 406.) See also West, *The Second Admiral,* p. 181.

52. *O.R., 24,* 616–617.

53. *O.R. Navies,* Ser. I, XXIII, 386, 546–547 (Walke's report).

54. *Ibid.*, Walke's report, p. 689 (the *Marmora*'s log); James R. Scoley, "Naval Operations in the Vicksburg Campaign," *B. and L.,* III, 551–570, especially p. 559; *O.R. Navies,* Ser. I, XXIII, 553–554 (report of Capt. Sunderland of the *Queen of the West*). West speaks of Walke's illness (*op. cit.,* p. 188).

In his report of the 17th Porter said, "The torpedo which blew up the *Cairo* was evidently fired by a galvanic battery. . . ." In a letter of the 20th, giving Gwin detailed instructions about removing mines, he said friction matches might be the means of detonation. (*O.R. Navies,* Ser. I, XXIII, 544–546, 567–568.)

In a short note "Confederate Torpedoes in the Yazoo," *B. and L.,* III, 580, Capt. I. N. Brown indicates that the mines were contact mines, but gives the impression that there were not many of them in the river at this time. The contemporary Federal reports indicate the explosion or removal of quite a number. A picture of one of the "infernal machines" is given in *O.R. Navies,* Ser. I, XXIII, 549.

A list of Union ships involved in the entire Vicksburg operations, properly classified, and with armaments listed, is given in *B. and L.*, III, 581.

55. Walke to Porter, *O.R. Navies*, Ser. I, XXIII, 540.

56. *O.R.*, *25*, 788.

57. *O.R.*, *25*, 485 (Sherman's order to Smith); Smith's and Burbridge's reports, *O.R.*, *24*, 627–628, 629–630. Burbridge's infantry marched 75 miles in 36 hours and his cavalry made an extra dash of 30 miles.

58. *O.R.*, *25*, 803, 804.

59. Pemberton's report, *O.R.*, *24*, 665–669; *25*, 804 (Pemberton to Maury). The dispatch to Maury is headed Vicksburg, Dec. 25, but would seem to be in error either as to place or date.

60. *O.R. Navies*, Ser. I, XXIII, 564; *O.R.*, *24*, 620–621; *25*, 805.

61. *O.R.*, *24*, 621–622; *O.R. Navies*, Ser. I, XXIII, 579. In his instructions to Steele (*O.R.*, *25*, 878–879) Sherman said, "There is a high, good levee back from the Yazoo River, along the Chickasaw Bayou, to the high land." The enemy of course was well aware of this and was prepared to protect it.

In the text of the *O.R.* the spelling is Haines, but in the Atlas it is Haynes, as it is in the Navy records.

62. Porter's report, *O.R. Navies*, Ser. I, XXIII, 572–574; Porter to Sherman, *ibid.*, pp. 577–578; Porter's report.

63. Sherman's, Morgan's, De Courcy's, Stuart's, Smith's, and Steele's reports, *O.R.*, *24*, 605–610, 637–638, 648–649, 634–637, 627–628, 650–652. Sherman spoke of a heavy fog enveloping the whole country.

64. Grant, *Memoirs*, I, 431 (Long, ed., p. 224). Grant also said, "The further north the enemy could be held the better."

In his instructions to Sherman on Dec. 8 Grant had said, "I will hold the forces here in readiness to co-operate with you in such manner as the movements of the enemy may make necessary." In his letter to Sherman on the 14th, he had said, "My headquarters will probably be in Coffeeville one week hence"—that is, 160 miles from Vicksburg and 10 miles north of the Yalobusha. To Halleck, Grant had said he intended to hold the Yalobusha, making a real attack if opportunity occurred. Sherman's instructions to his division commanders on Dec. 23 spoke of acting in "concert with General Grant against Pemberton's forces"—which was not saying against Vicksburg. He named one contingency in which they might meet on the Yazoo, but Sherman clearly expected no help from anyone in seizing the point behind Vicksburg. After that the gunboats were to help him take the city. He surely did not have in mind direct cooperation from other land forces when he wrote, "When we begin to act on the shore we must do the work quickly and effectually." (*O.R.*, *24*, 601; *25*, 412; *24*, 474, 616–617.)

65. Sherman's report; *O.R.*, *25*, 496–497.

66. *O.R.*, *24*, 622–623; Sherman's report.

67. Sherman's and Morgan's reports; Thayer's report, *ibid.*, pp. 658–659.

The main attack was made by Morgan supported by Steele. As a diversion, Smith on the right was to push across a sandbar. The 6th Missouri gallantly crossed, but sharp fire pinned the men down at the base of a high bank, into which they had to dig for protection (Smith's report; report of Col. Giles Smith,

O.R., 24, 633–634). For the criticisms that Sherman and Morgan subsequently made of each other, see George H. Morgan, "The Assault on Chickasaw Bluffs," *B. and L.*, III, 462–470.

68. *O.R., 24*, 625, 571, 643, 641; *O.R. Navies*, Ser. I, XXIII, 584–585, 586.

69. Martin L. Smith's report, *O.R., 24*, 671–674. The Confederate line was as follows, right to left: Lee, Barton, Vaughn, with Gregg in reserve, to be subsequently placed between Barton and Vaughn. For a postwar account of the defense, see S. D. Lee, "Chickasaw Bayou Campaign," *Publications of the Mississippi Historical Society*, IV (1901), 15–36.

70. *O.R. Navies*, Ser. I, XXIII, 587. Sherman said, "Unless Grant be near at hand, I can not promise success in a direct assault on Vicksburg," and ended by stating that both Grant and Banks "should now be heard from." He later pronounced such an idea ridiculous though he at the same time asserted it had never been contemplated that he would take Vicksburg alone (Thorndike, ed., *The Sherman Letters*, p. 173).

In a dispatch on the 29th to Fleet Captain Pennock at Cairo, Porter spoke of the impending attack against the hills back of Vicksburg as doubtful, then said, "This is a hard nut to crack, with so poor an army as we have" (*O.R. Navies*, Ser. I, XXIII, 586).

71. *Ibid.*, pp. 588, 593–594 (Ellet's report), 589. After saying that a new rake could be made if one were destroyed, Ellet commented, "The design was to obviate the necessity of sending men out in small boats to fish for torpedoes under tremendous fire from regiments of rebel sharpshooters stationed in rifle pits along either shore. This had been the plan hitherto pursued and found impracticable. The *Cairo* was blown up by a torpedo while protecting the men who were searching for them." On the 27th Steele, on a call from Porter, sent the 16th Missouri to the right bank of the Yazoo to disperse about 400 sharpshooters (Steele's report).

72. Sherman's report; *O.R. Navies*, Ser. I, XXIII, 597.

73. Sherman's report. Sherman spoke of hearing "cars coming and departing all the time," presumably with reenforcements, though making a noise with trains was a simple and favorite ruse.

74. *O.R., 25*, 528–530.

75. *Ibid.*, pp. 501–503.

76. Robert Todd Lincoln Collection, XCVII, 20572–4. McClernand said to Lincoln that it was doubtful if his officers would get through to Grant, because the road was "infested with guerrillas," and that it would be necessary for him "to run the gauntlet of the Miss. river, in a common steamer," to reach his command at Vicksburg. In his letter to Stanton he spoke of his officers riding through country "infested by guerrilla bands," but said they had reached Holly Springs on the night of the 28th, and there learned about the orders sent to Memphis for him, which he stated he received on the 29th.

77. *O.R., 25*, 510, 511. There was no legal basis for McClernand's having a staff of anything like fifty officers (adding the major sent to Washington), and if he had a group of that size, most of them must have been attached. Grant had a staff of only 17 officers, though Rosecrans had one of 30, several of Rosecrans's officers being detailed from regiments, while two of them were

volunteer aides (Grant's headquarters papers, G.O. 2, Oct. 26, 1862; *O.R., 30,* 215–216).

78. *O.R., 25,* 441, 491; *24,* 594.

79. *O.R., 25,* 498.

There is contradiction in the evidence as to whether the railroad from Paducah stopped at Fulton as shown on Map 14, or continued to the present Gibbs, three miles east of Union City on the road to McKenzie. At present the road is part of the Illinois Central line to Memphis and runs through Gibbs and Rives, the latter three miles south of Union City on the old Mobile and Ohio R.R.

Plate CLIII in the *O.R.* Atlas (a large-scale map for the area) shows the terminus at Fulton. Plates CXVII and CXVIII, both small scale, are in disagreement; the first has the road continuing to Gibbs, the second has it ending at the state line. Plates CLXII–CLXXI, which are basically the same, show the line terminating at Rives, and are therefore definitely incorrect. What should be the most authoritative map is the one that accompanied the final report of Brig. Gen. D. C. McCallum, director of U.S. Military Railroads, which is in the pocket in *O.R. 126.* It shows the "Paducah Branch" terminating at Fulton with double-dashed lines to Union City indicating projection or incomplete construction. As the part of the Mobile and Ohio south from Columbus through Union City for a short distance is indicated as an actual "military line," one would think that the status of the Paducah Branch would have been known and recorded with precision.

While it is stated in various places that the extension to present Gibbs was made as early as 1858, the *American Railroad Journal* for Sept. 8, 1860, contained a quotation from the *Paducah Herald* which shows conclusively that the road did not exist beyond Fulton at that time. But, if matters could be favorably arranged in Tennessee, it was hoped the road would be completed to a junction with the Mobile and Ohio by Jan. 1, 1861. The annual report of the latter road for 1866 shows conclusively that it was not completed between Columbus and Mobile until Apr. 22, 1861 (Lemly, *The Gulf, Mobile and Ohio,* p. 310).

The fact that the road in question was not chartered in Tennessee with authorization to extend the existing line in Kentucky from Fulton to Troy or Union City, until Apr. 19, 1866, points strongly to its non-existence below Fulton at the time of the war. In addition, there seems to be no indication in the *O.R.* that Paducah was a railhead. When Grant rushed Granger's division to Wright, it was to Columbus that the infantry went by rail (*supra,* p. 59).

A schedule in *Appleton's Guide* for December, 1864, of a daily mixed train each way between Paducah and Union City by way of Gibbs, must be challenged, even though local tradition gives it some support. It seems certain that in March the railroad was being operated from Paducah only as far as Mayfield, and Union City was not reoccupied by the Federals after it was captured by Forrest on March 24, the day before his attack on Paducah. A Federal detachment from Columbus had an encounter with a Confederate force in Union City on Sept. 2. (*O.R., 57,* 512, 515; *77,* 492.)

It is inconceivable that the Federals would allow a train to run into enemy-held territory; supplies were reaching the Confederates badly enough without any such facility. Thus the Appleton schedule cannot be taken as proof that the railroad existed beyond Fulton in 1864.

80. Fuller's, Dunham's, and Forrest's reports, *O.R.*, *24*, 568–572, 579–585, 594–597; Sullivan to Grant and Grant to Sullivan, *ibid.*, pp. 552, 553; Henry, *"First with the Most" Forrest*, p. 120. On the 26th Grant telegraphed to Sullivan (*O.R.*, *25*, 490): "Dodge learns from persons who saw Forrest cross the Tennessee River that he has but 3,500 men at the furthest. Act on the theory that he has no more."

The fact that Forrest was surprised resulted primarily from the inefficiency of four companies he had sent to Clarksburg to reconnoiter, but this does not explain why he had not kept in touch with Sullivan's column, which apparently got east of him without his knowledge. Dunham, who it may be recalled was captured and paroled at Munfordville on Sept. 17, had been exchanged in November (*O.R.*, *117*, 717).

81. *O.R.*, *25*, 493–494; *24*, 548–549.

82. Lord, ed., *The Fremantle Diary*, p. 121. Fremantle had entered the Confederacy from Mexico early in April.

NOTES TO CHAPTER VIII

1. *O.R.*, *30*, 3. On the 5th Gen. W. S. Smith, at Glasgow with his division, reporting on the sayings of three captured enemy cavalrymen, stated, "Bragg has been sent to Richmond, in arrest." Wisely he commented, "Except so far as the above statements refer to Breckinridge's division, they are, of course, mere camp rumors, entitled to credit only so far as concurrent circumstances may corroborate them." (*Ibid.*, p. 11.)

In spite of his general confidence in Bragg, Davis would not pass on Polk without talking to him, and Polk was called to Richmond to give his version of the recent campaign. Polk and Davis were personally well acquainted, the former having graduated from West Point in 1827, the latter the next year. See Horn, *The Army of Tennessee*, p. 190; W. M. Polk, *Leonidas Polk*, p. 165.

2. *O.R.*, *30*, 4, 7–8; Dyer, *Compendium*, p. 442. It is not possible to tell the date at which the cavalry organization Dyer gives was carried out. During the Perryville campaign the cavalry had been in three brigades, one of them under Capt. Ebenezer Gay. Gay remained in Kentucky and on Nov. 11 was under orders to go to Louisville with his cavalry—how large a force is not clear (*O.R.*, *30*, 37).

Dyer's remarkable book is indispensable for tracing the confusing shift of troops and reorganization of larger units in both Grant's and Rosecrans's commands. It would be impossible to give too great praise to the monumental compilation, and it has been used in the present book far more frequently than explicit references indicate.

3. *O.R.*, *30*, 9, 5.

4. *Ibid.*, p. 7.

5. *O.R., 21,* 589.

6. *O.R., 30,* 21.

7. *O.R., 30,* 11; Dyer, *op. cit.,* pp. 434–443. It may be recalled that Jackson's division of new regiments suffered badly at Perryville, Jackson himself being killed in the first minutes of the battle.

8. *O.R., 30,* 12, 10, 27.

9. *Ibid.,* pp. 12–13. In *Morgan's Cavalry* Duke says that Morgan left Kentucky with about 1,800 men but observes that they were joined at Gallatin by the 9th Tennessee Cavalry, which had been organized after they had left Hartsville in the summer and was to prove to be one of Morgan's best regiments (pp. 196, 207).

10. Duke, *op. cit.,* p. 210; *O.R., 30,* 388; *29,* 3–5, 6–7, 6. Col. R. F. Smith of the 16th Illinois put his loss at 5 wounded and 6 missing. He praised his command—an old regiment—and also said: "I cannot close my report without mentioning the excellent conduct of the mounted scouts belonging to Captain Twyman's independent company. I have rarely seen their equal for bravery and efficiency." (*O.R., 29,* 5.) The unit was from Kentucky.

Negley said the purpose of the enemy was to destroy the railroad and pontoon bridges. Breckinridge did not mention them in his order to Forrest, and the order to Morgan apparently does not survive. Duke speaks only of cars and locomotives being marked for destruction in the order he says was received at Gallatin. However, if Morgan had defeated Smith, he would certainly have also destroyed the bridges. Forrest evidently got pleasure out of the word Abolitionists; he used it six times. Two of the Federals evidently died, for Dyer gives the casualties as two killed and 24 wounded.

11. *O.R., 30,* 15.

12. *Ibid.,* pp. 22, 33.

13. *Ibid.,* p. 35. Cist is in error by ten days when he says that the advance of Rosecrans's army did not reach Nashville until Nov. 17 and that the general himself arrived a few days later. A more serious error, however, is his assertion that Bragg had left Breckinridge in front of Nashville when he went to Kentucky, for he uses it as a completely false argument as to what Bragg's potentialities were if he had not made the mistake. (*The Army of the Cumberland,* pp. 81, 78, 80.) Actually, Breckinridge did not reach Knoxville with his 2,500 men from Mississippi until Oct. 3 and did not assume command at Murfreesboro until the 28th (*O.R., 23,* 997, 1003).

14. *O.R., 30,* 35–36.

15. *Ibid.,* pp. 39, 56.

16. *Ibid.,* p. 59.

17. Ropes, *The Story of the Civil War,* II, 423. Steele, who unfortunately made no personal use whatever of the *Official Records* in writing his very readable *American Campaigns,* but accepted Ropes's use of them, speaks (p. 153) of Rosecrans as having the intention to accumulate 2,000,000 rations before moving, without, however, saying this purpose was announced to Halleck on Nov. 17.

18. *O.R., 30,* 60, 64. On the night of the 16th, fifteen minutes after a dis-

patch to Halleck in which he said, "General, we must have arms for our cavalry," Rosecrans sent another (*ibid.,* p. 58), saying he wanted to mount some infantry regiments, arm them with revolving rifles, and make sharpshooters out of them; he was willing to exchange old arms for the new ones.

19. *Ibid.,* p. 61.

20. *Ibid.,* pp. 403, 411, 412, 416–417. It would seem that it was originally intended to have Kirby Smith personally present with the major part of his corps, and this plan may have been changed by the interposition of Lee, who on Nov. 25 wrote to Cooper that Smith, in organizing his command to operate with Bragg in Middle Tennessee, had left Heth to command the Department of East Tennessee. Lee then said that Heth "for particular reasons" wanted active field service, that he could give such service to him, and that he understood another officer could take his place in Knoxville. On Dec. 23 Smith issued an order at Knoxville resuming command of the Department of East Tennessee. (*Ibid.,* pp. 425, 461.)

21. Duke, *op. cit.,* p. 218; *O.R., 30,* 33, 20.

22. *O.R., 30,* 37–38, 48, 58, 70–71, 44–45. Duke speaks (*op. cit.,* p. 217) about a strong force of Federals being posted at Jefferson, ten miles north of Murfreesboro, and that it required constant watching. The statement was probably an inaccurate recollection about the brigade at Rural Hill.

Unless there was a rise of the river considerably above the existing low stage, there was not much danger to the brigade on Rural Hill, for there was a ford and ferry two miles west of it and a ford and ferry ten miles farther down the river. See the excellent map in Plate XXX of the *O.R.* Atlas.

23. *O.R., 30,* 70, 73.

24. *Ibid.,* p. 64.

25. *Ibid.,* pp. 62–63.

26. *Ibid.,* pp. 67, 74, 125–126.

27. Duke, *op. cit.,* pp. 204, 206; *O.R., 30,* 46, 125–126.

28. *O.R., 30,* 79, 89.

29. *Ibid.,* pp. 97–98, 134, 310.

30. *Ibid.,* pp. 109–110.

31. *Ibid.,* pp. 67–68, 25, 26. After stating that he had seen Morgan at Gallatin, and estimating his force at between 2,000 and 3,000 men, the lieutenant said, "He is a very careless officer. I found no vedettes on any of the roads."

32. *Ibid.,* pp. 82, 82–83, 83.

33. *Ibid.,* pp. 94–95, 96. On Oct. 12 Stanton had written to Wright about extortions and oppressive measures of marshals. Wright forwarded a report on Nov. 25 by the provost marshal general for Kentucky, on which Boyle had indorsed his concurrence and said that guilty officers had long since been dismissed. On the same day the provost marshal furnished Boyle a report on the 3,030 prisoners, classified in nine categories, who had been received at the Louisville military prison since Oct. 30. On the 25th Wright sent Halleck an illuminating report from Boyle with inclosures. Boyle's chief concern was with boys 15 to 18 years of age, whom he pronounced "puppets of older heads"

who had joined the Confederates when they were in the state, but had deserted when Bragg was away. "What shall be done with them?" was a question that Wright repeated, saying that many of the class wanted to enlist in the Federal army. (*O.R.*, *117*, 616; *30*, 94–96; *117*, 752–753, 754–756.)

34. *O.R.*, *30*, 80–81. During their occupancy the Confederates had declared martial law in and around Lexington for a distance of ten miles (*ibid.*, *23*, 589–590).

35. *O.R.*, *30*, 93, 76–77.

36. *O.R.*, *30*, 44; *25*, 343; *30*, 94, 61–62, 71–72, 72–73, 104. In a dispatch to Halleck on Nov. 6 Grant had said: "Stanley is the only general in his division, and I have no one to take his place that can be spared. Will relieve him as soon as possible." (*O.R.*, *24*, 467–468.)

As a cure for getting paroled or straggling, Boyle suggested shaving half the offender's head. On Nov. 26 Col. G. St. Leger Grenfell, the British soldier of fortune who was Morgan's adjutant, reported that a large number of Federals, war-weary and homesick, were wandering about near the Cumberland River in search of a Confederate officer to parole them. (*O.R.*, *30*, 89, 427–428.)

Bruce reported the capture of numerous Confederates who had come home, and stated that many had voluntarily reported themselves. The Federals were compelled to be very watchful of all newcomers in a community. In a note warning commanders at four places that Morgan had "sent over a lot of soldiers in citizens' dress to loaf around and injure the railroad," Rosecrans said, "Whoever cannot give a good account of themselves shoot or hang on the nearest tree." (*Ibid.*, pp. 125–126, 108.)

37. *Ibid.*, pp. 83, 94, 96, 96–97, 98, 120, 133–134. In a second dispatch to Rosecrans (*ibid.*, p. 102) Cullum made it clear that he did not have in mind the pontoons that Buell built near Stevenson, for he said: "A large wooden pontoon train was taken by General Buell from Corinth, and used by him in crossing the Tennessee. What has become of it?" Cullum apparently thought Buell had crossed to the north side of the Tennessee by means of a pontoon bridge, whereas it has been seen that he used ferries. For the fate of the pontoon bridge he had had made in March and had had sent up the Tennessee River, see n. 28, Chap. II.

In his reply to Cullum's first dispatch, Rosecrans raised the question of canvas boats. Cullum's answer was that they were not dependable, while iron boats were not easily repaired without special workmen. That Rosecrans must have sent some message to Wright on the subject is indicated by Wright's dispatch contrasting canvas and wooden boats after he had telegraphed he had set his engineer to work. There seems to be no answer to Wright's second message.

In a dispatch to Rosecrans on Dec. 4 the commander of the 7th Tennessee said three of his acquaintances who lived near Chattanooga had come to his camp the day before and had reported that the Confederates were building four pontoon bridges over the Tennessee between Chattanooga and Bridgeport, and "had declined finishing the railroad bridge to Bridgeport" (*O.R.*, *30*, 121).

38. *O.R., 30*, 128, 111–112. As a result of Ripley's appeal, Halleck assigned Brig. Gen. William F. Barry to the position of chief of artillery, and Ripley drew up suggested instructions for him to issue (*ibid.*, p. 112).

39. *O.R., 30*, 91, 115; Pratt, *Stanton*, p. 252; *O.R., 30*, 124.

40. *O.R., 30*, 108–109, 109, 49–50, 113–114.

41. *O.R., 30*, 181; Horn, *The Army of Tennessee*, pp. 444–445.

42. *O.R., 30*, 102, 115–116, 117–118.

43. *Ibid.*, pp. 416–417, 118. Steele states (*op. cit.*, p. 159) that the whole country and all its future commanders owe Rosecrans's memory a debt of gratitude for his reply to Halleck. He came close to arguing that the government should not indicate dissatisfaction with an army commander. It should be noted that Steele does not give the letter of instructions that Rosecrans received when he took over command from Buell. It is possible that he never read it. Steele, however, was certainly familiar with Grant's *Memoirs*, and must have read his statement that he had intended to relieve Rosecrans of command the day he was called away, because Rosecrans would not obey orders.

44. *O.R., 30*, 123–124.

45. *Ibid.*, p. 125. The railroad was not opened on Nov. 20 as had been expected, but on the 26th (*O.R., 29*, 189). On Dec. 8 Mr. James Guthrie, president of the L. & N., wrote to Rosecrans at length about the rebuilding of the road and its condition. He indicated that lumber which Rosecrans had promised for relining the tunnels was not ready when needed, nor were the promised engines at hand. Not being able to find suitable mechanics in Louisville, New Albany, Jeffersonville, or Cincinnati to arch the tunnels, they had been brought from Virginia. He thought that eight of the eleven trestles built by the army workers would not stand freshets, though he thought he had those at the Louisville end in condition to do so. He would strengthen the others. When a sufficient supply of wood and water became available, Guthrie hoped to be able to deliver 70 to 80 cars a day at Nashville, and he said, "There have been some conflicting orders from the military, which we hope you will provide shall not happen in the future." (*O.R., 30*, 141.)

46. *Ibid.*, pp. 18–19.

47. *Ibid.*, pp. 116, 120, 127, 135. The statement about the 7th Michigan Cavalry is based on Dyer, *op. cit.*, p. 1273. Watson said 3,600 carbines and Colt revolving rifles had been sent; as Stanton had previously stated that 1,600 revolving rifles had gone forward, the breakdown is simple. Rosecrans's statement that only 3,038 cavalry were present must apply only to the cavalry division; on Dec. 15 Thomas reported 2,172 effective cavalry in the "Center" (*O.R., 30*, 185–186).

48. In his report dated Nov. 21, 1862 (*O.R., 123*, 849–859) Gen. Ripley put the number of carbines of American manufacture (eight varieties) purchased up to June 30 at 31,210, those of foreign make (mostly Bohemian) at 11,113, giving a total of 42,323. The number of revolvers of American make (eight varieties) he gave as 88,584 (including 1,977 smooth-bore horse pistols), those of foreign manufacture as 15,254, giving a total of 103,838. The number of Colt revolving rifles was 2,890.

In his report dated Oct. 27, 1863 (*O.R., 124,* 930–937) Brig. Gen. George D. Ramsay, the new Chief of Ordnance, gave the number of carbines on hand at the beginning of the "rebellion" and purchased up to June 30 as 111,443, and the number of revolvers and pistols as 257,953. He gave no figure for revolving rifles, but said, "As regards small-arms, we may now consider ourselves perfectly independent of foreign aid," and he put the yearly capacity for carbines at 100,000 and for revolvers at 300,000. He also made the interesting comment, "Iron of a quality fully equal to the celebrated irons manufactured in England and Norway is now produced in ample quantity to meet all our present wants, and the product can be increased to any desirable extent, thus relieving us entirely from our former dependence on European producers for this indispensable article."

While it would be impossible to say how many carbines had been procured up to, say, Oct. 31, 1862, it would seem that the number could not have been less than 60,000. Watson's statement to Rosecrans, "Lately you have received a far larger proportion of cavalry arms than any other commander," was probably entirely correct, as well as his statement that Rosecrans had been given all the swords (sabers) and pistols (revolvers) for which he had asked.

49. *O.R., 30,* 418, 420.

50. *Ibid.,* pp. 120, 411–412.

51. *Ibid., 29,* 63–64.

52. Various reports, *O.R., 29,* 45–72, and Duke, *op. cit.,* pp. 220–226. While Morgan said the infantry crossed in one boat, Hunt said two were used. The Federal strengths are based upon the casualty report, which included those missing or captured, not upon what Moore said in his belated report.

Horn's statement (*op. cit.,* p. 194) about Morgan making a brilliant swoop with 1,300 men hardly portrays the operation accurately. In his report Morgan said his attacking line was composed of 1,300 men. Moore's statement that he had only 1,200 men in line, largely because of much illness, is not trustworthy. The number of soldiers actually facing each other was probably not far from equal. The Federals had 58 killed and 204 wounded, while the Confederates had 21 and 104, respectively, all figures being compiled by the editors of the *O.R.* from "nominal lists."

The statement by Maj. Samuel Hill of the 2nd Indiana Cavalry that at 4 o'clock on the 6th Lebanon "was not occupied by the enemy, nor were there any indications of an advance of their forces," merely reveals how poor the cavalry patrolling had been. Duke says the column passed through Lebanon at 2:00 P.M. As the town was only ten miles from the starting point, this looks correct.

53. Harlan's report, *O.R., 29,* 47–51. Harlan said he "suggested the propriety" of Miller's marching toward Hartsville; as the senior officer he was certainly responsible that proper action be taken. He recaptured 11 of Moore's wagons and 13 of his mules, policed the battlefield, and sent back to his camp for 25 additional wagons to take away salvaged material. He largely rearmed the 10th Kentucky from recaptured weapons, because the Kentuckians had defective pieces and of a caliber for which he had no ammunition in his train. He saved a good stock of provisions, most of which he left for the hospital

he established for the wounded. In general, the information he obtained about the attack was accurate and complete; he correctly stated that Morgan used his cavalry horses to take his infantry back over the ford at Hartsville, and that a force had been left on the south bank—Morgan said a battalion and the two howitzers. But Harlan advisedly expressed no opinion "in regard to the causes which led to the unfortunate disaster."

54. *O.R., 29,* 673; *30,* 444–445; *29,* 62–63. Bragg's final figure for the number of Federals captured is certainly to be preferred to the 1,834 given for the "captured or missing" in the compilation of Federal casualties, though that is the figure given by Horn (*loc. cit.*). Johnston's statement that the prisoners exceeded Morgan's command was, of course, inaccurate.

55. *O.R., 30,* 127, 132, 132–133, 132.

56. *Ibid.,* pp. 139, 128–129, 138. On Nov. 28 Rosecrans had directed Thomas, "Order the Hartsville command to have scouts out, hired or otherwise, for 30 or 40 miles." This was not as a protection for the command, but to try to pick up information about a reported move of Kirby Smith into Kentucky "by some inland route, east of us." (*Ibid.,* p. 105.) Thomas said that about 700 wagons would suffice to supply him at Loudon "until the railroad could be opened." Supply by rail would naturally have necessitated possession of Chattanooga and the rebuilding of the bridge at Bridgeport, which would certainly be destroyed. A Confederate concentration against Thomas at Loudon would have been simple, but he could have withdrawn westward from before it, for in that friendly region he would be duly informed about it.

57. *Ibid.,* pp. 145, 146, 150. A dispatch to Thomas also spoke of the enemy feinting in front of Nashville and that it was thought he intended to attack Fort Donelson (*ibid.,* p. 145).

58. *O.R., 29,* 42–45. Moore said that civilians joined Morgan's force until it "numbered between 5,000 and 6,000 men."

59. Beatty, *Memoirs of a Volunteer,* p. 146; *O.R., 29,* 42. Rosecrans's dispatch informing Halleck of the capture of the brigade also bore the hour 11:00 P.M., Dec. 7 (*ibid.,* pp. 40–41).

60. *O.R., 30,* 151–152, 150.

61. *Ibid.,* pp. 151, 145, 149, 150.

62. *Ibid.,* pp. 177, 186, 184, 186. In an earlier dispatch on the 15th (*ibid.,* p. 180) to Boyle, Rosecrans said: "Morgan, with, perhaps, 2,000 or 3,000 men, now crossing river near Hartsville, to strike at railroad. Look out, and, if possible, aid me in destroying him." In his report to Halleck he stated that both sections of the bridge at Bridgeport were about finished. It may be recalled that the railroad bridge there took advantage of an island and was in two parts, and that Mitchel had saved one part from destruction (*supra,* III, 424).

63. *O.R., 30,* 179, 179–180.

NOTES TO CHAPTER IX

1. *O.R.*, *29*, 84, 84–85. A number of reports to Rosecrans by Federal officers are given (*ibid.*, pp. 80–81), but none of those to Bragg, upon which he said he based his reply.

2. *O.R.*, *30*, 200; Morgan's report, *O.R.*, *29*, 154–158; *30*, 218–219. In a message warning Wright about Morgan, Rosecrans said, "He is at Hartsville tonight." At 7:00 P.M. of the 23rd Brig. Gen. J. J. Reynolds, now commanding at Gallatin, reported to Garesché that Morgan had left Alexandria and would cross the river at Carthage or Gainesboro and go into Kentucky; at 10:30 he reported that "undoubted" information indicated a mounted force of 7,000 to 10,000 was moving on Gallatin. At 10:00 P.M. the next night he reported that Scout K. L. Carter saw Morgan cross the river at Sand Shoals near Carthage, put his force at 3,000—saying he could "be 200 out either way"—two guns, and about 25 mule teams. In a dispatch to Wright, Rosecrans accepted this report. (*O.R.*, *30*, 208, 217, 230, 240.)

Actually, Morgan started from Alexandria, crossed the river at dusk on the 22nd at Sand Shoals, and moved in the direction of Glasgow early the next day. His command was now organized into two brigades and numbered 3,100 men and seven guns. (Morgan's report, *O.R.*, *29*, 153–158; Duke, *Morgan's Cavalry*, p. 234.)

The *O.R.* calls Morgan's operation "Morgan's Second Kentucky Raid," the first being that of July 4–28. His operations during Bragg's invasion are not classed as a raid.

3. *O.R.*, *30*, 70, 207. Wright said that Gordon Granger did not have 500 mounted men left.

4. Carter's and Col. C. J. Walker's reports, *O.R.*, *29*, 88–94.

5. *O.R.*, *30*, 243; Morgan's reports.

6. Crittenden's and Wood's reports, *O.R.*, *29*, 446–453, 457–463; *30*, 223; McCook's and Thomas's reports, *29*, 251–258, 371–375. For the cavalry, see Kennett's report, *ibid.*, pp. 620–622.

7. *Supra*, I, 426; *O.R.*, *30*, 215–216.

8. Wood's report; Wheeler's reports, *O.R.*, *29*, 957–961. A fourth brigade of three Kentucky regiments under Brig. Gen. Abraham Buford was at Rover, 18 miles southwest of Murfreesboro on the Nashville-Shelbyville pike (Buford's report, *ibid.*, pp. 970–971).

A field return for Dec. 10 gives 360 cavalry—officers and men—present for duty in Polk's corps, 130 in Hardee's, 7,637 in Wheeler's "division," and 1,818 in Pegram's brigade, a note saying that Morgan's brigade is included in Wheeler's division. Forrest's command is not listed, and it is said that the artillery and cavalry with the portion of Smith's corps present were not reported. (*O.R.*, *30*, 446.)

A return dated Feb. 2, 1863, showing present for duty on Dec. 31, 1862, lists figures separately for the brigades of Wheeler, Wharton, Pegram, and Buford, and gives a cavalry total—officers and men—of 4,237 (*O.R.*, *29*, 674).

The two returns can be reconciled fairly well by assuming that the Dec. 10 figure for Wheeler's division also included Forrest's command. It would seem safe to say that the cavalry opposing Rosecrans's advance numbered about 4,200.

9. *O.R., 30,* 218. Rosecrans probably about doubled the actual cavalry force, which he said was foraging.

The roster for the 14th Army Corps included with the reports of the campaign give three regiments plus a company of cavalry to Minty, three regiments to Zahm, and three to the reserve, which, having no brigade commander, were directly under Stanley—a queer arrangement. In addition, the 4th U.S. Cavalry under Capt. Elmer Otis is listed as unattached. Johnson's division contained four companies of cavalry and Rousseau's contained six; their casualties being reported with the divisions, they were definitely organic. Two regiments of cavalry were in Mitchell's division that remained at Nashville and three with Brig. Gen. E. A. Paine at Gallatin (*ibid., 29,* 174–182).

Stanley, Kennett, and Minty did not state in their reports the strengths with which they left Nashville; Zahm very fortunately said his three regiments contained 950 men; equally happily Otis reported that six companies left after he had set up a courier line numbered 260 "rank and file." Taking 325 for the strength of a regiment, and considering the ten divisional companies as equivalent to a regiment, we would have for the eleven cavalry regiments a total strength of about 3,575, while Rosecrans reported his "effective" cavalry on Dec. 31 at 3,200. (Stanley's, Kennett's, Minty's, Zahm's, Otis's, and effective force reports, *ibid.,* pp. 617–620, 620–622, 623–626, 632–633, 648–650, 200–201.)

It would seem safe to say that Rosecrans left Nashville with about 3,600 cavalry.

10. Crittenden's, Thomas's, and McCook's reports.

11. McCook's report.

12. Hazen's and Hascall's reports, *O.R., 29,* 542–548, 464–466.

13. Thomas's report.

14. McCook's report; *O.R., 30,* 254. Stanley gives the impression that the reconnaissance was carried on solely by the cavalry, saying, "On the 28th we made a reconnaissance to College Grove, and found that Hardee's rebel corps had marched to Murfreesboro."

15. *O.R., 30,* 255, 255–256.

16. Wood's and Thomas's reports; *O.R., 30,* 256.

17. *O.R., 30,* 263–265; Wood's supplementary report, *O.R., 29,* 463–464.

18. *O.R., 30,* pp. 267, 269, 269–270. In a rather long dispatch to McCook at 4:02 P.M. (*ibid.,* pp. 268–269) Maj. Goddard, Rosecrans's senior aide, said, "Should it prove, as we now believe, the enemy has made a precipitate retreat from Murfreesborough, you had better move on Salem, where you will probably find forage, and where you can receive your supplies by Murfreesborough pike."

19. McCook's and Thomas's reports; Sheridan's report, *O.R., 29,* 347–352. In his article, "The Battle of Stone's River," *B. and L.,* III, 613–632, G. C. Kniffin says (p. 614), "The slumbers of the commanding general were dis-

turbed at half-past 3 on the morning of the 30th by a call from General McCook. . . ." McCook states in his report, "At 1 o'clock on the morning of the 30th I received an order from General Rosecrans to report in person at his headquarters on the Murfreesboro pike, and arrived there at 3:30 a.m." As McCook's report was submitted to Rosecrans, his placing of responsibility for the visit must be accepted.

20. *O.R., 29,* 661.

21. Wheeler's reports; Stanley's and Minty's reports. The report of Capt. J. A. S. Mitchell of the 2nd Indiana Cavalry (*ibid.,* p. 626) puts the La Vergne raid at 3:00 P.M. of Dec. 31. Confederate reports indicate no raid there on that date, but the first part of Walker's report (*ibid.,* pp. 441–445) speaks of a raid by from 1,000 to 2,000 Confederate cavalry upon La Vergne on the 31st, which must be the Wheeler raid of the 30th; and the date on the top of the second page of Walker's report shows the dates on the first page were incorrect. A good account of the raid is given by Kniffin, *op. cit.,* p. 614,n. He identifies the chief train destroyed at La Vergne as McCook's, as does Walker, which is additional proof that Walker's first date is incorrect.

22. *O.R., 30,* 275.

23. Carter's report, *O.R., 29,* 88–92.

24. Carter's and Morgan's reports; Marshall's report, *O.R., 29,* 95–118; *30,* 468, 470–472. Kirby Smith reported Carter's force to Cooper at 4,000; Marshall first gave that figure, but afterward reduced it. Carter reached Manchester, Ky., on Jan. 5; Morgan crossed the Cumberland at Burkesville on the 4th. There are numerous interesting Federal reports on Morgan's raid that describe efforts to intercept him. In a dispatch to Halleck on Dec. 31 Wright said, "The Cumberland is now navigable, and supplies are being sent that way to General Rosecrans, so that the result of the raid will not be very important." In an extended telegram to Lincoln the next day, Boyle said, "Morgan is flying precipitately," and told about supplies going to Rosecrans by water. (*O.R., 29,* 133–152.)

25. Crittenden's and Sheridan's reports; Davis's, Johnson's, Gibson's, and Baldwin's reports, *O.R., 29,* 261–266, 294–297, 303–309, 336–338; McCook's report. In the map that accompanied Rosecrans's report (*O.R.,* Atlas, Plate XXX–1), Willich is shown in conformity with the clear statement in the report of Col. E. H. Gibson, who succeeded to the command of the brigade; in the map with Kniffin's article the right of the Federal line is shown facing southeasterly.

26. Thomas's, Walker's, Otis's, Stanley's, Minty's, and Zahm's reports. Walker's report, rather than Thomas's, agrees with the order that went from Thomas's headquarters to Walker on the 30th (*O.R., 30,* 279–280). Thomas said Walker reached Stewartsburg about dark on the 29th; Walker stated he spent most of the night on the road.

27. Polk's, Hardee's, Cleburne's, Breckinridge's, and Trabue's reports, *O.R., 29,* 685–693, 771–779, 843–852, 781–788, 826–829. Breckinridge alludes to "the destroyed bridge on the Nashville turnpike" and to the nearby ford. The guns on the hill were all under the command of Capt. Cobb, who states in his report that he had his own battery and a section from each of two other

batteries. Assuming six guns for all batteries, this gives ten guns. Col. T. H. Hunt of the 9th Kentucky says that there were 12 guns. (*Ibid.*, pp. 826–838, 835–836.) An infantry officer—even a colonel—may overcount guns.

28. *O.R., 29,* 174–192, 658–661, 200–201, 674; *30,* 213. Rosecrans's figure of 43,400 effectives—after deducting a wagon guard of 1,600—has been increased by 1,600 for Walker's brigade and decreased by 812 for Spears's. (Spears did not arrive until the morning of Jan. 3, but he gave his strength as 1,450.) Livermore (*Numbers and Losses*, p. 97) is incorrect in saying that Rosecrans did not include Starkweather's brigade. The present-for-duty figure in the return for Dec. 20 was 81,729 officers and men.

29. Rosecrans's report, *O.R., 29,* 188–200; *30,* 381, 381–382.

Rosecrans undoubtedly did McCook damage by saying in his report that he asked him, "Can you hold your present position for three hours?" and that McCook responded, "Yes, I think I can." In his letter of Mar. 10 answering Rosecrans's abrupt note of that date—an unanswered one of the 4th had been milder—McCook said he did not remember that "three hours" had been mentioned in the conversation, and continued, "General Rosecrans did ask me if I thought I could hold my line. I replied, 'I think I can,' meaning, of course, if I were assailed by the enemy that I had fought during the day, but most certainly not meaning against the combined rebel army under General Bragg."

McCook likewise challenged Rosecrans's assertion that something was said to him about changing the line he held. Cist apparently accepts Rosecrans's complete statement as true, but criticizes him strongly for not having the line readjusted, if he thought it desirable (*The Army of the Cumberland*, pp. 130–131). Ropes also repeats without question Rosecrans's version of his conversation with McCook (*The Story of the Civil War*, II, 427–428). It might be noted that Rosecrans's full statement virtually confesses that he had never personally inspected the right of his line, so it is not clear on what he could have based any criticism of the position McCook held.

30. *O.R., 30,* 383. In his letter McCook, after noting that neither Crittenden nor Thomas made mention in their reports of a meeting of corps commanders on the night of the 30th, said, "I hope a similar letter to the one received by myself has been addressed to each of them." The next day Rosecrans sent a short note (*ibid.*, p. 382) to the two officers mentioned by McCook and to Stanley. Inasmuch as Rosecrans had said in his report that he had excused Crittenden from reporting in person, it required a good deal of nerve on Rosecrans's part to ask him whether he had listened to an explanation of the battle plan at army headquarters. Obviously he wanted to be favored with an affirmative answer by his subordinate, and such an effort justifies one in accepting McCook's rather than Rosecrans's account of their conversation.

31. McCook's report; *O.R., 30,* 275. His letter to Rosecrans of Mar. 10 indicated that the written instructions he received had come from Garesché and said they were "filed away" at his home in Ohio.

32. Rosecrans's and McCook's reports. It is to be noted that Rosecrans said clearly in his report that McCook and Stanley heard in full the detailed plan as he was setting it down.

33. Van Cleve's report, *O.R., 29,* 574–575; Wood's report. Wood knew

what should have been done—though there is no evidence that it was done—when he wrote, "I immediately dispatched the information to the headquarters of the left wing, and I doubt not it was sent thence to the commanding general, and by him distributed to the rest of the corps." It would look as if Wagner got some sort of late intelligence of the movement of Cleburne's division, which had been north of Murfreesboro with its left near the river, the order to move not being received until evening.

34. Hardee's report, *O.R., 29,* 771–779.

35. Johnson's report; McCown's report, *O.R., 29,* 911–916. In defending himself against Bragg's charge that the attack did not start until about 7 o'clock, McCown wrote that it began about 6; Brig. Gen. M. C. Ector, commanding one of McCown's brigades, gave 6:06 as the time of advance (*ibid.,* pp. 921, 923). Kniffin states (*op. cit.,* p. 618) that the men of both Johnson's and Davis's divisions were only preparing breakfast. Bragg speaks in his report (*O.R., 29,* 661–672) of "a hot and inviting breakfast of coffee and other luxuries" to which his "gallant and hardy men had long been strangers" being found unserved upon the fires, and that it was left behind while they "pushed on to the enjoyment of a more inviting feast."

Cist states that the fires built on McCook's right on the night of the 30th caused Bragg to prolong his lines and that Hardee thought the Federal lines extended a whole division to the right of where they did, and that this all resulted in a great advantage to the attackers (*op. cit.,* p. 131). There is nothing in Bragg's or Hardee's reports to substantiate this. McCown, who described the action of the 30th as "almost a battle," said, "During the night the enemy extended his lines, covering my front." This is quite different from saying that he did any shifting to the left.

Rosecrans's map is definitely incorrect as to the positions of McCown and Cleburne. Polk's map is much better than Bragg's, but shows Kirk's brigade south of the Franklin road and Willich facing a little west of South (*O.R.,* Atlas, Plate XXXII–1).

36. Baldwin's and Johnson's reports.

37. McCown's and Cleburne's reports.

38. Davis's report; Post's report, *O.R., 29,* 269–272.

39. Sheridan's report.

40. Rosecrans's report.

41. Rousseau's and Thomas's reports. Rousseau spoke of being on Negley's right, but must have been in error.

42. Sheridan's and Polk's reports.

43. Thomas's and Rousseau's reports; Negley's report, strength and casualty reports, *O.R., 29,* 406–410, 200–201, 207–215. Lt. Col. O. L. Shepherd, commanding the regular brigade, spoke in his report (*ibid.,* pp. 393–397) of losing nearly half his men, but said they were "too much engaged to know the full extent of their losses." He stated that some of his command was at first deceived by the enemy, "who advanced dressed in American uniforms."

44. Palmer's, Cruft's, and Grose's reports, *ibid.,* pp. 515–519, 525–531, 559–561; Hazen's and casualty reports.

45. Harker's report, *ibid.,* pp. 500–506; Hascall's report.

46. Wood's and Hascall's reports; Wagner's report, *O.R.*, *29*, 492–494.

47. Davis's, Johnson's, Harker's, Van Cleve's, Rosecrans's and Negley's reports; Bradley's report, *ibid.*, pp. 369–371. For comment about Murfreesboro, see Beatty, *Memoirs of a Volunteer*, p. 96. Polk's map shows the location of his own headquarters and those of Bragg.

48. Zahm's report. In speaking of a Federal train of several hundred wagons, Wharton included much more than those in McCook's ammunition train.

49. Stanley's, Minty's, Kennett's, and Otis's reports. Wheeler spoke of successfully engaging the Federals until dark, when he fell back to the left of Bragg's army.

50. Bragg's, Hardee's, Harker's, Van Cleve's, and Cleburne's reports.

51. Breckinridge's report, *O.R.*, *29*, 781–790; Bragg's report.

52. Bragg's report.

53. Hazen's report.

54. Cist, *op. cit.*, pp. 117, 116; Hazen's report.

55. Polk's and Cobb's reports.

56. Walker's report.

57. Sheridan, *Memoirs*, I, 232; *O.R.*, *22*, 578.

58. *O.R.*, *30*, 290; Starkweather's report, *O.R.*, *29*, 393.

According to Crittenden's account in his short article "The Union Left at Stone's River," in *B. and L.*, III, 632–634, the meeting that Rosecrans called was quite informal, and he says: "There was some talk of falling back. I do not remember who started the subject. . . ." On the other hand, John L. Yaryan, Wood's adjutant, portrays it as a formal council of war, with Rosecrans asking officers in turn for suggestions. He states that Thomas walked out of the room after saying he knew no better place to die. ("Stone River," *War Papers, Indiana Commandery Loyal Legion*, pp. 157–177.) It is impossible to believe that Thomas would have been so discourteous and insubordinate; nor is it clear why Wood should have attended the meeting when Hascall had relieved him of command early in the evening because of Wood's wound. Van Horne states in his life of Thomas (pp. 96–97) that the meeting was at McCook's headquarters, while Yaryan has it at those of Rosecrans. Van Horne says Thomas fell asleep again after saying the army could not retreat, while Stevenson in his book on the battle states (p. 120) that Thomas replied essentially that Rosecrans must make the decision, and he would abide by it, whatever it might be. Yaryan says Sheridan was at the meeting, but Sheridan's comment in *Memoirs*, I, 236–237, relative to the evening in question, shows that he was not. Cleaves in his book on Thomas and O'Connor in his work on Sheridan quote rather lengthily from Yaryan, as if accepting his story. Horn uses Stevenson's account (*The Army of Tennessee*, pp. 205–206).

59. *O.R.*, *30*, 280.

60. Beatty's report, *O.R.*, *29*, 575–578; Polk's, Thomas's, Sheridan's, and Bragg's reports.

61. Beatty (John), *op. cit.*, pp. 95, 156.

62. Bragg's and Breckinridge's reports.

63. Grose's, Beatty's, and Hazen's reports.

64. Mendenhall's report, *O.R.*, *29*, 453–457.

65. Mendenhall's and Cruft's reports. Capt. G. R. Swallow of the 7th Indiana Battery spoke of receiving galling artillery fire from three different points (*ibid.*, p. 579).

66. Mendenhall's, Beatty's, Davis's, and Hascall's reports. Davis said four guns were taken; Bragg reported that he lost only three.

67. Crittenden's, Johnson's, Palmer's, Sheridan's, and Walker's reports. Willich's brigade was now under Col. W. H. Gibson and had been in reserve in a central position; Gibson said he drove two enemy regiments back across the river (*O.R., 29*, 306–307).

68. Beatty, *op. cit.*, p. 154.

69. Spears's report, *O.R., 29*, 416–419. The roster of the 14th Corps shows Spears's brigade consisting of five Tennessee regiments. Apparently they were under the control of Andrew Johnson, for Spears says Johnson directed him to take the 1st and 2nd regiments and such other troops as Mitchell gave him, and convoy the train. In addition to the two Tennessee regiments, he was assigned the 14th Michigan, the 85th Illinois, two sections of guns, an unspecified company of cavalry, and the 3rd Tennessee Cavalry.

70. *N.Y. Tribune*, Jan. 6, 1863; Spears's and Polk's reports; Daniel McCook's report, *O.R., 29*, 445; Wheeler's and Zahm's reports. The 6th Tennessee of Spears's brigade was part of the escort. On Jan. 1 Zahm, with part of his brigade, escorted a train of empty wagons back to Nashville, successfully repulsing an attack by Wheeler below La Vergne.

Zahm's statement, "The Anderson Troop, I am sorry to say, were of very little benefit to me, as the majority of them ran as soon as we were attacked," makes it desirable to mention a very regrettable and difficult problem that soon confronted Rosecrans.

Upon taking command, Rosecrans found a Pennsylvania company of cavalry which had been serving as Buell's bodyguard, called the "Anderson Troop," because it had been recruited to serve with Robert Anderson when he commanded in Kentucky in 1861. On Nov. 2 he asked that the other companies of the regiment—called the 15th Pennsylvania Cavalry—be sent to him, Halleck replying promptly that this would be done as soon as they could be got "out of the hands of the Governor of Pennsylvania." After their arrival discontent soon began to appear, and when ordered forward on Dec. 26, all but some 200 men out of a total of nearly 1,000 refused to go. Shortage of competent officers was pleaded, though many of the men also believed they had been deceived when recruited. On succeeding days other men joined the group which had marched on the 26th, and some creditable service was performed by them in the battle. All were ordered back to Nashville and evidently served Zahm poorly on the way. By Jan. 5 a total of 415 were in confinement. There were protests from citizens of Philadelphia, the home of most of the men, lengthy reports by an inspector, and much work by other officers. The fifteen mutineers selected by Rosecrans for trial seem never to have been actually brought before a court, and in May, 1863, the regiment was reorganized. (*O.R., 30*, 5, 6, 345–382; *109*, 323–330—rosters of men who obeyed orders to go to the front and those who did not.)

71. *O.R., 29*, 184–185.

72. *O.R.*, *30*, 294, 297; *25*, 332–334. McClernand indicated that another separation would bring "endless collisions, which, after wasting all the States, must sink them in anarchy and wretchedness, like that which drapes Mexico in misery and mourning."

73. Rosecrans's report; *O.R.*, *30*, 298; *29*, 185. Crittenden stated in a dispatch to Rosecrans's adjutant (*O.R.*, *30*, 294) that all his division commanders thought the danger of a sudden rise of the river was imminent, and that he had ordered all troops back across the stream. He said, "The men must be located where they can build fires and dry their clothes and get some rest." Hascall said in his report that his division arrived near Rosecrans's headquarters "about 2 o'clock at night, completely drenched with mud and rain."

74. *O.R.*, *30*, 483.

75. *O.R.*, *30*, 485, 486; *29*, 186; *30*, 299–300, 301. Boyle said he thought the river was the quickest and cheapest way to send troops.

76. *O.R.*, *30*, 303; *29*, 186, 187. After beginning by telling Boyle to send reenforcements by the Cumberland, Rosecrans switched and said to send them by rail as far as the gap, whence they could march to Munfordville. He ended, "I hope you will soon open the road." In a dispatch to Rosecrans on the 3rd Boyle had said it would take four or five weeks to repair the damage done by Morgan—the most serious of which had been the destruction of bridges at Bacon Creek and Nolin Creek and the trestle work at Elizabethtown and Muldraugh Hill (*O.R.*, *30*, 296).

77. *O.R.*, *29*, 662. In a dispatch the day before (*ibid.*) Bragg had told Cooper that papers taken on the field indicated the Federals had from 60,000 to 70,000, while his force was not over half as great. As an apparent excuse for retreating he said in his report that McCook's captured papers, put in his hands on the night of the 2nd–3rd, showed the Federals' effective strength to be very near 70,000, clearly implying that this was the force on the field. Hardee, on the other hand, spoke in his report of the Federal force collected around Nashville being reported at 70,000.

78. *Ibid.*, pp. 215, 674. The Federal casualties are for the period Dec. 26–Jan. 5. For the small deductions needed for the minor engagements, see Livermore, *Numbers and Losses*, p. 97. The Confederate report acknowledges only 1,027 as missing, but Livermore, using a report by Rosecrans's provost marshal of the number of the enemy captured, puts the figure at "about 2,500." Rosecrans lost 28 guns captured and 1 disabled, while his losses in wagons and ambulances were 229 and 28, respectively (*O.R.*, *29*, 242, 228).

For comparative figures for Shiloh, see *supra*, III, 394.

79. *O.R.*, *29*, 187; Nicolay and Hay, *Lincoln*, VIII, 9–10; *O.R.*, *29*, 188.

80. *The Collected Works of Abraham Lincoln*, VI, 424–425.

81. On Dec. 6 Johnston said in a telegram to Cooper from Murfreesboro, "Two thousand cavalry will be sent to break up the Louisville and Nashville Railroad, and 4,000 will be employed in the same way in West Tennessee and Northern Mississippi. The latter may delay General Grant." (*O.R.*, *30*, 441.)

Because Bragg was subordinate to Johnston, full responsibility must be placed upon the latter for the use made of Bragg's cavalry after Dec. 6. J. E.

Dyer, however, puts it upon Bragg, though he notes that the detachment of Stevenson's division was done against Johnston's advice. Dyer's statement that Forrest's raid caused Grant to shift his base to Memphis is inaccurate. It was the combination of the raids by Forrest and Van Dorn that hurt Grant: neither alone would have compelled him to make a change of base. (Nor should one forget that Grant had planned to supply himself from Memphis after reaching Grenada, nor the influence upon his operations of the arrival of McClernand.) Inasmuch as Thomas had only five of the fourteen brigades composing his five divisions present at Stones River on Dec. 31, Dyer's statement that Thomas on that morning held Rosecrans's center with five divisions is a decided exaggeration. (J. E. Dyer, *"Fightin Joe" Wheeler*, pp. 72–73, 74, 84.)

In stating (p. 72) that the Confederate cavalry should have been able to keep the railroad to Louisville cut, and thus delay and discourage almost indefinitely the Federal advance, Dyer overlooks a number of things and forgets that the Cumberland soon became navigable, so that the railroad, though convenient, was no longer a necessity.

NOTES TO CHAPTER X

1. The army reports on the recapture of Galveston are full and interesting. See *O.R., 21,* 199–221. Naval reports are in *O.R. Navies,* Ser. I, XIX. Short accounts are in *B. and L.,* III, 571, 586.

The Confederates had withdrawn from the small town of Galveston near the eastern end of Galveston Island when the Federal fleet took a dominating position. The railroad bridge two miles to the west not having been destroyed, they still had direct access to the island and could easily attack the wharf. The power of defense was in the navy's guns, which for a while seemed to have broken the attack. Unfortunately, the flagship of Commander W. B. Renshaw grounded, and instead of moving to another vessel he superintended efforts to get her afloat. These having failed, the crew was removed and Renshaw himself lighted turpentine poured over the vessel. In a premature explosion he was killed. After a white flag was shown by the *Harriet Lane*—which will be remembered as one of the vessels that sought to take provisions to Fort Sumter—they were flown by other vessels, under which the Confederates claimed some of them escaped. Mahan states (*The Gulf and Inland Waters,* p. 108) that the affair caused Farragut "great indignation." In a letter to Porter on Feb. 6, 1863, Ass't Sec'y of the Navy Gustavus Fox said with reference to the loss of Galveston, "It is too cowardly to place on paper" (*O.R. Navies,* Ser. I, XXIV, 242–243).

Col. Fremantle of the British Army stopped at Galveston on his way from Brownsville to the theater of operations. He recorded in his diary, "The attack by Colonel Cook upon a Massachusetts regiment, fortified at the end of a wharf, also failed, and the Confederates thought themselves 'badly whipped.' But after daylight the fortunate surrender of the *Harriet Lane* to the cotton boat *Bayou City,* and the extraordinary conduct of Commodore Renshaw, converted a Confederate disaster into the recapture of Galveston." (Lord, ed., *The Fremantle Diary,* p. 56.)

2. *O.R., 25,* 828.

3. Reports on the capture of Van Buren, *O.R., 32,* 167–173. Curtis sent a dispatch to Halleck about the operation on Dec. 28. Herron called the march down and back "terrible."

4. Reports on Marmaduke's expedition, *ibid.,* pp. 178–211. In his indorsement to Marmaduke's report Holmes said the expedition had been devised by Hindman and had succeeded in its object of causing the retirement of the Federal forces in Arkansas. Of course, neither he nor Marmaduke knew that on Dec. 29 Curtis had closed a dispatch to Blunt, "You have finished the matter in Northwest Arkansas gloriously, and must come nearer supplies and nearer to other dangers" (*ibid.,* p. 883).

Stores were destroyed at Springfield as well as at several small forts the Federals had evacuated. Union casualties at Springfield and Hartville totaled 243; Marmaduke's loss was 262. The conspicuous bravery of Brig. Gen. Egbert B. Brown at Springfield elicited admiration from the Confederates; he was seriously wounded by a shot from a house. O'Flaherty (*General Jo Shelby,* pp. 165–166) gives Brown 2,099 men with benefit of protection, and Marmaduke 2,300.

The largest contingent in Marmaduke's command was Shelby's, whose six-page report began, "On the last day of December, 1862, when the old year was dying in the lap of the new, and January had sent its moaning winds to wail the requiem of the past, my brigade . . . were on the march for foray on the border's side." In addition to this poetical beginning the report contained three verses, that devoted to the battle at Springfield reading:

> I heard the cannon's shivering crash,
> As when the whirlwind rends the ash;
> I heard the muskets deadly clang,
> As if a thousand anvils rang!

O'Flaherty states that from the fall of 1862, the writing of Shelby's reports was done by his adjutant, Maj. John N. Edwards, because they were onerous to Shelby, and he indicates that Shelby read only a few of them. Leaving entirely aside the florid nature of the reports to which Shelby affixed his signature, and which O'Flaherty states were published after the war to discredit him, it can be said that Shelby's aversion to careful writing and reading is strong evidence that he reached his limit when he was commanding a division of cavalry. Higher commanders had to write many letters and dispatches. O'Flaherty states, however, that what was needed as commander for the Confederate Trans-Mississippi Department was a Napoleon, a Stonewall Jackson, or a Jo Shelby. (O'Flaherty, *op. cit.,* pp. 115, 116, 206, 384, 170.)

Napoleon was a voluminous writer, and Jackson, who had some traits that raise doubts as to his fitness for high, independent command, did not turn over part of his duty to a poetically minded adjutant.

5. *O.R., 24,* 480. After referring to the *Grenada Appeal,* Grant said, "If this statement is confirmed I will fall back to line of Memphis and Corinth."

A dispatch he sent to Dodge on the 4th also referred to the *Grenada Appeal* report (*O.R., 25*, 530).

6. *O.R., 25*, 542, 544, 550. Grant put Sherman at 32,000 men, less casualties, and said he could send 12,000 to 15,000 more. A telegram he had sent at 1:00 P.M. of the 9th said Sherman had returned to Napoleon and that his loss was small (*ibid.,* p. 549).

For orders with regard to Ewing's brigade, which contained 2,600 men, see *ibid.,* pp. 545, 550. Hugh Ewing, the commander, was the first of Sherman's three foster brothers who became brigadier generals.

7. *O.R., 24*, 481; *25*, 525, 522–523. In a dispatch to Gorman on the 3rd, Hurlbut said the railroad would connect with Grant's army "to-day or to-morrow." Replying to a suggestion from Halleck about abandoning the line to Columbus and supplying Corinth from Memphis, Grant told him on the 7th that he thought it advisable to finish repairs on the road to Columbus to get rolling stock "and possibly hold it for a short time." (*O.R., 25*, 526–527, 543; *24*, 480.)

8. *O.R., 25*, 524, 542.

9. *Ibid.,* pp. 540, 541, 833 (Pemberton to Van Dorn on Jan. 13, instructing him to report to Johnston "for operations in connection with Bragg's cavalry"), 532, 541. Some weeks passed before Van Dorn actually reported to Bragg.

On Jan. 6 Pennock at Cairo informed Grant that two light-draft gunboats were ordered up the Tennessee on the rise, and Grant instructed Col. Lowe at Fort Henry to request that they destroy flatboats and other craft that would facilitate a crossing of the river (*ibid.,* p. 541).

10. *Ibid.,* p. 543.

11. *O.R., 24*, 481; *109*, 323; *25*, 530 (Halleck's telegram directing the revoking of Grant's G.O. 11 of 1862, "if such an order has been issued"), 544 (Grant's circular revoking the order); Eaton, *Grant, Lincoln, and the Freedmen,* pp. 30–31.

It is hard to reconcile the wording of Halleck's telegram about G.O. 11 with the claim that he had directed its issuance. On the 21st he ended a letter to Grant with the statement: "It may be proper to give you some explanation of the revocation of your order expelling Jews from your department. The President has no objection to your expelling traitors [traders?] and Jew peddlers, which I suppose, was the object of your order; but, as it in terms proscribed an entire religious class, some of whom are fighting in our ranks, the President deemed it necessary to revoke it." (*O.R., 36*, 9.)

12. *O.R., 25*, 551. Grant also said: "This expedition must not fail. If there is force enough within the limits of my control to secure a certain victory at Vicksburg they will be sent there."

13. *Ibid.,* pp. 551–552; *O.R. Navies,* Ser. I, XXIII, 602–603. A longer quotation from Porter's letter will make the reader better acquainted with him. ". . . We have had lively times up the Yazoo. Imagine the Yazoo becoming the theater of war! We waded through 16 miles of torpedoes to get at the forts (seven in number) but when we got that far the fire on the boats from the riflemen in pits dug for miles along the river and from the batteries became very annoying, and that gallant fellow Gwin thought he could check them,

which he did until he was knocked over with the most fearful wound I ever saw. He could not advance, the torpedoes popping up ahead as thick as mushrooms, and we have had pretty good evidence of their power to do mischief. . . . The old war horse (*Benton*) retained her ancient renown, and, though much cut up, is ready for anything. . . . The same day the army made an assault on the forts back of Vicksburg. It was a fearful place they went through, with double their numbers opposed to them. They drove the rebels like sheep, who fired into their own fugitives and knocked them over like ninepins. That helped our party some but our reserve (a new regiment) fired into our own troops while they were going into the batteries, and the supporting brigade did not come up to the scratch. . . . Vicksburg was at one time ours, but we had not men enough to repeat the experiment. . . . Now it will take a large army to capture it; still it must be done, or the West will stampede. . . . The old ironclads are all breaking down, but in two months I expect to get some of the new ones, which are pretty good vessels. . . ."

No sailor was ever kinder to the army; perhaps no admiral ever had better qualifications for a newspaper correspondent.

Foote, to whom the letter was addressed, was now chief of the Bureau of Equipment and Recruiting.

14. *O.R., 33,* 31. The statement about Fisk's acquaintance with Grant is from *D.A.B.* Following his expression of discouragement Fisk said: "General, I wish you would put on your war harness again and come down this way to help us out. Harmony of action and hearty co-operation on the part of our double stars must be produced in some way. . . . I have been hammering knuckles all the way down; have requested several shoulder-straps to become better advised before they undertook to balance your accounts. I am after the rascals." Actually, Fisk said he was to take dispatches to Sherman. The records, however, contain no communication from Grant to Sherman, and on the 13th Fisk began a message to McClernand, "On the 10th instant, at Memphis, I received from General Grant the inclosed communication to yourself. . . ." (*O.R., 25,* 558). In his letter to Curtis, Fisk said that Grant had arrived in Memphis "this morning."

Soon after the end of the war Fisk was detailed to the Freedmen's Bureau, and during his work in Nashville founded a Negro school in 1866, which received a charter as Fisk University the next year.

15. *O.R., 25,* 546–547.

16. *Ibid.,* pp. 545–546, 552–553.

17. *Ibid.,* pp. 553–554.

18. *Encylopaedia Britannica,* 11th ed., article "Grant."

19. *O.R., 25,* 559 (explaining delay in the previous message), 553.

20. *Ibid.,* p. 555.

21. *Ibid.,* pp. 555, 543.

22. *Ibid.,* pp. 555, 554. Davies, who was directed to report in writing to the Headquarters of the Army for orders, was probably relieved because of his action at New Madrid when he became alarmed over Forrest's raid. On Dec. 26 six heavy guns at that place were spiked, their platforms burned, ammunition destroyed, as well as some barracks, and the small garrison removed to

Fort Pillow on the east bank of the Mississippi. Curtis had the officer in command arrested on the grounds that he should not have obeyed Davies's order, and Stanton ordered an investigation. The findings of Feb. 26, 1863, stated that Davies had acted prudently in view of the possibility that heavy ordnance might be captured, and the arrested officer was restored to duty. (*O.R.*, *32*, 173–177.)

23. McClernand's and Sherman's reports, *O.R.*, *24*, 700–709, 754–759.

24. Mahan, *op. cit.*, pp. 121, 161.

25. Sherman's report; De Courcy's and Lindsey's reports, *O.R.*, *24*, 753–754, 751–752.

26. McClernand's report; Ellet's report, *O.R.*, *24*, 779. Ellet spoke of a ferry six miles beyond the place he reached; he also said, "I notified the commander of the light-draught gunboats of this fact on my return, but am unaware whether any steps were taken to destroy the ferry." Mahan has the *Rattler, Glide,* and *Monarch* going to a ford 10 miles upstream; Porter spoke of the *Glide* going up to the ferry where 30 or 40 of the enemy escaped (*O.R. Navies,* Ser. I, XXIV, 118–119).

27. Sherman's and Lindsey's reports; Morgan's report, *O.R.*, *24*, 721–724; Thorndike, ed., *The Sherman Letters,* p. 181.

28. *O.R. Navies,* Ser. I, XXIV, 114–115; Mahan, *op. cit.*, p. 122.

29. Livermore, *Numbers and Losses,* p. 98; McClernand's report; *O.R. Navies,* Ser. I, XXIV, 108, 117, 108, 116.

30. Hovey's report, *O.R.*, *19*, 358–360; Sherman's report on Arkansas Post.

31. Churchill's report, *O.R.*, *24*, 780–782.

32. *O.R.*, *24*, 699; *25*, 559, 557. In his first report McClernand put the prisoners at from 7,000 to 10,000.

33. *O.R.*, *25*, 560.

34. *Ibid.*, pp. 561, 561–562, 562, 552, 579; *supra,* Chap. VI, p. 146. In a dispatch to Grant on the 10th, reporting his debarkation below Arkansas Post, McClernand said (*O.R.*, *25*, 552), "General Gorman sends word that he is moving with 12,000 men from Helena toward Devall's Bluff on the White River, and Brownsville" (between De Valls Bluff and Little Rock). In Grant's dispatch of the 10th—which was the one McClernand had received—Grant gave no order, because he did not yet know of McClernand's plan. It is not clear on what McClernand based his statement to Gorman about orders from Grant.

35. *O.R.*, *25*, 567, 566–567.

36. *Ibid.*, p. 569.

37. *Ibid.*, pp. 570–571. Sherman's statement that boats with guns could come out of the Arkansas is not convincing. Even after the capture of Arkansas Post rafts and small boats with field pieces could enter the Mississippi from the Arkansas or the White River, while such guns could be placed on the river bank and inflict damage on steamers. On Jan. 3 Porter had sent Shirk in the *Conestoga* "to keep the Arkansas and White rivers closed" (*O.R. Navies,* Ser. I, XXIV, 94).

On Jan. 1 Gorman reported to Hurlbut that the *Blue Wing* had been captured at or near Napoleon, with mail, artillery ammunition, and two barges of coal; he also thought the *Home* had been taken along with two barges of forage. Hurlbut forwarded the dispatch to Grant and in replying to Gorman on the 3rd said, "The *Blue Wing* was probably purposely surrendered; her captain has a bad reputation among loyal river men." In reply to a telegram Grant had sent on the 4th, the ordnance officer at St. Louis reported the next day that he was shipping a large quantity of small-arms ammunition to Memphis for Sherman as well as artillery ammunition to replace that captured on the *Blue Wing*. (*O.R., 25,* 522, 526–527, 536, 537.)

38. In a letter to his brother on Jan. 25, Sherman said he proposed the move against Arkansas Post to McClernand. In a letter to Porter on Feb. 1, in which he spoke of the malicious reports being made about him in the Northern press, he asked Porter to indicate among other things "whether I did not propose to you the attack on the Post of Arkansas as the best possible use we could make of time while awaiting the arrival of Grant and Banks." In a long letter to Sherman on Feb. 1, Brig. Gen. Frank Blair, who had been unjustly accused by Sherman of partial responsibility for what was said by a correspondent concerning the attack at Chickasaw Bluffs, stated, "I am well aware, also, that you planned and in a great measure executed the move against Arkansas Post, and have not failed to say what I knew of it on proper occasions." (Thorndike, ed., *op. cit.,* p. 183; *O.R. Navies,* Ser. I, XXIV, 216–217; *O.R., 25,* 582–586.)

On the other hand, McClernand said in the list of reasons for making the move that he attached to his report, "I had urged upon General Gorman, at Helena, on 28th of December, on my way down the river, either to reduce or invest the post." While the date is incorrect, McClernand accurately represented his feeling about Arkansas Post, as shown by a letter dated Dec. 31, 1862, to Curtis from Col. N. P. Chipman, Curtis's chief of staff, who was, along with McClernand, at Helena that day (*O.R., 32,* 887).

39. *O.R., 25,* 570.

40. Wilson, *The Life of John A. Rawlins,* p. 106.

41. *O.R., 25,* 572, 573. Grant assured Halleck that if Banks passed Port Hudson, his force would be ready to cooperate at any time.

42. *O.R., 36,* 8–9. In Halleck's letter of instructions to Banks on Nov. 9, 1862, the latter's seniority to Grant was plainly indicated (*supra,* Chap. VII, p. 195).

43. *Ibid.,* p. 9. The telegram began, "I found the Mississippi expedition at the mouth of the Arkansas, and started it from there immediately to Young's Point."

44. *Ibid.*

45. *Ibid., 25,* 578–579, 579.

46. *Ibid.,* p. 579.

47. *O.R., 36,* 10.

NOTES TO CHAPTER XI

1. *O.R., 38,* 18–19.

2. *O.R., 36,* 11–14.

3. Robert Todd Lincoln Papers, CI, 21431-2, 21488, 21489, 21504. McClernand's letter to Grant on the 1st does not seem to be in the *O.R.*

4. Grant, *Memoirs*, I, 441 (Long, ed., p. 230).

5. *O.R. Navies*, Ser. I, XXIV, 95; *O.R.*, 25, 827, 823.

6. *O.R.*, 25, 810–811, 831 (strength return for Confederate forces in and about Vicksburg on Jan. 10, 1863). Davis's letter to Holmes, written during his visit at Vicksburg, is in *O.R.*, 110, 397–399; the letter from Johnston that Davis forwarded is *ibid.*, 25, 800–801.

7. *O.R.*, 25, 839–840. For some interesting telegrams on the subject of salt, that passed between Davis and Gov. Pettus, see *O.R.*, 128, 126; 110, 393. A letter that Pettus wrote is apparently missing, but "arrangements" that he said in a telegram had been made were probably of the sort that Pemberton disliked.

8. J. C. Pemberton speaks on p. 224 of *Pemberton, Defender of Vicksburg,* of Pemberton's feat in holding back Grant's crushing numbers for nine months. It would be hard to find a statement that more completely ignores important realities. Vicksburg was a striking illustration of the way a defending force is greatly multiplied by unusually favorable terrain, complete acquaintance with it, and opportunity to fortify. It will appear later whether Grant really had "crushing numbers" at the really critical time of the campaign and whether Pemberton was adequate when he had lost the advantage of inaccessibility.

9. Thorndike, ed., *The Sherman Letters,* pp. 183. Sherman said the Confederates had the best Enfield rifles.

10. *O.R. Navies*, Ser. I, XXIV, 205, 204–205.

11. *Ibid.*, pp. 218, 219–220, 217–218.

12. *Ibid.*, pp. 223–224 (report by Ellet dated Feb. 5), 222.

13. *Ibid.*, pp. 323–324 (station list for the 54 vessels under Porter's command, which spoke of the *De Soto* having been turned over to the navy), 383–386 (Ellet's report; also in *O.R.*, 36, 341–344); Mahan, *The Gulf and Inland Waters,* p. 162. See n. 20 for reference to the correspondents aboard the *Queen.*

14. *O.R. Navies*, Ser. I, XXIV, 376–377 (Porter's instructions to Brown); Ellet's report; Brown's reports, *O.R. Navies*, Ser. I, XXIV, 377–379, 379–381.

15. Brown's and Ellet's reports; Ellet to Porter, *O.R. Navies*, Ser. I, XXIV, 382.

16. Brown's reports. In the second of his reports, which was written in Washington on May 28, after his exchange, Brown said the engagement lasted an hour and 27 minutes, that he lost 1 man killed, 1 wounded, and 7 missing, while the enemy lost 2 officers and 33 men killed, and many wounded. An entry in the log of the *Tuscumbia* for Apr. 20 located the wreck of the *Indianola* as "off Jeff Davis's plantation, at head of Palmyra Island" (*O.R. Navies*, Ser. I, XXIV, 704.)

17. *Ibid.*, pp. 686 (log of the *Black Hawk* for Feb. 27), 388, 388–389.

18. *Ibid.*, pp. 376–377; Mahan, *op. cit.*, pp. 133, 132–133. Mahan states that the dummy monitor was "built upon the hull of an old coal barge, with pork barrels piled to resemble smokestacks, through which poured volumes of smoke from mud furnaces." After passing the batteries the vessel "drifted into the lower end of the canal, and was again sent down stream by the amused

Union soldiers, who as little as the admiral dreamed of the good service the dummy was to do."

19. *O.R., 38,* 646. A telegram that Pemberton sent to Stevenson on the 27th began, "You must, if possible blow up the *Indianola.*"

20. Gosnell, *Guns on the Western Waters,* pp. 179–192 (accounts by Bodman, incorrectly stated as being with the *New York Tribune*); *O.R. Navies,* Ser. I, XXIV, 382–383. Porter said in his letter to Welles, "Had the commander of the *Queen of the West* waited patiently, he would, in less than twenty-four hours, have been joined by the *Indianola. . . .* My plans were well laid, only badly executed. I can give orders, but I can not give officers good judgment." It is questionable how much Ellet knew about the *Indianola's* mission. All that Porter seems to have told him was contained in a dispatch on Feb. 10, saying he hoped Ellet would get away as soon as it was dark, to which he added the postscript, "Don't be surprised to see the *Indianola* below. Don't mistake her for a rebel; she looks something like the *Chillicothe.* (*Ibid.,* p. 370.)

Bodman referred to J. B. McCullagh of the *Commercial* and Finley Anderson of the *Herald.* Anderson was a prisoner for eleven months (Starr, *Bohemian Brigade,* p. 193).

21. *O.R. Navies,* Ser. I, XXIV, 242–243. Fox said, "The disgraceful affair at Galveston has shaken the public confidence in our prestige," and continued in an unrestrained manner.

22. *O.R., 36,* 10. In a telegram on Feb. 3 that spoke of the work on the canal as progressing as rapidly as possible, Grant reported the running of the blockade by the *Queen of the West,* pronouncing it of "vast importance," because it cut Confederate communications with the west bank of the river (*ibid.,* p. 14).

23. *Ibid.,* pp. 14–16.

24. *O.R., 25,* 580–581 (Knox to Sherman), 889–892 (charges against Knox and the findings). The charges contain a long extract from Knox's story that had appeared in the *Herald* on Jan. 18. He was found not guilty of the charge of giving intelligence to the enemy, directly or indirectly, and also not guilty of the charge of being a spy. But he was found guilty of disobeying an order by Sherman and that by the War Department of Aug. 26, 1861, the latter having been violated when Knox wrote and caused to be printed information about the movement of the army "without the authority and sanction of the general commanding."

25. *Ibid.,* pp. 893–895 (Knox to Sherman with Lincoln's "Whom it may concern," Grant to Knox, Sherman to Knox, and Sherman to Grant).

26. Starr, *op. cit.,* pp. 279, 280; Miers, *The Web of Victory,* p. 55. According to Cadwallader, "several Cincinnati gentlemen of Hebrew persuasion" reached Oxford, Miss., a day or two after Grant's father. Jesse Grant was merely their cat's-paw; they were to furnish the capital; he was to get a permit from his son for cotton trading. The general's anger was bitter and malignant against the would-be traders and manipulators of his father; the first train for the north bore them swiftly homeward, "accompanied by 'Uncle Jesse' with a stupendous flea in his ear." It was after he had expelled his father that Grant—according

to Cadwallader—issued the expulsion order that he was presently directed to revoke.

It was seen *supra* p. 513 that Jesse Grant could not possibly have reached Oxford prior to Dec. 16, 1862, the day before the issuance of G.O. 11. John Eaton's statement about leaving Oxford on the same train with Grant's wife and father *after* the Holly Springs raid of the 20th shows that the spectacular part of the Cadwallader story is entirely false. The terminal date for his visit that Jesse Grant gave in his letter to Washburne would of course have sufficed to discredit what the onetime journalist wrote in his later years.

Cadwallader bitterly denounced Col. Dickey, who, it will be recalled, brought Grant the warning about Van Dorn's column. Cadwallader was with Dickey on his raid against the Mobile and Ohio R.R. and says that Dickey should have attacked the Confederate column even "at the cost of his entire command." In that way, valuable stores of great amount would have been saved. But, as Cadwallader plainly recognizes that Dickey's warning was in plenty of time and the destruction of the stores was Col. Murphy's fault, his reasoning was inconsistent.

One would think that a correspondent who had spent thirty months with Grant would have known that Grant had officially recorded his views about Holly Springs. While Grant's report strongly condemned Murphy, it spoke well of Dickey. With obvious approval Grant referred to Dickey's "passing safely" in the rear of Van Dorn, and he said what he had done upon learning that "Colonel Dickey was safe."

Cadwallader did not let Dickey off with saying he should have thrown his 800 men against a force reported to be from 7,000 to 8,000, and which actually numbered 3,500 men. In the same sentence in which he says that Murphy was openly disgraced, Cadwallader states that Dickey was "sent north on detached service until the close of the war," and he also says that Dickey as well as Murphy "failed on the crucial test." (Thomas, ed., *Three Years with Grant,* pp. 31–36.)

Later in this chapter we shall see Dickey still in command of the cavalry division; according to the *D.A.B.* he resigned from the army in the latter part of 1863, which one would hardly call the end of the war. Cadwallader's treatment of the Dickey case shows he had shortcoming as a military appraiser in addition to the indifference to facts that appears in his explanation of the "expulsion order."

27. Wilson, *The Life of John A. Rawlins,* p. 273.

28. Thorndike, ed., *op. cit.,* p. 185.

29. Wilson's report, *O.R., 36,* 386–389; *O.R., 38,* 38 (Grant's instructions of Feb. 7 to "Commanding Officer Yazoo Expedition"), 39 (Grant to Gorman, Feb. 8), 39 and 55 (order and Grant's letter to Porter referring to relief of Gorman).

On Nov. 28, I. N. Brown of the Confederate Navy had begun a letter to Pemberton from Yazoo City: "I beg leave respectfully to represent to the commanding officer that if the Yazoo Pass remains unobstructed it may at high water afford the enemy a passage for their gun-boats into the Coldwater River and thence to this place." While he was not sure a permanent obstruction could be built, Brown thought that trees felled from both sides of the stream would seriously impede navigation, the river seldom being over 100 feet wide. (*O.R., 110*, 392–393.)

30. Wilson's report. A map that Wilson sent to Rawlins on Feb. 24 (*O.R., 36*, 277) shows a new entrance into Moon Lake from the Mississippi in addition to the old one.

31. Deitzler's report, *O.R., 36*, 15.

32. *O.R., 38*, 33, 43–44.

33. *Ibid.*, pp. 40–41.

34. *O.R., 38*, 49; Thorndike, ed., *op. cit.*, p. 192; Thomas, ed., *op. cit.*, p. 56. For the change of command between Hamilton and Hurlbut in Memphis, see *O.R., 38*, 24 n.

35. *O.R., 38*, 58.

36. *Ibid.*, pp. 46, 50, 58. Hurlbut's dispatch to Rosecrans does not seem to be in the records, but in the one to Rawlins he said, "I have telegraphed to General Rosecrans and to the naval officer at Cairo to push a gunboat up."

37. *Ibid.*, p. 63.

38. *Ibid.*, p. 53.

39. *Ibid.*, pp. 56–57, 57, 63.

40. *O.R., 36*, 17. On Feb. 6 Grant had sent to Halleck the reports Wilson had written on the 2nd and 4th, in the second of which he had described the opening of the levee as a "perfect success" and had said that Confederate General Alcorn had stated they could reach the Yazoo (*ibid.*, pp. 17, 373).

41. *Ibid.*, p. 18.

42. *O.R., 36*, 19; *O.R. Navies*, Ser. I, XXIV, 448.

43. *O.R., 38*, 89–90; *36*, 19–20.

44. *O.R., 36*, 380–382. The mutual esteem that had already arisen between Rawlins and Wilson is revealed by the ending of the latter's letter: "Write me about affairs below and the prospect. Your letter of the latest day was very interesting. Accept my grateful acknowledgment of the kind sentiment manifested toward me, and believe me, dear Rawlins, very truly, your friend."

45. *Ibid.*, pp. 379, 385–386.

46. Mahan, *op. cit.*, pp. 146–147. Mahan states, "The difficulty of handling when fighting down stream prevented the vessels from getting that nearness to the enemy which is so essential in an attack by ships upon fortifications." He gives a fairly detailed account of the engagement of the 16th.

47. *O.R., 36*, 414–420. Loring's telegraphic reports began on Mar. 11. In one on the 13th he said, "Terrific fire from the enemy; four hours; uninterrupted; from ten to sixteen heavy caliber gunboat guns; two heavy guns on land, and a mortar. . . ." Pemberton forwarded this dispatch to Johnston at Chattanooga. (*Ibid.*, pp. 412–413.)

An excellent map by Wilson of the region about Fort Pemberton is in *ibid.*, p. 389. Ross sent several reports to Prentiss, beginning on Mar. 2. A report that he wrote on Apr. 18 was addressed to Rawlins. In it he said nothing of what had taken place during Quinby's command of the expedition, but closed, "Upon a full retrospect, with my present knowledge of the facts, I can discover nothing that the infantry force could have done, with the means at hand, more than they did to insure success." Brig. Gen. Frederick Salomon, who has been seen in the Indian Territory expedition and in southwest Missouri, was now a part of Ross's division, and he concluded his report, "I cannot close this report without mentioning the good effect obtained by the strict discipline under your command." (*Ibid.*, pp. 393–401.)

Quinby apparently made no final report, but sent several covering the beginning of his part in the operation, and two while on the Tallahatchie, the last dated Mar. 28 (*ibid.*, pp. 404–409).

In a letter on June 18 to Grant, Wilson said, "To the timidity, over cautiousness, and lack of interest displayed by Lieut. Commander Watson Smith, commanding the gunboats, and the delays growing out of them, is attributable the failure of the entire expedition." Wilson stated that he, Ross, and the commanders of the *Chillicothe* and *De Kalb* had all frequently urged Smith to move more rapidly. He commended the two gunboat commanders highly and said he was convinced that they would have "cheerfully obeyed any order from their superior officer." (*Ibid.*, pp. 390–391.)

Reports by Smith of Mar. 3 and 7 are in *O.R.*, *36*, 409–411. Porter's instructions to Smith of Feb. 6, Smith's final report to him, a letter from Grant to Porter of Feb. 6 about the operation, and several interim reports by Smith up to Mar. 16 are in *O.R. Navies*, Ser. I, XXIV, 243–278.

In his final report Smith said that his health had completely failed him and that he had been obliged to submit to the judgment of the medical officer. Command of the expedition then devolved upon the commander of the *Chillicothe*, and Smith stated, "At the time I had no fear for the final success of the expedition."

48. *O.R.*, *38*, 112 (Grant to McPherson, Mar. 16); *36*, 431–436 (Sherman's reports to Grant with regard to the Steele's Bayou expedition), 23–24 (Grant to Halleck).

Frank R. Smith, Congressman from Greenwood, Miss., speaks in *The Yazoo* (pp. 127–128) of the efforts that Sherman made to prevent looting, quoting a letter from Sherman to Steele, and saying that Sherman caused animals and equipment taken from plantations to be returned to their owners.

49. Mahan, *op. cit.*, pp. 136–138; Lewis, *David Glasgow Farragut*, II, Chap. XV; *O.R.*, *36*, 23–24; *O.R. Navies*, Ser. I, XX, 25–26. Failure of more ships to pass the batteries at Port Hudson was not so much because of the Confederate guns, though they scored good hits, as to other circumstances. The channel was near the eastern bank, and smoke from great fires built to illuminate the river made piloting very difficult. Ships grounded and were got off only after much labor.

Grant had closed a telegram to Halleck on the 24th: "Farragut holds the river above Port Hudson" (*O.R.*, *36*, 22).

When the Mississippi cut across the point opposite Vicksburg during high water in 1876, the channel it followed was not along the wartime Federal canal.

50. *O.R.*, *38*, 46–47.

51. Robert Todd Lincoln Collection, CVI, 22416-7; *O.R.*, *7*, 551–552. Grant stated that Kountz, recently sent to Cairo as master of transportation, "from his great unpopularity with river men and his wholesale denunciation of every-

body connected with the Government as thieves and cheats, was entirely unable to get crews for the necessary boats" [required by the demonstration Halleck had ordered], until he, Grant, intervened. For a study of Kountz, see Theodore R. Parker, "William J. Kountz, Superintendent of River Transportation under McClellan, 1861–1862," *Western Pennsylvania Historical Magazine,* XXI, 237–254.

Parker states that Grant acted in the public interest in the Kountz case and he also says that when the quartermaster general sent Kountz to the West, he cautioned him because of difficulties he had previously had with officers. In a letter to Kountz on Dec. 20, 1861 (not in the *O.R.* but in Grant's headquarters records in the Library of Congress), Grant took Kountz sharply to task for reportedly carrying on inspections without having reported to Grant for the purpose of showing the orders under which he was operating.

On Jan. 26, 1862, twelve days after Grant had put him in arrest, Kountz preferred charges against Grant for drunkenness. One specification was that Grant had been "beastly drunk" on a flag-of-truce boat from Cairo to Columbus on Dec. 6, 1861; another, that on Dec. 7 and diverse days afterward, he had been "intoxicated to drunkenness" at Cairo. The dates fall within a period specially emphasized by Rawlins in his letter to Washburne of Dec. 30 as one of abstinence by Grant (*supra,* III, 152), and Kountz's second specification can be accepted only by saying that Rawlins deliberately wrote falsely. (It may be recalled that Rawlins's letter had been in answer to an inquiry Washburne had made because of rumors that had been circulated about Grant, largely, according to Rawlins and Wilson, because Grant had prevented persons from defrauding the government by selling supplies at too high prices.)

There is strong reason to doubt that Grant was even on a flag-of-truce boat on Dec. 6, though Gen. Polk, commanding the Confederates at Columbus, spoke in a letter to his wife of Nov. 16 of having seen Grant on such boats prior to that date. A letter Grant wrote at Cairo to Polk on Dec. 5 indicates that a boat went to Columbus that day, and the next day Polk directed to Grant a letter that uses the "the memorandum herewith sent you" as a summary of all exchanges of prisoners that had been made and which spoke of other men Polk would return. (*Supra,* III, 100; *O.R., 114,* 528–529.) It is hard to reconcile the two letters with Grant's presence on a flag-of-truce boat on either Dec. 5 or 6. While it had been natural for him to go to see Polk personally immediately after the battle of Belmont, because higher authority had not yet fixed a policy for the exchange of prisoners, it was not natural for him to continue the practice.

Kountz sent his charges directly to Halleck at St. Louis, and Halleck referred them to Grant. On Jan. 29 Grant added the indorsement: "Capt Kountz will please furnish a copy of these charges for this office and one copy to be sent to Headquarters of the Dept." The next day Halleck telegraphed to Grant to make preparations to take Fort Henry, and Grant soon left Cairo. When Thomas A. Scott, Assistant Secretary of War, arrived in the town on Feb. 10, he found Kountz, whom he had known in Pennsylvania, in arrest. Two days later he discussed the case in a letter to Stanton, recommending that Kountz be released from arrest and that the charge against Grant "be suspended for the present." Scott sent the charge sheet to Stanton (it is in the Stanton Papers), Kountz on Feb. 12 having written below Grant's indc .e-ment, "I complied with the above at the time and gave the other to Maj. Rawlins on the 30th of Jan. 62." Whether or not Kountz actually gave a copy of the charges to Rawlins cannot be said. But it is certain that he did not return the original charge sheet to Grant's headquarters for resubmission to Halleck.

It is probable that Scott also forwarded to Stanton the scurrilous and anonymous sheet in the Stanton Papers dated Cairo, Feb. 8, 1862, charging Grant not only with drunkenness but with immoral conduct and playing cards for money while he was a disbursing agent of secret service funds.

From Parker we learn that Kountz, like Rawlins, was a teetotaler, his views on the subject of drinking being so extreme that he sometimes showed intolerance.

52. *O.R., 38,* 109–110. In *Memoirs,* I, 458 (Long, ed., p. 238), Grant speaks of the loss of life from disease having been much less than might have been expected, because the hospital arrangements and medical attendance were so perfect. He added, "Visitors to the camps went home with dismal stories to relate; Northern papers came back to the soldiers with these stories exaggerated."

53. Grant, *op. cit.,* p. 460 (Long, ed., p. 239); *O.R., 36,* 22.

54. *O.R., 36,* 19; *35,* 111 (Rosecrans's reply to Halleck); King, *The True Ulysses S. Grant,* p. 239.

55. *O.R., 36,* 22, 24, 27–28. After quoting a sentence from Halleck's telegram of the 24th, Miers speaks of him as being obviously irritated and on edge. He also refers to Grant as having been a desultory correspondent. (Miers, *op. cit.,* p. 118.)

In the letter in which he explained about the detention of boats, Grant said that he had been particular to write and telegraph, even when there was nothing important to say, knowing that Halleck wished to keep constantly posted. While he supposed that all his letters arrived, he thought the telegrams had in many cases failed to get through. To this Halleck also assented.

56. *O.R., 36,* 25 (Halleck to Grant); *38,* 168 (Grant to Porter). For a report on a reconnaissance of the bayous to the west of Milliken's Bend which Grant had ordered on Jan. 31, see Coryn to Grant, Feb. 5, *O.R., 38,* 33–34.

On Mar. 22 Grant wrote a rather long letter to Banks (*O.R., 38,* 125–126) which will appear in its proper setting in the next chapter. It had just become apparent that the Steele Bayou effort had failed, and Grant said: "This experiment failing, there is nothing left for me but to collect my strength and attack Haynes' Bluff. This will necessarily be attended with much loss, but I think it can be done." He ended by stating that because of the scattered situation of his forces and the difficulties of getting transportation, the attack could not possibly be made in less than two weeks, if then.

In spite of the positiveness of Grant's statement to Banks, the first steps in the move that was eventually used had been taken before the reconnaissance that led to the final and complete abandonment of the thought of an assault in the general region where Sherman had failed.

57. *O.R. Navies,* Ser. I, XXIV, 474–480. The folding map opposite p. 480

shows eight bridges between Black Bayou and Rolling Fork, the ones doubtless that the gunboats knocked down so effectively. The names of residents are given in the rich Deer Creek region, where Porter said the enemy had burned 20,000 bales of cotton.

58. *O.R., 38*, 151–152.

59. *O.R., 36*, 24.

60. *Ibid.*, pp. 25–26.

61. Greene, *The Mississippi*, p. 107.

62. Hale, *Horace Greeley*, pp. 252–253; Dana, *Recollections of the Civil War*, pp. 18–20; *O.R., 124*, 111–112 (Lincoln's proclamation, erroneously ascribed by Dana to Mar. 31).

It was Dana who had actually written the editorial in the *Tribune* demanding the resignation of the Cabinet after the first battle at Bull Run, although he was responsible for the slogan "Forward to Richmond" that the paper had carried at its masthead. Greeley, however, had at least not disapproved of the editorial, while he had definitely approved of the slogan. (Hale, *op. cit.*, p. 247.)

63. Dana, *op. cit.*, pp. 20–22.

64. *O.R., 36*, 69, 70. In his dispatch of Mar. 31 Dana reported: "Ten of the most prominent and wealthy secession families of Memphis yesterday received orders from Hurlbut to leave the city instantly. This is the consequence of orders in January notifying all such persons that their remaining here depended upon their friends beyond our lines leaving the railroad undisturbed. The attack of [the] 28th near Moscow is punished by this expulsion." (*O.R., 36*, 68–69.)

65. *O.R., 36*, 71–73; *38*, 179–180 (Sherman to Rawlins, Apr. 8). Sherman recommended that a return be made to an overland operation through Grenada. After listing seven points, he said: "I make these suggestions with the request that General Grant simply read them, and simply give them, as I know he will, a share of his thoughts. I would prefer he should not answer them, but merely give them as much or as little weight as they deserve. Whatever plan of action he may adopt will receive from me the same zealous co-operation and energetic support as though conceived by myself." Sherman closed by saying he did not believe Banks would make a serious attack on Port Hudson "this spring." In a letter to his brother written at Napoleon on Jan. 17 he had said, after referring to Banks, "Of ourselves we cannot take Vicksburg" (Thorndike, ed., *op. cit.*, p. 181).

Although Grant's force was larger than the one which Sherman had in mind in his letter to his brother, it is clear that he still held to the impossibility of taking Vicksburg except with substantial aid from the south or by an overland operation. In his *Memoirs* (I, 542–543; Long, ed., pp. 283–284) Grant describes a personal call that Sherman made on him after learning of his decision to go below Vicksburg. He states that he did not preserve the letter Sherman then wrote to Rawlins, not regarding it as official, but Sherman had furnished a copy of it to Badeau when Badeau was writing his history.

If Sherman had an inflexible loyalty for Grant, Sherman's soldiers had the same for him, as was demonstrated by a letter in the *Cincinnati Daily Com-*

mercial of Jan. 24, 1862, which had been written on the 13th, two days after the capture of Arkansas Post. The writer spoke of the abuse of Sherman in Ohio and said: "There is not a soldier in this entire army who does not love him as they love their own lives. They know that he is always near them in the hour of battle, ready to share their fate, if need be." The letter had been read to hundreds of soldiers from different states, and they had all wanted to sign it. Clearly the reverse that Sherman had suffered on the Yazoo had not hurt his standing with his men, and they went into the Vicksburg campaign with hearts filled with devotion to their commander.

An editorial in the *Commercial* on Jan. 23 had closed with a statement about the false light in which Grant had appeared before the public, "partly through his own indifference to what is said concerning him." Grant was not indifferent; he merely kept silent.

66. *O.R.*, *36*, 73–74, 25, 28.

67. *Ibid.*, pp. 74–75.

68. *Ibid.*, pp. 251, 252.

69. *O.R.*, *36*, 76, 78–79, 21; *38*, 231; *36*, 47, 31, 79–80.

70. *O.R.*, *36*, 38, 49–50, 58, 95, 202. For a detailed and interesting treatment of Grierson's raid, see Brown, *Grierson's Raid*. Brown's end maps show Grierson's route and the facing pages give explanatory chronology. A good map is also in McCormick's *Ulysses S. Grant*, facing p. 100.

71. *O.R.*, *36*, 47–48 (in Grant's general report), 142 (in McClernand's report); *38*, 231. In his letter to Halleck on Mar. 7 Grant had said, "The most ample provision that I ever saw has been made for the comfort of the sick." In *Memoirs*, I, 473 (Long, ed., p. 248), he states that the reason for continuing to Hard Times was inability to find a landing place above Grand Gulf.

72. *O.R.*, *124*, 100–101; Winther, ed., *With Sherman to the Sea* (letters and diaries of Upson), p. 55.

73. Porter, *Incidents and Anecdotes of the Civil War*, pp. 181–182; Wilson, ed., *Grant's Letters to a Friend*, pp. 23–26; Thomas, ed., *op. cit.*, p. 60.

Porter states that he gave Thomas a sharp warning against removing Grant, and although he concedes that Thomas replied that he had no intention of doing so because he was pleased with what he had seen, Porter still manages to emerge with much credit to himself. The great detail and the lively conversation given in the Porter book is alone sufficient to raise distrust about it, and it has previously been noted (*supra*, p. 509) that Porter has Grant make statements to him when they first met at Cairo that are completely irreconcilable with the situation at the time.

Sandburg accepts the Porter story apparently without question. Benjamin Thomas states that Lincoln sent Washburne, Yates, and Gen. Thomas to investigate Grant's conduct, but gives no authority. (Sandburg, *Abraham Lincoln, The War Years*, II, 120–121; Thomas, *Abraham Lincoln*, p. 373.)

The presence of Gov. Yates hardly needs an explanation if one recalls the large number of Illinois troops in Grant's army. An invitation to him from McClernand is not at all unlikely.

Cadwallader recognizes Thomas's mission as only secondarily concerned with Negro matters.

74. *O.R., 38,* 174, 186–187, 187.

75. *O.R., 36,* 518, 517, 564–565. For a detailed report to Lagow by Lieut. Col. W. S. Oliver of the 7th Missouri, who commanded the *Tigress,* see *ibid.,* pp. 566–567. Oliver said: "Not a man of my crew [all from his regiment] left his post until ordered so to do, the engineers and firemen being in water up to their knees before being relieved. I assembled my crew on the hurricane deck, and hailed the steamer *J. W. Cheesman,* which came alongside." Oliver estimated that the *Tigress* was struck 35 times, 14 of the hits being in the hull, "the last one causing her to fill and settle fast."

76. Letter from U. S. Grant, 3rd, to the author. In his article "With Grant at Vicksburg," Frederick Dent Grant passed over how he got below the city. He spoke of accompanying his father on a thirty-mile ride from Milliken's Bend to visit McClernand at New Carthage. After speaking of returning to Milliken's Bend, he said, "From there father moved to the head of the army, which now had advanced to Hard Times." He himself next appears on Apr. 29, when he was on the tug with his father observing the bombardment of Grand Gulf.

77. William Tecumseh Sherman Papers, Vol. XII, letters of Apr. 26 and 10, 1863; Dana, *op. cit.,* p. 76.

Sherman's statement about Grant being impelled by clamor in the rear does not appear in the letter as given by Thorndike. The sentence about Dana is limited to the first four words without indication of omission, the next sentence following immediately after those words. Statements highly derogatory to Lincoln are omitted from John Sherman's letter of May 7, as published by Thorndike. According to John Sherman, "anybody would be better," Lincoln's handling of the Knox affair being only one of a thousand evidences of his unfitness that could be named.

78. *O.R., 38,* 227.

79. *O.R., 36,* 80, 79–80, 78.

80. *Ibid.,* pp. 80, 80–81.

81. *O.R., 38,* 237–238. The directive said, "The first object is to get a foothold where our troops can maintain themselves." Although Grant spoke of only three signals, Porter described five in his order to the commander of the *Benton* (*O.R. Navies,* Ser. I, XXIV, 609).

82. *O.R., 36,* 48 (in Grant's report); *O.R. Navies,* Ser. I, XXIV, 628–629 (Alfred Mitchell to "Dear Ainsworth"), 610–612 (Porter's report dated the 29th), 616, 617, 621, 623 (other reports). Seven gunboats made the attack, and Porter evidently did not know he had done some serious damage to the enemy, for he said, "It was remarkable that we did not disable his guns, but though we knocked the parapets pretty much to pieces, the guns were apparently uninjured."

83. *O.R., 36,* 48 (in Grant's report).

84. *O.R., 38,* 246. Macfeely and Bingham have been already seen in Buell's campaign.

85. *O.R., 36,* 32.

86. *Ibid.,* p. 83.

87. *O.R., 124,* 106–107; *supra,* II, 577.

88. *O.R., 38,* 801, 802–803.

89. Brown, *op. cit.,* pp. 25, 56, 62–65; Grierson's report, *O.R., 36,* 522–529.

NOTES TO CHAPTER XII

1. Grant's and McClernand's reports, *O.R., 36,* 44–59, 137–157; *38,* 248.

2. McPherson's, Logan's, and Sherman's reports, *O.R., 36,* 633–642, 642–650, 751–758; *38,* 261; *36,* 576–577.

3. McClernand's report. At Arkansas Post, Hovey had commanded a brigade in Sherman's corps, but had since been advanced to division command and transferred to McClernand's corps.

4. Grant to Halleck, May 3, *O.R., 36,* 32–34; Bowen's report, *ibid.,* pp. 651–667; Grant's, McPherson's, and McClernand's reports.

5. McPherson's and Grant's reports. Grant put his casualties at 130 killed, 718 wounded, and 5 missing, making a total of 853. (A final tabulation in *O.R., 36,* 582–585, gives a total of 875, owing mostly to an increase of 20 in missing.) Bowen put his loss at 68 killed, 380 wounded, and 384 missing, giving a total of 832. Because Bowen left the field, many of his "missing" may have been killed or wounded.

6. *O.R., 36,* 660, 660–661.

7. *O.R., 36,* 661; *38,* 812–823, 811, 807.

8. *O.R., 38,* 808; *36,* 578; *38,* 808. For naval reports on the attack at Haynes Bluff, see *O.R. Navies,* Ser. I, XXIV, 583–596. Porter was much displeased over what had taken place, for it gave the Confederates a chance to boast of a victory. In a dispatch on May 14 to the officer left in command above, he said (*ibid.,* p. 596): "A feint means a pretended attack, whereas yours was a real one. When I told General Grant that he might have the squadron above to make a feint I never intended the vessels to go under fire, otherwise I would have written you. Under no circumstances, during my absence, will you permit the vessels to make any attack on land batteries without orders from me."

9. *O.R., 38,* 807, 808. Davis had sent Johnston to Tullahoma because he understood that the opinions that Bragg had solicited from his subordinates, as so far received, indicated a lack of confidence in him since his retreat from Murfreesboro (*O.R., 35,* 613–614).

10. McClernand's, McPherson's, and Logan's reports; Wilson's report, *O.R., 36,* 126–130. McPherson states that Logan's engineer and pioneer troops assisted Wilson.

11. Wilson's report.

12. McPherson's and Logan's reports; Grant's letter to Halleck of May 3, *O.R., 36,* 32–34. McPherson says Logan's division took the road to Grand Gulf, and Grant's statement in *Memoirs,* I, 489–490 (Long, ed., p. 257), agrees with this. Logan's report, however, indicates that only a brigade went in that

direction; and in his letter to Halleck, written at Grand Gulf, Grant said that upon arriving at Willow Springs, "I immediately started for this place with one brigade of Logan's division and some 20 cavalrymen."

In his report Wilson says Grindstone Ford was found to be practicable for infantry, but, because of bad approaches, "rather difficult for cavalry or artillery." He gives a full description of what was done in rebuilding the bridge, ending with the statement, "The pioneer company and detail did not report till 11.30 p.m. By 5.00 a.m. the next morning the bridge was completed and the army in full march."

13. *O.R., 38*, 816.

14. *Ibid.,* p. 266.

15. *Ibid.,* pp. 815, 821. On Apr. 20 Reynolds made a raid with three brigades of infantry and one of cavalry in the direction of McMinnville; on the 27th something of a demonstration was made in the direction of Van Dorn's main command south of Franklin (Cist, *The Army of the Cumberland*, p. 147).

16. *O.R. Navies,* Ser. I, XXIV, 626–627.

17. Grant, *Memoirs*, I, 490–491 (Long, ed., p. 257).

18. *O.R., 38*, 259–260 (Farragut to Grant), 182–183 (Banks to Grant). In *Memoirs*, I, 491 (Long, ed., p. 258), Grant says that while at Grand Gulf he heard from Banks, "who was on the Red River." He probably had in mind one of Banks's later communications, though Banks did not reach Alexandria on the Red River from Opelousas until May 7. On the other hand, Grant says in his report, the date referred to being May 3, "About this time I received a letter from General Banks, giving his position west of the Mississippi River. . . ." Greene states (*The Mississippi*, pp. 138–139), "On May 2, at Port Gibson, Grant received a letter from Banks, sent by Farragut on the ram Switzerland from the mouth of Red River."

19. Banks's report, *O.R., 41*, 5–21; Richard B. Irwin, "The Capture of Port Hudson," *B. and L.,* III, 586–598; Greene, *op. cit.,* Chap. VII; Mahan, *The Gulf and Inland Waters,* p. 164.

20. Parks, *General Edmund Kirby Smith,* pp. 257, 259; *O.R., 33,* 798 (Smith's order of Mar. 7 assuming command at Alexandria), 830 (order of Apr. 24 transferring headquarters to Shreveport), 780 (order of Jan. 30 directing Hindman to go to Vicksburg and await further orders), 781 (letter of Feb. 3 from Seddon to Smith about trying to arrange with Pemberton for an interchange of troops that would take Price and his men west of the Mississippi), 808 (order by Holmes of Mar. 30 assigning Price to command of a division), 911 (Price's order of Apr. 1 assuming command of the division at Little Rock).

Smith was first (Jan. 14, 1863) given command only of the Southwestern Army, embracing the Department of West Louisiana and Texas, which was to be broken off the Trans-Mississippi Department; on Feb. 9 his command was extended to the entire original department (*O.R., 21,* 948, 972).

A strength return for March (*O.R., 33,* 810) gives Holmes an aggregate present of 25,313 in the District of Arkansas, of which 8,543 were in the division given Price and 8,444 in that of Walker. Parks states that Smith found Holmes's strength had been greatly exaggerated in Richmond, which would confirm what Holmes had been saying. The condition of the command was, however, better than Smith had expected, because of Hindman's disappearance and Holmes's energy in getting absentees back. Any effect of Price's coming could not have appeared by Mar. 17, the day of Smith's arrival in Little Rock.

21. Grant to Banks of Mar. 22, Grant to Farragut (two letters) of Mar. 23, Banks to Grant of Apr. 23, *O.R.*, *38*, 125–126, 131, 223–225; Greene, *op. cit.*, pp. 221–222.

Greene has Grant's letter to Banks written on Mar. 23, both in the text and in the appendix, where it is given in full. In the *O.R.*, however, it is dated the 22nd. Since a letter that Farragut wrote to Grant on the 22nd (*O.R.*, *38*, 125) begins, "I have just received your several communications and one for General Banks. . . ." there is no question about the date of the dispatch to Banks— unless Farragut was confused as to the day on which he was writing. There being only one message from Grant to Farragut on the 22nd (*ibid.*, p. 126), the word "several" adds to the puzzle, as does also the fact that Banks in his letter of Apr. 23 spoke of Grant's dispatches of Mar. 23, which was, however, the date of the one to Farragut that had said Grant could send 20,000 men to Banks if he got the Ohio River steamers.

Reference has already been made (*supra*, p. 553) to Grant's statement in his letter to Banks that there was nothing left for him to do but attack Haynes Bluff.

22. *O.R.*, *38*, 182–183, 259–260; *O.R. Navies*, Ser. I, XX, 137–138, 138–139; *O.R.*, *41*, 10–11 (in Banks's final report—not written until Apr. 6, 1865).

An interesting account of Taylor's operations will be found in his *Destruction and Reconstruction*, a book of much literary merit, and containing interesting descriptions of various men—notably Bragg. While Taylor's challenge of Banks's statements is doubtless sound, some of his own must have been without foundation except conjecture, for instance the one (p. 135) that Banks was detained at Opelousas from Apr. 20 to May 5 "by fear of Mouton's horse to the west." Banks was having difficulty communicating with Farragut, with whom he wanted to operate. Taylor's book is undocumented; and while his memory of his own actions may have been fairly reliable in 1877, his feelings were also still doubtless very strong.

23. *O.R.*, *36*, 252; *21*, 1046; *41*, 10. In *Pemberton, Defender of Vicksburg*, J. C. Pemberton states (p. 110) that "the only commanders with available forces to distract Grant on the march to concentrate on Pemberton's left flank were appealed to in vain: Generals Kirby Smith and Richard Taylor." The support for the statement is that first cited above. No mention is made, however, of the fact that Taylor was retreating before Banks. His forces were hardly "available."

In a dispatch to Smith on May 1, reporting that the Federals had crossed to Bruinsburg and were pressing Bowen, Pemberton asked, "Cannot you do something to operate against them on your side of the river?" (*O.R.*, *38*, 808). By this time Pemberton should have known of Taylor's difficulties.

24. Greene, *op. cit.*, p. 222; Grant's report; Grant, *Memoirs*, I, 491–492 (Long, ed., p. 258); Halleck to Grant, Apr. 2, *O.R.*, *36*, 25.

25. In *Memoirs,* I, 499 (Long, ed., p. 262), Grant says he estimated Pemberton at 18,000 after he had moved out of Vicksburg and before the Battle of Champion's Hill. A garrison would have been left in the works, but Grant's statement that he afterward learned that Pemberton had 50,000 men is very puzzling. Pemberton's return for Mar. 31 is in *O.R., 38,* 702. The numbers given as present for duty in the whole department are 3,878 officers and 44,951 men; the aggregate present and absent is 82,318.

26. Liddell Hart, *Sherman,* p. 185; Fuller, *The Generalship of Ulysses S. Grant,* pp. 138, 139.

27. *O.R., 36,* 34, 32–35; Grant, *op. cit.,* p. 491 (Long, ed., p. 258); *O.R., 24,* 156, 470.

28. *O.R., 38,* 268, 268–269. The train of 120 wagons would at present be called a "service train," to distinguish from regimental "field trains."

29. Brown, *Grierson's Raid,* pp. 209–219, gives a vivid account of the last day's march and the parade of the tattered and weary troopers through Baton Rouge at the insistence of Gen. Augur, commanding the Federal garrison. In addition to referring to Grierson's raid in his letter, Grant devoted an entire telegram to it (*O.R., 36,* 34; incorrectly dated May 6 instead of May 3).

30. *O.R., 38,* 269, 246. Marmaduke's raid covered the period Apr. 17–May 2. Both Federal and Confederate reports are full and are in *O.R., 32,* 252–304. The total Federal casualties were 120; the Confederate, 161. The demand made on the Federal commander at Cape Girardeau said, "By order of Maj. Gen. Sterling Price, commanding, . . ." Price was probably in the vicinity of Little Rock.

31. Grant, *op. cit.,* p. 491 (Long, ed., p. 258).

32. McPherson's and Logan's reports; Force's report, *O.R., 36,* 650–651.

33. *O.R., 38,* 275, 272, 273, 274–275.

34. *Ibid.,* pp. 275, 275–276.

35. *Ibid.,* pp. 273, 273–274.

36. *O.R., 36,* 83–84.

37. *Ibid.,* p. 84.

38. *O.R., 38,* 279.

39. *Ibid.,* pp. 277–278, 827 (Pemberton to Cooper, reporting taking 25 prisoners from the barges and a tug, including four correspondents). Under the heading "The Press Gang Saved," The *N.Y. Tribune* on May 20 carried a letter A. D. Richardson had written at Jackson, saying they had been treated with kindness and courtesy, and would probably be taken to Richmond. See also Weisberger, *Reporters for the Union,* pp. 179–180; Starr, *Bohemian Brigade,* pp. 185–186; and Andrews, *The North Reports the Civil War,* pp. 393–395.

40. *O.R., 36,* 35.

41. *O.R., 36,* 35; *38,* 285, 281, 281–282.

42. *O.R., 36,* 85.

43. Sherman's, McPherson's, and McClernand's reports; *O.R., 38,* 284–285.

44. *O.R., 38,* 285–286.

45. Grant, *Memoirs,* I, 493 (Long, ed., p. 259).

46. *Ibid.,* p. 488 (Long, ed., p. 256).

47. *O.R., 38,* 286.

48. *Ibid.,* pp. 276, 288–289. Grant explained his situation at some length and indicated that he accepted as reliable the concurrent testimony of deserters and contrabands that Port Hudson was "almost entirely evacuated," though it might "not be true."

In a letter to Welles dated Alexandria, May 7, Porter said Banks had arrived that evening. He himself had reached the town on the 5th with four gunboats, a ram, and a tug, after the Confederates had evacuated Fort De Russy, a powerful work below Alexandria. The *Benton* had broken a heavy raft barrier in the river. Porter stated much cordiality had been shown them along the river, and that there had been great rejoicing among Union men in Alexandria, "and no indisposition on the part of anyone to meet us in a friendly manner." (*O.R. Navies,* Ser. I, XXIV, 645–646.)

49. *O.R., 36,* 36. The part of Halleck's dispatch unquoted in the text was, "General Hooker recrossed to the north of the Rappahannock, but he inflicted a greater loss upon the enemy than he received himself." Except in "missing," where the Federal figures were much the larger, it might be recalled that casualties in the Battle of Chancellorsville were about equal numerically, but in proportion to the two forces far heavier for the Confederates. Furthermore, they lost Stonewall Jackson.

50. Greene, *op. cit.,* p. 141; *O.R., 36,* 35–36; Sherman's report; *O.R., 38,* 297.

On May 11 Wilson made a very long entry in what was published years later as "A Staff-Officer's Journal on the Vicksburg Campaign." It is particularly rich in the matter of information about the enemy. A really full study of Grant's campaign should draw heavily upon it.

51. McPherson's report; Dana and Wilson, *The Life of Ulysses S. Grant,* p. 120; Gregg's report, *O.R., 36,* 736–739. Gregg put his "aggregate engaged" at 2,500; as some of his regiments were hardly in action, this should not be taken as his available strength. Johnston considered Gregg's force definitely larger the next day. McPherson gave his killed as 69, wounded as 341, and missing as 30. He stated that the enemy's loss in killed was 103, and put the number of Confederate wounded or captured at 720. Gregg, however, gave his killed, wounded, and missing as, respectively, 73, 229, and 204. An addition to Gregg's report, compiled by the editors of the *O.R.,* puts his total casualties at 514.

52. Hovey's report, *O.R., 37,* 40–46; Sherman's report.

53. *O.R., 38,* 300, 301.

54. Whitton, *The Decisive Battles of Modern Times,* p. 45.

55. *O.R., 38,* 301. Just what maps were being used it is impossible to say. In his letter to Blair on May 9, previously cited, Sherman said he was sending "a copy of Wilson's map, which is a little fuller than ours in the country south of the Big Black." *O.R.* Atlas, Plate XXXVI, gives a fine map "compiled, surveyed and drawn" under Wilson's direction that is the basis for maps commonly used for the campaign behind Vicksburg. This could hardly have been the map referred to by Sherman, but an earlier form of it may have been.

56. *O.R., 38,* 287, 845; *36,* 215.

57. *O.R., 36,* 215, 214; *38,* 859, 889; *110,* 474; Johnston, *Narrative of Military Operations,* p. 175. For the shooting of Van Dorn, see Horn, *The Army of Tennessee,* p. 453.

58. *O.R., 38,* 844; *36,* 215; Greene, *op. cit.,* pp. 146, 137.

59. McPherson's and Sherman's reports. In a letter to Grant on the 14th McClernand spoke of the "tremendous rainstorms of last evening and to-day" (*O.R., 38,* 310–311).

60. Gregg's and Sherman's reports; Grant, *op. cit.,* pp. 505–506 (Long, ed., p. 264). Gist's units were under the command of Col. P. H. Colquitt.

61. On Nov. 1, 1863, Johnston wrote that the force in Jackson upon his arrival consisted of Gregg's and Walker's brigades, reported at 6,000. Gregg stated in his report that Johnston informed him that the place would be evacuated and that he was to cover the withdrawal of the trains. Colquitt made a short report, but Gregg wrote that Walker declined to make one. In a letter to Beauregard on May 25, Gist explained that more of Beauregard's two brigades had not arrived because transportation was being used for removal of state and Confederate stores from Jackson. (*O.R., 36,* 238, 787; *38,* 919–920.)

McPherson gave his killed as 37, his wounded and missing as 228, and the enemy's total casualties as 845 (the figure must have included captured stragglers). Grant states that Sherman had 4 killed and 21 wounded or missing. Gregg put his casualties at 200, but a compilation for Colquitt's three regiments and battery—the only one in the *O.R.*—shows 198. Grant agrees with McPherson in saying the captured guns numbered 17, assigning 10 to Sherman and 7 to McPherson; Sherman put the number at 18.

Greene's statement (*op. cit.,* p. 146) that Gregg's brigade covered the road from Raymond is definitely contradicted by Gregg's report, which says that the force protecting that route consisted of the 3rd Kentucky Mounted Infantry and a battalion of sharpshooters with a battery from Walker's brigade.

62. *O.R., 36,* 85 (Dana to Stanton, May 24); Grant, *op. cit.,* pp. 507–508 (Long, ed., p. 266); *O.R., 36,* 261 (in Pemberton's report). In his report Johnston gives (*ibid.,* p. 239) the last four sentences combined into one with semicolons replacing periods. As given by Grant, the sentence "The troops here could co-operate," is missing, and there are other minor differences.

In January, 1874, Pemberton wrote to Grant, then President, inquiring as to Grant's receipt of Johnston's dispatch of May *14,* which he said did not reach him until the 16th, and received through a secretary a confirmatory reply. It is not strange that Grant did not recall the date on the message that he had received. But it is not clear why Pemberton—who received in good time a copy of the message one copy of which went to Grant—should have thought a dispatch was slow in reaching him because a copy of it had been delivered to Grant. In spite of the explicitness of Pemberton's statement in his letter to Grant, his grandson has him inquire of Grant about Johnston's dispatch of May 13. (*B. and L.,* III, 545; *O.R., 36,* 261; J. C. Pemberton, *op. cit.,* p. 155.)

63. *O.R., 38,* 310, 311. A return for Apr. 20 (*ibid.,* p. 249) gives the "present strength" of the force operating against Vicksburg as 52,596. This includes one of McPherson's divisions which had not yet joined. The present strength of Hurlbut's 16th corps, which was garrisoning many places, is given as 51,561.

Some of the corps was later called to Vicksburg. The Helena garrison from the 13th Corps amounted to 6,664 men.

64. Hovey's, McClernand's, and McPherson's reports.

65. *O.R., 38,* 310–311; McClernand to Lincoln, May 29, 1863, Robert Todd Lincoln Collection; *O.R., 38,* 313. In a directive to his own four division commanders (*ibid.,* p. 315), McClernand repeated the statement he made to Blair.

66. *O.R., 36,* 242 (in Johnston's report); *38,* 858; J. C. Pemberton, *op. cit.,* p. 141; *O.R., 36,* 261 (in Pemberton's report).

67. McClernand's report; *O.R., 36,* 262 (in Pemberton's report); S. H. Lockett, "The Defense of Vicksburg," *B. and L.,* III, 482–492. Lockett was a Virginian and second man in the West Point class of 1859.

68. Hovey's, Grant's, Logan's, and McClernand's reports; Crocker's and Holmes's reports, *O.R., 36,* 722–725, 773–777; Loring's reports, *O.R., 36,* 73–79; Grant, *op. cit.,* pp. 519–520 (Long, ed., pp. 271–272); John B. Sanborn, *The Crisis at Champion's Hill,* pp. 13–15.

Dispatches that Grant sent his corps commanders on the 16th, as well as some from them, are in *O.R., 38,* 319–320. In one to McClernand at 10:15 A.M. from west of Bolton, Grant said: "McPherson is now up with Hovey, and can support him at any point. Close up all your forces as expeditiously as possible, but cautiously." A better word than "cautiously" would have been "carefully," though McClernand was not to point to the word as an excuse for want of enterprise. A message that Grant sent him at 12:35 P.M. said, "As soon as your command is all in hand, throw forward skirmishers and feel the enemy, and attack him in force if an opportunity occurs. I am with Hovey and McPherson, and will see that they fully co-operate."

Bowen's division arrived on the Confederate left and attacked vigorously about 2:30 (Stevenson's report, *O.R., 37,* 92–99). Thus by that time McClernand was weakly opposed. Without noting that part of Loring's division became engaged on the Confederate left, Liddell Hart speaks of Pemberton's being saved by McClernand's inertia in allowing his four divisions to be held in play by a single enemy division (*op. cit.,* pp. 189–190).

69. Livermore, *Numbers and Losses,* pp. 99–100; *O.R., 37,* 7–10; Hovey's report; Loring's second report.

Pemberton put his force at only 17,500, but Livermore cites returns that indicate that he had at least 22,500 present for duty on May 16. He suggests that Pemberton counted "only the men bearing muskets."

A subtitle to Sanborn's article calls Champion's Hill "The Decisive Battle of the Civil War," and he quotes a supporting statement by Lord Wolseley in *The North American Review* and one from the Comte de Paris's *The Civil War in America* (III, 337).

70. *O.R., 36,* 215–216.

71. Grant's and McClernand's reports; *O.R., 36,* 266 (in Pemberton's report).

72. McClernand's, Logan's, and Sherman's reports; Quinby's report, *O.R., 37,* 59–60. Quinby had arrived on the morning of the 16th; but, being exhausted from a long ride, he left the command of his division with Crocker, though he remained on the field.

73. *O.R., 36,* 54.

74. Lawler's report, *O.R., 37,* 133–142.

75. Dana, *Recollections of the Civil War,* p. 65.

76. *O.R., 36,* 267 (in Pemberton's report).

77. Grant, *op. cit.,* I, 524 (Long, ed., p. 274). In his *Military History of Ulysses S. Grant* (I, 221), Badeau says that after learning of Grant's plan of campaign, "Halleck at once sent him orders to return and coöperate with Banks." As support, he quotes the first sentence of Halleck's telegram of May 11, italicizing the words "between Vicksburg and Port Hudson." More worthy of emphasis were the beginning words of the message—"If possible," for they kept the dispatch from being an out-and-out order. Furthermore, Halleck did not use the word "return," or the words "coöperate with Banks," which suggest a movement against Port Hudson before one against Vicksburg.

If it was sound for Grant to "earnestly request" Banks on May 10 to join him in whole or in part, and for him to throw all his force toward Jackson before moving against Vicksburg, it was equally sound for Halleck to say what he did on May 11. It is strange that Fuller should seemingly accept Badeau's tortured interpretation of Halleck's message (*op. cit.,* p. 140).

On the day that Halleck sent his message, Grant wrote him one from Cayuga (telegraphed from Memphis on the 18th) that ended, "As I shall communicate with Grand Gulf no more, except it becomes necessary to send a train with heavy escort, you may not hear from me again for several days." There is a dramatic touch in the last ten words, and they are sometimes given as a complete sentence or dispatch, the implication being that Grant first informed Washington of what he was doing on May 11. Years ago Nicolay and Hay quoted from Grant's letter of the 3rd—which they said marked a turning point in his career—and passed over the dispatch of the 11th (*Abraham Lincoln,* VII, 174).

The *N.Y. Tribune* for Sept. 12, 1863, spoke of the *Evening Star* having arrived from New Orleans after a trip of 5 days, 16 hours; the *N.Y. Times* for the 28th said the *Continental* had taken 6 days, 12 hours for the passage.

78. *O.R., 38,* 298–299, 303–304, 304. The Vicksburg volumes of the *O.R.* had not been published at the time of the writing of Grant's *Memoirs.*

79. Grant's report; *O.R., 38,* 321–322.

80. Sherman, *Memoirs,* I, 324.

81. Sherman's report.

82. Grant's report; Grant, *Memoirs,* I, 527–528 (Long, ed., pp. 275–276).

83. Sherman's and Grant's reports.

84. *O.R., 36,* 86. For Hovey's protest and an indorsement on it by McClernand, see addenda to Hovey's reports.

85. Grant, *op. cit.,* pp. 486–487 (Long, ed., p. 255); letter from U. S. Grant, 3rd, to author; Dana, *op. cit.,* pp. 45–46. Dana said the horses he and Fred Grant were riding when they reached Port Gibson were captured animals that had been given to them by some officers, but that they had had to find saddles and bridles. Veterans of the campaigns saw that the name Frederick Dent Grant was in the roster on the Illinois monument at Vicksburg.

86. *O.R., 110,* 472, 472–473. Under date of June 20, 1863, Col. Fremantle

said, after speaking of changing cars at Gordonsville, Va., on his way to join Lee's army: "Near this place I observed an enormous pile of excellent rifles rotting in the open air. These had been captured at Chancellorsville; but the Confederates have already such a superabundant stock of rifles that apparently they can afford to let them spoil." (Lord, ed., *The Fremantle Diary*, p. 176.)

A letter of May 20 from the commanding officer of the Selma, Ala., arsenal to Johnston's chief of staff is in *O.R., 38,* 902–903.

NOTES TO CHAPTER XIII

1. Grant, *Memoirs,* I, 530–531 (Long, ed., p. 277).

2. *O.R., 36,* 132 (reference to Marine Brigade). Dana later reported that the brigade was a useless and very costly institution (*ibid.,* pp. 96–97).

3. Grant's report, *O.R., 36,* 44–59; Prime and Comstock's reports, *O.R., 37,* 168–187. Prime stressed the point that the men would not have worked well if they had not first tried an assault.

4. Fuller, *The Generalship of Ulysses S. Grant,* p. 153; Livermore, *Numbers and Losses,* p. 100; *O.R., 36,* 86.

5. Livermore, *loc. cit.;* Grant's report.

6. *O.R., 38,* 337–338, 341.

7. *Ibid.,* pp. 342–343.

8. *Ibid.,* p. 343.

9. *O.R., 36,* 86–87, 87–88.

10. *O.R., 38,* 342.

11. *N.Y. Tribune,* May 24, 1863 (quoting *Richmond Enquirer* of the 21st in a Washington dispatch of the 22nd), May 21.

12. *N.Y. Tribune,* May 24, 26. Hurlbut's dispatch is in *O.R., 38,* 344; Porter's in *O.R. Navies,* Ser. I, XXV, 5–6. Porter at once sent vessels up the Yazoo and said that within three hours he had "received letters from Generals Grant, Sherman, and Steele, informing me of their vast successes and asking me to send up provisions, which was at once done." He reported on the enemy works at Haynes Bluff, saying they were very formidable with "14 of the heaviest kind of guns mounted, 8 and 10 inch and 7½-inch rifled guns, with ammunition enough to last a long siege."

On May 22 the *Tribune* reprinted a story from the *Galena Advertiser* of the 18th that told of Washburne's return from a visit with Grant. He had been with the general as far as Port Gibson. On the 25th the *Tribune* gave a summary of Grant's career, which ended, "He is held in the highest esteem by his men, who seem to place their unbounded confidence in him, not because of his political preferences or aspirations, but because he is emphatically a 'fighting general.' "

13. Hickenlooper's report, *O.R., 37,* 197–203; Prime and Comstock's reports.

14. Hickenlooper's and Prime and Comstock's reports; Lockett's, Wilson and Comstock's, and Hains's reports, *ibid.,* pp. 329–335, 178–180, 180–187. Grant's order that siege operations be started is in *O.R., 38,* 348.

15. Capt. O. R. Howard's report, *O.R.*, *36*, 130–137.

16. *O.R. Navies*, Ser. I, XXV, 146–147 (Porter's station list for June 1); Thorndike, ed., *The Sherman Letters*, p. 197; letter of Pvt. Richard Puffer, Co. E, 8th Illinois Infantry, in *Chicago History*, Vol. II, No. 4 (Summer, 1949), pp. 120–121. Of the 68 vessels in the Mississippi Squadron, 25 were listed as below or above Vicksburg, or in the Yazoo; 15 were in the Tennessee or Cumberland. Five tugs were given as above Vicksburg, with one below; seven boats belonging to the Mississippi Marine Brigade were set down as transporting troops for Grant.

In his letter of May 28 to his sister, R. Idelia Puffer, of Mount Palatine, Ill., Pvt. Puffer portrayed a good deal of siege activity, and said, "The rebs also keep firing and if a man shows himself in range he is sure to get shot at." The letter closed with a paragraph about a visit from Grant: "Gen. Grant came along the line last night. He had on his old clothes and was alone. He sat down on the ground and talked with the boys with less reserve than many a little puppy of a Lieutenant. He told us that he had got as good a thing as he wanted here. Said that Pemberton was a Northern man and had got into bad company and did not like to have us get him. . . ."

17. *O.R.*, *38*, 888. In *Memoirs*, I, 522 (Long, ed., p. 273), Grant says that a movement across the Big Black the night after the battle at Champion's Hill, then northward to join Johnston, would have been the proper one for Pemberton, and that it would have been what Johnston would have done, if he had been in Pemberton's place.

18. *O.R.*, *36*, 37–40.

19. *O.R.*, *38*, 919–920; *110*, 482, 484.

20. *O.R.*, *36*, 40. Grant had said Johnston's force is "reported to be 45,000, but may not be so large."

The correspondence between Grant and Banks involved no fewer than five letters between May 25 and June 4 inclusive (*O.R.*, *38*, 346–347, 353–354, 359–360, 367–368, 385–386).

In his letter of May 31 to Banks, Grant had said: "Our situation is for the first time during the entire Western campaign what it should be. We have, after great labor and extraordinary risk, secured a position which should not be jeopardized by any detachments whatever. On the contrary, I am now and shall continue to exert myself to the utmost to concentrate. The enemy clearly perceive the importance of dislodging me at all hazards." He said that Johnston, whose force was estimated at 40,000, was known to have at least 20,000; he put Pemberton at 18,000 effectives. He stated he could effect the reduction of Vicksburg within 20 days, but that if he detached 10,000 men he would "be crippled beyond redemption."

A return for May 31 (*O.R.*, *38*, 370–371) gives Grant an "aggregate present" at Vicksburg of 65,897 (engineer troops, 13th, 15th, and 17th corps, and one division of the 16th). Hurlbut's 16th Corps, with troops at Grand Junction, La Grange, Jackson (in process of abandonment), Memphis, Corinth, and Columbus, Ky., had a present strength of 44,384.

21. *O.R.*, *36*, 40; *38*, 377, 376, 376–377, 377, 383, 384; *37*, 318–319 (Herron's report). Halleck said to Grant that he had repeatedly directed Banks to

join him; this dispatch ended: "If possible, send him this. My last dispatch from him was of May 4." Burnside wanted to accompany his troops, but Halleck told him to remain in his department, one reason being that the organization of the Kentucky militia required his attention.

In a message to Dana on June 5, Stanton said: "Everything in the power of this Government will be put forth to aid General Grant. The emergency is not underrated here. Your telegrams are a great obligation, and are looked for with deep interest. I cannot thank you as much as I feel for the service you are now rendering." (*O.R., 36,* 93.)

22. *O.R., 38,* 386, 380. On June 5 Col. Stager, superintendent of telegraphs, reported to Stanton that he had just arrived in Memphis. He stated that the withdrawal of troops from the line of the road from Memphis to Cairo would make it "most certain" that telegraphic communications would be interrupted, adding: "Dispatches will have to be sent by river to Cairo until the line can be protected. Will make an effort to keep line open by running a hand-car." Stanton had on the 4th telegraphed to Hurlbut about aiding the telegraph corps in maintaining and extending lines. (*Ibid.,* pp. 386, 384.)

23. *O.R., 37,* 435–436.

24. *O.R. Navies,* Ser. I, XXV, 132–134.

25. *O.R., 38,* 375, 379.

26. *Ibid.,* p. 384.

27. *O.R., 37,* 436–437.

28. *Ibid.,* pp. 437, 438.

29. *O.R., 36,* 94; *38,* 387.

30. Miers, *The Web of Victory,* p. 223. On p. 243 Miers says that minor skirmishes at Mechanicsburg, Milliken's Bend, and Young's Point filled most of Dana's letter for June 6–8. There was a dispatch on each of the three days and they went by wire from Memphis. Apparently the very important sentence in the dispatch of the 6th explaining Grant's reason for going to Mechanicsburg was missed by Miers.

31. Dana, *Recollections of the Civil War,* pp. 82–84; *O.R., 37,* 438.

32. *O.R., 36,* 94, 94–95. As if foreseeing that Grant might wish to make use of Dana, Stanton said in his previously noted telegram to Dana of June 5: "You have been appointed an assistant adjutant-general, with rank of major, with liberty to report to General Grant, if he needs you. The appointment may be a protection to you." Had Dana been captured during his reconnaissance with the cavalry, he would have been in an embarrassing position.

33. *O.R., 38,* 385–386, 389. As a means of identifying the agent, Hurlbut sent Rawlins one of the agent's reports in his own handwriting. The postscript is a little vexing: "He goes by the name of ———. His name is ———."

34. *O.R., 36,* 41; *38,* 390. Blair's dispatch was received at the War Department at 2:45 A.M. of June 17. In addition to what is said in the text as to the contents of the letter from Banks that Grant forwarded, the following is quoted: "It seems to me that I have no other course than to carry my object here, thus crippling the enemy, and to join you with my whole strength as soon as possible. This I hope to accomplish in a few days. I believe, if uninterrupted by fresh attacks, this day week will see our flag floating over the fortifications

568

now occupied by the enemy." It would seem doubtful whether Blair actually saw this letter. Knowledge that Banks was not coming would have sufficed to start all sorts of talk about him.

35. *O.R., 38,* 378, 380, 356, 375.

36. *Ibid.,* pp. 301–303. The letter contained much information about the situation along the Yazoo, and said people at Yazoo City thought Grierson's raid "surpassed anything done by Morgan or Forrest."

37. Smith to Confederate Governor Reynolds of Missouri (who was at Camden, Ark.), June 4, and to Holmes, June 5, *O.R., 33,* 855–856, 857; Taylor's and Walker's reports, *O.R., 37,* 457–466. See also Parks, *General Kirby Smith,* pp. 269–271; the statement that Banks had "crossed to Grant's assistance," is not accurate, except that he did hold some of the garrison of Port Hudson, which Johnston had ordered abandoned. On June 22 Dana reported to Stanton that the bravery of the Negro troops at Milliken's Bend had revolutionized the sentiment in the army about them; prominent officers who formerly had sneered now favored the idea of using Negroes (*O.R., 36,* 105–106).

38. *O.R., 37,* 453, 454.

39. *O.R., 38,* 390; *36,* 42, 43–44. Brig. Gen. N. B. Mower was in command of the District of Northeastern Louisiana.

40. Eaton, *Grant, Lincoln and the Freedmen,* pp. 63–65.

41. *O.R., 36,* 42.

42. Dana, *op. cit.,* pp. 87–88, 70. *D.A.B.* states that Herron, who was born at Pittsburgh, Pa., on Feb. 17, 1837, was the youngest major general in the Civil War. He was one of 26 who held the rank from Nov. 29, 1862, Meade being one and Prentiss being the first in the list. George Custer, who was born on Dec. 5, 1839, was brevetted major general of volunteers in October, 1864, and received the full rank as of Apr. 15, 1865, after the war was virtually ended.

For remarks on the handling of the left of the Federal line, see Prime and Comstock's report.

43. *O.R. Navies,* Ser. I, XXV, 74.

44. *O.R., 37,* 317.

45. Grant's report; Grant to Parke, *O.R., 38,* 418; *37,* 219.

46. *O.R., 36,* 158–165, 43, 102–104. Wilson carried the order relieving McClernand (Wilson, *The Life of John A. Rawlins,* pp. 133–135). Dana ended his dispatch to Stanton on the 29th: "It appears that ten days ago he [McClernand] invited General M. K. Lawler to attend a meeting of officers from his corps, at which resolutions commendatory of himself (McClernand) were to be passed. Lawler refused, on the ground that it would be a mutinous proceeding, and does not know whether such a meeting was held." (*Ibid.,* pp. 104–105.)

47. *O.R., 36,* 101, 104.

48. *O.R., 37,* 444, 454–455; *38,* 406, 409. Porter said to Welles, "General Grant's position is a safe one, though he should have all the troops that can possibly be sent to him." Six heavy navy guns had been mounted in the rear of Vicksburg, and the army could have all it wanted.

49. *O.R., 38,* 422–423, 414, 415, 416, 437. A long letter of instructions of June 23 that Asboth gave the commander of an expedition he was sending out portrays the situation in western Kentucky (*ibid.,* p. 434).

50. *Ibid.,* pp. 422, 442, 429, 435. The Federals were not taking a purely passive attitude, but made expeditions into northern Mississippi. See *O.R., 37,* 484–507.

51. For Dodge's work of organizing secret service work under Grant's direction, see Chap. VIII in Perkins, *Trails, Rails and War.*

52. *O.R., 38,* 428, 448.

53. *Ibid.,* p. 439. Hurlbut had closed a dispatch to Grant on June 8, "It is important for this command that a close watch be kept on any northerly movements of the force under Johnston" (*ibid.,* p. 391).

54. *Ibid.,* p. 438.

55. *Ibid.,* pp. 442, 449–450, 449. See also Sherman to Grant, and Sherman to Rawlins, *O.R., 37,* 245–246, 246–248.

56. *O.R., 38,* 446; *37,* 454–455; *38,* 423–424. Dodge sent another long intelligence summary on the same day (*ibid.,* pp. 445–446). His scout put Johnston at not over 35,000 men and said it was believed Pemberton had provisions for sixty days. In a long letter to Dennis on the 22nd (*ibid.,* p. 426) Grant reported on a conversation between a Federal and a Confederate picket who had laid down their arms and apparently had had a good talk. The Confederate said 2,000 boats were to be constructed.

57. *O.R., 37,* 461.

58. *O.R., 38,* 445 (Prentiss to Hurlbut, June 27); *33,* 334 (Halleck to Schofield). Prentiss's latest information was that Price was moving toward the Red River, but for ten days his scouts had been unable to obtain information because three enemy regiments within twenty miles of Helena prevented communication with the interior.

59. *O.R., 37,* 248–249; *38,* 456; *37,* 203. In his article "The Defence of Richmond," *B. and L.,* III, 482–492, Lockett describes (p. 491) both the mines used by the Federals and the countermines of the Confederates. The Federal effort to enter the works after the explosion of a mine on June 26 resulted in a good many casualties; six Confederate counterminers were buried by the explosion. The mine exploded on July 1 was a great deal heavier, virtually destroying a redan, but though an assault was anticipated by the Confederates, none was made, the Federals having become cautious after the previous effort. Lockett speaks of a Negro being blown into the Federal lines, practically unhurt. Grant states in *Memoirs,* I, 553 (Long, ed., p. 288): "The enemy must have lost more in the two explosions than we did in the first. We lost none in the second."

60. *O.R., 38,* 457; *37,* 249.

61. *O.R., 38,* 458–459. Comstock, who had headed the West Point class of 1855, had reported for duty at Vicksburg on June 15. He has been mentioned earlier in this work in connection with the Fredericksburg and Chancellorsville campaigns.

62. *O.R., 36,* 113–114, 244, 198, 197.

63. *O.R., 38,* 447–448, 982–983, 982. The letter to Pemberton was signed

"Many Soldiers," and an editorial note in the *O.R.* says it was found among his papers. Thus he definitely saw it.

64. On June 30 Dana wrote to Stanton that Grant had that morning submitted the question of an assault to his corps and division commanders, and that the decision was in favor of "exhaustion of the garrison," and that since Grant had been inclined to that course, it would, "no doubt, be adhered to" (*O.R., 36,* 112–113). In his report Grant stated that he had notified Sherman he would make an assault at daylight on the 6th. Wilson and Comstock, after describing the situation, said in their report, "Accordingly, on July 1, it was decided to assault on the morning of July 6." Their statement about preparations agrees in general with Comstock's directive to Steele. It would have been possible to put the heads of regiments within from 5 to 120 yards of the enemy line.

65. *O.R., 37,* 180; *38,* 458.

66. *O.R., 38,* 461. Grant had not communicated the fact of receiving Pemberton's request to appoint commissioners merely for information; he had used it to deduce that Johnston was "not coming to Vicksburg," adding, "he must be watched, though."

67. *Ibid.,* pp. 463, 463–464, 460.

68. *Ibid.,* pp. 459, 460, 461. For accounts of the negotiations, see Grant, *op. cit.,* pp. 556–563 (Long, ed., pp. 290–294); *B. and L.,* III, 543–545; J. C. Pemberton, *Pemberton, Defender of Vicksburg,* pp. 225–236. Dana's dispatch to Stanton on the 4th (*O.R., 36,* 114–117) covered the negotiations, including the interchange of messages by Pemberton and Grant.

69. *O.R., 38,* 463–464; Winther, ed., *With Sherman to the Sea,* p. 61. Unfortunately, Upson's entries in his diary are often hard to date. The one quoted seems to have been made on July 3, because in the next entry he stated that he was one of the guards that accompanied the paymaster to Vicksburg on the 4th.

70. *O.R., 38,* 460, 466, 467. Grant's order of the 3rd directed each corps commander and Gen. Herron to "fire a national salute of thirty-four guns from each battery (not from each gun) they have in position on to-morrow, the eighty-seventh anniversary of American Independence, at 5 a.m."

71. *Ibid.,* pp. 470, 471–472.

72. *O.R., 36,* 44; *38,* 472. In his dispatch to Halleck, Grant pointed out the advantage of paroling prisoners because it made boats available, said that Sherman would move immediately against Johnston, that help would be sent to Banks, and Burnside's troops returned.

Sherman's statement looks a little as if July 4 were on Sunday; that was not the case; it was on Saturday.

73. *O.R., 38,* 473.

74. Grant, *op. cit.,* p. 564 (Long, ed., p. 295); *B. and L.,* III, 492; Grant, *op. cit.,* p. 570 (Long, ed., p. 298). J. C. Pemberton states (*op. cit.,* p. 237) that Steele's division occupied the city at 10:00 A.M., and omits Grant's statement about Logan from the quotation he makes from Grant.

On July 15 the *N.Y. Tribune* carried a dispatch from Vicksburg, dated July 4. It began, "The long agony is over," and stated, "Gen. Logan's division, with

Ransom's brigade temporarily detached, was marched into the city to take possession and guard it." The time of raising the Union flag was put at about 11 o'clock.

75. *O.R., 37,* 325, 178; Grant, *op. cit.,* p. 572 (Long, ed., pp. 299–300); *O.R., 36,* 285–286, 292; Dana, *op. cit.,* pp. 99–101; J. C. Pemberton, *op. cit.,* pp. 238–239. Commenting upon Grant's statement, "The enemy had generally new arms which had run the blockade and were of uniform caliber," Vandiver says in *Ploughshares into Swords,* p. 93: "Grant's views were an exaggeration, but not too large a one at that. He was wrong in broadly assuming that all Confederate arms were superior and that all were imported (he would have been right had he estimated that two-thirds of the Confederacy's stock of arms had come from abroad)." The precise facts about the Confederate arms at Vicksburg—the only ones about which Grant was speaking—are probably not determinate.

76. *O.R., 37,* 168; *supra,* III, 394; II, 720. Incomplete Confederate returns put casualties during the siege at 2,872 (*O.R., 37,* 328).

Without apparently noting what the Federal casualties in the campaign were, J. C. Pemberton observes (*op. cit.,* p. 239), that the total of Federal soldiers buried in the National Cemetery is 16,822, saying they lost their lives in and around Vicksburg. It would be incorrect to conclude that the total number is to be ascribed to the six months of operations that led to the capture of the city. The number of Federals who died of disease was about double the number killed in action or mortally wounded (Dyer, *Compendium,* p. 12).

77. *O.R. Navies,* Ser. I, XXV, 103; *Chicago Tribune,* July 8 and 9, 1863; *Diary of Gideon Welles,* entry for July 7, 1863; *O.R., 36,* 62.

The *Chicago Tribune* for the 8th carried a Cairo dispatch of noon of the 7th which identified the steamer bringing Porter's dispatch as the *V. F. Wilson.* A Cairo dispatch of 10:00 P.M. stated that no other news had arrived, nor need it be expected soon, because the *V. F. Wilson* was a very fast boat and had come "from below without stopping, at the top of her speed, to bring the news to the Navy Department."

The *Tribune* for the 9th gave a Cairo dispatch of the 8th which said the *Niagara,* from Memphis on the 7th, had brought Lieut. Dunn, and it stated, "Dunn came as far as Memphis on the *V. F. Wilson.*" Confirmation of this has not been found elsewhere, but it appears reasonable that an effort to telegraph from Memphis would have been made. The *Tribune* reporter saved Porter from the appearance of having deliberately arranged to have his message reach Washington first.

In *Memoirs,* I, 571–572 (Long, ed., p. 299), Grant quotes a dispatch from Halleck that he says was the first he received after the fall of Vicksburg. In his *B. and L.* article on the campaign (III, 492–539) he correctly says it was sent on the 8th. Whether or not the dispatch about his promotion to a major generalcy in the regular Army arrived first or not, it was sent a day before the other. Since Halleck raised the question in the dispatch of the 8th about the advisability of paroling prisoners, Grant's statement makes it appear as if the first thing the government did was to complain. If Grant had informed Halleck that there was a Confederate commissioner of prisoners in

Vicksburg, the latter would probably not have raised the question he did. On the 10th Halleck sent a message that Grant does not note either in the *Memoirs* or in his *B. and L.* article: "On a full examination of the question, it is decided that you, as the commander of an army, were authorized to agree upon the parole and release of the garrison of Vicksburg with the general commanding the place" (*O.R., 36*, 62). Irregularities in paroling were receiving attention at this time, and a new order on the subject had been issued on July 3.

Inasmuch as I have questioned the accuracy of two of Grant's statements in his *Memoirs*, I would like to give support that has come to me for an incident described in the *Memoirs* which I accepted in Vol. III, noting that Conger questioned it because of lack of corroboration. It had to do with Grant's personal reembarkation on a transport after the Battle of Belmont (*supra*, III, 84). Confirmation of the incident comes from Henry P. Stearns of the history department of the Taft School, Watertown, Connecticut. His grandfather, Dr. Henry Putnam Stearns, was Brigade Surgeon at Belmont and was on Grant's staff in the river campaigns up to and including Shiloh. I quote with Mr. Stearns's permission. Referring to his grandfather, Mr. Stearns says:

In his copy of Grant's *Memoirs,* which I have before me, he has written in the margin of page 278 (Volume I) as follows:

"I was an eye witness to the above occurrence and I can testify to its entire accuracy with one exception. I was a member of his staff on that occasion and was immediately behind him. I followed him on the plank of the boat. I also saw him go into the captain's room and at once come out. It is not surprising that he did not recall my presence when writing 30 years afterward, as we were in the midst of a constant firing of guns and cannon.

H. P. STEARNS, M.D."

78. *O.R., 36*, 244–245, 198, 199.

79. *The Collected Works of Abraham Lincoln,* VI, 230–231. Lincoln's entire letter is very interesting, being in reply to one from Arnold urging the dismissal of Halleck because the public believed he had driven from the service such men as Frémont, Butler, and Siegel.

80. *O.R., 38*, 470; *O.R. Navies,* Ser. I, XXV, 279–280. Sherman wrote a warm letter of appreciation to Porter on the 4th. It would be hard indeed to imagine smoother working together by the army and navy than was shown at Vicksburg. Referring to Porter, Grant had said in a letter to Farragut on Mar. 26, "I am happy to say the admiral and myself have never yet disagreed upon any policy." (*O.R., 38*, 473; *O.R. Navies,* Ser. I, XX, 26–27.)

81. *O.R., 109*, 406, 416. Lincoln's statement that when Grant first reached the vicinity of Vicksburg, he thought he should do what he finally did—run the batteries with transports and march the troops around—is in conflict with Halleck's statement to Grant on January 25 that the President attached much importance to the canal project.

Wilson later wrote that on the day Grant arrived at the Yazoo he (Wilson) suggested to Rawlins what was finally done and that Rawlins, after expressing some doubt at first, finally said he would advocate the plan (Wilson, *op. cit.*, pp. 108–110). One must be skeptical of Wilson's recollection of what he and Rawlins had said when seated on the trunk of a cottonwood tree fifty-three years after the incident. Porter's statement would indicate that the entire idea was Grant's, so far as he knew at the time. But it is not a question of where lies credit for the thought of running the batteries. (They had been first run by Farragut the summer before when he brought his fleet up to join Davis's gunboats.) The great question was how the army would be supplied after it got below. Fuller's description of Grant's situation at Grand Gulf is convincing, and Grant's statement to Banks that extraordinary risks had been run was no exaggeration. Sherman's reluctance did not come from fear that transports might not make a passage of the guns; he probably took it for granted that they would.

82. *Diary of Gideon Welles,* entry for July 31, 1863.

83. Washburne Papers, XXV, 4973. Joseph Medill was editor of the *Chicago Tribune.*

84. *O.R., 36,* 63.

85. *Ibid.,* p. 6.

86. Fuller, *op. cit.,* as previously quoted and elsewhere; Fuller, *Grant and Lee,* pp. 183–184; Greene, *The Mississippi,* pp. 170–171.

87. Liddell Hart, *Sherman,* p. 196.

88. Cramer, ed., *Letters of Ulysses S. Grant,* pp. 98–99.

NOTES TO THE APPENDIX

1. *O.R., 21,* 906–908; Coulter, *The Confederate States of America,* p. 72. Davis pronounced all of Butler's commissioned officers to be "criminals, deserving death," and said that "they and each of them be, whenever captured, reserved for execution." The proclamation was made part of a General Order of Dec. 24, which charged all officers with its observance and enforcement.

It is a little ironical that Butler had cast 57 votes for Davis as candidate for President in the Democratic Convention at Charleston in 1860.

2. *O.R. Navies,* Ser. I, XVIII, 229, 230–231, 231–232, 234–235.

3. *Ibid.,* pp. 237–238, 232–233. On May 31 Butler wrote to Stanton that he had arrested Pierre Soulé, one charge being that Soulé had actually written the "insolent letters" that Mayor Monroe signed and sent to Farragut. Soulé was sent north, and after being confined in Ft. Lafayette, N.Y., for a time, was paroled to Boston, whence he made his way to Nassau. Though he ran the blockade, Davis's strong hostility to him kept him from being used in any important position. While Minister to Spain in the Pierce Administration, Soulé had indulged in intrigues and was virtually author of the famous and embarrassing "Ostend Manifesto," which demanded that Cuba be wrested from Spain if it could not be bought. (*O.R., 116,* 612; *D.A.B.,* article on *Soulé;* Nevins, *Ordeal of the Union,* II, 348–363.)

4. Parton, *General Butler in New Orleans,* p. 351.

5. *N.Y. Herald,* May 30, 1862. The *N.Y. Tribune* for July 22 carried a dispatch from its Washington correspondent strongly condemning Butler's order and saying he should be rebuked.

6. De Forest, *A Volunteer's Adventures,* p. 22; Butler, *Butler's Book,* p. 419.

7. *O.R., 21,* 510–511, 511; *117,* 880–885.

8. Ross, *Rebel Rose,* pp. 166–167; Williams, ed., *A Diary from Dixie,* p. 10.

9. *O.R., 21,* 42–49.

10. Senate Reports, 37th Cong., 3rd Sess., Vol. 3, Pt. 4, pp. 353ff.

11. Flower, *James Parton, The Father of Modern Biography,* p. 71; Howard P. Johnson, "New Orleans Under General Butler," *The Louisiana Historical Quarterly,* XXIV (1941), 434–536.

Asbury in his *The French Quarter* (p. 167n.) calls Parton's book as thorough a piece of whitewashing as can be found in American literature. Such a broad statement cannot be accepted without convincing evidence of careful examination of the complicated issues in the Butler question. Flower's statement that the Butler book is "one of the least admirable volumes that Parton wrote" is certainly much more restrained.

Butler's New Orleans period is of course considered in Holzman's *Stormy Ben Butler,* as well as in Caskey's *Secession and Restoration of Louisiana.*

12. *O.R., 111.* 543–544; Holzman, *op. cit.,* pp. 251–252. Holzman states that while McClellan and Frémont held rank from May 14, 1861, they were not appointed until July 24, while Butler had been appointed on May 16.

War Department G.O. 14, of May 3, 1861, placed "Major General George B. McClellan, Ohio Volunteers," in command of the Department of the Ohio, and he assumed office on the 13th. The next day—May 14—McClellan was informed by telegraph that he had been made a major general in the regular Army, formal notification following promptly by mail. In a letter to Congressman I. N. Arnold on May 26, 1863, Lincoln said McClellan held the highest rank in the Army, with Frémont next. (*O.R., 107,* 376; Myers, *General George Brinton McClellan,* p. 163, with reference to McClellan's papers; *Collected Works of Abraham Lincoln,* VI, 230–231.)

The ultimately determining facts were dates and order of precedence assigned by Lincoln's recommendation to the Senate and its confirmation, to which Holzman makes no reference. In accordance with Lincoln's recommendation of July 16, 1861, McClellan and Frémont were confirmed as major generals of the regular Army on Aug. 3, to rank from May 14. On the same day Banks and Dix were confirmed as major generals of volunteers to date from May 16, in accordance with Lincoln's recommendation of July 29, which had asked for the appointments of Banks, Dix, and Butler, as of May 16, and *in that order of precedence.* Butler was not confirmed until August 5, there being opposition in his case with a recording of votes, doubtless because of his defeat at Bethel, Va., on June 10. (Senate Executive Journal, Vol. XI, 1858–1861.)

Butler was thus fifth, not first, by final Presidential and Senate action, and he never held even unconfirmed seniority over McClellan, though Holzman states that McClellan was still in private employment when Butler was appointed on May 16. While Frémont was, as Holzman states, in Europe at that time, he was appointed not on July 24, but about July 1, and a War Department order of July 3 put "Major General Frémont" in command of the Western Department (Nicolay and Hay, *Lincoln,* IV, 402; *O.R., 3,* 390).

It is notable that the War Department order of Aug. 20 listing officers of volunteers who had been appointed and confirmed or appointed by the President "alone" since the adjournment of the Senate (the latter carefully marked by an asterisk) did not contain Butler's name, probably because of the two-day delay in his confirmation. Banks's name headed the list followed by that of Dix. Apparently Butler's name was never officially published.

If Butler slipped from second to fifth as a major general, it was by no means the only instance of change in relative position, and there were more notable instances than his. As a lawyer, Butler should have known that Presidential appointment was merely temporary. And it is hard to believe he did not know that McClellan was exercising department command as a major general while he himself was only a brigadier, and hard to see why he was not aware of the Presidential appointment of the former to a regular army position two days before his own appointment as a volunteer.

13. *O.R.*, *38*, 18–19.

14. *Ibid.*, *25*, 866–867.

15. McClernand Papers.

16. *Ibid.* In a note the same day to his chief of staff, McClernand said he was leaving that night and would "necessarily be absent several days."

17. Sandburg, *Lincoln*, II, 109; Porter, *Incidents and Anecdotes of the Civil War*, pp. 122–123. Porter has Lincoln say that McClernand was a better general than either Grant or Sherman, and that McClernand, not Grant, had won Shiloh. It has already been noted that Porter had Grant say things at their first meeting at Cairo that do not fit the situation existing. One must suspect Porter of spinning another yarn in the case of Lincoln. A contemporary entry in Secretary Chase's diary seems to be the only reliable gauge of Lincoln's estimate of McClernand at the time. Under date of Sept. 27, 1862, Chase said McClernand had called on him and had impressed him favorably with the plan of operations he proposed. Then Chase saw Lincoln and asked for his opinion of the general. The President replied he thought McClernand brave and capable, but too desirous to be independent of everybody else. (Donald, ed., *Inside Lincoln's Cabinet*, p. 161.) Calling McClernand "capable" is a far cry from pronouncing him a "natural-born general," which were words Porter put into Lincoln's mouth.

While Porter said he had argued with Lincoln for Grant or Sherman as commander of the expedition, Secretary Welles ten months later (July 31, 1863) wrote in his diary (I, 386) that Porter had wanted a volunteer officer to work with, and had spoken very disparagingly of West Pointers. There can be no certainty as to what Porter said either to Lincoln or to Welles. But it is incontestable that immediately after McClernand relieved Sherman at the mouth of the Yazoo, Porter wrote to Foote that Sherman would "have all the brains" (*supra*, p. 292).

Welles went on to say that Stanton and Halleck supported the views of the President that it was a good time to bring forward McClernand. While this is perhaps true as far as Stanton is concerned, the charges that McClernand leveled at Halleck in his letter to Stanton of Jan. 3, 1863, previously referred to, are inconsistent with the claim that Halleck had ever favored him as commander of the Vicksburg expedition. Again the Chase diary gives an entry that is acceptable. Under date of Sept. 28, 1862, Chase recorded that he had called on Halleck and asked him his opinion of McClernand. Halleck had replied that McClernand was brave and able, but was no disciplinarian, and he illustrated the latter point. The "cause of the evil" Halleck attributed to the fact that McClernand's officers and men were his constituents. Being a professionally trained officer, Halleck would hardly have approved a poor disciplinarian for command of an important and difficult operation.

18. Phisterer, *Statistical Record*, p. 5; *O.R., 25*, 187; Dyer, *Compendium*, pp. 1077–1101 (historical sketches of 72nd–131st Illinois infantry regiments. The 121st Infantry did not complete organization.)

In a letter to Stanton on Nov. 10 (*O.R., 25*, 332–334) McClernand said he had left Washington on the 22nd, arrived at Indianapolis on the 23rd, left there on the 24th, and reached Springfield on the morning of the 25th. He spoke of completing the organization, mustering, and forwarding of twelve Illinois regiments of infantry. The regimental histories seem to indicate only three mustered between Oct. 25 and Nov. 10, the 130th Infantry being mustered on the 25th. The following regiments previously mustered were forwarded in the period: 103rd, 106th, 109th, 111th, 113th, 114th, 115th. Only the 120th and 128th were mustered and forwarded.

19. *O.R., 25*, 308; Dyer, *op. cit.*, pp. 1100, 1093.

20. *O.R., 25*, 332–334, 334–335, 349. In his letter to Stanton, McClernand dwelt at length on disaffection in the West because the Mississippi was closed, predicting that delay in opening it would cause the rise of a party calling for the recognition of the independence of the Confederacy, or bring another separation entailing "endless collisions, which, after wasting all the States, must sink them in anarchy and wretchedness, like that which drapes Mexico in misery and mourning."

Of the exchanged Indiana troops, only 3,122 officers and men had been captured at Richmond, Ky., on Aug. 30; 3,678 had been taken at Munfordville on Sept. 17; after being paroled, all were sent to Indianapolis for reorganization and exchange (*ibid., 117*, 717).

21. Dyer, *op. cit.*, Illinois regimental histories; Thorndike, *The Sherman Letters*, p. 109; *O.R., 25*, 371–372.

McClernand said in a telegram of Oct. 28 to Stanton, "At 11:30 o'clock a.m. to-day General Ketchum resigned his functions here to me" (*O.R., 25*, 300). Brig. Gen. W. Scott Ketchum, a regular officer, who had previously been on duty at St. Louis, was evidently mustering and dispatching troops at Springfield.

Halleck, who may never have seen Stanton's order to McClernand, wired to Gov. Yates on Oct. 30, "It seems that General Grant is likely to be hard pressed by the enemy and it is important that troops be sent to him as rapidly as possible." In reply to a query from McClernand as to where Indiana troops should go, Stanton telegraphed on Oct. 31, "Orders have been sent to Governor Morton to forward his regiments to Columbus, on the Mississippi, as fast as possible." (*Ibid.*, pp. 309, 310.) A similar telegram to the governor of Iowa would have taken care of the regiments from that state.

22. *Ibid.*, pp. 332–334, 345, 348–349.

23. *Ibid.,* pp. 371–372.

24. *Ibid.,* pp. 401, 413, 415. In his telegram to Stanton, McClernand raised the question whether the victory at Prairie Grove, Ark., would not make it possible to augment the Mississippi expedition, adding, "I only ask the question suggestively." His statement in his telegram to Halleck that his report to Stanton of the 1st had been turned over to Halleck would seem to have been a mere inference. Regimental histories as given by Dyer confirm the figure McClernand gave as to the number of regiments that had been forwarded.

25. *O.R., 25,* 462.

26. *Collected Works of Abraham Lincoln,* VI, 71, 70.

27. *Supra,* p. 374.

28. *O.R., 36,* 166–167, 167–168; *109,* 431.

29. *O.R., 109,* 437–438.

30. *O.R., 109,* 439–440; *36,* 168, 169.

31. *O.R., 36,* 169–186.

32. Wilson, *The Life of John A. Rawlins,* p. 132. Wilson said that McClernand declared emphatically that he would not obey the order, that he would not be dictated to any longer by Grant or anyone else, and that he intimated that he considered himself to be in command of the expedition. Wilson said that McClernand's violent language seemed intended for him as much as for higher authority.

33. McClernand also had the chance to read the indorsement written by Grant on his report: "Respectfully forwarded. This report contains so many inaccuracies that to correct it, to make it a fair report to be handed down as historical, would require the rewriting of most of it. It is pretentious and egotistical, as is sufficiently shown by my own and all other reports accompanying. The officers and men composing the Thirteenth Army Corps, throughout the campaign ending with the capture of Vicksburg, have done nobly, and there are no honors due the Army of the Tennessee in which they do not share equally." In addition, there was Grant's statement to Adj. Gen. Lorenzo Thomas when he transmitted the papers on the McClernand case: "A disposition and earnest desire on my part to do the most I could with the means at my command, without interference with the assignments to command which the President alone was authorized to make, made me tolerate General McClernand long after I thought the good of the service demanded his removal. It was only when almost the entire army under my command seemed to demand it that he was relieved." (*O.R., 36,* 157, 158–159.)

34. Douglas Southall Freeman, Untitled Address, *Civil War History,* I, 7–15 (March, 1955).

35. Thomas, ed., *Three Years with Grant,* xiii. Thomas states that about a third of the original manuscript was not used, and speaks of Cadwallader as sometimes wandering into the trite and trivial. In an announcement for the book he used the word "dross." A careful study of the omitted portions of the manuscript would be necessary for a full appraisal of Cadwallader's reliability.

36. A ledger, containing copies of dispatches from Grant to subordinates, that is in the manuscript division of the Library of Congress, covers the period Aug. 8, 1861, to June 25, 1862. One covering messages to higher headquarters

is for a longer period. The National Archives yielded nothing to fill the gap in Grant's messages to subordinates.

The figure 330 covers dispatches in *O.R., 24* and *25.* Six dispatches to Halleck and two to subordinates are headed "Grant's Headquarters." A short dispatch to Gen. Sullivan (*O.R., 25,* 477) gives neither place nor date—it was concerned with Forrest's raid and was probably sent on Dec. 24, 1862. On Dec. 26 Grant sent seven telegrams to Sullivan, three of which give the date of origin, the other four omitting it. Indorsements Grant put on three dispatches about Van Dorn's raid do not give the place of writing. In a message to Dodge and Hamilton on Jan. 1, 1863, that did nothing but transmit a telegram from Sullivan, Grant did not show his own position. Such seem to be the only instances where he failed to give his location.

37. The letters to Sherman are in *O.R., 25,* except that of Dec. 8, 1862, which is given in *O.R., 24,* 601. A dispatch of Nov. 1 addressed "Major-General Sherman, Memphis, Tenn." bears the notation, "Sent in cipher to Columbus to forward by first steamer." It is not included in the ten letters mentioned.

An examination of dispatches to officers other than Sherman, including Halleck, shows that Grant only occasionally failed to abbreviate rank when used with a name. He habitually abbreviated Tennessee, and seldom wrote "commanding" after his own name and rank.

38. *O.R., 25,* 178–179 (Sherman's letter). The Sherman journal is in the War Records Office (Old Army section), National Archives. Isham's explanation was received on the 16th, the day of writing; the entry says "filed." In his letter to Grant, Sherman said the correspondent was that day sending him "a long appeal" by mail and had asked him to stay proceedings until Grant was heard from. He had informed the man he would not do so.

39. Alton records in the National Archives show that Isham and six other prisoners were turned over to Col. Jesse Hildebrand, commanding the Alton Military Prison (Hildebrand was seen at Shiloh, *supra,* III, 367), at Memphis on Aug. 27 and was delivered at Alton on the 31st. On Sept. 11 Isham wrote to Col. G. Gantt, provost marshal general in St. Louis, requesting that he be paroled in the city; he denied having written the letter which had caused his arrest and believed some other correspondent was the guilty party. Hildebrand recommended that the parole be granted.

On Nov. 19 Capt. H. W. Freedley, a representative of the Commissary General of Prisoners, Col. William Hoffman, reported that Grant and Curtis (commanding in St. Louis) had been ordering that prisoners be released from Alton in opposition to regulations; although orders and letters were on his desk, Hildebrand pleaded want of information. On the 27th Hoffman wrote to Stanton that Grant had released eighty-six men, though the Alton prison was not under his command and such release was contrary to orders. On the 24th Freedley reported that Alton rolls showed the disposition made of prisoners without the dates; on the 27th he wrote of "a terrible lack of system" in the adjutant's office and said three men were in the prison whose names were not on any roll. Hildebrand was soon replaced by Freedley. (*O.R., 117,* 734–735, 761, 753–754, 763–764, 765.)

With such a record, one cannot be certain that Isham was arrested on Aug.

15, and not the next day as a result of Sherman's receipt of Grant's letter of the 4th. Hildebrand may have trusted to his memory of what had been told him at Memphis.

Cadwallader, it should be noted, interceded with Grant, through Col. Dickey, for Isham's release because Isham had been punished enough and his family was in distress, not because of his innocence. Had Cadwallader forgotten the man's claim, which must have been known to the editor of the *Chicago Times*? In the letter to Sherman, whose genuineness is being questioned, Grant directed that, unless sooner discharged by competent authority, Isham should be confined "until the end of the war." It is not clear then why Grant should have said to Dickey that confinement for two months was "severe discipline for the offense."

Unless there is good corroboration, one must doubt the confinement that Cadwallader has Grant specify, and he must regard the sending of a staff officer to secure Isham's release—which Cadwallader says Grant did—as just an instance of Cadwallader fiction. (Thomas, *ed., op. cit.,* pp. 5, 13, 14.)

40. *Supra,* pp. 340–341. Cadwallader is in irreconcilable disagreement with Frederick Dent Grant regarding actions in Jackson, Miss. He states (*ibid.,* pp. 73–74) that as soon as the Confederate batteries stopped their fire, he and Grant's son started at full speed for the capitol to secure the large Confederate flag that waved from a staff on the roof. They had reached the steps leading from the garret when they met a ragged and muddy cavalryman descending with the coveted prize under his arm. (Why they had not seen the sergeant on the roof while they were still on the ground is not explained.)

In his article "With Grant at Vicksburg," F. D. Grant says that, thinking the battle was over, he rode toward the state house, but he says nothing about Cadwallader and nothing about being intent on getting the Confederate flag. He saw some Confederate troops who paid no attention to him, and then a mounted officer with a Union flag advancing toward the capitol. He followed the officer into the building and went into the governor's office, where he confiscated a pipe, "primarily and ostensibly for the National service, but secondarily and actually for my own private and individual use." Upon returning to the street, he witnessed the raising of the Union flag by the officer, who "proved to be Captain, afterward Colonel, Cornelius Cadle." Brig. Gen. Marcellus Crocker said in his report that Capt. Cadle and Capt. Lucien Martin raised the flag of the 59th Indiana above the dome of the capitol (*O.R., 36,* 723–724).

Dispatches to the *Cincinnati Commercial* (quoted in the *N.Y. Tribune,* May 25) and the *N.Y. Herald* (May 30) spoke of raising the Union flag but said nothing of removing the Confederate colors. Dispatches from special correspondents of the *N.Y. Times* (May 26) and the *N.Y. Tribune* (June 1) said nothing about either flag.

Miss Charlotte Capers of the Department of Archives and History of the State of Mississippi has written me that they have no records showing that a Confederate flag that had been above the state capitol fell into Federal hands. I have been told by Gen. U. S. Grant, 3rd that he never heard his father speak of an expedition with Cadwallader that was frustrated on the threshold of success by an enterprising, trophy-minded sergeant of cavalry, and, in fact, that he has no recollection of ever hearing any member of the family or staff speak of this alleged intimate friend.

41. Thomas, ed., *op. cit.*, pp. 102–103, covers the two days, June 6–7. The situation at and east of Satartia and Grant's trip as revealed in the *O.R.* are discussed *supra*, pp. 400–402.

The *Diligent* is mentioned several times in *O.R. Navies*, Ser. I, XXIV and XXV, but its whereabouts on the dates in question are not indicated; there is no log for it in the National Archives, either in the Navy records or those of the Quartermaster General. The vessel is also referred to in *O.R. 36* in connection with the Steele Bayou expedition, and it is mentioned in *O.R. 38*.

42. *O.R., 37*, 437. Kimball had left Brig. Gen. J. A. Mower in command of the troops in Mechanicsburg.

43. Dana, *Recollections of the Civil War*, pp. 82–83.

44. *O.R., 37*, 440 (Jackson's report of June 7). It would be interesting to know the basis of the word "tactfully." It looks as if Cadwallader had been accepted as an unquestionable authority (and that in spite of the necessity to change the title of his book) against whom other writers could be judged. It may be recalled that when Grant became President, Dana expected to be appointed collector of customs in New York and was much displeased because he failed to secure the post. While he was not a man who years later would be spiteful or vengeful because of a disappointment which had not harmed a distinguished career, it is nevertheless true that Dana was under no obligation to Grant.

45. Starr, *op. cit.*, pp. 282–283. In a review of *Three Years* in the *Saturday Review* for Oct. 29, 1955, Starr speaks of having examined the original Cadwallader manuscript, which he characterized as "discursiveness gone mad."

46. Miers, *op. cit.*, pp. 232–238; *supra*, p. 402 (Grant's dispatch). While Miers's book appeared a few months before *Three Years*, he had had a typescript of *Four Years* (Miers, *op. cit.*, p. 307).

47. *Supra*, p. 353.

48. Wilson, *The Life of John A. Rawlins*, pp. 128–129. When Rawlins first directed that the box of wine be removed, he was told that Grant had said it was not to be taken away: he was keeping it to give to his friends when they got in Vicksburg.

How anything connected with drinking is almost certain to be exaggerated, is shown by Sandburg's reference to "this wine drunk" (*Abraham Lincoln, The War Years*, II, 117).

In his *The North Reports the Civil War* (p. 67), Andrews has Grant make his Yazoo trip near the end of 1862, that is, when Grant was writing messages in northern Mississippi.

49. Wilson changes Dana's words "was ill" to "fell sick" (quotation marks in Wilson), says nothing about meeting the gunboats, and has the trip to Satartia abandoned solely because of Grant's sickness.

In his *The Life of Charles A. Dana,* published nine years before the Rawlins book, Wilson states that an account of the trip to Satartia was given in great detail by S. Cadwallader in an unpublished manuscript. (It would thus seem that Wilson saw the Cadwallader work not long after it was written and again when he wrote the book about Rawlins.) Wilson states that the trip became the occasion of a very remarkable letter of remonstrance from Rawlins to Grant. The çhief point of difference between what he said in the Dana book and in the Rawlins book was in regard to the return to camp. In the Dana book Wilson has Dana not arrive back in camp with the entire party (again the trip was given up solely because of Grant's illness) until the next evening. This is also in contradiction with the Cadwallader claim.

Dana says specifically that Grant sent him from Haynes Bluff on the morning of the 7th with a party of cavalry toward Mechanicsburg, and states that they had a hard ride and did not get back to the headquarters camp until the morning of the 8th, a statement fully corroborated by the dispatch he sent Stanton at 10:00 A.M. that day (*O.R., 36*, 94–95).

It would be hard to imagine a greater distortion of Dana's page of clear, simple writing than Wilson contrived to make in his two accounts of Satartia. Wilson, it should be noted, like Dana, had been a disappointed office seeker, and the feeling of the very distinguished officer toward his old commander apparently changed when he was not appointed Secretary of War to succeed his close friend Rawlins, when the latter died in September, 1869, after having held the position for only six months.

50. Dana, *op. cit.*, pp. 72–73. Rawlins soon proved the truth of Dana's statement that he never lost a moment. Living in the house of the wealthy planter where Grant established headquarters after the capture of Vicksburg was a Connecticut-born governess—Emma Hurlbut. Rawlins, a widower, laid siege to her, but it seems not to be claimed that Grant brought a bottle of wine out of hiding to drink a toast to the couple when Rawlins announced Emma's capitulation. (Wilson, *op. cit.*, p. 150.)

Far too much has been made of a letter that Rawlins wrote to Miss Hurlbut on Nov. 16, 1863, from Chattanooga, expressing deep regret that he could not make her a contemplated visit. Liquor had reappeared at headquarters, Rawlins said, and events the night before showed it had reached Grant. Rawlins pictured himself as indispensable at headquarters; but he made no reference to Grant's Satartia trip. A jumbled sentence proves the truth of Dana's statement about Rawlins's English. In it Rawlins seemed to be trying to say in an impressive way that no one could understand his feelings on the subject of drinking unless he had been haunted by the fear of dying a drunkard. (Sandburg, *Lincoln Collector*, pp. 318–320.)

The article on Rawlins in *D.A.B.* says that the necessity of Rawlins as a control on Grant's drinking "has some times been greatly exaggerated." In a review of Miers's book in *American Heritage*, June, 1955, p. 51, Bruce Catton says of Grant: "He drank too much? To be sure: but, somehow, not when the chips were down." The word "somehow" shows that the *assumption* made had raised a difficulty. Since the time of the Greeks it has been common to disprove a false hypothesis by *reductio ad absurdum*.

51. Starr, *op. cit.*, p. 285n.

52. Thomas, ed., *op. cit.*, p. 110. Miers (*op. cit.*, p. 218) has the Rawlins letter a part of the aftermath of Grant's "drunk" as given by Cadwallader, the

statement being made by way of introduction to a quotation from Wilson's *Under the old Flag* (1912). In that book Wilson changed the box of wine into a case of champagne, and had Grant make a personal explanation to Rawlins about wanting to keep it for a celebration—but to no avail.

53. Thomas, ed., *op. cit.*, pp. 71, 116; Porter, *op. cit.*, p. 215. The invariability with which Cadwallader says Grant drank to excess if he took one glass cannot reasonably be restricted to the occasions of which Cadwallader speaks.

Cadwallader could not tell even the simple story of May 12 without making a major error about an important person. He says that the drink that Duff gave Grant came from a half-barrel of whisky that Gov. Oglesby of Illinois had recently left with Duff and Cadwallader upon returning home after visiting the army. A note in *Three Years* (p. 66) explains that it was really Gov. Richard Yates who had given the present and that Richard Oglesby did not become governor for over a year! More might appropriately have been said. At the time in question Oglesby was in Grant's army, not, it is true, in the campaign behind Vicksburg, but in command at Jackson, Tenn. After thirty years had passed, two Richards were too much for Cadwallader.

54. Winther, ed., *With Sherman to the Sea*, pp. 102–103.

A fundamental and important fact in the whole question is that charges of drinking to excess were circulated about Grant as early as the fall of 1861. Rawlins's letter to Washburne of Dec. 20, 1861, in which he went into the matter at length and stated that Grant had in fact been practically completely abstemious, was cited *supra*, III, 152. It was there noted that Rawlins assigned the rumors to enemies Grant had made because of his efforts "to guard against and ferret out frauds in his district."

In a note to Chapter XII there was given a comment that Dr. Henry P. Stearns, a surgeon on Grant's staff from Cairo days until after Shiloh, wrote in the margin of his copy of Grant's *Memoirs*, supporting Grant's statement about the manner of his embarking after the battle at Belmont. Dr. Stearns left Grant's staff to take charge of a large military hospital at Paducah, where he remained until the end of the war. His distinguished postwar career in the field of mental diseases is described in *D.A.B.* In transmitting the note referred to, Dr. Stearns's grandson, a teacher of history, wrote, after citing his grandfather's period of field service, "Incidentally, during those months my grandfather said that he never once saw Grant under the influence of liquor, although he was with him constantly." Thus the statement of an eminent physician and scientist, reliably transmitted, refutes the rumors about Grant for a longer period than Rawlins did, extending it past the time of Kountz's charges, as well as Fort Donelson and Shiloh, when accusations were again widely circulated.

55. *Supra*, III, 4 (quotation from Col. W. C. Church).

56. Eaton, *Grant, Lincoln and the Freedmen*, pp. 40–42. The dentist was working with one of the sanitary commissions, and was from Cincinnati, a place where Eaton says that stories of Grant's intemperance and general incompetence were numerous. He shared quarters with Eaton, and after he had had a hasty judgment corrected, became one of Grant's greatest admirers.

57. Agassiz, ed., *Meade's Headquarters, 1863–1865*, pp. 130, 354.

58. Porter, *op. cit.*, pp. 462–464; Thomas, ed., *op. cit.*, pp. 317–318; Grant, *Memoirs*, II, 484 (Long, ed., p. 533). In his *Military History of Ulysses S. Grant*, Badeau speaks (III, 594) of Grant's illness on the 8th and of his receiving Lee's message "while unable to sleep from pain."

59. Porter, *op. cit.*, pp. 471–476; Thomas, ed., *op. cit.*, pp. 326–327. Cadwallader states that after the ordinary civilities had been exchanged, the military secretaries were called upon to put the surrender terms in proper form. What Grant had himself written was merely copied in ink by a staff officer, including two or three pencil interlineations that Lee, with Grant's approval, had inserted as he read the original. Lee's acceptance was drafted by Col. Marshall after Lee had given some indications as to what he wished said.

Freeman's account in *R. E. Lee* (IV, 135–140) is based on the best authorities. He states that Babcock opened the door for Grant. An editorial note on p. 327 of *Three Years* says that Cadwallader's account of the occasion differs in some minor details from that of Freeman. As Freeman also says that it was Babcock who, after some whispered words with Grant, went to the door and summoned the other Federal officers, it must be insisted that the differences are in virtually every significant fact of the historic incident.

Porter's book is justly well regarded, and the part beginning with Apr. 7, 1865, down through Grant's second meeting with Lee on the 10th, is essentially the article written more than ten years before the publication of the book, the article having appeared in *B. and L.*, IV, 729–746. In the article Porter states that on the evening of the 9th he made full note of occurrences at the surrender and had based his account upon them.

60. A typed copy of Freeman's address was furnished by Robert Sanner.

61. *O.R.*, *35*, 836–837.

62. *O.R.*, *47*, 173–174; *35*, 837–838.

63. Longstreet, *From Manassas to Appomattox*, pp. 327–328, 331; *O.R.*, *26*, 1050; *40*, 790.

64. *O.R.*, *40*, 782–783 (Lee to Davis, May 7, 1863); Freeman, *R. E. Lee*, III, 19; *O.R.*, *40*, 841–843, 848–849.

65. *O.R.*, *47*, 173–174. The concluding question echoed what Beauregard had written on June 21 upon his original plan. Therein he said, "The whole of this brilliant campaign" could have been terminated by the end of June with the destruction of Rosecrans's and Grant's armies and the conquest of Tennessee and Kentucky. Then the offensive could have been assumed "in Ohio or Pennsylvania, as circumstances indicated." One might recall the vision of a move on St. Louis that Beauregard had had in February, 1862 (*supra*, III, 286).

66. *O.R.*, *40*, 832–833. In a dispatch to Secretary Seddon on June 2, Johnston put the number of troops received from Beauregard at 6,000 (*O.R.*, *36*, 195).

67. Davis, *The Rise and Fall of the Confederate Government*, II, 404–405.

68. Joseph E. Johnston, "Jefferson Davis and the Mississippi Campaign," *B. and L.*, III, 472–482.

69. For about a month after Johnston arrived at Jackson, he believed that his new assignment to the field in Mississippi had relieved him from command over Bragg, but the matter was cleared up in a dispatch from Seddon on June

8 which, however, Johnston could not decipher and asked to have repeated. A telegram he sent to Seddon on the 12th ended, "It is for the Government to decide between this State [Mississippi] and Tennessee." Davis saw this dispatch, and in replying on the 15th he said, "The order to go to Mississippi did not diminish your authority in Tennessee, both being in the country placed under your command in original assignment." On the 16th Johnston argued in a dispatch to Davis about the naturalness of his assumption, and Davis the next day asked for the date of a dispatch or letter that would warrant his position. In a message on the 20th Johnston said that he regretted his carelessness in his message of the 16th, but still held to the reasonableness of his interpretation of a dispatch Seddon had sent on the 5th. In a telegram on June 30 Davis stated that he was still at a loss to account for Johnston's "strange error." In replying on July 5, Johnston said, "I regret very much that an impression which seemed to me to be natural should be regarded by you as a strange error." On July 8 Davis countered by saying the mistakes in Johnston's message of the 5th would be considered in a letter, and then switched to "the disastrous termination of the siege of Vicksburg," announced by Johnston on the 7th in a message that was received the same day. (*O.R., 36,* 226, 196, 197, 224, 198, 199.)

The major point that Davis made for himself in his promised letter (dated July 15) was the dispatch that he had sent to Bragg on May 22, which he quoted, italicizing in part: ". . . Can you aid him [Johnston]? If so, *and you are without orders from General Johnston,* act on your judgment." Forgetting that Johnston had never seen the message, Davis wrote, "The words that I now underscore suffice to show how thoroughly your right of command of the troops in Tennessee was recognized." In his reply Johnston of course said that if he had received a copy of the dispatch, his error would have been corrected, adding, "but it was not sent to me, and I have its evidence for the first time in your letter." (*Ibid.,* pp. 202–207, 209–213.)

Johnston could be a querulous subordinate, but Davis certainly showed something akin to vindictiveness in pressing his claim that Johnston had erred. Davis should have furnished Johnston a copy of his dispatch to Bragg, and an ultimate but unadmitted realization that it was he who had been wrong may have been the cause of his continuing ill will toward Johnston.

70. J. C. Pemberton, *Pemberton, Defender of Vicksburg,* p. 252; Steele, *American Campaigns,* p. 205. J. C. Pemberton's categorical statement that Johnston neither heeded nor acknowledged authority is of course not true. Though sick, he went to Jackson without delay upon receiving Seddon's direction. Other instances of following orders could be cited.

How much of his force the Confederate general could have extricated is open to much doubt. Steele, it will be recalled, did not use the *O.R.* and he was handicapped in his appraisal of Vicksburg by want of knowledge of many important things. He states that Vicksburg did nothing to add to Johnston's fame as a general. One can ask the question, What chance did he have, when Pemberton disobeyed the first order he received from Johnston, though most of his officers in a council of war at Edwards on May 14 had favored the move to join Johnston that the latter had directed in his dispatch of the evening before? Upon receiving another message on the morning of May 16, Pemberton reversed his column, then moving toward Raymond to cut Grant's communications, and informed Johnston that he would join him by a route which he described. In his report he did not plead that the defeat he suffered at Champion's Hill had prevented the completing of the move. Nor did he say that he was under explicit orders from the government to defend Vicksburg at all costs. He stated merely that he "knew and appreciated the earnest desire of the Government and the people that it should be held"—something that he knew on the morning of the 16th when he informed Johnston that he would move to join him. (*O.R., 36*, 261, 263, 271—in Pemberton's report.)

Very much on the credit side of Johnston's record was the telegram he sent Pemberton on the morning of May 2, as well as his subsequent efforts to unite all Confederate forces outside Vicksburg. J. C. Pemberton makes the statement that Grant would have been glad if Gen. Pemberton had obeyed Johnston's order. Then Grant would have had Vicksburg without the heavy casualties of his two assaults and he would not have come close to the shattering of his entire career. Determined efforts, we are told, were made before the end of the siege to have Grant superseded. (J. C. Pemberton, *op. cit.,* p. 115.)

Grant's losses in the assaults were certainly heavy in comparison with those of the Confederates, but six weeks to the day after that of May 22, Pemberton met with Grant to surrender: one lieutenant general, 4 major generals, 10 brigadier generals, 49 colonels, 37 lieutenant colonels, a couple of thousand lesser officers, and 27,000 enlisted men, of whom 709 refused to give their paroles and were sent north (*O.R., 37*, 324–325).

The Vicksburg harvest was ten times Grant's losses in the two assaults. Had Pemberton heeded Johnston's order after Champion's Hill, and possessed the skill and steadiness of purpose to execute the movement that Grant said he should have made—which is open to doubt—and had thus eluded Grant at the last, then the criticism of the winter might have been renewed. As things were, any remaining opposition to Grant was of no consequence. The government had Dana's steady, illuminating dispatches, and the public knew of the three divisions that were sent early in June to draw the investing line tighter and hold off Johnston. The brilliance of the operation back of Vicksburg was well appreciated.

71. Liddell Hart, *Sherman,* p. 196.

72. J. C. Pemberton quotes (pp. 250–251) from a letter strongly critical of Johnston that he had received from Lieut. Col. John W. Thompson, Jr. It is of no force because it does not show that it was based on a knowledge of many of the realities of the campaign—the strength of Johnston's force and his difficulty in getting transportation to give mobility. The statement that if Jackson, Lee, or Longstreet had been sent to the West, Grant would not have been free to starve out fortresses is hardly impressive when it is recalled that within less than two months after Grant opened his 1864 campaign, Lee was under siege in Petersburg and Richmond.

Perhaps the most perplexing thing about Johnston's actions was some sentences in a dispatch he wrote to Pemberton on May 14 from seven miles north of Jackson. Referring to Grant, he said: "Can he supply himself from the

Mississippi? Can you not cut him off from it, and above all, should he be compelled to fall back for want of supplies, beat him?" Having written this, Johnston reverted to the thought of joining forces and closed by saying that the campaign would be decided if the Federal force at Jackson could be beaten, which, however, could only be done by "concentrating." Apparently Johnston had entirely forgotten about his suggestion of a move against Grant's supply line when he received the next morning the dispatch that Pemberton had written at Edwards on the 14th, that said he would move the next morning toward Dillon's on the road from Raymond to Port Gibson. In replying, Johnston said, "Our being compelled to leave Jackson makes your plan impracticable. The only move by which we can unite is by your moving directly to Clinton, informing me, that we may move to that point with about 6,000." This was the message which, received by Pemberton at 6:30 the next morning, caused him to countermarch. Johnston's dispatch of the 14th was not received until after Pemberton's defeat at Champion's Hill, but it was natural that Pemberton should regard it as sanctioning his move to the southeast even though Johnston's query had not caused it. That Pemberton thought about the "late" dispatch a good deal would seem indicated by his postwar letter to Grant. Johnston on his part certainly did not divine what Grant would do. In his message to Pemberton of the 15th, he said, after speaking of the uncertainty of the size of Grant's force in Jackson, "I fear he will fortify if time is left him." (*O.R.*, *38*, 878–879; *36*, 362; *38*, 882; *supra*, p. 562.)

In June, 1863, Gen. Richard Taylor sent Gen. C. LeD. Elgee on a mission to Johnston, and while en route back Elgee sent Taylor a dispatch in which he put Johnston's force at 25,000 men and said, "General Johnston's troops are far from being the best, owing to causes which you may easily conjecture." Unused were the 12,000 arms that Richmond had hopefully sent for the use of militia; as July ended, Johnston would say, "The militia won't serve," and add that many conscripts were keeping out of service on the plea of being in the militia under the authority of the War Department. (*O.R.*, *38*, 998–999, 1010, 1036.)

73. *O.R.*, *40*, 832–833.

74. On Aug. 4, 1863, a Confederate commissioner of conscription in Meridian, Miss., who stated that he was well known to Davis, wrote at length to Cooper about the situation in the state. Personally, he had no question of Pemberton's loyalty, but he said, "The soldiers now scattered over the Confederacy have lost all confidence in General Pemberton, and their determination is almost universal never to take the field under his lead." On the other hand he said, "General Johnston, I think, still enjoys the entire confidence of the people and soldiers of this department." (*O.R.*, *38*, 1043–1044.)

75. *Supra*, III, 448–452.

76. 45th Cong., 2nd Sess. (1877), House Mis. Doc. No. 58, 121. At least in this document the last seven words are italicized.

In connection with the distorted letter that Miss Carroll used to support her case, one can well mention untruthful words found in what the Greenbies call the original of the Tennessee plans, but do not quote, though they inaccurately state that it is addressed to Thomas A. Scott (*op. cit.*, pp. 496–497). The paper is dated Baltimore, Nov. 30, 1861, and it is in the Carroll collection in the Maryland Historical Society Library. It begins, "After a visit of three months to the West . . ." As the Greenbies place Miss Carroll in Washington on Oct. 2 (*ibid.*, p. 274), her trip did not last two months, and it did not even have parts in three different calendar months.

Sixteen typed pages analyzing Miss Carroll's statements in memorials and before congressional committees have been given me by a former judge of a higher court, who wishes to be anonymous. The pages also cover testimony by Miss Carroll's friend Judge L. D. Evans, and Pilot C. M. Scott, with whom she talked while in St. Louis. It seems unlikely that a more able study of the documents has been made or that anyone else so competent will soon go into the case as carefully. A letter explained: "I approached the problem just as I would a court record, and tried to weigh Anna's credibility as a witness. I concluded that it was practically *nil,* in view of the self-contradictions of herself and Judge Evans."

Added to the analysis of Miss Carroll's shifting position as memorial followed memorial are parenthetical comments expressing the writer's surprise at what he found. One will suffice: "Why was the lady unable ever to make her story consistent?"

77. S. and M. B. Greenbie, *op. cit.*, p. 442.

78. Lincoln, *Collected Papers,* V, 381.

79. Grant, *Memoirs,* II, 18 (Long, ed., p. 308); S. and M. B. Greenbie, *op. cit.*, pp. 368–369, 379–380.

80. S. and M. B. Greenbie, *op. cit.*, p. 383.

81. Casualties totaling 6,092 are given in reports, which do not, however, include Loring's at Champion's Hill (*O.R., 36,* 320, 667, 739, 787).

82. It seems to have not yet been claimed that Grant's quick seizure of Paducah on Sept. 6, 1861, was in response to some mysterious flash from Miss Carroll.

BIBLIOGRAPHY

(Only works quoted or cited as authority)

Agassiz, George R., ed., *Meade's Headquarters, 1863–1865: Letters of Colonel Theodore Lyman.* Boston, Atlantic Monthly, 1922.

American Heritage. New York, American Heritage Publishing Co.

Andrews, J. Coulter, *The North Reports the Civil War.* Pittsburgh, University of Pittsburgh Press, 1955.

Asbury, Herbert, *The French Quarter.* New York (Knopf, 1936), Pocket Book edition, 1949.

Badeau, Adam, *Military History of Ulysses S. Grant, from April, 1861, to April, 1865* (3 vols.). New York, Appleton, 1881.

B. and L. See next entry.

Battles and Leaders of the Civil War, Robert V. Johnson and C. C. Buel, eds. New York, Century, 1884–1888.

Beatty, John, *Memoirs of a Volunteer,* Harvey S. Ford, ed. New York, Norton, 1946.

Bradley, Omar N., *A Soldier's Story.* New York, Holt, 1951.

Brown, D. Alexander, *Grierson's Raid.* Urbana, University of Illinois Press, 1954.

Butler, Benjamin F., *Butler's Book.* Boston, Thayer, 1892.

Cadwallader, Sylvanus. See Thomas, Benjamin P., ed.

Carroll, Anna E., Papers of. MS. Collection in the Maryland Historical Society Library, Baltimore.

Caskey, Willie M., *Secession and Restoration of Louisiana.* Baton Rouge, Louisiana State University Press, 1938.

Chase, Salmon P. See Donald, David, ed.

Chesnut, Mary B. See Williams, Ben Ames, ed.

Chicago History (Chicago Historical Society Quarterly).

Chicago Tribune.

Cincinnati Daily Commercial.

Cist, Henry M., *The Army of the Cumberland* (Vol. VII of *Campaigns of the Civil War*). New York, Scribner, 1883.

Civil War History. Iowa City, State University of Iowa, 1955–.

Cleaves, Freeman, *Rock of Chickamauga: The Life of General George H. Thomas*. Norman, University of Oklahoma Press, 1948.

C.C.W. Report of the Committee on the Conduct of the War, Senate Document, 37th Congress, 3rd Session, 1862–1863, Vol. IV.

Conger, Arthur L., *The Rise of U. S. Grant*. New York, Century, 1931.

Coulter, E. Merton, *The Confederate States of America, 1861–1865* (Vol. VII of *A History of the South*, W. H. Stevenson and E. M. Coulter, eds). Baton Rouge, Louisiana State University Press, 1950.

Cramer, Jesse Grant, ed., *Letters of Ulysses S. Grant to His Father and His Youngest Sister, 1857–78*. New York, Putnam, 1912.

D.A.B. See Dictionary.

Dana, Charles A., *Recollections of the Civil War*. New York, Appleton, 1899.

————, and James H. Wilson, *The Life of Ulysses S. Grant, General of the Armies of the United States*. Springfield, Mass., Bill, 1868.

Davis, Jefferson, *The Rise and Fall of the Confederate Government* (2 vols.). New York, Appleton, 1881.

Dearing, Mary R., *Veterans in Politics: The Story of the G.A.R.* Baton Rouge, Louisiana State University Press, 1952.

De Forest, John W., *A Volunteer's Adventures,* James H. Croushore, ed. New Haven, Yale University Press, 1946.

Dictionary of American Biography. New York, Scribner, 1928–1936, 1948.

Donald, David, ed., *Inside Lincoln's Cabinet: The Civil War Diaries of Salmon P. Chase*. New York, Longmans, 1954.

Dyer, Frederick H., *A Compendium of the War of the Rebellion*. Des Moines, Dyer, 1908.

Dyer, John P., *"Fightin' Joe" Wheeler*. Baton Rouge, Louisiana State University Press, 1941.

Eaton, John, *Grant, Lincoln and the Freedmen: Reminiscences of the Civil War*. New York, Longmans, Green, 1907.

Encyclopaedia Britannica.

F(ield) M(anual) 100–5: Field Service Regulations—Operations. Washington, Government Printing Office, 1944.

Fiske, John, *The Mississippi Valley in the Civil War*. Boston, Houghton Mifflin, 1900.

Fitch, John, *Annals of the Army of the Cumberland, etc.* Philadelphia, Lippincott, 1864.

Flower, Milton E., *James Parton, The Father of Modern Biography*. Durham, Duke University Press, 1951.

Freeman, Douglas S., *R. E. Lee: A Biography* (4 vols.) New York, Scribner, 1935.

Fremantle, James A. L. See Lord, Walter, ed.

Fry, James B., *Operations of the Army Under Buell, from June 10th to October 30, 1862, and the "Buell Commission."* New York, Van Nostrand, 1884.

Fuller, J. F. C., *The Generalship of Ulysses S. Grant.* New York, Dodd, Mead, 1929.

Gosnell, H. Allen, *Guns on the Western Waters: The Story of the River Gunboats in the Civil War.* Baton Rouge, Louisiana State University Press, 1949.

Grant, Frederick Dent, "With Grant at Vicksburg," *The Outlook,* LIX, 522–544 (July 2, 1898).

Grant, Jesse R., *In the Days of My Father General Grant,* New York, Harper, 1925.

Grant, Ulysses S., Headquarters Papers of (63 vols.). MS. Collection, Library of Congress (received in 1953 from Maj. Gen. U. S. Grant 3rd).

———, *Personal Memoirs of U. S. Grant* (2 vols.). New York, Webster, 1885. See also Long, E. B., ed.

———. See Cramer, Jesse Grant, ed.

———. See Wilson, James Grant, ed.

Greeley, Horace, *The American Conflict: A History.* Hartford, Case, 1864–1866.

Greenbie, Sydney, and Marjorie Barstow Greenbie, *Anna Ella Carroll and Abraham Lincoln.* Tampa, University of Tampa Press, 1952.

Greene, Francis V., *The Mississippi* (Vol. VIII of *The Campaigns of the Civil War*). New York, Scribner, 1884.

Grimes, Absolom. See Quaife, M. M., ed.

Hale, William H., *Horace Greeley: Voice of the People.* New York, Harper, 1950.

Halleck, Henry W., *Elements of Military Art and Science, etc.* New York, Appleton, 1846.

Henry, Robert Selph, *"First with the Most" Forrest.* Indianapolis, Bobbs-Merrill, 1944.

Holland, Cecil F., *Morgan and His Raiders: A Biography of the Confederate General.* New York, Macmillan, 1942.

Holzman, Robert S., *Stormy Ben Butler.* New York, Macmillan, 1954.

Horan, James D., *Confederate Agent.* New York, Crown, 1954.

———, and Howard Swiggett, *The Pinkerton Story.* New York, Putnam, 1951.

Horn, Stanley F., *The Army of Tennessee.* Indianapolis, Bobbs-Merrill, 1941; Norman, University of Oklahoma Press, 1953.

Johnston, Joseph E., *Narrative of Military Operations.* New York, Appleton, 1874.

Journal of the Illinois State Historical Society.

King, Charles, *The True Ulysses S. Grant.* Philadelphia, Lippincott, 1914.

Korn, Bertram Wallace, *American Jewry and the Civil War.* Philadelphia, Jewish Publication Society, 1951.

Lemly, James H., *The Gulf, Mobile and Ohio.* Homewood, Ill., Irwin, 1953.

Lewis, Charles L., *David Glasgow Farragut: Our First Admiral.* Annapolis, United States Naval Institute, 1943.

Lewis, Lloyd, *Captain Sam Grant.* Boston, Little, Brown, 1950.

———, *Sherman, Fighting Prophet.* New York, Harcourt, Brace, 1932.

Liddell Hart, B. H., *Sherman: Soldier, Realist, American.* New York, Dodd, Mead, 1929.

Lincoln, Abraham, *Collected Works of Abraham Lincoln* (8 vols. and index), Roy P. Basler, ed. New Brunswick, Rutgers University Press, 1953–55.

Lincoln, Robert Todd, MS. Collection of Papers of Abraham Lincoln, Library of Congress.

Livermore, Thomas L., *Numbers and Losses in the Civil War in America, 1861–65.* Boston, Houghton Mifflin, 1901.

Long, E. B., ed., *Personal Memoirs of U. S. Grant.* Cleveland, World, 1952.

Longstreet, James, *From Manassas to Appomattox: Memoirs of the Civil War in America.* Philadelphia, Lippincott, 1896.

Lord, Walter, ed., *The Fremantle Diary.* Boston, Little, Brown, 1954.

Louisiana Historical Quarterly.

Lyman, Theodore. See Agassiz, George R., ed.

McClernand, John A., Papers of. MS. Collection in the Illinois State Historical Library, Springfield.

McCormick, Robert R., *Ulysses S. Grant: The Great Soldier of America.* New York, Appleton-Century, 1934.

McKee, Irving, *"Ben-Hur" Wallace: The Life of General Lew Wallace.* Berkeley, University of California Press, 1947.

Mahan, Alfred T., *The Gulf and Inland Waters* (Vol. III of *The Navy in the Civil War*). New York, Scribner, 1883.

Miers, Earl S., *The Web of Victory: Grant at Vicksburg.* New York, Knopf, 1955.

Monaghan, Jay, *Civil War on the Western Border, 1854–1865.* Boston, Little, Brown, 1955.

Myers, William S., *General George Brinton McClellan.* New York, Appleton-Century, 1934.

Nevins, Allan, *The Ordeal of the Union* (2 vols.). New York, Scribner, 1947.

New York Herald.

New York Times.

New York Tribune.

Nicolay, John G., and John Hay, *Abraham Lincoln: A History* (10 vols.). New York, Century, 1890.

O'Connor, Richard, *Sheridan, the Inevitable.* Indianapolis, Bobbs-Merrill, 1953.

O'Flaherty, Daniel, *General Jo Shelby, Undefeated Rebel.* Chapel Hill, University of North Carolina Press, 1954.

O.R. See *War of the Rebellion.*

O.R. Navies. See next entry.

Official Records of the Union and Confederate Navies in the War of the Rebellion. Washington, Government Printing Office, 1894–1927.

Parks, Joseph H., *General Edmund Kirby Smith, C.S.A.* Baton Rouge, Louisiana State University Press, 1954.

Parton, James, *General Butler in New Orleans.* Boston, Houghton Mifflin, 1868.

Patton, James W., *Unionism and Reconstruction in Tennessee, 1860–1869.* Chapel Hill, University of North Carolina Press, 1934.

Pemberton, John C., *Pemberton, Defender of Vicksburg.* Chapel Hill, University of North Carolina Press, 1942.

Perkins, J. R., *Trails, Rails and War: The Life of General G. M. Dodge.* Indianapolis, Bobbs-Merrill, 1929.

Phisterer, Frederick, *Statistical Record of the Armies of the United States* (supplementary volume of *Campaigns of the Civil War*). New York, Scribner, 1883.

Polk, William M., *Leonidas Polk, Bishop and General* (2 vols.), new edition. New York, Longmans, Green, 1915.

Porter, David, *Incidents and Anecdotes of the Civil War.* New York, Appleton, 1888.

Porter, Horace, *Campaigning with Grant.* New York, Century, 1897.

Pratt, Fletcher, *Stanton, Lincoln's Secretary of War.* New York, Norton, 1953.

Publications of the Mississippi Historical Society.

Quaife, M. M., ed., *Absolom Grimes, Confederate Mail Runner.* New Haven, Yale University Press, 1926.

Register of Graduates and Former Cadets. West Point, U.S. Military Academy, 1948.

Ropes, John C., *The Story of the Civil War* (4 vols.). New York, Putnam, 1891.

Ross, Ishbel, *Rebel Rose: The Life of Rose O'Neal Greenhow, Confederate Spy.* New York, Harper, 1954.

Russell, William H., *My Diary North and South,* Fletcher Pratt, ed. New York, Harper, 1954.

Sanborn, John B., *The Crisis at Champion's Hill, the Decisive Battle of the Civil War*. Pamphlet, St. Paul, Minn., 1903.

Sandburg, Carl, *Abraham Lincoln: The War Years* (4 vols.). New York, Harcourt, Brace, 1939.

————, *Lincoln Collector*. New York, Harcourt, Brace, 1949.

Saturday Review. New York, Saturday Review Associates.

Seitz, Don C., *Braxton Bragg: General of the Confederacy*. Columbia, S.C., The State Co., 1924.

Senate Executive Journal.

Senate Reports, 37th Congress, 3rd Session.

Sheridan, Philip H., *Personal Memoirs of P. H. Sheridan, General United States Army* (2 vols.). New York, Webster, 1888.

Sherman, John. See Thorndike, Rachel Sherman, ed.

Sherman, William T., Letters of. See Thorndike, Rachel Sherman, ed.

————, *Memoirs of William T. Sherman* (2 vols.). New York, Appleton, 1875.

————, Papers of. MS. Collection in the Library of Congress.

Smith, Frank E., *The Yazoo River*. New York, Rinehart, 1954.

Southern Bivouac, The. Louisville, Ky., 1882–1887.

Stampp, Kenneth M., *Indiana Politics and the Civil War*. Indianapolis, Indiana Historical Bureau, 1949.

Stanton, Edwin M., Papers of. MS. Collection in the Library of Congress.

Starr, Louis M., *Bohemian Brigade: Civil War Newsmen in Action*. New York, Knopf, 1954.

Steele, Matthew F., *American Campaigns*. Washington, Combat Forces Press, 1951.

Stevenson, Alexander F., *The Battle of Stone's River near Murfreesboro, Tenn., December 30, 1862, to January 3, 1863*. Boston, Osgood, 1884.

Taylor, Richard, *Destruction and Reconstruction*. New York, Appleton, 1893.

Thomas, Benjamin P., ed., *Three Years with Grant as Recalled by War Correspondent Sylvanus Cadwallader*. New York, Knopf, 1955.

Thorndike, Rachel Sherman, ed., *The Sherman Letters: Correspondence between General and Senator Sherman from 1837 to 1891*. New York, Scribner, 1894.

Turner, George E., *Victory Rode the Rails: The Strategic Place of the Railroads in the Civil War*. Indianapolis, Bobbs-Merrill, 1953.

Upson, Theodore F. See Winther, Oscar O., ed.

Vandiver, Frank E., *Ploughshares into Swords: Josiah Gorgas and Confederate Ordnance*. Austin, University of Texas Press, 1952.

Van Horne, Thomas B., *The Life of Major-General George H. Thomas*. New York, Scribner, 1882.

War Department General Orders.

War of the Rebellion: Official Records of the Union and Confederate Armies. Washington, Government Printing Office, 1882–1900.

References are by serial number in italic, and page, following the abbreviation *O.R.*: e.g., *O.R., 17,* 250. A key transferring serial numbers into series, volumes, and parts is given in the index of the complete work.

Washburne, Elihu B., Papers of. MS. Collection in the Library of Congress.

Weisberger, Bernard A., *Reporters for the Union.* Boston, Little, Brown, 1953.

Welles, Gideon, *Diary of Gideon Welles* (3 vols.). Boston, Houghton Mifflin, 1911.

West, Richard S., Jr., *Gideon Welles: Lincoln's Navy Department.* Indianapolis, Bobbs-Merrill, 1943.

——, *The Second Admiral: A Life of David Dixon Porter, 1813–1891.* New York, Coward-McCann, 1937.

Western Pennsylvania Historical Magazine.

Whitton, F. E., *The Decisive Battles of Modern Times.* London, Constable, 1923.

Williams, Ben Ames, ed., *A Diary from Dixie* (by Mary B. Chesnut). Boston, Houghton Mifflin, 1949.

Wilson, James Grant, ed., *General Grant's Letters to a Friend, 1861–1880.* New York, Crowell, 1897.

Wilson, James Harrison, *The Life of Charles A. Dana.* New York, Harper, 1907.

——, *The Life of John A. Rawlins.* New York, Neale, 1916.

——, "A Staff-Officer's Journal of the Vicksburg Campaign, April 30 to July 4, 1863," *Journal of the Military Service Institution of the United States,* XLIII (1908), 93–109, 261–275.

Winther, Oscar O., ed., *With Sherman to the Sea: Civil War Letters, Diaries, and Reminiscences of Theodore F. Upson.* Baton Rouge, Louisiana State University Press, 1933.

Yaryan, John L., "Stone River," *War Papers of the Indiana Commandery of the Loyal Legion.* Indianapolis, Indiana Commandery, 1898.

INDEX

Ranks shown are the highest held in connection with mention in this volume. The abbreviation C.S. denotes civil as well as military officers of the Confederate States; M.C. denotes a member of Congress; (k.) means killed, (d. w.), died of wounds. A hyphen is used between nonconsecutive page numbers to indicate scattered references to the subject as well as continuous treatment. No references are made to the notes, or to battles treated in former volumes and referred to in this.